Poland

MI JUL 2016

Gdańsk & Pomerania
p305

Warmia & Masuria
p369

Mazovia & Podlasie
p87

Wielkopolska
p281

Warsaw
p48

Silesia
p237

Małopolska
p159

Kraków
p118

Carpathian Mountains
p196

THIS EDITION WRITTEN AND RESEARCHED BY

Mark Baker, Marc Di Duca, Tim Richards

Contents

MARKET, OLD TOWN
SQUARE (P53), WARSAW

BADAHOS/GETTY IMAGES ©

BISONS, BIAŁOWIEŻA
NATIONAL PARK, P109

MAREMAGNUM/GETTY IMAGES ©

Contents

Welcome to Poland

Chic medieval hot spots such as Kraków and Gdańsk vie with energetic Warsaw for your urban attention. Outside the cities, woods, rivers, lakes and hills beckon for some fresh-air fun.

A Thousand Years

Poland's roots go back to the turn of the first millennium, leaving a thousand years of twists, turns, kings and castles to explore. WWII history buffs are well served. Tragically, Poland found itself in the middle of that epic fight, and monuments and museums dedicated to these battles – and to Poland's survival – can be seen everywhere. There's a growing appreciation, too, of the rich Jewish heritage. Beyond the affecting Holocaust memorials, synagogues are being sensitively restored, and former Jewish centres such as Łódź and Lublin have heritage trails, so you can trace this history at your own pace.

Castles to Log Cabins

The former royal capital of Kraków is a living lab of architecture over the ages. Its nearly perfectly preserved Gothic core proudly wears overlays of Renaissance, Baroque and Art Nouveau, a record of tastes that evolved over centuries. Fabulous medieval castles and evocative ruins dot hilltops around the country, and the fantastic red-brick fortresses of the Teutonic Knights stand proudly in the north along the Vistula. Simple but finely crafted wooden churches hide amid the Carpathian hills, and the ample skills of the highlanders are on display at the many skansens (open-air ethnographic museums).

Heart-Warming Food

If you're partial to good home cooking, the way your grandmother made it, you've come to the right place. Polish food is based largely on local ingredients such as pork, cabbage, mushrooms, beetroot and onion, combined simply and honed to perfection. Regional specialities, including duck, goose and trout, keep things from getting dull. As for sweets, it's hard to imagine a more accommodating destination. Cream cakes, apple strudel, pancakes, fruit-filled dumplings and a special mania for *lody* (ice cream) may have you skipping the main course and jumping straight to the main event.

Fresh-Air Pursuits

Away from the big cities, much of Poland feels remote and unspoiled. While large swathes of the country are flat, the southern border is lined with a chain of low-lying but lovely mountains that invite days, if not weeks, of splendid solitude. Well-marked hiking paths criss-cross the country, taking you through dense forest, along broad rivers and through mountain passes. Much of the northeast is covered by interlinked lakes and waterways ideal for kayaking and canoeing – no experience necessary. Local outfitters are happy to set you up for a couple of hours or weeks.

Why I Love Poland

By Mark Baker, Writer

I first travelled to Poland as a student in the 1980s and was touched by the humour, wit and kindness of people living under difficult circumstances. Over numerous return trips, I've been able to dive deeper and try to understand the culture, often formed in a crucible of torturous history. These days, what I'm impressed by is the verve and energy of the people as they've created arguably Central Europe's greatest post-communist success story. And then there's *kiełbasa* (Polish sausage), *pierogi* (dumplings) and quince-flavoured vodka. What more could you ask for?

For more about our writers, see page 456

Above: Royal Castle (p52), Warsaw

Poland

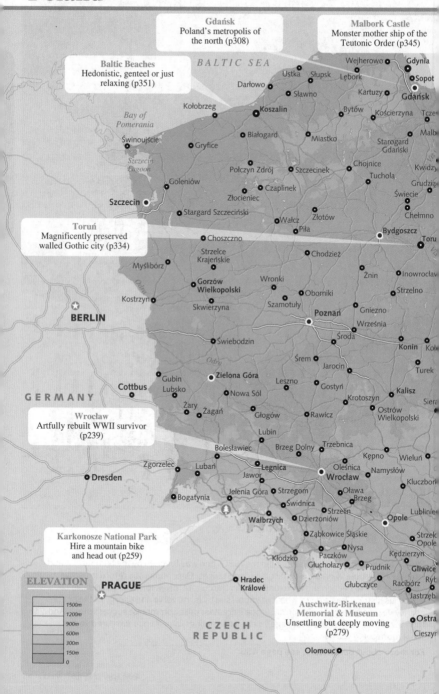

Gdańsk
Poland's metropolis of the north (p308)

Malbork Castle
Monster mother ship of the Teutonic Order (p345)

Baltic Beaches
Hedonistic, genteel or just relaxing (p351)

Toruń
Magnificently preserved walled Gothic city (p334)

Wrocław
Artfully rebuilt WWII survivor (p239)

Karkonosze National Park
Hire a mountain bike and head out (p259)

Auschwitz-Birkenau Memorial & Museum
Unsettling but deeply moving (p279)

BALTIC SEA

Bay of Pomerania

Szczecin Lagoon

BERLIN

GERMANY

Cottbus

Dresden

PRAGUE

ELEVATION

1500m
1200m
900m
600m
300m
150m
0

CZECH REPUBLIC

Wejherowo • Gdynia
Ustka • Słupsk • Lębork • Sopot
Darłowo • Sławno • Kartuzy • Gdańsk
Kołobrzeg • Koszalin • Bytów • Kościerzyna • Tcze
Świnoujście • Białogard • Miastko • Starogard Gdański • Malb
Gryfice • Szczecinek • Chojnice • Kwidzy
Połczyn Zdrój • Tuchola • Grudzią
Goleniów • Czaplinek • Świecie
Szczecin • Złocieniec • Chełmno
Stargard Szczeciński • Wałcz • Złotów • Bydgoszcz
Piła • Toru
Choszczno • Chodzież
Strzelce Krajeńskie • Znin • Inowrocław
Myślibórz • Wronki • Strzelno
Gorzów Wielkopolski • Oborniki • Gniezno
Kostrzyn • Skwierzyna • Szamotuły • Poznań • Września
Świebodzin • Środa • Konin • Koł
Śrem • Jarocin • Turek
Zielona Góra • Leszno • Gostyń • Kalisz
Gubin • Nowa Sól • Krotoszyn • Siera
Lubsko • Głogów • Rawicz • Ostrów Wielkopolski
Żary • Żagań • Lubin • Kępno • Wieluń
Bolesławiec • Brzeg Dolny • Trzebnica • Namysłów
Zgorzelec • Lubań • Jawor • Legnica • Oleśnica • Wrocław • Kluczbor
Jelenia Góra • Strzegom • Oława • Brzeg • Opole • Lublinie
Bogatynia • Świdnica • Strzelin • Strzelc Opole
Wałbrzych • Dzierżoniów • Ząbkowice Śląskie • Kędzierzyn
Nysa • Gliwice
Kłodzko • Paczków • Prudnik • Raciborz • Ryb
Głuchołazy • Jastrzęb
Hradec Králové • Głubczyce • Ostra
Cieszyr
Olomouc

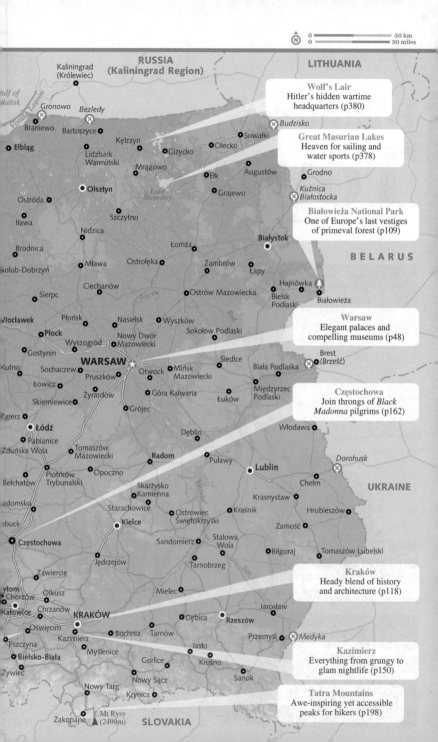

Poland's
Top 17

Stately Kraków

1 A unique atmosphere drifts through the attractive streets and squares of this former royal capital (p118), with its heady blend of history and harmonious architecture. From the vast Rynek Główny, Europe's largest medieval market square (pictured below left), to the magnificent Wawel Castle on a hill above the Old Town, every part of the city is fascinating. Add to that the former Jewish district of Kazimierz and its scintillating nightlife (and then contrast it with the communist-era concrete structures of Nowa Huta), and it's easy to see why Kraków is an unmissable destination.

Warsaw's Museums & Palaces

2 Poland's capital (p48) has an extravagantly dramatic history, and its best museums reflect that complex past. The city's darkest hour in the revolt against German Nazi rule is powerfully retold at the Warsaw Rising Museum; while Poland's long Jewish presence is related with energy at the Museum of the History of Polish Jews. Beautiful music can be heard at the Chopin Museum, and the Neon Museum presents a riot of communist-era colour. For stately charm, head to Wilanów Palace (pictured below), or Łazienki Park's lovely Palace on the Water.

S-F/SHUTTERSTOCK ©

MARCIN KRZYŻAK/SHUTTERSTOCK ©

Gdańsk

3 Colossal red-brick churches peer down on slender merchants' townhouses (pictured below), wedged ornately between palaces that line wide, ancient thoroughfares and crooked medieval lanes. A cosmopolitan residue of art and artefact left behind by a rich maritime and trading past packs whole museums, and tourists from around the world compete with amber stalls and street performers for cobblestone space. This is Gdańsk (p308); it was once part of the Hanseatic League, but now it's in a league of its own.

Wrocław

4 Throughout its turbulent history the former German city of Breslau (pictured bottom) has taken everything invaders could throw at it, and survived. Badly damaged in WWII, it was rebuilt around its main square. Another attraction is the *Panorama of Racławice*, a vast 19th-century painting hung about the walls of a circular building. Beyond historical gems, however, Wrocław (p239) has a vibrant nightlife, with plenty of dining and drinking options throughout the narrow streets of its lively Old Town. Cathedral of St John the Baptist (p244)

MANFRED GOTTSCHALK/GETTY IMAGES ©

WITOLD SKRYPCZAK/GETTY IMAGES ©

Malbork Castle

5 Medieval mother ship of the Teutonic order, Gothic blockbuster Malbork Castle (p345; pictured above) is a mountain of bricks held together by a lake of mortar. It was home to the all-powerful order's grand master and later to visiting Polish monarchs. They have all now left the stage of history, but not even the shells of WWII could dismantle this baby. If you came to Poland to see castles, this is what you came to see; catch it just before dusk when the slanting sunlight burns the bricks kiln-crimson.

Great Masurian Lakes

6 Sip a cocktail on the deck of a luxury yacht, take a dip, or don a life-jacket, grab your paddle and slide off into a watery adventure on one of the interconnected lakes (p378; pictured top right) that make up this mecca for Polish sailing and water-sports fans. Away from the water, head for one of the region's buzzing resorts, where the slap and jangle of masts competes with the clinking of glasses and the murmur of boat talk. In winter, when the lakes freeze over, cross-country skis replace water skis on the steel-hard surface.

Baltic Beaches

7 The season may be brief and the sea one of Europe's nippiest, but if you're looking for a dose of sand, there are few better destinations than the Baltic's cream-white beaches. Many people come for the strands along one of the many coastal resorts, be it hedonistic Darłówko, genteel Świnoujście (p361; pictured above right) or the spa town of Kołobrzeg (p358); others opt to flee the masses and head out instead for the shifting dunes of the Słowiński National Park (p353), where the Baltic's constant bluster sculpts mountains of sifted grains.

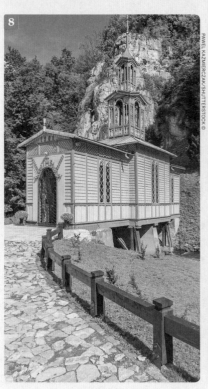

PAWEL KAZMIERCZAK/SHUTTERSTOCK ©

Folk Architecture

8 If the word 'skansen', referring to an open-air museum of folk architecture, isn't a part of your vocabulary yet, it will be after your trip to Poland. These great gardens of log cabins and timbered chalets make for a wonderful ramble and are testament to centuries of peasant life in Poland. The country's reputedly largest skansen is in Sanok (p214) in the Carpathians, but there are remnants of old wooden churches (pictured above) and other buildings at other open-air museums around the country. Chapel on the Water (p161)

Wolf's Lair

9 Wolf's Lair (p380; pictured top right), Hitler's headquarters during WWII, was so well designed that the Allies had no idea it existed until it was overrun by the Red Army in 1945. They might not have needed to had one of Hitler's own men, Colonel Claus von Stauffenberg, been more successful in his bid to assassinate the Führer here six months earlier. The ramshackle location, rapidly being reclaimed by nature, takes a little imagination to appreciate fully, but it's still one of Poland's most fascinating WWII heritage sites and marks a significant chunk of 20th-century history.

Sampling Vodka

10 For most Poles, the day-to-day tipple of choice is beer. But when it comes time to celebrate, someone's bound to break out the vodka (p39). And once that bottle is on the table, you can put to rest any notion about having a convivial cocktail. No one leaves until the bottle is finished. Poles make some of the world's best versions of the stuff and are not afraid to experiment. Proof of this: Żubrówka ('bison vodka'; pictured above) is flavoured with grass from the Białowieża Forest on which bison feed.

Gothic Toruń

11 While many of northern Poland's towns went up in a puff of red-brick dust in WWII's end game, Toruń (p334) miraculously escaped intact, leaving today's visitors a magnificently preserved, walled Gothic city by the swirling Vistula. Wander through the Old Town (pictured below), crammed with museums, churches, grand mansions and squares, and when you're all in, perk up with a peppery gingerbread cookie, Toruń's signature snack. Another treat is the city's Copernicus connections in one of Toruń's Gothic townhouses.

Black Madonna Pilgrimage

12 In many parts of Europe, religious buildings are often little more than historical sights or curiosities. It's refreshing, then, in Poland to find churches and monasteries that still feel lived in, and an integral part of everyday life. Nowhere is this more apparent than at the Jasna Góra monastery (p163) in Częstochowa. To see what we mean, pay a visit on 15 August, when the Feast of the Assumption (pictured bottom) draws hundreds of thousands of pilgrims to this relatively small city.

Nightlife in Kazimierz

13 Once a lively blend of both Jewish and Christian cultures, the western half of Kazimierz has become one of Kraków's nightlife hubs (p150; pictured below). Hidden among its narrow streets and distressed facades are numerous small bars, ranging from grungy to glamorous. The centre of all this activity is Plac Nowy, a small, atmospheric square dominated by a circular central building that was once the quarter's meat market. If Kraków's Old Town is becoming a bit staid for your taste, a night in Kazimierz will revive your spirits.

Hiking in the Tatras

14 In many ways, the Tatras (p198; pictured bottom) are the perfect mountain range: awe-inspiring yet accessible, with peaks that even ordinary folks – with a little bit of extra effort – can conquer. That doesn't diminish their impact, especially on a summer day when the clouds part to reveal the mountains' stern rocky visage climbing up over the dwarf pines below. The best approach to the peaks is from the Polish mountain resort of Zakopane.

PARIS/GETTY IMAGES ©

KEVIN CLOGSTOUN/GETTY IMAGES ©

Cycling in the Karkonosze

15 Slung between Mt Wielki Szyszak (1509m) to the west, and Mt Śnieżka (1602m) to the east, the Karkonosze National Park (p259) is not only a treat for hikers. Through its leafy expanse are threaded several mountain-biking trails, covering some 450km, that are easily accessed from the mountain towns of Szklarska Poręba (p260) or Karpacz (p262; pictured above). Pick up a free bike-trail map from the tourist office, hire a bike and head on out through the trees, passing impressively lofty cliffs carved by ice-age glaciers.

Białowieża National Park

16 That bison on the label of a bottle of Żubr beer or Żubrówka vodka starts to make a lot more sense once you've visited this little piece of pristine wood on the Belarus border. The Białowieża National Park (p109; pictured top right) holds one of Europe's last vestiges of primeval forest, which you can visit in the company of a guide. Nearby there's a small reserve with another survivor from a bygone era: the once-mighty European bison.

Auschwitz-Birkenau

17 This former ex-termination camp (p279; pictured above) is a grim reminder of a part of history's greatest genocide and the killing of more than a million people here. Now it's a museum and memorial to the victims. Beyond the infamous 'Arbeit Macht Frei' sign at the entrance to Auschwitz are surviving prison blocks that house exhibitions as shocking as they are informative. Not far away, the former Birkenau camp holds the remnants of the gas chambers used for mass murder. Visiting the complex is an unsettling but deeply moving experience.

Need to Know

For more information, see Survival Guide (p419)

Currency
Polish złoty (zł)

Language
Polish

Visas
Generally not required for stays up to 90 days.

Money
ATMs widely available. Credit cards accepted in most hotels and restaurants.

Mobile Phones
Local SIM cards can be used in European, Australian and some American phones. Other phones set to roaming.

Time
Central European Time (GMT/UTC plus one hour)

When to Go

Gdańsk •
GO Jun–Aug

• Poznań
GO May–Sep

• Warsaw
GO Sep–Oct

• Wrocław
GO May–Sep

• Kraków
GO May–Sep

Warm to Hot Summers, Cold Winters

High Season
(May–Sep)

➡ Expect sunny skies in June and July, but prepare for rain.

➡ Museums, national parks and other attractions are open for business.

➡ Expect big crowds, especially over holidays and at weekends.

Shoulder
(Mar & Apr, Oct)

➡ Some attractions may be closed or have shorter hours.

➡ April and October are cool, but expect some sunny days.

➡ Easter weekend can be very crowded; book in advance.

Low Season
(Nov–Feb)

➡ Snow in the mountains brings skiers to the southern resorts.

➡ The week between Christmas and New Year can be crowded.

➡ Museums and castles in smaller towns may be closed.

Useful Websites

Lonely Planet (www.lonely planet.com/poland) Destination information, hotel bookings, traveller forum and more.

Polish National Tourist Office (www.poland.travel) Official tourist site.

New Poland Express (www. newpoland express.pl) Overview of top news.

Warsaw Voice (www.warsaw voice.pl) Covers Polish current affairs.

Warsaw Tourist Information (www.warsawtour.pl) Official Warsaw tourist website.

InfoKraków (www.infokrakow. pl) Official Kraków tourist website.

Important Numbers

When calling between cities, it's no longer necessary to first dial ✆0.

Ambulance	✆999
Fire	✆998
Police	✆997
Emergency from mobile phone	✆112
Poland's country code	✆48

Exchange Rates

Australia	A$1	2.73zł
Canada	C$1	2.88zł
Europe	€1	4.12zł
Japan	¥100	3.02zł
New Zealand	NZ$1	2.50zł
UK	£1	5.82zł
USA	US$1	3.73zł

For current exchange rates, see www.xe.com.

Daily Costs

Budget: Less than 150zł

➡ Hostel dorm room or low-cost guesthouse: 50zł

➡ Meals in milk bars and self-catering: 40zł

➡ Train/bus tickets: 30zł

➡ Sundries: 10zł

Midrange: 200–300zł

➡ Room in a midrange hotel or pension: 100–120zł

➡ Lunch and dinner in decent restaurants: 80zł

➡ Train/bus tickets: 30zł

➡ Sundries: 20zł

Top End: More than 350zł

➡ Room in the best place in town: 200zł

➡ Lunch and dinner in the best restaurants: 100zł

➡ Train/bus/taxi: 50zł

➡ Sundries: 20zł

Business Hours

Shopping centres and malls are generally open longer hours than below, and from 9am to 8pm on Saturday and Sunday. Museums are almost invariably closed on Mondays, and have shorter hours outside high season.

See p422 for more information.

Arriving in Poland

Frédéric Chopin Airport (p428), Warsaw

Train 4.40zł, 20 minutes to Warszawa Centralna station

City Bus 4.40zł; bus 175 to the Old Town

Taxi About 60zł; 20 minutes to the Old Town

John Paul II International Airport (p428), Kraków

Train 10zł; 18 minutes to Kraków Główny station

City Bus 4zł; bus 292 or 208 to the bus station

Taxi About 80zł; 20 minutes to the Old Town

Lech Wałęsa Airport (p428), Gdańsk

City Bus 3zł; bus 110 to the suburb of Wrzeszcz

Taxi About 70zł; 30 minutes to the centre

Getting Around

Poland has an extensive network of trains and buses, though connections are most reliable between big cities. Transport is reasonably priced, though it's not always terribly quick or efficient.

Train Polish Rail/PKP Intercity trains offer affordable and fast service between major cities. For a handy train timetable, try Polish Rail's website: www. rozklad-pkp.pl.

Bus National Polski Bus (www. polskibus.com) service links big cities and can be faster than trains on some routes. Elsewhere, buses are useful for remote towns and villages that aren't serviced by trains.

Car Always handy for travelling at your own pace, but Polish highways can be narrow and crowded. Cars can be hired in many towns and cities. Drive on the right.

For much more on **getting around**, see p430

PLAN YOUR TRIP NEED TO KNOW

If You Like...

Castles

If there's a hilltop, you can bet there's a castle. Poland has some humdingers: everything from aristocratic, 19th-century piles to more sombre – and often more elegant – ruins.

Wawel Royal Castle The granddaddy of them all, the mighty Kraków Castle is the symbol of the Polish nation. (p120)

Malbork It took about a zillion red bricks to build Europe's biggest medieval fortress. (p345)

Książ Silesia's largest castle is a splendid edifice that holds a curious wartime secret beneath its foundations. (p255)

Krzyżtopór What you get when you cross magic, money and a 17th-century Polish eccentric. (p174)

Museums

Whether it's art, history, folk architecture or science, Poles are collectors at heart. Warsaw and Kraków, in particular, have some world-class collections.

Schindler's Factory Evocative museum within Oskar Schindler's former enamel factory tells the story of Kraków under German occupation in WWII. (p132)

Rynek Underground This museum lies beneath Kraków's vast market square and uses audiovisual wizardry to illuminate the city's trading history. (p126)

National Maritime Museum If maritime flotsam and jetsam float your boat, you'll love this museum complex in Gdańsk. (p315)

Chopin Museum A high-tech, interactive homage to Poland's greatest composer. (p59)

Communist Architecture

From the stern socialist-realist buildings of the 1950s to the wacky retro-futurist '60s and '70s, there's no denying that 40 years of communist rule made a mark on the country's built environment.

Kielce Bus Station Check out this flash, *Jetsons*-style bus station in a country where a handsome bus station is, admittedly, hard to find. (p170)

Palace of Culture & Science Stalin's 'gift' to the Polish people continues to shock and awe. (p61)

Nowa Huta This sprawling 1950s suburb makes a startling contrast to Kraków's Old Town. (p136)

Monument to the Victims of June 1956 Dramatic monument to the Poznań workers killed in a brutal crackdown. (p288)

Hiking

With everything from mountain treks to traversing a farmer's field, Poland is criss-crossed by thousands of kilometres of marked hiking trails.

Zakopane Just outside the door of your hotel, you'll find Poland's highest and most dramatic walks in the Tatras. (p198)

Bieszczady Green, clean and remote. This little corner wedged by Ukraine is as close to the end of the world as it gets in Poland. (p214)

Karkonosze National Park Hike the ridge between Mt Szrenica and Mt Śnieżka in this Silesian national park for views of forests and mighty cliffs. (p259)

Góry Stołowe Explore the strange and fascinating rock formations of this national park within the Sudetes Mountains. (p268)

Nightlife

Poles love to party. In summer, town squares across

the country are filled with tables and late-night revellers.

Praga Warsaw's 'right bank' is where the city goes to let down its hair. (p78)

Wrocław Thousands of university students have to have something to do on a Friday night. (p248)

Kazimierz This Kraków district is home to a plethora of cool, small bars, tucked behind attractive old facades in narrow streets. (p150)

Poznań A magnet for business people and local students, the city's Old Town is packed with lively pubs, clubs and eateries. (p293)

Folk Culture

Interest in folkways is growing. Skansens (open-air ethnographic museums) dot the landscape and the summer calendar is filled with folk-music fests.

Sanok The Museum of Folk Architecture here is the biggest in the country. (p215)

Tarnów The Ethnographic Museum here specialises in the folk history of the minority Roma. (p204)

Katowice This industrial city isn't the obvious place to find a skansen, but the Upper Silesian Ethnographic Park is spread over 20 hectares of city parkland. (p275)

Kashubia Traditional region of drowsy villages and ethnographic museums provides folksy contrast to the brashness of the coast. (p333)

Top: Wawel Cathedral (p121), Kraków
Bottom: Museum of Folk Architecture (p215), Sanok

Month by Month

January

January normally starts with a bang at midnight , but don't expect services to be fully restored until after the first week of the year.

✸ Kraków New Year

New Year's Eve celebrations are held around the country with fireworks and drinking. In Kraków there's that and also a classier alternative: a New Year's concert at the Teatr im Słowackiego. (p152)

🏃 Head for the Hills

Poland's festival pulse is barely beating. A better idea is to head south for a bit of skiing, such as to the country's main winter resort of Zakopane. (p200)

February

The winter ski season reaches its peak this month. The crowds on slopes worsen about mid-month, when schoolkids get the week off.

✸ Shanties in Kraków

In case you were wondering, a 'shanty' is a traditional sailor's song. Kraków's held this international shanty fest (shanties. pl) since 1981 and it's still going strong – in spite of Kraków's landlocked locale!

April

With ever-lengthening days, budding trees, and warm, sunny afternoons that promise better days ahead, Easter is a big travel weekend.

✸ Easter & Beethoven

Easter weekend is celebrated around the country, usually with a big dinner and lots of drinking. The annual Beethoven Easter festival (beethoven.org. pl) in Warsaw brings two weeks of concerts over the holiday season.

🏃 Cracovia Marathon

Kraków's marathon (zis. krakow.pl) has become an increasingly popular running event and now draws more than a thousand runners to its scenic course, which heads out from the Old Town.

May

May brings the return of reliably decent weather and the sound of students about to be freed from school. In Kraków, during Juvenalia, the students actually take over the city.

✸ Baltic Music

The Probaltica Music & Art Festival (probaltica.art.pl) in Toruń brings together traditional musicians from across the Baltic region.

✸ Sacral Music

Częstochowa is known as a Catholic pilgrimage site, but each May it shows off its ecumenical side with the 'Gaude Mater' Festival (gaudemater.pl), highlighting religious music from Christian, Jewish and Islamic faiths.

June

Summer gets rolling while festivals marking Corpus Christi (usually June, but sometimes May) can be raucous. The biggest is in Łowicz.

✯ Four Cultures

Each year, Łódź celebrates its historic role as a meeting place of Polish, Jewish, Russian and German cultures with this suitably named festival (4kultury. pl). There's theatre, music, film and dialogue.

☆ Theatre in Poznań

Poznań's Malta Festival (malta-festival.pl) is the country's biggest theatre and dramatic arts event. Expect a week of entertaining street theatre – and thousands of people competing for hotel rooms.

✯ Jewish Culture Festival

Kraków's Jewish Culture Festival (jewishfestival.pl), at the end of June and start of July, is one of the leading events of the year and ends with a grand open-air klezmer concert on ul Szeroka in Kazimierz.

July

Resorts are crowded, but not as bad as they will be in August. Festival season kicks into high gear.

✯ Rock around the Airport

Gdynia's Open'er Festival (opener.pl) of pop and indie rock is *the* summer event everyone in the Tri-City talks about. It's held

Top: Christmas market, Castle Sq (p52), Warsaw
Bottom: Cracovia Marathon, Kraków

the first week of July at the city's Kosakowo Airport. (p319)

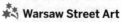 **Warsaw Street Art**

Warsaw's annual street arts festival (sztukaulicy.pl) brings five days of theatre, open-air art installations and 'happenings', staged in public places.

August

Expect big crowds at the sea as well as lake and mountain resorts, which worsen at weekends. You'll get sunshine, lots of festivals – and a *pierogi* (dumpling) fair in Kraków.

Getting Down with Highlanders

Zakopane's International Festival of Mountain Folklore (zakopane.pl) draws highlanders (mountain folk) from around Europe and the world for a week of music, dance and traditional costume.

St Dominic's Fair

Gdańsk's biggest bash (jarmarkdominika.pl) of the year has been held since 1260. Launched by Dominican monks as a feast day, the fun has spread to streets all around the Main Town. (p320)

September

Autumn arrives early in the month as kids return to school and life returns to normal. There's usually a long patch of sunshine in September.

Wratislavia Cantans

The unforgettably named Wratislavia Cantans (wratislaviacantans.pl) is Wrocław's top music and fine-arts confab. The focus is on sacral music but given a high-brow twist.

'Old' Jazz

Poznań's Old Jazz Festival (oldjazzfestival.pl), in late September, features a range of local and international jazz performers, both old and young, strutting their stuff at venues around town.

October

Tourist season is officially over, and castles and museums revert to winter hours or fall into a deep slumber.

Warsaw Reeling

The Warsaw Film Festival (wff.pl) highlights the world's best films more than 10 days in October. There are screenings of the best Polish films and plenty of retrospectives.

November

The first significant snowfalls begin in the mountains, though the ski season doesn't begin in earnest until December. Elsewhere, cool temps and darkening afternoons herald the coming of winter.

All Souls' Jazz

Cracovians fight the onset of the winter blues with the week-long Zaduszki Jazz Festival, which commences every year around All Souls' Day (2 November). Look for performances all over town, in clubs, bars and even churches.

St Martin's Day Croissants

Polish Independence Day falls on 11 November, but in Poznań it's also St Martin's Day, a day of parades and merriment. The real treat, though, is the baking and eating of special St Martin's Day croissants.

December

The air turns frosty and ski season in the south begins around the middle of the month.

Capital Christmas Market

Christmas markets are found around the country, but arguably the most evocative is in Warsaw's Old Town. A Christmas tree brightens Castle Sq (Plac Zamkowy) and market stalls, filled with mostly tat, spring up all around.

Kraków Christmas Cribs

December kicks off an unusual contest to see who can build the most amazing Christmas crèche. The *szopki* (Nativity scenes) are elaborate compositions in astonishing detail fashioned from cardboard, wood and tinfoil. (p141)

Itineraries

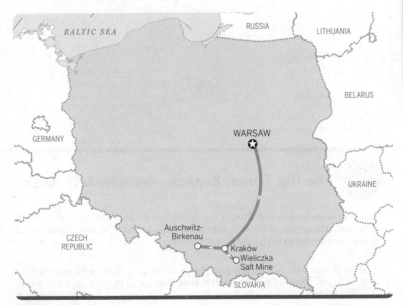

 Essential Poland

Poland's a big country with lots to see, so travellers with limited time will have to choose their destinations carefully. For first-time visitors, especially, the places to start are the capital, Warsaw, and the country's most popular city, Kraków. For a week-long tour, budget roughly three days in each, and a day for travel.

Warsaw is an eye-opener, a scintillating mix of postwar Soviet-style reconstruction and a lovingly restored Old Town, with Baroque and Renaissance architecture.

Leave at least a day for museum-hopping, particularly to the breathtaking Warsaw Rising Museum or newer attractions like the Chopin Museum and the Museum of the History of Polish Jews.

From Warsaw, the former royal capital of **Kraków** is a 180-degree turn. If Warsaw is 'old overlaid on new', Kraków is new on top of ancient. Spend a day in the Old Town and the Wawel Royal Castle, a second day around the former Jewish quarter of Kazimierz and the third day with a side trip to the **Wieliczka Salt Mine** (if you have kids in tow) or the memorial and museum of **Auschwitz-Birkenau**.

The Big Three: Kraków, Warsaw & Gdańsk

This tour visits Kraków and Warsaw before heading to the ravishing Baltic port city of Gdańsk. Though the tour can be done in 10 days, adding extra days allows for more travel time (needed to bridge the long distances) and a chance to tack on some more day trips.

Allow at least four days for **Kraków**, one of the most perfectly preserved medieval cities in Europe. As with the 'Essential Poland' tour, spend the first day meandering around Kraków's delightful Old Town. Don't miss the Rynek Underground museum and, naturally, St Mary's Basilica. The second day will be taken up with the sights of the Wawel Royal Castle. Spend the third day exploring the former Jewish quarter of Kazimierz. For the last day, plan a side trip to either the **Wieliczka Salt Mine** or **Auschwitz-Birkenau**. If you have an extra day, consider the mountain resort of **Zakopane**, two hours away by bus.

Take the train to **Warsaw** and plan to stay put another three to four days. The extra day leaves more time to see the city's amazing museums, as well as to enjoy the sights of the Old Town and stroll down elegant ul Nowy Świat. If you're up for a night of drinking, the gritty dive-bar hood of Praga beckons from across the Vistula. A more sedate pleasure involves a walk through lovely Łazienki Park. For day trips, consider **Wilanów Palace**, 6km south of the centre, or a full-day journey to the former Nazi-German extermination camp at **Treblinka**.

From Warsaw, take the train to **Gdańsk** and prepare to be dazzled by the stunningly restored Main Town, which, like Warsaw, was reduced to ruins in WWII. Proceed down the Royal Way and don't miss the Amber Museum. Then there's the waterfront district and pretty ul Mariacka.

If it's summer and you're lucky enough to get a warm day, spend your last full day on the water, at either the brash but popular beach resort of **Sopot** or the quieter, more refined strand on the **Hel Peninsula**.

Along the Vistula

The Vistula is Poland's greatest river, winding its way from the foothills of the country's southern mountain range to the Baltic Sea. It's played a key role in Poland's very identity, as it passes through – or close to – many of its oldest and most important settlements.

Ideally suited to roaming, this tour is for visitors who are not on a strict timetable and are looking for an unusual approach to Poland's core. The four-week schedule assumes that you rely on buses (train services to many of these towns have been cut back in recent years). Naturally, if you have your own wheels, you could cover the terrain in three weeks or even less.

Begin upstream with two or three days at the former royal capital of **Kraków** and take a day tour to the memorial and museum at **Auschwitz-Birkenau** in Oświęcim. From Kraków, make your way by bus to beautiful **Sandomierz**, one of Poland's undiscovered delights, with its impressive architectural variety and position on a bluff overlooking the river. From here, it's worth taking a detour, again by bus, to the Renaissance masterpiece of **Zamość**, a nearly perfectly preserved 16th-century town.

Back on the path along the Vistula, stop in at the former artists colony – now a popular weekend retreat – of **Kazimierz Dolny**, before hitting **Warsaw** and indulging in its attractions for a few days. Next, call in at **Płock**, Poland's Art Nouveau capital, then follow the river into Pomerania and through the heart of medieval **Toruń**, another nicely preserved Gothic town that also boasts being the birthplace of stargazer Nicolaus Copernicus.

Soon after Toruń, the river heads directly for the sea. In former times, the Vistula's path was guarded by one Teutonic Knight stronghold after another. Today, these Gothic gems silently watch the river pass by. You can see the knights' handiwork at **Chełmno**, **Kwidzyn** and **Gniew**, but the mightiest example resides at **Malbork**, on the banks of one of the river's side arms. End your journey in the port city of **Gdańsk**, where the river meets the sea.

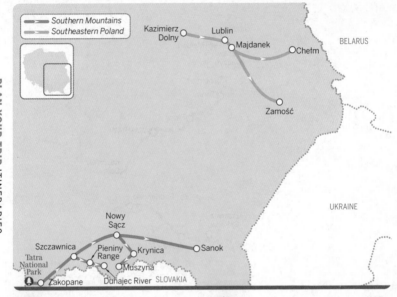

Southern Mountains

1 WEEK

Poland's southern border is lined with mountains end to end. This itinerary is ideal for walkers who want to escape the city. Though this trip can be done in a week, bus transport can be spotty in parts.

Start in the mountain resort of **Zakopane**, easily reached by bus from Kraków. Allow at least a day to see the town's historic wooden architecture and the Museum of Zakopane Style, and another for a walk into the **Tatras** (or more for a longer trek).

From here you'll have to make some tough choices. We like the **Pieniny** range, east of the Tatras. The spa town of **Szczawnica** makes a good base for hikes, as well as biking and the ever-popular rafting ride down the **Dunajec River**.

From Szczawnica, the medium-sized city of **Nowy Sącz** offers urban comforts, or opt for **Krynica** or **Muszyna**, two popular spa resorts and good jumping-off points for more hikes.

A long bus ride from Nowy Sącz brings you to **Sanok**, with its amazing skansen (open-air ethnographic museum) and access to the 70km Icon Trail and its wooden churches.

Southeastern Poland

1 WEEK

The southeastern corner of Poland is seldom explored and a good place to see the country off the beaten path. Begin in **Lublin**, whose Old Town has been much spruced up in recent years, with some great places to see and eat. Don't miss Lublin Castle or the chance to clamber up the Trinitarian Tower for a commanding view of the countryside. Spend a half-day at the enormous **Majdanek** concentration camp on the outskirts of the city.

Use Lublin as a base to explore **Chełm**, best known for its underground Chalk Tunnels. It also has some very worthwhile Jewish heritage sights and restaurants.

Lublin also makes a nice base for visiting the popular riverside artists retreat at **Kazimierz Dolny**. The town is filled with museums and charming galleries, and the surrounding fields and forests make for a perfect day out on a bike or on foot.

From Lublin, head south to the self-proclaimed (with justification) 'Pearl of the Renaissance': **Zamość**. This perfectly preserved 16th-century Renaissance town has a lively central square, which hosts summertime concerts and music fests.

Cities of the West

1 WEEK

Western Poland is borderland terri-tory, straddling a region hotly contested between Poland and Germany over the centuries. **Wrocław**, with its good trans-port connections, makes a logical start and merits at least two days. This was the former German city of Breslau, and the architecture retains a Germanic flavour with a Polish pulse. After WWII, Wrocław was repopulated by refugees from Poland's eastern lands lost to the Soviet Union, giv-ing the city an added ethnic dimension.

From here make your way to **Poznań**, a thriving commercial hub with an in-toxicating mix of business and pleasure, the latter fortified by a large student popu-lation. It was in Poznań that the Polish kingdom got its start a millennium ago.

After Poznań, the beautifully preserved Gothic town of **Toruń** is a short bus or train ride away. It boasts enchanting red-brick architecture and gingerbread cookies.

Finish the tour in either **Gdańsk** or **Szczecin**, the latter adding a gritty contrast to the architectural beauty of the other cities.

Eastern Borderlands

3 WEEKS

Poland's eastern border region feels especially remote. Indeed, this swath of natural splendour is largely cut off from the day-to-day goings-on in the rest of Poland. This itinerary will appeal to wan-derers who prefer the solitude of nature to the hustle-bustle of the big city.

Start in **Kraków** for convenience's sake, but head quickly to **Sanok**, with its skansen and icon museum, and then head deeper into the **Bieszczady National Park**. Turn north and take the back roads to the Renaissance town of **Zamość**, via **Przemyśl**. Continue on to **Chełm** to see the underground chalk tunnels and then to the big-city comforts of **Lublin**.

Strike out north through rural back-waters to **Białowieża National Park** and its primeval forest and bison herd. Head north again to the provincial city of **Białystok** and the hamlet of **Tykocin**, with its unforgettable synagogue.

From here is a wealth of parklands: the **Biebrza** and **Wigry National Parks**, and the **Great Masurian Lakes**, all with excellent hiking and boating possibilities.

Plan Your Trip

Outdoor Activities

Poland is not widely known as a haven for adrenalin junkies, but perhaps it should be. What better way could there be to slow down, meet some of the locals and leave the beaten track far behind? Why experience Poland through the window of a train, pickled in a museum or through the lens of a camera when you can hire a bike, grab a paddle or put on a pair of walking boots and get some fresh air?

Best Outdoor Activities

Best Hiking
Tatra Mountains (p201), Pieniny Mountains (p234), Bieszczady Mountains (p221)

Best Kayaking
Krutynia River (p373), Drawa Route (p33), Brda River (p33)

Best Cycling
Bieszczady Mountains (p214), Sudetes Mountains (p255)

Best Skiing
Tatra Mountains (p198), Sudetes Mountains (p255)

Best Water Sports
Great Masurian Lakes (p378), Augustów and around (p112)

Best Time to Go

Summer (June to August) The best time for walking, cycling and kayaking

Late spring (May) and early autumn (September) The months either side of summer can be sunny and the trails, lakes and waterways less frequented

Winter (November to March) The best time for skiing and snowboarding in the mountain ranges of the south

Then & Now

Poles have a tradition of outdoor fun going back to the 19th century, when the first walking trails were marked out through the mountain ranges in the south. Polish hikers and climbers can always be found in the world's mountaineering hot spots, and the country has financed many expeditions around the world, including to the Himalayas.

Foreign travellers started to get in on the action decades ago, but it's only since the fall of communism that Poland has been discovered as an outdoor destination. Tour operators are increasingly catering to the demands of adventurers from around the world, offering improving facilities and serving up a wider range of adrenalin hits.

Cycling

Almost every region of Poland now has well-signposted cycling routes, from short and easy circuits to epic international routes, and the situation is improving by the year. It's possible to restrict yourself to the flatter regions of the country and travel the rest by train, but if you're not deterred by gradients you can cycle some of the more riveting (and relatively unexplored) regions. Maps showing cycling trails can be hard to source outside Poland, but tourist offices can normally supply good cartography.

Where to Cycle

Carpathian Mountains

Some epic bicycle adventures are waiting in the Bieszczady ranges. These tracks will roll you through a montage of deep forest green and rippling meadows, opening up intermittently to postcard-perfect natural and architectural panoramas. Part of the 70km **Icon Trail** (p216) near the town of Sanok is accessible to cyclists and rewards pedalling with views of old timber churches and castles. The town of Sanok lies astride a sprawling network of bike-friendly roads and pathways that covers hundreds of kilometres in Poland and extends to neighbouring Slovakia and Ukraine. The town's municipal website (www.gminasanok.com) maintains a good overview of the trails in English.

The region around the Dunajec River |in the Pieniny isn't just for rafting. **Szczawnica** (p233), in particular, is a great cycling centre. It's the starting point for several rewarding rides and is blessed with numerous bike-rental outfits. One of the region's best rides follows the Dunajec River for around 15km all the way to the Slovak town of Červený Kláštor.

Białowieża Forest

There are some enchanting routes (starting near the village of Białowieża) through the northern part of the Białowieża Forest and the large stretches of undisturbed woods that lie to the north and west of **Białowieża National Park** (p110), including detours into parts of the park itself. Pick up a map from the park's information centre and head off. If you need wheels, try **Rent a Bike** (p110).

> ## CYCLING WEBSITES
> **Cities for Bicycles** (www.rowery.org.pl)
>
> **Cycling Holidays Poland** (www.cyclingpoland.com)
>
> **EuroVelo** (www.ecf.com)
>
> **Central & Eastern European Greenways** (www.greenways.by)

The Northeast

Cycling in the Masuria region is rewarding, and also pretty easy as the terrain is as flat as a board. The town of **Węgorzewo** (p381) on Lake Mamry is a convenient base from which to access 18 marked routes ranging from 25km to 109km circuits. The **Augustów Forest** (p114) and the areas around **Suwałki** (p115) are also great biking territories. You'll find a few bike-rental outfits in Augustów, including locally run rental Jan Wojtuszko (p113).

Sudetes Mountains

The Sudetes, especially the area around the town of **Szklarska Poręba** (p260), are a jackpot for mountain bikers. Stretching to the Czech border, **Karkonosze National Park** (p259) offers myriad marked mountain-biking trails and is popular with Polish extreme-sports enthusiasts. Some of the trails now cross over into the Czech Republic. The **Szklarska Poręba tourist office** (p261) can help with maps and advise on rentals.

Cycling Tours

Most cyclists go it alone in Poland, but if you fancy joining an organised group, UK-based Cycling Holidays Poland (p104) is the leading specialist company to contact. Otherwise you could try **Hooked on Cycling** (UK +44 1506 635 399; www.hooked

> ## SAFE CYCLING
> ➡ Where possible, stay on marked cycling trails. Motorists are rarely cycle-conscious, while Poland's roads, especially away from major routes, can be atrocious. Ride defensively.
>
> ➡ Among the big cities, Kraków appears to be making the best inroads for cyclists, and the cycling routes along the river are scenic and safe.
>
> ➡ Even small towns have at least one cycle shop selling spare parts and offering a cheap repair service.

oncycling.co.uk), which specialises in self-guided two-wheeled tours across Europe.

Walking & Hiking

Poland's mountainous areas are a joy to explore on foot and attract thousands of hikers every year and in every season. There are around 2000km of walking trails sliced through the country's national parks, and many are well marked and well equipped with shelters. Nature's repertoire of heights, gradients, climates and terrains is showcased in Poland: hiking options range from week-long treks for the hardcore hiker to hour-long rambles for the ascent averse. The **PTTK** (Polish Tourist and Sightseeing Society, Polskie Towarzystwo Turystyczno-Krajoznawcze; 📞22 826 2251; www.pttk.pl) has a notoriously wonky website, but it's still an excellent resource for hiking and walking in all parts of the country. The website has a list of PTTK-run mountain huts and info centres, and lots of other useful info for planning a trek.

Where to Walk & Hike

The southern mountain ranges are best for exhilarating high-altitude hikes, but low-level walks can be found across the country.

Carpathian Mountains

The **Tatra Mountains** (p201) in the south are the most notable region for hiking Polish-style. The West and the High Tatras offer different scenery; the latter is more challenging and as a result more spectacular. One of the most popular climbs in the Tatras is Mt Giewont (1894m). The cross at the peak attracts many visitors, though the steep slopes deter some.

The valleys around Zakopane offer walks of varying lengths for walkers of

varying fitness levels (some take less than an hour). Similarly, trails around the nearby **Pieniny** (p234) and the **Bieszczady** (p221) in the east offer exciting hiking experiences – even for those who prefer to stroll. Another great option is **Beskid Sądecki** (p230), which has convenient paths dotted with mountain hostels. Muszyna and Krynica are popular bases from which to access this region.

The lower **Beskid Niski** (p224) mountain range offers less arduous walks and less spectacular views.

Your first port of call in each of these areas should be the local tourist information office.

Sudetes Mountains

The **Karkonosze National Park** (p259) offers a sterling sample of the Sudetes. The ancient and peculiar 'table top' rock formations of the Góry Stołowe (Table Mountains) are among the highlights of the Sudetes. The area is easily accessed from the town of Szklarska Poręba at the base of Mt Szrenica (1362m), and there is a choice of walking trails from Karpacz to Mt Śnieżka (1602m). Further south, the village of Międzygórze is another well-kitted-out base for Sudetes sojourns. Tourist offices in Karpacz and Szklarska Poręba stand ready to point you to suitable trails and mountain hostels.

Other Regions

➡ The **Augustów Forest** (p114) in the Augustów-Suwałki region has 55 lakes and many well-paved roads and dirt tracks. Diverse wildlife can be found in various stretches of the forest. There are numerous bays and peninsulas to explore around nearby Lake Wigry in the **Wigry National Park** (p117), and the 63-sq-km **Suwałki Landscape Park** (p116) offers drop-dead-gorgeous views from its picturesque terrain.

➡ The lowest mountain range in the country is in the **Świętokrzyski National Park** (p170) in Małopolska, near Kielce. There's a 17km walk here that takes you past an ancient hilltop holy site that's now a picturesque monastery.

➡ **Roztocze National Park** (p194) offers a range of light walks through gentle terrain, and the landscape park surrounding **Kazimierz Dolny** (p185) offers some easy but worthwhile rambles.

MOUNTAIN GUIDES

Two commendably practical walking guides for the Tatras are *High Tatras: Slovakia and Poland*, by Colin Saunders and Renáta Nároźná, published in 2012, and the harder-to-find but still excellent *Tatra Mountains of Poland and Slovakia*, by Sandra Bardwell, published in 2006.

POLAND'S NATIONAL PARKS: TOP 10 FOR ACTIVITIES

Poland has 23 national parks featuring a wide variety of landscapes. Check their websites for more information on hiking and cycling routes. Ask in person before you assume any route is open.

NATIONAL PARK	FEATURES	ACTIVITIES	BEST TIME TO VISIT	WEBSITE
Białowieża (p109)	primeval forest; bison, elk, lynx, wolf	wildlife watching, hiking	spring, summer	www.bpn.com.pl
Biebrza (p106)	river, wetland, forest; elk, great snipe, aquatic warbler	birdwatching, canoeing	spring, autumn	www.biebrza.org.pl
Kampinos (p85)	forest, sand dunes	hiking, mountain biking	summer	www.kampinoski-pn.gov.pl
Karkonosze (p259)	mountains; dwarf pine, alpine flora	hiking, mountain biking	summer, winter	www.kpnmab.pl
Narew (p108)	river, reed beds; beaver, waterfowl	birdwatching, canoeing	spring, autumn	www.npn.pl
Ojców (p161)	forest, rock formations, caves; eagle, bat	hiking	autumn	www.ojcowskipark narodowy.pl
Roztocze (p194)	forest; elk, wolf, beaver, tarpan	hiking	spring, autumn	www.roztoczanskipn.pl
Słowiński (p353)	forest, bog, sand dunes; white-tailed eagle, waterfowl	hiking, birdwatching	all year	www.slowinskipn.pl
Tatra (p201)	alpine mountains; chamois, eagle	hiking, climbing, skiing	all year	www.tpn.pl
Wolin (p352)	forest, lake, coast; white-tailed eagle, bison	hiking, birdwatching	spring, autumn	www.wolinpn.pl

➡ There is also Kampinos National Park (p81) just outside Warsaw, with its famed sand dunes, Wielkopolska National Park (p297) in Wielkopolska, and the compact Wolin National Park (p352) in northwest Poland.

Walking Tours

Many local companies and individual guides operate along the tracks and trails of Poland's wild side. If you are looking to organise a guided trek from home, UK-based **Venture Poland** (☏UK +44 20 7558 8179; www.venturepoland.eu) specialises in organised walking tours of the Carpathian Mountains, while **Walks Worldwide** (☏UK +44 1962 737 565; www.walksworldwide.com; ⊙8am-6pm Mon-Fri, 9am-5pm Sat) covers all the southern mountain ranges.

Canoeing, Kayaking & Rafting

Choices of where to kayak in Poland flow freely: the lowlands of Masuria, Warmia and Kashubia in Poland's north offer literally thousands of lakes and rivers to choose from. Further to the east is the **Augustów Canal** (p113), and the lakes and rivers connected to it. Just south of Augustów there's a series of seldom-visited national parks that offer more kayaking opportunities in a protected and isolated environment of river tributaries and bogs.

There's no need to haul your kayak through airports either, as there are plenty of hire centres, where boats, paddles and life jackets can be rented for very reasonable rates, as well as numerous tour companies

Top: Danajec Gorge (p235), from Mt Sokolica

Left: Kayaking, Krutynia River (p373)

POSZTOS/SHUTTERSTOCK ©

and guides. Local tourist offices can usually point you in the right direction.

Where to Get Paddling

Great Masurian Lakes

The town of **Olsztyn** (p371) is a handy base for organising adventures on water, particularly kayaking. **PTTK Mazury** (p432) here organises trips, equipment and guides. From Olsztyn it's possible to canoe the Łyna River to the border of Russia's Kaliningrad enclave, or spend a couple of laid-back hours floating closer to the city.

The most popular kayaking route in the Great Masurian Lakes area runs along the **Krutynia River** (p373), originating at Sorkwity, 50km east of Olsztyn, and follows the Krutynia River and Lake Bełdany to Ruciane-Nida. Some consider Krutynia the most scenic river in the north and the clearest in Poland. It winds through 100km of forests, bird reserves, meadows and marshes. To get a taste of the river (hopefully not literally), PTTK Mazury in Olsztyn runs popular 10-day kayaking tours along the Krutynia, starting at the **Stanica Wodna PTTK** (www.sorkwity.pttk. pl) in Sorkwity. Tours depart at regular intervals from June to August, and the price (1190zł) includes a kayak, food, insurance, lodging in cabins and a Polish-, English- or German-speaking guide. You can also do the trip on your own, hiring a kayak (30zł to 40zł per day) from the Stanica Wodna PTTK in Sorkwity, but check availability in advance.

Koch (☑89 751 1093; www.masuren2.de; ul Sportowa 1) is a tour company based at Kętrzyn's Hotel Koch that can arrange all kinds of adventures in the Great Masurian Lakes.

Augustów-Suwałki Region

Less visited than the renowned Great Masurian Lakes (and arguably cooler than them, too), the lakes of the **Augustów-Suwałki region** (p112) are not connected, but their waters are crystal clear. The river to paddle in these parts is the Czarna

Hańcza, generally from Augustów along the Augustów Canal, all the way to the northern end of Lake Serwy. This route takes in the 150-year-old Augustów Canal, the Suwałki Lake District and the Augustów Forest. Numerous tour operators cover this loop, but it is also possible to do this and other routes independently.

Close to the city of Suwałki, Lake Wigry in the **Wigry National Park** (p117) offers surprisingly pristine paddling. In the Augustów-Suwałki region, check in with **Szot** (p114) in Augustów, which offers an excellent selection of short and long trips and English-friendly guides.

South of the Masurian Lakes, the Biebrza River runs through the scenic splendour of the Podlasie region and through **Biebrza National Park** (p106), with its varied landscape of river sprawls, peat bogs, marshes and damp forests. The principal kayaking route here flows from the town of Lipsk downstream along the Biebrza to the village of Wizna, for a distance of about 140km (seven to nine days). While this is longer than most people will have time for, shorter stretches are also possible and camping sites dot the river along the way to allow for overnight stops.

The **Narew National Park** (p108), further south, is just as interesting as the Biebrza National Park, but not as geared toward visitors. This park protects an unusual stretch of the Narew River that's nicknamed the 'Polish Amazon', where the river splits into dozens of channels. For adventures in this part of Podlasie, check in with **Kaylon** (p108) for canoeing and kayaking adventures.

Pomerania

The most renowned kayaking river in Pomerania is the Brda, which leads through forested areas of the **Bory Tucholskie National Park** (www.pnbt. com.pl) and past some 19 lakes.

The Drawa Route, which runs through **Drawa National Park** (www.dpn.pl), is an interesting trip for experienced kayakers. The Drawa Route is believed to have been a favourite kayaking jaunt of Pope John Paul II when he was a young man.

Carpathian Mountains

The organised rafting trip to do in Poland is the placid glide through the **Dunajec Gorge** (p235) in the Pieniny. The river

---

RESCUE SERVICES
....
General emergency ☑112

Mountain rescue ☑601 100 300

Water rescue ☑601 100 100

PLAN YOUR TRIP OUTDOOR ACTIVITIES

TREK SAFE

To ensure you enjoy your walk or hike in comfort and safety, put some thought into your preparations before hitting the trail.

➡ Obtain reliable information about the conditions and characteristics of your intended route from local national-park authorities.

➡ Buy a suitable map from the local bookshop or tourist office.

➡ If possible, always inform someone of your route and when you expect to be back.

➡ Weather conditions can be unpredictable in mountainous areas, so pack appropriate clothing and equipment and check the weather forecast.

➡ Be aware of the local laws, regulations and etiquette about flora and fauna.

➡ Always be ready to turn back if things start to go wrong.

➡ If planning to overnight in a mountain hut, try to reserve in advance or at least let someone know you're coming. Otherwise you risk not having a place to sleep.

snakes from Czorsztyn Lake (Jezioro Czorsztyńskie) west between several steep cliffs, some of which are over 300m high. The river is narrow, in one instance funnelling through a 12m-wide bottleneck, and changes incessantly from majestically quiet, deep stretches to shallow mountain rapids. Be advised, however, that this is not a white-water experience but a leisurely pleasure trip. The outing begins in the small village of Sromowce Wyżne-Kąty, at the **Raft Landing Place** (p235). You'll take an 18km-long float and disembark in Szczawnica. The journey takes about 2¼ hours, depending on the level of the river. Some rafts go further downstream to Krościenko (23km, 2¾ hours), but there's not very much to see on that stretch of the river.

Skiing & Snowboarding

If you haven't skied before, perhaps Poland is the place to start, if only because you'll pay less for the privilege here than elsewhere in Europe. Accommodation in ski-resort areas can range from 50zł for rooms in private homes up to the more luxurious 300zł hotel options. Ski-lift passes cost around 100zł per day.

Southern Poland is well equipped for cross-country and downhill skiers of all abilities and incomes, though there's nothing budget about the scenery.

Where to Ski

Obviously, the mountain ranges of southern Poland are the places to snap on skis, though there's plenty of cross-country skiing in other flatter locations, especially around (and on) the lakes of Masuria.

Tatra Mountains

The Tatras are the best-equipped skiing area and the country's winter-sports capital of Zakopane is the most popular place to slither. The slopes of this region, which peak at **Kasprowy Wierch** (p200) (1987m), are suitable for all skill levels, and Zakopane has good equipment and facilities. As well as challenging mountains (such as Kasprowy Wierch and **Gubałówka** (p200), with runs of 4300m and 1500m respectively), the varied terrain around Zakopane offers flat land for beginners and plenty of time to learn, with a generous ski season lasting into April some years.

Sudetes Mountains

Another centre of outdoor action is **Szklarska Poręba** in Silesia, at the foot of Mt Szrenica (p260; 1362m). The city offers almost 15km of skiing and walking routes, and great cross-country skiing. The nearby town of Karpacz on the slopes of Mt Śnieżka (1602km) enjoys around 100 days of snow per year. The **Karpacz Tourist Office** (p263) website has an excellent round-up of downhill and cross-country skiing options, as well as options for snowboarding and snow tubing. The town of Międzygórze also hosts ski enthusiasts, who venture out to the **ski centre** (p264) at the 'Black Mountain' of Czarna Góra.

Beskid Śląski

The village of Szczyrk, at the base of the Silesian Beskids, has less severe slopes and far shorter queues than elsewhere in the country. Szczyrk is home to the Polish Winter Olympics training centre and has mild enough mountains for novice skiers and snowboarders. See Szczyrk's official website (www.szczyrk.pl) for information on ski routes, ski schools, equipment hire and tourist services.

Other Outdoor Activities

Horseback Riding

It's worth spending some time in the saddle in Poland – a country that has enjoyed a long and loyal relationship with the horse. National parks, tourist offices and private equestrian centres have become quite proficient in marking routes and organising horseback holidays along them.

The **PTTK** (p30) can assist with organising independent horse riding through its Mountaineering and Horse Riding division. There are many state-owned and private stables and riding centres throughout the country, from rustic agrotourism establishments to luxurious stables fit for a Bond film. It's also possible to organise riding tours of a few hours, or a few days, through numerous private operators. The cost of undertaking these experiences varies depending on duration and level of luxury. A down-to-earth horseback ride on a pony for a week can cost around €800, while a weekend at a fine estate with access to steed-studded stables can cost upwards of €500. Shop around until you find something that suits your taste, ability and budget.

For more on horse-riding holidays, take a look at the **Polish Equestrian Association** (🖉22 417 6700; www.pzj.pl). There's lots of information here, but note that it's all in Polish.

Boating & Sailing

There's an underexplored seafaring culture in Poland. It's possible to hire yachts or sailing ships complete with their own shanty-singing skipper. The Baltic coast attracts some craft, but the summer crowds testify to the sailing suitability of the Great Masurian Lakes, which truly live up to their name. This sprawling network of interconnected lakes allows sailors to enjoy a couple of weeks on the water without visiting the same lake twice.

You can hire sailboats in Giżycko, Mikołajki and several smaller villages. In Giżycko, the **tourist office** (p384) maintains a list of boats and yachts for hire on its web page, and also offers good first-hand advice in person. In Mikołajki the **Wioska Żeglarska** (p384), on the waterfront, has sailing boats for hire, and staff may be able to advise you on other companies if their boats are booked out.

Boat enthusiasts will get a particular thrill from excursions on the **Elbląg-Ostróda Canal** (p376) in the Olsztyn region. The 82km canal is the longest navigable canal still in use in Poland. It's also the most unusual. The canal deals with the 99.5m difference in water levels by means

---

WHERE TO RIDE

Białowieża National Park Offers the chance to ride (or use horse-drawn carriages and sleighs in winter) on nondesignated routes through forests. Contact the National Park Information Centre (p111) for details.

The Bieszczady Several bridle paths cross the Bieszczady range, including within Bieszczady National Park. The best place to organise a trip is in the town of Ustrzyki Dolne. The town's helpful tourist office (p220) is a good place to get started.

Lower Silesia Offers the 360km Sudety Horse-Riding Route. The privately operated **Horse Ranch Sudety-Trail** (www.sudety-trail.eu) runs all kinds of equestrian packages, suited to both novices and experienced riders, for two to six people from May to November.

Masurian Lake District Ride horses around the lakes. For some inspiration, check out the Masurian Lake District tourist website (www.masurianlakedistrict.com). The **Old Smithy Inn** (Karczma Stara Kuźnia; www.starakuznia.com.pl), near Giżycko, is housed in a 19th-century Prussian manor house, and offers guided rides as well as meals and overnight stays.

of a unique system of slipways, where boats are physically dragged across dry land on rail-mounted trolleys. The canal follows the course of a chain of six lakes, most of which are now protected conservation areas. From May to September, pleasure boats operated by **Żegluga Ostródzko-Elbląska** (p376) sail the main part of the canal between Ostróda and Elbląg. Trips of various durations are offered. For a nice taste of canal life, try the run from Elbląg as far as Buczyniec (from 99zł, 4½ hours), which covers the most interesting part of the canal, including all five slipways.

Baltic Sea sailing takes place on the bay at **Szczecin** (p363), shared by Germany and Poland. Sailors can visit **Wolin Island and National Park** (p352) when sailing this 870-sq-km bay. The bay in Gdańsk also offers access to sea harbours and quaint fishing towns.

In the Carpathian Mountains, **Solina Lake** (p222) is the Bieszczady region's most important centre for water sports, including boating and recreation. It's about 30km southwest of Ustrzyki Dolne and accessible by bus. The **Solina Lake tourist office** (p222), just off Hwy 894 on the way to Lesko, can supply you with all the details.

Windsurfing & Kitesurfing

Windsurfing and kitesurfing are mostly done in the same areas that attract sailors, but the true heartland is Hel – the Gulf of Gdańsk between Władysławowo and Chałupy along the Baltic coast. The arbitrary dance of wind and currents constantly changes the shape of the enticingly named **Hel Peninsula** (p331). The Great Masurian Lakes may be popular, but there's no place like Hel. Gdańsk-based **JoyTrip** (p325) is a good tour company to contact for equipment hire etc.

Hang-Gliding & Paragliding

Hang-gliding and paragliding are taking off in Poland, particularly in the southern mountains, starting around Zakopane and moving eastward. The website www.paraglidingmap.com/sites/Poland maintains a good list of launch sites, complete with pictures and weather forecasts. A popular place from which to start is the top of **Kasprowy Wierch** (p200), south of Zakopane, though bear in mind that at 1967m, the elevation is high and winds can be strong. For more information, enquire at tourist offices and tour operators in **Zakopane** (p198).

Climbing & Caving

The Tatras offer opportunities for beginner and advanced climbers. Contact the Polish Mountain Guides Society (www.pspw.pl, in Polish only, though you can send an email in English) for further information and a list of qualified guides.

There are more than 1000 caves in the country, but few are ready for serious spelunking. A good one is **Bear's Cave** (www.jaskinia.pl), near the village of Kletno, in Silesia, southeast of the city of Kłodzko. It's reachable by car and is situated on the elevation of Śnieżnik Kłodzki, on the right slope of the Kleśnica valley. Check the website for details, and note that you must reserve a tour in advance.

There are two caves in the Kraków-Częstochowa Upland. **King Łokietek Cave** (p161) stretches over 270m through several passages and can be visited on a 30-minute tour. Nearby **Wierzchowska Górna Cave** (p162) is the longest in the region and goes on for nearly 1km.

Geocaching

This newish sport/activity, a GPS-based treasure-hunting game, may not be as popular in Poland as it is in other countries such as the UK, but an ever-increasing number of Poles are now finding their way to it. The websites www.opencaching.pl and www.geocaching.pl are good places to start. Fans may also want to check out the Twitter feed of geocachingpl (www.twitter.com/geocachingpl) for a great source on current trends and trails. Tweets are normally in Polish but can be deciphered fairly easily with an online translator.

Plan Your Trip

Eat & Drink Like a Local

Polish food, with its reliance on local ingredients such as potatoes, cucumbers, beets, mushrooms, buckwheat and apples, reflects the country's long agrarian tradition. The necessity of making food last the winter means the cuisine is rich in pickles, preserves, smoked fish and meat. Foraged wild foods, such as mushrooms and berries, add seasonal character to dishes in uniquely Polish ways.

Polish Specialities

Bread

Chleb (bread) has always meant more than sustenance to Poles. It's a symbol of good fortune and is sacred to many; some older people kiss a piece of bread if they drop it on the ground. Traditional Polish bread is made with rye, but bakeries nowadays turn out a bewildering array of loaves, including those flavoured with sunflower, poppy and sesame seeds, and raisins and nuts.

Soup

Every substantial meal in Poland traditionally begins with *zupa* (soup), and Poland has some good ones. Rye is a staple ingredient in what will likely become a staple order of yours: *żurek*. This soup is made with beef or chicken stock, bacon, onion, mushrooms and sour cream, and given a distinctive tart flavour through the addition of *kwas* (a mixture of rye flour and water that has been left to ferment for several days). It's often accompanied by a hard-boiled egg or *kiełbasa* (Polish sausage) and served inside a hollowed-out loaf of bread.

As Polish as *żurek,* but not as unique, is *barszcz* (or *barszcz czerwony*), a red beetroot soup known in Russia as borscht that can be served as *barszcz czysty* (clear borscht), *barszcz z uszkami* (borscht with tiny ravioli-type dumplings stuffed with meat) or *barszcz z pasztecikiem* (borscht with a hot meat- or cabbage-filled pastry).

Best Seasonal Foods

While many Polish staples are served year-round, each season brings something a little special.

Spring

Strawberries Strawberry season arrives in late spring; look for them layered on ice cream, poured over cakes and stuffed inside *pierogi* (dumplings).

Summer

Berries The Polish summer yields raspberries, blackberries and blueberries. These national treasures are usually poured over pancakes or stuffed inside *pierogi*.

Autumn

Mushrooms Poles are crazy about mushrooms, and the cool, damp mornings of early autumn are perfect for picking. Mushrooms are used in soups, as a stuffing for pastries and in sauces.

Winter

Beetroot soup Beets are a staple of Polish cooking and the cold winters bring a renewed appreciation for this oft-overlooked red root. Beetroot soup is a cherished part of the traditional Christmas Eve meal.

Pierogi

Pierogi (or 'Polish raviolis') are square- or crescent-shaped dumplings made from dough and stuffed with anything from cottage cheese, potato and onion to minced meat, sauerkraut and fruit. They are usually boiled and served doused in melted butter.

Pierogi are highly versatile and can be eaten as a snack between meals or as a main course for lunch or dinner. They're a budget traveller's dream. No matter how fancy a restaurant is, the chef will usually be able to whip up an order of *pierogi* for anything from 15zł to 25zł.

They can also be a vegetarian's best friend: many of the more popular versions, especially the ubiquitous *pierogi ruskie* (Russian *pierogi),* stuffed with cottage cheese, potato and onion, are meatless. Just remember to tell the waiter to hold the bacon bits. Popular variations to look for:

➡ *pierogi z mięsem* – stuffed with spicy minced meat, normally pork

➡ *pierogi z serem* – with cottage cheese

➡ *pierogi z kapustą i grzybami* – with cabbage and wild mushrooms

➡ *pierogi z jagodami* – with blueberries

➡ *pierogi z truskawkami* – with wild strawberries

Kiełbasa

What would a trip to Poland be without sampling some of the country's signature sausages? *Kiełbasa* is normally eaten as a snack or as part of a light lunch or dinner, served with a side of brown bread and mustard. It's usually made with pork, though other meats, like beef and veal, can be added to lend a distinctive flavour. The sausages are generally seasoned with garlic, caraway and other spices.

The most popular type, *Wiejska kiełbasa,* is a thick cylinder of pork, spiced with garlic and marjoram, that probably comes closest to the type of *kiełbasa* known outside of Poland. Some other popular varieties:

➡ *kabanosy* – thin pork sausages that are air-cured and seasoned with caraway seeds

➡ *krakowska* – as the name implies, these originated in Kraków, though they're found throughout the country; usually thick and seasoned with pepper and garlic

➡ *biała* – thin white sausages sold uncooked and then boiled in soups such as *żurek staropolski* (sour barley soup with white sausage)

Bigos

If there's one dish more genuinely Polish than any other, it might just be *bigos*. It's made with sauerkraut, chopped cabbage and meat, including one or more of pork, beef, game, sausage and bacon. All the ingredients are mixed together and cooked over a low flame for several hours, then put aside to be reheated a few more times.

As with French cassoulet, this process enhances the flavour. The whole operation takes a couple of days and the result can be mouth-watering. Every family has its own well-guarded recipe, and you will never find two identical dishes.

Because it's so time-consuming, *bigos* does not often appear on a restaurant menu and the version served in cheap eateries and cafes is often not worth its name – though you can find worthy variations at Polish festivals and fairs.

Pork

Polish menus appear to be an egalitarian lot, usually featuring a range of dishes made from beef, chicken and pork, as well as other meats like turkey or duck. But don't let that fool you. The main event is almost always *wieprzowina* (pork), and Poles have come up with some delicious ways to prepare it:

➡ *golonka* – boiled pig's knuckle, usually served with horseradish and sauerkraut

➡ *kotlet schabowy* – breaded pork chops

➡ *schab wieprzowy* – succulent roast loin of pork

➡ *dzik* – wild boar, a rare treat but one worth trying if you get the chance

Regional Dishes

There are regional specialities across the country – freshwater fish dishes in the north, aromatic duck preparations in Wielkopolska, large dumplings called *kluski* in Silesia that are often served with bacon *(kluski śląskie ze słoniną)* – but nowhere are these regional dishes so well defined as in the Podhale at the foot of the Tatras. Among some of the things to try here are *kwaśnica* (sauerkraut soup), *placki po góralsku* (potato pancakes served with goulash) and the many types of *oscypek* (smoked sheep's-milk cheese) that come in oblong shapes with distinctive stamps on the rind. Buckwheat groats *(kasza gryczana)* are a delicious side dish – and a nice change of pace from the more common rice or potatoes. They are typically found in rural areas or in simpler restaurants around the country.

Vodka

Poles love their *wódka* (vodka) – only the Russians drink more per capita – and make some of the best in the world. While drinking habits are evolving in Poland, and most Poles normally relax over a glass of beer or wine, vodka remains the drink of choice when it comes to holidays, special occasions, or simply times when only vodka will do.

The most popular type of vodka in Poland, as with much of the rest of the world, is *czysta* (clear) vodka, but this is not the only species of the *wódka* family. Look around for some of these varieties:

➡ *wyborowa* – wheat-based clear vodka

➡ *żytnia* – rye-based vodka, with a whole spectrum of varieties, from sweet to extra dry

➡ *myśliwska* – means 'hunter's vodka' and tastes not unlike gin

➡ *pigwówka* – flavoured with quince (not too tart, not too sweet and our favourite of the moment)

➡ *wiśniówka* – flavoured with cherries

➡ *cytrynówka* – flavoured with lemon

➡ *pieprzówka* – flavoured with pepper

➡ *żubrówka* – ('bison vodka') flavoured with grass from the Białowieża Forest on which bison

---

MEALS OF A LIFETIME

Poland is filled with great restaurants, and some of the very best meals can be found in some of the country's tiniest hamlets.

Restauracja Tejsza (p106) The Talmudic house behind the synagogue in the eastern town of Tykocin is home to Poland's best home-cooked kosher – and arguably the best *pierogi* (dumplings), too.

W Starym Siole (p222) Open-air dining in the Carpathian village of Wetlina, with grilled fish and great wines.

Restauracja Jadka (p248) This Wrocław treasure presents impeccable modern takes on Polish classics, silver-service table settings and Gothic surrounds.

Warszawa Wschodnia (p76) Housed within an atmospheric former factory in Warsaw's grungy Praga district, this eatery brings a 21st-century sensibility to Polish classics, melding them with a French influence.

Carska (p111) Silver-service restaurant in what was once the tsar's private railway station in Białowieża.

Bajeczny (p303) In Kalisz, a great example of how an old communist-era *bar mleczny* (milk bar) can be updated to become an attractive budget option.

Gothic (p347) Conveniently (and surprisingly) situated in Malbork Castle itself, this is one of the north's top restaurants.

Sąsiedzi (p147) High-end Polish restaurant in Kraków's Kazimierz district with a lovely, secluded garden.

Velevetka (p322) The best place in Gdańsk to sample authentic Kashubian fare such as duck with apple sauce and Baltic fish dishes.

Spiżarnia Warmińska (p373) Great new organic place in Olsztyn where most of the ingredients are locally sourced and seasonal.

HOW TO DRINK VODKA IN POLAND

Vodka is usually drunk from a 50mL shot glass called a *kielisze* and downed in a single gulp – *do dna* (to the bottom). A small snack (often a pickle or piece of pickled herring) or a sip of mineral water is consumed just after drinking to give some relief to the throat. Glasses are immediately refilled for the next drink and so on until the bottle is empty. Poles say, 'The saddest thing in the world is two people and just one bottle'.

As you may expect, unless you're a seasoned drinker, at this rate you won't be able to keep up for long. Go easy and either miss a few turns or sip your drink in stages. Though this will be beyond the comprehension of a 'normal' Polish drinker, you, as a foreigner, will be treated with due indulgence. If you do get tipsy, take comfort in the fact that Poles get drunk, too – and sometimes rip-roaringly so. *Na zdrowie!* (Cheers!)

feed (or as local wags have it, 'on which bison peed')

Generally, clear vodka should be served chilled. Flavoured vodkas don't need as much cooling, and some are best drunk at room temperature. While all vodkas were traditionally drunk neat and – horror of horrors – *never* mixed as cocktails, that too is changing and some experiments have been very successful. *Żubrówka* and apple juice – known as a *tatanka* (buffalo) – is a match made in heaven.

Beer

There are several brands of locally brewed Polish *piwo* (beer); the best include Żywiec, Tyskie, Okocim and Lech. Beer is readily available in shops, cafes, bars, pubs and restaurants – virtually everywhere – and is almost always lager (as opposed to dark or wheat beer).

In addition to Polish beer, labels from the neighbouring Czech Republic, such as Staropramen, Pilsner Urquell, Bernard, Holba and Primátor, have become quite popular. We're not choosing sides here, but even Poles generally regard Czech beer as (slightly) superior. There's a small but growing microbrew community in large cities like Warsaw, Kraków and Gdańsk.

Don't ask us why, but you'll soon see that Poles (particularly women) like to flavour their beer with fruit juice, usually *sok malinowy* (raspberry juice). It's then drunk through a straw.

How to Eat Like a Local

When to Eat

Poles tend to be early risers and *śniadanie* (breakfast) is taken between 6am and 8am.

Polish breakfasts are similar to their Western counterparts and may include *chleb z masłem* (bread and butter), *ser* (cheese), *szynka* (ham), *jajka* (eggs) and *herbata* (tea) or *kawa* (coffee). Hotels and pensions normally offer a *szwedzki bufet* (Swedish-style buffet), consisting of these items as well as slices of cucumber and tomatoes, pickles and occasionally something warm like a pot of scrambled eggs, *kiełbasa, parowki* (frankfurters) or pancakes. Normally, the only coffee available is instant, but some places are starting to offer mini espresso machines (hoorah!).

Obiad (lunch) normally kicks off a bit later than you might be used to, around 1pm or 2pm, and can stretch to as late as 3pm or 4pm. It's traditionally the most important and substantial meal of the day.

The evening meal is *kolacja* (supper). The time and menu vary greatly: sometimes it can be nearly as substantial as *obiad,* but more often it's just sliced meats with salad, or even lighter – a pastry and a glass of tea.

Where to Eat

Normally you'll eat in a *restauracja* (restaurant), a catch-all expression referring to any place with table service. They range from unpretentious eateries where you can have a filling meal for as little as 20zł, all the way up to luxurious establishments that may leave a big hole in your wallet.

The menus of most top-class restaurants are in Polish with English translations, but don't expect foreign-language listings in cheaper eateries (nor waiters speaking anything but Polish).

A cheaper but usually acceptable alternative to a restaurant is a *bar mleczny* (milk bar). This is a no-frills, self-serve cafeteria that offers mostly meat-free dishes at very low prices. The 'milk' part of the name reflects the fact that no alcohol is served. You can fill up for around 15zł to 20zł.

Milk bars open around 8am and close at 6pm (3pm or 4pm on Saturday); only a handful are open on Sunday. The menu is posted on the wall. You tell the cashier what you want, then pay in advance; the cashier gives you a receipt, which you hand to the person dispensing the food. Once you've finished your meal, return your dirty dishes (watch where other diners put theirs). Milk bars are very popular and there are usually queues.

Menu Advice

Polish menus can be quite extensive and go on for several pages. You'll soon get a general feel, though, for how they're organised, and that doesn't change much from place to place. Menus are normally split into sections, including *zakąski* (hors d'oeuvres), *zupy* (soups), *dania drugie* or *potrawy* (main courses), *dodatki* (side dishes), *desery* (desserts) and *napoje* (drinks). The main courses are often split further into *dania mięsne* (meat dishes), *dania rybne* (fish dishes), *dania z drobiu* (poultry dishes) and *dania jarskie* (vegetarian dishes).

The name of the dish on the menu is accompanied by its price and, in milk bars in particular, by its weight. The price of the main course doesn't normally include side orders such as potatoes, chips and salads; these must be chosen from the *dodatki* section. Only when all these items are listed together is the price that follows for the whole plate of food. Also note that for menu items that do not have a standard portion size – most commonly fish – the price given is often per 100g. When ordering, make sure you know how big a fish (or piece of fish) you're getting.

Etiquette

Dining out in Poland is fairly straightforward and not much different from eating out anywhere else. Expect slower service, perhaps, than you might get in other destinations, particularly if it's a crowded place. To speed things up, you're welcome (even encouraged) to grab your own menus when you enter a restaurant; there will likely be a stack by the door.

Many places, particularly outdoor cafes, are self-service, so if no one comes to your table right away, it might be a sign you're expected to fetch your own drinks and make food orders at the counter.

Polish restaurants are not particularly kid-friendly. Children are always welcome, of course, and some places even have special children's menus, but you won't usually find high chairs or even lots of room to push a stroller through in many places.

Service leans toward the officious, rather than the overly friendly. Expect competent and often excellent results from the kitchen. Occasionally, though, your order may be misunderstood by the server or botched in the kitchen. Unless it's a major mistake, though, refrain from sending food back as it inevitably creates ill will and will delay the meal even more. Tip 10% of the tab for good service (slightly more for an extraordinary experience).

CHEAP TREATS

There are some uniquely Polish snacks to sample on the go. While strolling the *ulica*, look for the following:

➡ *zapiekanki* – the street snack of choice, 'Polish pizza' is an open-faced baguette topped with melted cheese, chopped mushrooms and ketchup, and best (or only) eaten after a heavy night on the town.

➡ *naleśniki* – perfect any time, these are pancakes stuffed with fruit or cottage cheese and topped with a strip of jam, powdered sugar and a dollop of sour cream.

➡ *obwarzanek* – an irresistible cross between a pretzel and a bagel topped with poppy seeds, sesame or salt. Native to Kraków but occasionally found elsewhere.

➡ *oscypek* – smoked highlander sheep's-milk cheese, usually found in mountain areas south of Kraków. Usually grilled and served with *żurawiny* (cranberry jam).

➡ *lody* – ice cream isn't native to Poland, but it's cheap and Poles can't get enough of the stuff.

Regions at a Glance

Which region of Poland you choose to focus on will depend on whether you prefer an active holiday, centred on hiking, boating and biking, or one involving more sedentary, urban-based pursuits, such as museums, cafes and clubs.

For the latter, Poland's trilogy of great cities, Kraków, Warsaw and Gdańsk, offers excellent museums, restaurants and other urban amenities. Kraków, in particular, escaped damage in WWII and is an unmissable mix of modern and medieval.

If sports are on the card, consider the regions of Warmia and Masuria, and Mazovia and Podlasie. Both of these are considered lake country, with abundant kayaking, hiking and biking opportunities. The mountains in the south are covered in hiking paths and the place to go to get away from it all.

Warsaw

History
Nightlife
Food

Engaging Museums

In Warsaw, the conflicts of WWII are not just the stuff of dusty history tomes but events that resonate to the present and are brought to life in thought-provoking, interactive museums.

Dives to Cocktail Bars

With tens of thousands of students, Warsaw has it all when it comes to whiling away the hours between sundown and sunup, with classic dives, funky coffee shops, trendy cocktail bars and happening clubs.

Culinary Capital

Warsaw is the food capital of Poland. Not only are the best Polish restaurants here, but there's a thriving international food scene too, along with a surprising number of new and trendy vegan places.

p48

Mazovia & Podlasie

Nature
Water Sports
Museums

Primeval Forest

Podlasie is home to three of the country's best national parks, including Białowieża, which claims a small patch of Europe's last remaining primeval forest. Birders will appreciate the abundant waterfowl at Biebrza National Park.

River Paddling

The Suwałki region in the extreme northeast is a quieter version of the Masurian Lakes and is home to canals, rivers and lakes that invite hours of canoeing and kayaking.

Film History

The city of Łódź may not be much to look at, but there's a lot to see, including two great art museums, a stunning history museum and a quirky museum to the greats of Polish cinema.

p87

Kraków

Museums
Nightlife
Food

Schindler's Factory

Poland's former royal capital has plenty of excellent museums, including several on Wawel Hill. Newer, high-tech institutions include the Rynek Underground and Oskar Schindler's old enamel factory.

Kazimierz Crawls

From quiet bars to nightclubs, Kraków has it all. The best options are its Old Town cellar pubs and the character-packed bars and cafes of Kazimierz.

Street Eats

Kraków has argu-ably Poland's best street-food scene, complete with late-night sausage stands, food trucks, an open-faced cheese baguette known as *zapie-kanka* (or, tongue in cheek, 'Polish pizza') and the humble pretzel-bagel hybrid, *obwarzanek*.

p118

Małopolska

Religious History
Heritage
Architecture

Place of Pilgrimage

Częstochowa's Jasna Góra monastery is one of the most important pilgrim-age destinations for Catholics, and the monastery retains a feeling of hushed holiness, even for nonbelievers.

Jewish Remnants

Pre-WWII, Lublin was a leading centre for Jewish scholars, and there is now a fascinating self-guided Jewish herit-age trail. Chełm was similarly important. The region was, sadly, home to three of Nazi Germany's most notorious ex-termination camps.

Gothic & Renaissance

Sandomierz is one of Poland's Gothic treasures, with a beautifully pre-served town square; the city of Zamość calls itself the 'Pearl of the Renaissance', with good reason.

p159

Carpathian Mountains

Hiking
Architecture
Spas

Tranquil Treks

Walkers are spoilt with choice in the Carpathians. Want drama? Go for the Tatras. Solitude? Head for the Bieszc-zady. The chance to mix a bit of boating with a hike? The Pieniny.

Wooden Treasures

The Carpathians are sprinkled with the traditional wooden architecture of the country's indigenous highlander popula-tion. In Zakopane, this architecture was raised to an art form. Beyond this, old wooden churches dot the countryside.

Hot Springs

The Carpathian region is blessed with abundant hot springs, and that means spas. Krynica is one of the largest and most popular. Szczawnica, on the Dunajec River, is smaller and quieter.

p196

Silesia

Mountains
Nightlife
Architecture

Rock Climbing

Bordered by the Sudetes Mountains, Silesia is a hiker's dream. The Karkon-osze National Park offers hikes among craggy cliffs, while the Góry Stołowe mountains are dot-ted with strange rock formations perfect for climbing.

Student Pubs

Silesia's cultural capital, Wrocław, is a major university town, and thou-sands of students translate into hun-dreds of bars, pubs and clubs.

Gothic to Modern

Silesia's tumultu-ous history has left its mark on the diverse built envi-ronment, including the bizarre Chapel of Skulls at Kudowa-Zdrój, the grand facades of Wrocław and the modernist lines of Katowice.

p237

Wielkopolska

History
Cycling
Food

Poland's Birthplace

Wielkopolska's deep history is seen every where: from the cathedrals of Poznań and Gniezno to the plentiful museums across the region that document events from the Middle Ages to the communist era.

Country Roads

One of the flattest parts of Poland, the region is a great place to hire a bike and hit the road, whether it be in Poznań or in the rural countryside.

Cutting-Edge Cuisine

Poznań has as sophisticated and varied a restaurant scene as any big city in Poland, from cheapie milk-bar survivors to cutting-edge casual dining.

p281

Gdańsk & Pomerania

Architecture
Beaches
Folk Festivals

Red-Brick Churches

Medieval Poland's masons must have been busy building the north's hundreds of churches, castles, walls and town halls. Even the Red Army couldn't put a dent in this red-brick wealth, and postwar reconstruction restored many buildings to their former glory.

Baltic Bathing

Poland's Baltic sea coast may be chilly, but when the sun shines and the winds abate, there's no better place for a spot of beach fun than the stretches of white sand along the northern coast.

Kashubian Culture

Inland from the coast you'll find the local Kashubian culture thriving at festivals, celebrations and the open-air museum in Wdzydze Kiszewskie.

p305

Warmia & Masuria

Lakes
Water Sports
Architecture

Sailing

Poland has more lakes than any other country in Europe except Finland – and most are in Masuria. The Great Masurian Lake area boasts Poland's biggest body of water, Lake Śniardwy.

Swimming & Rowing

Where there's water, there's sport, and the Great Masurian Lakes are no exception. This is the best place in Poland to don flippers, grab a paddle or hire a yacht for a bit of waterborne R&R.

Architecture

Away from watery attractions, the region has some remarkable architecture, starting with the Baroque church at Święta Lipka and followed by the red-brick majesty of Lidzbark Warmiński's castle.

p369

On the Road

Historic Cities

Poland has been around more than a millennium, and its cities reflect the architectural and economic changes over the centuries. Many important cities, including Warsaw, Gdańsk and Wrocław, were damaged in WWII and rebuilt. Others, such as Kraków and Toruń, emerged unscathed and look and feel much as they always have.

FOTOLUPA/SHUTTERSTOCK ©

PATRYK KOSMIDER/SHUTTERSTOCK ©

1. Kraków (p118)
Wawel Royal Castle (p120) incorporates 14th-century Gothic structures and 16th-century Renaissance and Baroque styles.

2. Wrocław (p239)
A view over the Old Town of Wrocław.

3. Warsaw (p48)
Although much of the city was destroyed during WWII Warsaw's Old Town was reconstructed to look as it was.

4. Gdańsk (p308)
The Żuraw (Crane) was built in the mid-15th century and was the largest medieval crane in Europe.

JEROEN P/GETTY IMAGES ©

Warsaw

POP 1.74 MILLION

Best Places to Eat

→ Charlotte (p75)

→ Mango (p74)

→ Cô Tú (p74)

→ Warszawa
Wschodnia (p76)

→ Dwie Trzecie (p76)

Best Places to Stay

→ Castle Inn (p71)

→ Hotel Rialto (p73)

→ Hotel Bristol (p72)

→ Oki Doki Hostel (p71)

→ New World Street
Hostel (p71)

Why Go?

Once you've travelled around Poland, you realise this: Warsaw is different. Rather than being centred on an old market square, the capital is spread across a broad area with diverse architecture: restored Gothic, communist concrete, modern glass and steel.

This jumble is a sign of the city's tumultuous past. Warsaw has suffered the worst history could throw at it, including virtual destruction at the end of World War II – and survived. As a result, it's a fascinating collection of neighbourhoods and landmarks. Excellent museums interpret its complex story, from the joys of Chopin's music to the tragedy of the Jewish ghetto.

It's not all about the past, however. Warsaw's restaurant and entertainment scene is the best in Poland. You can dine well and affordably here on cuisines from around the world, and take your choice of lively bars and clubs. This gritty city knows how to have fun.

When to Go
Warsaw

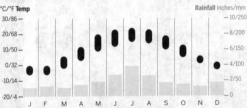

Mar–May Watch the trees bud and flowers bloom on a stroll through bucolic Łazienki Park.

Jun & Jul Midsummer brings a week of happenings around town during the Street Art Festival.

Oct Film buffs will enjoy 10 days of Polish and international film at the Warsaw Film Festival.

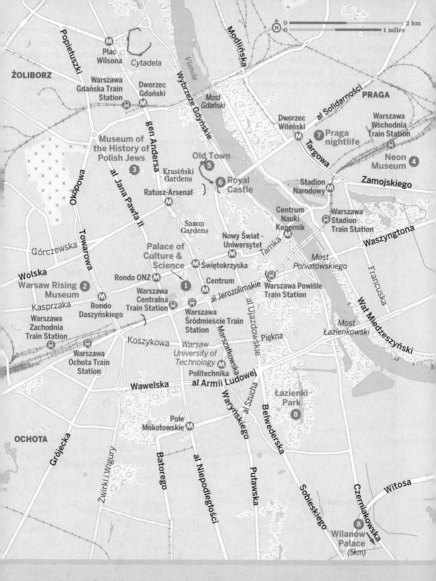

Warsaw Highlights

1 Taking in Warsaw and beyond from the **Palace of Culture & Science** (p61).

2 Listening to first-hand accounts of WWII at **Warsaw Rising Museum** (p64).

3 Learning about Poland's long Jewish history at the **Museum of the History of Polish Jews** (p64).

4 Exploring the **Neon Museum** (p68) and restaurants at the Soho Factory complex in Praga.

5 Marvelling at the quality of the restoration work in the **Old Town** (p52).

6 Taking in the regal splendour of the **Royal Castle** (p52).

7 Tapping into the capital's nightlife, whether it's clubbing with the beautiful people in the city centre or exploring the gritty bar scene of **Praga** (p78).

8 Admiring Warsaw's palaces at **Łazienki Park** (p66) and **Wilanów** (p69).

History

Warsaw's history has had more than its share of ups and downs. But like the essence of the Polish character, Warsaw has managed to return from the brink of destruction time and time again.

The first semblance of a town sprang up around the beginning of the 14th century, when the dukes of Mazovia built a stronghold on the site of the present Royal Castle. In 1413 the dukes chose Warsaw as their seat of power, and things went swimmingly for over 100 years until, in 1526, the last duke died with-

Warsaw

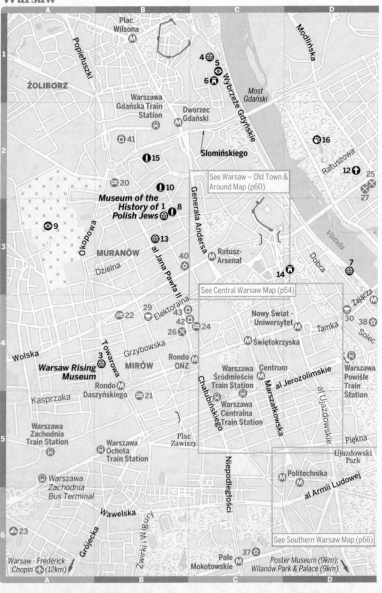

out an heir. The burgeoning town – and the whole of Mazovia – fell under the direct rule of the king in Kraków and was incorporated into royal territory.

Warsaw's fortunes took a turn for the better after the unification of Poland and Lithuania in 1569, when the Sejm (the lower house of parliament) voted to make Warsaw the seat of its debates because of its central position in the new, larger country. The ultimate ennoblement came in 1596, when King Zygmunt III Waza decided to move his capital from Kraków to Warsaw.

The Swedish invasion from 1655 to 1660 was not kind to Warsaw, but the city recovered and continued to develop. Paradoxically, the 18th century – a period of catastrophic decline for the Polish state – witnessed Warsaw's greatest prosperity. A wealth of palaces and churches was erected, and cultural and artistic life flourished, particularly during the reign of the last Polish king, Stanisław August Poniatowski.

In 1795 the city's prosperity was again shattered. Following the partition of Poland, Warsaw's status was reduced to that of a provincial town of the Russian Empire. When Napoleon arrived in 1806 on his way to Russia, things started looking up. The warring Frenchman created the Duchy of Warsaw and the city became a capital once more. The celebrations were brief, however, as in 1815 Warsaw, and much of the rest of Poland, fell back under Russian rule.

After WWI Warsaw was reinstated as the capital of newly independent Poland, and the urban development and industrialisation begun in the late 19th century continued. By 1939 the city's population had grown to 1.3 million. This included 380,000 Jews, who had long been a significant part of Warsaw's population.

German bombs began to fall on 1 September 1939 and a week later the city was besieged; despite brave resistance, Warsaw fell in a month. The conquerors terrorised the local population with arrests, executions and deportations, and a Jewish ghetto was built. The city's residents rebelled against the Germans twice; first came an eruption in the Jewish ghetto in April 1943, followed by the general Warsaw Rising in August 1944. Both revolts were cruelly crushed.

At the end of the war, the city of Warsaw lay in ruins and 800,000 people – more than half of the prewar population – had perished. (By comparison, the total military casualties for US forces in WWII was 400,000, for UK forces 326,000.) A massive rebuilding project was undertaken soon after, including the meticulous reconstruction of the historic Old Town. Despite more than 40 years of Communist rule, the city adapted well to the fall of the regime. As the business centre of Poland, Warsaw became the focus of economic growth,

Warsaw

and now corporate towers have joined Stalin's Palace of Culture on the city skyline.

◎ Sights

◎ Old Town

Though it's a relatively recent reconstruction, Warsaw's Old Town (Stare Miasto) looks as though it's been there for centuries. It's the first (and sometimes only) part of the city tourists hit, and with good reason: this small quarter holds numerous historic attractions, including the Royal Castle and St John's Cathedral. It's also fun just to hang around here; the attractive Old Town Square is always buzzing.

Sigismund III Vasa Column   MONUMENT
(Kolumna Zygmunta III Wazy; Map p60; Plac Zamkowy) A natural spot from which to start exploring the Old Town is triangular Castle Sq (Plac Zamkowy). Attracting tourists by the hundreds each day is the square's centrepiece, the Sigismund III Vasa Column. This lofty 22m-high monument to the king who

moved the capital from Kraków to Warsaw was erected by the king's son in 1644 and is Poland's second-oldest secular monument (after Gdańsk's Neptune fountain).

It was knocked down during WWII, but the statue survived and was placed on a new column four years after the war. The original, shrapnel-scarred granite column now lies along the south wall of the Royal Castle.

★ Royal Castle   CASTLE
(Zamek Królewski; Map p60; www.zamek-krolewski.pl; Plac Zamkowy 4; adult/concession 23/15zł; ⊙10am-6pm Mon-Sat, 11am-6pm Sun) This massive brick edifice, a copy of the original blown up by the Germans in WWII, began life as a wooden stronghold of the dukes of Mazovia in the 14th century. Its heyday came in the mid-17th century, when it became one of Europe's most splendid royal residences. It then served the Russian tsars and, in 1918, after Poland regained independence, became the residence of the president. Today it is filled with period furniture and works of art.

Highlights of the castle tour include the Great Apartment and its magnificent Great

Assembly Hall, which has been restored to its 18th-century decor of dazzling gilded stucco and golden columns. The enormous ceiling painting, *The Disentanglement of Chaos*, is a postwar re-creation of a work by Marcello Bacciarelli showing King Stanisław bringing order to the world. The king's face also appears in a marble medallion above the main door, flanked by the allegorical figures of Peace and Justice.

The neighbouring National Hall was conceived by the king as a national pantheon; the six huge canvases (surviving originals) depict pivotal scenes from Polish history. A door leads off the hall into the smaller Marble Room, decorated in 16th-century style with coloured marble and trompe l'oeil paintwork. The room houses 22 portraits of Polish kings, from Bolesław Chrobry to a gilt-framed image of Stanisław August Poniatowski himself.

Further on from the National Hall is the lavishly decorated Throne Room. Connected by a short corridor is the King's Apartment, the highlight of which is the Canaletto Room at the far end. An impressive array of 23 paintings by Bernardo Bellotto (1721–80), better known in Poland as Canaletto, captures Warsaw's mid-18th century heyday in great detail. The works were of immense help in reconstructing the city's historic facades.

★**Old Town Square**   SQUARE
(Rynek Starego Miasta; Map p60) At the centre of the partially walled Old Town (Stare Miasto), the Old Town Sq is, for those with an eye for historic buildings, the loveliest square in Warsaw. It's lined with tall houses exhibiting a fine blend of Renaissance, Baroque, Gothic and neoclassical elements; aside from the facades at Nos 34 and 36, all were reconstructed after destruction in WWII.

Warsaw Museum   MUSEUM
(Muzeum Warszawy; Map p60; www.muzeum warszawy.pl; Rynek Starego Miasta 28-42) On the northern side of the Old Town Sq, this museum tells Warsaw's dramatic story. Its film covering the reconstruction of the city, screened several times daily (the English version at noon), is fascinating.

The museum is currently closed for a major renovation and modernisation, and is due to reopen in 2016. Check with the tourist office for updated hours and entry fees.

St John's Cathedral   CATHEDRAL
(Archikatedra Św Jana; Map p60; ul Świętojańska 8; crypt 2zł; ⊘10am-1pm & 3-5.30pm Mon-Sat) Considered the oldest of Warsaw's churches, St John's was built at the beginning of the 15th century on the site of a wooden church, and subsequently remodelled several times. Razed during WWII, it regained its Gothic shape through postwar reconstruction. Look for the red-marble Renaissance tomb of the last dukes of Mazovia in the right-hand aisle, then go downstairs to the crypt to see more tombstones, including that of Nobel Prize–winning writer Henryk Sienkiewicz.

Barbican   FORTRESS
(Barbakan; Map p60; ul Nowomiejska) Heading north out of the Old Town along ul Nowomiejska you'll soon see the redbrick Barbican, a semicircular defensive tower topped with

WARSAW IN...

One Day
Start a tour of Warsaw at the **Royal Castle** (p52), a former Mazovian stronghold. Spend the rest of the morning exploring the evocative backstreets of the **Old Town** (p52), then head to the New Town for lunch. Enjoy the attractive facades along ul Krakowskie Przedmieście and ul Nowy Świat, before crossing town to the **Warsaw Rising Museum** (p64). Wait until late afternoon to take in the view from the top of the **Palace of Culture & Science** (p61), then round the day off with dinner at one of the many good restaurants south of al Jerozolimskie.

Two Days
Begin the day with one of the big museums. Depending on your interests, it could be the **Museum of the History of Polish Jews** (p64), the **Chopin Museum** (p59) or the quirky **Neon Museum** (p68). Head back toward ul Nowy Świat for lunch before travelling south of al Jerozolimskie to pass the early afternoon in beautiful **Łazienki Park** (p66). Late afternoon explore Warsaw's markets and craft shops. End your second day with dinner and drinks, then perhaps a classical music concert at the **Filharmonia Narodowa** (p79) or a pub crawl in Praga.

WARSAW SIGHTS

Central Warsaw

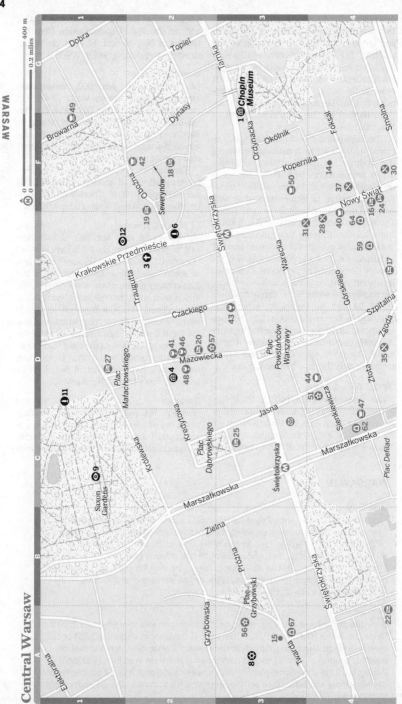

WARSAW

Ujazdowski Park

Prusa

Wiejska

al Ujazdowskie

Plac Trzech Krzyży

10

Mokotowska

Pękna

Książąca

7

61

Wspólna

Hoża

Wilcza

23

Bracka

45
36

al Jerozolimskie

Krucza

Żurawia

63

Plac Konstytucji

54

Widok

Chmielna

26

Marszałkowska

Motobuss Bus Stop

66

Centrum

33

Wspólna

65

Poznańska

29

39

38

32

58

Nowogrodzka

5

55

13

34

Emilii Plater

Hoża

Wilcza

21

Palace of Culture & Science

2

52

53

Warsaw Tourist Office

Warszawa Śródmieście Train Station

Emilii Plater

Niepodległości

Koszykowa

68

60

Warszawa Centralna Train Station

Chałubińskiego

Sienna

Złota

Ocza

Central Warsaw

a decorative Renaissance parapet. It was partially dismantled in the 19th century, but reconstructed after WWII, and is now a popular spot for buskers and art sellers.

◉ New Town

The New Town (Nowe Miasto) is something of a misnomer, considering it was founded at the end of the 14th century and after 1408 had its own administration. It contains similar architectural styles to those found in the Old Town, but lacks any defensive walls, as historically it was inhabited by poor folk.

Nuns of the Holy Sacrament CHURCH
(Kościół Sakramentek; Map p60; Rynek Nowego Miasta 2) Even by Polish standards, the New Town has a lot of churches; this church, which dominates New Town Sq, is one of the most interesting. It's the work of prominent architect Tylman van Gameren and has a fine Baroque exterior and clean white interior.

Field Cathedral of the Polish Army CHURCH
(Katedra Polowa Wojska Polskiego; Map p60; www.katedrapolowa.pl; ul Długa 13/15) As the name implies, this has been a traditional place of worship for soldiers. There's no homage to the glory of war here; inside the main doors, which feature bas-reliefs of

major battles fought by Polish forces, is a gruesome crucifix, with heads protruding from solid metal blocks on all sides of a ruined Jesus. Inside there are numerous plaques to fallen Polish soldiers.

Monument to the Warsaw Rising
MONUMENT

(Pomnik Powstania Warszawskiego; Map p60; Plac Krasińskich) One of Warsaw's most important landmarks, this striking bronze tableau depicts Armia Krajowa (AK; Home Army) fighters emerging ghostlike from the shattered brickwork of their ruined city, while others descend through a manhole into the network of sewers. The monument was unveiled on 1 August 1989, the 45th anniversary of the doomed revolt against German military occupation in 1944.

Marie Skłodowska-Curie Museum
MUSEUM

(Muzeum Marii Skłodowskiej-Curie; Map p60; www.muzeum-msc.pl; ul Freta 5; adult/concession 11/6zł; ⊙10am-7pm Tue-Sun) Marie Curie was born in 1867 along ul Freta, the main street of the New Town. This museum chronicles the life and work of the distinguished scientist, and is situated a test tube's throw from her birthplace.

⊙ Citadel

Citadel
FORTRESS

(Cytadela; Map p50; ul Skazańców) North of the New Town, the Citadel is a massive 19th-century fortress overlooking the Vistula, built by the Russian tsar to intimidate Warsaw following the November Insurrection of 1830. It served as a notorious political prison for years and is now used by the military. The huge gate overlooking the river is known as **Brama Straceń** (Gate of Execution; Map p50; ul Skazańców), a spot where political prisoners were executed all too frequently after the later 1863 uprising.

Block 10 Museum
MUSEUM

(Muzeum Pawilon-X; Map p50; www.muzeum niepodleglosci.art.pl; ul Skazańców 25; adult/concession 8/5zł, Thu free; ⊙10am-5pm Wed-Sun) Within Warsaw's Citadel, this museum preserves a wing of a former political prison. Cells are labelled with names of the more famous prisoners incarcerated here, including Józef Piłsudski, who did time in cell 25. Inside are paintings by Alexander Sochaczewski (1843–1923), a former inmate who, along with 20,000 other anti-Russian insurgents, was transported to the labour camps of Siberia in 1866. The paintings, such as the huge

---

A PHOENIX FROM THE FLAMES

Warsaw's German occupiers did a good job of following Hitler's instructions to raze the city after the 1944 Warsaw Rising – at the end of WWII, about 15% of the city was left standing. So complete was the destruction that there were even suggestions that the capital should be moved elsewhere, but instead it was decided that parts of the prewar urban fabric would be rebuilt.

According to plan, the most valuable historic monuments were restored to their previous appearance, based on original drawings and photographs. Between 1949 and 1963 work was concentrated on the Old Town, aiming to return it to its 17th- and 18th-century appearance – today not a single building in the area looks less than 200 years old. So complete was the restoration that Unesco granted the Old Town World Heritage status in 1980.

The Royal Castle took a little longer. It wasn't until 1971 that reconstruction began, and by 1984 the splendid Baroque castle stood again as if it had never been destroyed. Although the brick structure is a copy, many original architectural fragments have been incorporated into the walls.

The authorities also had to build, from scratch, a whole new city capable of providing housing and services to its inhabitants. This communist legacy is less impressive. The city centre was, until quite recently, a blend of bunker-like Stalinist structures and equally dull edifices of a later era, while the outer suburbs, home to the majority of Warsaw's inhabitants, were composed almost exclusively of anonymous, prefabricated concrete blocks.

The city's skyline is still marred by ugly high-rises, but things have improved markedly since 1989. Newly constructed steel-and-glass towers have begun to break up the monotony, and the city outskirts are steadily filling up with aesthetically pleasing villas and family houses. Warsaw may never regain an architectural landscape that truly appeals, but it certainly contains an interesting diversity of styles.

Pożegnanie Europy (Farewell to Europe), depict the suffering of his fellow prisoners.

☉ South of the Old Town

Running south from Castle Sq to busy al Jerozolimskie is the stamping ground of Warsaw's students, shoppers and socialites. For much of the 19th century it was the commercial and cultural heart of Warsaw, and is still generally thought of as the city centre.

UL KRAKOWSKIE PRZEDMIEŚCIE

This wide boulevard, running from Castle Sq to ul Nowy Świat, marks the start of the so-called Royal Way and makes a great walk. The boulevard is lined by evocative churches and two important monuments, one to Polish writer Adam Mickiewicz, the author of *Pan Tadeusz,* and the other to immortal astronomer Nicolaus Copernicus, who proved that the earth revolved around the sun. This is also the site of **Warsaw University** (Uniwersytet Warszawski; Map p54; www.uw.edu.pl; ul Krakowskie Przedmieście 26/28), whose entrance is marked by a decorative gate topped with the Polish eagle.

Church of the Holy Cross   CHURCH
(Kościół św Krzyża; Map p54; ul Krakowskie Przedmieście 3; ☉10am-4pm) **FREE** Of Warsaw's many impressive churches, this is the one most visitors want to visit. Not so much to admire the fine Baroque altarpieces that miraculously survived the War-

saw Rising reprisals, but to glimpse a small urn by the second pillar on the left side of the nave. This urn, adorned with an epitaph to Frédéric Chopin, contains what remains of the composer's heart. It was brought here from Paris after the great man's death.

St Anne's Church   CHURCH
(Kościół Św Anny; Map p60; ul Krakowskie Przedmieście 68) Marking the start of the Royal Way, this is arguably the most ornate church in the city. It escaped major damage during WWII, which explains why it sports an original trompe l'oeil ceiling, a Rococo high altar and a gorgeous organ. The facade is also Baroque in style, although there are neoclassical touches here and there.

Carmelite Church   CHURCH
(Kościół Karmelitów; Map p60; ul Krakowskie Przedmieście 52/54) Fortunately this church escaped the ravages of war and contains 18th-century fittings, including a high altar designed by Tylman van Gameren.

Museum of Caricature   MUSEUM
(Muzeum Karykatury; Map p60; www.muzeum karykatury.pl; ul Kozia 11; adult/concession 7/4zł, Tue free; ☉10am-6pm Tue-Sun) A refreshing break from history museums and churches, this quirky museum holds thousands of original works by Polish and foreign caricaturists dating from the 18th century onwards, plus satirical and humorous books and magazines. Displays are rotated on a regular basis.

WARSAW FOR CHILDREN

Warsaw is not the best travel destination for infants and small children. Distances are vast and transport options such as trams and buses are often packed and not particularly pram- or child-friendly. Exercise caution on public transport that can make sudden stops and unexpected turns. On the streets, traffic can be heavy and many corners lack kerb cuts. You'll find escalators and lifts in metro stations and some central underpasses, but outside the centre you'll have to negotiate lots of steps.

That said, there are plenty of parents with prams in Warsaw, and kids seem to do just fine. As for sights, there are a handful of crowd-pleasers for young visitors. Topping the list of attractions would be the **Copernicus Science Centre** (p59), followed by the **Zoological Gardens** (p69). Kids young and old will enjoy the illuminated signage in and around the **Neon Museum** (p68) in Praga. Older children might also enjoy the visual and sound effects of the highly interactive **Warsaw Rising Museum** (p64), though parental guidance is recommended in explaining its dark story. Parks abound. **Łazienki Park** (p66) has plenty of space to run, plus peacocks to spot, hungry ducks to feed, and a boat trip to take, while the **Saxon Gardens** (p59) has a good playground. There are boat trips at **Wilanów Park** (p69) too. The view from the **Palace of Culture & Science** (p61) is impressive for all ages.

The city's tourist information offices can help out. They offer a colourful, fold-out *Free Map for Young Travellers* aimed primarily at teens and students, but with some hints for younger travellers as well.

Monument to Adam Mickiewicz MONUMENT
(Pomnik Adama Mickiewicza; Map p60; ul Krakowskie Przedmieście) This monument to Poland's great Romantic poet was unveiled on the 100th anniversary of his birth in 1898.

Radziwiłł Palace PALACE
(Pałac Radziwiłłów; Map p50; www.president. pl; ul Krakowskie Przedmieście 48/50) This neo-classical palace is guarded by stone lions and an equestrian statue of Prince Józef Poniatowski. The prince was the nephew of the last Polish king, Stanisław August Poniatowski, and commander in chief of the Polish army of the Duchy of Warsaw, created by Napoleon. The Warsaw Pact Treaty was signed here in 1955, creating the Cold War military alliance to rival NATO. Today the palace is the Polish president's official residence, and is not open to the public.

Monument to Nicolaus Copernicus MONUMENT
(Pomnik Mikołaja Kopernika; Map p54; ul Krakowskie Przedmieście) Tribute to the great astronomer Mikołaj Kopernik (1473–1543), better known outside Poland as Nicolaus Copernicus, who proved conclusively that the earth revolves around the sun. The Latin inscription on one side translates as 'A grateful nation honours Mikołaj Kopernik', and the Polish inscription on the other side says 'To Mikołaj Kopernik from his countrymen'.

UL NOWY ŚWIAT
Running south from the junction of ul Świętokrzyska and ul Krakowskie Przedmieście to al Jerozolimskie, New World Street is the busiest pedestrian thoroughfare in Warsaw outside the Old Town. It's long been a fashionable shopping zone, and is lined with restaurants, shops and cafes. Most of the buildings date from after WWII, but the restoration was so complete that the predominant style of architecture is 19th-century neoclassical. Aside from shopping, eating and drinking, the best thing to do here (and in the side streets ul Foksal and ul Chmielna) is find a comfy seat and watch the parade of people.

★**Chopin Museum** MUSEUM
(Map p54; ☑ 22 441 6251; www.chopin.museum; ul Okólnik 1; adult/concession 22/13zł, Sun free; ⊙ 11am-8pm Tue-Sun) High-tech, multimedia museum within the Baroque Ostrogski Palace, showcasing the work of the country's most famous composer. You're encouraged to take your time through four floors of displays, including stopping by the listening booths in the basement where you can browse Chopin's oeuvre to your heart's content. Limited visitation is allowed each hour; your best bet is to book your visit in advance by phone or email.

Copernicus Science Centre MUSEUM
(Centrum Nauki Kopernik; Map p50; www.kopernik.org.pl; ul Wybrzeże Kościuszkowskie 20; adult/concession 25/16zł; ⊙ 9am-7pm Tue-Sun; Ⓜ Centrum Nauki Kopernik) For a kid-friendly attraction, try this over-the-top, fully interactive, push-the-buttons-and-see-what-happens science museum. There are too many attractions to list here, but all branches of science are represented. Most exhibits are suited for kids 12 to 18 years old, though there's plenty on hand to amuse younger – and older – visitors. The location is a bit out of the way, several blocks due east of ul Nowy Świat, but easily accessible via the metro.

SAXON GARDENS & AROUND

Saxon Gardens GARDENS
(Ogród Saski; Map p54) Stretching out a couple of blocks west of ul Krakowskie Przedmieście, these magnificent gardens date from the early 18th century and were the city's first public park. Modelled on the French gardens at Versailles, the gardens are filled with chestnut trees and Baroque statues (allegories of the Virtues, the Sciences and the Elements), and there's an ornamental lake overlooked by a 19th-century water tower in the form of a circular Greek temple.

If it looks to you as though the gardens are missing a palace, you'd be right. The 18th-century Pałac Saski (Saxon Palace), which once occupied Plac Piłsudskiego (Piłsudski Sq), was, like so many other buildings, destroyed during WWII. All that survived were three arches of a colonnade, which have sheltered the Tomb of the Unknown Soldier since 1925. There are plans to rebuild Saxon Palace from scratch at fabulous expense, but so far they remain unfulfilled.

Tomb of the Unknown Soldier MONUMENT
(Grób Nieznanego Żołnierza; Map p54; Ogród Saski) Inside the Saxon Gardens is this military memorial. The guard is changed every hour, and groups of soldiers marching back and forth between the tomb and the Radziwiłł Palace are a regular sight, though the big event is the ceremonial changing of the guard that takes place every Sunday at noon.

WARSAW SIGHTS

Ethnographic Museum   MUSEUM
(Muzeum Etnograficzne; Map p54; www.ethno
museum.pl; ul Kredytowa 1; adult/concession
12/6zł, Sat free; ☉9am-5pm Tue-Sat, noon-5pm
Sun) Provides a good introduction to the
country's rural heart via its small but fine
assembly of Polish folk art and crafts – but
it's the portrait shots of indigenous people
from around the world steal the show.

PLAC BANKOWY

Due west of the Old Town, Plac Bankowy
(Bank Sq) is too big and busy to be very appealing. However, the **City Hall** (Ratusz; Map
p60; Plac Bankowy 3/5) and the former stock

exchange and Bank of Poland building, both
grand neoclassical structures that were designed by Antonio Corazzi in the 1820s, lend
the square some architectural heft.

Museum of the
John Paul II Collection   MUSEUM
(Muzeum Kolekcji im Jana Pawła II; Map
p60; www.mkjp2.pl; Plac Bankowy 1; adult/
concession 10/5zł; ☉9am-4pm Tue-Sun) Housed
in the Bank of Poland building, this amazing
art collection was donated to the Catholic
Church by the Carrol-Porczyński family. It's
quite a surprise to find the likes of Dalí, Van
Gogh, Constable, Rubens, Goya and Renoir

Warsaw – Old Town & Around

gracing the walls of a fairly nondescript museum, and to often have them all to yourself. Enter from ul Elektoralna.

Jewish Historical Institute MUSEUM
(Żydowski Instytut Historyczny; Map p60; www.jhi.pl; ul Tłomackie 3/5; adult/concession 10/5zł, Sun free; ☉10am-6pm Sun-Fri) Just behind a blue skyscraper, this institute houses a library and paintings, sculptures, and old religious objects related to Jewish culture. However, it's the exhibition on the Warsaw Ghetto (p65) that sticks with you when you leave. Black-and-white photos and 40 minutes of original film footage from the ghetto hit home – the images of the atrocious conditions Jews were forced to endure, with starvation and death part of everyday life, tell a disturbing tale.

Museum of Independence MUSEUM
(Muzeum Niepodległości; Map p60; www.muzeum niepodleglosci.art.pl; al Solidarności 62; adult/concession 6/4zł, Thu free; ☉10am-5pm Wed-Sun) Stranded on a traffic island in the middle of al Solidarności, this museum has a small room devoted to the Solidarity movement and stages temporary exhibitions related to Poland's struggle for independence. This

was once home to Warsaw's Lenin museum and still has some interesting displays of socialist realist artwork.

◉ **Financial District**

The open expanses and tall buildings that are bounded by ul Marszałkowska, al Jerozolimskie, ul Jana Pawła II and al Solidarności collectively constitute Warsaw's financial zone.

★**Palace of Culture & Science** HISTORIC BUILDING
(Pałac Kultury i Nauki; Map p54; www.pkin.pl; Plac Defilad 1; observation terrace adult/concession 20/14zł; ☉9am-8.30pm) Love it or hate it, every visitor to Warsaw should visit the iconic, socialist realist PKiN (as its full Polish name is abbreviated). This 'gift of friendship' from the Soviet Union was built in the early 1950s, and at 231m high remains the tallest building in Poland. It's home to a huge congress hall, theatres, a multiscreen cinema and museums. Take the high-speed lift to the 30th-floor (115m) observation terrace to take it all in.

(Continued on p64)

Communist Architecture

Much of Poland was reconstructed after WWII according to plans drawn up in Moscow, in keeping with the then communist and socialist-realist aesthetic. The result was some fantastic follies, including Warsaw's Palace of Culture & Science, and more serious efforts that reflect a very different reality only a few decades ago.

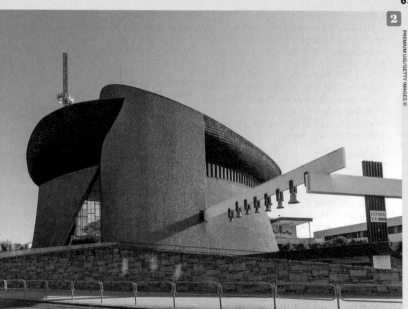

1. Warsaw (p48)
Congress Hall, part of the Palace of Culture & Science (p161), a gift of friendship from the Soviet Union.

2. Kraków (p118)
The Arka Pana church (p136) located in the newest of Kraków's suburbs, Nowa Huta (New Steelworks).

3. Łódź (p89)
An apartment block in the former industrial city.

4. Rzeszów (p207)
The *Monument of the Revolutionary Deed* by Marian Konieczny (p208) is dedicated to the fight against Nazi Germany.

(Continued from p61)

The building has never sat well with the locals, who have branded it with one uncomplimentary moniker after another; the 'Elephant in Lacy Underwear', a reference both to the building's size and the fussy sculptures that frill the parapets, is a particular favourite. However, though there are occasional calls for it to be demolished, the Palace is gradually becoming accepted (even embraced) as a city icon.

Fotoplastikon PHOTOGRAPHY

(Map p54; www.fotoplastikonwarszawski.pl; al Jerozolimskie 51; adult/concession 4/2zł, Sun free; ◷10am-6pm Tue-Sun) Photo and film buffs will be intrigued by this late-19th-century forerunner of the cinema. It's reputedly the last working example of its kind in Europe, and consists of a large rotating drum set with individual eyepieces displaying stereoscopic 3D photos, some of them in colour. Each session consists of 48 pictures and takes about 20 minutes.

◉ Former Jewish Ghetto

Before WWII, Warsaw had a thriving Jewish population. Much of this community lived in Mirów and Muranów, two districts to the west of al Jana Pawła II. It was here that the Germans created the Warsaw Ghetto in 1940, which was razed after the 1943 Ghetto Uprising. Today the area is characterised by cheap, communist-era apartment buildings, but a few remnants of Jewish Warsaw survive.

★ Warsaw Rising Museum MUSEUM

(Muzeum Powstania Warszawskiego; Map p50; www.1944.pl; ul Grzybowska 79; adult/concession 18/14zł, Sun free; ◷8am-6pm Mon, Wed & Fri, to 8pm Thu, 10am-6pm Sat & Sun; Ⓜ Rondo Daszyńskiego, ⓐ9, 22 or 24 along al Jerozolimskie) One of Warsaw's best, this museum traces the history of the city's heroic but doomed uprising against the German occupation in 1944 via three levels of interactive displays, photographs, film archives and personal accounts. The volume of material is overwhelming, but the museum does an excellent job of instilling in visitors a sense of the desperation residents felt in deciding to oppose the occupation by force, and of illustrating the dark consequences, including the Nazis' destruction of the city in the aftermath.

The ground floor begins with the division of Poland between Nazi Germany and the Soviet Union in 1939 and moves through the major events of WWII. A lift then takes you to the 2nd floor and the start of the uprising in 1944. The largest exhibit, a Liberator bomber similar to the planes that were used to drop supplies for insurgents, fills much of the 1st floor.

★ Museum of the History of Polish Jews MUSEUM

(Polin; Map p50; www.polin.pl; ul Anielewicza 6; adult/concession 25/15zł, incl temporary exhibits 30/20zł; ◷10am-6pm Mon, Wed-Fri & Sun, to 8pm Sat; ⓐ4, 15, 18 or 35 along ul Marszałkowska) This exceptional museum's permanent exhibition opened in late 2014. Impressive multimedia exhibits document 1000 years of Jewish history in Poland, from accounts of the earliest Jewish traders in the region through waves of mass migration, progress and pogroms, all the way to WWII and the destruction of Europe's largest Jewish community. It's worth booking online first, and you can hire an audio guide (10zł) to get the most out of the many rooms of displays, interactive maps, photos and videos.

Ghetto Heroes Monument MONUMENT

(Pomnik Bohaterów Getta; Map p50; cnr uls Anielewicza & Zamenhofa) FREE In a shady park just behind the Museum of the History of Polish Jews, this stern memorial commemorates the thousands who lost their lives in the ill-fated Ghetto Uprising of 1943. In the northwest corner of the park is Skwer Willy Brandta (Willy Brandt Sq), with another memorial marking the visit of German chancellor Willy Brandt to this spot on 7 December 1970. Brandt famously fell to his knees in a gesture of contrition for Germany's crimes against Polish Jews.

Monument to Mordechaj Anielewicz MONUMENT

(Pomnik Mordechaja Anielewicza; Map p50; ul Miła) This mound topped by a simple limestone block forms a memorial paying tribute to Mordechaj Anielewicz, the leader of the Ghetto Uprising, who perished in a bunker on this site in 1943.

Umschlagplatz MONUMENT

(Map p50; ul Stawki near ul Dzika) A moving monument marks the site of the *umschlagplatz*, the railway terminus from which Warsaw's Jews were transported by the German military to Treblinka. The rectangular monument's marble walls are carved with more than 3000 Jewish forenames, from Aba to Zygmunt, and the stark message: 'Along this path of suffering and death over

300,000 Jews were driven in 1942–43 from the Warsaw Ghetto to the gas chambers of the Nazi extermination camps'. Its shape is symbolic of the cattle trucks into which the prisoners were herded.

Jewish Cemetery CEMETERY

(Cmentarz Żydowski; Map p50; ul Okopowa 49/51; adult/concession 10/5zł; ⊘10am-5pm Mon-Thu, 9am-1pm Fri, 11am-4pm Sun) Founded in 1806, Warsaw's main Jewish Cemetery incredibly suffered little during WWII and contains more than 150,000 tombstones, the largest collection of its kind in Europe. A notice near the entrance lists the graves of many eminent Polish Jews, including Ludwik Zamenhof, creator of the international artificial language Esperanto. Be sure to look for the tomb of Ber Sonnenberg (1764–1822); take the first paved path on the left beyond the ticket office and when you arrive at a junction on your right, look left: it's the roofed structure over by the wall.

Nożyk Synagogue SYNAGOGUE

(Synagoga Nożyków; Map p54; www.warszawa. jewish.org.pl; ul Twarda 6; admission 10zł; ⊘9am-7pm Mon-Fri, 11am-7pm Sun) This is the city's only synagogue to survive WWII. Built between 1898 and 1902 in neo-Romanesque style, its interior features heavy metal chandeliers and tall vaulted colonnades. It's still used for religious purposes.

Pawiak Prison Museum MUSEUM

(Muzeum Więzienia Pawiak; Map p50; www. muzeum-niepodleglosci.pl; ul Dzielna 24/26; adult/concession 6/4zł; ⊘10am-5pm Wed-Sun) Dating from the 19th century, this former prison was built to incarcerate enemies of the Russian tsar. During WWII it was used by the Gestapo to imprison and torture mostly Polish political prisoners. It's estimated that around 100,000 prisoners passed through these sinister gates from 1939 to 1944, of whom around 37,000 were executed. The prison was blown up by the Germans in 1944, but half of the mangled gateway, complete with rusting, barbed wire, and three detention cells (which you can visit) survive.

⊙ South of al Jerozolimskie

Al Jerozolimskie is a big, busy thoroughfare that creates a physical east–west border through the city. The area to its south was

---

THE WARSAW GHETTO

At the outbreak of WWII Warsaw was home to about 380,000 Jews (almost 30% of the city's total population), more than in any other city in the world except New York.

In October 1940 the Germans established a ghetto in the predominantly Jewish districts of Muranów and Mirów, west of the city centre, sealed off by a 3m-high brick wall. In the following months about 450,000 Jews from the city and its surroundings were crammed into the area within the walls, creating the largest and most overcrowded ghetto in Europe. By mid-1942 as many as 100,000 people had died of starvation and epidemic diseases, even before deportation to the concentration camps had begun.

In a massive liquidation campaign in the summer of 1942, about 300,000 Jews were transported from the ghetto to the extermination camp at Treblinka. Then in April 1943, when only 50,000 people were left, the Nazis began the final liquidation of the ghetto. In a desperate act of defiance, the survivors took up arms in a spontaneous uprising, the first in any European ghetto.

From the outbreak of the uprising on 19 April it was clear that the Jews had little chance of victory against the heavily armed Nazi forces. German planes dropped incendiary bombs, turning the entire district into a chaos of burning ruins. Fierce fighting lasted for almost three weeks until, on 8 May, the Nazis surrounded the Jewish command bunker and tossed in a gas bomb.

Around 7000 Jews were killed in the fighting and another 6000 perished in fires and bombed buildings. The Germans lost 300 men and another 1000 were injured. The ghetto was razed to the ground except for a few scraps of wall, which survive to this day.

A number of personal accounts provide written testament to the brutality of life within the ghetto walls. For further reading pick up a copy of any of the following: *A Square of Sky: A Jewish Childhood in Wartime Poland*, by Janina David; *Beyond These Walls: Escaping the Warsaw Ghetto*, by the late Janina Bauman; and *The Diary of Mary Berg: Growing Up in the Warsaw Ghetto*, by Mary Berg.

Southern Warsaw

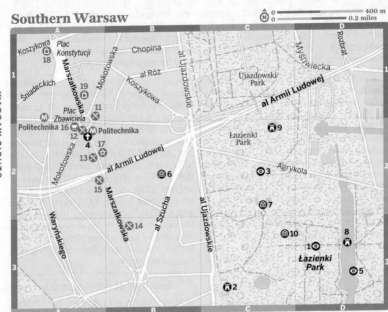

earmarked by the communists for post-WWII development, and some of the city's boldest socialist realist architecture can be found here. Ul Marszałkowska, a broad avenue running south from near the financial district, contains the most impressive examples; the stretch between Plac Konstytucji (Constitution Sq) and Plac Zbawiciela is lined with arcades bearing giant reliefs of heroic workers.

Al Ujazdowskie, the continuation of the Royal Way as it leaves ul Nowy Świat, is a wide, tree-lined boulevard with many old mansions, now often housing foreign embassies. Near its northern section the road passes through Plac Trzech Krzyży (Three Crosses Sq), a square centred on 19th-century **St Alexander's Church** (Kościół Św Aleksandra; Map p54; Plac Trzech Krzyży), which is modelled on the Roman Pantheon.

National Museum MUSEUM
(Muzeum Narodowe; Map p54; www.mnw.art.pl; al Jerozolimskie 3; adult/concession 15/10zł, Tue free; ☉ 10am-6pm) Containing almost 800,000 items in its permanent galleries, this is the largest museum in the country. Highlights include the Faras Collection, a display of early Christian art originating from a town on the banks of the Nile that was rescued by Polish archaeologists from the rising waters of the Aswan High Dam, the extensive gallery of medieval art, and the best of Polish art, housed in the upper floors.

★ **Łazienki Park** GARDENS
(Park Łazienkowski; Map p66; www.lazienki-krolewskie.pl; ul Agrykola 1; ☉ dawn-dusk) Pronounced wah-*zhen*-kee, this park is a beautiful place of manicured greens and wild patches. Its popularity extends to families, peacocks and fans of classical music, who come for the al fresco Chopin concerts on Sunday afternoons at noon and 4pm from mid-May through September. Once a hunting ground attached to Ujazdów Castle, Łazienki was acquired by King Stanisław August Poniatowski in 1764 and transformed into a splendid park complete with palace, amphitheatre, and various follies and other buildings.

➡ **Palace on the Water**
Łazienki Park's centrepiece is a neoclassic **palace** (Pałac Na Wyspie; adult/concession 25/18zł; ☉ 11am-6pm Mon, 9am-6pm Tue-Sun), the former residence of the Polish King Stanisław August Poniatowski. It straddles an ornamental lake and, like most other Łazienki buildings, was designed by the court architect Domenico Merlini. Renovated and refurbished, the palace is open to

Southern Warsaw

guided tours – highlights include the 17th-century marble reliefs depicting scenes from Ovid's *Metamorphoses* gracing the original bathhouse (*łazienki* in Polish, hence the name) and the ornate ballroom.

➡ **Island Amphitheatre**

This amphitheatre (Amfiteatr na Wyspie) was built in 1790 and is based on the appearance of the Roman theatre at Herculaneum, Italy. It is set on an islet in the park's lake, allowing part of performances to take place on the water.

➡ **White House**

No relation to its Washington namesake, this **pavilion** (Biały Dom; adult/concession 6/4zł; ☺11am-6pm Mon, 9am-6pm Tue-Sun) was erected in 1774 as a temporary residence until Łazienki Park's palace was finished. It's quite small for a royal home and has managed to retain most of its original 18th-century interior.

➡ **Old Orangery**

West of the Palace on the Water, this elegant structure was completed in 1788 and sheltered exotic trees in the winter. It's now the home of a **gallery** (Stara Pomaranczarnia; adult/student 20/10zł, Thu free; ☺11am-6pm Mon, 9am-6pm Tue-Sun), featuring an impressive selection of sculpture collected from across Europe by King Stanisław August Poniatowski; and of the Royal Theatre, an 18th-century auditorium featuring beautiful wood panelling.

Belvedere Palace   PALACE
(Pałac Belweder; Map p66; ul Belwederska 52) A stately home with a history, this 18th-century palace at the southern limit of al Ujazdowskie served as the official residence

of Marshal Józef Piłsudski (from 1926 to 1935) and Polish presidents from 1945 to 1952 and 1989 to 1994. It's not open to the public, but can be admired from afar; the best views are from al Ujazdowskie.

Ujazdów Castle   CASTLE
(Map p66; ul Jazdow 2) Erected in the 1620s for King Zygmunt III Waza as his summer residence, the castle was burned down by the Germans in 1944, blown up by the communists in 1954 and eventually rebuilt in the 1970s. Now it houses changing exhibitions of modern art from the **Centre for Contemporary Art** (Map p66; www.csw.art.pl; ul Jazdów 2; adult/concession 12/6zł, Thu free; ☺10am-6pm Wed-Mon).

Botanical Gardens   GARDENS
(Ogród Botaniczny; Map p66; www.ogrod.uw.edu.pl; al Ujazdowskie 4; adult/concession 8/4zł; ☺9am-8pm Mon-Fri, 10am-8pm Sat & Sun) Warsaw's Botanical Gardens was established in 1818. Its diverse collection of species ranges from European trees such as the beech, to exotic specimens such as the gingko biloba tree from China.

**Mausoleum of Struggle &
Martyrdom**   MUSEUM
(Mauzoleum Walki i Męczeństwa; Map p66; www.muzeum-niepodleglosci.art.pl; al Szucha 25; ☺10am-4pm Wed-Sun) **FREE** Once used by the Gestapo for interrogation, torture and murder, this building now stands as a memorial to the thousands of Poles who passed through its doors. With its depressing basement holding cells and a Gestapo

OVER THE RAINBOW

You wouldn't think that a colourful piece of street art could provoke much passion. But *Rainbow* (Tęczy), a large rainbow arch situated in recent years in Warsaw's hip Plac Zbawiciela, managed just that. Sitting to one side of the grassy area in the centre of the square (which is actually circular), the rainbow arch seemed a cheerful multicoloured installation at first glance, something pleasant to look at while sipping a coffee outside one of the plaza's popular bars or cafes.

However, the arch was also caught up in the tide of social change gradually flowing through the Polish capital since the fall of communism. Given its similarity to the rainbow symbol adopted by gay people around the world, many Poles interpreted *Rainbow* as a work promoting equal rights for the LGBTIQ community. And artist Julita Wójcik, who created the work to mark the Polish presidency of the EU in 2011, has described the piece as representing openness and diversity. With its steel frame stretching 26m wide and standing 9m high, and being covered with 16,000 artificial flowers, it was a challenge to assemble. The flowers were attached by hand to prefabricated segments of the metal frame in Sopot, which were then shipped to Brussels to be pieced together there.

It was such a hit in the EU capital that it was returned to Poland in 2012 to be installed in Plac Zbawiciela, decked out with new flowers to replace those souvenired by appreciative Belgian passers-by.

In Warsaw, however, it took on a new aura of controversy, situated as it was in front of the **Church of the Holy Redeemer**. Some felt its installation was a provocative riposte to the Catholic Church's conservative social stance; others that it merely brightened a square which had become a lively hub of food and drink as well as worship.

Rainbow was targeted by right-wing extremists, being set ablaze on several occasions (though, to be fair, some of these fires may have been caused by rowdy revellers). After an Independence Day rally in 2013, it was burned to the ground.

However, it also became a rallying point for acceptance and diversity. Not only did Warsaw's long-running mayor Hanna Gronkiewicz-Waltz commit to rebuilding the rainbow after any damage, but the arch became a focus of campaigns for equality and acceptance. In June 2015 the route of Warsaw's annual **Equality Parade** (p70) was altered by popular demand to pass the arch on its march through the city streets.

Sadly, the rainbow's adventurous stay in the centre of Plac Zbawiciela came to an end. The agreement on its placement between the city authorities and the Adam Mickiewicz Institute, which originally commissioned the work, expired at the end of 2015. In late August that year it was dismantled, and placed into storage at the Centre for Contemporary Art. *Rainbow*, however, will survive, though in what form was unclear at the time of research. Ask at the tourist office for details of its current location.

officer's interrogation room (complete with original bullwhips, coshes, knuckledusters etc), it's a grim place to visit.

Church of the Holy Redeemer CHURCH
(Kościół Najświętszego Zbawiciela; Map p66; www.parafiazbawiciela.org; ul Marszałkowska 37) Built from 1901 to 1911, this elegant place of worship borrows from both the Renaissance and Baroque periods. Demolished by the German occupiers during WWII, the church was rebuilt after the war – though the communist authorities weren't happy with its prominence, and withheld permission for its towers to be reconstructed until 1955. Highlights include statues of St Peter and St Paul on the facade, and the chapel of Our Lady of Częstochowa within.

⊙ Praga

Crossing the Vistula from the Old Town into Praga, Warsaw's eastern suburb, is like entering another city. Clean, level streets and renovated buildings are replaced by broken roads and crumbling facades, and much of the populace is working class and poor. Despite the grit, Praga is *the* place to be. The area is slowly being gentrified as artists, musicians and entrepreneurs move in, attracted by its pre-WWII buildings (as it was not directly involved in the battles of 1944, Praga didn't suffer much damage) and cheaper rent.

★ Neon Museum MUSEUM
(Muzeum Neonów; Map p50; www.neonmuzeum. org; ul Mińska 25; adult/concession 10/8zł; ⊙12-

5pm Wed-Sun; 🚃 22 from al Jerozolimskie) Situated within the cool Soho Factory complex of old industrial buildings housing designers and artists, this museum is devoted to the preservation of the iconic neon signs of the communist era. The collection is arrayed within a historic factory, with many large pieces fully lit. Other exhibits are dotted around the complex and are illuminated after dark. It's well worth the trek across the river. Alight the tram at the Bliska stop.

National Stadium STADIUM
(Stadion Narodowy; Map p50; www.stadion narodowy.org.pl; al Poniatowskiego 1; observation point adult/concession 10/5zł, guided tours adult/concession 20/12zł; ☉ 9am-9pm; Ⓜ Stadion Narodowy, 🚃 7, 22 or 25 from al Jerozolimskie) This prominent landmark on the east bank of the Vistula was constructed for the Euro 2012 football championships on the site of a defunct communist-era stadium. Its red-and-white patterning references the Polish flag, and the interior can seat 58,000 spectators for either sporting or entertainment events. Visitors can access an observation point for a view of the interior, or join a daily tour in English; times vary, so check out the website for the day you prefer to go.

Zoological Gardens ZOO
(Ogród Zoologiczny; Map p50; www.zoo.waw. pl; ul Ratuszowa 1/3; adult/concession 20/15zł; ☉ 9am-6pm) Established in 1928, this zoo has some 5000 animals representing 500 species from around the world, including apes, bears, wolves and elephants.

Orthodox Church CHURCH
(Cerkiew Prawosławna; Map p50; al Solidarności 52) Close to Warsaw's zoo, rising from behind a clump of trees just off Praga's main thoroughfare, al Solidarności, are the five onion-shaped domes of this church. Built in the 1860s in Russo-Byzantine style, its small nave still retains original Byzantine portraits and gold upon gold.

⊙ Outside the Centre

★ Wilanów Palace PALACE
(Pałac w Wilanowie; ☎ 22 544 2850; www. wilanow-palac.pl; ul Potockiego 10/16; adult/concession 20/15zł; ☉ 10am-7pm Tue-Sun; 🚃 116 or 180) Warsaw's top palace is Wilanów (vee-*lah*-noof), 6km south of Łazienki. It dates to 1677, when King Jan III Sobieski bought the land and turned an existing manor house into an Italian Baroque villa fit for a royal summer residence (calling it in Italian 'villa nuova', from which the Polish name is derived). Wilanów changed hands several times over the centuries, and with every new owner it acquired a bit of Baroque here and a touch of neoclassical there.

Miraculously, Wilanów survived WWII almost unscathed, and most of its furnishings and art were retrieved and reinstalled after the war.

The highlights of a visit include the two-storey Grand Entrance Hall, the Grand Dining Room, and the Gallery of Polish Portraits, featuring a collection of paintings from the 16th to 19th centuries. The exterior of the palace is adorned with impressive murals, including a 17th-century sundial with a bas-relief of Chronos, god of time. An audio guide (12zł) is a worthwhile enhancement to your visit here. You can book ahead for entry tickets via phone or online.

Wilanów Park GARDENS
(Park Wilanowski; www.wilanow-palac.pl; ul Potockiego 10/16; adult/concession 5/3zł, Thu free; ☉ 9am-dusk Apr-Sep; 🚃 116 or 180) This splendid 45-hectare park adjoins Wilanów Palace and contains a variety of landscaping. The central part comprises a manicured, two-level Baroque Italian garden, which extends from the palace down to the lake; the south is Anglo-Chinese in design; the northern section is an English landscape park. There's also a Renaissance-inspired rose garden. The last tickets each day are sold 30 minutes before closing time.

Also in the park is the **Orangery** (admission varies; ☉ 9am-dusk Apr-Sep; 🚃 116 or 180), which houses an art gallery displaying temporary exhibitions.

Poster Museum MUSEUM
(Muzeum Plakatu; www.postermuseum.pl; adult/concession 10/7zł, Mon free; ☉ noon-4pm Mon, 10am-4pm Tue-Sun; 🚃 116 or 180) Standing near Wilanów Palace, this museum houses some tens of thousands of Polish posters – one of the largest poster collections in the world – but only a fraction of these are shown at any one time. Exhibitions change regularly, making it a museum to visit time and time again.

🍴 Courses

Polish Your Cooking COOKING COURSE
(☎ 501 598 681; www.polishyourcooking.com) Gives a lesson in creating Polish cuisine, during

which students cook two classic dishes and sample several others. Includes breakfast and lunch for 199zł per person. Classes take place in a range of locations across Warsaw.

Academia Polonica LANGUAGE COURSE
(Map p54; ☑ 22 629 9311; www.academia polonica.com; al Jerozolimskie 55/14) Offers highly rated Polish language courses aimed at students, business people and expats, as well as short crash courses for visitors.

IKO LANGUAGE COURSE
(Map p54; ☑ 22 826 2259; www.iko.com.pl; ul Kopernika 3) Offers four-day crash courses in Polish on various dates over the summer; 490zł per person.

☞ Tours

Adventure Warsaw BUS TOUR
(Wycieczki po Warszawie; Map p50; ☑ 606 225 525; www.adventurewarsaw.pl; ul Mińska 25; from 149zł) Funky Praga-based tour company offering offbeat tours of Warsaw in communist-vintage vans and buses. Topics include the communist era, Warsaw's nightclubs, and districts 'off the beaten track'.

Warsaw City Tours BUS TOUR
(☑ 22 826 7100; www.warsawcitytours.info; per person €35) Offers three-hour coach sightseeing tours of the major sights, with hotel pick-up and drop-off. Book over the phone, online or through your hotel reception desk.

Our Roots CULTURAL TOUR
(Map p54; ☑ 22 620 0556; www.our-roots. jewish.org.pl; ul Twarda 6) Specialises in tours of Jewish sites; the Jewish Warsaw tour lasts five hours and costs around 500zł. Other tours, including to Auschwitz-Birkenau and Treblinka, can be organised on request.

✸ Festivals & Events

Warsaw has an active social calendar and you'll find fests and concerts at nearly any time of year. Autumn is the high point, both for classical music and for film. Check the official city tourism website www.warsaw tour.pl for an extensive list.

Beethoven Easter Festival MUSIC
(Wielkanocny Festiwal Ludwiga van Beethovena; www.beethoven.org.pl; ☉ Mar-Apr) A series of concerts celebrating the work of the great composer.

Equality Parade PARADE
(Parada Równości; www.paradarownosci.eu; ☉ Jun) Annual march through the city's streets in mid-June, in support of social equality and diversity.

Mozart Festival MUSIC
(Festiwal Mozartowski; www.operakameralna.pl; ☉ Jun-Jul) Staged annually from mid-June to the end of July and organised by the Warsaw Opera Kameralna. Features performances of all 26 of Mozart's stage productions, plus a selection of his other works.

Street Art Festival THEATRE
(Festiwal Sztuka Ulicy; www.sztukaulicy.pl; ☉ Jun-Jul) Held from late June to early July, this week-long festival features street theatre, open-air art installations and 'happenings' staged unpredictably in public places such as Old Town Sq, the Royal Way, public parks and even bus stops.

Warsaw Summer Jazz Days JAZZ
(www.adamiakjazz.pl; ☉ Jul) Series of July concerts brings leading international jazz stars to town, mixed in with performances by local talent. Major gigs are held in the Congress Hall at the Soho Factory complex in Praga.

Chopin and His Europe MUSIC
(Chopin i Jego Europa; en.chopin.nifc.pl/festival; ☉ Aug) Two-week festival of orchestral and chamber music held in August, presenting the works of Chopin and other great European composers.

Warsaw Autumn Festival of Contemporary Music MUSIC
(Warszawska Jesień Międzynarodowy Festiwal Muzyki Współczesnej; www.warsaw-autumn.art.pl; ☉ Sep) This 50-year-old festival, held over nine days in September, is the city's pride and joy. It offers a chance to hear the world's best avant-garde music, including new works by major Polish composers.

Warsaw Film Festival FILM
(Warszawski Festiwal Filmowy; www.wff.pl; ☉ Oct) Screenings of the year's best international films over 10 days in October, plus Polish film highlights and plenty of retrospectives.

⌯ Sleeping

An overnight stay in Warsaw can bust a tight budget. Forget about those tidy 200zł-a-night hotels that Poland seems to have in abundance elsewhere. Many Warsaw hotels are geared toward business travellers and are priced accordingly.

That's not to say things haven't improved. Hostels catering to international tourists have grown steadily in number, and room rates have stabilised in recent years. Try to time your visit for a weekend, as many hotels discount rates then.

Don't neglect the internet; you have a good chance of snagging a bargain online, rather than just fronting up to the reception desk. Warsaw's tourist information offices can also help find and book accommodation.

🛏 Old Town & Around

Hostel Kanonia
HOSTEL €

(Map p60; ☑ 22 635 0676; www.kanonia.pl; ul Jezuicka 2; dm 50-60zł, s 100-180zł, d 180-200zł; ☎) Well-run private hostel offering dorm accommodation as well as private singles and doubles at reasonable prices, given the romantic Old Town location. The simple, functional rooms won't win a beauty contest, but the friendly reception and bar go a long way toward fulfilling most backpackers' needs.

Dom Przy Rynku Hostel
HOSTEL €

(Map p60; ☑ 22 831 5033; www.cityhostel.net; Rynek Nowego Miasta 4; dm 50zł, r 110zł; ☎) Located in a quiet corner of the busy New Town, Przy Rynku is a neat, clean and friendly hostel occupying a 19th-century house. Its dorms sleep two to five people, and there's a big kitchen and laundry facilities for guest use.

★ Castle Inn
HOTEL €€

(Map p60; ☑ 22 425 0100; www.castleinn. pl; ul Świętojańska 2; s/d from 280/300zł; ✳☎) Nicely decorated 'art hotel', housed in a 17th-century town house. All rooms overlook either Castle Sq or St John's Cathedral, and come in a range of playful styles. Our favourite would be No 121, 'Viktor', named for a reclusive street artist, complete with tasteful graffiti and a gorgeous castle view. Breakfast costs an extra 35zł.

Mamaison Hotel Le Regina
HOTEL €€€

(Map p60; ☑ 22 531 6000; www.leregina.com; ul Kościelna 12; r from 400zł; ℙ☎) Housed in a lovely arcaded 18th-century-style palace just a few minutes' walk from the Old Town, the Regina manages a successful combination of traditional architecture and contemporary design. Rooms are light and airy, and decorated in shades of chocolate and vanilla, with lots of polished walnut, gleaming chrome and marble in the more expensive rooms.

Dom Literatury
HOTEL €€€

(Map p60; ☑ 22 635 0404; www.fundacjadl.com; ul Krakowskie Przedmieście 87/89; s/d 255/405zł; ☎) A plush, old-fashioned, hotel with a wonderful location and too many stairs. It's the headquarters of the Polish PEN Club, a writers' organisation. If you're happy to lug your bags to the 3rd floor, you'll enjoy views over the Old Town, and rooms with formal decor, deep sofas and wooden beams on the ceiling.

🛏 South of the Old Town

★ Oki Doki Hostel
HOSTEL €

(Map p54; ☑ 22 828 0122; www.okidoki.pl; Plac Dąbrowskiego 3; dm 29-90zł, r 128-260zł; ☎) Arguably Warsaw's most popular hostel, and certainly one of the best. Each of its bright, large rooms is individually named and decorated. Accommodation is in three- to eight-bed dorms, with a special three-bed dorm for women only. The owners are well travelled and know the needs of backpackers, providing a kitchen and a laundry service. Breakfast available (15zł).

New World Street Hostel
HOSTEL €

(Map p54; ☑ 22 828 1282; www.nws-hostel.pl; ul Nowy Świat 27; dm 42-67zł, r 178zł; ☎) Conveniently located amid the dining and shopping delights of ul Nowy Świat, this hostel has named its clean, bright dorms after the cities of the world, from Amsterdam to Sydney. Every bed has an individual lamp, and there's a lounge and kitchen available. The hostel also stocks a limited amount of groceries for guests to purchase.

Hostel Helvetia
HOSTEL €

(Map p54; ☑ 22 826 7108; www.hostel-helvetia.pl; ul Sewerynów 7; dm 35-49zł, r 129-237zł; ☎) Hostel with spick-and-span rooms, painted in warm, bright colours, with wooden floors and a good amount of space. Choose from three- to eight-bed dorms or good-value private singles and doubles. Laundry and kitchen facilities are in top order, and with a limited number of beds, it's best to book ahead in summer.

Hotel Harenda
HOTEL €€

(Map p54; ☑ 22 826 0071; www.hotelharenda. com.pl; ul Krakowskie Przedmieście 4/6; s/d from 310/340zł; ☎) Housed in an elegant neoclassic building, the Harenda boasts a quiet location close to the Old Town and an appealing, old-fashioned ambience. Single rooms are on the small side but the bathrooms are spotless; you're paying for the location here.

Chmielna Guest House
GUESTHOUSE €€

(Map p54; ☑ 22 828 1282; www.chmielnabb. pl; ul Chmielna 13; r 190-210zł; ☎) Handily situated in the middle of a bustling shopping and restaurant zone, this sister property of New World Hostel offers a small number of

RENTING YOUR OWN PAD

A short-term rental in a private apartment can be cheaper than a full-scale hotel; if you're staying longer than a couple of days, it's an excellent option. Short-term rentals usually have one or two bedrooms (for up to four people), plus a small kitchen with a few handy appliances such as a toaster and a coffee maker, not to mention a washing machine, a handy solution to Poland's lack of laundromats. Since there's no reception desk, you'll usually have to phone in advance and set up a meeting place to get the keys. Normally you book online with a credit card or pay in cash on the spot.

Apartments Apart (Map p54; ☑ 22 351 2260; www.apartmentsapart.com; ul Nowy Świat 29/3; apt from 200zł; ☎ ✿) Offers several attractive apartments in the Old Town and city centre, at prices ranging from around 200zł for a tiny studio to 300zł to 500zł per night for larger places.

Warsaw Apartments (☑ 22 550 4550; www.warsawapartments.com.pl; ul Augustówka 9; apt from 150zł; P) This agency manages three modern apartment blocks on the outskirts of Warsaw, all are in good order. The apartments have phones, TVs, cookers and refrigerators, and can be rented by the night; for stays of over a month the nightly rate falls by around half.

Residence St Andrew's Palace (Map p54; ☑ 22 826 4640; www.residencestandrews.pl; ul Chmielna 30; apt from 300zł; P @ ☎) Something a little different; exquisitely appointed luxury apartments in a refurbished building on central ul Chmielna. Worth a look and a splurge for something really special.

comfortable budget rooms, some of which have shared bathrooms. Rooms are decked out in colourful contemporary decor, and there's a basic kitchen for guest use. Note that the rooms are on the 3rd floor, and reception is located at New World Street Hostel (p71).

Hotel Mazowiecki
HOTEL €€

(Map p54; ☑ 22 827 2365; www.hotelewam.pl; ul Mazowiecka 10; s/d from 150/190zł; ☎) Once reserved as military accommodation, this hotel now offers its rooms to all and sundry. It's a basic but comfortable option, with the added bonus (or drawback, depending on how you look at it) of a location on one of the city centre's nightlife strips. About three-quarters of its rooms have no bathroom, so be aware when booking.

Hotel Bristol
HOTEL €€€

(Map p60; ☑ 22 551 1000; www.hotelbristol warsaw.pl; ul Krakowskie Przedmieście 42/44; r from 560zł; ✱ ☎ ✿) If you've got it, flaunt it. Established in 1899 and restored to its former glory after a massive renovation, the Bristol is touted as Poland's most luxurious hotel. Its neoclassical facade conceals a feast of original Art Nouveau features, and huge rooms that are both traditional and comfortable. Attentive staff cater to every whim, and the Old Town is only a few minutes' walk away.

Sofitel Victoria
HOTEL €€€

(Map p54; ☑ 22 657 8011; www.sofitel.com; ul Królewska 11; r from 450zł; ☎ ✿) Conveniently located between the Old Town and the Palace of Culture & Science, this hotel offers real comfort at rates a bit lower than competing five-star properties. With all the extras you'd expect from a top hotel (concierge service, wellness centre, the occasional celebrity), it's a fine choice, and an even better one with a discount from the website.

Financial District

The Financial District is home to some of the city's swankiest five-star hotels, including outposts of luxury chains such as **Inter-Continental** (Map p54; ☑ 22 328 8888; www. warsaw.intercontinental.com; ul Emilii Plater 49) and **Radisson Blu** (Map p50; ☑ 22 321 8888; www.radissonblu.com/hotel-warsaw; ul Grzybowska 24), to name but a couple. While these are normally targeted at business clients with deep expense accounts, they occasionally offer deals online or drop rates on weekends. It never hurts to try.

Hotel Premiere Classe
HOTEL €

(Map p50; ☑ 22 624 0800; www.premiere-classe-warszawa.pl; ul Towarowa 2; r from 145zł; ☎) Rooms – and especially the baths – at this modern, purpose-built budget chain hotel are tiny, but standards are relatively high given what you pay. It's not very handy for the city's attractions, but the trams that cruise al Jerozolimskie are only a few minutes' walk away.

Ibis Warszawa Centrum
HOTEL €€

(Map p50; ☏22 520 3000; www.ibis.com; al Solidarności 165; r from 160zł; P ✱ @ 🛜) Clean, compact budget chains such as Ibis make sense in Warsaw, where reasonably priced hotels with character are in short supply. This one, a little away from the action but well connected by trams, offers tidy, well-appointed rooms, and inviting modern baths. Book online for the best rate.

Hotel Maria
HOTEL €€

(Map p50; ☏22 838 4062; www.hotelmaria.pl; al Jana Pawła II 71; s/d 323/384zł; P ✱ 🛜) Rambling old house masquerading as a hotel set on three floors (no lifts, just steep wooden stairs), with friendly staff, a delightful restaurant and breakfast nook, and spacious rooms. The location is outside the centre, but convenient to the Jewish sights and just a few tram stops away from the Old Town. Rooms at the back are slightly quieter than those at the front, along busy al Jana Pawła II. Weekend bookings slice about 100zł off the price.

🛌 South of al Jerozolimskie

Nathan's Villa Hostel
HOSTEL €

(Map p54; ☏22 622 2946; www.nathansvillahostel. com; ul Piękna 24/26; dm from 47zł, r 175zł; 🛜; 🚊131 or 522 from Warszawa Centralna train station) Established hostel set in a quiet courtyard, south of the centre. Like any good hostel, it has a kitchen, a common room and a reading room, but it also offers a laundry service and entertainment in the form of DVDs and games. Alight the bus at Plac Konstytucji.

Majawa Camping 123
CAMPGROUND, HOTEL €

(Map p50; ☏22 822 9121; www.majawa.pl; ul Bitwy Warszawskiej 1920r 15/17; site per person/car/tent 25/20/20zł, hotel s/d 100/150zł; P 🛜 ⛶) Set in extensive grounds near the Warszawa Zachodnia bus terminal, this camping ground has well-tended grass, tree-shaded areas and good facilities, including a tennis court and laundry. Simple hotel rooms and wood-panelled, two-person bungalows are also available, but beware, the walls are paper-thin. Rates given here include bathrooms; to save even more money, ask for a room or bungalow without.

★ Hotel Rialto
HOTEL €€€

(Map p54; ☏22 584 8700; www.rialto.pl; ul Wilcza 73; r from 500zł; P ✱ 🛜) This converted town house is a monument to early 20th-century design. Each room is individually decorated in Art Nouveau or Art Deco style, with antique and reproduction furniture, period fittings, and tiled or marbled baths. There are plenty of modern touches where it counts, such as power showers, and a sauna and steam room. Cheaper rates click into place at weekends.

🛌 Praga

Krokodyl
HOSTEL €

(☏22 810 1118; www.hostelkrokodyl.com; ul Czapelska 24; dm 45-60zł, s/d 150/160zł; P 🛜) Just what a party spot like Praga needs: a decent, private hostel with no lockout and a pleasant setting to crash in after a night out. There are lots of pluses here: cheerful rooms, a clean common cooking area, and free laundry. A short tram ride brings you into the heart of Warsaw.

Hotel Hetman
HOTEL €€

(Map p50; ☏22 511 9800; www.hotelhetman. pl; ul Kłopotowskiego 36; s/d 290/340zł; P 🛜; Ⓜ Dworzec Wileński, National Stadium, 🚊25) In a quiet location across the river in Praga, but only just over a kilometre's walk or bus ride from the Old Town, the Hetman sports English-speaking staff, fresh rooms decked out in soothing neutral tones, and gleaming bathrooms. It's well serviced by public transport.

Hotel Hit
HOTEL €€

(Map p50; ☏22 618 9470; www.hithotel.pl; ul Kłopotowskiego 33; s/d 175/209zł, ste from 300zł; P 🛜; Ⓜ Dworzec Wileński, 🚊25) A pleasing budget option not far from the best bars of Praga, as well as a tram stop and the metro. The clean, snug digs are on the bland side, but excellent value for money. In addition to singles and doubles there are a few apartments available.

✗ Eating

Of all the cities in Poland, you'll eat best in Warsaw. It's not just hearty Polish cuisine on offer, either – you'll find a growing selection of European, Southeast Asian, Indian, Middle Eastern and Japanese restaurants worthy of your hard-earned cash. Prices have risen with the increased variety, but you can still find some good, cheap eats in the centre, particularly in the form of Poland's classic milk bars.

The largest concentration of eateries exists on and around ul Nowy Świat and south of al Jerozolimskie. The Old Town generally houses expensive tourist traps, but there is a handful of quality spots if you take the time to look.

✖ Old Town & Around

Fret Á Porter   POLISH €€
(Map p60; ul Freta 37; mains 23-57zł; ☺noon-11pm; 🛜) One of a number of attractive restaurants on tree-lined New Town Sq. The menu is a mix of Polish and international favourites, so you can start out with an appetiser of *pierogi* (dumplings) and choose something such as salmon or steak for a main dish. The terrace is perfect for a meal on a nice evening; there's live entertainment – usually a singer – some nights.

Restauracja Pod Samsonem   JEWISH €€
(Map p60; ul Freta 3/5; mains 12-40zł; ☺11am-11pm) Situated in the New Town, Pod Samsonem is frequented by locals and tourists looking for inexpensive and tasty Polish food infused with a Jewish flavour, such as marinated herring, gefilte fish and *kawior po żydowsku* ('Jewish caviar' – chopped chicken liver with garlic).

Podwale Piwna Kompania   POLISH €€
(Map p60; Podwale 25; mains 24-60zł; ☺11am-11pm) The motto here is 'a lot of good food for a reasonable price' and that's exactly what you can expect from this lively beerhouse, just outside the Old Town.

★Restauracja Polka   POLISH €€€
(Map p60; ul Świętojańska 2; mains 24-68zł; ☺noon-11pm) Celebrity chef Magda Gessler loves to fit out her restaurants with folksy floral wallpaper and rustic wooden tables, and this Old Town venue is no exception. The decor accentuates the high-quality versions of traditional Polish food which issue from the kitchen, including blood sausage, pork shanks on cabbage, and crispy duck in honey. Some tables have views of Castle Sq.

✖ South of the Old Town

★Mango   VEGAN €
(Map p54; ul Bracka 20; mains 13-20zł; ☺11am-11pm; 🛜🍴) Mango is a stylish all-vegan eatery with a simple contemporary interior and pleasant outdoor seating. Excellent menu items range from vegie burgers to mango sticky rice. The 'Mango Plate' (Talerz Mango) of hummus, mango, falafel, eggplant, olives, sweet peppers and harissa paste served with pita bread is top value at 22zł.

Cô Tú   ASIAN €
(Map p54; Hadlowo-Usługowe 21; mains 15-23zł; ☺10am-9pm Mon-Fri, 11am-7pm Sat & Sun) The wok at this simple Asian diner never rests as hungry Poles can't get enough of the excellent dishes coming from the kitchen. The menu is enormous, covering all the main bases (seafood, vegetable, beef, chicken, pork), and you'll never have to wait more than 10 minutes for your food despite the queues. Accessed via the archway at ul Nowy Świat 26.

Krokiecik   CAFETERIA €
(Map p54; ul Zgoda 1; mains 10-14zł; ☺11am-11pm) Modern take on the classic milk bar, serving tasty inexpensive soups, salads and hot dishes such as *fasolka po bretońsku* (sausage and bean casserole), *strogonow z wołowiny* (beef stroganoff) and *ragout z kurczaka* (chicken ragout).

Petit Appetit   FRENCH €€
(Map p54; ul Nowy Świat 27; mains 14-39zł; ☺11am-11pm; 🛜) Appealing French bistro with timber tables and chequerboard tiles. Serves tasty light meals, including several all-day breakfast options. Try the 'hedgehogs' (baked potatoes with various fillings).

Socjal   MEDITERRANEAN €€
(Map p54; ul Foksal 18; mains 18-39zł; ☺noon-midnight) Hypercool restaurant and bar with pared-back interiors and an open kitchen. The menu is Mediterranean-influenced, with piadinas, pasta, and pizzas of a more adventurous stripe (asparagus pizza, anyone?). The outdoor deck is a great people-watching space.

Giovanni Rubino   ITALIAN €€
(Map p60; ul Krakowskie Przedmieście 37; mains 24-69zł; ☺10am-midnight) The outdoor seating at this classy Italian restaurant has a pleasant view over Herbert Hoover Sq. There's a fine range of pasta and pizzas on the menu, and a long wine list. From 10am to noon you can choose a set breakfast for 17zł.

Dawne Smaki   POLISH €€€
(Map p54; ul Nowy Świat 49; mains 39-95zł; ☺noon-11pm; 🛜) An excellent, easy-to-reach place at which to try Polish specialities such as herring in cream, stuffed cabbage rolls, *pierogi* (dumplings) and all the rest. The interior is traditional white walls, wood and lace, without being overly hokey. Try the good-value lunch specials.

Restauracja 99   POLISH €€€
(Map p50; al Jana Pawła II 23; mains 35-95zł; ☺8am-11pm; 🛜) A favourite of Warsaw business folk since 1997, this stylish white-toned restaurant serves updated Polish dishes

MORE THAN MILK

Capitalism has been rough on Warsaw's milk bars (*bar mleczny*), the dirt-cheap, canteen-like holdovers from communist times where hearty Polish meals – many vegetarian or dairy-based, hence the name – are dished out from bains-marie to appreciative, hungry customers. Though their ranks have thinned since their glory days, there are several survivors around town, popular with Poles as much as with visitors.

Bar Mleczny Pod Barbakanem (Map p60; ul Mostowa 27; mains 7-10zł; ⊙ 8am-4pm Mon-Fri, 9am-4pm Sat; 🖉) In the Old Town, just outside the Barbican, look for Bar Mleczny Pod Barbakanem, a staple that's been around for decades. Don't be put off by the faded exterior; this remains a popular place for lunch.

Bar Mleczny Familijny (Map p54; ul Nowy Świat 39; mains 4-10zł; ⊙ 7am-8pm Mon-Fri, 9am-5pm Sat & Sun; 🖉) In the swanky part of Warsaw, south of the Old Town, Bar Mleczny Familijny is a sentimental favourite, known around the city for its *zupa szczawiowa* (sorrel soup) and *pierogi z truskawkami* (strawberry fruit dumplings).

Prasowy (Map p66; ul Marszałkowska 10/16; mains 6-19zł; ⊙ 9am-8pm Mon-Fri, 11am-7pm Sat & Sun; 🖉) This milk bar in the sprawling area south of al Jerozolimskie has a classy '60s interior so retro, it could feature on the cover of *Wallpaper* magazine.

Rusałka (Map p50; ul Floriańska 14; mains 6-10zł; ⊙ 7am-6pm Mon-Fri, 9am-5pm Sat; 🖉) Praga's favourite milk bar, attracting a devoted blue-collar clientele and workers from the nearby hospital.

such as rabbit and potato pie, and dumplings stuffed with lamb and buckwheat; though there's not much on offer for vegetarians. There's also a breakfast menu, and live music on Friday nights. The bar has big TV screens for viewing major sports events.

🍴 South of al Jerozolimskie

★ **Charlotte Chleb i Wino** FRENCH € (Map p66; al Wyzwolenia 18; mains 9-25zł; ⊙ 7am-midnight Mon-Fri, 9am-1am Sat, 9am-10pm Sun; 🖘) Dazzling French bakery and bistro facing Plac Zbawiciela. It dishes up tantalising croissants and pastries at the break of dawn, then transitions to big salads and crusty sandwiches through the lunch and dinner hours, and finally to wine on the terrace in the evening. Great value for money.

Krowarzywa VEGAN € (Map p66; ul Marszałkowska 27; mains 10-16zł; ⊙ noon-11pm; 🖉) So much for vegan establishments being humourless and bland – this vegan burger specialist has a hip up-to-date interior with funky light fittings, minimalist furniture, and beardy tattooed customers. Serves a variety of meat-free burgers, along with house-made juices.

Beirut MIDDLE EASTERN € (Map p54; ul Poznańska 12; mains 10-25zł; ⊙ noon-1am; 🖘🖉) Hip and informal, this popular place serves chicken shashlik, beef kofta and lamb burgers, in addition to a long list of vegetarian items including hummus varieties and other Middle Eastern dishes. Choose from the menu above the counter and then find a table. There's a turntable on hand for later in the evening, when music kicks in.

Tel Aviv VEGETARIAN € (Map p54; ul Poznańska 11; mains 10-34zł; ⊙ 9am-midnight; 🖘🖉) Warm, welcoming Tel Aviv offers vegetarian, vegan and gluten-free mains, including lots of salads and vegan burgers. Where this place especially excels is in its comfortable interior, where you can relax with a book or laptop.

Flambéeria FRENCH €€ (Map p54; ul Hoża 61; mains 14-27zł; ⊙ noon-midnight) Slick modern restaurant serving a range of savoury tarts based on crème fraiche, in the style of Alsace. The cool interior is fitted with artistically cracked tiles and bare light bulbs. Enter from ul Emilii Plater.

Dżonka ASIAN €€ (Map p54; ul Hoża 54; mains 17-27zł; ⊙ 11am-8pm Mon-Fri, 12-6pm Sat & Sun; 🖘🖉) With only eight indoor tables, Dżonka is small in size but big on Asian cuisine, serving up steaming Thai soups, Mandarin chicken and spicy (by Polish standards) beef Szechwan. Good selection for vegan and vegetarian eaters.

Tandoor Palace INDIAN €€

(Map p66; ul Marszałkowska 21/25; mains 22-48zł; ☉11am-11pm; ☑) A long-time stalwart on Warsaw's Indian food scene and still one of the best in the city, at the Palace food is prepared by experienced North Indian chefs using a genuine tandoor. The extensive menu ranges from classics such as butter chicken, *shahi korma* (chicken or lamb in a mild, creamy sauce with crushed almonds) and biryani to Kashmiri balti dishes and sizzling platters.

Warsaw Tortilla Factory MEXICAN €€

(Map p54; ul Wilcza 46; mains 22-79zł; ☉noon-1am) Lively Mexican place south of the border...well, south of al Jerozolimskie. This is the place to enjoy Mexican and Tex-Mex favourites, including quesadillas, tacos, fajitas and ribs. More than a culinary destination, this is a party spot, with a lively atmosphere.

Izumi Sushi JAPANESE €€

(Map p66; ul Mokotowska 17; mains 18-55zł; ☉11am-11pm) Facing hip Plac Zbawiciela, this restaurant serves an array of sushi along with larger dishes such as teriyaki chicken. Its elegant black and white interior is complemented by a mellow outdoor terrace, with views of the passing parade.

Dwie Trzecie MEDITERRANEAN €€€

(Map p54; ul Wilcza 50/52; mains 28-70zł; ☉noon-11pm; ☎) It's worth splurging on the well-turned-out dishes here, such as spicy pumpkin soup, flavoured with beetroot and shrimp, followed by slow-roasted veal cheeks and polenta. The interior is formal without a hint of fussiness, and the warm brick-lined walls and plank flooring lend a calming feel. The wine list is excellent, including a good choice of wine by the glass.

🍴 Praga

Le Cedre 61 LEBANESE €€

(Map p50; al Solidarności 61; mains 15-59zł; ☉11am-11pm; ☑; Ⓜ Dworzec Wileński, ☷4) This Lebanese restaurant with colourful interiors serves authentic Middle Eastern food opposite Park Praski on the eastern side of the Vistula. Choose from an array of hot and cold dishes, with a fair number of vegetarian options. A belly dancer performs every Friday evening. It's a short walk from trams and the metro station.

★**Warszawa Wschodnia** MODERN EUROPEAN €€€

(Map p50; ul Mińska 25; mains 25-80zł; ☉24hr; ☎) Fabulous restaurant within a huge industrial building in the Soho Factory complex,

---

COFFEE & A GOOD READ

Poles have had a long love affair with literature, but a relatively recent love is coffee. It was only a matter of time before someone came up with the cafe-bookshop, thus providing locals with a practical ménage à trois involving these two loves. These intellectual establishments have sprung up across town, offering racks of books alongside coffee, tea and snacks. They're wonderful places to spend a few hours, dipping into a book or catching the occasional literary event or concert.

Kafka (Map p54; ul Oboźna 3; ☉9am-10pm; ☎) This quiet cafe serving healthy cakes, quiches and sweet-and-sour pancakes is our top pick. Choose from its big selection of secondhand books, and kick back on its low couches or outdoor seating.

Chłodna 25 (Map p50; www.klubchlodna25.pl; ul Chłodna 25; ☉9am-11pm Mon-Fri, 10am-11pm Sat & Sun; ☎) Bohemian haunt attracting journalists, artists, musicians and anyone else who can fit through the door. Concerts, films, debates and lecturers feature regularly; wine, beer and homemade cakes are available.

Wrzenie Świata (Map p54; ul Gałczyńskiego 7; ☉9am-10pm; ☎) Small, peaceful bookshop and coffee house that draws journalists and those interested in Polish and world affairs. The location is on a quiet backstreet behind ul Nowy Świat.

Czuły Barbarzyńca (Map p50; www.czuly.pl; ul Dobra 31; ☉8.30am-8.30pm Mon-Thu, 10am-10pm Fri & Sat, to 8.30pm Sun; ☎) Stripped-back space where books, discussions and readings come first and coffee (albeit good coffee) is just along for the ride. The 'Gentle Barbarian' was the city's first cafe-bookshop.

Tarabuk (Map p54; www.tarabuk.pl; ul Browarna 6; ☉10am-10pm Mon-Fri, 11am-10pm Sat & Sun; ☎) This cosy cafe provides space not only for books and coffee, but also for concerts, readings, lectures and vodka.

taking its name from a neon sign salvaged from the nearby train station of the same name. Serves a modern interpretation of Polish cuisine, with French influences. Mains are priced between 60zł and 80zł, so you can't beat the 25zł three-course set lunch menu served noon to 4pm Monday to Friday.

 Drinking & Nightlife

Varsovians don't generally distinguish between places that serve coffee and those that serve alcohol. Most places do both, starting the day pushing caffeine, and ending it selling beer and cocktails. Most drinking establishments open at 11am or noon and close when *ostatni gość* (the last guest) leaves – in practice, any time between midnight and 4am. Cafe culture has become phenomenally popular in Warsaw in recent years. You'll find plenty of places to caffeinate across the city, and new ones pop up on a regular basis.

If you're up for some clubbing, check out ul Mazowiecka in the city centre, and ul Ząbkowska in Praga.

Old Town & Around

Polyester CAFE, BAR
(Map p60; ul Freta 49/51; noon-midnight; 🛜) Smooth establishment with fashionably retro furnishings and a laid-back vibe – arguably the hippest cocktail bar in the vicinity of the Old Town. Serves excellent cocktails, as well as a full range of coffee drinks and light food. Also hosts jazz and other live music on a regular basis.

Pożegnanie z Afryką CAFE
(Map p60; ul Freta 4/6; 10am-7pm Mon-Fri, to 5pm Sat & Sun) 'Out of Africa' is a tiny cafe offering nothing much beyond coffee – but what coffee! Choose from around 50 varieties, served in a little pot, and a range of tempting cakes. This is the original shop in a small chain of cafes scattered across Poland's major cities.

Same Fusy TEAHOUSE
(Map p60; ul Nowomiejska 10; 1-11pm) Head downstairs to find the stylish tea room belonging to this multilevel bistro-cafe. More than 100 different types of tea are served, from the accepted norm to the out of the ordinary.

South of the Old Town

Relax CAFE
(Map p54; ul Złota 8; 8am-11pm Mon-Fri, 10am-11pm Sat & Sun; 🛜) Compact Relax, at the back

of a former cinema, has a retro-grungy charm. It serves a range of Polish microbrews, as well as good coffee, cake and sandwiches.

Cafe Blikle CAFE
(Map p54; ul Nowy Świat 35; 9am-8pm Mon-Sat, 10am-8pm Sun; 🛜) The mere fact that Blikle has survived two world wars and the challenges of communism makes it a household name locally. But what makes this legendary cafe truly famous is its doughnuts, for which people have been queuing up for generations. Enter its cake shop via the separate entrance to the right, and find out why.

Między Nami BAR
(Map p54; ul Bracka 20; 10am-11pm; 🛜) A mix of bar, restaurant and cafe, 'Between Us' attracts a trendy set with its designer furniture, whitewashed walls and excellent drinks list.

Paparazzi BAR
(Map p54; ul Mazowiecka 12; 6pm-late Mon-Sat; 🛜) A long-time mainstay on the popular ul Mazowiecka scene, Paparazzi somehow manages to retain a whiff of fashionable exclusivity. Its speciality is cocktails, and with talented and friendly bar staff, it remains one of the best bars in town.

Lemon CAFE, BAR
(Map p54; ul Sienkiewicza 6; 24hr; 🛜) Cool split-level venue down a relatively quiet side street. The lime-green interior and brown couches make a dramatic statement, best countered by an alcoholic beverage. There's coffee on offer too, as well as light meals. As this place never closes, it's ideal for late starters or the terminally energised. But is it a bar or a cafe? You decide.

Enklawa CLUB
(Map p54; ul Mazowiecka 12; 10pm-4am Tue-Sat) Blue and purple light illuminates this space with comfy plush seating, mirrored ceilings, two bars and plenty of room to dance. Check out the extensive drinks menu, hit the dance floor or observe the action from a stool on the upper balcony. Wednesday night is 'old school' night, with music from the '70s to the '90s.

Klubokawiarnia CLUB
(Map p54; ul Czackiego 3/5; 6pm-late) Under the steady gaze of communist icons, dance the night away to great music with a chilled party crowd at this basement club. Regular fancy-dress events are held to spice up an already funky night.

Capitol
CLUB

(Map p60; ul Marszałkowska 115; ⊘10pm-late Fri & Sat) If scarcity excites you, squeeze through the doors of this oh-so-cool club on the two nights of the week it's open – Friday and Saturday. Low lighting gleams off pillars, retro decor and the shining faces of Warsaw's beautiful people as they gyrate within the dance floor throng.

Room 13
CLUB

(Map p54; ul Mazowiecka 13; ⊘10pm-late Thu-Sun) Lively nightclub on a popular nightlife strip.

South of al Jerozolimskie

Plan B
BAR

(Map p66; al Wyzwolenia 18; ⊘11am-late) Phenomenally popular, this upstairs bar on Plac Zbawiciela draws a mix of students and young office workers. Find some couch space and relax to smooth beats from regular DJs. On warm summer evenings the action spills out onto the street, giving the square the feel of a summer block party.

Coffee Karma
CAFE

(Map p66; Plac Zbawiciela 3/5; ⊘7.30am-10pm Mon-Fri, 10am-10pm Sat & Sun; ☜) Laid-back Coffee Karma has an enviable perch on Plac Zbawiciela, comfy couches and a light menu. The cavernous, dimly lit interior is a fine place to work through a morning-after slump with the aid of caffeine.

Praga

★Kofi
CAFE

(Map p50; ul Mińska 25; ⊘9am-5pm; ☜) If you're weary of the weak filtered coffee of Central Europe, you'll shed a happy tear when you enter this cool cafe within the sprawling Soho Factory compound in Praga. Excellent coffee is served in an atmospheric industrial interior, enhanced by the aroma of coffee beans being roasted on the premises.

Po Drugiej Stronie Lustra
PUB

(Map p50; ul Ząbkowska 5; ⊘6pm-late) Start a night of carousing at this pub, with its inviting garden and dozens of different beers, including many hard-to-find microbrews.

W Oparach Absurdu
BAR

(Map p50; ul Ząbkowska 6; ⊘noon-late) Contains an eclectic bric-a-brac interior, and hosts occasional live bands from countries such as Belarus and Ukraine.

Łysy Pingwin
PUB

(Map p50; ul Ząbkowska 11; ⊘noon-late) The 'Bald Penguin' is a classic old-school Praga bar – grungy but fun.

Sen Pszczoły
CLUB

(Map p50; ul Grochowska 301/305; ⊘9pm-late) The name of this nightclub translates loosely as 'The Dream of Bees' – a reference to a Salvador Dalí painting. The slightly surreal reality is a chilled-out dance club and bar.

CONCENTRATED DRINKING

Warsaw's nightlife is as dispersed as it is diverse, but there are a few central points where bar-hopping doesn't require taking the bus.

Arguably, the best grouping of nightspots per square metre can be found along ul Mazowiecka, a couple of blocks west of ul Krakowskie Przedmieście.

➡ **Paparazzi** (p77)

➡ **Room 13** (p78)

➡ **Tygmont** (p79)

If your taste runs to dive bars and holes in the wall, look no further than the happening district of Praga, across the Vistula. There are several bars and clubs within easy walking distance of each other and enough going on that you could easily spend the whole evening (and the wee hours of the morning) on this side of the river.

➡ **Po Drugiej Stronie Lustra** (p78)

➡ **W Oparach Absurdu** (p78)

➡ **Łysy Pingwin** (p78)

➡ **Sen Pszczoły** (p78)

☆ Entertainment

Warsaw's range of classical and contemporary entertainment options is the best in the country. The city is home to many classical music, opera and theatre venues, and the list of clubs grows longer every year. Film is also well represented at both mainstream and art-house cinemas.

Detailed listings of museums, art galleries, cinemas, theatres, musical events and festivals (in Polish only) can be found in the Friday edition of *Gazeta Wyborcza*. A free what's-on monthly, *Aktivist* (www.aktivist. pl), is distributed through restaurants, bars and clubs, though the listings are only in Polish. Another useful source of listings in Polish (but it can be deciphered with some effort) is the website www.kulturalnie.waw.pl.

As for useful English-language listings, the monthly *Warsaw Insider* (www.warsaw insider.pl) and the entertainment columns of the weekly *Warsaw Voice* (www.warsaw voice.pl) provide some information on cultural events, as well as on bars, pubs and other nightspots.

Tickets for theatre, opera, musical events and visiting shows can be bought from **Eventim** (☑ 22 590 6915; www.eventim.pl; al Jerozolimskie 25; ☺ 9am-7pm Mon-Fri), and from some Empik shops (www.empik.com).

Live Music

Fabryka Trzciny   LIVE PERFORMANCE
(Map p50; ☑ 22 619 0513; www.fabrykatrzciny. pl; ul Otwocka 14; ☺ box office 9.30am-5pm) Located in a revamped factory in the heart of Praga, this arts centre hosts a range of events, including live music performances. Call or check the website before heading out, since this place is only open for events.

Stodoła   LIVE MUSIC
(Map p50; ☑ 22 825 6031; www.stodola.pl; ul Batorego 10; ☺ 9am-9pm Mon-Fri, to 2am Sat) Originally the canteen for builders of the Palace of Culture & Science, Stodoła is one of Warsaw's biggest and longest-running live music venues. A great place to catch touring bands.

Tygmont   LIVE MUSIC
(Map p54; ☑ 22 828 3409; www.tygmont.com.pl; ul Mazowiecka 6/8; ☺ 7pm-late) Hosting both local and international acts, the live music here (occasionally including jazz) is both varied and plentiful. Concerts start around 9pm; it fills up early, so either reserve a table or turn up at opening time. Dinner is also available.

Classical Music & Opera

Warsaw is a great music city, with regular offerings from the symphony orchestras supplemented by lively music fests and church concerts. Buy tickets, which run anywhere from 20zł to 130zł, at venue box offices. Note that many venues take a summer break in July and August.

The Chopin Society brings in pianists from around the world for its free Chopin recitals in Łazienki Park from mid-May until the end of September at noon and 4pm.

Filharmonia Narodowa   CLASSICAL MUSIC
(National Philharmonic; Map p54; ☑ 22 551 7128; www.filharmonia.pl; ul Jasna 5; ☺ box office 10am-2pm & 3-7pm Mon-Sat) Home of the world-famous National Philharmonic Orchestra and Choir of Poland, founded in 1901, this venue has a concert hall (enter from ul Sienkiewicza 10) and a chamber-music hall (enter from ul Moniuszki 5), both of which stage regular concerts. The box office entrance is on ul Sienkiewicza.

Warszawa Opera Kameralna   OPERA
(Warsaw Chamber Opera; Map p50; ☑ 22 831 2240; www.operakameralna.pl; al Solidarności 76b; ☺ box office 11am-7pm Mon-Fri, 3 hrs before performance Sat & Sun) Performs a repertoire ranging from medieval mystery plays to contemporary works, but is most famous for its performances of Mozart's operas – the annual Mozart Festival (p70) is staged here.

Teatr Wielki   OPERA
(National Opera; Map p60; ☑ 22 826 5019; www.teatrwielki.pl; Plac Teatralny 1; ☺ box office 9am-7pm Mon-Fri, 11am-7pm Sat & Sun) This magnificent neoclassical theatre, dating from 1833 and rebuilt after WWII, is the city's main stage for opera and ballet. The repertoire includes international classics anmd works by Polish composers.

Cinemas

Most films (except for children's films, which are dubbed into Polish) are screened in their original language with Polish subtitles. Admission prices range from 15zł to 35zł.

Kinoteka   CINEMA
(Map p54; www.kinoteka.pl; Plac Defilad 1) Multiplex cinema housed in the Palace of Culture & Science; its entrance faces al Jerozolimskie. It's worth seeing a movie here just for the splendid decor.

GAY & LESBIAN WARSAW

Attitudes toward gays and lesbians are gradually evolving, and Warsaw even successfully hosted the international EuroPride festival in 2010. That said, many Poles still are not accepting of gay culture. Given the prevailing attitude, Warsaw does not have the kind of well-developed scene you might expect of a city its size. For an up-to-date listing of clubs, check out www.warsaw.gayguide.net, www.gay.pl or www.innastrona.pl (a Polish-language gay and lesbian listings site).

Fantom (Map p54; www.facebook.com/fantomwarsaw; ul Bracka 20b; ⊘2pm-3am) Poland's longest-running gay club, Fantom has been on the scene since 1994. It's more than just a bar and a club; it also offers a sauna, sex shop and video lounge. The inconspicuous entrance is in the courtyard behind Między Nami.

Galeria (Map p50; www.clubgaleria.pl; Plac Mirowski 1; ⊘8pm-5am Tue-Sun) Popular late-night gay nightclub, offering midweek karaoke and DJs at the weekend. Ring the bell at the mirrored door to get inside.

Kino.Lab   CINEMA
(Map p66; www.kinolab.art.pl; Ujazdów Castle, ul Jazdów 2) Art-house film brought to you by the Centre for Contemporary Art (p67), including cutting-edge cinematic creations from Poland and the world.

Kino Luna   CINEMA
(Map p66; www.kinoluna.pl; ul Marszałkowska 28) Mainly art-house films from around the globe.

Muranów Cinema   CINEMA
(Map p60; www.muranow.gutekfilm.pl; ul Generala Andersa 1) Screens art-house films.

Theatre

Polish theatre has long had a high profile in the capital, and continues to do so. Warsaw's theatres include some of the best in the country. Note that most close in July and August for their annual holidays.

Teatr Ateneum   THEATRE
(Map p50; ☑22 625 2421; www.teatrateneum.pl; ul Jaracza 2) Founded in 1928, the Ateneum leans towards contemporary productions in Polish.

Teatr Dramatyczny   THEATRE
(Map p54; ☑22 656 6844; www.teatrdramatyczny.pl; Plac Defilad 1) Situated within the grand edifice of the Palace of Culture & Science.

Teatr Polonia   THEATRE
(Map p54; ☑22 622 2132; www.teatrpolonia.pl; ul Marszałkowska 56) Run by Krystyna Janda, winner of Best Actress at Cannes in 1990. Often stages productions with strong social themes.

Teatr Powszechny   THEATRE
(Map p50; ☑22 818 2516; www.powszechny.com; ul Zamojskiego 20) With three auditoriums of different sizes, this Praga-based company stages plays from both international and local playwrights.

Teatr Roma   THEATRE
(Map p54; ☑22 628 0360; www.teatrroma.pl; ul Nowogrodzka 49; ⊘box office 10am-7pm Mon-Sat, 1-6pm Sun) Theatre staging big-budget Broadway-style musicals, such as *Mamma Mia*, or the ever-popular *Deszczowa Piosenka* (aka *Singin' in the Rain*).

Teatr Żydowski   THEATRE
(Theatre; Map p54; ☑22 850 5656; www.teatr-zydowski.art.pl; Plac Grzybowski 12/16; ⊘box office 11am-2pm & 3-6pm Mon-Fri, 12.30-7pm Sat, 2.30-6pm Sun) This theatre company derives its inspiration from Jewish culture and traditions. Some of its productions are performed in Yiddish; Polish and English translations are provided through headphones.

🔒 Shopping

Warsaw has all the brand-name shops and malls you'd expect in any European city. For the most part, prices are a little cheaper here.

The main shopping area lies in the maze of streets between the Palace of Culture & Science and ul Nowy Świat, and along the eastern section of al Jerozolimskie and the southern section of ul Marszałkowska.

Lapidarium   ARTS
(Map p60; www.lapidarium.pl; ul Nowomiejska 15/17; ⊘10am-9pm Mon-Sat, 1-7pm Sun) One of the most interesting shops in the Old Town,

81

WARSAW INFORMATION

Lapidarium sells jewellery, folk art, religious art and militaria, including communist-era collectables such as medals and badges.

Cepelia   HANDICRAFTS
(Map p54; www.cepelia.pl; ul Chmielna 8) Long-established organisation dedicated to promoting Polish arts and crafts, stocking its shops with woodwork, pottery, sculpture, fabrics, embroidery, lace, paintings and traditional costumes. There are other branches at **Plac Konstytucji** (Map p66; www.cepelia.pl; Plac Konstytucji 5), **ul Krakowskie Przedmieście** (Map p60; www.cepelia.pl; ul Krakowskie Przedmieście 39) and **ul Marszałkowska** (Map p54; www.cepelia.pl; ul Marszałkowska 99/101).

Neptunea   JEWELLERY, CRAFTS
(Map p60; www.neptunea.pl; ul Krakowskie Przedmieście 47/51; ⊙11am-7pm Mon-Fri, to 5pm Sat) Talk about a mishmash of items: this shop sells Polish jewellery, carved stoneware and crafts, along with furniture, shells and even musical instruments from across the globe.

Galeria Grafiki i Plakatu   ARTS
(Map p54; www.galeriagrafikiiplakatu.pl; ul Hoża 40; ⊙11am-6pm Mon-Fri, 10am-3pm Sat) Small gallery stocking the best selection of original prints and graphic art in Poland. It also has a good range of posters.

Galeria Art   ARTS
(Map p60; www.galeriaart.pl; ul Krakowskie Przedmieście 17; ⊙11.30am-7pm Mon-Fri, to 5pm Sat) Owned by the Association of Polish Artists and Designers, this gallery offers a broad range of contemporary Polish art for sale.

Desa Unicum   ANTIQUES
(Map p66; www.desa.pl; ul Marszałkowska 34/50; ⊙11am-7pm Mon-Fri, to 4pm Sat) Art and antiques dealership Desa Unicum sells a range of old furniture, silverware, watches, paintings, icons and jewellery.

Atlas   BOOKS
(Map p50; www.ksiegarniaatlas.pl; al Jana Pawła II 26; ⊙10am-7pm Mon-Fri, 11am-3pm Sat) Specialises in maps (particularly for hiking and national parks), atlases and travel guides.

Empik   BOOKS
(Map p54; www.empik.com; ul Nowy Świat 15/17; ⊙9am-10pm Mon-Sat, 11am-7pm Sun) Empik stocks a decent selection of English-language books and magazines, along with useful maps. There are other handy central branches at the **Wars Sawa Junior** (Map p54; www. empik.com; ul Marszałkowska 116/122; ⊙9am-10pm

Mon-Sat, 11am-8pm Sun) and **Złote Tarasy** (Map p54; www.empik.com; ul Złota 59; ⊙9am-10pm Mon-Sat, to 9pm Sun) shopping malls.

Koło Bazaar   MARKET
(Bazar na Kole; ul Obozowa; ⊙6am-2pm Sun; 🚌12, 23 or 24) This antiques and bric-a-brac market, held on Sundays in the western suburb of Koło, sells everything from old farm implements and furniture to WWII relics such as rusted German helmets, ammo boxes and shell casings. You have to pick through the junk to find a bargain, but that's half the fun.

Hala Mirowska   MARKET
(Map p50; Plac Mirowski 1; ⊙dawn-dusk) Despite being converted into a modern supermarket, Hala Mirowska is worth visiting for its architecture alone. The redbrick pavilion of this 19th-century marketplace is in exceptional condition, and there's still a semblance of market atmosphere here; stalls selling fresh flowers, fruit and vegetables line its south and west sides.

Złote Tarasy   MALL
(Map p54; www.zlotetarasy.pl; ul Złota 59; ⊙10am-10pm Mon-Sat, to 8pm Sun) Popular, very central mall behind Warszawa Centralna station, with almost every chain shop you can think of. Its distinctive curved glass roof is clearly visible near the Palace of Culture & Science.

Wars Sawa Junior   MALL
(Map p54; www.warssawajunior.pl; ul Marszałkowska 104/122; ⊙10am-9pm) Sprawling modern shopping mall in the city centre; tenants range from Polish chains including Empik to internationals such as Marks & Spencer.

Arkadia   MALL
(Map p50; www.arkadia.com.pl; al Jana Pawła II 82; ⊙10am-10pm Mon-Sat, to 9pm Sun; Ⓜ Dworzec Gdański) Largest shopping mall in Poland, with some 200 shops under one roof. It's handy to the metro.

Sadyba Best Mall   MALL
(www.sadyba.pl; ul Powsińska 31; ⊙10am-9pm Mon-Sat, 8pm Sun) A modern mall housing a wide range of fashion, shoe, jewellery and perfume shops, a multiplex cinema and numerous eating places.

ⓘ Information

DANGERS & ANNOYANCES
➡ Warsaw is no more dangerous than any other European capital city, but you should take precautions while walking at night, and watch

FINELY CRAFTED

Forget the malls and generic chain shops. *Real* shoppers should take to the backstreets of Warsaw, where the art of handmaking products is still alive, and quality over quantity is paramount.

Jan Kielman (Map p54; www.kielman.pl; ul Chmielna 6; ⊘11am-7pm Mon-Fri, to 2pm Sat) The Kielman clan has been making shoes since 1883. Their leather footwear starts at 1900zł, but you'll probably have them for life.

Wyrobów Oświetleniowych (Map p54; www.oswietlenie.strefa.pl; ul Emilii Plater 36; ⊘9am-5pm Mon-Fri) Need an exquisite chandelier? Pick up a Gothic or *fin-de-siécle* number here. Most end up in museums and palaces, but there are a few pieces available (wall lamps start at 700zł) for the average Joe.

Pracownia Sztuki Dekoracyjnej (Map p54; www.lopienscy.pl; ul Poznańska 24; ⊘8am-5pm Mon-Fri) The oldest bronze-metal foundry in Warsaw, in business since 1862. Pick up exceptional pieces in the shape of candleholders, mirror and picture frames and wall lamps.

your possessions on public transport and in other crowded places.

➤ Bikes are particularly at risk; try not to leave your bike out of sight for too long, and always lock it firmly with the strongest lock you can find. Beware also of unauthorised 'mafia' taxis.

➤ Praga has improved but still has a reputation as a rough area at night. Follow the lead of the locals and use taxis as transport in and out of the neighbourhood.

INTERNET ACCESS

Be forewarned: internet cafes in Warsaw come and go.

Arena Cafe (Plac Konstytucji 5; per hr 6zł; ⊘24hr) Internet cafe open all hours.

Verso Internet (ul Freta 17; per hr 6zł; ⊘8am-8pm Mon-Fri, 9am-5pm Sat, 10am-4pm Sun) Online access in the New Town. Enter from ul Świętojerska.

MEDICAL SERVICES

➤ For an ambulance call ☑999, or ☑112 from a mobile phone. English-speaking dispatchers are rare, however, so you're probably better off phoning a medical centre with multilingual staff.

➤ For nonurgent treatment, you can go to one of the city's many *przychodnia* (outpatient clinics). Your hotel or embassy can provide recommendations.

➤ There are plenty of pharmacies in Warsaw where you can get medical advice; look or ask for an *apteka*.

Apteka 21 (al Jerozolimskie 54; ⊘24hr) All-night pharmacy at Warszawa Centralna train station.

Damian Medical Centre (☑22 566 2222; www.damian.pl; ul Wałbrzyska 46; ⊘7am-9pm Mon-Fri, 8am-8pm Sat, 10am-3pm Sun) Reputable private outpatient clinic with hospital facilities.

EuroDental (☑22 380 7000; www.eurodental.com.pl; ul Śniadeckich 12/16; ⊘8am-8pm Mon-Fri) Private dental clinic with multilingual staff.

Lux Med (☑22 332 2888; www.luxmed.pl; Marriott Hotel Bldg, al Jerozolimskie 65/79; ⊘7am-8pm Mon-Fri, 8am-4pm Sat) Private clinic with English-speaking specialist doctors and its own ambulance service; carries out laboratory tests and arranges house calls.

MONEY

Kantors (currency-exchange offices) and ATMs are easy to find around the city centre. There are 24-hour *kantors* at the Warszawa Centralna train station and either side of the immigration counters at the airport, but exchange rates at these places are about 10% lower than in the city centre. Avoid changing money in the Old Town, where rates can be poor.

Bank Pekao (ul Krakowskie Przedmieście 1) Bank Pekao cashes travellers cheques and has several branches in the city centre; other locations include the Marriott Hotel (al Jerozolimskie 65/79) and Plac Bankowy (Plac Bankowy 2).

Western Union (Bank Pekao; www.western union.pl; al Jerozolimskie 44; ⊘8am-7pm Mon-Fri, 10am-2pm Sat) Money-transfer service within branches of Bank Pekao throughout Warsaw; this is the most central outlet.

POST & TELEPHONE

Main Post Office (Map p54; ul Świętokrzyska 31/33; ⊘24hr) Warsaw's head postal facility, which never closes its doors.

TOURIST INFORMATION

Warsaw is blessed with a useful network of tourist information centres, staffed with cheerful English speakers with oodles of free brochures on what to do, where to stay, where to eat, and just about everything else. They can help you sort out transport and make accommodation recommendations.

There are several free monthly tourist magazines worth seeking out. Some of the better ones include *Poland: What, Where, When; What's Up in*

Warsaw; and *Welcome to Warsaw.* All are mines of information about cultural events and provide reviews of new restaurants, bars and nightclubs. They're available in the lobbies of most top-end hotels. The comprehensive monthlies *Warsaw Insider* (10zł) and *Warsaw in Your Pocket* (5zł) are also useful, and are sometimes free for the asking at hotel reception desks.

Warsaw Tourist Office (Map p54; www. warsawtour.pl; Plac Defilad 1, enter from ul Emilii Plater; ⊙8am-8pm May-Sep, to 6pm Oct-Apr; 🐾) The Palace of Culture & Science branch of Warsaw's official tourist information organisation is a central resource for maps and advice. The staff can also help with accommodation. There's no phone number, so visit in person or contact via email.

Also note the other helpful branches at the airport (www.warsawtour.pl; Terminal A, Warsaw Frédéric Chopin Airport, ul Żwirki i Wigury 1; ⊙8am-8pm May-Sep, to 6pm Oct-Apr) and the Old Town (Map p60; www.warsawtour.pl; Rynek Starego Miasta 19/21; ⊙9am-8pm May-Sep, to 6pm Oct-Apr; 🐾).

TRAVEL AGENCIES

Almatur (📞22 826 3512; www.almatur.com.pl; ul Kopernika 23; ⊙9am-7pm Mon-Fri, 10am-3pm Sat) Handles student travel.

Kampio (📞601 775 369; www.kampio.com.pl) Focuses on ecotourism, organising kayaking, biking, walking and birdwatching trips.

WEBSITES

www.um.warsaw.pl Official website of the city of Warsaw.

www.inyourpocket.com/warsaw Highly opinionated and often amusing reviews.

www.local-life.com/warsaw Eating, sleeping, drinking and shopping reviews.

www.warsawtour.pl Official website of the Warsaw Tourist Office.

www.warsawvoice.pl Online version of the English-language magazine.

🔵 Getting There & Away

AIR

Warsaw Frédéric Chopin Airport (Lotnisko Chopina Warszawa; 📞22 650 4220; www. lotnisko-chopina.pl; ul Żwirki i Wigury 1) Warsaw's main airport lies in the suburb of Okęcie, 10km south of the city centre; it handles most domestic and international flights.

The airport has an outpost of the Warsaw Tourist Office, which sells city maps and can help visitors find accommodation. You will also find currency-exchange counters, ATMs, and several car-hire agencies. Buy tickets for public transport from the tourist office or from one of several newsagents.

Warsaw Modlin Airport (📞801 80 1880; www. modlinairport.pl; ul Generała Wiktora Thommée 1a) Airport 35km north of Warsaw that handles budget carriers, including frequent Ryanair flights to and from the UK.

BUS

➝ West of the city centre, **Warszawa Zachodnia bus terminal** (Map p50; 📞708 208 888; www.dworzeconline.pl; al Jerozolimskie 144; ⊙ information & tickets 6am-9pm) handles the majority of international and domestic routes in and out of the city, run by various bus operators. Bus tickets are sold at the terminal.

➝ The private bus company Polski Bus (www. polskibus.com) operates buses to cities across Poland and beyond from the **Młociny bus station** (Dworzec Autobusowy Młociny; ul Kasprowicza 145) north of the city centre, and the **Wilanowska bus station** (Dworzec Autobusowy Wilanowska; ul Puławska 145), south of the centre. Each station is next to the Metro station of the same name. Book on its website for the lowest fares.

CAR

All the major international car-hire companies have offices in Warsaw, many of which are based at the airport. Polish companies offer cheaper rates, but may have fewer English-speaking staff and rental options. One dependable local operator is **Local Rent-a-Car** (📞22 826 7100; www. lrc.com.pl; ul Marszałkowska 140), which offers a midsized Opel in the summer months for €43 a day, or €273 a week, which includes tax, collision damage waiver (CDW), theft protection and unlimited mileage.

TRAIN

Warsaw has several train stations, but the one most travellers use is **Warszawa Centralna** (Warsaw Central; 📞22 391 9757; www.pkp.pl; al Jerozolimskie 54; ⊙24hr). You can travel by rail from Warsaw to every major Polish city and many other places in between; check the useful online timetable in English at www.rozklad-pkp.pl for details of times and fares.

Centralna was built in the 1970s as a major communist-era project, but had become pretty seedy by the 2000s. In response to Poland cohosting the Euro 2012 international football (soccer) tournament, officials embarked on an enormous clean-up. This restored the main hall to its original gleam, and rendered the underground platforms several degrees less sinister.

In the still confusing maze of passages between the above-ground main hall and the subterranean platforms, you'll find a shopping concourse with ticket counters, ATMs and snack bars, and several newsagents where you can buy public transport tickets. There are also money-changing *kantors* (one of which is open 24 hours), a left-luggage office, self-service luggage lockers, cafes, and minisupermarkets.

The process for buying tickets, both for international and domestic destinations, has eased considerably in recent years. The easiest option is to use one of the ticket machines along the walls, which provide instructions in English.

Otherwise, line up at one of the many ticket counters found in both the main hall and the shopping concourse. Though, in theory, most ticket agents should be able to handle some English, not all can. It's still best to write down your destination, and travel dates and times for the ticket seller.

Some domestic trains also stop at **Warszawa Zachodnia train station** (al Jerozolimskie), next to Warszawa Zachodnia bus terminal, and at **Warszawa Wschodnia** (ul Kijowska), in Praga, on the east bank of the Vistula.

ℹ Getting Around

TO/FROM THE AIRPORT
Warsaw Frédéric Chopin Airport

Train The easiest way of getting from Warsaw Frédéric Chopin Airport to the city (and vice versa) is by train. Regular services run between **Warszawa Lotnisko Chopina** (ul Żwirki i Wigury) and Warszawa Centralna stations every 30 minutes between about 5am and 10.30pm (4.40zł, 20 minutes). Some trains also link the airport to **Warszawa Śródmieście station** (al Jerozolimskie), next to the Palace of Culture, on a roughly hourly frequency.

Bus A more frequent bus 175 (4.40zł, every 15 minutes, 5am to 11pm) also runs from the airport, passing along ul Jerozolimskie and ul Nowy Świat before terminating at Plac Piłsudskiego, within walking distance of the Old Town. Don't forget to buy a ticket at a newsagent in the airport arrivals hall, then validate your ticket in one of the machines aboard the bus.

Taxi The taxi stand is right outside the door of the arrivals hall and handles taxis run by several local companies. They all have desks inside the terminal, so you can ask about the fare to your destination – it should be around 40zł to Centralna station and 60zł to the Old Town.

Warsaw Modlin Airport

Train From Warsaw Modlin airport, a train can take you from nearby **Modlin station** (ul Mieszka I) to Warszawa Centralna and Warszawa Zachodnia stations at least once an hour throughout the day (13.80zł, 41 minutes); a shuttle bus transfers passengers between the airport and Modlin station.

Bus The other alternative from Modlin airport is the **Modlin Bus** (☑ 22 535 3381; www.modlin bus.com), which travels between the airport and major landmarks, such as the Palace of Culture, along three different routes (33zł, 40 minutes,

twice an hour). Fares can drop to as low as 9zł when purchased online.

Taxi From Modlin airport, a taxi to the city centre will cost 159zł between 6am and midnight, and 199zł in the wee small hours.

BICYCLE

➤ Cycling in Warsaw is a mixed blessing. The city is generally flat and easy to navigate, distances aren't too great, and cycle paths are on the increase. However, Warsaw drivers don't give a toss about cyclists and you'll soon be following the locals' lead and sharing the footpath with pedestrians.

➤ From March to November Warsaw operates a public bike hire system, similar to those found in other European cities, known as Veturilo (www. veturilo.waw.pl). It's free to use a bicycle for up to 20 minutes, then the fee rises by ascending amounts per hour up to a maximum of 12 hours' use. Visit the website to register, and to find pick-up and drop-off locations.

CAR & MOTORCYCLE

➤ Warsaw's street surfaces are not the most well-maintained in Europe, so driving demands constant attention.

➤ The city's local government oversees paid parking on central streets. You pay using coins in the nearest ticket machine (parkomat) and get a receipt that you display in the windscreen.

➤ For security, try to park your car in a guarded car park (parking strzeżony). There are some in central Warsaw, including one on the aptly named ul Parkingowa, parallel to ul Marszałkowska.

➤ The Polish Automobile Association, **PZM** (Polski Związek Motorowy; ☑ 196 37; www.pzm. pl), operates a 24-hour road breakdown service (pomoc drogowa).

PUBLIC TRANSPORT

Warsaw's integrated public-transport system is operated by **Zarząd Transportu Miejskiego** (Urban Transport Authority; ☑ 19 115; www.ztm. waw.pl) and consists of tram, bus and metro lines, all using the same ticketing system.

Operating Hours

Main routes operate from about 5am to 11pm, and services are frequent and pretty reliable, though often crowded during rush hours (7am till 9am and 3.30pm till 6.30pm Monday to Friday). Friday and Saturday nights the Metro runs until 2.30am. After 11pm several night bus routes link major suburbs to the city centre. The night-service hub is at ul Emilii Plater, next to the Palace of Culture & Science, from where buses depart every half-hour.

Ticketing

➤ Buy a ticket before boarding buses, trams and metros. Tickets are sold at Ruch and Relay news stands, some hotels, post offices, Metro stations and various general stores – look for a sign saying 'Sprzedaży Biletów ZTM'.

→ Tickets, timetables and information are available at ZTM information desks at several underground stations, as well as at Chopin Airport and Warzawa Wschodnia train station in Praga. Some of the more central information desks are located at metro stations including **Ratusz-Arsenał** (Punkt Informacji ZTM; Ratusz-Arsenał Metro station, al Solidarności; ☺7am-8pm Mon-Fri, 9am-4pm Sat), **Centrum** (Punkt Informacji ZTM; Centrum Metro station, ul Marszałkowska; ☺7am-8pm Mon-Sat) and **Świętokrzyska** (Punkt Informacji ZTM; Świętokrzyska Metro station, ul Świętokrzyska; ☺12-7pm Mon-Fri).

→ Several ticket prices and packages are available depending on your needs. For most trips, a *jednorazowy* bilet (single-journey ticket) is sufficient. It costs 3.40zł and is only valid for 20 minutes, though it can be used for more than one service within that period.

→ For several journeys within a longer period of time, consider a 40- or 90-minute ticket, which cost 4.40zł and 7zł respectively. These tickets also allow unlimited transfers.

→ If you're travelling a lot, it might be more convenient to purchase a 24-hour unlimited transfer ticket for 15zł. Another good deal is the weekend ticket for 26zł, which is valid from 7pm Friday to 8am Monday.

→ Note that all these tickets include night buses. Foreign students under 26 years of age who have an International Student Identity Card (ISIC) get a discount of around 50%.

→ There are no conductors onboard vehicles. Validate your ticket by feeding it (magnetic stripe facing down) into the yellow validator machine on the bus or tram or in the Metro station lobby the first time you board; this stamps the expiry time and date on it. Inspections are common and fines are high (up to 266zł!), so don't take the risk of riding unvalidated.

→ Watch out for pickpockets on crowded buses and trams.

Warsaw's Metro

→ Construction of Warsaw's Metro system began in 1983 and there are now two lines. The oldest and longest line (M1) runs from the southern suburb of Ursynów (Kabaty station) to Młociny in the north via the city centre. The newer east–west line (M2) runs from Rondo Daszyńskiego, west of the city centre, to Dworzec Wileński in Praga, though it's likely to be extended in the future. The lines intersect at Świętokrzyska station.

→ Yellow signs with a big red letter 'M' indicate the entrances to Metro stations. You'll find it hard to miss the station entrances on the east-west line, which each resemble a giant letter 'M' made from coloured glass.

→ Every Metro station has a public toilet.

→ There are lifts for passengers with disabilities.

→ Riding the Metro, you use the same tickets as on trams and buses, but validate the ticket at the gate at the entrance to the platform, not inside the vehicle. Trains run approximately every eight minutes (every four minutes during rush hours).

TAXI

→ Taxis in Warsaw are easily available and not too expensive, costing 8zł flag fall and 3/4.50zł per kilometre during the day/night within the centre.

→ Reliable companies include **MPT Radio Taxi** (☎22 191 91), which has English-speaking dispatchers, **Super Taxi** (☎22 196 22; www.supertaxi.pl), and **Halo Taxi** (☎22 196 23). All are recognisable by signs on the taxi's roof with the company name and phone number.

→ Beware of 'pirate' or 'mafia' taxis, which do not display a phone number or company logo – the drivers may try to overcharge you and turn rude and aggressive if you question the fare. They are becoming less common, but still occasionally haunt tourist spots looking for likely victims.

→ All official taxis in Warsaw have their meters adjusted to the appropriate tariff, so you just pay what the meter says. When you board a taxi, make sure the meter is turned on in your presence, which ensures you don't have the previous passenger's fare added to yours.

→ Taxis can be waved down on the street, but it's easier to order a taxi by phone; there's no extra charge for this service.

AROUND WARSAW

Kampinos National Park

Popularly known as the **Puszcza Kampinoska**, **Kampinos National Park** (Kampinoski Park Narodowy; www.kampinoski-pn.gov.pl; ul Tetmajera 38, Izabelin) begins just outside Warsaw's northwestern administrative boundary and stretches west for about 40km. It's one of the largest national parks in Poland, with around three-quarters of its area covered by forest, mainly pine and oak.

Kampinos is popular with Warsaw's hikers and cyclists, who take advantage of its 300km of marked walking and cycling trails. If you plan on exploring the park, buy a copy of the *Compass Kampinoski Park Narodowy* map (scale 1:30,000), available from bookshops in Warsaw.

The park includes Europe's largest area of inland sand dunes, mostly tree-covered and up to 30m high; it's a strange feeling to have sand between your toes so far from the sea. Other parts of the park are barely accessible peat bogs that shelter much of its animal life.

The eastern part of the park, closer to the city, is favoured by walkers as it's accessible by public transport; the western part is less visited. As well as half- and one-day hikes, there are two long trails that traverse the entire length of the park, both starting from Dziekanów Leśny on the eastern edge of the park. The red trail (54km) ends in Brochów, and the green one (51km) in Żelazowa Wola.

Bivouac sites designated for camping are the only accommodation options within the park's boundaries, but there are hotels close by in Czosnów, Laski, Leszno, Tułowice and Zaborów. Warsaw's tourist information centres have a list of places to stay near the park.

ℹ Getting There & Away

The most popular jumping-off point for walks in the eastern part of the park is the village of Truskaw. To get there from central Warsaw, take the Metro to its northern end at Młociny, then catch city bus 708 (two or three an hour on weekdays, hourly on Saturday).

Regular buses operated by Motobuss (www. motobuss.eu) run to Kampinos from a **stop** (Map p54; ul Marszałkowska) next to the Wars Sawa Junior mall, near the intersection with ul Złota (9zł, one hour, 10 daily).

Żelazowa Wola

If it wasn't for Poland's most famous musician, Żelazowa Wola (zheh-lah-*zo*-vah *vo*-lah) wouldn't be on the tourist map. This tiny village 53km west of Warsaw is the **birthplace of Frédéric Chopin** (Dom Urodzenia Fryderyka Chopina; www.chopin.museum; Żelazowa Wola 15; adult/concession museum & park 23/14zł, park only 7/4zł; ⊙ 9am-7pm Tue-Sun), and the house where he was born on 22 February 1810 has been restored and furnished in period style to create a museum. It's a lovely little country house with beautiful gardens, and the exhibits examine the story of the Chopin family's time here. The tranquillity and charm of the place make it a pleasant stop.

Piano recitals, often performed by top-rank virtuosos, are normally held here each Sunday from the first Sunday in May to the last Sunday in September. There are usually two concerts, up to an hour long, at noon and 3pm; there's no fee other than the park entry ticket. The program can be found at www.en.chopin.nifc.pl.

ℹ Getting There & Away

The private bus company Motobuss (www. motobuss.eu) runs buses between central Warsaw and Sochaczew that stop in Żelazowa Wola (19zł, two hours, 10 daily). Buses depart from a stop (p86) adjacent to the Wars Sawa Junior mall, near the intersection with ul Złota.

Mazovia & Podlasie

POP 5.3 MILLION

Best Places to Eat

➡ Restauracja Art Deco (p100)

➡ Restauracja Tejsza (p106)

➡ Ato Sushi (p94)

➡ Ogródek Pod Jabłoniami (p115)

➡ Carska (p111)

Best Places to Stay

➡ Hotel Tumski (p99)

➡ Andel's Hotel (p93)

➡ Hotel Żubrówka (p111)

➡ Hotel Branicki (p104)

➡ Velvet Hotel (p116)

Why Go?

The rolling landscape of Mazovia (Mazowsze in Polish) may look blissful, but this central region has had an eventful history. Once a duchy, Mazovia is dotted with castles, cathedrals and palaces, the biggest of which reside in the riverside towns of Płock and Pułtusk. Łódź is the provincial capital, with more going for it than meets the eye. It's Poland's third-largest metropolis and reflects the ups and downs of its industrial past in its mix of gritty and restored architecture. If you take the time to discover its charms, you'll be happy you did.

To the east, the Podlasie region acts as the green lungs of Poland. Aside from a few urban centres, this province abutting the Lithuanian and Belarusian borders is a paradise of farmland, forest and lakes. Its four national parks are splendid: Narew and Biebrza for their marshlands; Wigry for its lakes; and Białowieża for its primeval forest and wild European bison, the kings of Polish fauna.

When to Go
Łódź

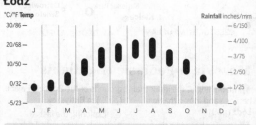

May & Jun Celebrate spring amid the lush primeval greenery of Białowieża National Park.

Jun Visit Łódź for the 'Four Cultures' (Polish, Russian, Jewish, German) festival.

Sep Enjoy the last of the warm weather while kayaking in and around the Augustów Canal.

Mazovia & Podlasie Highlights

① Marvelling at the industrial heritage and movie magic of **Łódź** (p89).

② Harking back to a time of romance at **Arkadia & Nieborów** (p96).

③ Wondering how **Płock** (p97) got hold of so many Art Nouveau treasures.

④ Strolling the attractive grounds of the Branicki Palace (p102) in **Białystok**.

⑤ Exploring the last remnants of Poland's Tatar culture at **Kruszyniany & Bohoniki** (p108).

⑥ Searching primeval forest for a glimpse of the rare European bison at **Białowieża National Park** (p109).

⑦ Relaxing the mind and exercising the body kayaking the Rospuda and Czarna Hańcza in the **Augustów-Suwałki region** (p113).

⑧ Catching your breath as sunshine reveals the stunning scenery of the **Suwałki Landscape Park** (p116).

WESTERN MAZOVIA

Łódź

POP 706,000

Poland's third-largest city grew fabulously wealthy in the 19th century on the backs of its massive textile mills – and on the labour of the thousands of workers who toiled inside them. That wealth was shattered in waves: by the Great Depression of the 1930s, the tragic German occupation during WWII, and the inept communist regime that came after. By 1990, the city was an industrial ruin, on par in some ways with present-day Detroit or the former industrial powerhouses in the British Midlands. The future looked bleak.

But Łódź (woodge) is not just a story of decline, but one of rebirth. In recent years, millions of euros have been poured into the city in an effort to spur one of the country's, and continent's, biggest renovation efforts. The investments have led to the rejuvenation of ul Piotrkowska, the main pedestrian thoroughfare, and to the creation of malls and business centres within the decaying husks of old industrial complexes.

However, the grit of the past isn't that easy to hide; step away from ul Piotrkowska and within a few streets you'll see distressed facades. The city has come a long way, but there's more distance to cover – and this mix of renewal and decay is one of the things that makes it a fascinating place to visit.

Beyond textiles, Łódź's other famous industry is movie-making. The city has long been the centre of the Polish film industry, and directorial giants like Andrzej Wajda, Roman Polański and Krzysztof Kieślowski honed their talents here. It's not for nothing that it's nicknamed 'Holly-woodge'.

Travellers interested in Jewish heritage also have a reason to visit. Before WWII, Łódź was Poland's second-largest Jewish city, after Warsaw, with a community numbering some 230,000. During the war, the Germans created Poland's second-biggest Jewish ghetto in a depressed section north of the centre, and its cemetery and monuments stand as a grim reminder of those dark days.

History

Although the first account of its existence dates from 1332, Łódź remained an obscure settlement until the beginning of the 19th century. In the 1820s the government of the Congress Kingdom of Poland, eyeing the town's advantageous position between Russia and Prussia, chose Łódź as a new textile centre. Enterprising industrialists (primarily Jews, but also Poles, Germans and Russians) rushed in to build textile mills, closely followed by thousands of workers. The wealthy mill owners built opulent palaces (the Historical Museum of Łódź and the Cinematography Museum currently fill two of them), while workers occupied purpose-built tenements surrounding the factories. By the outbreak of WWI, Łódź had grown a thousandfold, reaching a population of half a million.

Following WWI, the city's growth began to slow. With the newly created independent Poland, the city lost access to the huge Russian market, and then came the Great Depression. WWII tragically changed the city forever, as the Nazis first incarcerated Łódź's massive Jewish community, and then gradually shipped the residents to extermination camps. More than 200,000 people passed through Łódź's wartime ghetto, and only a few thousand survived.

The communists continued textile production into the modern age, but skimped on investment and the city lost its competitive advantage. The fall of the regime in 1989 left a city in decline, with a largely impoverished population dependent on an industry that was rapidly disappearing.

Around the year 2000, the city's leaders decided to embark on a path of renewal, embracing the city's industrial heritage and carving out today's quirky, likeable and historically complex destination.

⊙ Sights

◎ City Centre

MS1 Museum of Art MUSEUM
(MS1 Muzeum Sztuki; www.msl.org.pl; ul Więckowskiego 36; adult/concession 10/5zł; Thu free; ⊗11am-7pm Tue-Sun) Original branch of the Art Museum, a few blocks' walk west of ul Piotrkowska. On hand is an extensive collection of 20th-century paintings, drawings, sculpture and photography from Poland and abroad. There are also works by Picasso, Chagall and Ernst (though these are not always on display).

★ Cinematography Museum MUSEUM
(Muzeum Kinematografii; www.kinomuzeum.pl; Plac Zwycięstwa 1; adult/concession 10/7zł; Tue free; ⊗10am-4pm Tue-Fri, to 6pm Sat & Sun) Housed

Łódź

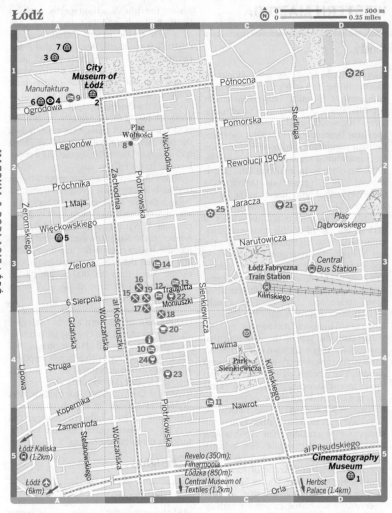

in the palatial home of 'Cotton King' Karol Scheibler, this attraction is actually two museums in one. The basement and 1st floor are devoted to Polish cinema and contain props, film posters and archaic camera equipment connected to the city's cinematic past. Everything changes, however, once you reach the ground floor – here the wealth of 19th-century Łódź is plain to see. At ground level, room after room is filled with extravagant boiserie (elaborately carved wood panelling), dreamy ceiling frescoes and elaborate ceramic stoves. The 'Mirror Room' is a particular delight, with three crystal mirrors and angels coated in 24-carat gold.

Central Museum of Textiles MUSEUM
(Centralne Muzeum Włókiennictwa; www.muzeum wlokiennictwa.pl; ul Piotrkowska 282; adult/concession 10/6zł; ⊙9am-5pm Tue, Wed & Fri, 11am-7pm Thu, to 4pm Sat & Sun) Those wishing to dig a little deeper into Łódź's industrial past should take a gander at this museum. It's located within Ludwig Geyer's gorgeous White Factory, the city's oldest textile mill, dating from 1839. The collection consists of textile machinery, early looms and fabrics, clothing and other objects related to the industry.

Łódź

Herbst Palace MUSEUM

(Pałac Herbsta; www.msl.org.pl; ul Przędzalniana 72; adult/concession 10/5zł; ☺10am-5pm Tue-Sun) Now a branch of the Museum of Art, this building started life in 1875 as a grand villa of the Herbst family. Although the owners fled before WWII, taking all the furnishings and art with them, the interior has been restored and furnished like the original, giving an insight into how barons of industry once lived. The area around it, known as the Priest's Mill (Księży Młyn), once hosted a model 19th-century mill town, created by Herbst's father-in-law Karol Scheibler.

◎ Manufaktura

The sprawling **Manufaktura** (www.manufaktura.com; ul Karskiego 5; ☺9am-10pm) shopping, entertainment and office complex deserves to be listed as a tourist attraction in its own right. While most of the enormous (more than 100,000 sq metres) structure is a standard shopping mall, the sheer size and the setting – within a once-abandoned 19th-century textile mill – are extraordinary. In addition to nearly every conceivable retail outlet, there are bowling lanes, a multiplex cinema, a video game arcade and a handful of worthwhile museums. Trams 3 and 11 run from near ul Piotrkowska to Manufaktura.

★ City Museum of Łódź MUSEUM

(Muzeum Miasta Łodzi; www.muzeum-lodz.pl; ul Ogrodowa 15; adult/concession 9/5zł, Sun free; ☺10am-2pm Mon, 2-6pm Wed, 11am-4pm Tue,

Thu, Sat & Sun) Historical museum adjacent to the Manufaktura mall, housed in the impressive palace of 19th-century textile baron Izrael Kalmanowicz Poznański. The opulent interior is a clear indication of the Poznańskis' wealth: it's bedecked with elaborate dark-wood wall panelling, delicate stained-glass windows and a suitably grand ballroom. Despite the exhibitions taking a back seat to the building, they're nonetheless interesting, covering Łódź's history, the Łódź ghetto, and famous Łódź citizens including pianist Artur Rubinstein, writer Jerzy Kosiński and poet Julian Tuwim.

MS2 Museum of Art MUSEUM

(MS2 Muzeum Sztuki; www.msl.org.pl; ul Ogrodowa 19; adult/concession 10/5zł; ☺11am-7pm Tue-Sun) A worthy adjunct to the city's main art museum (MS1), this campus focuses on experimental and avant-garde works from the 20th and 21st centuries. The setting, an abandoned weaving mill on the edge of the Manufaktura mall, is a treat. There's a good in-house cafe.

Experymentarium MUSEUM

(www.experymentarium.pl; ul Drewnoska 58; adult/concession 12/8zł; ☺10am-9pm) Seemingly designed for kids and high-school science nerds, this modern, interactive science museum, in fact, is a blast at any age. The exhibits are built around staid subjects such as chemistry and astronomy, but the displays encourage visitors to touch and play, and learn in the process. There's a cosmic tunnel, laser games and optical illusions to keep things moving.

Museum of the Factory MUSEUM
(Muzeum Fabryki; www.muzeumfabryki.pl; ul Drewnowska 58; adult/concession 4/3zł; ⊘9am-7pm Tue-Fri, 11am-7pm Sat & Sun) This industrial museum within the Manufaktura complex is not as impressive as other museums in town but is nevertheless a passable rainy-day attraction with some old textile machines, fascinating maps and a short video of the textile king himself, Izrael Kalmanowicz Poznański.

⊙ Jewish Ghetto

The rapid industrial expansion of Łódź in the 19th century attracted Jews to the city; starting in the 1830s, and as early as the 1840s, Jews accounted for around 20% of the population. Many settled in the northern half of the city, in the area around today's Stary Rynek (Old Town Sq). By the time Germany invaded Poland in 1939, their numbers had grown to 230,000. In May 1940 the Germans sealed off the northern part of Łódź to create the second-biggest Jewish ghetto in Poland, after the Warsaw ghetto.

The tourist information office hands out a useful free booklet *Jewish Landmarks in Łódź*, which traces out a 10km-long walking tour of the former ghetto and identifies the main sites, beginning at the **Bałucki Rynek**, the administrative centre of the ghetto, all the way to Radegast station and the Jewish Cemetery.

To reach this area, take tram 6 in a northerly direction from al Kościuszki to its terminus at Strykowska.

Jewish Cemetery CEMETERY
(Cmentarz Żydowski; www.jewishlodzcemetery.org; ul Bracka 40; admission 6zł, first Sun of month free; ⊘9am-5pm Sun-Fri) Łódź's Jewish cemetery was founded in 1892. The largest Jewish graveyard in Europe, it contains around 68,000 surviving tombstones, some of which are very beautiful. It's been partially cleaned up, particularly the area known as Ghetto Field (Polem Gettowym), which is the final resting place for 43,000 victims of the wartime ghetto. Enter from ul Zmienna.

Radegast Station MEMORIAL
(Stacja Radegast; al Pamięci Ofiar; ⊘10am-5pm) FREE North of the Jewish Cemetery was the main deportation centre for Jews sent to the death camps at Chełmno and Auschwitz-Birkenau. The station, about 3km northeast of Bałucki Rynek, has been preserved and now holds a moving memorial to those lost in the Holocaust. Three original Deutsche Reichsbahn cattle cars used for the deportations stand silently next to the now-defunct station, and original deportation lists (some headed with '*Zur Arbeit*' – 'to work') line a long concrete tunnel nearby.

⌕ Tours

Dętka Canal Tour TOUR
(www.muzeum-lodz.pl; Plac Wolności 2; adult/concession 5/3zł; ⊘noon-7pm Thu-Sun Apr-Sep, 10am-2pm Fri, 2-6pm Sat & Sun Oct) Guided tours every half-hour through the old brick sewer system beneath the city's streets, with exhibits en route. Operated by the City Museum.

✸ Festivals & Events

Łódź Ballet Meetings DANCE
(www.operalodz.com; ⊘May) Dance and ballet festival that includes both Polish and foreign groups, and runs for two weeks in May every odd-numbered year. Performances are staged in the Grand Theatre.

Fotofestiwal PHOTOGRAPHY
(www.fotofestiwal.com; ⊘May-Jun) Held annually from May to June, this is one of Poland's most prominent festivals of photography and visual arts.

Four Cultures PERFORMING ARTS
(www.4kultury.pl; Plac Wolności 5; ⊘Jun) Theatre, music, film and visual arts festival held each year in June, celebrating the city's historic role as a meeting place of four cultures: Polish, Jewish, Russian and German.

⌅ Sleeping

Music Hostel HOSTEL €
(⌨53 353 3263; www.music-hostel.pl; ul Piotrkowska 60; dm 39-45zł, s/d 85/118zł; P ⊛) Enter through the passageway at ul Piotrkowska 60 and walk right to the back of the alley to find this clean and hip hostel. The theme here is music, with albums and posters of Hendrix, the Beatles and everyone else on the walls. Light, airy rooms feature wooden bunks and big windows. There's a communal kitchen too.

Flamingo Hostel HOSTEL €
(⌨42 661 1888; www.lodz.flamingo-hostel.com; ul Sienkiewicza 67; dm 29-42zł, r 99-119zł; ⊛) This chic, centrally located hostel offers a glamorous shared modern kitchen, handsome room decor – think minimalist boutique rather than youth hostel – and nice extras such as free hot beverages, secure lockers and city maps. The downside, and it's a deal-breaker if you hate to climb stairs, is that the rooms are a five-floor walk up.

HOLLY-ŁÓDŹ BOULEVARD

Ul Piotrkowska began life in the 19th century as the road to Piotrków Trybunalski (hence its name), then the major town of the region. By the beginning of the 20th century Piotrkowska was an elegant boulevard, lined with Art Nouveau buildings and expensive restaurants, but in the wake of WWII it became a gloomy, grey street of soot-blackened facades and half-empty shops.

Its revival began in the 1990s, when the Piotrkowska Street Foundation was created by a group of local artists and architects with the aim of turning the derelict thoroughfare into a lively European avenue. It has also become a sort of homage to successful locals, hosting statues and stars dedicated to the city's most famous sons and daughters.

In front of the Grand Hotel is the Avenue of the Stars (Aleja Gwiazd), a series of bronze stars set in the pavement in imitation of Los Angeles' Hollywood Boulevard, each dedicated to a well-known name in Polish film.

Further south in front of the house (at No 78) where the eminent Polish pianist Artur Rubinstein once lived, is Rubinstein's Piano, a bronze monument much loved by snap-happy tourists. A few paces down the street (at No 104) is Tuwim's Bench, a monument created in memory of local poet Julian Tuwim. Touch his nose – it's supposed to bring good luck. The last of the series is Reymont's Chest (at No 135), showing the Nobel Prize winner for literature, Władysław Reymont, sitting on a large travel trunk.

Although much of ul Piotrkowska is pedestrianised, public transport is provided by a fleet of *riksza* (bicycle rickshaws) for around 10zł they will whisk you from one end to the other.

City Center Rooms
HOTEL €€

(☑42 208 0808; www.citycenterrooms.pl; ul Piotrkowska 91; s/d 130/190zł; Ⓟ ⓦ) Reasonably priced accommodation just off the main drag, with entry via a pleasant courtyard. Rooms are clean and bright, with modern furnishings, and come with extras such as electric kettles. Some rooms have kitchenettes for self-catering; ask for these upon booking. Top value for the quality and location.

Revelo
HOTEL €€

(☑42 636 8686; www.revelo.pl; ul Wigury 4/6; r 250zł; Ⓟ ⓦ) Accommodation mixing old and new in a beautifully preserved villa dating from 1925. Staff greet you dressed in 1920s' outfits and lead you up dark-wood stairs to immaculate rooms with period furniture, brass bedsteads and thoroughly modern bathrooms. Downstairs is a quality restaurant and attached garden. With only six rooms, it's best to book ahead.

Hotel Savoy
HOTEL €€

(☑42 632 9360; www.centrumhotele.pl; ul Traugutta 6; s/d 115/170zł; ⓦ) Good trade-off between price and location, just a block from the choicest section of ul Piotrkowska. While the faded exterior and sizable lobby hint at a glorious past, the rooms themselves are a plain beige. That said, they are big and clean. Austrian writer Joseph Roth used this hotel as the setting for his 1924 novel of the same name.

Grand Hotel
HOTEL €€

(☑42 633 9920; www.grandlodz.pl; ul Piotrkowska 72; s/d/ste 220/260/400zł; Ⓟ ⓦ) If you enjoyed *The Grand Budapest Hotel* at the cinema, this is the hotel for you. Although this regal, 19th-century edifice was acquired by luxury hotel group Likus in 2009, the expected upgrade has not yet materialised. The lobby and corridors exude faded grandeur, though the extravagant dining room is a wonder to behold. Rooms, while comfortable, are modern and bland.

★ Andel's Hotel
HOTEL €€€

(☑42 279 1000; www.andelslodz.pl; ul Ogrodowa 17; s/d 330/410zł; Ⓟ ⓦ ⓦ ⓦ) The owners of this property could write the book on how to turn a drab, red-brick mill into a postmodern palace. The sleek lobby wows on entry, as do the beanbag chairs for casual lounging. Rooms are smoothly contemporary, with stylish bathrooms containing big tubs. There are on-site restaurants and a pool, and the Manufaktura complex is on the doorstep.

✕ Eating

Greenway
VEGETARIAN €

(ul Piotrkowska 80; mains 12-20zł; ⓧ9am-9pm; ⓓ) Part of a Polish vegetarian chain, Greenway is an attractive, modern cafe-bar serving a range of appealing dishes such as Mexican goulash (with beans and sweet corn), Indian vegetable kofta and spinach dumplings.

MAZOVIA & PODLASIE ŁÓDŹ

THE 'LITZMANNSTADT' GHETTO

Award-winning films such as *Schindler's List* and *The Pianist* have helped to communicate the plight of Poland's Jews during WWII in Kraków and Warsaw, but the story of the Łódź – or Litzmannstadt – ghetto remains relatively obscure.

Litzmannstadt was the first of the big urban Jewish ghettos to be set up by the Germans, in 1940, and the last of these ghettos to be liquidated, in 1944. At its height, the ghetto held around 200,000 people – mostly local Jews but also sizable groups from Prague, Vienna, Berlin, Hamburg and Luxembourg, as well as 5000 Roma from Austria.

The Litzmannstadt ghetto was not a typical ghetto. It was not used primarily as a holding centre, as in Warsaw, but as a forced labour camp harnessed directly to the German war effort. In Łódź, Jews were obliged to barter their labour in exchange for the shred of hope they might survive the war. In the end, only a handful managed to do so. For four long years, the ghetto survived under the highly controversial leadership of Jewish elder Mordechai Chaim Rumkowski. Rumkowski led a policy of collaboration with the Germans as a way of prolonging the lives of ghetto inhabitants. When in 1942 the Germans demanded more victims to clear space in the ghetto, Rumkowski infamously pleaded with mothers to give up their children. The mothers refused, but in the end 7000 children were rounded up and shipped to the Chełmno extermination camp.

The Łódź ghetto was liquidated in August 1944, just as the Warsaw Rising was underway and the Soviet Red Army was approaching from the east. The Nazis sent 73,000 Jews to Auschwitz-Birkenau in a 20-day period that year from 9 August to 29 August. Rumkowski himself was one of the last to go. He died at Birkenau on 28 August. When the Red Army liberated Łódź in 1945, only 880 Jewish survivors remained.

After the war, few of the survivors elected to return to Łódź, and the tragic story of the ghetto was eventually buried under a mountain of communist propaganda.

There's also a handy breakfast menu, featuring muesli with yoghurt and fruit.

Ato Sushi
JAPANESE €€

(ul 6 Sierpnia 1; mains 30-46zł; ☉noon-11pm) Offers the best sushi in this part of Poland, served in a welcoming setting. The menu is a mix of traditional nigiri sushi and rolls, plus a few inventive, more-modern creations, like the 'Fusion Roll' involving basil.

Anatewka
JEWISH €€

(ul 6 Sierpnia 2; mains 29-58zł; ☉11am-11pm) This Jewish restaurant, just off ul Piotrkowska, is often packed with expats and young Poles eager to sample excellent duck and goose mains. The atmosphere is warm and convivial, and the dining experience is rounded off with live music some nights.

Ganesh
INDIAN €€

(ul Piotrkowska 69; mains 26-39zł; ☉noon-11pm; 🖉) One of the country's best Indian restaurants just happens to be inside this passageway at ul Piotrkowska 69. The kitchen is open, allowing you to see the Indian chefs work their way with the chicken tikka masalas and other curries on offer.

Presto
PIZZA €€

(ul Piotrkowska 67; pizzas 15-39zł; ☉noon-11pm) Simple eatery with a pizza list almost as long as ul Piotrkowska, and a few pasta dishes thrown in for good measure. What makes it stand out from the crowd? The pizzas are cooked in a wood-fired oven.

🍷 Drinking & Nightlife

Łódź is well known as Poland's centre for electronic music, but DJs at its bars and clubs regularly mix it up with hip-hop, house and drum 'n' bass.

★Łódź Kaliska
CLUB

(ul Piotrkowska 102; ☉1pm-late Mon-Sat, 4pm-late Sun; 🖗) With its open-door policy, this renowned nightclub attracts a broad cross-section of Łódź society. The unusual decor – stripped-back walls covered in cheeky semi-erotic photos from the bar's namesake art group – fits well with the dim red lighting and slightly seedy atmosphere. In summer the crowds spill onto an outdoor terrace above the alleyway.

Affogato
CAFE

(ul Piotrkowska 90; ☉noon-10pm Mon-Sat, to 6pm Sun; 🖗) Classy cafe tucked away in a courtyard behind ul Piotrkowska's most beautiful facade. Serves quality coffee within a slick modern interior, along with a range of teas and alcoholic beverages.

Bagdad Café
BAR

(ul Jaracza 45; ⊘9.30am-10pm Mon-Thu, to 3am Fri, 6pm-3am Sat) Housed in the basement of a crumbling mansion, the Bagdad is the place to head for a cheap, booze-infested night out. The city's top DJs regularly feature on the decks, and a motley crew of students cram the place to overflowing.

Bedroom
CLUB

(ul Moniuszki 4a; ⊘10pm-5am Fri & Sat) Glamorous weekend-only nightclub with a lavish interior influenced by the Far East – think large busts of Buddha and loads of red in the decor. A cool space in which to strut your stuff.

Piotrkowska Klub
BAR

(ul Piotrkowska 97; ⊘11am-10pm Sun-Thu, to 2am Fri & Sat) Easily recognisable by the two-storey, wrought-iron-and-glass drinking area that stands outside the front door, this joint has great views up and down its namesake street. Inside it's more sedate, with wood panelling and cosy booths tucked into quiet corners.

☆ Entertainment

Check with the Tourist Information Centre for information about what's on.

Teatr Wielki
OPERA

(Grand Theatre; ☑42 633 7777; www.operalodz.com; Plac Dąbrowskiego; ⊘box office noon-7pm Mon-Sat) The city's main venue for opera and ballet also stages festival events and touring shows.

Filharmonia Łódzka
CLASSICAL MUSIC

(Łódź Philharmonic; ☑42 664 7979; www.filharmonia.lodz.pl; ul Narutowicza 20/22; ⊘box office 10am-6pm Mon-Fri) Stages regular concerts of classical music, from chamber music to the full orchestral experience.

Teatr Muzyczny
MUSICALS

(Musical Theatre; ☑42 678 1968; ul Północna 47/51; ⊘box office 11am-6.30pm Mon-Fri, noon-6.30pm Sat, 3-6.30pm Sun) Stages mostly operettas and musicals. The theatre is located east of the northern end of ul Piotrkowska.

Teatr Jaracza
THEATRE

(☑42 662 3333; www.teatr-jaracza.lodz.pl; ul Jaracza 27; ⊘box office noon-7pm Mon-Fri) Among the most respected drama theatres in Poland.

ⓘ Information

POST

Main Post Office (ul Tuwima 38; ⊘8am-8pm Mon-Fri, to 2pm Sat)

TOURIST INFORMATION

Tourist Information Centre (Centrum Informacji Turystycznej; ☑42 638 5955; www.cit.lodz.pl; ul Piotrkowska 87; ⊘9am-7pm Mon-Fri, 10am-4pm Sat & Sun;) Provides general tourist information; has a number of worthwhile free booklets in English, including *Jewish Landmarks in Łódź*, *Industrial Architecture* and *Villas and Palaces*. Visitors enjoy free wi-fi access within its premises. There are other branches at Łódź Kaliska train station (ul Karolewska 55; ⊘9am-5pm Mon-Fri, 10am-4pm Sat & Sun) and the airport (ul Maczka 35; ⊘9am-5pm Mon-Fri).

TRAVEL AGENCIES

Airport Travel Centre (☑42 638 5256; ul Maczka 35; ⊘10am-6pm Mon-Fri) Specialises in low-cost air travel inside and outside of Poland. Located at Łódź airport.

Eurotravel (☑42 630 4488; al Kościuszki 28; ⊘9.30am-5.30pm Mon-Fri, 10am-1pm Sat) Youth travel, domestic and international bus tickets.

Fabricum (☑42 636 2825; www.fabricum.pl; ul Drewnowska 58; ⊘9am-5pm Mon-Fri) Offers guided tours of Łódź and the surrounding region.

ⓘ Getting There & Away

AIR

Łódź's **airport** (www.airport.lodz.pl; ul Maczka 35) is a small but potentially useful alternative to Warsaw. It's serviced by a few budget carriers, including Ryanair, and there's regular service to destinations in the UK (London Stansted, Liverpool and East Midlands) and continental Europe (Munich, Prague and Oslo).

BUS

The city's **central bus station** (Dworzec Centralny PKS; Plac Sałacińskiego 1) was located next to the central Łódź Fabryczna station; but as that train station has been undergoing a total rebuild, at the time of research, most buses departed instead from Łódź Kaliska station to the west of the city centre. Expect this situation to reverse once Łódź Fabryczna reopens. There are buses to Płock (30zł, 2½ hours, nine daily), as well as many other destinations both inside and outside Poland.

Private company **Polski Bus** (www.polskibus.com) heads to Warsaw (2¼ hours, hourly), Poznań (three hours, three daily) and Berlin (seven hours, twice daily); fares vary, so you get the best deal by booking online before you ride.

TRAIN

At the time of research the city's most central train station, **Łódź Fabryczna** (Plac Sałacińskiego 1), was closed for a massive reconstruction project, expected to be completed by late 2015. In the meantime **Łódź Kaliska** (al Unii Lubelskiej

THE ROMANCE OF ARKADIA & NIEBORÓW

It's hard to imagine anything of interest in the tiny, rural villages of Arkadia and Nieborów (nyeh-*bo*-roof), southeast of Łowicz. But hiding among the trees are two perfect backdrops for a Jane Austen novel.

With its overgrown ruins, peeling pavilions, temples and follies, the landscaped garden at **Arkadia Park** (www.nieborow.art.pl; adult/concession 10/6zł; ☉10am-dusk) is a romantic pagan enclave in a sea of Catholicism. The park was laid out by Princess Helena Radziwiłł in the 1770s to be an 'idyllic land of peace and happiness', but after the princess' death the park fell into decay. Most of the works of art were taken to Nieborów's palace and can be seen there today, and the abandoned buildings fell gradually into ruin.

Nowadays, an air of decay only adds to the charm of the place. Tree-shrouded ruins are dotted throughout the park, including a red-brick Gothic House (Domek Gotycki) perched above Sybil's Grotto, a 'Roman' aqueduct, and the impressive Archpriest's Sanctuary (Przybytek Arcykapłana), a fanciful mock ruin dominated by a classical bas-relief of Hope feeding a chimera. The focus of Arkadia is Diana's Temple (Świątynia Diany), which overlooks the lake and houses a display of Roman sculpture and funerary monuments.

About 4km further along the main Łowicz–Skierniewice road (No 70) brings you to Nieborów and its stunning, late-17th-century palace, a classic example of Baroque architecture. The palace was designed by Tylman van Gameren for Cardinal Radziejowski, the archbishop of Gniezno and primate of Poland. In 1774 Prince Michał Hieronim Radziwiłł bought the palace, and he and his wife Helena set about cramming it with as much furniture and works of art as they possibly could.

More than half of the palace rooms are occupied by the **Nieborów Museum** (www. nieborow.art.pl; adult/concession 20/10zł, park only 10/6zł; ☉10am-4pm Mar-Apr & Jul-Oct, to 6pm May-Jun). Part of the ground floor features 1st-century Roman sculpture and bas-reliefs collected by Helena, and highly unusual black-oak panelling from the late 19th century. The stairwell leading to the 1st floor, with its ornamental Dutch tiles dating from around 1700, is worth the entry fee alone.

Arkadia is on the Łowicz–Skierniewice road, about 4km southeast of Łowicz; Nieborów is on the same road, 4km beyond Arkadia. Both are reachable by bus from Łowicz.

You can also hike or bike along a specially marked cycling path, known as the 'Prince Bike Trail' (Szlak Książęcy). The blue-marked path runs about 14km and starts at the Stary Rynek in Łowicz, near the entrance to the museum.

3/5) is the most convenient station; tram 12 connects it to the top of ul Piotrkowska. Trains depart for Łowicz (20zł, two hours, six daily), Warsaw (25zł, two hours, at least hourly), Kraków (45zł, three to five hours, five daily), Częstochowa (30zł, two hours, nine daily), Wrocław (35zł, four hours, six daily), Kalisz (22zł, two hours, 10 daily) and Poznań (54zł, 3½ hours, four daily).

ⓘ Getting Around

For airport transfers, city buses 55 and 65 run from the airport to the centre of town, with bus 65 connecting to Łódź Kaliska train station. Otherwise, a taxi to the centre will cost about 40zł.

Łódź's public transport system includes trams and buses, both of which use the same ticket system. A ticket becomes valid for a set length of time after you validate it in the machine on board, and remains valid for unlimited transfers between bus and tramlines. Tickets valid for 40/60 minutes cost 2.60/3.40zł; a 24-hour ticket costs 12zł.

Order a taxi through **MPT** (☏42 19191) or **Merc Radio** (☏42 650 5050). *Riksza* (bicycle rickshaws) ply ul Piotrkowska and cost about 10zł per trip (two passengers maximum).

Rent bikes from **Dynamo** (☏42 630 6957; www.dynamo.com.pl; ul Kilińskiego 3; ☉11am-8pm Mon-Fri, 10am-3pm Sat, 11am-2pm Sun).

Łowicz

POP 29,000

For much of the year Łowicz (*wo*-veech) is close to slipping into a permanent coma, but when Corpus Christi (Boże Ciało) comes around, it's *the* place to be. It can also boast a long and important connection to the Catholic Church – it was for over 600 years the seat of the archbishops of Gniezno, the supreme Church authority in Poland. It's also a regional centre for folk arts and crafts, although you'll see little of this outside Łowicz's museum.

◉ Sights

Łowicz Cathedral CHURCH
(Katedra w Łowiczu; Stary Rynek 24/30) Origi-nally Gothic, this vast 15th-century build-ing underwent several renovations and is now a mishmash of styles, including Re-naissance, Baroque and Rococo. Twelve archbishops of Gniezno and primates of Poland are buried in the church.

Piarists' Church CHURCH
(Kościół Ojców Pijarów; ul Pijarska) Near Łowicz's grand cathedral is this similarly impressive church. It's a Baroque marvel which can be viewed during mass times, generally 7am and 5.30pm on weekdays and several times during the day on Sundays.

Łowicz Museum MUSEUM
(Muzeum w Łowiczu; www.muzeumlowicz.pl; Stary Rynek 5/7; adult/concession 10/6zł; ⊙10am-4pm Tue-Sun) Museum housed in a 17th-century missionary college designed by Dutch ar-chitect Tylman van Gameren; its highlight is the former priests' chapel, with its fading Baroque frescoes (1695) by Italian artist Mi-chelangelo Palloni and finely carved ivory tusks. The 1st floor features archaeological finds from the region such as Stone Age tools and more tusks, this time from mammoths.

In the back garden are two old farmsteads from the region, complete with original fur-nishings, implements and decoration.

✿ Festivals & Events

Corpus Christi RELIGIOUS
(Boże Ciało; ⊙May/Jun) This feast in honour of the Holy Eucharist falls on a Thursday in May or June, depending on the date for Easter, and is celebrated with gusto in Łow-icz. It is marked by a large procession that circles the main square and the cathedral, and participants dress in brightly coloured and embroidered traditional costumes and carry elaborate banners.

Corpus Christi falls on these dates for the next few years: 26 May 2016, 15 June 2017, 31 May 2018 and 20 June 2019.

⌂ Sleeping & Eating

Dom Wycieczkowy GUESTHOUSE €
(☑46 837 3433; www.lowickie.eu; Stary Rynek 17; s 40-49zł, d 80-98zł; 🅿🛜) The Tourist Informa-tion Bureau offers rooms on two floors above the main office. The accommodation, a mix of singles and doubles with and without bath-rooms, couldn't be cleaner or cheerier, with

simple pinewood beds and desks. Book in advance if you plan on arriving any time near the Corpus Christi holiday. No breakfast.

Hotel Eco HOTEL €€
(☑46 830 0005; www.hotel-eco.pl; ul Podrzeczna 22; s/d 150/200zł; 🅿🛜) Located 150m west of the Stary Rynek and along one of the main roads, this is easily the nicest hotel in town. The rooms are plain but spotlessly clean with big comfortable mattresses and modern bathrooms. The restaurant is a de-cent place to eat.

Café Bordo CAFE €
(Stary Rynek 8; snacks 10-12zł; ⊙10am-7pm) Good coffee and cakes are served at this family cafe on the main square, with a small but pleasant outdoor seating area.

Polonia POLISH €€
(Stary Rynek 4; mains 20-40zł; ⊙10am-11pm; 🛜) This is the most attractive restaurant in town, cooking up a variety of Polish dishes in a restored 18th-century building. Treat yourself to the one non-Polish dish on the menu, Chicken Provençal, served in memo-ry of Napoleon's 1806 visit to Łowicz.

ℹ Information

Tourist Information Bureau (Biuro Informacji Turystycznej; ☑46 837 3433; www.lowicz. eu; Stary Rynek 17; ⊙9am-6pm) Offers many brochures and much good advice, and even maintains clean, reasonably priced accommo-dation on the floors above.

ℹ Getting There & Away

The **bus station** (ul 3 Maja 1) and **train station** (ul Dworcowa) are side by side, about a five-minute walk east from the Stary Rynek. There are trains to Łódź (20zł, two hours, six daily) and Warsaw (23zł, one hour, hourly). There are regular bus services to many outlying towns and villages, including seven buses running from Monday to Friday to Skierniewice which pass through Nie-borów (4zł, 20 minutes). To reach Arkadia, board a bus headed to Nieborów and ask the driver to drop you near the Arkadia Park (3zł, 15 minutes).

Płock

POP 122,000

Płock (pwotsk), dramatically perched on a cliff high above the Vistula, has a long his-tory and a pleasing old centre. It also boasts the remnants of a Gothic castle, a glorious cathedral and the finest collection of Art Nouveau art and architecture in the country.

Płock

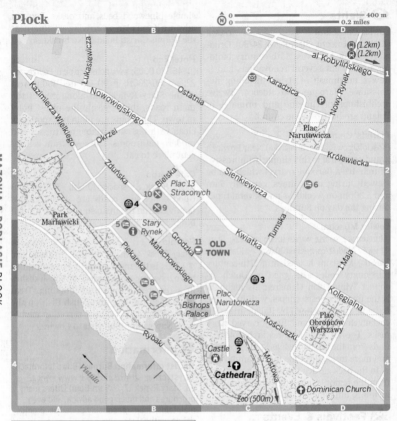

Płock was a royal residence between 1079 and 1138 and the first Mazovian town to be given a municipal charter (in 1237). Its city walls were built in the 14th century and the town developed as a wealthy trading centre until the 16th century. The flooding of the Vistula in 1532, when half the castle and part of the defensive walls slid into the river, was merely a portent of further disasters to come, and the wars, fires and plagues that struck the town in the following centuries brought its importance to an end.

These days, it's first and foremost a refinery town, with a working-class, blue-collar feel, though there are enough sights to hold a visitor's interest for a day or so.

◎ Sights

Most of the main attractions are grouped to the southeast of the Stary Rynek along a picturesque ridge overlooking the Vistula. The dominating features of Płock are two redbrick towers: the **Clock Tower** (Wieża Zegarowa) and the **Noblemen's Tower** (Wieża

Szlachecka) – the last vestiges of the original Gothic castle that once protected the city. You're free to gaze at them from the outside, but these are not open to the public.

To the northwest of the castle stretches the Old Town. At the northern end of ul Grodzka is the Stary Rynek, formerly the heart of 14th-century Płock.

Town Hall   HISTORIC BUILDING
(Ratusz; Stary Rynek 1) The old market square is dominated by this attractive building at its northwest end. From atop the town hall, a trumpeter plays at noon and 6pm each day, and spectators below are treated to the automated spectacle of King Władysław Herman knighting his son Bolesław Krzywousty.

Mazovian Museum   MUSEUM
(Muzeum Mazowieckie; www.muzeumplock.art.pl; ul Tumska 8; adult/concession 10/5zł; ⏱10am-5pm Tue-Sun) Holds a highly worthy collection of Art Nouveau furniture, decorative items, paintings and glassware. Exhibits show the influence here of both the florid Parisian style of Art Nouveau as well as its sterner, more geometric Viennese cousin, Secession. Newer holdings have added an Art Deco room.

★**Cathedral**   CHURCH
(Katedra w Płocku; ul Tumska; ⏱10am-5pm Mon-Sat, 2-5.30pm Sun) FREE This 12th-century cathedral is topped with a 16th-century Renaissance dome. Its interior boasts a number of tombstones and altarpieces, and tasteful Art Nouveau frescoes. The royal chapel holds the sarcophagi of two Polish kings, Władysław Herman and his son Bolesław Krzywousty, who lived in Płock during their reigns. Both are in immaculate condition (the tombs, not the kings).

Take time to note the bronze doors at the southern end of the cathedral – copies of the original 12th-century doors commissioned by the local bishops. The originals disappeared in mysterious circumstances and reappeared in Novgorod, Russia, where they remain today.

Diocesan Museum   MUSEUM
(Muzeum Diecezjalne; ul Tumska 3a; adult/concession 10/5zł; ⏱10am-3pm Tue-Sat, 11am-4pm Sun) Exhibits a large collection of manuscripts, paintings, sculpture, vestments and tapestries. Most of the exhibits are religious in nature, but there are a few secular items, such as the Charter of Płock from 1237, Stone Age archaeological finds, ceramics and coins from across the globe, and medieval weaponry.

A few select pieces steal the show – look for the delicately gilded 12th-century ciborium (metal carved cup) from Czerwińsk, and a first edition of Adam Mickiewicz's *Pan Tadeusz*.

Zoo   ZOO
(Ogród Zoologiczny; www.zoo.plock.pl; ul Norbertańska 2; adult/concession 10/8zł; ⏱9am-6pm) Further to the east from the cathedral, beyond the road bridge, is the city zoo. It has a picturesque wooded setting above the river and is reputedly home to the country's biggest collection of reptiles.

🛏 Sleeping

Hostel Kamienica   HOSTEL €
(✆24 268 8977; www.hostel-kamienica.pl; ul Tumska 16; dm 80zł, s/d 150/250zł; ⓟ🛜) Decent budget lodgings in a 19th-century building, an easy walk from the Rynek, with colourful dorms and attractively appointed private rooms. There's a fully equipped kitchen on the premises for guest use, and a grocery store across the road.

Dom Darmstadt   GUESTHOUSE €
(✆24 367 1922; darmstadt@pokis.pl; Stary Rynek 8; r 150zł; ⓟ🛜) Centrally situated above the tourist information centre in a historic townhouse, this is a quiet, cosy place with three rooms sharing a bathroom and a kitchen. Book in advance to be sure of a place.

★**Hotel Tumski**   HOTEL €€
(✆24 262 9060; www.hoteltumski.pl; ul Piekarska 9; s/d 299/349zł; ⓟ✳🛜) Rooms at the city's nicest hotel have price tags to match the dramatic riverside views. There's much attention to detail here, from the crisp period styling of the rooms to the elegant dining room. Weekends bring big discounts.

Hotel Starzyński   HOTEL €€
(✆24 366 0200; www.starzynski.com.pl; ul Piekarska 1; s/d from 190/235zł; ⓟ✳🛜) This accommodation sprawls through two wings and has a spa and fitness room. The rooms are comfortable and well appointed; ask for one connecting onto the broad riverside terrace for spectacular views. Room prices are discounted at weekends.

🍴 Eating & Drinking

Sempre   CAFE €
(ul Grodzka 9; snacks 10-15zł; ⏱10am-8pm) Elegant cafe on a lively restaurant strip, serving a range of top-quality cakes and beverages in an interior littered with comfy couches.

WORTH A TRIP

REMEMBERING 800,000 AT TREBLINKA

In a peaceful clearing, hidden in a Mazovian pine forest, stands a granite monolith; around it is a field of 17,000 jagged, upright stones, many engraved with the name of a town or village. Beneath the grass, mingled with the sand, lie the ashes of some 800,000 human beings.

Treblinka, the site of the Nazi Germanys' second-largest extermination camp after Auschwitz-Birkenau, is another name that will forever be associated with the horror of the Holocaust. Between July 1942 and August 1943, on average more than 2000 people a day, mostly Jews, were gassed in the camp's massive gas chambers and their bodies burnt on huge, open-air cremation pyres.

Following an insurrection by the inmates in August 1943, the extermination camp was demolished and the area ploughed over and abandoned. The site of the camp is now the **Museum of Struggle & Martyrdom** (Muzeum Walki i Męczeństwa; www.treblinka-muzeum. eu; admission 6zł; ⊙ 9am-6.30pm).

Access is by a short road that branches off the Małkinia-Sokołów Podlaski road and leads to a car park and a kiosk that provides information and sells guidebooks. Across from the kiosk, the ground floor of a white building houses a small exhibition with factual yet chilling explanations of the camp (for example, the fact that its gas chambers could hold up to 5000 people at one time) and a handful of the personal belongings of prisoners found at the site.

It's a 10-minute walk from the car park to the site of the Treblinka II extermination camp, alongside a symbolic railway representing the now-vanished line that brought the cattle trucks full of Jews from the Warsaw Ghetto. A huge granite monument, 200m east of the ramp, stands on the site where the gas chambers were located. Around it is a vast symbolic cemetery in the form of a forest of granite stones representing the towns and villages where the camp's victims came from. Unlike Auschwitz-Birkenau, nothing remains of the extermination camp, but the labels on the plan showing the original layout speak volumes.

A further 20-minute walk leads to another clearing and the site of Treblinka I, a penal labour camp that was set up before Treblinka II, where remains of the camp, including the concrete foundations of the demolished barracks, have been preserved.

Treblinka is about 100km northeast of Warsaw, a two-hour drive. By train, the nearest station is in Małkinia, about 15km southeast of Ostrów Mazowiecka, and 8km from Treblinka. There are trains from Warszawa Centralna every two hours (24zł, 1¾ hours). Once in Małkinia, there are no buses to Treblinka so your only option other than walking is to take a taxi from the train station; a round trip by taxi will cost up to 200zł, depending on how long you want the taxi to wait.

Restauracja Art Deco POLISH €€
(Stary Rynek 17; mains 15-45zł; ⊙ 10am-11pm) Set in the middle of the sunny side of the Stary Rynek, this place has the comfiest outdoor tables on the square, and a menu of Polish favourites including *czernina staropolska* (ducks'-blood soup), a *pierogi* (dumpling) platter, roast duck, roast pork, and potato dumplings with pork crackling.

Browar Tumski POLISH €€
(www.browartumski.pl; Stary Rynek 13; mains 15-46zł; ⊙ 11am-8pm Mon-Sat; 🐾🖉) Tasty food served in a location on the main square, with the added benefit of craft beer brewed on the premises. The menu holds few surprises, with the usual items like pork cutlets, duck and fish, but the list of vegetarian meals is longer than usual.

ℹ Information

Main Post Office (ul Bielska 14b; ⊙ 8am-8pm Mon-Fri, to 2pm Sat)

Tourist Information Centre (Centrum Informacji Turystycznej; 🖉 24 367 1944; www. turystykaplock.eu; Stary Rynek 8; ⊙ 9am-6pm Mon-Fri, 10am-4pm Sat & Sun May-Sep, 8am-4pm Mon-Fri Oct-Apr; 🐾) Provides a wealth of information on the town and its region, and has free internet access.

ℹ Getting There & Away

The combined **train and bus station** (ul Chopina) is nearly 2km northeast of the Old Town, in a colourful new building that looks as though it was built from Lego bricks. Though buses are the more direct option, there are six trains each day to the busy rail hub Kutno (13zł, 1¼ hours), from where you can catch onward trains to almost anywhere in Poland.

There are frequent PKS buses to Warsaw (25zł, two hours, at least hourly) and Toruń (32zł, 2½ hours, hourly). Buses also head to Łódź (30zł, 2½ hours, nine daily), Gdańsk (60zł, six hours, four daily) and Poznań (51zł, six hours, one daily).

NORTHERN & EASTERN MAZOVIA

Pułtusk

POP 19,000

A sleepy town with a splendid castle and the longest market square in the country, Pułtusk (*poow*-toosk) is a fine place to stop for a few hours if your travels happen to lead you this way.

Today, Pułtusk is just another dot on the Polish map, but the town's history is long and varied – its roots date back to the 10th century, making it one of Mazovia's oldest towns. It enjoyed its golden age in the 15th and 16th centuries, when it was the residence of the bishops of Płock and an important trade and cultural centre. In 1806 Napoleon's army fought one of its toughest battles in the campaign against Russia here. In 1944 Pułtusk was on the frontline of WWII for several months, during which time 80% of its buildings were destroyed.

◉ Sights & Activities

The town's historic core, set on an island, is laid out around a 400m-long cobbled Rynek. It still operates as a marketplace on Tuesday and Friday, when stallholders selling local farm produce and piles of junk overrun its northern half.

Regional Museum   MUSEUM
(Muzeum Regionalne; www.muzeum.pultusk. pl; Rynek 43; adult/concession 6/4zł; ☉10am-4pm Tue-Sun) This museum sits within the 15th-century brick tower of the town hall in the middle of the market square. It presents archaeological finds (many from inside the castle grounds) and ethnographic exhibits, along with fragments of a meteorite which fell from the skies in 1868. Nearby, at house No 29, Napoleon recuperated after the Battle of Pułtusk.

Collegiate Church   CHURCH
(Kościół Kolegiata; ul Marii Konopnickiej 1) At the northern end of the market square is this church, erected in the 1440s. It underwent the usual architectural makeover every few centuries, and contains a dozen Baroque altars, Renaissance stucco decoration on the nave's vault, and aisles with original Gothic features. Note the 16th-century wall paintings in the chapel at the head of the right-hand aisle.

Pułtusk Castle   CASTLE
(Zamek w Pułtusku; ul Szkolna 11) At the southern end of the market square stands the castle, looking more like a palace nowadays. It was built in the late 14th century as an abode for bishops, and rebuilt several times in later periods. It now hosts the Hotel Zamek, a plush hotel and conference centre.

Narew River   BOATING
(rowboats per hr 12zł, kayaks per hr/day 7/65zł, cruises per 30min/1hr 90/150zł) A cobbled road leads around the east side of the castle to a little harbour on the river, where you can hire rowing boats and kayaks, and organise boat trips.

🛏 Sleeping & Eating

Pułtusk's best eating options are inside the castle. For lunch, try its riverside eatery, Kasztelanka.

Hotel Baltazar   HOTEL €
(✐23 692 0475; www.hotel-baltazar.com.pl; ul Baltazara 41; s 100zł, d 120-160zł; P 🛜) Hidden away at the end of a minor road, 1km north of the Rynek, this family-run hotel is an attractive, modern option with bright, spacious rooms and friendly service. There's a restaurant on the premises.

Hotel Zamek Pułtusk   HOTEL €€
(✐23 692 9000; www.zamekpultusk.pl; ul Szkolna 11; s 145-180zł, d 180-230zł, ste 320zł; P 🛜) Housed in the restored and much-converted castle, this hotel offers atmospheric accommodation in sepia-tinted rooms redolent of past elegance. For a treat, pay a bit extra to book a room with a fireplace. There are numerous restaurants, bars and cafes on site, and spa treatments can be arranged.

❶ Getting There & Away

Pułtusk lies on the road from Warsaw to the Great Masurian Lakes. There's no railway in town, but there are regular buses to and from Warsaw (10zł, 1¼ hours, half-hourly). Pułtusk's **bus station** (Nowy Rynek 2) is just off the main road through town, about 750m southwest of the Rynek.

MAZOVIA & PODLASIE PUŁTUSK

SOUTHERN PODLASIE

Southern Podlasie (pod-*lah*-sheh) fills a large swath of northeastern Poland, hogging much of the country's border with Belarus. More than any other region in this vast country, it is here that the influence of foreign cultures can be felt the strongest. The closer you get to the last dictatorship in Europe, the more onion-shaped Orthodox domes you'll see and Belarusian language you'll hear. You'll also be witness to remnants of 17th-century Tatar settlements. Jews, who once populated the region, have left traces of their presence too.

Despite its rich cultural make-up, the main attraction here is nature. Podlasie literally means 'the land close to the forest', a moniker it has for good reason. This part of the world was once covered in primeval forest, and while much of it has fallen to the woodcutter's axe, a rich pocket still remains within the Białowieża National Park. Southern Podlasie is also home to unique lowland marshes, which fall under the protection of the Biebrza and Narew National Parks.

Białystok

POP 295,000

Białystok (byah-*wi*-stok) is Podlasie's metropolis and a large, busy city for these parts. Attractions are limited, but its proximity to the region's national parks makes it a good base, and the historic mix of Polish and Belarusian cultures gives it a special atmosphere found in no other Polish city.

The city may have been founded in the 16th century but it didn't begin to develop until the mid-18th century, when Jan Klemens Branicki, the commander of the Polish armed forces and owner of vast estates – including the town – established his residence here and built a palace. A century later the town received a new impetus from the textile industry, and eventually became Poland's largest textile centre after Łódź. The textile boom attracted an ethnic mix of entrepreneurs, including Poles, Jews, Russians, Belarusians and Germans, and by the outbreak of WWI, Białystok had some 80,000 inhabitants and more than 250 textile factories. It was growing up in this multilingual mix which later inspired Ludwik Zamenhof to create his artificial language Esperanto, and you'll see his name and that of the language dotted around town.

During WWII the Nazis practically destroyed the city, murdering half its population, including almost all of the Jews, and razing most of the industrial base and central district. Post-war reconstruction concentrated on tangible issues such as the recovery of industry, infrastructure and state administration. As you can still see today, historic and aesthetic values somewhat receded into the background. Still, it's a friendly city, surprisingly laid-back for its size and a good place to relax.

⊙ Sights

The centre of the city and the locus of evening activity is the triangular Rynek Kościuszki, the former market square, with its 18th-century town hall in the middle.

Podlasie Museum   MUSEUM
(Muzeum Podlaskie; www.muzeum.bialystok. pl; Rynek Kościuszki 10; adult/concession 6/3zł; ⊙10am-5pm Tue-Sun) Rebuilt from scratch after the war, the town hall now houses this museum. It features a modest collection of Polish paintings on the ground floor, including some important names such as Jacek Malczewski and Stanisław Ignacy Witkiewicz (Witkacy), and archaeological finds from a Viking village unearthed near Elbląg.

★Branicki Palace   HISTORIC BUILDING
(Pałac Branickich; www.umb.edu.pl; ul Kilińskiego 1) In Park Pałacowy stands this grand former residence of Jan Klemens Branicki. Though he lost to his brother-in-law Stanisław August Poniatowski in the 1764 royal elections, he built a luxurious palace on a scale to rival the king's. Burned down in 1944 by the retreating Germans, it was restored to its 18th-century form, but the interior was largely modernised. The palace now houses a medical university, but tours of the grand interior are run by the onsite **Museum of the History of Medicine & Pharmacy** (Muzeum Historii Medycyny i Farmacji; www.umb. edu.pl; ul Kilińskiego 1; adult/concession including palace tour 10/5zł; ⊙10am-5pm Tue-Fri, to 6pm Sat & Sun). The landscaped gardens are free for you to wander through.

Ludwik Zamenhof Centre   CULTURAL CENTRE
(Centrum Ludwika Zamenhofa; www.centrum zamenhofa.pl; ul Warszawska 19; adult/concession 8/4zł; ⊙10am-5pm Tue-Sun) Across the narrow Biała River from the Branicki Palace, this cultural centre dedicated to the creator of Esperanto hosts a range of art exhibitions, concerts, lectures, and performing arts events. Its interesting permanent exhibition,

Białystok

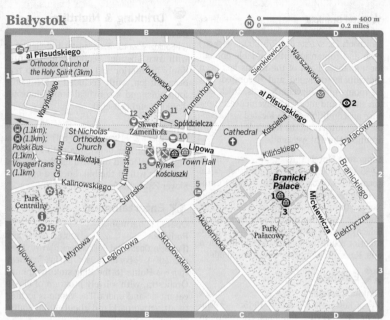

Białystok

⦿ Top Sights
1 Branicki Palace C2

⦿ Sights
2 Ludwik Zamenhof Centre D1
3 Museum of the History of
   Medicine & Pharmacy C2
4 Podlasie Museum B2

🛏 Sleeping
5 Esperanto Hotel C2
6 Hotel Branicki C1
7 Podlasie Hostel A1

✗ Eating
8 Chilli Pizza B2
9 Esperanto Café B2

⦿ Drinking & Nightlife
10 Bella Vita B2
11 Castel B1
12 M7 Club B1
13 Pijalnia Czekolady B2

⊕ Entertainment
14 Białostocki Teatr Lalek A2
15 Opera i Filharmonia Podlaska A3

The Białystok of Young Zamenhof, brings to life the multicultural city of the 19th century via sound, light and photography of the era.

Orthodox Church of the Holy Spirit
CHURCH

(Cerkiew Św Ducha; ul Antoniuk Fabryczny 13) It's worth making a detour 3km northwest of the centre to this modern church. Begun in the early 1980s, this monumental building is Poland's largest Orthodox church. The huge central onion-shaped dome is topped with a large cross (weighing 1500kg) symbolising Christ, while 12 smaller crosses around it represent the apostles. The spacious interior boasts a spectacular main iconostasis with two smaller ones on either side, and a fantastic giant chandelier. Bus 5 from ul Sienkiewicza in the city centre will let you off nearby.

🛏 Sleeping

Podlasie Hostel
HOSTEL €

(☑ 85 652 4250; www.hostelpodlasie.pl; al Piłsudskiego 7b; dm 28-33zł; [P][⊕]) This modern hostel, housed in an old-style villa, is incongruously set amid concrete apartment blocks (it's tucked away from the street behind block No 7). It offers accommodation in pine bunk beds in wood-panelled dorms of six to 16 beds, with a kitchen and 24-hour reception.

★ **Hotel Branicki** HOTEL €€

(☑85 665 2500; www.hotelbranicki.com; ul Zamenhofa 25; s/d/ste 325/375/800zł; P✳🕲) Posh and romantic, but affordable enough for a splurge. Each of the rooms has been individually designed and decorated, but all rooms offer big comfy beds, thick cotton sheets and modern conveniences; most have air-conditioning. It's located just a couple of minutes from the Rynek. Prices fall by around a third at weekends.

Esperanto Hotel HOTEL €€

(☑85 740 9900; www.hotelesperanto.net; ul Legionowa 10; s/d from 300/340zł; P✳🕲) Comfortable modern hotel with a restaurant and bar on the premises, located a short walk from the Rynek on the edge of the Branicki Palace grounds. It's worth shelling out for the superior rooms, which are big and include a sofa. Rates drop impressively at weekends.

✗ Eating

Pijalnia Czekolady CAFE €

(Rynek Kościuszki 17; snacks 10-15zł; ⊙9am-10pm; 🕲) Serving fabulous chocolate in the form of drinks, cakes and sweets, this cafe is a chocolate-lover's dream come true. There's outdoor seating overlooking the main square.

Bella Vita CAFE €

(Rynek Kościuszki 22; snacks 10-15zł; ⊙9am-10pm) Old-fashioned ice-cream counter. Big booth seating gives it a vaguely diner-style look and provides a comfy seat for coffee and ice cream.

Chilli Pizza PIZZA €€

(Rynek Kościuszki 17; mains 11-54zł; ⊙8am-11pm Mon-Sat, 10am-11pm Sun; 🕲) Białystok's best pizza (and arguably its best pastas and salads) can be found at this popular venue. If in the mood for something beyond pizza, try the grilled meat dishes served on a heated slab of stone. The terrace is popular in summer and affords a wonderful view over the pretty town square. Breakfast also available.

Esperanto Café INTERNATIONAL €€

(Rynek Kościuszki 10; mains 21-55zł; ⊙9am-10pm Mon-Fri, 10am-10pm Sat & Sun; 🕲) Central cafe and restaurant named in honour of Białystok's own LL Zamenhof, the inventor of Esperanto, who was born in Białystok in 1859. The menu is eclectic, with Polish staples sharing space with more inventive international items such as baked turkey breast (in this case served with cranberry sauce).

🍷 Drinking & Nightlife

Castel BAR

(ul Spółdzielcza 10; ⊙noon-late) Excellent bar with two distinct sections: a romantic, dimly lit interior and an over-the-top rear beer garden, with secluded tables, little fountains, and a convivial atmosphere for drinking and chit-chat.

M7 Club CLUB

(ul Malmeda 7; ⊙9pm-late Thu-Sat) If you feel like hitting the dance floor, this central nightclub decked out with black glass and red sofas will fit the bill. Located opposite Skwer Zamenhofa.

☆ Entertainment

Opera i Filharmonia Podlaska OPERA, CLASSICAL MUSIC

(Podlasie Opera and Philharmonic; www.oifp.eu; ul Odeska 1; ⊙box office 9am-7pm Tue-Thu, 11am-7pm Fri) Home to the Białystok Symphony Orchestra, with a lively program of classical music and opera. The venue is located in attractive parkland about 500m southwest of the Rynek.

Białostocki Teatr Lalek THEATRE

(Bialystok Puppet Theatre; ☑85 742 5033; www.btl.bialystok.pl; ul Kalinowskiego 1; ⊙box office 8am-noon Tue & Wed, to noon & 3.30-7pm Thu & Fri, 3.30-7pm Sat) One of Poland's best puppet theatres, this venue stages children's shows, such as *Pinocchio* or *Punch & Judy*, as well as traditional Polish stories, at least three or four times a week.

ℹ Information

Main Post Office (ul Warszawska 10; ⊙24hr)

Tourist Information Point (Punkt Informacji Turystycznej; ☑85 732 6831; www.podlaskieit.pl; ul Odeska 1; ⊙9am-5pm Mon-Fri) Located inside the opera house. The gatehouse of the Branicki Palace contains another tourist information point (Punkt Informacji Turystycznej; www.odkryj.bialystok.pl; ul Kilińskiego 1; ⊙9am-5pm Mon-Fri).

ℹ Getting There & Away

The very ugly **bus station** (www.pks.bialystok.pl; ul Bohaterów Monte Cassino 10) and rather attractive **train station** (ul Dworcowa 1), built in the 1860s on the Warsaw to St Petersburg line, are next to each other and connected via a pedestrian overpass about 1.5km west of the city centre. Walk to the centre in 25 minutes, or take bus 2 to Rynek Kościuszki.

BUS

Białystok's bus station is relatively orderly as far as Polish bus stations go, with a helpful information counter and a large publicly posted timetable. There are eight buses each day to Warsaw (25zł, 3½ hours). Nine buses head to Augustów (20zł, two hours), of which seven continue to Suwałki (30zł, 2½ hours). Other long-haul destinations include Lublin (52zł, 5½ hours, two daily), Rzeszów (72zł, nine hours, one daily), Kraków (70zł to 88zł, nine to 12 hours, two daily) and Gdańsk (69zł, eight hours, two daily). Buses to Grodno, Belarus depart five times a day (40zł, two hours).

Polski Bus (www.polskibus.com) leaves from a stand between the bus station and ul Bohaterów Monte Cassino, travelling to Warsaw (three hours, eight daily) and Vilnius (nine hours, two daily). It's best to book these tickets online in advance, as fares widely vary from day to day.

To get to Białowieża, take the minibus operated by VoyagerTrans (p111; 15zł, two hours, six daily). It departs from the minibus stand to one side of the bus station. Alternatively, take a regular bus to the Kościoł stop at Hajnówka (9zł, 1½ hours, hourly), where many buses terminate, and change to one of the frequent minibuses to Białowieża (6zł, 30 minutes, half-hourly).

TRAIN

The main intercity rail services are to Warsaw, calling first at Warszawa Wschodnia station then stopping at Warszawa Centralna (30zł, 2½ hours, five daily). There are three daily trains to Suwałki (24zł, 2½ hours), with a stop in Augustów (22zł, two hours) along the way. Trains also head across the border to Grodno, Belarus (28zł, 2½ hours, two daily). You can book this journey online via the Belarusian Railway site (www.poezd.rw.by).

Tykocin

POP 2000

Like so many of the region's sleepy towns, Tykocin's (ti-*ko*-cheen) importance lies in its past. It started life as a stronghold of the Mazovian dukes, began to grow in the 15th century, and was further accelerated after the town became the property of King Zygmunt II August in 1543. It was during this period that Jews started to settle in Tykocin, and their community grew to define the town's character for the next four centuries. They also built the town's greatest monument, a 17th-century synagogue that miraculously survived WWII.

The slaughter of the town's Jewish residents in the summer of 1941 is a tragic story and one that lends a visit here poignancy. On 25 August, shortly after Nazi Germany declared war on the Soviet Union, the Ger-

mans called the town's nearly 2000 Jewish residents to the Rynek (Old Town Sq), from where they were marched (or trucked in the case of women and children) to the Łopuchowo Forest, about 8km west of Tykocin, and shot. They were buried in mass graves.

Though today the village appears relatively prosperous, it's fair to say that Tykocin has never recovered from the massacre. In 1950, owing to the loss of half of its population, it was deprived of its town charter, to become an ordinary village. It recovered its charter in 1994, but remains a sleepy backwater.

⊙ Sights

Tykocin is relatively compact. The eastern section of town, as you enter from Białystok, was the traditional Catholic part, centred on Plac Czarnieckiego. The Jewish section is 500m to the west, beyond the Rynek. Here you'll find the former synagogue. About 500m further west is the old Jewish cemetery (Cmentarz Żydowski), though today it's nothing more than an abandoned field with a couple of headstones popping up through the weeds.

Tykocin Museum   MUSEUM
(Muzeum w Tykocinie; www.muzeum.bialystok. pl; ul Kozia 2; adult/concession 12/6zł; ⊙10am-6pm Tue-Sun) Tykocin's former synagogue, erected in 1642, is considered to be the best-preserved Jewish house of worship in Poland and is home to this highly worthwhile museum. Much of the original interior has been preserved. Adjacent to the former prayer room is a small exhibition containing photos and documents of Tykocin's Jewish community and objects related to religious ritual, such as elaborate brass and silver *hanukiahs* (candelabras), Talmudic books and liturgical equipment.

Talmudic House   MUSEUM
(ul Kozia 2; adult/concession 12/6zł; ⊙10am-6pm Tue-Sun) Standing opposite the synagogue, this structure houses a wing of the Tykocin Museum (tickets are valid for both buildings). The permanent exhibition is a reconstructed old-fashioned pharmacy, but the real treats are the rotating photo and art exhibitions.

🛏 Sleeping & Eating

Villa Regent   HOTEL €
(☑85 718 7476; www.villaregent.eu; ul Sokołowska 3; s 115zł, d 120-150zł; 🅿🛜) Standing just to the northeast of the former synagogue, this is a smart-looking, relatively new hotel that offers the best accommodation in town. The

rooms are clean and well-appointed, and excellent value at this price. The restaurant is good, serving a mix of traditional Jewish and Polish cooking.

Kiermusy Dworek Nad Łąkami RESORT €€
(☑ 85 718 7444; www.kiermusy.com.pl; Kiermusy 12, Kiermusy; s/d 180/290zł, house 320-680zł; P ☀)
This relatively isolated resort, about 4km west of Tykocin in Kiermusy village, defies easy description. It's part traditional inn and part bungalow accommodation, though the bungalows border on luxurious. The inn is decorated in traditional style, while the houses have a distinctive rustic look. The on-site tavern, Karczma Rzym (p106), is worth seeking out even if you're not staying here.

To find it from the synagogue, walk (or drive) south on ul Kozia for a couple of blocks and turn right (west) at ul Holendry and keep heading straight for 4km.

★ Restauracja Tejsza JEWISH €
(ul Kozia 2; mains 9-18zł; ☉ 10am-7pm Mon-Fri, to 9pm Sat & Sun) In the basement of the Talmudic House (enter from the back), this basic eatery serves excellent and inexpensive home-cooked kosher meals, including some of the best *pierogi* in the country, and a tasty beef goulash stewed in a sauce of carrots and plums. There's also an outdoor seating area.

Karczma Rzym POLISH €€
(☑ 85 718 7444; www.kiermusy.com.pl; Kiermusy 12, Kiermusy; mains 16-30zł; ☉ noon-10pm) Atmospheric tavern with a hyper-rustic interior of timber beams and deer antlers, serving old-school Polish cuisine. Located in the Kiermusy Dworek Nad Łąkami resort, about 4km west of Tykocin in Kiermusy village.

❶ Getting There & Away

Tykocin is served by hourly buses from Białystok (4zł, 40 minutes); buses stop at the Rynek, 100m from the synagogue.

Biebrza National Park

The **Biebrza National Park** (Biebrzański Park Narodowy; www.biebrza.org.pl; Osowiec-Twierdza 8, Goniądz; adult/concession 6/3zł) is Poland's largest and longest, stretching more than 100km from close to the Belarus border to the Narew River near Tykocin. Established in 1993, Biebrza (*byehb*-zhah) is a relatively new park but an important one, protecting the Biebrza Valley, Central Europe's largest area of natural bog.

The varied landscape consists of river sprawls, peat bogs, marshes and damp forests. Typical local flora includes numerous species of moss, reed grass and a range of medicinal herbs. The fauna is rich and diverse, and features mammals such as wolves, wild boar, foxes, roe deer, otters and beavers. The king of the park, however, is the elk: about half of the country's population, around 600 animals, live within the park's borders. Birdwatchers flock to Biebrza to glimpse the 270 or so bird species (over half of all species recorded in Poland) that call the park home.

◉ Sights & Activities

The park can be broadly divided into three areas: the **Northern Basin** (Basen Północny), the smallest and least-visited area of the park; the **Middle Basin** (Basen Środkowy), stretching along the river's broad middle course and featuring a combination of wet forests and boglands; and the equally extensive **Southern Basin** (Basen Południowy), where most of the terrain is taken up by marshes and peat bogs.

The showpiece is the Red Marsh (Czerwone Bagno) in the Middle Basin, a strictly protected nature reserve encompassing a wet alder forest that is inhabited by about 400 elk.

With more than 200km of water trails criss-crossing the length of the valley, the best way to explore the park is by boat. The principal water route flows downstream from the town of Lipsk along the Biebrza to Wizna. This 140km stretch can be paddled at a leisurely pace in seven to nine days. Campsites along the river allow for overnight stops, and food is available in towns on the way.

The visitor information centre in Osowiec-Twierdza can provide maps and information. You can also hire a kayak for a few hours or a day and cover part of the route; a handy two-hour stretch runs from Goniądz to Osowiec-Twierdza (kayaks can be rented from Goniądz's camping ground). Access to kayak trails costs 6zł for adults and 3zł for students and children per day on top of hire charges (kayaks per hour/day 6/30zł).

Despite its overall marshy character, large parts of the park can be explored by bicycle and on foot. About 250km of signposted trails have been tracked through the most interesting areas, including nearly 50km through the Red Marsh alone. Dikes, boulders and dunes among the bogs provide access to some splendid birdwatching sites.

THE TATARS OF POLAND

In the 13th century, large parts of Eastern and Central Europe were ravaged by hordes of fierce Mongol horsemen from Central Asia. These savage nomadic warriors (commonly, though confusingly, referred to as the Tatars) came from the great Mongol empire of Genghis Khan, which at its peak stretched from the Black Sea to the Pacific Ocean.

They first invaded Poland in 1241 and repeatedly overran and destroyed much of Silesia and Małopolska, including the royal city of Kraków. They withdrew from Europe as fast as they came, leaving few traces other than some folk stories. Not long after, the Mongol empire broke up into various independent khanates.

By the end of the 14th century, Poland and Lithuania were facing a different threat, from the Teutonic Knights, who were swiftly expanding southward and eastward. As a measure of protection, Lithuania (which was soon to enter into a political alliance with Poland) began looking for migrants to settle its scarcely inhabited borderlands. To that end, it welcomed refugees and prisoners of war from the Crimean and Volgan khanates, offspring of the once-powerful Golden Horde state ruled by the heirs of Genghis Khan. These new settlers were Muslim Tatars.

The Tatars' military involvement in Polish affairs began in 1410 at the Battle of Grunwald, where King Władysław II Jagiełło defeated the Teutonic Knights; in this battle, a small unit of Tatar horsemen fought alongside Polish-Lithuanian forces. From that time on, the numbers of Tatar settlers grew, and so did their participation in battles to defend their adopted homeland. By the 17th century, they had several cavalry formations to reinforce Polish troops in the many wars of that time.

In 1683, after the victory over the Turks at the Battle of Vienna, Jan III Sobieski granted land in the eastern strip of Poland to those Tatars who had fought under the Polish flag. The Tatars founded new settlements and built their mosques. Of all these villages, only Kruszyniany and Bohoniki have preserved some of their Tatar inheritance, though apart from their mosques and cemeteries not much else remains.

🛏 Sleeping

The nearest camping grounds and hotels outside the park are in Goniądz, Mońki and Rajgród. Youth hostels in the region include those in Goniądz, Grajewo, Osowiec-Twierdza and Wizna; all are open in July and August only. There are also about 70 agrotourist farms (rooms 40zł to 50zł) in the region – the park's information centre can provide details, as can its website (most listings are in the Polish-language section).

Biebrza National Park Campsites CAMPGROUND €
(☑85 738 3035; www.biebrza.org.pl; per person 12zł) There are several campsites within the park, and more outside its boundaries. The three most strategically located are in Osowiec-Twierdza (2km from the information centre), Grzędy (a gateway to the Red Marsh) and Barwik. All three are accessible by road and have car parks.

Biebrza National Park Hunting Lodge LODGE €
(☑85 738 3035; www.biebrza.org.pl; per person 35zł) The park has this five-room hunting lodge for up to 16 people in Grzędy.

ℹ Information

Park admission can be paid at the **visitor information centre** (☑85 738 3035; www.biebrza.org.pl; Osowiec-Twierdza 8, Goniądz; ⊙8am-5pm May-Aug, 7.30am-3.30pm Mon-Fri Sep-Apr), just along the road from Osowiec-Twierdza train station. The helpful English-speaking staff will provide information about the park and its facilities. The centre provides information on where to find guides (35 to 40zł an hour per group), kayaks (per hour/day 6/30zł) and canoes (7/35zł). The office is stocked with maps and brochures on the park. The 1:100,000-scale *Biebrzański Park Narodowy* map (10zł) is among the best, with descriptions of half- and full-day hiking and kayaking trips in several languages.

ℹ Getting There & Around

Osowiec-Twierdza is 50km northwest of Białystok, and sits on the railway line between Białystok (15zł, one hour, four daily) and Ełk (12zł, 40 minutes, four daily). The park office is just 200m from **Osowiec station** (Osowiec-Twierdza), and there are hiking trails and look-out towers within a few kilometres.

Having your own transport is a huge advantage, as you can easily access most of the park's major attractions.

Narew National Park

Narew National Park (Narwiański Park Narodowy; www.npn.pl; Kurowo 10, Kurowo; adult/concession 4/2zł) is just as interesting as Biebrza, but is not as geared towards visitors. Narew (*nah*-ref) protects an unusual stretch of the Narew River that's nicknamed the 'Polish Amazon', where the river splits into dozens of channels that spread out across a 2km-wide valley, forming a constellation of swampy islets in between. Most of the park's 73 sq km is comprised of rivers, feeder streams and bogs, and much of it is inaccessible to visitors, though you can kayak on stretches of the Narew River and some of its tributaries. There's also a network of paths and dirt and gravel roads that encircle the park and which can be hiked or biked.

The park's **headquarters** (☎85 718 1417; www.npn.pl; Kurowo 10, Kurowo; kayak per hr/day 5/30zł, tent per person 6zł; ⊙7.30am-3.30pm Mon-Fri, 9am-5pm Sat & Sun) is in the tiny hamlet of Kurowo in the northwestern section of the park, where the watery labyrinth of channels is most extensive. The helpful staff here provide maps and can advise on walks and hikes. They also rent out kayaks and space to pitch a tent. There's no restaurant, so bring your own food.

Kurowo lies 5km south of the town of Stare Jeżewo, which is 30km west of Białystok along busy highway No 8 to Warsaw. Stare Jeżewo is serviced by frequent buses from Białystok (12zł, 30 minutes, hourly), but from there you'll have to hoof it along a 5km dirt track to Kurowo.

The park can also be accessed at its southern end, from the town of Suraż. This is the home base of **Kaylon** (☎502 508 060; www.kaylon.pl; ul Piłsudskiego 3, Suraż; ⊙May-Sep), an agency that organises multiday canoeing expeditions from May to September. Prices start at around 200zł per day for a guide, 30zł to 40zł per day for kayak hire, and around 2zł per kilometre for transport.

Kruszyniany & Bohoniki

These two small villages, close to the Belarusian border to the east and northeast of Białystok, are noted for their timber mosques, the only surviving historic mosques in Poland. They were built by the Muslim Tatars who settled here at the end of the 17th century.

Kruszyniany (kroo-shi-*nya*-ni) is the larger of the two villages and contains the larger mosque. Its green **mosque** (Meczet w Kruszynianach; ☎502 543 871; www.kruszyniany.com.pl; Kruszyniany; adult/concession 5/3zł; ⊙9am-7pm May-Sep, by appointment Oct-Apr) is an 18th-century rustic wooden construction, in many ways similar to old timber Christian churches. You'll find it hidden in a cluster of trees, set back from the main road in the central part of the village.

The mosque's modest interior, made entirely from pine, is divided into two rooms; the smaller one is designed for women, who are not allowed into the main prayer hall (unless they're a tourist). The latter, with carpets covering the floor, has a small recess in the wall, the mihrab, in the direction of Mecca. Next to it is the minbar, a pulpit from which the imam says prayers. The painted texts hanging on the walls, the Muhirs, are verses from the Quran.

Kruszyniany's **Mizar** (Muslim cemetery) is located in the patch of woodland 100m beyond the mosque. The recent gravestones are Christian in style, showing the extent of cultural assimilation that has taken place, and are on the edge of the graveyard. Go deeper into the wood, where you'll find old tombstones hidden in the undergrowth. Some of them are inscribed in Russian, a legacy of tsarist times.

The Bohoniki **mosque** (Meczet w Bohonikach; www.bohoniki.eu; Bohoniki) is similar to Kruszyniany's in its decoration and atmosphere. Bohoniki's Mizar is about 1km north of the mosque at the edge of a tree grove; walk to the outskirts of the village then turn left up a tree-lined dirt road.

Sleeping & Eating

Kruszyniany offers decent sleeping and eating options.

Dworek Pod Lipami HOTEL €
(☎85 722 7554; www.dworekpodlipami.pl; Kruszyniany 51, Kruszyniany; s/d 65/130zł; P 📶) Lovely manor house with comfortable rooms and friendly staff. Traditional Tatar food and drink from the region are served in its restaurant, such as *babka ziemniaczana* (potato cakes) and *barszcz* (hot beetroot soup).

Tatarska Jurta TATAR €€
(Kruszyniany 58, Kruszyniany; mains 15-25zł; ⊙11am-6pm) Restaurant that serves traditional Tatar dishes and wonderful home-

made cakes. Take some time to check out the yurt in the backyard.

❶ Getting There & Away

Kruszyniany and Bohoniki are 37km apart, each about 50km from Białystok. They're best reached by car, though Kruszyniany is directly accessible by bus from Białystok (17zł, 1¾ hours, three daily).

Białowieża National Park

Białowieża (byah-wo-*vyeh*-zhah) National Park (**Białowieski Park Narodowy**; ☑ 85 681 2295, 85 681 2624; www.pttk.bialowieza.pl; 20km E of Hajnówka; zł12.00, licensed guides zł195.00, horse-drawn carts zł162.00, bikes zł25.00; 🚐 from Hajnówka or Białystok) was established in 1921 and is Poland's oldest national park. It covers an area of about 105 sq km and is part of a bigger forest known as the Białowieża Forest (Puszcza Białowieska), which straddles the border between Poland and Belarus.

The national park is famous for two reasons. First, it's the home of the European bison, the continent's largest land mammal. Though the bison died out in the wild in 1919, it's been successfully reintroduced here. The park contains several bison breeding reserves, where animals can be viewed living more or less a natural existence.

Second, much of the park shelters what's considered to be Europe's largest swath of original lowland forest, known in Polish as *puszcza* (primeval forest). It's debatable whether the word 'primeval' can accurately be used to describe this, since there's inevitably been human interaction over the millennia, but much of the park has been undisturbed for centuries, leaving a fascinating mix of old- and new-growth forest, and all of the various flora and fauna that flourish in such a special environment.

The park is divided into three zones: a strictly protected area *(Obręb Ochronny Orłówka)* of old growth that's accessible only under the supervision of a guide; an area of secondary protection *(Obręb Ochronny Hwoźna)* that does not require a guide and has abundant hiking and biking paths; and several small bison reserves *(Ośrodek Hodowli Żubrów)*.

The park owes its existence largely to royalty. It was a private hunting ground for the Polish monarchs and later for Russian tsars, and as such was protected for centuries by royal patronage.

These days, Białowieża is a popular weekend destination in summer. People come mainly for the chance to hike, bike and, hopefully, spot a bison (aside from the one on the label of a bottle of Żubr beer).

The starting point for excursions into the national park is the village of Białowieża, 85km southeast of Białystok. It has information points, accommodation, food, and travel agencies that can organise visits to the strictly protected area of the park. The village straggles along for about 3km on the southern edge of the national park, centred on the rectangular Palace Park (Park Pałacowy). The helpful PTTK office, which can organise guides, and the Hotel Żubrówka are at the southern entrance to Palace Park; the national park's own tourist information centre is near the eastern entrance.

If you're arriving by bus, there are three bus stops in Białowieża: one at the entrance to the village, one just after Hotel Żubrówka (closest to the PTTK office), and one just past the post office (near the eastern gate of Palace Park).

◉ Sights

Strictly Protected Area FOREST
(Obręb Ochronny Orłówka; www.bpn.com.pl; adult/child 6/3zł) This is the oldest section of the Białowieża national park and covers an area of around 47.5 sq km, bordered to the north and west by the marshy Hwoźna and Narewka Rivers, and to the east by the Belovezhskaya Pushcha National Park in Belarus.

This part of the park can only be entered in the company of an official guide, who can be hired through the PTTK office (p111) or any one of several private tourist agencies.

Guides typically offer two types of tours. A shorter 'standard' tour takes about three hours and covers about 8km. Prices vary, but it will cost about 225zł regardless of the size of the group (note it's perfectly fine to 'share' guides and split the costs with other travellers). A longer tour lasts about six hours, covers around 20km and costs about 450zł.

The terrain is mostly flat, swampy in parts, and covered with mixed forest of oak, hornbeam, spruce and pine. Ancient trees reach spectacular sizes uncommon elsewhere, with spruce 50m high and oak trunks 2m in diameter; some of the oak trees are more than 500 years old. The forest is home to a variety of large mammals, including elk, roe deer, wild boar, lynx, wolves, beavers and the uncontested king of the *puszcza*, the bison. There are about 120 species of birds, including owls, cranes, storks, hazelhens and nine species of woodpecker.

The reserve gets pretty swampy in spring (March to April) and may be closed at times to visitors. Mosquitoes can be a problem throughout the summer, so be sure to cover your arms and legs and bring along some mosquito repellent.

Palace Park
PARK

(Park Pałacowy; www.bpn.com.pl; ⊗24hr) **FREE** Palace Park was laid out in the 19th century around a splendid residence built for the Russian tsar, on the site of an ancient royal hunting lodge once used by Polish kings. The southern entrance, beside the PTTK office, leads across a pond past a stone obelisk, which commemorates a bison hunt led by King August III Saxon in 1752. The royal bag that day was 42 bison, 13 elk and two roe deer.

From the eastern entrance, past the national park's tourist information centre, the main path leads uphill past a red-brick gate, which is all that remains of the tsar's palace – it was burned to the ground by retreating Germans in 1944. The palace site is now occupied by the Natural History Museum.

Natural History Museum
MUSEUM

(Muzeum Przyrodniczo-Leśne; www.bpn.com.pl; Park Pałacowy; adult/concession 13/9zł; ⊗9am-4pm Tue-Sun) Located on the site of the former palace, this museum features exhibitions relating to the park's flora and fauna (mostly forest scenes with stuffed animals and a collection of plants), the park's history, and the archaeology and ethnography of the region. The viewing tower provides terrific views, and just north of the museum you will find a grove of 250-year-old oaks.

European Bison Show Reserve
WILDLIFE RESERVE

(Rezerwat Pokazowy Żubra; www.bpn.com.pl; adult/concession 9/5zł; ⊗9am-5pm daily May-Sep, 8am-4pm Tue-Sun Oct-Apr) This enclosed animal park around 4km west of Palace Park is your best chance to see an actual bison. It also holds several other species that are typical of the *puszcza*, including elk, wild boar, wolves and roe deer. You can also see the *żubroń*, a cross between a bison and cow, which has been bred so successfully in Białowieża that it is even larger than the bison itself, reaching up to 1200kg.

Another peculiarity is the tarpan *(Equus caballus gomelini)*, a small, stumpy, mouse-coloured horse with a dark stripe

running along its back from head to tail. The tarpan is a Polish cousin of the wild horse *(E ferus silvestris)* that once populated the Ukrainian steppes but became extinct in the 19th century.

To reach the reserve by car, follow the main road, No 689, in the direction of Hajnówka for about 3km and look for the turn-off to the parking lot. By foot, take the green- or yellow-marked trails, both starting from the PTTK office, or the trail called Żebra Żubra (Bison's Ribs). You can also get here by horse-drawn cart – ask at the PTTK office (p111) for details.

🏃 Activities

The secondary protected zone of the park that lies largely to the north of the strictly protected area, and the vast *puszcza,* to the west and north of the park proper, do not require a guide to enter and are criss-crossed by hundreds of kilometres of wonderful, well-marked hiking and cycling paths.

Maps are available for sale at both the PTTK office and the Białowieża National Park Information Centre, as well as at hotels and shops around Białowieża. The 1:50,000 *Puszcza Białowieska* map (16zł) by Compass has a street plan of Białowieża, and marked cycle and walking paths through the forest.

Most hotels and pensions in Białowieża have bikes available for guests. Otherwise, try **Rent a Bike** (⊋660 451 540; ul Olgi Gabiec 11; bicycle hire per hr/day 5/30zł) across the street from Hotel Żubrówka.

🛏 Sleeping

Apart from the places listed here, the road approaching Białowieża is lined with dozens of signs advertising *pokoje gościnne* (guest rooms) in private homes (30zł to 40zł per person).

Gawra
GUESTHOUSE **€**

(⊋85 681 2804; www.gawra.bialowieza.com; ul Polecha 2; s 90-100zł; d 90-180zł; P🖥) Quiet homely place just behind the Hotel Żubrówka, with large rooms lined with timber in a hunting-lodge style, overlooking a pretty garden. Rooms are spread across three different sections, so sizes and facilities vary; some even have their own chimneys. Breakfast is an extra 18zł.

Wejmutka
GUESTHOUSE **€€**

(⊋85 681 2117; www.wejmutka.pl; ul Kolejowa 1a; s 140zł; d 170-300zł; P🖥) Rambling hunting lodge which features a beautiful dining and sitting area, plus clean, cosy rooms. The location is ideal, within easy walking distance of both the PTTK office and the National Park Information Centre. The welcome is warm and the breakfast above average.

Pensjonat Unikat GUESTHOUSE €€
(☑85 681 2109; www.unikat.bialowieza.pl; ul Waszkiewicza 39; s 120zł; d 145-190zł; **P** 🛜) This timber guesthouse has clean, functional and sizable rooms, and a good restaurant serving *pierogi* (dumplings) and venison. It's a comfortable option, about 400m east of the National Park Information Centre.

★ Hotel Żubrówka HOTEL €€€
(☑85 682 9400; www.hotel-zubrowka.pl; ul Olgi Gabiec 6; s/d 420/460zł, ste 600-1100zł; **P** ❄ 🛜 ⚛) Białowieża's plushest hotel, with a big atmospheric lobby leading to a bar and an excellent restaurant serving regional specialties. Rooms are comfortable and modern, and suites have open fireplaces. There's also a spa centre and sauna onsite, accompanied by a spectacular swimming pool.

✗ Eating

In addition to these, there are good restaurants at the Unikat and Żubrówka hotels, and at the Natural History Museum.

Pokusa POLISH €€
(ul Olgi Gabiec 15; mains 22-38zł; ⊙11am-10pm) One of the better choices in the village, this eatery offers decent Polish cooking, including good fried fish, in comfortable digs across the street from the Hotel Żubrówka. There's a small garden at the back.

Carska POLISH €€€
(ul Stacja Towarowa 4; mains 30-90zł; ⊙10am-11pm) Silver-service restaurant in what was once the tsar's private railway station, 2km southeast of the village centre. Specialises in game, such as *polędwiczka z dzika* (tenderloin of wild boar).

ⓘ Information

MONEY
ATM (ul Olgi Gabiec 6) Right outside the entrance of the Hotel Żubrówka.

POST
Post Office (ul Parkowa 2; ⊙8am-5pm Mon-Fri) Located just outside the eastern entrance of Palace Park.

TOURIST INFORMATION
National Park Information Centre (Punkt Informacji Turystycznej BPN; ☑85 681 2901; www. bpn.com.pl; Park Pałacowy; ⊙8.30am-4.30pm) Dispensing information from a small wooden hut at the eastern entrance to Palace Park.

PTTK Tourist Office (☑85 681 2295; www.pttk. bialowieza.pl; ul Kolejowa 17; ⊙8am-6pm) At the southern entrance to Palace Park; can help arrange guides and accommodation.

TRAVEL AGENCIES
Each of the following agencies offers guides for visiting the strictly protected area of the national park. The major operator is PTTK, which organises guides (225zł for up to three hours) for visits to the Strictly Protected Area, and trips by *britzka* (horse-drawn cart) or sledge in winter (from 230zł for four people). Weekends are the best times to join English-speaking tours.

Other agencies with English-speaking guides:

Biuro Turystyki Ryś (☑85 681 2249; www. turystyka-rys.pl; ul Krzyże 22)

Puszcza Białowieska (☑601 931 787; bup@ tlen.pl)

Pygmy Owl Nature Tours (☑669 774 777; www.bialowiezaforest.net; Park Dyrekcyjny 11)

ⓘ Getting There & Away

It's far more difficult to get to and from this World Heritage site by public transport than it should be, but it can be done. Frequent buses and minibuses (6zł, 30 minutes, half-hourly) connect Białowieża to the larger regional city of Hajnówka, from where you can make onward connections. Buses run hourly from Hajnówka to Białystok (9zł, 1½ hours). To travel by rail from Hajnówka to Warsaw, catch a train to Siedlce (22zł, two hours, two daily) then change to a Warsaw train (26zł, one hour, four daily).

One bus per day travels all the way between Białowieża and Warsaw (44zł, 4½ hours); it leaves Białowieża at an ungodly 4.59am, and heads the other way from a stand outside Warszawa Wschodnia train station at 2.50pm. To travel directly from Białowieża to Białystok, take a minibus operated by **VoyagerTrans** (www. voyagertrans.pl; ul Bohaterów Monte Cassino 6) (15zł, two hours, six daily).

In June 2015, Belarus started offering limited visa-free entry to the Belovezhskaya Pushcha National Park on its side of the border, when crossing by foot or bicycle at the border crossing point 4km south of Białowieża. Individual visitors must apply ahead of time by following the 'Visa-Free' link at the National Park's website www.npbp.brest.by.

The special-entry permit lasts for up to three days, and visitors using it are not allowed to travel further into Belarus without an appropriate visa. At the time of research the details of how this would work in practice were still unclear, so enquire at the PTTK office when you arrive in Białowieża; it's possible that local tour companies or your hotel may be able to complete the formalities for you.

AUGUSTÓW-SUWAŁKI REGION

The northern stretch of Podlasie, known as Suwalszczyzna, is an area of outstanding natural beauty, with large swaths of pristine forest and, towards the north, rugged hills and deep valleys. Its defining feature, though, is water: it is a notable lakeland region, with around 200 lakes, and its rivers and canals are among the most paddled in the entire country.

Like the rest of Poland, the modern population here consists predominantly of Poles, but it was for centuries an ethnic and religious mosaic comprising Poles, Lithuanians, Belarusians, Tatars, Germans, Jews and Russians. Traces of this complex cultural mix can still be found, at least in the local cemeteries.

Despite its natural beauty and historical ethnic make-up, the region attracts few visitors from outside Poland's borders. It is therefore the perfect place to avoid the summer crowds that swamp the Great Masurian Lakes to the west; find your own peaceful pocket and kick back for a couple of days.

Augustów
POP 30,000

Augustów (aw-*goos*-toof) is a small but appealing town straddling the Netta River as it enters Lake Necko. It's the gateway to the Suwałki region and, with its close proximity to a number of natural wonders, it's a popular base for holidaymakers.

The town itself has retained little historical character due to WWII effectively

The Augustów-Suwałki Region

0 — 10 km
0 — 6 miles

RUSSIA (Kaliningrad Region)

Wiżajny
Żytkiejmy

Gołdap (5km)

Bledzianka River

Suwałki Landscape Park
Smolniki

Dubeninki
Stańczyki
Lake Hańcza

LITHUANIA

Szypliszki
Puńsk
Trakiszki

Mt Cisowa Góra (256m)

Vilnius (250km)

Lake Rospuda
Turtul
Jeleniewo

Filipów

Krasnopol

Lake Gaładuś
Ogrodniki

Suwałki
Stary Folwark

Sejny

Giżycko (51km); Olsztyn (150km)

Krzywe
Wysoki Most

Olecko

Lake Wigry

Wigry National Park

Fracki

Raczki
Rospuda

Lake Serwy
Lake Paniewo
Jałowy Róg

Augustów Canal

Mikołajki (70km); Olsztyn (161km)

Kalinowo
Lake Necko

Lake Studzieniczne

Ełk

Augustów

Augustów Forest

Rajgród
Warsaw (220km)

Augustów Canal

Białobrzegi

Białystok (71km)

Lipsk

Vilnius (200km)

resetting the clock – during a two-month battle in 1944, the town switched hands several times and 70% of it was destroyed.

Its history, however, dates back to the time of King Zygmunt II August, who in 1557 founded the town and modestly named it after himself. Despite the strategic location, its development only really began in the 19th century after the construction of the canal bearing the town's name, and was further boosted when the Warsaw to St Petersburg railway was completed in 1862.

Today, Augustów largely survives on tourism, booming in the summer and effectively dying in the winter. Bear in mind that it's a highly popular Warsaw weekend destination during the summer, so book in advance for Friday and Saturday night accommodation to avoid disappointment.

Sights

Regional Museum   MUSEUM
(Muzeum Ziemi Augustowskiej; ul 29 Listopada 5a; adult/concession 3/2zł; ⊙ 9am-4pm Tue-Sun) Augustów's regional museum is housed in two locations. The most interesting collection is dedicated to the history of the Augustów Canal and is housed in this quaint, 19th-century wooden cabin a short walk from the pleasure boat wharf. The other section, several blocks from the Rynek, features a small **ethnographic exhibition** (Muzeum Ziemi Augustowskiej, Dział Etnograficzny; ul Hoża 7; adult/concession

3/2zł; ⊙ 9am-4pm Tue-Sun). You'll find it on the upper floor of the public library.

Activities

Augustów is an active destination. The city's perch on Lake Necko and its flat terrain make it ideal for biking. One of the most enjoyable, family-friendly pedals is to head out along the shoreline of the lake, where a bike trail follows the edge for a few kilometres. Most hotels have bikes for guests or try **Jan Wojtuszko** (☑604 958 673; www.kajaki.augustow. pl; ul Nadrzeczna 62; per day 25zł), a family-run enterprise with bikes (and kayaks) for hire.

There's also swimming – though water temps in summer rarely rise above 20°C – at the City Beach (Plaża Miejska), north of the centre along the southern shore of Lake Necko.

Kayaking

Kayaking is one of the most popular pursuits in Augustów, whether it be a couple of hours of paddling in Lake Necko or a multiday expedition on the region's lakes and rivers. Numerous local operators, including many hotels and hostels, offer package tours that run anywhere from a day to two weeks, depending on the river and the operator. Alternatively, kayaks can be hired individually (25 to 30zł per day), to head out on your own.

The Czarna Hańcza River is the most popular kayaking destination in the

---

AUGUSTÓW CANAL

Built in the 1820s, the Augustów Canal (Kanał Augustowski) is a 102km-long waterway connecting the Biebrza and Niemen Rivers. Linking lakes and stretches of river via artificial channels, it's a picturesque route marked by old locks and floodgates. No longer used commercially, it's experiencing a renaissance as a tourist attraction and kayak route.

The canal was built by the short-lived Congress Kingdom of Poland. It was intended to provide the country with an alternative outlet to the Baltic Sea, since the lower Vistula was in the hands of a hostile Prussia. The project aimed to connect the tributaries of the Vistula with the Niemen River and to reach the Baltic at the port of Ventspils in Latvia.

The Polish part of the waterway was designed by an army engineer, General Ignacy Prądzyński, and built in just seven years (1824–30), though final works continued until 1839. The Russians were meant to build their part from the town of Kaunas up to Ventspils around the same time, but the work was never completed.

The Augustów Canal ended up as a regional waterway, and though it contributed to local development, it never became an international trade route. Its route includes 28km of lakes, 34km of canalised rivers and 40km of canal proper. There are 18 locks along the way (14 in Poland), whose purpose is to bridge the 55m change in water level. The lock in Augustów itself has an extra twist to its history: badly damaged in WWII, it was rebuilt in 1947 in a different place.

The whole Polish stretch of the canal is navigable, but tourist boats from Augustów go only as far east as Lake Studzieniczne – the locks beyond this point are inoperative. By kayak, you can continue to the border with Belarus.

THE DEEP, DARK AUGUSTÓW FOREST

The Augustów Forest (Puszcza Augustowska) stretches east of Augustów as far as the Lithuania–Belarus border. At 1100 sq km, it's Poland's largest continuous forest after the Bory Dolnośląskie in Lower Silesia. It's a remnant of the vast primeval forest that once covered much of eastern Poland and southern Lithuania.

The forest is mainly made up of pine and spruce, with colourful deciduous species such as birch, oak, elm, lime, maple and aspen. The wildlife is rich and diverse, and includes beavers, wild boar, wolves, deer and even some elk. Birds are also well represented and the 55 lakes abound in fish. It was virtually unexplored until the 17th century, but today is criss-crossed by paved roads, dirt tracks, and walking and cycling paths. Despite this, there are large stretches that are almost untouched, and if you want to get firmly off the beaten track in Poland then this is a great swath of nature in which to do it.

You can explore part of the forest using private transport; roads will take you along the Augustów Canal to the Belarus border. Many of the rough tracks are perfectly OK for bikes and horses, and on foot you can get almost everywhere except the swamps.

region. The traditional route normally starts at Lake Wigry and follows the river downstream through the Augustów Forest to the Augustów Canal. The trip takes six to eight days, depending on how fast you paddle. Various shorter trips are also available.

Other rivers used for kayaking trips include the Rospuda (four to six days) and the Biebrza (seven to 10 days); some companies also offer trips to rivers in neighbouring Lithuania (seven days).

The tourist information centre has information and brochures on various outfitters. Opening hours of the following operators vary, so it's best to phone first.

PTTK Augustów　　　　　　　　KAYAKING
(☏ 87 643 3455; www.pttk.augustow.pl; ul Nadrzeczna 70a) Easy to get to from the centre, though mainly serves Polish school groups and is less adept at handling walk-ins.

Szot　　　　　　　　　　　　　　KAYAKING
(☏ 87 643 4399; www.szot.pl; ul Konwaliowa 2) Has an excellent selection of short and long trips and English-friendly guides, though the offices are a 30-minute walk south of the city centre.

Pleasure Boat Excursions

If big boat outings are not your thing, take a walk along ul Rybacka on the southern shore of the Netta River (that links the lake to the Augustów Canal) to find several private operators offering smaller trips for two to eight people at prices starting at about 20zł per person.

Żegluga Augustowska　　　　　BOAT TOUR
(☏ 87 643 2881; www.zeglugaaugustowska.pl; ul 29 Listopada 7) From May to September, pleas-

ure boats operated by Żegluga Augustowska ply the surrounding lakes and a part of the Augustów Canal. Boats depart around once an hour from 10am to 4pm in July and August, and between 10am and 3pm the rest of summer. The shortest trips (30zł, one hour) ply Lake Necko and Lake Białe.

More interesting are the cruises further east along the canal system; the longest is a trip to Lake Studzieniczne (40zł, three hours).

🎭 Festivals & Events

Augustów Theatre Summer　　　THEATRE
(☉ Jul-Aug) Features open-air live performances and movie screenings.

Polish Sailing in Anything Championships　　　　　　　　BOATING
(Mistrzostwa Polski w Pływaniu na Byle Czym; ☉ Aug) Highly bizarre and entertaining open event for homemade vessels, held on the Netta River.

🛏 Sleeping

Hotel Szuflada　　　　　　　　HOTEL €€
(☏ 87 644 6315; www.szuflada.augustow.pl; ul Skorupki 2c; s 140zł, d 170-220zł; 🛜) Quality offering just a couple of steps away from the Rynek, but within easy walking distance of the lake. Rooms are on the ordinary side, but tidy and comfortable. There's a great little cafe on the ground floor, with the city's best coffee.

Hotel Logos　　　　　　　　　HOTEL €€
(☏ 87 643 2021; www.augustow-logos.pl; ul 29 Listopada 9; s/d 140/200zł; 🅿🛜) Right by the pleasure-boat wharf, this is a neat and reasonable option with high standards. Where it excels is on small details, such as comfortable beds and low noise levels away

from Augustów's busy main road. It has its own restaurant and a travel agency offering all the usual regional activities.

Hotel Warszawa
HOTEL €€€

(☑ 87 643 8500; www.hotelwarszawa.pl; ul Zdrojowa 1; s 270-315zł, d 385-430zł, ste 520-890zł; P ☎ ⚡) Quality luxury hotel with plenty of trimmings such as a restaurant, a bar, a sauna, bikes and boats. Rooms are suitably comfortable and the entire complex is discreetly hidden among trees near the lake. Note that the city centre is about 2km away, either by foot along a busy road or following a more looping – and picturesque path – along the lake's perimeter.

✖ Eating & Drinking

★ Ogródek Pod Jabłoniami
POLISH €€

(ul Rybacka 3; mains 9-49zł; ⊙ 11am-11pm) The best meal in a town that doesn't offer much in the way of good eating. The draws here are the grilled meats, including pepper steak, pork and chicken, but it also does good pizza and a whole range of cheap and filling Polish treats. The terrace affords a beautiful view of Lake Necko.

Greek Zorbas
GREEK €€

(ul Kościelna 4; mains 15-49zł; ⊙ 11am-11pm; 🛜) This popular restaurant and occasional music club offers an eclectic menu, with Greek dishes like moussaka sharing space with Polish favourites and pizza. A lively place to have a bite to eat.

Beer Gardens
BEER GARDEN

(ul Mostowa; ⊙ 10am-midnight) In summer, head to these semi-permanent beer gardens, by the Netta bridge and strung out along the Netta River, for cheap food and drink in a festive atmosphere.

ⓘ Information

Main Post Office (Rynek Zygmunta Augusta 3; ⊙ 7am-7pm Mon-Fri, 8am-2pm Sat)

Tourist Information Centre (Centrum Informacji Turystycznej; ☑ 87 643 2883; www. augustow.eu; Rynek Zygmunta Augusta 44; ⊙ 8am-8pm Mon-Fri, 10am-6pm Sat & Sun; 🛜) Friendly and helpful, with plentiful information on the city and its surrounds.

ⓘ Getting There & Away

BUS

The **bus station** (Rynek Zygmunta Augusta 19) is on the southern side of the Rynek and handles roughly hourly services to Białystok (20zł, two hours) and Suwałki (9zł, 30 minutes). There are five buses directly to Warsaw (38zł, five hours);

all come from Suwałki and can be full. Two buses a day run to Sejny (12zł, one hour).

TRAIN

Augustów's **train station** (ul Kolejowa) is a long way from the town centre; a taxi from here to the Rynek will cost about 25zł. There's one train daily to Warsaw (60zł, 4½ hours), going via Białystok. There are two more direct trains to Białystok (22zł, 1½ hours), and three heading north to Suwałki (10zł, 30 minutes).

Suwałki

POP 69,000

Suwałki (soo-*vahw*-kee) is the largest town in the region, but lacks Augustów's charm and immediate proximity to lakes and rivers. There's also little in the way of tourism infrastructure, so if you view it as a gateway to the surrounding countryside, particularly the nearby Wigry National Park, rather than as a destination in itself, you're on the right track.

The town first appeared on the map at the end of the 17th century as one of the villages established by the Camaldolese monks from Wigry. The small multinational community grew slowly; at different times it included Jews, Lithuanians, Tatars, Russians, Germans and Old Believers, a religious group that split off from the Russian Orthodox Church in the 17th century. Very few members of any of these groups are still present in the town today.

⊙ Sights

Cemetery
CEMETERY

(ul Zarzecze) One way to get a flavour of the town's former ethnic mix is to visit the sprawling cemetery about 1km west of the tourist office. It comprises several separate burial grounds for people of different creeds, including those following the Catholic, Orthodox, Old Believer, and Muslim faiths.

Begin your exploration at the doorway to the tiny Muslim graveyard, the last remnant of the Tatars. The gate, situated just to the right of ul Zarzecze 12, is locked and the graves are hardly recognisable. The only way you'd know it's a Muslim graveyard is the crescent symbol etched in the wall at the gate.

About 30m along, opposite ul Zarzecze 29, is the entry to the relatively large Jewish cemetery, reflecting the one-time size of the community. Their cemetery was destroyed in WWII and only a memorial stands in the middle, assembled from fragments of old grave slabs. The gate is normally locked, but you can get the key at the Town Hall office at

THE GORGEOUS SUWAŁKI LANDSCAPE PARK

The **Suwałki Landscape Park** (Suwalski Park Krajobrazowy; ✆ park office 87 569 1801; www. spk.org.pl; Suwałki Landscape Park Office, Malesowizna-Turtul; ◉ park office 8am-7pm Mon-Fri, 10am-5pm Sat Jul & Aug, 8am-4pm Mon-Fri Sep-Jun), about halfway between Suwałki and the Lithuanian border, is a cluster of pristine lakes and rugged hills that certainly merits a detour. Covering some 63 sq km, a healthy portion of the park is either lakes (26 in all, totalling 10% of the park's area) or fine forest (another 24%). It's a perfect place for walking or cycling. The village of Smolniki, 20km north of Suwałki, is probably the most convenient base for the park.

There are three good viewpoints in the village, which allow you to enjoy some of this landscape. One of the numerous walking options is an hour's walk west to Lake Hańcza, the deepest lake in the country. With its steep shores, stony bottom and amazing crystal-clear water, it's like being up in the mountains.

Three buses make the 35-minute trip each day (10zł) between Suwałki and Smolniki. For accommodation options, enquire at the Suwałki **tourist information office** or contact the park office on the southern edge of the park.

One special sleeping option to consider, but only feasible if you've got your own wheels since the location is so remote, is the **Jaczno guest lodge** (✆ 87 568 3590; www.jaczno. com; Jaczne 3, Jeleniewo; s 235zł, d 285-350zł, ste 420-510zł; ☻ 🀢 🖵 🐾), near the tiny village of Udziejek, about 6km south of Smolniki. This place is a series of timbered mountain chalets built around a beautifully restored stone farmhouse.

The 1:50,000 map *Suwalski Park Krajobrazowy* (10zł) is good for exploring the area. It has all the hiking trails marked on it, and sightseeing information in English on the reverse.

---

ul Mickiewicza 1. Opposite ul Zarzecze 19 is the Orthodox cemetery, marked by a wooden church, and behind this stands the Old Believers' graveyard; both are largely wild and unkempt. The Catholic cemetery begins here and stretches for a good long way.

🏃 Activities

PTTK Office   KAYAKING
(✆ 87 566 5961; www.suwalki.pttk.pl; ul Kościuszki 37; ◉ 8.30am-11am Mon-Tue & Thu-Fri) Operates kayak trips down the Czarna Hańcza and Rospuda Rivers, and hires out kayaks (around 35zł per day).

🛏 Sleeping & Eating

Hotel Logos   HOTEL €
(✆ 87 566 6900; www.logos-hotel.pl; ul Kościuszki 120; r 150zł; ☻ 🖥) Two-star hotel offering simple but comfortable accommodation in the centre of Suwałki. There's a bar and restaurant on the premises.

★ Velvet Hotel   HOTEL €€
(✆ 87 563 5252; www.hotelvelvet.pl; ul Kościuszki 128; s/d 300/350zł; ☻ ✳ 🖥) As smooth as the name suggests, this impressive new hotel at the north end of ul Kościuszki contains slick, well-appointed rooms with contemporary decor. There's a spa on the premises, as well as a fitness club and a good restaurant.

Klubokawiarnia Poduszka   CAFE €
(ul Kościuszki 82; snacks 12-15zł; ◉ noon-10pm) Elegant cafe serving a selection of cakes with tea or coffee, in an interior full of classy timber furniture. A great spot for partaking of afternoon tea.

Restauracja Rozmarino   INTERNATIONAL €€
(ul Kościuszki 75; mains 14-38zł; ◉ 11am-11pm) Never has so much been crammed into so little space with so few negative results. As pizzeria-cum-piano bar-cum-art gallery-cum-restaurants go, this is an amazing place, boasting a two-tiered rainbow-hued summer garden for live music, a menu that looks like a newspaper, and dishes beyond the usual Italian suspects.

ℹ Information

Post Office (ul Sejneńska 13; ◉ 8am-7pm Mon-Fri, to 2pm Sat)

Tourist Office (✆ 87 566 2079; www.um. suwalki.pl; ul Hamerszmita 16; ◉ 8am-6pm Mon-Fri, 9am-3pm Sat & Sun) Helpful tourist office one block west of ul Kościuszki, on the western edge of Park Konstytucji 3 Maja.

ℹ Getting There & Away

The **train station** (ul Kolejowa) is 1.5km northeast of the centre; the **bus station** (ul Utrata) is closer to the central area. Trains are useful mostly for longer journeys, with three daily departures to

Białystok (24zł, two hours) via Augustów (10zł, 30 minutes), and one to Warsaw (70zł, five hours) which passes through Białystok.

Hourly buses run to Augustów (9zł, 45 minutes), Sejny (12zł, 45 minutes) and Białystok (30zł, 2½ hours).

Around Suwałki

Wigry National Park

On the northern fringes of Augustów Forest is arguably the most beautiful lake in Podlasie. At 21 sq km, **Lake Wigry** is also the largest in the region and one of the deepest, reaching 73m at its greatest depth. Its shoreline is richly indented, forming numerous bays and peninsulas, and there are 15 islands on the lake. The lake is the dominating feature of **Wigry National Park** (Wigierski Park Narodowy; www.wigry.win.pl), a small park to the east of Suwałki whose dense forest and plethora of smaller lakes make it a popular destination for kayakers, cyclists and hikers. The Czarna Hańcza River flows through the park, connecting with the Augustów Canal (p113) further downstream.

Access is easiest from the Suwałki–Sejny road, which crosses the northern part of the park. The **park headquarters** (☑87 563 2540; www.wigry.win.pl; Krzywe 82, Krzywe; ☺7am-4pm Mon-Fri, 9am-4pm Sat & Sun) are on this road in Krzywe, which is 5km from Suwałki.

There are marked trails throughout the park, leading to some truly remote corners. The *Wigierski Park Narodowy* map (available at the park headquarters for 10zł) shows all the necessary detail.

The park's attractions are not restricted to nature. Spectacularly located on a peninsula in the lake, in the village of Wigry, is a former **Camaldolese monastery** (Pokamedulski Klasztor; www.wigry.pro; Wigry 11, Wigry), built by the death-obsessed Camaldolese monks soon after they were brought to Wigry by King Jan II Kazimierz Waza in 1667. The whole complex, complete with a church and 17 hermitages, was originally on an island, which was later connected to the shore. It has now been turned into a hotel and restaurant, providing an atmospheric base for exploring the park.

Train lovers can get a fix riding the **narrow-gauge train** (Wigierska Kolej Wąskotorowa; www.augustowska.pl; Płociczno Tartak 40, Płociczno; adult/concession 25/18zł; ☺1pm May & Sep, 10am & 1pm Jun, 10am, 1pm & 4pm Jul & Aug) that skirts the southern fringes of the park from Płociczno-Tartak to Krusznik. The trip takes about 2½ hours, passing through lush forest and providing views of Lake Wigry.

There's also the **Wigry Museum** (Muzeum Wigier; Stary Folwark 48, Stary Folwark; adult/concession 10/5zł; ☺10am-3pm) in the village of Stary Folwark, with exhibitions on the flora and fauna to be found in the park and lake.

The little village of Wigry is arguably the most atmospheric place to stay overnight, with the first choice being the former monastery, **Pokamedulski Klasztor w Wigrach** (☑87 566 2499; www.wigry.pro; Wigry 11, Wigry; s 100zł, d 110-180zł, apt 300-400zł; P ❧). Outside the monastery there are smaller guesthouses. **U Haliny** (☑875637042; Wigry 12, Wigry; r 60zł; P) is a friendly homestay with an onsite camping ground.

The Suwałki–Sejny road is serviced by regular buses. If you want to go directly to the monastery, take the daily bus to Wigry, which departs Suwałki at 3.45pm (1¾ hours, 21zł).

Sejny

POP 5600

Sejny, 30km east of Suwałki, is the last Polish town before the Ogrodniki border crossing to Lithuania, 12km beyond. The town grew up around the Dominican monastery, which was founded in 1602 by monks from Vilnius. The order was expelled by the Prussian authorities in 1804 and never returned, but the proud two-towered silhouette of their **Church of St Mary** (Bazylika Mniejsza Nawiedzenia NMP; www.sejny.diecezja.elk.pl; Plac Św Agaty 1) still dominates the town from its northern end. It dates from the 1610s, but the facade was thoroughly remodelled 150 years later in the so-called Vilnius Baroque style. Its pastel interior has harmonious Rococo decoration.

At the opposite, southern end of the town is a large synagogue built by the sizable local Jewish community in the 1880s. During the German occupation it served as a fire station, and after the war as a storage room. Today it's an art gallery operated by the **Borderland Centre** (Ośrodek Pogranicze; ☑87 516 2765; www.pogranicze.sejny.pl; ul Piłsudskiego 37), focusing on the arts and culture of the various ethnic and religious traditions of the region. In summer, the foundation regularly hosts evenings of klezmer music. Concert schedules are normally posted on the door of the synagogue; otherwise check the website for details.

Hourly buses run from Sejny to Suwałki (12zł, 45 minutes).

Kraków

POP 761,000

Best Places to Eat

➜ Ed Red (p145)

➜ Glonojad (p144)

➜ Sąsiedzi (p147)

➜ Marchewka z Groszkiem (p147)

➜ ZaKładka Food & Wine (p148)

Best Places to Drink

➜ Forum Przestrzenie (p150)

➜ Ambasada Śledzia (p149)

➜ Café Bunkier (p148)

➜ Café Camelot (p148)

➜ Cheder (p150)

Why Go?

If you believe the legends, Kraków was founded on the defeat of a dragon, and it's true a mythical atmosphere permeates its attractive streets and squares.

Wawel Castle is a major drawcard, while the Old Town contains soaring churches, impressive museums and the vast Rynek Główny, Europe's largest market square. In the former Jewish quarter, Kazimierz, remnant synagogues reflect the tragedy of the 20th century, just as its lively squares and backstreets symbolise the renewal of the 21st. Here and throughout the Old Town are hundreds of restaurants, bars and clubs.

However, there's more to the former royal capital than history and nightlife. As you walk through the Old Town, you'll sometimes find yourself overwhelmed by the harmony of a quiet back street, the 'just so' nature of the architecture and light. It's at times like these that Kraków reveals its harmonious blend of past and present, an essential part of any visit to Poland.

When to Go

Kraków

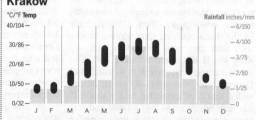

May or Jun As spring ends, the Lajkonik Pageant features a parade.

Jul The Jewish Culture Festival is the highlight of the Kazimierz calendar.

Dec Christmas sees the *szopki* (Nativity scenes) competition.

Kraków Highlights

1 Immersing yourself in Polish history at the multiple museums within the grand **Wawel Castle** (p120).

2 Heading beneath the vast Rynek Główny to experience the multimedia **Rynek Underground** (p126) exhibition.

3 Learning about WWII history in the magnificent museum inside **Schindler's Factory** (p132).

4 Marvelling at the amazing underground salt sculptures within the **Wieliczka Salt Mine** (p137).

5 Viewing the city from the heights of the **Kościuszko Mound** (p135).

6 Absorbing the startling contrasts presented by the communist-era architecture of **Nowa Huta** (p136).

7 Spending an evening carousing in the clubs and bars of lively **Kazimierz** (p150).

8 Taking in the sights of the **Old Town** on a bicycle tour (p139).

History

The history of Poland's former royal capital reads like an epic novel. Kraków became the capital of Poland in 1038, but was burned to the ground in 1241 by marauding Tatars. Under the enlightened leadership of Kazimierz III Wielki (Casimir III the Great; 1333–70), the city again thrived in the 14th century, symbolised by the founding in 1364 of Jagiellonian University. The city's status slipped badly in 1596 when Zygmunt III Waza moved Poland's capital to Warsaw, though Kraków remained the site of coronations and burials. In the 19th century the then-occupying Austrian Empire relegated the city to the peripheral province of Galicia.

After independent Poland was restored following WWI, Kraków thrived until WWII. The German occupation during the war led to the murder of the city's academic elite and the slaughter of tens of thousands of its Jewish citizens in the Holocaust. The communist government that came after the war heaped on more misery by building a massive and heavily polluting steelworks at Nowa Huta, just 10km east of the Old Town.

Kraków, particularly its most famous resident Karol Wojtyła, who would later become Pope John Paul II, played an important role in the anticommunist movement of 1970s and '80s. The former pope remains a great source of pride for the city's residents. Today, Kraków is again on the upswing. It's now the country's leading tourist destination and its second-biggest city.

⊙ Sights

◉ Wawel Hill

This hilltop location is enveloped in the heady atmosphere of Polish history perhaps more than any other site in the country. Its great castle was the seat of the kings for over 500 years from the early days of the Polish state, and even after the centre of power moved to Warsaw in the late 16th century, it retained much of its symbolic power. Today, Wawel Hill is the silent guardian of a millennium of Polish history, and one of the nation's most popular drawcards for Poles and foreigners alike.

Plan on at least four hours here if you want anything more than just a glance over the place. In summer, it's best to come early as there may be long queues for tickets later in the day. Buy your tickets at the **Wawel Visitor Centre** (Map p122; ☑ guides 12 422 1697, info 12 422 5155; www.wawel.krakow.pl; Wawel Hill ; ⊙ 9am-6pm; 🚊 6, 8, 10, 13, 18), which also houses a gift shop, post office and cafe. Alternatively, you can prebook your tickets by email or phoning at least one day ahead. If possible, avoid weekends, when Wawel is besieged by visitors.

★ **Wawel Royal Castle**   CASTLE
(Zamek Królewski na Wawelu; Map p122; ☑ Wawel Visitor Centre 12 422 5155; www.wawel.krakow.pl; Wawel Hill; grounds admission free, attractions priced separately; ⊙ grounds 6am-dusk; 🚊 6, 8, 10, 13, 18) As the political and cultural heart of Poland through the 16th century, Wawel Castle is a potent symbol of national identity. It's now a museum containing five separate sections: Crown Treasury & Armoury; State Rooms; Royal Private Apartments; Lost Wawel; and the Exhibition of Oriental Art. Each requires a separate ticket. Of the five, the State Rooms and Royal Private Apartments are most impressive. There's also a special display here of the city's most valuable painting, Leonardo da Vinci's *The Lady with an Ermine.*

The Renaissance palace you see today dates from the 16th century. An original, smaller residence was built in the early 11th century by King Bolesław I Chrobry. Kazimierz III Wielki (Casimir III the Great) turned it into a formidable Gothic castle, but when it burned down in 1499, Zygmunt I Stary (Sigismund I the Old; 1506–48) commissioned a new residence. Within 30 years, the current Italian-inspired palace was in place. Despite further extensions and alterations, the three-storey structure, complete with a courtyard arcaded on three sides, has been preserved to this day.

Repeatedly sacked and vandalised by the Swedish and Prussian armies, the castle was occupied in the 19th century by the Austrians, who intended to make Wawel a barracks, while moving the royal tombs elsewhere. They never got that far, but they did turn the royal kitchen and coach house into a military hospital and raze two churches. They also built a new ring of massive brick walls, largely ruining the original Gothic fortifications.

After Kraków was incorporated into re-established Poland after WWI, restoration work began and continued until the outbreak of WWII. The work was resumed after the war and has been able to recover a good deal of the castle's earlier external form and interior decoration.

➡ **State Rooms**

(Map p122; adult/concession 18/11zł; ⊙ 9.30am-1pm Mon, to 5pm Tue & Fri, to 4pm Wed & Thu,

11am-6pm Sat & Sun) The State Rooms constitute the largest and most impressive exhibition of Wawel Castle; the entrance is in the southeastern corner of the courtyard, from where you'll ascend to the 2nd floor. Proceed through a never-ending chain of two-dozen rooms and chambers of the castle, restored in their original Renaissance and early-Baroque style and crammed with period furnishings, paintings, tapestries and works of art.

The two most memorable interiors are on the 2nd floor. The **Hall of Senators**, originally used for senate sessions, court ceremonies, balls and theatre performances, houses a magnificent series of six 16th-century Arras tapestries following the story of Adam and Eve, Cain and Abel or Noah (they are rotated periodically).

The **Hall of Deputies** has a fantastic coffered ceiling with 30 individually carved and painted wooden heads staring back at you. Meant to illustrate the life cycle of man, from birth to death, they are all that have survived from a total of 194 heads, which were carved around 1535 by Sebastian Tauerbach. There's also a tapestry with the Polish insignia dating from 1560.

➤ **Royal Private Apartments**
(Map p122; adult/concession 25/19zł; ☺9.30am-5pm Tue-Sun Apr-Oct, to 4pm Tue-Sat Nov-Mar) This tour lends insight into how the monarchs and their families once lived. You'll see plenty of magnificent old tapestries, mostly northern French and Flemish, hanging on the walls. The collection was largely assembled by Zygmunt II August (Sigismund II Augustus; 1548–72). Other highlights include the so-called **Hen's Foot**, Jadwiga's gemlike chapel in the northeast tower, and the sumptuous Gdańsk-made furniture in the **Alchemy Room** and annexe.

The dozen or so apartments are visited with a guide, which is included in the ticket price. English-language tours depart at least once an hour.

➤ **Crown Treasury & Armoury**
(Map p122; adult/concession 18/11zł; ☺9.30am-1pm Mon, to 5pm Tue-Sun Apr-Oct, to 4pm Tue-Sun Nov-Mar) Housed in vaulted Gothic rooms surviving from the 14th-century castle, the most famous object in the treasury is the Szczerbiec (Jagged Sword), dating from the mid-13th century, which was used at all Polish coronations from 1320 onward. The armoury features a collection of old weapons from various epochs – from crossbows, swords, lances and halberds from the 15th to 17th centuries to muskets, rifles, pistols and cannon from later years.

➤ **Lost Wawel**
(Map p122; adult/concession 10/7zł; ☺9.30am-1pm Mon, to 5pm Tue-Sun Apr-Oct, to 4pm Tue-Sun Nov-Mar) Accommodated in the old royal kitchen, this exhibition features remnants of the late-10th-century Rotunda of Saints Felix and Adauctus, reputedly the first church in Poland, as well as various archaeological finds (including colourful ceramic tiles from the castle stoves) and models of previous Wawel churches.

➤ **Exhibition of Oriental Art**
(Map p122; adult/concession 8/5zł; ☺9.30am-5pm Tue-Fri, 10am-5pm Sat & Sun) A collection of 17th-century Turkish banners and weaponry, captured after the Battle of Vienna and displayed with a variety of old Persian carpets, Chinese and Japanese ceramics, and other Asian antiques.

★**Wawel Cathedral** CHURCH
(Map p122; ☎12 429 9515; www.katedra-wawelska.pl; Wawel 3, Wawel Hill; cathedral free, combined entry for crypts, bell tower & museum adult/concession 12/7zł; ☺9am-5pm Mon-Sat, from 12.30pm Sun; ☒6, 8, 10, 13, 18) The Royal Cathedral has witnessed many coronations, funerals and burials of Poland's monarchs and strongmen over the centuries. This is the third church on this site, consecrated in 1364. The original was founded in the 11th century by King Bolesław I Chrobry and replaced with a Romanesque construction around 1140. When that burned down in 1305, only the Crypt of St Leonard survived. Highlights include the Holy Cross Chapel, Sigismund Chapel, Sigismund Bell, and the Crypt of St Leonard and Royal Crypts.

The present-day cathedral is basically a Gothic structure, but chapels in different styles were built around it later. Before you enter, note the massive iron door and, hanging on a chain to the left, huge prehistoric animal bones. They are believed to have magical powers; as long as they are here, the cathedral will remain. The bones were excavated on the grounds at the start of the 20th century. Once inside, you'll get lost in a maze of sarcophagi, tombstones and altarpieces scattered throughout the nave, chancel and ambulatory.

Among a score of chapels, a highlight is the **Holy Cross Chapel** (Kaplica Świętokrzyska) in the south-western corner (to the right as you enter). It's distinguished by the 15th-century Byzantine frescoes and the red

Kraków – Old Town & Wawel

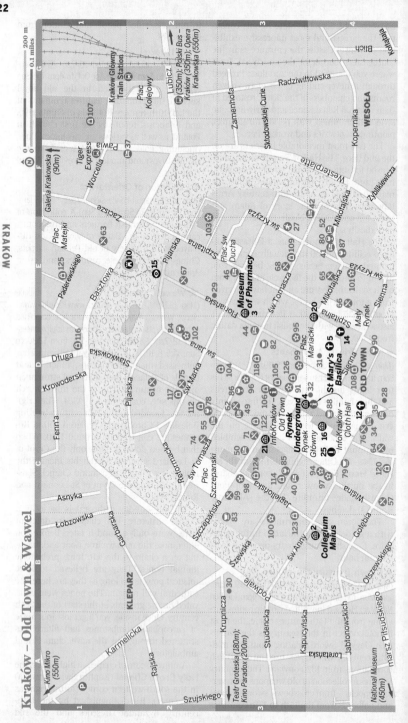

200 m
0.1 miles

Kraków Train Station

Plac Kolejowy

Lubicz

(350m); Polski Bus –
Kraków (350m); Opera
Krakowska (550m)

Radziwiłłowska

WESOŁA

Zamenhofa

Składowskiej-Curie

Westerplatte

Kopernika

Bilch

Kołłątaja

Zybłikiewicza

Sienna

Mały Rynek

Sienna

OLD TOWN

Tiger Express

Pawia

Worcela

Zacisze

Galeria Krakowska (90m)

107

37

Plac Matejki

Paderewskiego

Basztowa

125

10

15

Pijarska

Szpitalna

Plac Ducha

św Krzyża

63

Floriańska

Museum of Pharmacy

67

29

46

68

109

św Tomasza

41 80 52

87

101

65

66

Mikołajska

42

27

103

116

Długa

Krowoderska

Sławkowska

św Jana

84

102

44

82

105

99

Plac Mariacki

St Mary's Basilica

20

5

14

Fenn'a

Pijarska

św Marka

75

61

117

112

55

74

50

104

118

86

96

49

62

122

106

126

InfoKraków – Old Town

91

32

Rynek Underground

4

16

InfoKraków – Cloth Hall

88

12

90

31

108

28

64 34 35

76

120

57

Reformacka

Plac Szczepański

św Tomasza

71

21

85

40

114

124

94

97

79

Wiślna

Asnyka

Łobzowska

Szczepańska

Garbarska

59

98

83

100

123

2

Collegium Maius

św Anny

Gołębia

KLEPARZ

30

Szewska

Podwale

Krupnicza

Studencka

Kapucyńska

Loretańska

Jabłonowskich

Olszewskiego

marsz Piłsudskiego

Teat Groteska (180m);
Kino Paradox (200m)

Karmelicka

Rajska

Szujskiego

National Museum (450m)

Kino Mikro (550m)

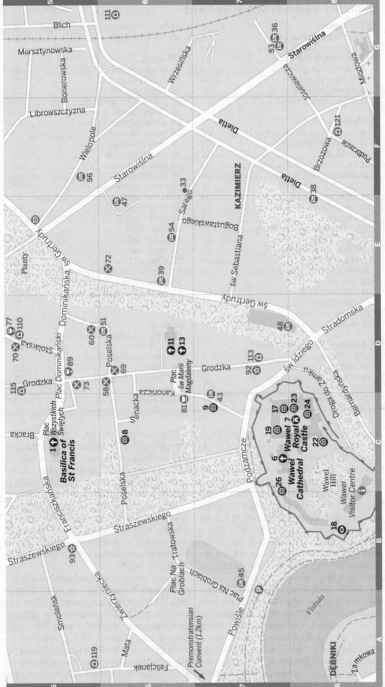

Kraków – Old Town & Wawel

marble sarcophagus (1492) in the corner by Veit Stoss, the Nuremberg sculptor known to Poles as Wit Stwosz.

Ascend the tower accessible through the sacristy via 70 steps to see the **Sigismund Bell** (Dzwon Zygmunta). Cast in 1520, it's 2m high and 2.5m wide, and weighs 11 tonnes, making it the largest historic bell in Poland. Its clapper weighs 350kg, and eight strong men are needed to ring the bell, which happens only on the most important church holidays and for significant state events. The views from here are worth the climb.

From the nave, descend from the left-hand aisle to the **Crypt of St Leonard**, the only remnant of the 12th-century Romanesque cathedral extant. Continue to the **Royal Crypts** (Groby Królewskie) where, along with kings such as Jan III Sobieski, many national heroes and leaders, including Tadeusz Kościuszko, Józef Piłsudski and WWII General Władysław Sikorski, are buried.

The showpiece chapel is the **Sigismund Chapel** (Kaplica Zygmuntowska) up the aisle and on the southern wall. It's often referred to as the most beautiful Renaissance chapel north of the Alps and is recognisable from the outside by its gilded dome.

Diagonally opposite the Sigismund Chapel is the **Tomb of St Queen Hedwig** (Sarkofag Św Królowej Jadwigi), a much beloved and humble 14th-century monarch whose unpretentious wooden coronation regalia is on display nearby.

In the centre of the cathedral stands the flamboyant Baroque **Shrine of St Stanislaus** (Konfesja Św Stanisława), dedicated to the bishop of Kraków, canonised in 1253 and now the patron saint of Poland. The silver sarcophagus, adorned with 12 relief scenes from the saint's life, was made in Gdańsk between 1663 and 1691; note the engravings on the inside of the ornamented canopy erected about 40 years later.

KRAKÓW SIGHTS

Wawel Cathedral Museum   MUSEUM
(Map p122; ☑12 429 9515; www.katedra-wawel ska.pl; Wawel 3, Wawel Hill; adult/concession 12/7zł, ticket covers admission to Royal Crypt & Sigismund bell; ☺9am-5pm Mon-Sat; 🚎6, 8, 10, 13, 18) Diagonally opposite the cathedral is this treasury of historical and religious objects from the cathedral. There are plenty of exhibits, including church plate and royal funerary regalia, but not a single crown. They were all stolen from the treasury by the Prussians in 1795 and reputedly melted down.

Dragon's Den   CAVE
(Smocza Jama; Map p122; www.wawel.krakow.pl; Wawel Hill; admission 3zł; ☺10am-6pm Apr-Oct; 🚎6, 8, 10, 13, 18) If you've had enough of high art and Baroque furnishings, complete your Wawel trip with a visit to the cheesy Dragon's Den, former home of the legendary Wawel Dragon and an easy way to get down from Wawel Hill. The entrance to the cave is next to the **Thieves' Tower** (Baszta Złodziejska) at

the southwestern end of the complex. From here you'll have a good panorama over the Vistula River and the suburbs further west.

After you buy your ticket from a coin-operated machine at the entrance, you descend 130 steps into the cave, then stumble some 70m through its damp interior and emerge onto the bank of the Vistula next to a distinctive fire-spitting bronze dragon, the work of contemporary sculptor Bronisław Chromy.

Old Town

Curiously, the disastrous Tatar invasions of the 13th century were also a gift to Kraków, allowing the city to implement a harmonious street layout in the aftermath of the devastation. It took almost two centuries to envelop the town with a powerful, 3km-long chain of double defensive walls complete with 47 towers and eight main entrance gates, as well as a wide moat.

The major alteration to this set-up took place at the beginning of the 19th century, when the obsolete walls were demolished, except for a small section to the north. The moat was filled up and a ring-shaped park called the Planty was laid out on the site, surrounding the footprint-shaped Old Town with the parkland that is still one of the city's most attractive features.

The Old Town is packed with historical buildings and monuments, including several museums and many churches. It's been included on Unesco's World Heritage List since 1978, and is largely car-free.

RYNEK GŁÓWNY

Measuring 200m by 200m, the Rynek Główny (main square) is the largest medieval town square in Europe and one of the finest urban designs of its kind. Its layout, based on that of a *castrum* (Roman military camp), was drawn up in 1257 and has been retained to this day, though the buildings have changed over the centuries. Most of them now look neoclassical, but don't let the facades confuse you – the basic structures are much older, as can be seen by their doorways, architectural details and interiors. Of particular note are the sloping buttresses you'll spot outside many of the square's older buildings; these were an early way of adding extra support to a building's foundations.

Cloth Hall   HISTORIC BUILDING

(Sukiennice; Map p122; www.museum.krakow.pl; Rynek Główny 1/3; 🚊1, 6, 8, 13, 18) FREE Dominating the middle of Rynek Główny, this building was once the centre of Kraków's medieval clothing trade. Created in the early 14th century when a roof was put over two rows of stalls, it was extended into a 108m-long Gothic structure, then rebuilt in Renaissance style after a 1555 fire; the arcades were a late-19th-century addition. The ground floor is now a busy trading centre for crafts and souvenirs; the upper floor houses the recently renovated Gallery of 19th-Century Polish Painting.

The gallery's collection features works by Józef Chełmoński, Jacek Malczewski, Aleksander Gierymski and the leader of monumental historic painting, Jan Matejko.

★ Rynek Underground   MUSEUM

(Map p122; ☑12 426 5060; www.podziemiarynku. com; Rynek Główny 1; adult/concession 19/16zł, Tue free; ⏰10am-8pm Mon, to 4pm Tue, to 10pm Wed-Sun; 🚊1, 6, 8, 13, 18) This fascinating attraction beneath the market square consists of an underground route through medieval market stalls and other long-forgotten chambers. The 'Middle Ages meets 21st century' experience is enhanced by holograms and audiovisual wizardry. Buy tickets at an office on the western side of the Cloth Hall (Sukiennice 21), where an electronic board shows tour times and tickets available. The entrance to the tunnels is on the northeastern end of the Cloth Hall.

★ St Mary's Basilica   CHURCH

(Basilica of the Assumption of Our Lady; Map p122; ☑12 422 0737; www.mariacki.com; Plac Mariacki 5, Rynek Główny; adult/concession church 10/5zł, tower 15/10zł; ⏰11.30am-5.30pm Mon-Sat, 2-5.30pm Sun; 🚊1, 6, 8, 13, 18) Overlooking Rynek Główny, this striking brick church, best known simply as St Mary's, is dominated by two towers of different heights. The first church here was built in the 1220s and following its destruction during a Tatar raid, construction of the basilica began. Tour the exquisite interior, with its remarkable carved wooden altarpiece, and in summer climb the tower for excellent views. Don't miss the hourly *hejnał* (bugle call) from the taller tower.

The main church entrance, through a Baroque portal added to the southwestern facade in the 1750s, is used by worshippers; tourists must enter through the side door to the southeast.

The chancel is illuminated by magnificent stained-glass windows dating from the late 14th century; the blue star vaulting of the nave is breathtaking. On the opposite side of the church, above the organ loft, is a fine Art Nouveau stained-glass window by Stanisław Wyspiański and Józef Mehoffer. The colourful wall paintings, designed by Jan Matejko, harmonise beautifully with the medieval architecture and are an appropriate background for the high altar, which is acclaimed as the greatest masterpiece of Gothic art in Poland and allegedly designated the eighth wonder of the world by Pablo Picasso.

The altarpiece is a pentaptych (an altarpiece consisting of a central panel and two pairs of side wings), intricately carved in lime wood, then painted and gilded. The main scene, visible when the pentaptych is open, represents the Dormition (or Assumption) of the Virgin surrounded by the Apostles. The outside has a dozen sections portraying scenes from the life of Christ and the Virgin. The altarpiece is topped with the Coronation of the Virgin in Heaven and, on both sides, the statues of the patron saints of Poland, St Stanislaus and St Adalbert.

Measuring about 13m high and 11m wide, the pentaptych is the country's largest and most important piece of medieval art. It took a decade for its maker, Veit Stoss (known in Poland as Wit Stwosz), to complete this monumental work before it was consecrated in 1489.

The pentaptych is opened daily at precisely 11.50am and closed at 5.30pm, except for Saturday when it's left open for the Sunday morning mass. The altarpiece apart, don't miss the delicate crucifix on the Baroque altar in the head of the right-hand aisle, another work by Veit Stoss, and the still larger crucifix placed on the rood screen, attributed to pupils of the master.

Church of St Barbara
CHURCH

(Kościół Św Barbary; Map p122; ☑12 428 1500; www.swietabarbara.jezuici.pl; Plac Mariacki; ⊙8am-6pm; ☐1, 6, 8, 13, 18) South of St Mary's is this sombre 14th-century church sited on the small, charming Plac Mariacki, which until the early 19th century was a churchyard. St Barbara's was the cemetery chapel and served the Polish faithful during the Middle Ages (the Mariacki was for Germans). Note the skull and crossbones on the north exterior; just inside the entrance is an open chapel featuring stone sculptures of Christ and three of the Apostles, also attributed to the Stoss school.

Historical Museum of Kraków
MUSEUM

(Map p122; ☑12 619 2335; www.mhk.pl; Rynek Główny 35; adult/concession 12/8zł, Sat free; ⊙10am-5.30pm Tue-Sun; ☐2, 4, 14, 19, 20, 24) At the northern corner of the square, the collection within the 17th-century Krzysztofory Palace is home to *Cyberteka*, an interactive exhibition which charts the city from the earliest days to WWI. The museum features a bit of everything related to the city's past,

including old clocks, armour, paintings, Kraków's celebrated *szopki* (Nativity scenes), and the costume of the Lajkonik.

Church of St Adalbert
CHURCH

(Kościół Św Wojciecha; Map p122; ☑12 422 8352; Plac Mariacki; ☐1, 6, 8, 13, 18) In the southern corner of the square is this small domed building. It's one of the oldest churches in the Old Town, dating from the 11th century. The original foundations of the building are located 2m below the surface. The church was closed to the public at the time of research and it wasn't clear when it would reopen.

Hipolit House
MUSEUM

(Kamienica Hipolitów; Map p122; ☑12 422 4219; www.mhk.pl; Plac Mariacki 3; adult/concession 9/7zł, Wed free; ⊙10am-5.30pm Wed-Sun; ☐3, 10, 19, 24, 52) Next to St Mary's Basilica, this branch of the Kraków City History Museum contains faithful recreations of townhouse interiors from the 17th to early 19th centuries.

Town Hall Tower
TOWER

(Wieża Ratuszowa; Map p122; Rynek Główny 1; adult/concession 7/5zł; ⊙10.30am-6pm Apr-Oct; ☐1, 6, 8, 13, 18) Southwest of the Cloth Hall, this soaring tower is all that is left of the 15th-century town hall which was dismantled in the 1820s. The 70m-tall tower can be climbed in the warmer months.

NORTH OF THE RYNEK

★ Collegium Maius
HISTORIC BUILDING

(Map p122; ☑12 663 1521; www.maius.uj.edu.pl; ul Jagiellońska 15; adult/concession 16/12zł; ⊙10am-2.20pm Mon-Fri, to 1.20pm Sat; ☐2, 13, 18, 20) The Collegium Maius, built as part of the Kraków Academy (now the Jagiellonian University), is the oldest surviving university building in Poland, and one of the best examples of 15th-century Gothic architecture in the city. It has a magnificent arcaded **courtyard**

FOLLOW YOUR NOSE

Kraków is a wonderful city to explore on your own. The streets are well-marked, the buses and trams easy to negotiate, and the locals friendly. While there are plenty of great sights to see, don't forget to give yourself time to wander about and make your own discoveries. If you get some sunshine on your trip, be certain to stroll the Planty, a green belt of trees and benches that encircles the Old Town. Or take in the walks along the river, with dramatic views of Wawel Royal Castle. Want to see a grungier Kazimierz with every-day residents? Head south over the bridge to working-class Podgórze. Or just go blindly into that great maze of streets and rail lines beyond the Old Town, poking your head into little shops, joining in a game of *piłka nożna* (football) in a park or having beer in a local *piwnica* (pub).

KRAKÓW'S CALL

Every hour on the hour the *hejnał* (bugle call) is sounded four times on a trumpet from the higher tower of St Mary's Basilica. Now a musical symbol of the city, this simple melody, based on only five notes, was played in medieval times as a warning call. Intriguingly, it breaks off abruptly in midbar. Legend links it to the Tatar invasions; when the watchman on duty spotted the enemy and sounded the alarm, a Tatar arrow pierced his throat mid-phrase. Because the town was awakened from its collective slumber and defended itself successfully, the tune has stayed that way ever since. The job is now done by a handful of firemen in costume – at least from the waist up. The *hejnał* is also broadcast on Polish Radio every day at noon.

(7am–dusk) and a fascinating university collection. Visit is by guided tour only.

On the tour you'll be shown half-a-dozen historic interiors, featuring rare 16th-century astronomic instruments used by star pupil Copernicus, as well as some of his manuscripts; a fascinating alchemy room; old rectors' sceptres; and, the highlight of the show, the oldest existing globe (c 1510) depicting the American continent. You'll also visit an impressive Aula, a hall with an original Renaissance ceiling, and crammed with portraits of kings, benefactors and rectors of the university (five of whom were sent to Sachsenhausen concentration camp in 1939). The treasury contains everything from copies of the 1364 university foundation papers and Jan III Sobieski's hammered silver table to film awards (including an Oscar) given to director Andrzej Wajda.

All visits are guided in groups; tours begin every half-hour and there are usually a couple of daily tours at 11am and 1pm in English. In summer it's advisable to reserve in advance, either personally or by phone. The courtyard can be entered free of charge. Try to visit at 9am, 11am, 1pm or 3pm, when the 14th-century replica clock on the south side chimes and its cast of characters go through their paces.

★ **Museum of Pharmacy** MUSEUM
(Muzeum Farmacj; Map p122; ☎12 421 9279; www.muzeumfarmacji.pl; ul Floriańska 25; adult/concession 9/6zł; ☺noon–6.30pm Tue, 10am–2.30pm Wed–Sun; ☐2, 4, 14, 19, 20, 24) The name of this museum doesn't sound that exciting, but the Jagiellonian University Medical School's Museum of Pharmacy is one of the largest museums of its kind in Europe and arguably the best. Accommodated in a beautiful historic townhouse worth the visit alone, it features a 22,000-piece collection, which includes old laboratory equipment,

rare pharmaceutical instruments, heaps of glassware, stoneware, mortars, jars, barrels, medical books and documents.

Several pharmacies dating back to the 19th and early 20th centuries, including one from Lesko, have been painstakingly recreated here, and the garret is crammed with elixirs and panaceas, including vile vials or dried mummy powder. Much attention is given to the 'righteous gentile' Tadeusz Pankiewicz and the Pharmacy Under the Eagle (p135) he courageously kept in operation in the Jewish ghetto during the German occupation.

City Defence Walls HISTORIC SITE
(Mury Obronne; Map p122; ☎12 421 1361; www.mhk.pl; ul Pijarska; adult/concession 8/6zł; ☺10.30am–6pm May–Oct; ☐2, 4, 14, 19, 20, 24) This small museum includes entry to both the **Florian Gate** (Brama Floriańska) and **Barbican** (Barbakan), among the few surviving remnants of the city's medieval defence walls. The Florian Gate was once the city's main entrance and dates from the 14th century. The Barbican, a circular bastion adorned with seven turrets, was built at the turn of the 16th century to lend additional protection. It was once connected to the gate by a narrow passage running over a moat.

SOUTH OF THE RYNEK

★ **Basilica of St Francis** CHURCH
(Bazylika Św Franciszka; Map p122; ☎12 422 5376; www.franciszkanska.pl; Plac Wszystkich Świętych 5; ☺10am–4pm Mon–Sat, closed Sun during mass; ☐1, 6, 8, 13, 18) Duck into the dark basilica on a sunny day to admire the artistry of Stanisław Wyspiański, who designed the fantastic Art Nouveau stained-glass windows. The multi-coloured deity in the chancel above the organ loft is a masterpiece. From the transept, you can also enter the Gothic cloister of the Franciscan Monastery to admire the fragments of 15th-century frescoes.

Church of SS Peter & Paul CHURCH
(Map p122; ☑12 350 6365; www.apostolowie.pl; ul Grodzka 52a; ☺9am-5pm Tue-Sat, 1.30-5.30pm Sun; ☒6, 8, 10, 13, 18) The Jesuits erected this church, the first Baroque building in Kraków, after they had been brought to the city in 1583 to do battle with supporters of the Reformation. Designed on the Latin cross layout and topped with a large sky-lit dome, the church has a refreshingly sober interior, apart from some fine stucco decoration on the vault.

Church of St Andrew CHURCH
(Map p122; ☑12 422 1612; ul Grodzka 54; ☺8am-6pm Mon-Fri; ☒6, 8, 10, 13, 18) Breathtakingly, this church is almost a thousand years old. Built towards the end of the 11th century, much of its austere Romanesque stone exterior has been preserved. As soon as you enter, though, you're in a totally different world; its small interior was subjected to a radical Baroque overhaul in the 18th century.

Archdiocesan Museum MUSEUM
(Muzeum Archidiecezjalne; Map p122; ☑12 421 8963; www.muzeumkra.diecezja.pl; ul Kanonicza 21; adult/concession 5/3zł; ☺10am-4pm Tue-Fri, to 3pm Sat & Sun; ☒6, 8, 10, 13, 18) This collection of religious sculpture and paintings, dating from the 13th to 16th centuries, is located in a 14th-century townhouse. Also on display is the room where Karol Wojtyła (the late Pope John Paul II) lived from 1958 to 1967, complete with his furniture and belongings – including his skis. There's a treasury of gifts he received here too.

Archaeological Museum MUSEUM
(Map p122; ☑12 422 7100; www.ma.krakow. pl; ul Poselska 3; adult/concession 9/6zł, Sun free; ☺9am-3pm Mon, Wed & Fri, 9am-6pm Tue & Thu, 11am-4pm Sun, closed Sat; ☒1, 6, 8, 13, 18) You can learn about Małopolska's history from the Palaeolithic period up until the early Middle Ages here, but you'll be most enthralled by the collection of ancient Egyptian artefacts, including both human and animal mummies. There are also more than 4000 iron coins from the 9th century. The gardens are a lovely place for a stroll afterwards.

WEST OF THE OLD TOWN
There are a couple of important sights worth the easy walk west from the Old Town.

Manggha Centre of Japanese Art & Technology MUSEUM
(Map p132; ☑12 267 2703; www.manggha.pl; ul Konopnickiej 26; adult/concession 20/15zł, Tue free; ☺10am-6pm Tue-Sun; ☒11, 18, 22, 52) This museum is the brainchild of Polish film director Andrzej Wajda, who donated the Kyoto Prize money he received in 1987 to fund a permanent home for the National Museum's extensive collection of Japanese art, ceramics and scrolls. The bulk of the collection is made up of several thousand pieces assembled by Feliks Jasieński (1861–1929), an avid traveller and essayist, known as Manggha. Note the location is across the river from the Old Town.

National Museum MUSEUM
(Muzeum Narodowe w Krakowie; Map p119; ☑12 433 5540; www.muzeum.krakow.pl; Al 3 Maja 1; adult/concession 28/19zł, Sun free; ☺10am-6pm Tue-Sat, to 4pm Sun; ☒20) Three permanent exhibitions – the Gallery of 20th-Century Polish Painting, the Gallery of Decorative Art, and Polish Arms and National Colours – are housed in this main branch of the National Museum in Kraków, 500m west of the Old Town down ul Piłsudskiego. The most notable collection is the painting gallery, which houses an extensive collection of Polish painting (and some sculpture) covering the period from 1890 until the present day.

There are several stained-glass designs (including the ones for Wawel Cathedral) by Stanisław Wyspiański, and an impressive selection of paintings by Witkacy (Stanisław Ignacy Witkiewicz). Jacek Malczewski and Olga Boznańska are also well represented. Of the postwar artists, take particular note of the works by Tadeusz Kantor, Jerzy Nowosielski and Władysław Hasior.

☺ Kazimierz

For much of its early history, Kazimierz was an independent town with its own municipal charter and laws. Its mixed Jewish and Christian population created a pair of distinctive communities side by side (p130). Though the ethnic make-up of Kazimierz is now wholly different, the architecture gives hints of the past, with clearly distinguishable elements of what were Christian and Jewish quarters. Located within walking distance of Wawel Hill and the Old Town, the suburb these days does double duty. It is home to many important tourist sights, including churches, synagogues and museums. And it's also the site of some of the city's liveliest and best cafes, clubs and restaurants.

WESTERN KAZIMIERZ
Corpus Christi Church CHURCH
(Parafia Bożego Ciała w Krakowie; Map p132; ☑12 430 5995; www.bozecialo.net; ul Bożego Ciała 26;

KRAKÓW SIGHTS

⊘7am-7pm; 🚌6, 8, 10, 13) In the northeastern corner of Plac Wolnica and founded in 1340, this was the first church in Kazimierz and for a long time the town's parish church. Its interior has been almost totally fitted out with Baroque furnishings, including the huge high altar, extraordinary massive carved stalls in the chancel and a boat-shaped pulpit. Note the surviving early-15th-century stained-glass window in the sanctuary and the crucifix hanging above the chancel.

Ethnographic Museum
MUSEUM

(Muzeum Etnograficzne; Map p132; ☑12 430 5575; www.etnomuzeum.eu; Plac Wolnica 1; adult/concession 13/7zł, Sun free; ⊘11am-7pm Tue, Wed, Fri & Sat, to 9pm Thu, to 3pm Sun; 🚌6, 8, 10, 13) This interesting museum is housed within the former town hall of Kazimierz. It was built in the late 14th century then significantly extended in the 16th century, at which time it acquired its Renaissance appearance. The permanent exhibition features the reconstructed interiors of traditional Polish peasant cottages and workshops, folk costumes, craft and trade exhibits, extraordinary nativity scenes, and folk and religious painting and woodcarving.

Pauline Church of SS Michael & Stanislaus
CHURCH

(Skalka Kościół Paulinów Św Michała i Stanisława; Map p132; ☑12 619 0900; www.skalka.paulini.pl; ul Skałeczna 15; adult/concession 3/2zł; ⊘9am-5pm; 🚌6, 8, 10, 13) This mid-18th-century Baroque church is associated with Bishop Stanisław (Stanislaus) Szczepanowski, patron saint of Poland. In 1079, the bishop was beheaded by King Bolesław Śmiały (Boleslaus the Bold): the tree trunk where the deed was done is beside the altar. The crypt shelters tombs of 12 eminent cultural figures, including Nobel-winning writer and poet Czesław Miłosz.

St Catherine's Church
CHURCH

(Kościół św. Katarzyny; Map p132; www.parafia-kazimierz.augustianie.pl; ul Augustiańska 7; ⊘10am-4pm Mon-Fri, 11am-2pm Sat; 🚌6, 8, 10, 13) One of the most monumental churches in the city, and possibly the one that has best

THE RISE & FALL (& RISE) OF KAZIMIERZ

Kazimierz was founded in 1335 by Kazimierz III Wielki on the southern fringe of Kraków. Thanks to privileges granted by the king, the town developed swiftly and soon had its own town hall, a market square almost as large as Kraków's, and two huge churches. The town was encircled with defensive walls and by the end of the 14th century was Małopolska's most important and wealthiest city after Kraków.

The first Jews settled in Kazimierz soon after its foundation, but it wasn't until 1494, when they were expelled from within the walls of Kraków by King Jan Olbracht, that their numbers rapidly rose. They settled in a prescribed area of Kazimierz, northeast of the Christian quarter, with the two sectors separated by a wall.

The subsequent history of Kazimierz was punctuated by fires, floods and plagues, with both communities living side by side, though confined to their own sectors. The Jewish quarter became home to Jews fleeing persecution from all corners of Europe, and it grew particularly quickly, gradually determining the character of the whole town. It became the most important Jewish centre of all Poland.

At the end of the 18th century Kazimierz was administratively incorporated into Kraków, and in the 1820s the walls were pulled down. At the outbreak of WWII Kazimierz was a predominantly Jewish suburb, with a distinctive culture and atmosphere. During the war, the Germans forcibly moved Jewish residents across the river to a purpose-built restricted ghetto in Podgórze. From there, the Jews were eventually dispersed to labour and concentration camps, where they were murdered by the Nazi regime. Of the 65,000 Jews living in Kraków (most of whom lived in Kazimierz) in 1939, only about 6000 survived the war.

During communist rule, Kazimierz was largely a forgotten district of Kraków, and descended into something of a slum. Then in the early 1990s along came Steven Spielberg to shoot Schindler's List and everything changed overnight.

Kazimierz was actually not the setting of the movie's plot – most of the events portrayed in the film took place in or near the Podgórze ghetto, Oskar Schindler's factory and the Płaszów extermination camp, all of which were further southeast beyond the Vistula. Though Kazimierz is a fascinating place, it's worth crossing the river to grittier Podgórze to get a feel for the whole story.

retained its original Gothic shape, St Catherine's was founded in 1363 and completed 35 years later, though its planned towers were never built. The lofty and spacious white-washed interior boasts the imposing, richly gilded Baroque high altar from 1634 and some flamboyant choir stalls.

JEWISH QUARTER

The eastern part of Kazimierz became, over the centuries, a centre of Jewish culture equal to no other in the country. However, with the mass deportation and extermination of the Jewish people of Kraków by the German occupiers during WWII, the folklore, life and atmosphere of the quarter was tragically extinguished. Kazimierz became a run-down area after WWII, but in recent years this area has regained some of its Jewish character via the establishment of kosher restaurants complete with live klezmer music, along with museums devoted to Jewish culture. Miraculously, seven synagogues survived the war, and most are available to visit.

The heart of the Jewish quarter is ul Szeroka. Short and wide, it looks more like an elongated square than a street, and is often packed with tourists and coaches.

★ **Galicia Jewish Museum**   MUSEUM
(Map p132; ☑ 12 421 6842; www.galiciajewish museum.org; ul Dajwór 18; adult/concession 15/10zł; ☉ 10am-6pm; ☐ 3, 9, 19, 24, 50) This museum both commemorates Jewish victims of the Holocaust and celebrates the Jewish culture and history of the former Austro-Hungarian region of Galicia. It features an impressive photographic exhibition depicting modern-day remnants of southeastern Poland's once-thriving Jewish community, called 'Traces of Memory', along with video testimony of survivors and regular temporary exhibits. The museum also leads guided tours of the Jewish sites of Kazimierz. Call or email for details.

Jewish Museum   MUSEUM
(Old Synagogue; Map p132; ☑ 12 422 0962; www.mhk.pl; ul Szeroka 24; adult/concession 9/7zł, Mon free; ☉ 10am-2pm Mon, 9am-5pm Tue-Sun; ☐ 3, 9, 19, 24, 50) This museum is housed in the Old Synagogue, which dates to the 15th century. The prayer hall, complete with a reconstructed *bimah* (raised platform at the centre where the Torah is read) and the original *aron kodesh* (the niche in the eastern wall where Torah scrolls are kept), houses an exhibition of liturgical objects. Upstairs there's a photographic exhibit.

The Old Synagogue is the oldest Jewish house of worship in the country. Damaged by fire in 1557, it was reconstructed in Renaissance style by the Italian architect Matteo Gucci. It was plundered and partly destroyed by the Nazis but later restored.

Remuh Synagogue   SYNAGOGUE
(Map p132; ☑ 12 430 5411; www.remuh.jewish.org. pl; ul Szeroka 40; adult/concession 5/2zł; ☉ 9am-6pm Sun-Thu; ☐ 3, 9, 19, 24, 50) Near the northern end of ul Szeroka is the district's smallest synagogue and one of only two in the area that is regularly used for religious services. The synagogue was established in 1558 by a rich merchant, Israel Isserles, and is also associated with his son Rabbi Moses Isserles, a philosopher and scholar.

Remuh Cemetery   CEMETERY
(Map p132; ☑ 12 430 5411; ul Szeroka 40; ☉ 9am-6pm Mon-Thu; ☐ 3, 9, 19, 24, 50) **FREE** Just behind the Remuh Synagogue and founded in the mid-16th century, this cemetery was closed for burials in the late 18th century, when a new and larger graveyard was established. During WWII the German occupiers vandalised and razed the tombstones, but during postwar conservation work some 700 gravestones, many outstanding Renaissance examples and dating back four centuries, were uncovered. The tombstones have been meticulously restored, making the place one of the best-preserved Renaissance Jewish cemeteries anywhere in Europe.

Isaac Synagogue   SYNAGOGUE
(Synagoga Izaaka; Map p132; ☑ 12 430 2222; ul Jakuba 25, enter from Kupa 18; adult/concession 10/7zł; ☉ 9am-7pm Sun-Thu, to 2.30pm Fri; ☐ 3, 9, 19, 24, 50) Near the southwestern edge of the Remuh Cemetery is Kraków's largest synagogue, completed in 1644. In the wake of WWII, it was finally returned to the Jewish community in 1989. Inside you can see the remains of the original stuccowork and wall-painting decoration. The synagogue was recently restored and now houses a permanent exhibition titled 'In Memory of Polish Jews'.

High Synagogue   SYNAGOGUE
(Synagoga Wysoka; Map p132; ☑ 12 430 6889; www.austeria.eu; ul Józefa 38; adult/concession 9/6zł; ☉ 9.30am-7pm; ☐ 3, 9, 19, 24, 50) This place of worship was built around 1560, and is the third-oldest synagogue after the Old and Remuh Synagogues. The High Synagogue takes its name from the fact that the

Kraków – Kazimierz

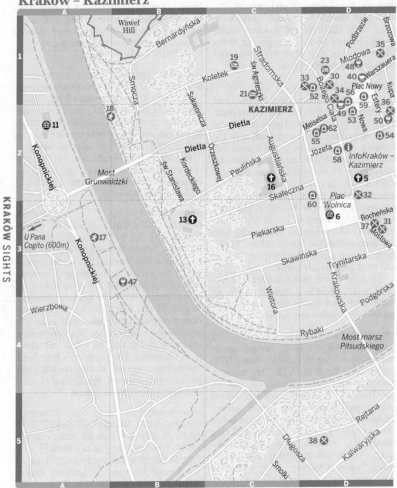

prayer hall was situated on the 1st floor, while the ground floor was given over to shops. These days, the ground floor holds arguably the city's best Jewish bookshop, Austeria (p154).

◉ Podgórze

This gentrifying but still largely working-class suburb would pique few travellers' curiosities if it wasn't for the notorious role it played during WWII. It was here that the Nazis herded some 16,000 Jews into a ghetto, centred around today's Plac Bohaterów Getta, and gradually emptied it via deportations to the concentration camps, including one located a short distance to the southwest in Płaszów. Both ghetto and camp were chillingly recreated in the movie *Schindler's List*.

Beyond the former wartime ghetto, Podgórze is surprisingly green and hilly, with one of the city's most mysterious mounds and a tiny church whose origins remain unknown to this day.

★**Schindler's Factory**   MUSEUM
(Fabryka Schindlera; Map p132; ☎12 257 0096; www.mhk.pl; ul Lipowa 4; adult/concession 21/16zł, Mon free; ⊙10am-4pm Mon, 9am-8pm Tue-Sun; 🚊3, 9, 19, 24, 50) This impressive interac-

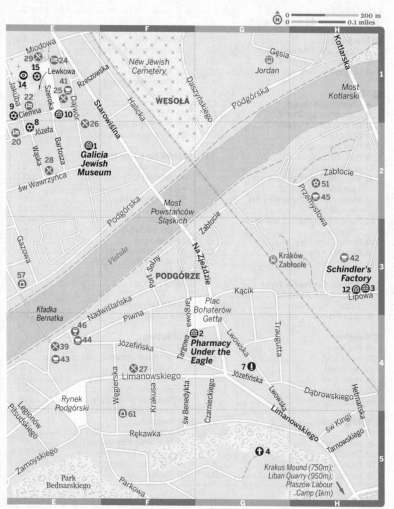

tive museum covers the Nazi occupation of Kraków in WWII. It's housed in the former enamel factory of Oskar Schindler, the Nazi industrialist who famously saved the lives of members of his Jewish labour force during the Holocaust. Well-organised, innovative exhibits tell the moving story of the city from 1939 to 1945.

From the main post office in the Old Town, catch any tram down ul Starowiślna and alight at the first stop over the river at Plac Bohaterów Getta. From here, follow the signs east along ul Kącik, under the railway line to the museum.

★ **Pharmacy Under the Eagle** MUSEUM

(Apteka Pod Orłem; Map p132; ☑12 656 5625; www.mhk.pl; Plac Bohaterów Getta 18; adult/concession 10/8zł, Mon free; ⊙9am-5pm Tue-Sun, 10am-2pm Mon; ☑3, 9, 19, 24, 50) On the south side of Plac Bohaterów Getta is this museum in a former pharmacy, which was run by the non-Jew Tadeusz Pankiewicz during the Nazi German occupation. The interior has been restored to its wartime appearance and tells the story of the ghetto and the role of the pharmacy in its daily life.

Kraków – Kazimierz

Ghetto Wall MONUMENT
(Map p132; ul Lwowska 25-29; ᵍ3, 9, 19, 24, 50) Just south of Plac Bohaterów Getta are the remains of the wartime Jewish ghetto wall from WWII, with a plaque marking the site.

Museum of Contemporary Art in Kraków MUSEUM
(MOCAK; Map p132; ☎12 263 4000; www.mocak.pl; ul Lipowa 4; adult/concession 10/5zł, Tue free; ☉11am-7pm Tue-Sun; ᵍ3, 9, 19, 24, 50) Opened in 2011, MOCAK (as it's known for short) is a major museum of modern art, and the first such building in Poland to be constructed from scratch. As it's right next to Schindler's Factory, the two attractions could be combined for an absorbing day out.

Płaszów Labour Camp HISTORIC SITE
(ul Jerozolimska; ☉dawn-dusk; ᵍ3, 6, 13, 23, 24, 50, 69) The former Płaszów forced-labour and concentration camp was built by occupying Germans during WWII to facilitate liquidation of the nearby Podgórze Jewish ghetto. At its height in 1943–44, the camp held some 25,000 people. These days, almost nothing of the camp survives with the exception of a few plaques. It's not easy to find. Enter via ul Jerozolimska (off ul Wielicka) or follow a path leading south from the Krakus Mound along the edge of the Liban Quarry.

Krakus Mound MONUMENT
(Kopiec Krakusa; ul Maryewskiego; Map p119; ☉dawn-dusk; ᵍ3, 6, 9, 13, 23, 24, 50) Nobody

knows the exact origins of the 16m mound that towers over Podgórze. According to legend, it was the burial site of the city's founder, Prince Krak. Excavations in the 1930s could not confirm this story, but they did discover artefacts dating to the 8th century. The mysterious mound offers 360-degree panoramic views, including the Old Town, Kazimierz, Nowa Huta and Płaszów.

Church of St Benedict CHURCH
(Kościółek Św Benedykta; Map p132; ul Rękawka, Lasota Hill; 3, 6, 9, 13, 23, 24, 50) Tucked into a wooded hillside above Podgórze, this mysterious little church is one of the oldest in Kraków. Historians are not certain of its origin, though archaeologists estimate that it was built in the 12th century. Although the interior has been restored, the church is open only once a year on the first Tuesday after Easter, when the spring festival of Rękawka is celebrated.

Liban Quarry RUIN
(ul Za Torem; Map p119; ☉dawn-dusk; 3, 6, 9, 13, 23, 24, 50) This former limestone quarry was used by the occupying Germans during WWII as a labour camp. It was later employed extensively in the film *Schindler's List* as a stand-in for the Płaszów concentration camp. These days it's abandoned, overgrown and more than a little bit creepy, but a fascinating place to stroll and ponder modern history. To find it, follow the path south from the Krakus Mound or simply follow the street ul Za Torem into the woods.

◎ Outer Kraków

These sights outside central Kraków are worth a half- or full-day excursion.

ZWIERZYNIEC

★ Kościuszko Mound MONUMENT
(Kopiec Kościuszki; Map p119; ☑12 425 1116; www.kopieckosciuszki.pl; Al Waszyngtona 1; adult/concession 12/10zł; ☉9am-dusk; 1, 2, 6) The mound, dedicated to Polish (and American) military hero Tadeusz Kościuszko, was erected between 1820 and 1823, soon after the great man's death. The mound stands 34m high, and soil from the Polish and American battlefields where Kościuszko fought was placed here. The views over the city are spectacular. The memorial is located in the suburb of Zwierzyniec, just under 3km west of the Old Town.

The entrance is through a small neo-Gothic chapel, which holds an exhibition of memorabilia related to Kościuszko; there's also a separate waxworks exhibition featuring Polish heroes across the ages. The large brick fortification at the mound's foothill is a fortress built by the Austrians in the 1840s.

LAS WOLSKI

The 485-hectare Las Wolski (Wolski Forest), west of Zwierzyniec, is the largest forested

---

DARKNESS & LIGHT WITHIN THE GHETTO

At Jerusalem's Yad Vashem, a museum dedicated to the Holocaust, there's a row of trees called the 'Avenue of the Righteous Among the Nations'. They represent some of the 21,000-odd Gentiles (non-Jews) who either saved Jews during the Holocaust or came to their defence by putting their own lives at risk. Among those so honoured is the German factory owner Oskar Schindler, probably the best known of the so-called 'Righteous Gentiles' thanks to author Thomas Keneally's book *Schindler's Ark* (1982), made into the award-winning film *Schindler's List* (1993) by Steven Spielberg.

But alongside Schindler's name are the names of some 6000 Poles – almost one-third of the worldwide total – named in this roll of honour. Schindler was something of an antihero, a heavy-drinking profiteer who originally saved the lives of Jews only because he needed their cheap labour at his enamelware factory in Podgórze (now a museum).

More altruistic was the pharmacist Tadeusz Pankiewicz, who cajoled the authorities into letting him keep his business, the Pharmacy Under the Eagle (p133), open in the ghetto until the final deportation. He dispensed medicines (often without charge), carried news from the 'outside world', and even allowed use of the establishment as a safe house on occasion.

Pankiewicz's harrowing memoir, *The Cracow Ghetto Pharmacy*, describes many of these deeds in measured detail without bravado or boast, and provides an eyewitness account of the short and tragic history of the Kraków ghetto from beginning to liquidation. It's a remarkable story from a Kraków resident who acted according to the most noble principles of humanity during the city's darkest days.

area within the city limits and a popular weekend destination for city dwellers. It's possible to walk between the three main attractions via forest trails.

Piłsudski Mound
MONUMENT

(Kopiec Piłsudskiego w Krakowie; Map p119; ⊘ 24hr; 🚌 134) FREE This mound-based memorial was erected in honour of Marshal Józef Piłsudski after his death in 1935; it was formed from soil taken from WWI Polish battle sites. The views of the city are excellent. Bus 134, which terminates at the zoo, is the nearest public transport. You can also reach the mound from the Kościuszko Mound on foot via a well-marked trail, taking about 2½ hours.

Zoological Gardens
ZOO

(Ogród Zoologiczny; Map p119; ☎ 12 425 3551; www.zoo-krakow.pl; Al Kasy Oszczędności Miasta Krakowa 14; adult/concession 18/10zł; ⊘ 9am-6pm; 🚌 134) The 20-hectare zoological gardens are well-tended and home to about 1500 animals. Highlights include a pair of Indian elephants, pygmy hippopotamuses, and a herd of rare Asian horses (Przewalski) that once roamed the Mongolian steppes. Bus 134 heads to the zoo from its terminus near the National Museum.

NOWA HUTA

The youngest and largest of Kraków's suburbs, Nowa Huta (New Steelworks) is a result of the postwar rush toward industrialisation. In the early 1950s, a gigantic steelworks was built 10km east of the centre of Kraków, along with a new town to serve as a dormitory community for its workforce. The steel mill accounted for nearly half the national iron and steel output, and the suburb became a vast urban sprawl populated by over 200,000 people. The steelworks' operations have been scaled back since the fall of communism, and it's now owned by the giant ArcelorMittal steel company.

The steelworks can't be visited, but you may want to have a peek at the suburb's austere socialist-realist lines (certainly a shock after the Old Town's medieval streets). In its day, Nowa Huta was held up as a model of communist-era town planning, and the architectural symmetry lends a funky retro feeling that lingers to this day. Tram 4 from Kraków Główny train station will drop you at Plac Centralny, the suburb's central square. From here, the best bet is to wander amid the stone-grey housing projects – remarkably still

in good shape – where families continue to live and raise their children.

Outside of the planned community, the history of the Nowa Huta area stretches back centuries. About 1km east of Nowa Huta, you'll find the sprawling Cistercian Monastery and a remarkable wooden church from the 15th century that's still standing.

Muzeum PRL-u
MUSEUM

(☎ 12 446 7821; www.mprl.pl; os Centrum E1; adult concession 6/4zł; ⊘ 9am-5pm Mon-Fri; 🚌 4, 10, 16, 21) This museum and exhibition space launched in 2015 and focuses on the communist history of Nowa Huta and of Poland in general. Rotating exhibitions highlight various aspects of life under communism, with plenty of local tie-ins to life in Nowa Huta. The setting is perfect in the socialist-realist Światowid cinema. There's even a nuclear bunker in the basement.

Nowa Huta Museum
MUSEUM

(☎ 12 425 9775; www.mhk.pl; os Słoneczne 16; adult/concession 6/4zł, Wed free; ⊘ 9.30am-5pm Tue-Sun; 🚌 4, 10, 16, 21) Two blocks north of Plac Centralny, the Nowa Huta Museum is more like a glorified tourist office, but there is a small, well-curated exhibit space. Rotating exhibits incorporate multimedia to explore the neighbourhood's history and contemporary development.

Arka Pana
CHURCH

(Lord's Ark; ☎ 12 644 0624; www.arkapana.pl; ul Obrońców Krzyża 1; ⊘ 9am-6pm; 🚌 1, 5) The retro-modern Arka Pana was the first church in Nowa Huta, built in 1977 after much controversy. Authorities had intended the suburb to be a church-free zone, and it required protests and politicking by the local bishop (one Karol Wojtyła, who would later become pope) to get the job done.

Church of St Bartholomew
CHURCH

(Kościół Św Bartłomieja; ☎ 12 644 2331; www.mogila. cystersi.pl; ul Klasztorna 11; ⊘ 10am-6pm Thu-Sat, noon-5pm Sun; 🚌 10, 16) The small, shingled Church of St Bartholomew dates from the mid-15th century, which makes it Poland's oldest surviving three-nave timber church. It was one of only two churches available to workers in Nowa Huta, until the Arka Pana church was built in 1977.

Cistercian Abbey
MONASTERY

(Opactwo Cystersów; ☎ 12 644 2331; www.mogila. cystersi.pl; ul Klasztorna 11; ⊘ 9am-5pm; 🚌 10, 16) The Cistercian Abbey consists of a church and monastery with a large garden-park be-

MONASTERY ON THE SILVER MOUNTAIN

The **Monastery of Camaldolese Monks** (Klasztor Kamedułów; Map p119; www.kameduli.info; Srebrna Góra, Western Kraków; ⊙8-11am & 3-4.30pm; 🚌1,2, 6) sits atop Silver Mountain, overlooking the Vistula (Wisła) River, in an outlying suburb west of the Old Town. It's well worth a few hours to visit. Men can visit the church and crypt any day from 8am to 11am and 3pm to 4.30pm. Women can enter only on certain feast days, including Easter, Easter Monday, the second and fourth Sundays in July, Assumption of Mary (15 August), and Christmas.

The order, part of the Benedictine family of monastic communities, with its very strict rules and Memento Mori ('remember you must die') motto, attracts curiosity regarding its members' ascetic way of life. It was brought to Poland from Italy in 1603 and in time founded a dozen monasteries throughout the country. Today there are just two in Poland, including one in Masuria. The monks live in seclusion in hermitages and contact each other only during prayers; some have no contact with the outside world at all.

The monks are vegetarian and have solitary meals in their 'homes', with only five common meals a year. The hermits don't sleep in coffins as rumoured, but they do keep the skulls of their predecessors in the hermitages.

You approach the complex through a long walled alley that leads to the main gate, the ceiling of which is covered in naive frescoes. Once you are let in, you walk to the massive white limestone facade of the monastery church (50m high and 40m wide). A spacious, single-nave interior is covered by a barrel-shaped vault and lined on both sides with eight ornate Baroque chapels. The Baroque main altar is impressive.

Underneath the chancel of the church is a large chapel used for prayers and, to its right, the crypt of the hermits. Bodies are placed into niches without coffins and then sealed. Latin inscriptions state the age of the deceased and the period spent in the hermitage. The niches are opened after 80 years and most of the remains moved to a place of permanent rest. It's then that the hermits take the skulls to keep in their shelters.

In the garden behind the church are 14 surviving hermitages where several monks live (others live in the building next to the church), but the area is off limits to tourists. You may occasionally see hermits in the church, sporting long bushy beards and fine white cassocks.

The hermitage is 7km west of the city centre. Take tram 1, 2 or 6 to the end of the line at Salwator and change for any westbound bus. The bus will let you off at the foot of Srebrna Góra (Silver Mountain), then it's a 200m walk up the hill to the church.

hind it. The Cistercians came to Poland in 1140 and founded abbeys around the country, including this one in 1222. The church has a large three-nave interior with a balanced mix of Gothic, Renaissance and Baroque furnishings and decoration. Have a look at the Chapel of the Crucified Christ (in the left transept), the polyptych in the high altar and the beautiful stained-glass windows behind it.

WIELICZKA

★**Wieliczka Salt Mine** UNDERGROUND MUSEUM
(📞12 278 7302; www.kopalnia.pl; ul Daniłowicza 10; adult/concession 79/64zł; ⊙7.30am-7.30pm Apr-Oct, 8am-5pm Nov-Mar) Some 14km southeast of Kraków, Wieliczka (vyeh-leech-kah) is famous for its deep salt mine. It's an eerie world of pits and chambers, and everything within its depths has been carved by hand from salt blocks. The mine has a labyrinth of tunnels, about 300km distributed over nine levels, the

deepest being 327m underground. A section of the mine, some 22 chambers connected by galleries, from 64m to 135m below ground, is open to the public by guided tour, and it's a fascinating trip.

The mine is renowned for the preservative qualities of its microclimate, as well as for its health-giving properties. An underground sanatorium has been established at a depth of 135m, where chronic allergic diseases are treated by overnight stays.

The salt-hewn formations include chapels with altarpieces and figures, while others are adorned with statues and monuments – and there are even underground lakes. The showpiece is the ornamented Chapel of St Kinga (Kaplica Św Kingi), which is actually a fair-sized church measuring 54m by 18m, and 12m high. Every single element here, from chandeliers to altarpieces, is of salt. It took over 30 years (1895) for one man and then his

NOWA HUTA: SOCIALIST DREAM TURNED NIGHTMARE

The postwar communist regime deliberately built the Nowa Huta steelworks in Kraków to administer a 'healthy' injection of industrial workers as an antidote to the strong aristocratic, cultural and religious traditions of the city. It was of no interest to city planners that Kraków had neither ore nor coal deposits and that virtually all raw materials had to be transported from great distances. The project also did not take into account that the site had one of the most fertile soils in the region, nor that construction of the complex would destroy villages that could trace their histories back to the early Middle Ages.

Perhaps not surprisingly, the communist dream didn't materialise as planned. Rather than threatening the traditional roots of Kraków, it actually became a threat to its creators. Strikes broke out here as frequently as anywhere else, paving the way for the eventual fall of communism. The steelworks also caused catastrophic environmental pollution that threatened its citizens' health, the natural environment and the city's historical monuments.

Nowadays Nowa Huta has been fully integrated into Kraków, and the steelworks operate at higher environmental standards. The greatest indications of change, however, are Nowa Huta's street signs, now divested of communist notables and bearing such names as Pope John Paul II and Ronald Reagan.

brother to complete this underground temple, and about 20,000 tonnes of rock salt had to be removed. Other highlights are the salt lake in the Erazm Barącz Chamber, whose water contains 320g of salt per litre, and the 36m-high Stanisław Staszic Chamber.

Included in the entry price is a visit to the Kraków Saltworks Museum, accommodated in 14 worked-out chambers on the third level of the mine, where the tour ends, but most visitors appear to be 'over-salted' by then. From here a fast mining lift takes you back up to the real world.

Visitors are guided in groups and the tour takes about two hours. You walk about 2km through the mine, so wear comfortable shoes. The temperature in the mine is 14°C. In July and August English-language tours depart every half-hour from 8.30am to 6pm. During the rest of the year there are between six and eight daily tours in English.

Minibuses to Wieliczka (3zł) depart Kraków frequently between 6am and 8pm from makeshift bus stands along ul Pawia, across the street from the Galeria Krakowska shopping mall (adjacent to Kraków Główny train station). Several tour operators, including Cracow City Tours (p139), run bus tours to the mine for around 130zł, including admission.

🏃 Activities

Hiflyer Balon Widokowy
BALLOONING

(Hiflyer Viewing Balloon; Map p132; ☑ 511 802 202; www.hiflyer.pl; Bulwar Wołyński; adult/concession 42/34zł; ⊙10am-8pm Apr-Sep; ☐18, 19, 22) For fabulous views of Wawel Castle and the Old Town, it's hard to beat the Hiflyer hot-air balloon. Moored along the Vistula (Wisła) River, near the Grunwald Bridge, across the river from Kazimierz, the enormous balloon takes passengers for a 15-minute float 150m over the city. On a clear day you can see the Tatras.

Park Wodny
SWIMMING

(☑ 12 616 3190; www.parkwodny.pl; ul Dobrego Pasterza 126; per hr adult/concession Mon-Fri 23/19zł, Sat & Sun 25/22zł, all day incl sauna weekdays 52/40zł, weekend 58/45zł; ⊙8am-10pm; ☐129, 152) Your skin will be wrinkled and prune-like by the time you leave this fun-filled aqua park, located 2.5km northeast of the Old Town. For endless hours of wet and wild, there are paddling pools, watersports, 800m of water slides, saltwater hot tubs, saunas and more.

Statek Nimfa
CRUISE

(Map p132; ☑ 505 102 677; www.statekkrakow.com; Wawel pier; 1hr cruise adult/concession 25/20zł, 3hr cruise 60/50zł; ⊙10am-6pm; ☐11, 18, 22, 52) The pleasure boat *Nimfa* cruises along the Vistula River, departing from the pier below Wawel Castle, and motoring past sights such as Kościuszko Mound, Skałka and Plac Bohaterów Getta, with up-close views of all six bridges. The three-hour tour goes all the way to Tyniec. Book tickets online or by email.

👉 Tours

Free Walking Tour
WALKING TOUR

(Map p122; ☑ 513 875 815; www.freewalkingtour.com; ☐1, 6, 8, 13, 18) These free walking tours of the Old Town and Kazimierz are provided by licensed tour guides who make their money from tips. Tours depart daily (May to October) at 10am and 3.30pm from in front of St Mary's Basilica on the Rynek Główny. Look for the tour guide holding the sign 'Free Walking Tour'.

Cracow Tours TOUR

(Map p122; ☑ booking 12 430 0726; www.cracow tours.pl; ul Krupnicza 3; Kraków city tour 145zł; ☺ 8am-4pm Mon-Fri; ☒ 2, 4, 8, 13, 14, 18, 20, 24) Offers a four-hour bus and walking tours of the city. English tours depart at 9am from ul Powiśle 11, which runs alongside the river to the northwest of Wawel Castle. Tour price includes admission prices.

Crazy Guides HISTORY

(☑ 500 091 200; www.crazyguides.com) Highly entertaining tours of the city's communist-era suburbs, including a 2½-hour tour to Nowa Huta (139zł), in a restored East German Trabant car. Book online or by phone.

Cool Tour Company BICYCLE TOUR

(Map p122; ☑ 12 430 2034; www.krakowbiketour. com; ul Grodzka 2; ☒ 1, 6, 8, 13, 18) Cool Tour Company offers a four-hour spin on wheels around town (90zł) that departs twice daily from May through September at 10am and 3pm. The tour takes in everything from the Old Town walls and Wawel Hill to Oskar Schindler's factory in Podgórze.

Krak Tour TOUR

(☑ 886 664 999; www.kraktour.pl) No bus can get you around the narrow streets and hidden courtyards of the Old Town and Kazimierz like these five-seater golf carts. Expect to pay about 160zł per person for an hour's run-around with taped commentary. Book by telephone.

Cracow City Tours TOUR

(Map p122; ☑ 12 421 2864; www.cracowcitytours. pl; ul Floriańska 44; city tour adult/concession 120/100zł; ☺ 9.30am-9.30pm May-Sep, 10am-8pm Oct-Apr; ☒ 2, 4, 14, 19, 20, 24) A decent range of city walking and bus tours, including a popular four-hour bus tour, as well as longer day excursions to the Wieliczka Salt Mine (130zł) and the Auschwitz-Birkenau Memorial & Museum (130zł). Note that bus tours depart from a branch office at Plac Matejki 2, just to the north of the Florian Gate.

Horse-Drawn Carriages CARRIAGE

(Map p122; Rynek Główny; half/full hour 150/250zł; ☒ 1, 6, 8, 13, 18) The most romantic

way to tour Kraków is by the horse-drawn carriages that line up at the northern end of Rynek Główny. You decide which route you want to take, or leave it up to the driver to take you for a trot round the sights of the Old Town or even down to Kazimierz. Negotiate the price in advance.

Marco der Pole TOUR

(Map p122; ☑ 12 430 2117; www.krakow-travel. com; ul Sarego 22; ☒ 6, 8, 10, 13, 18) Runs a range of walking and golf-cart tours of the Old Town and Kazimierz, as well as longer trips throughout the city and around Poland. Book tours in advance over the website.

Jarden Tourist Agency JEWISH HERITAGE

(Map p132; ☑ 12 421 7166; www.jarden.pl; ul Szeroka 2; ☒ 3, 9, 19, 24, 50) Mainly Jewish-themed tours, including two- and three-hour walking tours of Kraków's Kazimierz and Podgórze, as well as a popular two-hour driving tour of places made famous by the film *Schindler's List*. Tours are priced per person, ranging from 40zł to 90zł, depending on the number participating.

Cracow Sightseeing Tours BUS

(☑ 795 003 231; www.cracow-redbus.com; 48-hr ticket adult/concession 90/70zł) A 'jump-on, jump-off' doubledecker red bus, with departure points around the city. Consult the website for a full map. The first bus leaves from ul Grodzka (near Wawel Castle) at 9.30am.

Bird Service ECOTOUR

(Map p122; ☑ 12 292 1460; www.bird.pl; ul Św Krzyża 17; ☒ 3, 10, 19, 24, 52) A specialist in birdwatching tours, this company organises birding trips throughout eastern Poland, including the Białowieża and Biebrza National Parks. Bird Service also offers week-long bicycle tours along the Dunajec River in the Carpathian Mountains and other places around the country. See the website for tours and prices.

✯ Festivals & Events

Kraków has one of the richest cycles of annual events in Poland. The first port of call for information is the nearest branch of the InfoKraków tourist office. The Kraków Festival Guide website (www.krakowfestival.com) maintains a handy list in English.

Shanties International
Festival of Sailors' Songs FOLK MUSIC

(www.shanties.pl; ☺ Feb) Going strong since 1981, despite Kraków's inland location. Held in February.

Bach Days
CLASSICAL MUSIC

(www.bach-cantatas.com; ☉ Mar) Baroque fugues presented at the Academy of Music in mid-March.

Cracovia Marathon
RUNNING

(www.zis.krakow.pl; ☉ Apr) Increasingly popular international running event, in April.

Juvenalia
YOUTH

(www.juwenalia.krakow.pl; ☉ May) During this student carnival, students receive symbolic keys to the town's gates and take over the city for four days and three nights. There's live music, street dancing, fancy-dress parades, masquerades and lots of fun. Held in May.

Krakow Film Festival
FILM

(www.kff.com.pl; ☉ May-Jun) Film festival that's been going for more than half a century screens hundreds of movies from various countries. Held in late May and early June.

Lajkonik Pageant
HISTORIC

(www.mhk.pl; ☉ May-Jun) Takes place seven days after Corpus Christi (usually in June, but possibly in late May). This colourful pageant is headed by the Lajkonik, a comical figure disguised as a bearded Tatar. It's organised each year by the Historical Museum of the City of Kraków.

Jewish Culture Festival
JEWISH

(www.jewishfestival.pl) Features a variety of cultural events including theatre, film, music and art exhibitions, and concludes with a grand open-air klezmer concert on ul Szeroka. Held in late June and early July.

International Festival of Street Theatre
THEATRE

(www.teatrkto.pl; ☉ Jul) Takes place on the Rynek in July.

Festival of Music in Old Cracow
MUSIC

(www.capellacracoviensis.pl; ☉ Jul-Aug) This important musical event goes on for two weeks, spans five centuries of musical tradition from medieval to contemporary, and is presented in concert halls, churches and other historic interiors. Usually in July and August.

Summer Jazz Festival
JAZZ

(www.cracjazz.com; ☉ Jul-Aug) Featuring the best of Polish modern jazz, in July and August.

International Summer Organ Concert Festival
MUSIC

(www.dworek.krakow.pl; ☉ Jul-Aug) Organ recitals, taking place in several city churches from July to August.

Pierogi Festival
FOOD

(www.biurofestiwalowe.pl; ☉ Aug) Three-day celebration of the mighty dumpling, held in Mały Rynek (Small Market Sq) east of St Mary's Church in August.

Sacrum Profanum
CLASSICAL MUSIC

(www.biurofestiwalowe.pl; ☉ Sep) Classical-music festival dedicated to the composers of a dif-

---

ICONIC LAJKONIK: KRAKÓW'S COLOURFUL HORSEMAN

A curious symbol of Kraków is the Lajkonik, a bearded man dressed in richly embroidered garments and a tall pointed hat, riding a hobbyhorse. He comes to life on the Thursday after Corpus Christi (late May or June) and heads a joyful pageant from the **Premonstratensian Convent** (Map p119; ☑ 12 427 1318; www.norbertanki.w.krakow.pl; ul Kościuszki 88) in Zwierzyniec to the Old Town's Rynek Główny.

Exact details of the Lajkonik's origins are hard to pin down, but one story involves a Tatar assault on Kraków in 1287. A group of raftsmen discovered the tent of the commanding khan on a foray outside the city walls and dispatched the unsuspecting Tatar leader and his generals in a lightning raid. The raftsmen's leader then wore the khan's richly decorated outfit back to the city.

The pageant, accompanied by a musical band, lasts about six hours, during which the Lajkonik takes to dancing, jumping, greeting passersby, popping into cafes en route, collecting donations and striking people with his mace, which is said to bring them good luck. Once the pageant reaches the main square, the Lajkonik is greeted by the mayor and presented with a symbolic ransom and a goblet of wine.

The Lajkonik's garb and his hobbyhorse were designed by Stanisław Wyspiański; the original design is kept in the Kraków City History Museum. It consists of a wooden frame covered with leather and embroidered with nearly a thousand pearls and coral beads. The whole outfit weighs about 40kg.

ferent nominated country each year. Held in September.

Zaduszki Jazz Festival   JAZZ
(⊙ Oct-Nov) This popular festival is held in a range of venues around the city in late October and November.

Kraków Christmas Crib
Competition   CHRISTMAS
(www.szopki.eu; ⊙ Dec) This competition is held on the main square beside the statue of Adam Mickiewicz on the first Thursday of December. The 'cribs' are nativity scenes, but different from those elsewhere in the world – Kraków's *szopki* are elaborate compositions built in an architectural, usually churchlike form, and made in astonishing detail from cardboard, wood, tinfoil and the like.

🛏 Sleeping

Kraków is Poland's premier tourist destination, so it has plenty of accommodation options. However, advance booking during the busy summer season is recommended for anywhere central. The Old Town has a selection of accommodation across all budget ranges. Kazimierz also has a number of hostels and atmospheric hotels, in a relatively quiet location. Note that the more expensive hotels sometimes quote prices in euros.

Modern hostels, geared towards the needs and expectations of Western backpackers, have sprung up everywhere. While mainly serving the budget-traveller market, nearly all of them also have private rooms in the midrange price bracket.

Private rooms and apartments can also be a good option if you're intending to stay a bit longer. International room-booking services like Airbnb (www.airbnb.com) list dozens of affordable options in and around central Kraków. **Hamilton Suites** (✑ 12 426 5126; www.krakow-apartments.biz; apt 300-600zł; 🖭) is a locally based firm offering good-value, short-term apartment rentals.

🛏 Old Town & Around

The Old Town has a plentiful supply of budget places, typically bright, clean, modern hostels with multilingual staff and extras such as washing machines and dryers. They also offer private rooms at midrange rates. There are a decent number of midrange hotels within walking distance of Rynek Główny and other major sights, and no shortage of places for a top-end splurge.

★ Mundo Hostel   HOSTEL €
(Map p122; ✑ 12 422 6113; www.mundohostel.eu; ul Sarego 10; dm 60-65zł, d 170-190zł; @ 🖭; 🚌 6, 8, 10, 13, 18) Attractive, well-maintained hostel in a quiet courtyard location neatly placed between the Old Town and Kazimierz. Each room is decorated for a different country; for example, the Tibet room is decked out with colourful prayer flags. Barbecues take place in summer. There's a bright, fully equipped kitchen for do-it-yourself meals.

Hostel Flamingo   HOSTEL €
(Map p122; ✑ 12 422 0000; www.flamingo-hostel.com; ul Szewska 4; dm 47-65zł, d 158zł; 🖭; 🚌 2, 4, 14, 18, 20, 24) Highly rated hostel with an excellent central location, just a couple steps from the main square. Pluses – in addition to the expected amenities – include free breakfast, an in-house cafe and a cheeky attitude. Sleeping in six- to 12-bed dorms plus a few private doubles.

Cracow Hostel   HOSTEL €
(Map p122; ✑ 12 429 1106; www.cracowhostel.com; Rynek Główny 18; dm 40-70zł, ste 260zł; 🖭; 🚌 1, 6, 8, 13, 18) Location, location, location. This standard hostel on three floors may not be the best in town, with somewhat cramped rooms of between four and 18 beds. But it's perched high above Rynek Główny, with an amazing view from the comfortable lounge. There's also a pretty apartment on offer with big windows that's very attractively priced for the locale.

Pink Panther's Hostel   HOSTEL €
(Map p122; ✑ 12 422 0935; www.pinkpanthershostel.com; ul Św Tomasza 8/10; dm 50-60zł, d 190zł; 🖭; 🚌 2, 4, 14, 18, 20, 24) A self-described 'party' hostel, this is a good choice for budget travellers in town to enjoy the nightlife. Simple dorm accommodation in 4- to 14-bed dorms, with some private doubles. The staff put on organised pub crawls, as well as themed nights, in the public area and small terrace. It's a two-floor walk-up if you're travelling with big bags.

Greg & Tom Hostel   HOSTEL €
(Map p122; ✑ 12 422 4100; www.gregtomhostel.com; ul Pawia 12/7; dm 57zł, d from 150zł; 🖭) This well-run hostel is spread over three locations, though all check-in is handled at the main branch on ul Pawia. The staff are friendly, the rooms are clean, and laundry facilities are included. On Tuesday and Saturday evenings, hot Polish dishes are served.

KRAKÓW SLEEPING

Hostel Centrum Kraków
HOSTEL €

(Map p122; ☑12 429 1157; www.centrumkrakow.pl; ul Św Gertrudy 10; dm 50-70zł, s/d 100/170zł; @ 🛜; 🚌6, 8, 10, 13, 18) This large hostel is bare-bones but offers an excellent location, just off the Planty and a few minutes walk to the main square. The rooms are clean and quiet, but sparsely furnished and a bit dated. The breakfast is mainly bread and cereal. The private singles and doubles are excellent value.

Hostel Atlantis
HOSTEL €

(Map p122; ☑12 421 0861; www.atlantishostel.pl; ul Dietla 58; dm from 35-50zł, d/tr 150/195zł; 🛜; 🚌3, 9, 11, 19, 22, 24, 50, 52) Colourful, well-maintained hostel situated on the southern end of the Old Town, within easy walking distance of both Kazimierz and Wawel Hill. The prices for a bunk in a four-, six- or eight-bed dorm room are some of the cheapest in the city, so a great choice for travellers on a tight budget.

★Wielopole
HOTEL €€

(Map p122; ☑12 422 1475; www.wielopole.pl; ul Wielopole 3; s/d 260/360zł; ❀🛜; 🚌3, 10, 19, 24, 52) Wielopole's selection of bright, modern rooms – all of them with spotless bathrooms – is housed in a renovated block with a great courtyard on the eastern edge of the Old Town, within easy walk of Kazimierz. The breakfast spread here is impressive.

U Pana Cogito
HOTEL €€

(☑12 269 7200; www.pcogito.pl; ul Bałuckiego 6; s/d/q 240/290/390zł; P❀@🛜; 🚌11, 18, 22, 52) White and cream seem to be the colours of choice at this friendly 14-room hotel in a lovely mansion across the river and southwest of the centre. All rooms have big bathrooms and refrigerators, and for extra privacy, the one apartment has a separate entrance. The hotel also has its own restaurant, also done out in fresh, minimalist white.

Dom Polonii
ROOM €€

(Map p122; ☑12 422 4355; www.wspolnota-polska.krakow.pl; Rynek Główny 14; s/d 180/250zł, ste 250-350zł; 🚌1, 6, 8, 13, 18) You couldn't ask for a more central location. The Dom has two high-ceilinged double rooms (overlooking the Rynek) and one double suite, all on the third floor (no lift). Rooms are sparsely furnished but great value given the locale. They get booked out far in advance. A small breakfast is included. Inquire by phone or email.

Hotel Pollera
HOTEL €€

(Map p122; ☑12 422 1044; www.pollera.com.pl; ul Szpitalna 30; s/d/tr 299/399/480zł; P@🛜; 🚌2, 3, 4, 10, 14, 19, 20, 24, 52) The Pollera is a classy place dating from 1834, containing 42 large rooms crammed with elegant furniture. The singles are unexciting, but the doubles are far nicer, and it's central and quiet.

Hotel Royal
HOTEL €€

(Map p122; ☑12 421 3500; www.hotelewam.pl; ul Św Gertrudy 26-29; s/d from 249/360zł; P@🛜; 🚌6, 8, 10, 13, 18) This large and impressive Art Nouveau edifice could use an update but will appeal to travellers who love period details like high ceilings, crown moldings and spiral staircases. The location is excellent, just a few minutes walk to Wawel Hill. The in-house restaurant, featuring traditional Polish cooking, and garden get high marks.

Hotel Pod Wawelem
HOTEL €€

(Map p122; ☑12 426 2626; www.hotelpodwawelem.pl; Plac Na Groblach 22; s 280zł, d 380-410zł, ste 460zł; ❀@🛜; 🚌1, 2, 6) This hotel, at the foot of Wawel and overlooking the river, gets high marks for crisp, up-to-date design and excellent breakfast buffet. The rooms are generously proportioned and look either onto the river or the castle. The view from the rooftop cafe is stunning. Not suited for drivers, as parking in this part of town is difficult.

Hotel Campanile
HOTEL €€

(Map p122; ☑12 424 2600; www.campanile.com.pl; ul Św Tomasza 34; r 369zł; 🛜; 🚌3, 10, 19, 24, 52) Part of a French chain, this modern hotel has somehow succeeded in nestling in the Old Town, just a few blocks from the Rynek. Its attractive, bright rooms are done out with an unremarkable corporate decor, but still excellent value given the quality and location. Breakfast is an extra 35zł.

Hotel Saski
HOTEL €€

(Map p122; ☑12 421 4222; www.hotelsaski.com.pl; ul Sławkowska 3; s/d 295/395zł; @🛜; 🚌2, 4, 14, 19, 20, 24) If you're in the mood for a touch of belle époque Central European style, but without the hefty price tag, this grand old establishment occupies a historic mansion just off Rynek Główny. The uniformed doorman, rattling century-old lift and ornate furnishings lend the place a certain glamour, and though the rooms themselves are comparatively plain, most have modern bathrooms.

★Hotel Pugetów
BOUTIQUE HOTEL €€€

(Map p122; ☑12 432 4950; www.donimirski.com; ul Starowiślna 15a; s/d 290/500zł; P❀🛜; 🚌1, 3, 19, 24, 52) This charming boutique hotel stands proudly next to the 19th-century neo-Renaissance palace of the same name. It offers just seven rooms with distinctive names (Conrad, Bonaparte) and identities. Think embroidered bathrobes, black-marble baths and a fabulous breakfast room in the basement.

Hotel Pod Różą
HOTEL €€€

(Map p122; ☑12 424 3300; www.podroza. hotel.com.pl; ul Floriańska 14; s 650zł, d 650-720zł; ❄@🛜) A hotel that has never closed, even in the dark, dreary days of communism, 'Under the Rose' offers antiques, oriental carpets, a wonderful glassed-in courtyard restaurant and state-of-the-art facilities. Breakfast costs an extra 50zł.

Hotel Wit Stwosz
HOTEL €€€

(Map p122; ☑12 429 6026; www.wit-stwosz.com. pl; ul Mikołajska 28; s/d 330/420zł; @🛜; 🚊3, 10, 19, 24, 52) Wit Stwosz occupies a renovated 14th-century townhouse in a serene location just off the Planty, east of the main square. The medieval origins are seen in the high ceilings and big windows, though the rooms themselves have been given a blander, modern makeover. Staff are unusually helpful and can organise day trips. The breakfast buffet is fresh and diverse.

Hotel Amadeus
HOTEL €€€

(Map p122; ☑12 429 6070; www.hotel-amadeus. pl; ul Mikołajska 20; s/d 540/620zł; @🛜; 🚊3, 10, 19, 24, 52) Amadeus, with its Mozartian flair, is one of Kraków's most refined hotels. Its rooms are tastefully furnished (if somewhat small) and service is of a high standard. There's a sauna and a small fitness centre, and a well-regarded gourmet restaurant. Check out the photos of famous guests in the lobby.

Hotel Stary
HOTEL €€€

(Map p122; ☑12 384 0808; www.stary.hotel.com. pl; ul Szczepańska 5; s/d 800/900zł; ❄🛜🏊; 🚊2, 4, 14, 18, 20, 24) Setting a high standard, the Stary is housed in an 18th-century aristocratic residence that exudes charm. But the only thing 'old' about this chic place is its name and the building it's in. The fabrics are all natural, the bathroom surfaces are Italian marble, and the internet service is fast.

Hotel Copernicus
HOTEL €€€

(Map p122; ☑12 424 3400; www.hotel.com.pl/copernicus/; ul Kanonicza 16; s 800zł, d 900-980zł; ❄🛜🏊; 🚊6, 8, 10, 13, 18) Nestled in two beautifully restored buildings in one of Kraków's most picturesque and atmospheric streets, the Copernicus is one of the city's finest and most luxurious hotels. The rooftop terrace, with spectacular views over Wawel, and the swimming pool, accommodated in a medieval vaulted brick cellar, add to the hotel's allure.

Hotel Wawel
HOTEL €€€

(Map p122; ☑12 424 1300; www.hotelwawel. pl; ul Poselska 22; s/d 340/480zł; ❄🛜; 🚊1, 2, 6) Ideally located off of central ul Grodzka, this hotel contains large, comfortable and stylish rooms. It's set far enough back from the main drag to avoid most Old Town noise, but the peeling of church bells in the morning is still audible. Nevertheless, it's a romantic splurge given a playful twist by the fairytale murals along the corridors.

🛏 Kazimierz

In addition to some hostels in the vicinity of busy ul Dietla, Kazimierz has a small selection of interesting midrange hotels, some with a distinctive Jewish flavour. It's a pleasant and peaceful area in which to stay.

Good Bye Lenin Hostel
HOSTEL €

(Map p122; ☑12 421 2030; www.goodbyelenin.pl; ul Joselewicza 23; dm 40-55zł, d 140zł; 🅿🛜; 🚊3, 9, 19, 24, 50) This cheerful place has a cheeky communist theme with absurd paintings and statues mocking the imagery of the era. Most dorm rooms have four to six beds and a small garden out front is popular for lounging and barbecue. The hostel can be tricky to find. It's located in an alley to the right as you approach from ul Starowiślna.

Ars Hostel
HOSTEL €

(Map p132; ☑533 966 522; www.arshostel.pl; ul Koletek 7; dm 45-55zł, d/tr 160/255zł; 🅿@) This unfortunately named hostel is famed as much for its moniker (it means 'art' in Latin) as its handy location below Wawel. Accommodation is in well-kept four- to 10-bed dorms, with some private doubles and triples at affordable rates.

Hotel Kazimierz
HOTEL €€

(Map p132; ☑12 421 6629; www.hk.com.pl; ul Miodowa 16; s/d 320/380zł; 🅿@🛜; 🚊6, 8, 10, 13) Friendly accommodation offering a number of modern, comfortable rooms above a popular restaurant.

Hotel Eden
HOTEL €€

(Map p132; ☑12 430 6565; www.hoteleden.pl; ul Ciemna 15; s/d 240/320zł; 🛜; 🚊3, 9, 19, 24, 50) Located within three meticulously restored 15th-century townhouses, the Eden has comfortable rooms and comes complete with a sauna and the only *mikvah* (traditional

Jewish bath) in Kraków. Kosher meals are available on request.

Hotel Klezmer-Hois
HOTEL €€

(Map p132; ☑ 12 411 1245; www.klezmer.pl; ul Szeroka 6; s €52-60, d €65-74, ste €123; 🚌 3, 9, 19, 24, 50) This uniquely stylish little hotel has been restored to its pre-war character. Its airy rooms are each decorated differently, though the cheaper rooms don't have private bathrooms. There's a good-quality Jewish restaurant on-site, as well as an art gallery, and live music at 8pm nightly.

Hotel Abel
HOTEL €€

(Map p132; ☑ 12 411 8736; www.abelkrakow.pl; ul Józefa 30; s/d 150/190zł; 🕿; 🚌 3, 9, 19, 24, 50) Reflecting the character of Kazimierz, this modest, good-value hotel has a distinctive personality, evident in its polished wooden staircase, arched brickwork and age-worn tiles. The rooms are clean but simply furnished. The hotel makes a good base for exploring the historic Jewish neighbourhood.

Hotel Alef
HOTEL €€

(Map p132; ☑ 12 424 3131; www.alef.pl; ul Św Agnieszki 5; r 195zł; 🅿 🕿; 🚌 6, 8, 10, 13) This affordable hotel within the shadow of Wawel Hill has large, charming rooms, furnished with antiques and paintings.

★ Metropolitan Boutique Hotel
BOUTIQUE HOTEL €€€

(Map p122; ☑ 12 442 7500; www.hotelmetropolitan.pl; ul Joselewicza 19; s/d 575/650zł; 🅿 ❄ @ 🕿; 🚌 3, 9, 19, 24, 50) An excellent choice for travellers who prefer a Kazimierz location but who want more comfort than hotels in this part of town usually offer. This luxury boutique fuses modern design within the confines of a 19th-century townhouse. The rooms are done out in chocolate browns, enlivened by bold stripes and patterns. Service is excellent, as is the in-house 'Fusion' restaurant.

Outer Kraków

Camping Smok
CAMPGROUND €

(☑ 12 429 8300; Map p119; www.smok.krakow.pl; ul Kamedulska 18; site per person/tent 26/20zł, d/tr 180/240zł; 🚌 1, 2, 6) This quiet camping ground is around 4km west of the Old Town in leafy Zwierzyniec. Also on offer are good-value double and triple rooms. To get here from the train station, take tram 1, 2 or 6 to the end of the line at Salwator and change for any westbound bus, asking the driver to stop at the campground.

Eating

By Polish standards, Kraków is a food paradise. The Old Town is tightly packed with gastronomic venues, serving a wide range of international cuisines and catering for every pocket. Kazimierz also has a number of restaurants, some of which offer Jewish-style cuisine and are worth a visit.

Self-caterers can stock up at the supermarket within the Galeria Krakowska shopping mall next to the main train station.

Old Town & Around

★ Glonojad
VEGETARIAN €

(Map p122; ☑ 12 346 1677; www.glonojad.com; Plac Matejki 2; mains 16-20zł; ⊗ 8am-10pm; 🕿 🗷; 🚌 2, 4, 14, 19, 20, 24) Attractive modern vegetarian restaurant with a great view onto Plac Matejki, just north of the Barbican. The diverse menu has a variety of tasty dishes including samosas, curries, potato pancakes, burritos, gnocchi and soups. There's also an all-day breakfast menu, so there's no need to jump out of that hotel bed too early.

U Babci Maliny
POLISH €

(Map p122; ☑ 12 422 7601; www.kuchniaubabci maliny.pl; ul Sławkowska 17; mains 12-25zł; ⊗ 11am-9pm Mon-Fri, noon-9pm Sat & Sun; 🚌 2, 4, 14, 19, 20, 24) This rustic basement restaurant is partly hidden in a courtyard. Simply descend the stairs like you know where you're going and follow your nose toward the dumplings, meat dishes and salads. One of the specialties here, definitely worth a try, is the house *żurek* – a sour rye soup flavoured with sausage – served here in a bread bowl.

Milkbar Tomasza
POLISH €

(Map p122; ☑ 12 422 1706; ul Św Tomasza 24; mains 10-18zł; ⊗ 8am-10pm Mon-Sat, 9am-10pm Sun; 🕿; 🚌 3, 10, 19, 24, 52) A modern take on a traditional Polish milkbar, where panini sit proudly beside the *pierogi* (dumplings). It's a clean casual space, with lots of light, bright colours and exposed brick walls.

Green Day
VEGETARIAN €

(Map p122; ☑ 12 431 1027; www.greenday.pl; ul Mikołajska 14; mains 9-22zł; ⊗ 11am-10pm Mon-Sat, to 9pm Sun; 🗷; 🚌 3, 10, 19, 24, 52) Some of Kraków's best-value vegetarian and vegan fare is on offer at this branch of a vegie chain, with meat-free burgers, wraps and salads on the menu.

Antler Poutine & Burger
BURGERS €

(Map p122; ☑ 12 349 0757; Gołębia 10; burgers 10-15zł; ⊗ 11am-10pm; 🕿; 🚌 2, 13, 18, 20) A must for homesick Canadians: a firmly tongue-in-cheek burger joint (the 'Edmonton' burger comes topped with cranberries and mayo), plus authentic poutine (fries covered in gravy and smothered in cheese). Order at the counter and sit at one of the few stools or take away.

★Charlotte Chleb i Wino   BAKERY €€

(Map p122; ☑600 807 880; www.bistrocharlotte.pl; Plac Szczepański 2; salads & sandwiches 10-20zł; ☺7am-midnight Mon-Thu, to 1am Fri & Sat, 9am-10pm Sun; ☎; 🖫2, 4, 14, 18, 20, 24) This is the Kraków branch of a popular Warsaw restaurant serving croissants, French breads, salads and sandwiches. The crowd on artsy Plac Szczepański is suitably stylish as they tuck into their croque monsieurs and sip from excellent but affordable French wines. The perfect stop for morning coffee.

Trufla   ITALIAN €€

(Map p122; ☑12 422 1641; www.truflakrakow.pl; ul Św Tomasza 2; mains 22-35zł; ☺9am-11pm Mon-Fri, 10am-11pm Sat & Sun; ☎; 🖫2, 4, 14, 18, 20, 24) Affordable yet quality Italian food, including steaks, seafood, pasta and risotto – but no pizza. The decor is uncluttered: think hardwood floors and simple, wooden tables. Yet the overall ambience is relaxing. In summer, there's a pretty garden out back (to access the garden, walk through a corridor to the left of the main entrance).

Restauracja Pod Gruszką   POLISH €€

(Map p122; ☑12 346 5704; www.podgruszka.pl; ul Szczepańska 1; mains 12-29zł; ☺noon-midnight; 🖫2, 4, 14, 18, 20, 24) A favourite haunt of writers and artists back in the day, this is the eatery that time forgot, with its elaborate old-fashioned decor, featuring chandeliers, lace tablecloths, age-worn carpets and sepia portraits. The menu covers a range of Polish dishes, including a very good *żurek staropolski* (sour barley soup with white sausage and cottage cheese).

Gospoda CK Dezerter   POLISH €€

(Map p122; ☑12 422 7931; www.ckdezerter.pl; ul Bracka 6; mains 35-40zł; ☺9am-midnight; 🖫2, 13, 18, 20) Dezerter is a pleasantly decorated place, conveniently close to the main square, which focuses on traditional, meaty Galician specialties, including some Austrian and Hungarian choices.

Il Forno   ITALIAN €€

(Map p122; ☑12 421 6498; www.ilforno.pl; Mały Rynek 2; mains 20-35zł; ☺noon-late; ☎; 🖫3, 10, 19, 24, 52) An amenable and unpretentious place

away from the bulk of the tourist traffic, Il Forno has a very long menu of pizza and pasta dishes, along with weightier meat and fish selections. Eat outdoors on the lovely terrace with a view of Mały Rynek. The downstairs bar section is the Arabian-styled Shisha Club, serving Middle Eastern food.

Jama Michalika   POLISH €€

(Map p122; ☑12 422 1561; www.jamamichalika.pl; ul Floriańska 45; mains 18-35zł; ☺9am-11pm; 🖫2, 4, 14, 19, 24) Established in 1895, this cavernous place was a hang-out for writers, painters, actors and other artistic types, and the birthplace of the Młoda Polska artistic movement. Today it's a grand, Art Nouveau restaurant with a very green interior and lots of theatrical etchings adorning the walls. The traditional Polish food is reasonable value.

Balaton   HUNGARIAN €€

(Map p122; ☑12 422 0469; www.balaton.krakow.pl; ul Grodzka 37; mains 19-40zł; ☺noon-10pm; 🖫1, 6, 8, 13, 18) The long-standing Balaton has gotten a spiffy renovation and the old shabby restaurant most people remember is long gone. These days, waiters serve up plates of chicken paprikas and bowls of goulash in a clean, spare space free from kitsch. It's a popular spot in the evening, so best to book in advance.

Smak Ukraiński   UKRAINIAN €€

(Map p122; ☑12 421 9294; www.ukrainska.pl; ul Grodzka 21; mains 18-30zł; ☺noon-10pm; 🖫1, 6, 8, 13, 18) This countrified oasis, perched on one of the city's busiest pedestrian thoroughfares, presents authentic Ukrainian dishes in a cosy dining room decorated with predictably folksy flair. Expect lots of dumplings, borscht (the Ukrainian variety) and waiters in waistcoats.

★Miód Malina   POLISH €€€

(Map p122; ☑12 430 0411; www.miodmalina.pl; ul Grodzka 40; mains 30-70zł; ☺noon-11pm; ☎; 🖫1, 6, 8, 13, 18) The charmingly named 'Honey Raspberry' serves Polish dishes in colourful surrounds. Grab a window seat and order the wild mushrooms in cream, and any of the duck or veal dishes. There's a variety of beef steaks on the menu as well. The grilled sheep's cheese appetiser, served with cranberry jelly, is a regional speciality. Reservations essential.

★Ed Red   STEAK €€€

(Map p122; ☑690 900 555; www.edred.pl; ul Sławkowska 3; mains 35-60zł; ☺7am-11pm; ☎; 🖫2, 4, 14, 19, 20, 24) This is a solid splurge option for the steaks – cuts include New

THE KING OF PRETZELS

One of the unmistakable signs that you've arrived in Kraków are the stalls placed seemingly at every street corner selling the *obwarzanek* (ob-va-zhan-ek), a hefty pretzel. This street snack resembles its German cousins, though is somewhat larger and denser than the average Germanic bread-based snack and is created by entwining two strands of dough before baking.

This popular ring of baked bread, traditionally encrusted with poppy seeds, sesame seeds or salt, gives daily employment to myriad men and women while ensuring them a dose of fresh outdoor air (though selling it in winter must, admittedly, be less fun).

It's also a historic curiosity that has outlived numerous kings, republics and military occupiers. There's evidence of *obwarzanki* (the plural) being baked as far back as the 14th century, and Cracovians still happily purchase them in large numbers as a quick bite on the way to work or study – in fact 150,000 are baked every day. Feel free to join in the pretzel celebration, though note that they're definitely much better in the morning than the afternoon, a promising sign perhaps that they contain little in the way of artificial preservatives.

While munching, you'll be enjoying an officially unique Kraków experience – the European Union has agreed to register the humble *obwarzanek* on its list of protected regional products, barring anyone but the city's bakers from producing a pretzel and calling it by that name.

York strip, ribeye and T-bone – made from dry-aged beef and using only local producers. Other mains include beef cheeks served on buckwheat, wild boar and free-range chicken. The interior, with walls painted in muted blues and browns, is straight out of a magazine.

Cyrano de Bergerac FRENCH €€€
(Map p122; ☑12 411 7288; www.cyranodebergerac.pl; ul Sławkowska 26; mains 50-90zł; ⊗noon-11pm; ⬛2, 4, 14, 19, 20, 24) One of Kraków's top eateries, this restaurant serves fine, authentic French cuisine in one of the most beautiful cellars in the city. Artwork and tapestries add to the romance and in warmer months there's seating in a covered courtyard.

Corse CORSICAN €€€
(Map p122; ☑12 421 6273; www.corserestaurant.pl; ul Poselska 24; mains 40-70zł; ⊗1-11pm; ☎; ⬛1, 6, 8, 13, 18) This Corsican restaurant serves one of the more unusual cuisines available in Kraków. Its nautical decor, with white-canvas sail material hanging from the ceiling, feels upscale but comfortable, and the dishes – baked sea bream, veal with grapes, beef fondue – are well prepared.

Wentzl FRENCH, POLISH €€€
(Map p122; ☑12 429 5299; www.restauracjawentzl.com.pl; Rynek Główny 21; mains 60-80zł; ⊗1-11pm; ⬛1, 6, 8, 13, 18) This historic eatery, dating back to 1792, is perched above the Rynek, with timbered ceilings, Oriental carpets and fine oil paintings all around. The

food is sublime – cognac-flavoured foie gras, duck fillet glazed with honey, Baltic cod served with lentils and spinach – and the service is of a high standard.

Pimiento ARGENTINIAN €€€
(Map p122; ☑12 422 6672; www.pimiento.pl; ul Stolarska 13; mains 50-80zł; ☎; ⬛1, 6, 8, 13, 18) This upmarket grill serves a dizzying array of steaks to suit both appetite and budget, and offers some reasonable vegetarian alternatives for the meat-averse. Factor the South American wine list into your calculations, and you have a classy night out.

Sakana Sushi Bar JAPANESE €€€
(Map p122; ☑12 429 3086; www.sakana.pl; ul Św Gertrudy 7; mains 30-50zł; ⊗noon-11pm Mon-Sat, 1-10pm Sun; ☎; ⬛6, 8, 10, 13, 18) With sushi and sashimi floating around in little boats which loop around a 'canal' encircling a curvy communal table, the Sakana is different from the usual Kraków offerings. There's also tempura and some unusual soups.

✗ Kazimierz

Momo VEGETARIAN €
(Map p132; ☑609 685 775; ul Dietla 49; mains 12-19zł; ⊗11am-8pm; ✗; ⬛11, 12, 22, 52) Vegans will cross the doorstep of this restaurant with relief – the majority of the menu is completely animal-free. The space is decorated with Indian craft pieces, and serves up subcontinental soups, stuffed pancakes and rice dishes, with a great range of cakes – some gluten-free. The

momo (Tibetan dumplings; 15zł) are a treat worth ordering.

Bagelmama
BAGELS €

(Map p132; ☑12 346 1646; www.bagelmama.com; Dajwór 10; sandwiches 15zł; ☉9am-7pm; ☎; ☒3, 9, 19, 24, 50) How clever of someone to think of selling bagels in the Jewish quarter. Whether you are a bagel traditionalist (lox and cream cheese) or a bagel innovator (warm brie and tomato), you'll find something you like. There are also soups, salads, and wraps for a perfect easy lunch.

Pierogi Mr Vincent
POLISH €

(Map p132; ☑506 806 304; Bożego Ciała 12; mains 10-15zł; ☉11am-9pm; ☒6, 8, 10, 13) There are only a few scattered tables in this place, but there are about 40 kinds of dumplings on the menu; sweet and savoury, classic and creative. Maybe you thought you were tired of *pierogi,* but Vincent will convince you to eat one more plate!

Młynek Café
VEGETARIAN €

(Map p132; ☑12 430 6202; www.cafemlynek.com; Plac Wolnica 7; mains 15-20zł; ☉8am-11pm; ☎☑; ☒6, 8, 10, 13) This vegetarian cafe is the perfect pit stop on the 'other' side of Kazimierz. It offers delectable, animal-free soups and sandwiches; occasional concerts, poetry readings and art exhibits; a collection of typewriters and coffee grinders to admire; and outdoor seating overlooking the square.

★ Marchewka z Groszkiem
POLISH €€

(Map p132; ☑12 430 0795; www.marchewkaz groszkiem.pl; ul Mostowa 2; mains 20-30zł; ☉9am-10pm; ☎; ☒6, 8, 10, 13) Traditional Polish cooking, with hints of influence from neighbouring countries like Ukraine (beer), Hungary (wine) and Lithuania. Excellent potato pancakes and a delicious boiled beef with horseradish sauce highlight the menu. There's are a few sidewalk tables to admire the parade of people down one of Kazimierz's up-and-coming streets.

Hamsa
JEWISH €€

(Map p132; ☑515 150 145; www.hamsa.pl; ul Szeroka 2; mains 30-50zł; ☉10am-11pm; ☎☑; ☒3, 9, 19, 24, 50) How can a place miss when it calls itself a 'hummus and happiness' restaurant? The light, uncluttered interior is a welcome tonic to the, admittedly kitschy, Jewish-themed restaurants in the area. The menu features a full range of Middle Eastern salads, plus spicy grilled chicken and fish. Good selection of vegetarian and gluten-free options.

Well Done
BARBECUE €€

(Map p132; ☑607 132 001; ul Mostowa 2; mains 15-30zł; ☉10am-11pm; ☎; ☒6, 8, 10, 13) Very likable barbecue and burger joint poised along shady ul Mostowa, a string of restaurants and cafes that locals regard as the centre of Kazimierz's emerging hipsterdom. The grillmasters know how to impart that smoky flavour to burgers, steaks and chicken breasts. The interior is kind of retro-diner, while there are a few picnic tables out front.

Warsztat
ITALIAN €€

(Map p132; ☑12 430 1451; www.restauracja warsztat.pl; ul Izaaka 3; mains 22-43zł; ☉10am-10pm; ☎; ☒3, 9, 19, 24, 50) Warsztat takes the concept of 'piano bar' to a whole new level. Horns, harps and accordions adorn the walls, while the centrepiece is a piano submerged into the floor. Delicious pizzas, pastas and salads constitute the bulk of the menu.

Ariel
JEWISH €€

(Map p132; ☑12 421 7920; www.ariel-krakow.pl; ul Szeroka 18; mains 20-60zł; ☉10am-midnight; ☎; ☒3, 9, 19, 24, 50) One of a number of Jewish restaurants in and around ul Szeroka, this atmospheric joint is packed with old-fashioned timber furniture and portraits, and serves a range of kosher dishes. Try the Berdytchov soup (beef, honey and cinnamon) for a tasty starter. There's often live klezmer music here at night.

Manzana
MEXICAN €€

(Map p132; ☑12 422 2277; www.manzanarestaurant.com; ul Miodowa 11; mains 25-40zł; ☉4-10pm Mon-Fri, 10am-11pm Sat, 10am-10pm Sun; ☎; ☒6, 8, 10, 13) Manzana is slightly more upscale than is usual for a Mexican restaurant in this part of the world, with a sleek interior and enormous bar. That said, the menu features the same mix of tacos, burritos, and quesadillas you're used to, at reasonable prices for the quality. Creative mains like 'fiesta chicken pasta' use tequila as a cooking ingredient. Reservations recommended.

Sąsiedzi
POLISH €€€

(Map p132; ☑12 654 8353; www.sasiedzi.oberza.pl; ul Miodowa 25; mains 30-50zł, milk bar 10-20zł; ☉10am-10pm; ☎; ☒3, 9, 19, 24, 50) A perfect combination: on the left side a high-end Polish restaurant with a lovely, secluded garden, while on the right a clean, friendly milk bar, serving well-above-average steamtable food at affordable prices. We love the roast duck in apple with pearl barley (47zł). Evening meals are accompanied by live piano music.

KRAKÓW EATING

Reservations (for the fancier side) are recommended.

Podgórze

Delecta
PIZZA €

(Map p132; ☑12 423 5001; www.restauracja-delecta.pl; ul Limanowskiego 11; mains 17-24zł; ☺11am-10pm Sun-Thu, to 11pm Fri & Sat; ☐3, 9, 19, 24, 50) There are not a huge number of restaurants in Podgórze, but there is pizza. Tasty pies come with all kinds of toppings: some are authentic while others are inventive (the Delecta specialty pizza features ham, bacon and corn kernels). The place goes all out for Italy, with its Tuscan-sun decor.

★ ZaKładka Food & Wine
BISTRO €€€

(Map p132; ☑12 442 7442; www.zakladkabistro.pl; ul Józefińska 2; mains 35-50zł; ☺noon-11pm; ☎; ☐6, 13, 19, 23) This Parisian-style bistro specialises in simple French cooking centred around veal, rabbit, fresh fish and mussels and is one of the best places in this part of town. Expect courteous but formal service and an excellent wine list, featuring bottles from around Europe. The simplicity of the presentation extends to the decor: beige walls, black tables and wooden floors.

With Fire & Sword
POLISH €€€

(Ogniem i Mieczem; Map p132; ☑12 656 2328; www.ogniemimieczem.pl; Plac Serkowskiego 7; mains 40zł; ☺noon-midnight Mon-Sat, to 10pm Sun; ☐8, 10, 11, 23) Named after the historical novel by Henryk Sienkiewicz, this dark, atmospheric restaurant re-creates the Poland of yesteryear. The wood interior is made even more rustic with animal pelts and a roaring fire. The menu features well-researched old-time recipes, such as the succulent roasted pig that comes stuffed with fruit.

Drinking & Nightlife

You'll be spoiled for choice when heading out for a drink in Kraków. The Rynek Główny is literally ringed on all sides by cafes, usually serving a complement of cakes and ice cream. Bars and pubs seem to lie down every street and hide behind every facade. Kazimierz also has a lively bar scene, centred on Plac Nowy and its surrounding streets. The area around Plac Wolnica in the western part of Kazimierz has blossomed in recent years into another cafe/bar cluster.

Note that the difference between a cafe and bar or pub can be thin indeed. Many cafes will offer alcoholic beverages, and you'd be hard pressed to find a bar in Kraków that couldn't also whip up a coffee on demand. Many cafes and bars also offer snacks or meals, while others are just watering holes. If food is also on the agenda, it pays to check the website or call ahead.

Old Town

★ Café Camelot
CAFE

(Map p122; ☑12 421 0123; www.camelot.pl; ul Św Tomasza 17; ☺9am-midnight; ☐2, 4, 14, 19, 20, 24) For coffee and cake, try this genteel haven hidden around an obscure street corner in the Old Town. Its cosy rooms are cluttered with lace-covered candle-lit tables, and a quirky collection of wooden figurines featuring spiritual or folkloric scenes. Also a great choice for breakfasts and brunches.

★ Café Bunkier
CAFE

(Map p122; ☑12 431 0585; http://en.bunkiercafe.pl; Plac Szczepański 3a; ☺9am-late; ☎; ☐2, 4, 14, 18, 20, 24) The 'Bunker' is a wonderful cafe with a positively enormous glassed-in terrace tacked onto the Bunkier Sztuki (Art Bunker), a cutting-edge gallery northwest of the Rynek. The garden space is heated in winter and seems to always have a buzz. Excellent coffee, non-filtered beers, and homemade lemonades, as well as light bites like burgers and salads. Enter from the Planty.

Noworolski
CAFE

(Map p122; ☑515 100 998, 12 422 4771; www.noworolski.com.pl; Rynek Główny 1, Sukiennice; ☺8.30am-midnight; ☐1, 6, 8, 13, 18) Even if you don't stop for a coffee or small bite to eat, at least pause to admire the stunning Art Nouveau interiors by Polish artist Józef Mehoffer. As the sign outside says, the Noworolski has been here since 1910, serving the likes of Lenin in the early years, and later becoming a favourite haunt of occupying Nazi officers.

Arlekin
CAFE

(Map p122; ☑12 430 2457; www.arlekin-krakow.pl; Rynek Główny 24; ☐2, 13, 18, 20) There are plenty of larger and more attractive cafes on the main square, but locals – particularly older Cracovians – consider this small, narrow space to serve the best and most authentic cakes and pastries.

Bona
CAFE

(Map p122; ☑12 430 5222; www.bonamedia.pl; ul Kanonicza 11; ☺11am-8pm; ☎; ☐1, 6, 8, 13, 18) Pleasant combination of cafe and bookshop, with its bookshelves sandwiched between the interior and outdoor seating. Great choice for a pit stop on the way from the Old Town to

STREET FOOD: POLISH 'PIZZA' & BELGIAN FRIES

Kraków has loads of restaurants, but alas come 11pm, most serious food options close down. Thankfully, street-food purveyors extend those hours, giving you ample opportunity to quash the late-night munchies. Kazimierz, specifically **Plac Nowy** (p154), is ground zero for 'Polish pizza' – otherwise known as *zapiekanka*. It's essentially half of a baguette, topped with cheese, ham and mushrooms. Other varieties are available (the Hawaiian has ham and pineapple), but nothing beats the classic. It's a cheap, filling snack that tastes especially delicious after midnight. Indeed, there may be no reason to eat it before midnight. Not your cup of tea? No worries. Try out the various **food trucks** (Map p132; ul Św Wawrzyńca 16 – Skwer Judah); most items 5-15zł; ☺noon-10pm Tue-Thu, to 1am Fri-Sun; ☒3, 9, 19, 24, 50) that have set up shop on an isolated square a couple blocks southeast of Plac Nowy. There you'll find burgers, ice cream, stuffed baked potatoes and the current craze: Belgian fries. A more traditional option is to have a grilled sausage, served nightly (except Sunday) till 3am from a sidewalk vendor at **Hala Targowa** (p154).

Wawel. Buy a book and sip a coffee with a view of the Church of SS Peter & Paul across the way.

Ambasada Śledzia
BAR

(Map p122; ☏662 569 460; ul Stolarska 8-10; ☺noon-midnight; ☒1, 6, 8, 13, 18) The 'Herring Embassy' sits neatly, if cheekily, on this street lined with consulates. It's pioneered an unlikely but successful concept – herring and vodka shots. Sit at the bar and order tasty snack-sized servings of *śledź* (herring) or *kiełbasa* (sausage) to go with your vodka. A second branch across the street (ul Stolarska 5) stays open until 5am.

Tram Bar
BAR

(Map p122; ☏12 423 2255; Stolarska 5; ☺11am-2am; ☒1, 6, 8, 13, 18) Quirky bar in the middle of the Old Town's most popular drinking street. True to its name, Tram Bar is dedicated to the street car, with old maps and memorabilia on the walls and even seats made from old tram cars. Since it's not as overrun at night compared with neighbouring pubs, it's often possible to find a seat here.

Movida Cocktail Bar
BAR

(Map p122; ☏12 429 4597; www.movida-bar.pl; ul Mikołajska 9; ☺4pm-late; ☎; ☒3, 10, 19, 24, 52) This bright, modern cocktail bar has an inventive drinks menu that includes concoctions like the 'Bull Ride' – a heady mix of bison-grass vodka, cinnamon and egg white. There's also inexpensive bar food.

Antycafe
BAR

(Map p122; ☏506 481 888; www.antycafe.pl; ul Sławkowska 12; ☺noon-late; ☎; ☒2, 4, 14, 18, 20, 24) This popular Old Town student bar serves a full range of drinks and stays open late. Good place to start off or finish up the night.

Black Gallery
PUB

(Map p122; ☏724 630 154; ul Mikołajska 24; ☺noon-late Mon-Sat, 2pm-late Sun; ☎; ☒3, 10, 19, 24, 52) Underground pub-cum-nightclub with a modern aspect: split levels, exposed steel frame lighting and a metallic bar. It really gets going after midnight. During the day, relax over beers in the courtyard.

Prozak 2.0
CLUB

(Map p122; ☏733 704 650; Plac Dominikański 6; ☺8pm-late; ☎; ☒1, 6, 8, 13, 18) A legend in its own time, this nightlife giant entices revellers into its labyrinth of passageways, nooks and crannies. It specialises in presenting international DJs.

Hush Live
CLUB

(Map p122; ☏604 943 400; www.hushlive.pl; ul Św Tomasza 11; ☺8pm-3am Sun-Thu, to 5am Fri & Sat; ☒2, 4, 14, 19, 20, 24) The latest incarnation at this legendary subterranean club space in the Old Town features DJs and bands that play a style of music called 'Disco Polo' – essentially a Polish take on cheesy dance pop from the 1990s. Very popular and more fun than it sounds.

Frantic
CLUB

(Map p122; ☏12 423 0483; www.frantic.pl; ul Szewska 5; ☺10pm-4am Wed-Sat; ☎; ☒2, 13, 18, 20) With two dance floors, three bars, a chillout room and top Polish and international DJs, Frantic is regularly packed out with smart young locals. There's sniffy door selection, so don't be too scruffy.

Cień
CLUB

(Map p122; ☏12 422 2177; www.cienklub.com; ul Św Jana 15; ☺10.30pm-late Thu-Sat; ☎; ☒2, 4, 14, 19, 20, 24) The enormous 'Shadow' attracts a perfect (as in perfectly tanned) crowd with house sounds, produced by DJs fresh in from Ibiza, and great decor.

 ## Kazimierz

★ Cheder
CAFE

(Map p132; ☑515 732 226; www.cheder.pl; ul Józefa 36; ☺10am-10pm; ☒3, 9, 19, 24, 50) Unlike most of the other Jewish-themed places in Kazimierz, this one aims to entertain *and* educate. Named after a traditional Hebrew school, the cafe offers access to a decent library in Polish and English, regular readings and films, as well as real Israeli coffee, brewed in a traditional Turkish copper pot with cinnamon and cardamom, and snacks such as homemade hummus.

Alchemia
CAFE

(Map p132; ☑12 421 2200; www.alchemia.com.pl; ul Estery 5; ☺9am-late; ☒3, 9, 19, 24, 50) This Kazimierz venue exudes a shabby-is-the-new-cool look with rough-hewn wooden benches, candlelit tables and a companionable gloom. It hosts occasional live-music gigs and theatrical events through the week.

Mleczarnia
CAFE

(Map p132; ☑12 421 8532; www.mle.pl; ul Meiselsa 20; ☺10am-midnight; ☒6, 8, 10, 13) Wins the prize for best courtyard cafe – located across the street. Shady trees and blooming roses make this place tops for a sunny-day drink. If it's rainy, never fear, for the cafe is warm and cosy, with crowded bookshelves and portrait-covered walls. Self service.

Artefakt Cafe
CAFE

(Map p132; ☑535 799 666; www.artefakt-cafe.pl; ul Dajwór 3; ☺4pm-2am; ☒3, 9, 19, 24, 50) This much-loved student cafe has two front rooms and a small garden at the back. Bookshelves line the walls of one room, while big photos – part of a rotating photo exhibition – hang in the other. In addition to coffee drinks, they have a large selection of bottled craft beers and decent Czech lagers such as Holba on tap.

Singer Café
BAR

(Map p132; ☑12 292 0622; ul Estery 20; ☺9am-late; ☎; ☒3, 9, 19, 24, 50) A laid-back hang-out of the Kazimierz cognoscenti, this relaxed cafe-bar's moody candlelit interior is full of character. Alternatively, sit outside and converse over a sewing machine affixed to the table.

Miejsce Bar
BAR

(Map p132; ☑600 960 876; www.miejsce.com.pl; ul Estery 1; ☺10am-2am; ☎; ☒11, 12, 22, 52) Trendy bar that draws an eclectic mix of intellectual types, hipsters, students and generally anyone who enjoys good cocktails and a relaxed vibe. Quiet during the day; rowdier and more adventurous by night.

Podgórze

★ Forum Przestrzenie
BAR

(Map p132; ☑514 342 939; www.forumprzestrzenie.com; ul Konopnickiej 28; ☺10am-2am; ☎; ☒11, 18, 22, 52) In a highly creative re-use of an old communist-era eyesore, the Hotel Forum has been repurposed as a trendy, retro coffee and cocktail bar – and occasional venue for DJs, live music and happenings. In warm weather, lounge chairs are spread out over a patio overlooking the river.

Coffee Cargo
CAFE

(Map p132; ☑604 576 339; www.coffeeproficiency.com; Przemysłowa 3; ☺8am-6pm Tue-Sat; ☎; ☒3, 9, 19, 24, 50) Steampunkish cafe and coffee roaster, occupying a warehouse space in an industrial part of Podgórze. In addition to the home-roasted Guatemalan, it serves sweets including cheesecake and ice cream. The coffee is excellent but probably not worth the walk over from Kazimierz. It's an easy stroll, though, from Schindler's Factory or MOCAK for an after-visit pick-me-up.

Drukarnia
CLUB

(Map p132; ☑12 656 6560; www.drukarniaclub.pl; ul Nadwiślańska 1; ☺10am-last guest; ☎; ☒6, 13, 19, 23) Old typewriters and newsprint wallpaper evoke the namesake 'printhouse', creating an arty atmosphere at this riverside venue. Upstairs, there are two spacious bars and pavement seating; downstairs is where the music goes down (jam sessions on Tuesday evenings, dance parties on Friday and Saturday).

Cawa
CAFE, WINE BAR

(Map p132; ☑12 656 7456; www.cawacafe.pl; ul Nadwiślańska 1; ☺8.30am-9.30pm Sun-Thu, to midnight Fri & Sat; ☎; ☒6, 13, 19, 23) In up-and-coming Podgórze, one does not expect to see such a chic little wine bar, but here it is, complete with post-industrial decor and spiffy waitstaff. Come for cappuccino or cava (duh). If you're hungry, there are sophisticated, Med-style tapas listed on the slate board.

BAL
CAFE

(Map p132; ☑734 411 733; Ślusarska 9, enter from Przemysłowa; ☺8.30am-9pm; ☎; ☒3, 9, 19, 24, 50) This trendy industrial-style cafe and breakfast bar is tucked into a re-purposed warehouse space in Podgórze's up-and-coming Zabłocie district. Great for coffee as well as light eats, sandwiches and salads throughout the day. BAL is popular among the city's start-up and design crowd who work nearby. It's just around the corner from Schindler's Factory (about five minutes' walk).

Cafe Rękawka   CAFE
(Map p132; ☑ 12 296 2002; ul Brodzinskiego 4b; ⊙ 8am-7pm; ☜; ☒ 6, 13, 19, 23) The smell of fresh-brewed java and the sounds of jazz music entice you into this sweet sanctuary. It's a funny mismatch of burlap coffee bags, lace curtains and leafy plants, creating the perfect atmosphere to sink into a comfortably worn armchair and warm up with a cuppa.

☆ Entertainment

Kraków has a lively cultural life, particularly in theatre, music and visual arts, and there are numerous annual festivals. The city is also rich in jazz clubs and art-house cinema. The comprehensive Polish and English monthly magazine *Karnet* (www.karnet.krakow.pl), available at any branch of the tourist office, lists almost every event in the city.

For tickets, the Old Town InfoKraków branch (p157) at ul Św Jana 2 specialises in cultural events and 14 can help arrange bookings.

For other sources of information, bimonthly *Kraków In Your Pocket* (www.inyourpocket.com), which has a cover price of 5zł but is often free at large hotels and tourist-information offices, also has excellent coverage of entertainment, including bars, pubs and clubs. For additional online resources, the websites Cracow Life (www.cracow-life.com) and Krakow Post (krakowpost.com) are good for general info. For clubbing and parties, check out www.krakownightlife.com and www.where2b.org.

Jazz & Live Music

Kraków has a lively jazz scene and a number of clubs present live music year-round.

★ Harris Piano Jazz Bar   JAZZ
(Map p122; ☑ 12 421 5741; www.harris.krakow.pl; Rynek Główny 28; ⊙ 1pm-late; ☒ 1, 6, 8, 13, 18) This active jazz haunt is housed in an atmospheric, intimate cellar space. Harris hosts jazz and blues bands most nights of the week from around 9.30pm, but try to arrive an hour earlier to get a seat (or book in advance by phone). Wednesday nights see weekly (free) jam sessions.

Piec' Art   JAZZ
(Map p122; ☑ 12 429 1602; www.piecart.pl; ul Szewska 12; performances 15-20zł; ⊙ noon-late; ☜; ☒ 2, 13, 18, 20) Dark and inviting, this intimate basement bar is a seductive place for a drink even when it's quiet. Several times a week, there's live acoustic jazz, which makes it all the more appealing.

Piano Rouge   JAZZ
(Map p122; ☑ 12 431 0333; www.thepianorouge.com.pl; Rynek Główny 46; ⊙ 10am-late; ☒ 1, 6, 8, 13, 18) This sumptuous cellar jazz club and restaurant is decked out with classic sofas, red velvets, louche lampshades and billowing lengths of colourful silk. Live jazz every night at 10pm.

Fabryka Klub   LIVE MUSIC
(Map p132; ☑ 530 053 551; Zabłocie 23; ☒ 3, 9, 19, 24, 50) This former factory in Podgórze has become the city's leading venue for indie and experimental live music. Shows vary from metal to electronica and are held in the hulking main hall of the plant or on the lawn. For concert info and tickets, check TicketPro (www.ticketpro.pl). Plenty of tables in warm weather and it's also great just for drinks.

Jazz Club U Muniaka   JAZZ
(Map p122; ☑ 12 423 1205; www.umuniaka.pl; ul Floriańska 3; ⊙ 7pm-late; ☜; ☒ 2, 4, 14, 19, 20, 24) Housed in a fine cellar, this is one of the best-known jazz outlets in Poland, the brainchild of saxophonist Janusz Muniak. There are concerts most nights from 8.30pm.

Re   LIVE MUSIC
(Map p122; ☑ 12 431 0881; www.klubre.pl; ul Św Krzyża 4; ⊙ noon-2am; ☒ 3, 10, 19, 24, 52) You can't beat Re for its excellent line-up of live music, which features indie rock bands from all over the world, playing up close and in your face. Even if you're not into the music, you'll love the shady courtyard.

Stalowe Magnolie   LIVE MUSIC
(Map p122; ☑ 12 422 8472; www.stalowemagnolie.pl; ul Św Jana 15; ⊙ 7pm-late; ☜; ☒ 2, 4, 14, 18, 19, 24) 'Steel Magnolias' is a brightly decorated venue with an emphasis on live music, presenting pop, rock and jazz. It's a party inside every night of the week, with the music starting up around 9pm. Thursday night is ladies night.

Classical Music & Opera

Filharmonia Krakowska   CLASSICAL MUSIC
(Filharmonia im. Karola Szymanowskiego w Krakowie; Map p122; ☑ reservations 12 619 8722, tickets 12 619 8733; www.filharmonia.krakow.pl; ul

Zwierzyniecka 1; ☺ box office 10am-2pm & 3-7pm Tue-Fri; 🚌 1, 2, 6) Home to one of the best orchestras in the country.

Opera Krakowska
OPERA

(☎ 12 296 6260; www.opera.krakow.pl; ul Lubicz 48; tickets 20-200zł; ☺ 10am-7pm Mon-Fri, or two hours before performances at box office; 🚌 4, 10, 14, 20, 52) The Kraków Opera performs in the strikingly modern red building at the Mogilskie roundabout. The setting is decidedly 21st century, but the repertoire spans the ages, incorporating everything from Verdi to Bernstein.

Cinemas

Kraków is a great film city and has several cinemas around town devoted to independent and arthouse cinema. Check the website for screenings and note that foreign films are almost always shown in their original language with Polish subtitles. This may or may not be English, depending on the film's origin.

Kino Pod Baranami
CINEMA

(Map p122; ☎ 12 423 0768; www.kinopodbaranami.pl; Rynek Główny 27; tickets 12-20zł; ☎; 🚌 1, 6, 8, 13, 18) The 'Cinema Under the Rams' is hidden inside a historic palace on a corner of the Rynek Główny. There are three screening rooms given over to the best independent Polish and international cinema. Popular with expats, and Polish films are occasionally screened with English subtitles. The website is English-friendly.

Kino Ars
CINEMA

(Map p122; ☎ 12 421 4199; www.ars.pl; ul Św Tomasza 11, cnr ul Św Jana; tickets 18-20zł; 🚌 3, 10, 19, 24, 52) This Old Town art cinema features the best indie and international films. Films are normally screened in their original languages (often English), with Polish subtitles.

Kino Mikro
CINEMA

(☎ 12 341 4332; www.kinomikro.pl; ul Lea 5; tickets 10-16zł; 🚌 4, 13, 14, 24) Small, student-orientated cinema that's still going strong. Films are shown in their original language, with Polish subtitles. Buy tickets online through the website or at the cinema before the show (though arrive early since popular films often sell out).

Kino Paradox
CINEMA

(☎ 12 430 0015; www.kinoparadox.pl; Centrum Młodzieży im H Jordana, ul Krupnicza 38; tickets 10-12zł; 🚌 2, 4, 8, 13, 14, 18, 20, 24) Popular arthouse cinema features independent European, Polish and international films that will likely never make it to the multiplex.

Theatre

Narodowy Stary Teatr
THEATRE

(Map p122; ☎ 12 422 8020; www.stary.pl; ul Jagiellońska 5; tickets adult/concession 55/35zł; ☺ box office 10am-1pm, 5-7pm Tue-Sat; 🚌 2, 4, 14, 18, 20, 24) This is the city's best-known theatre company and it has attracted the cream of its actors. To overcome the language barrier, pick a Shakespeare play you know well from the repertoire, and take in the distinctive Polish interpretation. The box office is off of Plac Szczepański.

Teatr im Słowackiego
OPERA, THEATRE

(Map p122; ☎ information 12 424 4528, tickets 12 424 4526; www.slowacki.krakow.pl; Plac Św Ducha 1; tickets 20-80zł; ☺ box office 10am-2pm & 2.30-6pm Mon, 9am-2pm & 2.30-7pm Tue-Sat, 3-7pm Sun; 🚌 2, 3, 4, 10, 14, 19, 24, 52) This important theatre focuses on Polish classics and large-scale productions. It's in a large and opulent building (1893) that's patterned on the Paris Opera, and is northeast of the Rynek Główny.

CHURCH & CHAMBER MUSIC

The Baroque interior of a church can be an uplifting venue for classical music. During the summer tourist season (May to September), church and chamber concerts are staged all around town. Buy tickets at the door before the concert or at any InfoKraków (p156) tourist office. The best venues include the **Church of SS Peter & Paul** (Map p122; ☎ 695 574 526; ul Grodzka 52a; tickets adult/concession 60/40zł; ☺ 8pm Wed, Fri, Sat, Sun; 🚌 1, 6, 8, 13, 18), south of the main square, which hosts evening concerts of Vivaldi, Bach, Chopin and Strauss performed by the Cracow Chamber Orchestra of Saint Maurice. For Frédéric Chopin, Poland's best-known composer, head to the Renaissance Hall of the **Bonerowski Palace** (Map p122; ☎ 604 093 570; www.cracowconcerts.com; ul Św Jana 1; tickets 60zł; ☺ 7pm Tue-Sun; 🚌 1, 6, 8, 13, 18). Another reliable option is the **Church of St Giles** (Kościół św Idziego; Map p122; ☎ 695 574 526; ul Grodzka 67 ; tickets adult/concession 60/40zł; ☺ 5pm Tue-Fri ; 🚌 6, 8, 10, 13, 18), home to intimate, late-afternoon organ concerts.

Teatr Groteska   THEATRE

(📞12 633 4822; www.groteska.pl; ul Skarbowa 2; ⊙box office 8am-noon & 3-5pm Mon-Fri; 🚌2, 4, 8, 13, 14, 18, 20, 24) The 'Grotesque Theatre' stages mostly puppet shows and is well worth a visit. It's 450m west of the Planty along ul Krupnicza. Note the troupe takes an annual summer break in July and August.

🛍 Shopping

Kraków's Old Town has a vast array of shops, selling everything from tacky T-shirts to exquisite crystal glassware, and all within a short walk from Rynek Główny. The obvious place to start (or perhaps end) your Kraków shopping is at the large souvenir market within the Cloth Hall in the centre of Rynek Główny, which sells everything from fine amber jewellery to tacky plush dragons. If you're in a mall mood, **Galeria Krakowska** (📞12 428 9900; ul Pawia 5; ⊙9am-10pm Mon-Sat, 10am-9pm Sun; 🚌2, 3, 4, 10, 14, 19, 24, 52), next to the train station, has hundreds of shops.

🏛 Old Town & Around

⭐**Galeria Plakatu**   ART

(Map p122; 📞12 421 2640; www.cracowposter gallery.com; ul Stolarska 8-10; ⊙11am-6pm Mon-Fri, to 2pm Sat; 🚌1, 6, 8, 13, 18) Poland has always excelled in the underrated art of making film posters and this amazing shop has the city's largest and best choice of posters, created by Poland's most prominent graphic artists.

⭐**Galeria Dyląg**   GALLERY

(Map p122; 📞12 431 2521; www.dylag.pl; ul Św Tomasza 22; ⊙noon-6pm Mon-Fri, 11am-2pm Sat; 🚌3, 10, 19, 24, 52) This small private art gallery features modern Polish artists from the 1940s to the 1970s. Look for the Polish drip paintings, reminiscent of Jackson Pollock, from the late '50s. Many of the pieces on sale here are from artists now displayed in museums.

Krakowska Manufaktura Czekolady   FOOD

(Map p122; 📞502 090 765; www.chocolate. krakow.pl; ul Szewska 7; ⊙10am-10pm; 🚌2, 4, 14, 18, 24) Beautiful figurines made of white and dark chocolate, as well as a range of wrapped chocolate candies and caramels, including a life-sized chocolate Labrador (dog) that would take at least a month to eat. Upstairs there's a small cafe for perfectly executed hot chocolate drinks as well as cakes, candies and coffee.

Boruni Amber Museum   JEWELLERY

(Map p122; 📞513 511 512; www.ambermuseum. eu; ul Św Jana 4; ⊙10am-9pm; 🚌1, 6, 8, 13, 18) One-stop shopping for amberphiles. Cases and cases of amber rings, necklaces, broaches and earrings, plus a 'museum' (free admission) at the back, where you can see how amber is cut, polished and set. Boruni includes a certificate of quality with each purchase.

Stary Kleparz   MARKET

(Map p122; 📞12 634 1532; www.starykleparz.com; ul Paderewskiego, Rynek Kleparski; ⊙6am-6pm Mon-Fri, to 4pm Sat, 8am-3pm Sun; 📱; 🚌2, 4, 14, 19, 20, 24) The city's most atmospheric and historic place to shop for fresh fruits, vegetables and flowers is this sprawling covered market, which dates back to the 12th century. You'll also find meats, cheeses, spices and bread, as well as clothes and other necessities.

Antykwariat Stefan Kamiński   BOOKS

(Map p122; 📞12 422 3965; www.krakow-antykwariat.pl; ul Św Jana 3; ⊙9am-5pm Mon-Fri, 10am-1.30pm Sat; 🚌1, 6, 8, 13, 18) Evocative, dusty antiquarian bookshop with plenty of old postcards, prints, books and posters to rummage through.

Jan Fejkiel Gallery   GALLERY

(Map p122; 📞12 429 1553; www.fejkielgallery.com; ul Sławkowska 14; ⊙11am-6pm Mon-Fri, to 3pm Sat; 🚌2, 4, 14, 19, 20, 24) Jan Fejkiel was trained as an art historian, but his gallery specialises in contemporary prints and drawings, with a focus on emerging artists. This place claims the country's largest stock of contemporary graphic art, so he's not messing around.

Wedel Pijalnia Czekolady   FOOD & DRINK

(Map p122; 📞12 429 4085; www.wedelpijalnie. pl; Rynek Główny 46; ⊙9am-10pm; 🚌1, 6, 8, 13, 18) The name E Wedel means only one thing: chocolate. This 'chocolate lounge' is the place to buy a box of handmade pralines to take home to your sweetheart.

My Gallery   JEWELLERY

(Map p122; 📞12 431 1344; www.mygallery.pl; ul Gołębia 1a; ⊙9am-7pm Mon-Fri, 10am-4pm Sat; 🚌2, 13, 18, 20) This one little room has such an eclectic assortment you could do all your souvenir shopping here. Choose from dramatic, nature-inspired jewellery, handmade scarves and sweaters, and stained-glass sun catchers, as well as the odd pair of soft slippers.

La Mama   CLOTHING

(Map p122; 📞602 396 230; www.lamama.sklep.pl; ul Sławkówska 24; ⊙10am-7pm Mon-Fri, 11am-4pm

Sat; 🚊2, 4, 14, 19, 20, 24) Local designer Monika shows off her funky children's fashions. Everything is made from natural fabrics and the designs are simple and clean.

Hala Targowa
MARKET

(Map p122; Ul Grzegórzecka 3; ⊙7am-3pm; 🚊1, 9, 11, 22, 50) An outdoor flea market, where you'll find lots of old books with yellowed pages, postcards depicting the Kraków of yesteryear, paintings and icons, and loads of other trash and treasure. Vendors set up here daily but Sunday before noon is best. There's also a popular sausage stand here for late-night street food (8pm to 3am Monday to Friday).

Salon Antyków Pasja
ANTIQUES

(Map p122; ☑12 429 1096; www.antykwariat-pasja.pl; ul Jagiellońska 9; ⊙11am-7pm Mon-Fri, 10am-3pm Sat; 🚊2, 13, 18, 20) This well-established antique salon is like a minimuseum; its three rooms are stuffed with clocks, maps, paintings, lamps, sculptures and furniture. Come to think of it, it's better than a museum, because if you see something you like, you can take it home.

Kobalt
CERAMICS

(Map p122; ☑798 380 431; www.kobalt.com.pl; Grodzka 62; ⊙10am-8pm; 🚊6, 8, 10, 13, 18) Sells eye-poppingly beautiful ceramic designs from the western Polish city of Bolesławiec. The dishes, plates and bowls are all hand-painted with a unique stamping and brush technique, and can be found in kitchens around the country.

Krakowski Kredens
FOOD & DRINK

(Map p122; ☑12 423 8159; www.krakowskikredens.pl; ul Grodzka 7; ⊙10am-8pm Mon-Sat, 11am-6pm Sun; 🚊1, 6, 8, 13, 18) If you love *żurek* like we love *żurek,* you'll want to take some home. Peek inside the 'Kraków cupboard' and you'll find a jar of this traditional sour soup, as well as loads of edible souvenirs, such as marinated mushrooms, herb honey, spicy mustard and gooseberry preserves.

Andrzej Mleczko Gallery
ART

(Map p122; ☑12 421 7104; www.mleczko.pl; ul Św Jana 14; ⊙10am-6pm; 🚊2, 4, 14, 19, 20, 24) The gallery displays and sells comic drawings and other articles, like coffee mugs and T-shirts, by popular satirical cartoonist Andrzej Mleczko.

Rubin
ANTIQUES

(Map p122; ☑12 422 9140; www.rubin.com.pl; ul Sławkowska 1; ⊙11am-5pm Mon-Fri; 🚊2, 4, 14, 18, 20, 24) Beautiful selection of antique jewellery, including many amber pieces, silver spoons, rings and watches.

Lulu Living
HOMEWARES

(Map p122; ☑12 421 0472; www.lululiving.pl; ul Św Tomasza 17; ⊙10am-7pm; 🚊2, 4, 14, 19, 20, 24) Hidden above the Camelot Cafe, find a set of stairs inside the cafe and ascend to this light, airy, contemporary home-furnishings store. Modern designs in glass, lighting, textiles and ceramics sit comfortably alongside retro posters and signs, to lend a surprisingly cohesive effect.

Galeria Bukowski
GIFTS

(Map p122; ☑12 433 8855; www.galeriabukowski.pl; ul Sienna 1; ⊙10am-7pm Tue-Sat, to 6pm Sun-Mon; 🚊1, 6, 8, 13, 18) This unbearably cute shop specialises in *miś pluszowy* (teddy bears) of all shapes, sizes, hues and descriptions.

🄰 Kazimierz

For everything from rusty war relics to attractive collectables, check out the flea market held each Saturday morning in **Plac Nowy** (Jewish Market; Map p132; ⊙from 6am; 🚊6, 8, 10, 13) in Kazimierz. For galleries, the most fertile hunting ground is along ul Josefa.

★ Błażko Jewellery Design
JEWELLERY

(Map p132; ☑508 646 298; www.blazko.pl; ul Józefa 11; ⊙11am-7pm Mon-Fri, to 3pm Sat; 🚊6, 8, 10, 13) The eye-catching creations of designer Grzegorz Błażko are on display in this small gallery and workshop, including his unique range of chequered enamel rings, pendants, bracelets, earrings, and cufflinks. Most are silver.

Austeria
BOOKS

(Map p132; www.austeria.pl; ul Józefa 38; ⊙9am-7pm; 🚊3, 9, 19, 24, 50) Best collection of Jewish-themed books and Judaica in Kraków.

Antykwariat na Kazimierzu
ANTIQUES

(Map p132; ☑12 292 6153; www.judaica.pl; ul Meiselsa 17; ⊙10am-5pm Mon-Fri, to 2pm Sat & Sun; 🚊6, 8, 10, 13) In the basement of the Judaica Foundation in Kazimierz, this Aladdin's cave is a jumble of antique china, glass, paintings, books and other assorted goodies.

Vanilla
CLOTHING

(Map p132; ☑500 542 114; ul Meiselsa 7; ⊙11am-7pm Mon-Fri, to 4pm Sat, 10am-3pm Sun; 🚊6, 8, 10, 13) High-end, secondhand women's clothing store featuring well-chosen tops, skirts, dresses, and shoes from luxury labels, but at a fraction of the original price. The selections tend toward retro, giving this shop a vintage feel.

Produkty Benedyktyńskie — FOOD & DRINK
(Benedictine Products; Map p132; ✆12 422 0216; www.produktybenedyktynskie.com; ul Krakowska 29; ◷9am-6pm Mon-Fri, to 3pm Sat; ⧉6, 8, 10, 13) The Benedictine monks are nothing if not industrious. Here you can buy cheeses, wines, cookies, honey…all the goodies that are produced by the holy men up the river in Tyniec, as well as some products from monasteries further afield.

Raven Gallery — ARTS
(Map p122; ✆12 431 1129; www.raven.krakow.pl; ul Brzozowa 7; ◷11am-6pm Mon-Fri, to 3pm Sat; ⧉11, 12, 22, 52) This small private art gallery features the work of well-known Polish painters working from the 1930s to the present day. The gallery is particularly strong on cubist paintings from the 1920s and '30s, as well as abstract and socialist-realist painting from the 1950s and '60s.

Antyki Galeria Retro — ANTIQUES
(Map p132; ✆691 803 863; www.antykiretro.pl; ul Miodowa 4; ◷11am-6pm Mon-Fri, 10.30am-3pm Sat; ⧉6, 8, 10, 13) Bustling junk shop, featuring stacks of antique porcelain plates, silver sets, and candelabras on the tables, plus rows of big wooden clocks on the walls. There's also a small but valuable selection of paintings from the 1960s and '70s.

By Insomnia — CLOTHING
(Map p132; ✆881 228 122; www.byinsomnia.com; ul Meiselsa 7; ◷10am-6pm Mon-Fri, to 3pm Sat; ⧉6, 8, 10, 13) Natural materials and subtly sexy styles characterise the designs for women's clothing on display at this tiny boutique. The flagship designer is Warsaw-based 'By Insomnia', and all of the clothing is made in Poland.

Marka — HOMEWARES
(Map p132; ✆12 422 2965; ul Józefa 5; ◷noon-6pm; ⧉6, 8, 10, 13) This self-described 'concept' store opened at the start of 2015 with a mission to bring to market art, furniture, accessories, lighting, and glassware made exclusively by Polish designers. Standouts include the retro lighting fixtures, beautifully sculpted vases, and crystal decanters and bowls.

Danutta Hand Gallery — SOUVENIRS
(Map p132; ✆733 466 277; www.danuttahandgallery.pl; ul Meiselsa 22; ◷10am-7pm Mon-Sat; ⧉6, 8, 10, 13) What appears to be an ordinary souvenir shop from the street is actually a highly personalised boutique, featuring a range of handicrafts made by local artists and artisans. Everything from the refrigerator magnets to the cuff links made from watch parts, and earrings made from found objects, is from a Kraków-based gallery or designer.

Klubczyk — FOOD & DRINK
(Map p132; ✆692 428 510; Mostowa 14; ◷10am-5pm Mon-Fri, 11am-6pm Sat & Sun; ⧉6, 8, 10, 13) This tiny deli and packaged food shop on Kazimierz's blossoming ul Mostowa specialises in organic foods, including meats, cheeses, grains and beans of Polish origin. It's a handy shop for picking up picnic provisions. There's also a tiny retro-style cafe, with a few tables where you can sample the products in-house.

Jarden Jewish Bookshop — BOOKS
(Map p132; ✆12 421 7166; www.jarden.pl; ul Szeroka 2; ◷9am-6pm Mon-Fri, 10am-6pm Sat & Sun; ⧉3, 9, 19, 24, 50) This small bookshop is dedicated to titles on Jewish heritage, with a decent selection on local history and lore, as well as Holocaust literature. It also sells Jewish-themed music on CDs, and offer tours of sites of Jewish interest.

🔒 Outside The Centre

★Massolit Books & Cafe — BOOKS
(Map p122; ✆12 432 4150; www.massolit.com; ul Felicjanek 4; ◷10am-8pm Sun-Thu, to 9pm Fri & Sat; 🛜; ⧉1, 2, 6) Highly atmospheric book emporium selling English-language fiction and nonfiction, both new and secondhand. There's a cafe area with loads of character, starting among the bookshelves and extending into a moody back room. The collection is particularly strong on Polish and Central European authors in translation.

Cepelix — CRAFTS
(✆12 644 1571; os Centrum B1, Nowa Huta; ◷10am-6pm Mon-Fri, to 1pm Sat; ⧉4, 10, 16) The local branch of a national chain of Polish handcrafts and souvenirs, specialising in leather, lace and various local mementoes. The highlight of a stop here is to view the interior. The metal chandeliers, cabinets, ceiling and furnishings retain the feel of a shopping experience during Nowa Huta's socialist-realist heyday in the 1960s and '70s.

Empik — BOOKS
(Map p122; ✆22 451 0385; www.empik.com; ul Pawia 5; ◷9.30am-9pm; ⧉2, 3, 4, 10, 14, 19, 24, 52) Big chain bookshop, also good for maps, newspapers, magazines and hard-to-find Polish films on DVD to take back home. This branch, on the first floor of the Galeria Krakowska shopping centre, has arguably the best selection.

Starmach Gallery   GALLERY

(Map p132; ☑ 12 656 4317; www.starmach.com.
pl; ul Węgierska 5, Podgórze; ☺11am-6pm Mon-Fri;
🚊3, 6, 11, 23) Starmach is among the city's
most prestigious galleries of contemporary
painting and sculpture, exhibiting both
emerging and established Polish artists. The
striking modern gallery is housed in the
former Jewish Zucher prayer house, a 19th-
century neo-Gothic brick beauty.

🛈 Information

DANGERS & ANNOYANCES

Kraków is generally a safe city for travellers,
although as a major tourist spot it has its fair
share of pickpockets; be vigilant in crowded
public areas.

   If you're staying in the centre of the Old Town,
especially near the main square, you may experience late-night noise from the area's many restaurants, bars and clubs; ask for a room at the
back if this is going to be an issue. In summer,
the large numbers of tourists in town can be a
little overwhelming and mean long queues for
top sights such as the Wawel Royal Castle and
scarce seating in the more popular restaurants.
Keep a wary eye out for the many horse-driven
carriages that cart tourists around the Old Town,
including along the pedestrianised streets.

INTERNET ACCESS

Internet Café Hetmańska (☑ 12 430 0108;
www.hetmanska24.com; ul Bracka 4; per hr
4zł; ☺24hr; 🚊1, 6, 8, 13, 18) Well-placed Old
Town internet cafe that's conveniently open day
and night.

Klub Internetowy Planet (☑ 12 432 7631; 1st
fl, Rynek Główny 24; per hr 4zł; ☺10am-10pm;
🚊1, 6, 8, 13, 18) Handy internet cafe just off
the Rynek Główny. Enter the passageway and
find the flight of stairs up.

Blich Internet (☑ 12 391 6111; ul Blich 5; per
hr 4zł; ☺10am-9pm Mon-Sat, noon-9pm Sun;
🚊1, 9, 11, 12, 22, 50) Internet cafe about 600m
south of the main train station.

MAPS

The free map from the tourist offices should be
sufficient for a short visit. If you want something
more detailed, one of the best is the 1:10,000
scale *Kraków Plan Miasta* (9zł) published by
Demart, which usefully includes all tram and bus
routes along with their stops. Big bookstores like
Empik (p155) and **Księgarnia Pod Globusem**
(Map p122; ☑ 12 422 1739; www.liberglob.pl;
ul Długa 1; ☺10am-7pm Mon-Fri, to 2pm Sat;
🚊2, 4, 14, 19, 20, 24) carry a large selection of
maps. Another good place to check is the travel
specialist **Sklep Podróżnika** (Map p122; ☑ 12
429 1485; www.sp.com.pl; ul Jagiellońska 6;

☺11am-7pm Mon-Fri, 10am-2pm Sat; 🚊2, 13,
18, 20).

MEDICAL SERVICES

Apteka Pod Opatrznością (☑ 12 631 1980; ul
Karmelicka 23; ☺24hr; 🚊4, 13, 14, 24) This
24-hour pharmacy is west of the Old Town.

AstraDent Kraków (☑ 12 421-8948; www.
astradent.pl; Plac Szczepański 3; ☺8.30am-7pm
Mon-Fri; 🚊2, 4, 14, 18, 20, 24) Reliable dental
clinic in the Old Town.

Medicina (☑ 12 266 9665; www.medicina.
pl; ul Barska 12; ☺7.30am-8pm Mon-Fri, 8am-
2pm Sat; 🚊11, 18, 22, 52) Private healthcare
provider.

Medicover (☑ 500 900 500; www.medicover.pl;
ul Podgórska 36; ☺7.30am-8pm Mon-Fri, 8am-
2pm Sat; 🚊3, 9, 19, 24, 50) Private clinic with
English-speaking specialist doctors. Provides
24-hour emergency service.

LAUNDRY

Most hostels have washing machines (and sometimes even dryers) that you can use, though they
may charge a fee.

Betty Clean (☑ 12 430 1563; www.bettyclean.
pl; ul Zwierzyniecka 6; ☺7.30am-7.30pm Mon-
Fri, 8am-3.30pm Sat; 🚊1, 2, 6) Branch of a
chain of drycleaners near the southwest edge
of the Old Town, which will also accept general
laundry.

MONEY

Kantors (private currency-exchange offices),
banks and ATMs can be found around the centre.
It's worth noting that many *kantors* close on
Sunday, and areas near Rynek Główny and the
main train station offer poor exchange rates.
Make a point of comparing rates and check
whether a commission is being charged.

POST

Main Post Office (Poczta Polska; Map p122;
☑ 12 421 0348; www.poczta-polska.pl; Westerplatte 20; ☺7.30am-8.30pm Mon-Fri, 8am-
2pm Sat; 🚊3, 10, 19, 24, 52) The main post
office is located just east of the Old Town.

TELEPHONE

The best place to pick up a Polish SIM card for
your mobile phone is at the Galeria Krakowska
(p153) shopping mall next to the train station.
All the telecommunications companies have
outlets here, right next to each other, so you can
easily compare rates and offers.

TOURIST INFORMATION

The official tourist information office, InfoKraków (www.infokrakow.pl), maintains
branches around town, including at the **Cloth
Hall** (Map p122; ☑ 12 433 7310; Cloth Hall,
Rynek Główny 1/3; ☺9am-7pm May-Sep, to 5pm

Oct-Apr; 🚇; 🚋1, 6, 8, 13, 18), **Kazimierz** (Map p132; 📞12 422 0471; ul Józefa 7; ⊙9am-5pm; 🚋6, 8, 10, 13), **Old Town** (Map p122; 📞12 421 7787; ul Św Jana 2; ⊙9am-7pm; 🚋1, 6, 8, 13, 18) and the **Airport** (📞12 285 5341; www. en.infokrakow.pl; John Paul II International Airport, Balice; ⊙9am-7pm). Expect cheerful service, loads of free maps and promotional materials, help in sorting out accommodation and transport, and a computer on hand (in some branches) for free, short-term web-surfing.

The good-value **Kraków Card** (www.krakow card.com; 2/3 days 100/120zł) can make sense if you plan on visiting many museums in a short span of time. It's available from tourist offices, travel agencies and hotels. It offers free entry to dozens of museums (though not those on Wawel Hill), unlimited travel on public transport, including the Wieliczka bus, and discounts on organised tours and at certain restaurants.

TRAVEL AGENCIES

Bocho Travel (📞12 421 8500; www.krakow. travel; ul Stolarska 8-10; 🚋1, 6, 8, 13, 18) Sells air tickets and intercity train tickets.

WEBSITES

In Your Pocket (www.inyourpocket.com/ poland/krakow) Irreverent reviews of accommodation, sights and entertainment.

Kraków Info (www.krakow-info.com) An excellent source for news and events.

Kraków Post (www.krakowpost.com) English-language resource with local news, interviews, features and listings.

Local Life (www.local-life.com/krakow) Heaps of information on eating, drinking and entertainment.

Magical Kraków (Magiczny Kraków; www. krakow.pl) Good general information direct from city hall.

❶ Getting There & Away

AIR

Kraków's **John Paul II International Airport** (KRK; 📞information 12 295 5800; www.krakow airport.pl; Kapitana Mieczysława Medweckiego 1, Balice; 🚇) is located in the town of Balice, about 15km west of the centre. The airport terminal hosts several car-hire desks, bank ATMs, a branch of the InfoKraków tourist information office and currency exchanges offering unappealing rates. At the time of research the airport was undergoing massive reconstruction, but was expected to return to normal sometime in 2016. Flights were operating as scheduled, but expect delays.

The main Polish carrier **LOT** (📞12 285 5128, help line 22 577 9952; www.lot.com; ul Basztowa

15; ⊙9am-5pm Mon-Fri; 🚋2, 4, 14, 19, 20, 24) flies to Warsaw and major cities around Europe.

A range of other airlines, including several budget operators, connect Kraków to cities in Europe. There are direct flights daily to and from London via EasyJet and Ryanair. Dublin is serviced by Ryanair.

BUS

Kraków's modern **bus station** (Map p119; 📞703 403 340; www.mda.malopolska.pl; ul Bosacka 18; ⊙information 7am-8pm; 🚋2, 3, 4, 10, 14, 19, 24, 52) is conveniently located next to the main train station on the fringe of the Old Town. Bus travel is the best way to reach Zakopane (16zł, two hours, hourly). Modern **Polski Bus** (📞emergencies 703 502 504; www. polskibus.com) coaches depart from here to Warsaw (five hours, several daily) and Wrocław (three hours, several daily); check fares and book tickets online.

Polski Bus offers a few international connections to nearby countries, including to Berlin (99zł, eight hours, four daily). Other leading international coach services include **Eurolines** (📞14 657 1777; www.eurolines.pl) and **Jordan** (Map p132; 📞12 422 4278; http://autobusy. jordan.pl; ul Gęsia 8; ⊙8am-5pm Mon-Fri). Most of these arrive at and depart from the main bus station. Buy tickets at the station ticket office or in some cases from the driver. **Tiger Express** (Map p122; 📞608 921 919; www.tiger express.eu; ul Worcella 12; ⊙8am-7pm; 🚋3) minibuses run to and from major destinations in the Czech Republic, including Prague (99zł, six hours). Buses depart from a small station across the street from the Galeria Krakowska (p153) shopping centre. Buy tickets online.

TRAIN

Newly remodeled and gleaming **Kraków Główny Train Station** (Dworzec Główny; Map p119; 📞information 22 391 9757; www.pkp.pl; Plac Dworcowy; 🚋2, 3, 4, 10, 14, 19, 24, 52), on the northeastern outskirts of the Old Town, handles all international trains and most domestic rail services. The station is beautifully laid out, with ample ticketing counters and machines, left-luggage office, lockers, bank ATMs and many restaurants and shops. Enter the station through the Galeria Krakowska (p153) shopping centre.

Useful domestic destinations include Gdańsk (80zł, eight hours, three daily), Lublin (62zł, four hours, two daily), Poznań (80zł, eight hours, three daily), Toruń (73zł, seven hours, three daily), Warsaw (60zł to 130zł, three hours, at least hourly) and Wrocław (50zł, 5½ hours, hourly). Popular international connections include Bratislava (seven hours, one daily), Budapest (10½ hours, one daily), Lviv (7½ to 9½ hours, two daily) and Prague (10 hours, one daily).

KRAKÓW GETTING THERE & AWAY

ⓘ Getting Around

TO/FROM THE AIRPORT

A regular train service, departing once or twice an hour between 4am and 11.30pm, runs to Kraków Główny station, though the train was temporarily suspended for repairs during the time of research. On exiting the terminal, take a free shuttle bus from the airport to a nearby train station. Buy tickets on board the train from a vending machine or the conductor (10zł) for the 18-minute journey.

Public buses 292 and 208 both run from the airport to Kraków's main bus station (p157) (and back) and require a 4zł ticket.

A taxi between the airport and the city centre should cost about 80zł.

If you need to transfer between Kraków and Katowice airport, **Matuszek** (☑ 32 236 1111; www.matuszek.com.pl; single/return 44/88zł) offers regular shuttle service to/from the Kraków bus terminal (two hours). Buy tickets over the website.

BICYCLE

Every year, Kraków gets easier to negotiate by bike. Bike paths follow both sides of the river throughout most of the centre. More-ambitious bike paths are under construction to connect the Old Town with Nowa Huta. InfoKraków tourist offices have free cycling maps. Reliable renters:

Krk Bike Rental (☑ 509 267 733; www.krkbike rental.pl; ul Św Anny 4; per hour/day 9/50zł; ⊞ 2, 13, 18, 20) Old Town bike-rental outfit offers city bikes for puttering around town, or better-equipped mountain bikes for longer, more adventurous hauls. It also runs a three- to four-hour city tour (per person 90zł, minimum three persons), though these must be booked in advance.

Dwa Koła (☑ 12 421 5785; ul Józefa 5; per 3hr/day 20/40zł; ☉ 10am-6pm; ⊞ 6, 8, 10, 13) Rents bikes, including bikes with children's seats, by the hour or the day.

CAR & MOTORCYCLE

With limited parking, and much of the Old Town a car-free zone, driving in Kraków will be more of a hindrance than a help. If you are travelling by car, the major route into the city is the A4; note a 9zł toll is paid when you enter and exit the highway. Street parking in the area outside the Old Town requires special tickets (karta postojowa), which you buy from ticket machines and then display on your windscreen. They cost 3zł for the first hour and rates rise from there. Tickets must be displayed from 10am to 6pm Monday to Friday.

Many of the big international car-rental firms have offices in Kraków and/or at Kraków's airport. Local companies often offer a better deal:

Joka Rent a Car (☑ 12 429 6630; www.joka. com.pl; ul Zacisze 7; ⊞ 2, 3, 4, 14, 19, 20, 24)

PUBLIC TRANSPORT

Kraków is served by an efficient network of buses and trams that run between 5am and 11pm. Two types of individual tickets are available: short-term tickets (2.80zł) are valid for 20 minutes and are fine for short journeys. Normal 40-minute tickets cost 3.80zł. You can also buy one-/two-/three-day (15/24/36zł) passes for longer stays. Buy tickets from machines located onboard vehicles (have coins ready) or from news kiosks at important stops. Remember to validate your ticket in stamping machines when you board; spot checks are frequent.

Most tourist attractions are in the Old Town or within easy walking distance from them, so you probably won't use buses or trams very often unless you're staying outside the centre. Transport information was accurate at the time of research, but note that trams are often re-rerouted in summer as lines are upgraded and repaired.

Kraków Public Transport Authority (Miejskie Przedsiębiorstwo Komunikacyjne/MPK; ☑ 19150; www.mpk.krakow.pl) Operates all city trams and buses. The website has an online timetable.

TAXI

While the number of rogue taxi drivers has decreased in recent years, it's still better to order a taxi by phone rather than hail one off the street. The following companies employ reliable drivers and are prepared to take a phone taxi request in English. In an honest cab, the meter starts at 7zł and rises by 2.30zł per kilometre travelled. Note that rates rise to 3.50zł per kilometre from 10pm to 6am and on Sundays.

iTaxi (☑ 737 737 737; www.itaxi.pl) From the website, you can download the app to your smartphone.

Radio Taxi Barbakan (☑ 12 357 2003, 12 19661; www.barbakan.krakow.pl)

Euro Taxi (☑ 12 266 6111, 12 19664)

Lajkonik Taxi (☑ 12 19628)

Małopolska

POP 5.1 MILLION

Best Places to Eat

➡ Lapidarium pod
Ratuszem (p173)
➡ U Braci (p166)
➡ Calimero Cafe (p169)
➡ Pivovaria (p175)
➡ Kardamon (p181)

Best Places to Stay

➡ Hotel Korunny (p193)
➡ Hostel-Art (p168)
➡ Eger Pensjonat (p185)
➡ Vanilla Hotel (p180)
➡ Hostel Zamość (p193)

Why Go?

Małopolska, known in English as Lesser Poland, is the sprawling region surrounding Kraków, running from Częstochowa in the west to Lublin in the east. It's played an outsized role in Polish history, forming the core of the ancient Polish kingdom. These days, though, it's mostly passed over by travellers who make a beeline for Kraków and then move on.

That's a pity. While Małopolska lacks truly world-class sights, the region is rich in natural beauty, with rolling hills and several national parks. Sandomierz, an ancient Gothic town on a bluff overlooking the Vistula River, is one of Poland's prettiest places.

The region is also rich in cultural diversity. The Jasna Góra monastery in Częstochowa is a major pilgrimage site for Roman Catholics. To the east, cities such as Lublin and Chełm were once home to large Jewish communities, and moving traces of that centuries-long existence can still be found.

When to Go
Lublin

May & Jun The Corpus Christi holiday is marked by massive weekend festivals.

Aug Thousands of pilgrims gather at the Jasna Góra monastery.

Aug & Sep The International Meeting of Jazz Singers comes to Zamość.

Małopolska Highlights

1 Joining throngs of *Black Madonna* pilgrims in **Częstochowa** (p162).

2 Appreciating the perfection of 16th-century town planning in **Zamość** (p190).

3 Blushing as portraits peer down at you in **Kielce**'s Kraków Bishops' Palace (p167).

4 Revelling in the grandeur of **Pieskowa Skała Castle** (p162) in Ojców National Park.

5 Chatting to a ghost in the chalk tunnels of **Chełm** (p188).

6 Saying 'they don't make them like they used to' at the fairytale Krzyżtopór Castle (p174) in **Ujazd.**

7 Wondering why it happened, at Majdanek extermination camp (p179) in **Lublin.**

8 Being dwarfed by ancient nature in **Roztocze National Park** (p194).

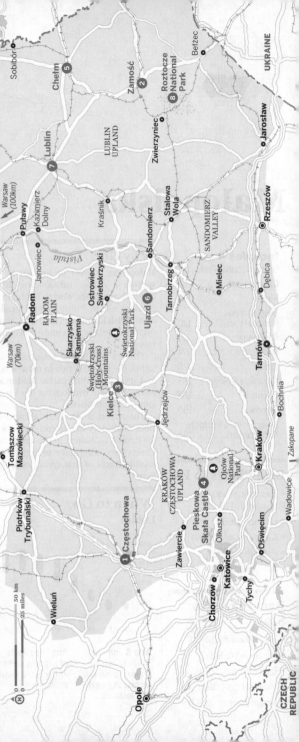

THE KRAKÓW–CZĘSTOCHOWA UPLAND

When Silesia fell to Bohemia in the 14th century, King Kazimierz III Wielki (Casimir III the Great, 1333–70) fortified the frontier by building a chain of castles from Kraków to Częstochowa. This 100km stretch comprises the Kraków–Częstochowa Upland (Wyżyna Krakowsko–Częstochowska).

The plan worked and the Bohemians were never able to penetrate the wall. Centuries later, in 1655, however, the Swedes invaded and destroyed many castles. More turbulence in the 18th century completed the process, leaving impressive ruins for the 21st-century traveller.

The upland region is also known as the Jura, having been formed from limestone in the Jurassic period some 150 million years ago. Erosion left hundreds of caves and oddly shaped rock formations, which can still be enjoyed in the Ojców National Park.

An excellent way to explore the upland is by hiking the Trail of the Eagles' Nest (Szlak Orlich Gniazd), which winds 164km from Kraków to Częstochowa. Tourist offices in Kraków and Częstochowa can provide more information.

Ojców National Park

Perhaps size doesn't matter after all. Ojców National Park (Ojcowski Park Narodowy) may be the smallest in Poland, but it packs two castles, several caves and countless rock formations into its 21.5 sq km. The flora in the park is beech, fir, oak and hornbeam forest, and the fauna a diverse mix of small mammals, including badgers, ermines and beavers. This postcard-worthy park is one of the most beautiful areas of the Kraków–Częstochowa Upland.

Most tourist attractions line the road running along the Prądnik River between Ojców and Pieskowa Skała. There is no direct bus connecting these villages, but the flat 7km between them is well worth walking. The Trail of the Eagles' Nest also follows this road.

🔵 Sights & Activities

The narrow village of Ojców is located in the national park, and is popular with day trippers from Kraków. There are a couple of museums in town, but the true allure of Ojców is its access to the tourist trails running through the national park.

Before you embark on a hike, buy a map of the park in Kraków or at the Ojców PTTK office. There are a couple of versions, but Compass' *Ojcowski Park Narodowy* (scale 1:20,000, 11zł) stands out for detailing every trail, road and rock.

Pieskowa Skała Castle CASTLE
(🖉 12 389 6004; www.ojcowskiparknarodowy.pl; ul Ojcowska; adult/concession 10/7zł; ⊙10am-4pm Tue-Thu, 9am-1pm Fri, 10am-6pm Sat & Sun May-Sep, to 3.30pm Tue-Sun Oct-Apr, closed Mon) If you can only do one thing in Ojców National Park, visit this 14th-century castle, one of the best-preserved castles in the upland. The castle was rebuilt in the 16th century in imitation of the royal residence of Wawel and now serves as a branch of the Wawel Royal Castle museum, with a large collection of art and artefacts from the 15th to 19th centuries. The castle is near the northern end of the park, about 8km north of Ojców village.

From the castle, the red trail along the road toward Ojców takes you to a 25m-tall limestone pillar; it's called Hercules' Club (Maczuga Herkulesa), despite obvious temptations to name it after something else.

Ojców Castle RUIN
(Zamek w Ojcowie; www.ojcowskiparknarodowy. pl; ul Ojcowska; adult/concession 3/2zł; ⊙10am-4.45pm Apr-May & Aug-Sep, to 5.45pm Jun & Jul, to 3.45pm Oct, to 3pm Nov, closed Mon) Ojców Castle was deserted in 1826, and has since fallen into ruin. The 14th-century entrance gate and octagonal tower are original, but there's little else to explore. The view of the wooden houses scattered across the slopes of Prądnik valley is worth the little money and effort. Access the castle by trail from the PTTK car park.

Chapel on the Water CHURCH
(Kaplica na Wodzie; www.ojcowskiparknarodowy.pl; ul Ojcowska) About 100m north of Ojców Castle is the frequently photographed Chapel on the Water, which was fashioned in 1901 from the bathhouse that originally stood in its place. In keeping with its exterior simplicity, the three altars inside are shaped as peasants' cottages. You may sneak a peek inside when the doors open for religious service.

King Łokietek Cave CAVE
(Grota Łokietka; 🖉 12 419 0801; www.grotalokietka. pl; Czajowice; adult/concession 8/6zł; ⊙9am-3.30pm Apr, to 6.30pm May-Sep, to 5.30pm Oct, to 4.30pm Sat & Sun Nov-Mar) Stretching over 270m through several passages, Łokietek

Cave is accessible from the black trail heading south from Ojców Castle and can be visited on a 30-minute tour. Legend has it that before he became king in the 14th century, Władysław Łokietek hid from the Bohemian ruler Václav II in the cave. Chambers are named for the various uses made of them by Łokietek. The temperature of the cave remains between 7°C and 8°C all year.

Wierzchowska Górna Cave CAVE
(☑12 411 0721; www.gacek.pl; ul Wł Bandurskiego 16/11, Wierzchowie; adult/concession 15/13zł; ⊙9am-4pm Apr, Sep & Oct, to 5pm May-Aug, to 3pm Nov) Just outside the park boundaries, Wierzchowska Górna Cave is in the village of Wierzchowie, 5km southwest of Ojców. At 950m long, Wierzchowska is the largest cave in the Kraków–Częstochowa highlands. Artefacts from the late Stone Age and pottery from the middle Neolithic period were uncovered here during excavations after WWII.

🛏 Sleeping & Eating

There are several sleeping and eating options near the Pieskowa Skała Castle and Ojców, and more along the road between them.

Ask about private rooms (40zł to 60zł per person) at the PTTK office, or wander through Ojców village and look for 'noclegi' (accommodation) signs.

Dom Wycieczkowy PTTK Zosia HOSTEL €
(☑12 389 2008; www.dwzosia.pl; Ojców-Złota Góra 4; per person without/with bathroom 30/40zł) You can't beat the value or the vibe at this casual place, just 1km west up the hill from Ojców Castle. It offers well-kept rooms and facilities, and friendly common areas.

Camping Złota Góra CAMPGROUND €
(Złota Góra; ☑12 389 2014; Ojców 8; per person/tent/car/trailer 7/7/10/12zł; ⊙19 Apr–15 Oct) A few hundred metres from the PTTK, near the centre of the park, this camping ground has a bonfire at its heart and trees all around. The expanding dining area lures passers-by with its snug seating and fast-flowing beer. It's BYO tent only.

Agroturystyka Glanowski GUESTHOUSE €
(☑12 389 6212; agroglanowski.tur.pl; Pieskowa Skała, Podzamcze 2; per person 40-50zł) Half a kilometre from Pieskowa Skała Castle, with a range of clean, rustic rooms, a simple restaurant and camping facilities.

Zajazd Zazamcze GUESTHOUSE €€
(☑12 389 2083; www.zajazdzazamcze.ojcow.pl; Ojców 1b; s/d/tr 100/160/200zł; @🛜) An easy walk from the Ojców turn-off, Zajazd Zazamcze offers bland but airy rooms. The restaurant turns out hearty and wholesome fare in its cosy dining room and boasts a lovely garden.

Pieskowa Skała Castle POLISH €€
(☑12 389 6004; www.ojcowskiparknarodowy.pl; Ojcowska; mains 20-30zł; ⊙10am-8pm) The restaurant-cafe at Pieskowa Skała Castle is accessible without a museum ticket; the restaurant interior is castle-kitsch, and the upstairs terrace affords regal views.

ℹ Information

The small **PTTK office** (☑12 389 2010; www.ojcow.pttk.pl; Ojców 15; ⊙9am-5pm) is in the car park at the foot of Ojców Castle.

ℹ Getting There & Away

A sporadic minibus service links Kraków and Ojców (6zł, 45 minutes). Buses depart from Kraków at a small stop at Ogrodowa 4 (next to Galeria Krakowska) and arrive near the PTTK office at the base of Ojców Castle. At the time of writing, five minibuses departed from Kraków each weekday from 6am to 7.05pm, and four returned from Ojców between 9.35am and 6.20pm. Weekend timetables are nearly the same, with the first bus leaving Kraków at 8am.

Częstochowa
POP 246,225

Every year, Częstochowa (chen-sto-*ho*-vah) attracts four to five million visitors from 80 countries who come to fall at the feet of the *Black Madonna*. Some walk for 20 days over hundreds of kilometres with offerings for the Virgin. Others take a bus from Kraków.

Poland's spiritual heartland is not just for the faithful. The Monastery of Jasna Góra is the country's national shrine and one of the highlights of the region. Following an influx of resources from the EU, renovations have been working their way up the main thoroughfare towards the monastery, adding new pride to ancient reverence.

During pilgrimage times – particularly the day of Assumption on 15 August – hordes of devotees become a main attraction for people-watchers, and a deterrent for crowd-weary wanderers.

THE BLACK MADONNA OF CZĘSTOCHOWA

Unlike other pilgrimage sites, Jasna Góra has never claimed the appearance of apparitions. Its fame is attributed to the presence of the *Black Madonna*, a 122cm by 82cm painting of the Virgin Mary with the Christ Child on a panel of cypress timber, which was crowned 'Queen of Poland' in 1717.

It is not known for sure when or where the *Black Madonna* was created, but some say she was painted by St Luke the Evangelist on a table in the house of the Holy Family and was brought to Częstochowa from Jerusalem via Constantinople. It arrived in Częstochowa in 1382.

In 1430 the face of the Madonna was slashed by Hussite warriors, battling against what they saw as papal abuses in Rome. The painting still bears the scars, either because they were left as a reminder of the sacrilegious attack or, as legend has it, because they continually reappeared despite attempts to repair them.

Legends about the *Black Madonna's* role in saving Jasna Góra from the Swedish Deluge in 1655, and in keeping the Russians at bay in 1920, are still extolled today. The widespread belief in the legends is evident from the votive offerings – from crutches and walking canes to jewellery and medals – which are still presented to the Virgin by devoted pilgrims today.

History

The first known mention of Częstochowa dates to 1220, with the monastery appearing about 150 years later. The name 'Jasna Góra' means Bright Hill, and the fact that the monastery was one of the few places in the country to survive Swedish aggression in the 17th century sealed it as a holy spot in the minds of many.

The town's foundational charter was granted in the 14th century under German law by King Kazimierz III Wielki, placing Częstochowa on an important trade route from Russia. Agricultural and industrial development, aided by the Warsaw to Vienna railway line, saw Częstochowa evolve into an established industrial centre by the end of the 19th century. By the outbreak of WWII the city had some 140,000 inhabitants.

As with many Polish cities of its size, Częstochowa had a sizeable Jewish community until the German occupation during WWII. Most of the Jews were clustered in the neighbourhood around the Stary Rynek (the town's old market square) at the eastern end of al Najświętszej Marii Panny (NMP), which was also where the Nazis built their wartime ghetto. At its peak it held nearly 50,000 Jews. The ghetto was liquidated in September and October of 1942, when around 40,000 Jews were deported to the extermination camp at Treblinka (p100).

◉ Sights

★ Paulite Monastery of Jasna Góra
MONASTERY

(☑ 34 365 3888; www.jci.jasnagora.pl; ul Kordeckiego 2; ⊘ 8am-5pm Mar-Oct, to 4pm Nov-Feb) **FREE** Poland's spiritual capital began with the arrival of the Paulite order from Hungary in 1382, who named the 293m hill in the western part of the city 'Jasna Góra' (Bright Hill) and erected this monastery. Believers are drawn to the site for miracles credited to the *Black Madonna* painting in the Chapel of Our Lady, though there are many other sights worth seeing, too. The information centre arranges hour-long guided tours in English.

In the oldest part of the complex, the **Chapel of Our Lady** (Kaplica Cudownego Obrazu) contains the revered *Black Madonna*. The picture is ceremoniously unveiled at 6am and 1.30pm (2pm Saturday and Sunday) and veiled at noon and 9.20pm (1pm and 9.20pm Saturday and Sunday). Be sure to note the walls displaying votive offerings brought by pilgrims. Adjoining the chapel is the impressive **basilica** *(bazylika)*. Its present shape dates to the 17th century and the interior has opulent Baroque furnishings.

On the northern side of the chapel, paintings in the **Knights' Hall** (Sala Rycerska) depict key events from the monastery's history; there's also an exact copy of the *Black Madonna*. Upstairs, the **Golghota Gallery** contains a series of unique paintings by celebrated local painter and cartoonist Jerzy

Częstochowa

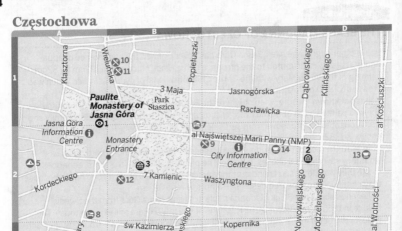

Duda Gracz (1941–2004), whose evocative works are indicative of the monastery's ability to preserve its historical heritage while maintaining modern relevance.

The 106m **bell tower**, the tallest historic church tower in Poland, offers views over the monastery complex and the expanse of al NMP. With many fallen predecessors, the current tower dates to 1906.

The **600th Anniversary Museum** contains fascinating artefacts, including the founding documents of Jasna Góra from 1382 and a cross made from the steel of the World Trade Center, destroyed in New York on 11 September 2001. Particularly moving are rosaries made from breadcrumbs by concentration camp prisoners. Lech Wałęsa's 1983 Nobel Peace Prize, donated by its recipient, can be found beyond the Father Kordecki Conference Room.

The **arsenal** contains military mementos including spoils of battle, offerings from soldiers, and an impressive collection of Turkish weapons from the 1683 Battle of Vienna.

The 17th-century **treasury** contains votive offerings dating back to the 15th century. Since the 17th century, records have been kept of gifts given to the Madonna.

Częstochowa Museum   MUSEUM
(Muzeum Częstochowskie; ☑ 34 360 5631; www.muzeumczestochowa.pl; al NMP 45; adult/concession 12/6zł, Wed free; ⊙ 11am-5pm Tue-Fri, to 6pm Sat & Sun) In the neoclassical town hall on al NMP, this museum contains paintings of Polish artists as well as extensive documentation detailing the history of Częstochowa and the region. Some of the collection is housed in the **Częstochowa Museum outlet** (☑ 34 360 5631; www.muzeumczestochowa.pl; Park Staszica; adult/concession 12/6zł, Wed free; ⊙ 11am-5pm Tue-Fri, to 6pm Sat & Sun), close to the monastery.

Jewish Memorial   MONUMENT
(Umschlagplatz; ul Strażacka) A small landmark near the Stary Rynek marks the deportation zone, the *Umschlagplatz,* from where tens of thousands of Jews were transported to their deaths at Treblinka in 1942. The memorial includes a copy of a hauntingly precise train timetable showing trains departing Częstochowa at 12.29pm and arriving at Treblinka at 5.25am the next morning.

🎇 Festivals & Events

**Gaude Mater Festival
of Religious Music**   MUSIC
(☑ 34 324 3638; www.gaudemater.pl; ⊙ early May) Focuses on religious music from Christian,

Jewish and Islamic traditions. Held annually the first week of May.

Marian Feasts   RELIGIOUS
(www.jasnagora.pl; ⊙ 3 May, 16 Jul, 15 Aug, 26 Aug, 12 Sep & 8 Dec) Draws believers in the tens of thousands, who camp out, sing songs and attend massive open-air masses.

Assumption   PILGRIMAGE
(www.jasnagora.pl; ⊙ 15 Aug) Pilgrims have been travelling by foot to Jasna Góra for Assumption since 1711.

🛏 Sleeping

During pilgrimage periods (such as the Marian feast days) book well ahead, or stay elsewhere and make a day trip into Częstochowa.

**Pokoje Gościnne
Pod Klasztorem**   GUESTHOUSE €
(☑ 34 324 7991; www.podklasztorem.pl; ul Św Barbary 13; s/d/tr 80/150/180zł; @) Without a hostel in town, these plain, tidy rooms about 100m from the monastery complex are the best value in town. Don't expect much more than a pinewood bed and basic furnishings, but all rooms have separate baths and everything is well-tended. There's a garden at the back, and some units come with kitchens.

Camping Oleńka   CAMPGROUND €
(☑ 34 360 6066; www.mosir.pl; ul Oleńki 22; car/tent 15/20zł, 4-person bungalow with bath 140zł) This camping ground behind the monastery has space for around 400 people. Those who forget to bring tents can enjoy great value in the self-contained bungalows. The campground is located about 100m southwest of the monastery complex.

Hotel Wenecki   HOTEL €€
(☑ 34 324 3303; www.hotelwenecki.pl; ul Joselewicza 12; s/d/tr 140/170/190zł; P@🛜) The Wenecki is the nicest hotel at its price point in town, with the only drawback being the location, about 20 minutes' walk from the monastery (though close to the train and bus stations). Rooms are slightly frayed, but clean. The beds are firm and the baths have handy extras, such as hair dryers. Breakfast costs an additional 20zł.

Mercure   HOTEL €€
(☑ 34 360 3100; www.accorhotels.com; ul Popiełuszki 2; s/d/apt 320/380/580zł; P🌐@🛜) The local member of the Mercure upmarket hotel chain offers clean, smartly appointed rooms with all modern conveniences. It also has one of the best locations in town, straddling the monastery to the west and the town centre to the east. Breakfast costs 44zł and

parking adds another 40zł a night (though street parking nearby is free).

🍴 Eating & Drinking

U Braci
ITALIAN €€

(☎ 515 314 190; 7 Kamienic 17; mains 25-35zł; ⊙ noon-10pm; 🛜) For pizza and pasta near the monastery, you could hardly do better than this authentic Italian restaurant, just a few minutes walk from the main monastery entrance. Expect wood-fired pizzas, inventive pastas, and delicious mains such as tender chicken breast, cooked sous-vide and served with risotto. An intensely flavoured espresso coffee rounds out the perfect lunch.

Dobry Rok
POLISH €€

(☎ 533 950 533; www.dobry-rok.pl; al NMP 79; mains 25-45zł; ⊙ 8am-10pm Mon-Fri, 9am-midnight Sat, 10am-10pm Sun; 🛜) Easily the best of a string of restaurants that line the upper end of al NMP toward the monastery. There's a mix of Polish and international dishes, with the local favourite being a plate of glazed and baked salmon and shrimp. The service is polite, and though the menu and website are not English-friendly, the servers are happy to translate.

Pireus
GREEK €€

(☎ 34 368 0680; www.restauracja-pireus.com. pl; ul Wieluńska 12; mains 25-50zł; ⊙ noon-10pm; 🛜) Pireus is a welcome oasis of excellent, simple Greek food, such as tzatziki and fried calamari, in a refined but still relaxed setting. The restaurant is within easy walking distance of the Jasna Góra monastery. Book ahead.

Twierdza
POLISH €€

(☎ 34 361 2828; www.twierdza.czest.pl; ul Wieluńska 10; mains 30-50zł; ⊙ 11am-11pm) Twierdza is close enough to the monastery to make for an easy lunch break. The menu has a decent mix of international standards such as steaks, and harder-to-find items such as venison and duck liver. We liked the chicken breast, served with smoked highlander sheep's cheese *(oscypek)*.

Caffe del Corso
CAFE

(☎ 723 191 974; al NMP 53; coffee 8 zł, ice cream 20zł; ⊙ 8am-10pm Mon-Sat, 10am-10pm Sun; 🛜) *The* place on al NMP for excellent coffees and extravagant ice-cream concoctions and cakes, with a handsome terrace for people watching. Also has a range of salads, toasted sandwiches and pancakes for a light meal.

Café 29
CAFE

(☎ 34 361 2355; www.cafe29.pl; al NMP 29; mains 10-25zł; ⊙ 10am-10pm Mon-Thu, to 11pm Fri & Sat, noon-10pm Sun; 🛜) Walk through the passageway at al NMP 29 to find Café 29, a popular student cafe with salads and light bites, as well as the usual coffee and beer. Café 29 shares garden space with the Flash Pub and with the Galeria Café and Carpe Diem club across the yard, so head here after sundown for drinks and more.

ℹ️ Information

There are a number of *kantors* (private currency-exchange offices) and ATMs on al NMP.

City Information Centre (Miejskie Centrum Informacji; ☎ 34 368 2250; www.czestochowa. pl; al NMP 65; ⊙ 9am-5pm Mon-Sat) Maps and sights information. Has a computer for checking email.

Jasna Gora Information Centre (Jasnagórskie Centrum Informacji; ☎ 34 365 3888; www. jasnagora.pl; ul Kordeckiego 2; ⊙ 9am-5pm Mar-Oct, to 4pm Nov-Feb) Information centre inside the Jasna Góra monastery. Organises guided tours of the major sites at the monastery (100zł, minimum of five people).

ℹ️ Getting There & Away

BUS

The **bus terminal** (☎ information 34 379 1149; www.pks-czestochowa.pl; al Wolności 45; ⊙ information counter 9am-5pm) is close to the main train station (both are about 2km east of the monastery) and serves mainly towns in the region including Jędrzejów (14zł, two hours) and Opole (15zł, two hours).

Polski Bus (www.polskibus.com) runs services to a number of Polish towns; buy tickets online.

Katowice 20zł, one hour, five per day

Kraków 27zł, three hours, two per day

Łódź 20zł, two hours, two per day

Warsaw 33zł, three hours, four per day

TRAIN

The **train station** (☎ information 19 757; www. pkp.pl; al Wolności) handles half a dozen daily fast trains to Warsaw (40zł, 3½ hours) and about four trains to Kraków (34zł, three hours).

There are about eight trains to Kielce (28zł, two hours 20 minutes) throughout the day. Several trains run to Katowice (20zł, 1½ hours) between 3am and 9pm, from where there are connections to Kraków. There are only a few trains to Zakopane, and these often depart in the inconvenient wee hours (35zł, seven hours).

THE MAŁOPOLSKA UPLAND

The Małopolska Upland is skirted by the Vistula and Pilica Rivers, but the centrepiece of this expanse is the Holy Cross Mountains (Góry Świętokrzyskie), a repository of abundant natural beauty, witness to harrowing episodes in the country's history, and object of religious reverence. The main urban centre of Kielce, which sits at the foot of the mountains, is a convenient base from which to access this varied cultural landscape and the surrounding mountain ranges.

Kielce

POP 203,800

First impressions of Kielce (kyel-tseh) are not likely to be positive. The town is ringed by postwar housing projects that on a rainy day, or any day, can look downright dispiriting. But dig a little deeper and you'll find a lively city with a surprisingly elegant core, centred on the cathedral, the remarkable Palace of the Kraków Bishops, and a pretty expanse of parkland surrounding both of them.

Kielce is not resting on its laurels. The city is still in the throes of a multiyear renovation effort that has scrubbed the central areas and restored the Rynek to its former lustre. The main thoroughfare, ul Sienkiewicza, has been spruced up and stretches as far as the eye can see with cafes, shops and bars.

◎ Sights

★ **Kraków Bishops' Palace** MUSEUM
(Pałac Biskupów Krakówskich; ☑ 41 344 4015; www.mnki.pl; Plac Zamkowy 1; adult/concession 10/5zł; ◎10am-6pm Tue-Sun) Kielce was the property of the Kraków bishops from the 12th century through to 1789. This palace was built (from 1637 onwards) as one of their seats and remains a testament to the richness of that era. The highlight of a visit are the restored 17th- and 18th-century interiors, which still feel very lived in. The only drawback is a shortfall of information in English. Be sure to ask at the admission counter for a free (and excellent) English-language booklet on the sights.

The centrepiece of the permanent exhibition is the former dining hall, where the whole brood of bishops stare down from their 56 portraits. The rest of this cavernous, multilevel museum leads through collections of porcelain and historical armour, and various centuries and genres of Polish painting.

Kielce Cathedral BASILICA
(☑ 41 344 6307; www.wrota-swietokrzyskie.pl; Plac NMP 3; ◎8am-7pm) Kielce's cathedral looks nothing like the Romanesque church first erected here in 1171; it was rebuilt in the 17th century and dressed in Baroque decorations. The cathedral's underground crypts are the final resting place for many bishops. Pope John Paul II celebrated Mass here in 1999. It was given a massive overhaul in 2012 and has emerged gleaming.

Museum of Toys and Play MUSEUM
(Muzeum Zabawek i Zabawy; ☑ 41 344 4078; www.muzeumzabawek.eu; Plac Wolności 2; adult/concession 10/5zł; ◎9am-5pm Tue-Sun; ⊕) This delightful museum offers the chance to reminisce about toys you forgot you wanted. The room full of frogs somehow makes sense when you're there.

Jewish Pogrom Memorial MEMORIAL
(☑ 41 344 7636; Planty 7/9; ◎9am-5pm Mon-Fri) A small plaque signed by former president Lech Wałęsa identifies the site of a tragic post-WWII pogrom in 1946 committed by Poles against Jews who had survived the Holocaust. The origins of the pogrom are unclear – some believe it was instigated by communist authorities to discredit nationalist Poles – but the violence ended with around 40 Jewish deaths. Inside there's a small but moving photo exhibition of Jewish life in Poland in the run-up to WWII.

Nine Poles were executed for taking part in the killings. The pogrom is often cited as the reason so few surviving Jews decided to remain in Poland after the war.

Museum of the Dialogue of Cultures MUSEUM
(Muzeum Dialogu Kultur; ☑ 41 344 4014; www.mnki.pl; Rynek 3/5; ◎9am-5pm Tue-Sun) This tiny, uplifting museum is dedicated to global efforts to promote peace and dialogue across cultural and ethnic groups. The museum also holds interesting temporary exhibitions, such as a fascinating display of Central European political posters from WWII to the present.

Open-Air Museum of the Kielce Village MUSEUM
(Muzeum Wsi Kieleckiej; ☑ 41 315 4171; www.mwk.com.pl; Tokarnia 303, Chęciny; adult/concession 12/6zł; ◎10am-6pm Tue-Sun Apr-Oct, 9am-4pm Mon-Fri Nov-Mar; ⊕) This 80-hectare skansen (open-air museum of traditional architecture) is located in the village of Tokarnia, about 20km from Kielce. It's a pleasant

Kielce

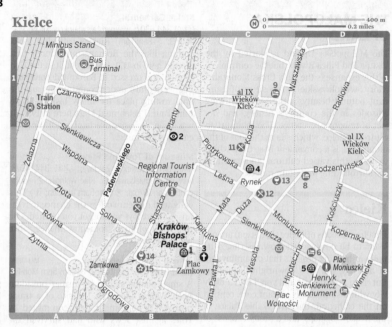

half-day outing, particularly for kids. Several minibuses from Kielce pass Tokarnia on their way to other destinations, as do five normal buses (4zł, 30 minutes) between 10.40am and 8.40pm on their way to destinations such as Jędrzejów. Get off at the village of Tokarnia and continue in the same direction on foot for around 1km to the entrance of the skansen.

Note that on Sundays, a special bus, marked 'T', runs to Tokarnia four times a day (3zł), departing from various bus stops around the centre. Check in with the Regional Tourist Information Centre (p170) for precise information on timetables and stops.

🎆 Festivals & Events

Days of Kielce
FAIR

(⊙May/Jun) Kielce has an active social calendar year-round, but the best fest by far is the annual Days of Kielce, which takes place every year in late May or June over the weekend of the Corpus Christi holiday. The whole town shuts down for four days of street food, live music and general merriment.

🛏 Sleeping

★ Hostel-Art
HOSTEL €

(☑41 344 6617; www.hostel-art-kielce.pl; ul Sienkiewicza 4c; s/d/tr 79/118/147zł; @🛜) This

design-conscious hostel is more boutique hotel than student flophouse, though rates are much lower than what you'd pay for a comparable room at a hotel. There are no multibed dorm rooms, rather there's a small number of private singles, doubles and triples (though baths are shared). A common kitchen will make self-caterers happy, and everything is spotlessly clean.

Hotel Śródmiejski
HOTEL €

(☑41 344 1507; www.hotelsrodmiejski.pl; ul Wesoła 5; s/d/tr 130/150/170zł; P@🛜) Every town should be so lucky as to have a small, family-run hotel so close to the action, yet still reasonably priced. Don't be put off by the run-down street – the hotel is clean and secure. The rooms are large and tastefully furnished; some have balconies out over the street. The room price includes breakfast and parking.

Hotel Pod Złotą Różą
HOTEL €€

(☑41 341 5002; www.zlotaroza.pl; Plac Moniuszki 7; s/d 200/280zł, ste 400-600zł; P@🛜) The small but meticulously refurbished rooms shine with a rich brown finish and are good value for money. There's no unnecessary ostentation here; it's just a compact, stylish place with an elegant restaurant.

Kielce

Ibis Hotel HOTEL €€

(☎ 41 340 6900; www.ibis.com; ul Warszawska 19; s/d 139/169zł; P@🛜) Kielce has the distinction of being home to Poland's cheapest Ibis chain hotel. This paired with the fact that the hotel opened a few years ago means excellent value in what still feels like a new hotel. The rooms are small and boxy, but clean and well appointed. Breakfast costs an extra 30zł and parking 15zł, which can jack up prices quickly.

🍴 Eating

Finding good food in Kielce is surprisingly hard for such a large city. The main drag, ul Sienkiewicza, is lined with kebab joints and pizza places, but little of any substance. The refurbished Rynek (town square) is worth a look.

★ Calimero Cafe CAFE €€

(☎ 519 820 320; www.calimerocafe.pl; ul Solna 4a; mains 20-25zł; ☺10am-10pm; 🛜) Plan to lunch at this casual bakery and cafe that specialises in healthy, delicious soups, sandwiches and salads, including our favourite: the house salad with dried ham, goat's cheese and pomegranate seeds. It serves homemade lemonade, green smoothies and just-baked breads and cakes. One of a kind and one of the best places for light, simple meals in this part of Poland.

Siesta Ristorante e Bar ITALIAN €€

(☎ 41 341 5426; Rynek 12; mains 25zł; ☺10am-11pm Sun-Thu, to 2am Fri & Sat) This little pizza and ice-cream joint is a good choice in a city with few decent dining options. Great wood-fired pizzas (our favourite is the 'classic': just tomato sauce and mozzarella, topped with fresh basil), but there are also good pastas, salads, and meat and fish dishes. Eat on the Rynek in fine weather.

Si Señor SPANISH €€€

(☎ 41 341 1151; www.si-senor.pl; ul Kozia 3; mains 35-50zł; ☺noon-10pm Mon-Sat, to 7pm Sun; 🛜) Arguably Kielce's best restaurant, with an intimate, upscale dining room of brown leather chairs, subdued lighting and dark walls. The Spanish-influenced menu is strongest on fish and seafood, though there are a couple of good steaks. The wine list, heavy on Spanish labels, is the best in Kielce. There's a small terrace out front.

🍷 Drinking & Entertainment

CKM BAR

(☎ 41 344 7959; www.ckm.kielce.com; ul Bodzentyńska 2; ☺2pm-1am Sun-Thu, to 3am Fri & Sat; 🛜) CKM is something between a club, a pub, a lounge and a cafe. It draws a mostly student-aged crowd for a night of foosball, pool, drinking and chit-chat.

Galery Café BEER GARDEN

(☎ 41 341 5223; ul Zamkowa 2; ☺10am-late) Popular beer garden located at the tail end of Zamkowa toward the park. Fetch a Lech at the bar and then find a picnic table outside.

Dom Środowisk Twórczych LIVE MUSIC

(☎ 41 368 2054; www.palacykzielinskiego.pl; ul Zamkowa 5; ☺11am-11pm) One of the best music venues in town, offering temporary exhibitions and live music (depending on the night, from classical to rock and jazz) in a resplendent but relaxed open-air space in a backyard garden. There's also a decent restaurant and cafe here.

ℹ Information

There are plenty of *kantors* on ul Sienkiewicza. The main post office is next to the train station, and there's another on Sienkiewicza.

Bank Pekao (ul Sienkiewicza 18; ⊙8am-6pm Mon-Fri, 10am-2pm Sun) Advances on Visa and MasterCard; 24-hour ATM.

Regional Tourist Information Centre (ROT Świętokrzyskie; ☑41 348 0060; www.swietokrzyskie.travel; ul Sienkiewicza 29; ⊙9am-6pm Mon-Fri, to 5pm Sat & Sun) Impressively helpful tourist office in a remodelled space in the centre of town.

ℹ Getting There & Away

BUS

Kielce is home to what is arguably Poland's coolest **bus station** (ul Czarnowska 12) – a retro-futuristic, UFO-shaped building that dates from the 1970s. Unfortunately, the station is partially closed and awaiting an uncertain fate. In the meantime, some intercity bus services are operating from temporary stops around the station. Your best bet is to check in with the Regional Tourist Information Centre (p170), which can advise on transport.

Buses to Święty Krzyż (5zł, one hour, four daily) leave between 6.45am and 3.40pm; to Łódź (30zł, 3½ hours, around 10 daily) between 6am and 8.20pm; to Sandomierz (20zł, two hours, 10 daily) between 7am and 7.40pm; and to Kraków (25zł, 2½ hours, 13 daily) between 2am and 5.35pm.

Polski Bus (www.polskibus.com) runs to Kraków (20zł, two hours, 10 daily), Radom (14zł, one hour, six daily), Warsaw (20zł, three hours, eight daily), and a handful of other cities. Consult the website for tickets and bus departure points in Kielce.

TRAIN

The train station (the key landmark at the western end of ul Sienkiewicza) services many destinations. There are around 15 trains per day to Radom (26zł, two hours), which continue on to Warsaw (40zł, 3½ hours); several to Kraków (35zł, three hours); four to Lublin (45zł, three hours); and five to Częstochowa (30zł, 1½ hours).

Świętokrzyski National Park

The 60 sq km **Świętokrzyski National Park** (Świętokrzyski Park Narodowy; ☑41 311 5106; www.swietokrzyskipn.org.pl) covers a stretch of low-lying hills known as the Świętokrzyski Mountains. It offers the perfect full-day, back-to-nature respite from urban Kielce. This is Poland's oldest mountainous geological formation (and lowest, due to erosion over more than 300 million years). Unusual piles of broken *gołoborza* (quartzite rock) on the northern slopes hint at how ancient this mountain range is.

The most popular activity is hiking, and ambitious visitors usually opt to follow the ancient pilgrimage route from the town of Nowa Słupia to a Benedictine monastery high in the hills at Święty Krzyż (Holy Cross) and then continue onward to the hamlet of Święta Katarzyna. The trail, of moderate difficulty, runs about 18km and takes from six to seven hours to complete.

◉ Sights

Benedictine Monastery
of Holy Cross   MONASTERY
(Święty Krzyż; ☑41 317 7021; www.swietykrzyz.pl; Święty Krzyż 1) This hilltop monastery got its name from the segment of Jesus' cross that was supposedly kept here. The abbey is at the top of Łysa Góra (595m) – the second-highest peak in the Świętokrzyski range after Łysica (612m). It has a fascinating history going back nearly a millennium. Most sources estimate it was built in the 11th century on an 8th- and 9th-century pagan worship site.

In more recent times, with the abolition of the Benedictine Order by the Russians in 1819, the abbey was converted into a prison. After a brief period of restoration, under Nazi Germany the buildings were reconverted into prisons. The Gestapo tortured many monks here before transporting them to Auschwitz-Birkenau, and many Soviet prisoners of war were executed and buried in mass graves near the peak. Under communism, the abbey was transferred to the national park and renovations commenced.

Holy Cross Church   CHURCH
(Bazylika na Świętym Krzyżu; ☑41 317 7021; www.swietkrzyz.pl; Święty Krzyż 1; crypts adult/concession 3/2zł; ⊙9am-5pm Mon-Sat, noon-5pm Sun & holidays) The Holy Cross Church in the Benedictine Monastery of Holy Cross (p170) was rebuilt several times over the years. The present-day church and its mainly neoclassical interior date to the late 18th century. In addition to the church, you can also take a peek at the crypts, where you'll see the mummified remains of nobleman Jeremi Michal Korybut, who died in 1651 at the ripe old age of 39.

Museum of the Holy Cross Ancient Metallurgy
MUSEUM
(Muzeum Starożytnego Hutnictwa Świętokrzyskiego; ☑690 900 871; www.mtip.pl; ul Świętokrzyska 59, Nowa Słupia; adult/concession 6/3zł; ⊙9am-5pm) Although it may not look like it, the area around the Świętokrzyski National Park is home to the largest ancient metallurgical centre discovered in Europe to date. This museum was established on the site of primitive 2nd-century smelting furnaces *(dymarki)* discovered in 1955. The entrance to the museum is about 300m from the national park gate, just outside the village of Nowa Słupia.

📩 Sleeping

The tourist information centre in Nowa Słupia can help find agroturist accommodation.

Youth Hostel
HOSTEL €
(Szkolne Schronisko Młodzieżowe w Nowej Słupi; ☑41 317 7016; ul Świętokrzyska 61, Nowa Słupia; dm 25zł, d 40-50zł) This hostel in Nowa Słupia is well tended and has 60 beds in double and dorm rooms. The location is convenient for entering the national park.

Jodłowy Dwór
HOTEL €€
(☑41 302 5028; www.jodlowydwor.com.pl; Huta Szklana 34; d/tr 160/210zł; 🅿🛜) Though the exterior looks more like a modern housing estate, this faux rustic lodge in a village along the road between Święty Krzyż and Święta Katarzyna offers arguably the best digs in the immediate area. There's a garden with a playground and a decent in-house restaurant.

❶ Information

There is a small **tourist information centre** (Informacja Turystyczna; ☑41 317 7626; www. nowaslupia.pl; ul Świętokrzyska 18, Nowa Słupia; ⊙9am-4pm Tue-Thu, to 5pm Fri, 10am-4pm Sat, to 2pm Sun) about 500m from the entrance to the national park, which has hiking maps and can offer advice and brochures on places to stay.

❶ Getting There & Away

The park is 25km east of Kielce. Buses leave every hour or so from Kielce to Święta Katarzyna (7zł, 30 minutes) roughly between 5am and 7pm, with some stopping at Święty Krzyż on the way. To get to Nowa Słupia (7zł, one hour), take a bus bound for either Jeziórko or Rudki (around 10 per day until 6pm or so).

There are frequent buses from both Nowa Słupia (7zł, one hour) and Święta Katarzyna (7zł, 30 minutes) back to Kielce, but from Święty Krzyż there are buses only every few hours.

THE SANDOMIERZ VALLEY

The Sandomierz Valley (Kotlina Sandomierska) covers an extensive area in and around the fork of the Vistula and San Rivers. In the heart of the valley is the hilltop town of Sandomierz – an underrated gem of Gothic splendour. Nearby are the fantastic fairytale ruins of Ujazd castle.

Sandomierz
POP 24,330
Tourists really should be rolling down the sloping Rynek of Sandomierz and piling up at the town hall. But the grandeur of the Old Town, with the impressive Gothic town hall propped upright in its centre, remains relatively undiscovered. Immaculate buildings painted warming hues of brown, orange and yellow, many festooned with elegant wrought-iron balconies, line the lanes as locals nonchalantly wander by, apparently oblivious to their good fortune in not being overrun by hordes of visitors.

History

No one is certain of precisely when Sandomierz came to life, but as far back as the 11th century the town was classified (by chronicler Gall Anonim) as a major settlement of the Polish kingdom, along with Kraków and Wrocław.

In the 13th century repeated assaults by Tatar raiders meant that Sandomierz had to be resurrected several times, most significantly in 1260 when it was rebuilt uphill at the site it occupies today. During the reign of Kazimierz III Wielki (1333–70), Sandomierz became a significant trade hub and saw the construction of the Royal Castle, Opatów Gate and town hall. The town prospered until the mid-17th century, which saw both the arrival of the Jesuits and the invasion of the Swedes – an onslaught from which it never completely recovered.

After having survived WWII with its historic architecture relatively unscathed, the next threat came in the 1960s when the town's most significant buildings started sliding into the river. The soft silt on which Sandomierz is built (and from which its underground cellars were carved) began to give way, necessitating a large-scale rescue operation. The injection of concrete and steel into the slippery soil stabilised the

MAŁOPOLSKA SANDOMIERZ

365 REASONS NOT TO BE MARTYRED

The interiors of Sandomierz **cathedral** give a pleasant first impression, but focus on the details beyond the initial ostentation and you discover the macabre side of Sandomierz.

The paintings on the walls of the cathedral are by 18th-century artist Karol de Prevot (1708–37), who was apparently not of a cheery disposition. The four paintings on the back wall under the organ depict historic scenes such as the 1656 destruction of Sandomierz castle by the Swedes. But it is the series of 12 paintings on the side walls that are a real argument for checking ID at the cathedral's door.

The series, *Martyrologium Romanum,* depicts the martyrdom of the Dominican Fathers and other people of Sandomierz at the hands of the Tatars between 1259 and 1260. The unfortunate subjects are being sawn, burned, hanged, whipped, quartered, sliced, diced and otherwise discourteously treated.

The 12 paintings are supposed to symbolise the 12 months of the year; next to each image of torture a number represents the day of the month. Legend has it that if you find the day and month on which you were born, you'll discover how you're going to die. Let's hope not.

city and securely tethered its architectural assets.

◉ Sights & Activities

Sandomierz's market square (Rynek), distinctive for its earthen tones and slope, is ringed with houses from different stylistic periods. Today, only Nos 10 and 27 have the arcades typical of 16th-century houses. The red rectangular **Town Hall**, erected in the 14th century, is the oldest building on the Rynek; the white **Clock Tower** was added in the 17th century, and the sundial on the southern wall (the work of Tadeusz Przypkowski) in 1958. Both are closed to the public.

Knights' Armoury   MUSEUM
(Zbrojownia; ☏728 382 531; www.rycerstwo. sandomierskie.pl; Rynek 5; adult/concession 7/5zł; ☺10am-4pm) This small exhibition of medieval armour, weaponry and torture instruments is actually a lot more fun than it seems at first glance. Unlike many similar types of museums, you're not only allowed to touch and photograph the objects, you can try them on if you want. The exhibition's director, Lukas, is a fount of knowledge on the subject and happy to demonstrate how the weapons were used.

Opatów Gate   GATE
(Brama Opatowska; www.sandomierz.travel; ul Opatowska; adult/concession 4/3zł; ☺9am-7pm) The main entrance to the Old Town, and the only surviving gate of the four originally built, is 14th-century Opatów Gate. You can climb to the viewing platform at the top for a pleasant (though by no means bird's-eye) view of surrounding terrain.

Cathedral   CHURCH
(☏15 832 7343; www.katedra.sandomierz.org; ul Mariacka; ☺9am-6pm Tue-Sun, closed Mon) Built between 1360 and 1382, this massive church has retained much of its Gothic exterior, apart from the Baroque facade added in the 17th century. The Russo-Byzantine frescoes in the chancel were painted in the 1420s but later whitewashed. They were only revealed again at the beginning of the 20th century. Also note the impressive Baroque organ gallery of the late 17th century, the marble altar dating to the 18th century, and the rather macabre paintings on the interior walls (p172).

Diocesan Museum   MUSEUM
(Muzeum Diecezjalne; ☏15 832 2304; www. domdlugosza.sandomierz.org; ul Długosza 9; adult/concession 6/3zł; ☺9am-4.30pm Tue-Sat & 1.30-4.30pm Sun Apr-Oct, 9am-3.30pm Tue-Sat & 1.30-3.30pm Sun Nov-Mar) The quintessential example of Sandomierz's underrated assets, the medieval **Długosz House** (Dom Długosza) was built in 1476 for Poland's first historian, Jan Długosz. Today it houses the Diocesan Museum, with a rich collection of medieval artwork, sculpture, tapestries, clothing, coins and ceramics.

Royal Castle and Regional Museum CASTLE
(Muzeum Okręgowe – Zamek; ☏15 832 2265; www.zamek-sandomierz.pl; ul Zamkowa 12; adult/ concession 10/6zł, Mon free; ☺1.30-3pm Mon, 10am-5pm Tue-Sun) The Royal Castle was built

in the 14th century on the site of a previous wooden stronghold and was gradually extended during the next three centuries. It now accommodates the regional museum, which contains modest ethnographic, archaeological and art collections.

Underground Tourist Route TOUR
(Podziemna Trasa Turystyczna; ☑15 832 3088; ul Oleśnickich; adult/concession 10/6zł; ☉10am-6pm) A 40-minute guided tour (in Polish) leads through a chain of 30-odd cellars tidily connected over 500m, beneath the Old Town. The cellars – originally used for storage and sometimes for shelter during times of conflict – were built between the 13th and 17th centuries. The deepest point is about 12m below ground, but it feels like more, because of disorienting twists, turns and Escher-esque staircases.

🛏 Sleeping

In addition to Sandomierz' hotels, there are several houses on side streets around the Rynek offer private rooms. Some of the best are on pretty ul Forteczna, a cobblestoned lane just behind the Rynek. Try **Zielone Wzgórze** (☑519 182 376; ul Forteczna 6; per person 50-60zł; ℗) or **Willa na Skarpie** (☑665 445 180; www.naskarpie.nocowanie.pl; ul Forteczna 8; per person 50-60zł; ℗🖤)

Jutrzenka PENSION€
(☑15 832 2219; ul Zamkowa 1; s/d/tr 60/100/120zł; ℗) You'll find the cheapest rooms in town at the back of this small, private home, just up from the castle and about five minutes' walk southwest of the Rynek following ul Zamkowa. There are few facilities, but the rooms themselves are freshly painted, clean, and filled with country bric-a-brac.

Hotel Basztowy HOTEL €€
(☑15 833 3450; www.hotelbasztowy.pl; pl Ks J Poniatowskiego 2; s/d/ste 200/240/450zł; ℗@🖤) The refined Basztowy is prime splurge material, catering both to business types and holidaymakers. Added touches including a spa and billiard room. The lobby feels fresh and welcoming; rooms are simple, and filled with elegant touches such as early modernist ceiling lamps. The breakfast buffet has seldom-seen extras such as mozzarella with tomato slices. It's a two-minute walk southwest of the Rynek, following ul Zamkowa.

Hotel Pod Ciżemką HOTEL €€
(☑15 832 0550; www.hotelcizemka.pl; Rynek 27; s/d/ste 250/270/350zł; ℗🖤) Pod Ciżemką is the grandest place in the Old Town and has been extensively refurbished. Set in a 400-year-old house with a perch over the main square, the stylish rooms are commendable renditions of old-world elegance, as is the on-site restaurant. Note there's no elevator, making this a slog if you're physically impaired or carrying lots of luggage.

🍴 Eating & Drinking
The Rynek is lined with places to eat and drink, so walk around and see what looks good.

Café Mała CREPERIE €
(☑602 102 225; ul Sokolnickiego 3; mains 15-25zł; ☉8.30am-9pm Mon-Thu, to 10pm Fri-Sun; 🖤☑) This cosy, French Provincial style cafe just around the corner from the Rynek is perfect for a cup of coffee or a small meal such as a salad or savoury crêpe. Even if you don't eat a full meal here, stop by for arguably the only real cup of coffee in town and a scrumptious dessert: strawberry shortcake, perhaps?

⭐Lapidarium pod Ratuszem BURGERS €€
(☑787 646 484; Rynek 1; mains 15-30zł; ☉11.30am-10pm; 🖤) Grilled meats, big salad plates, craft beers and very good burgers are the major draw cards at this cheery restaurant and cafe located in the town hall tower. Dine right on the Rynek during the summer, though try to time your arrival outside of usual meal times (or book in advance) as this place gets crowded.

Restauracja Trzydziestka '30' POLISH €€
(☑15 644 5312; Rynek 30; mains 20-30zł; ☉10am-11pm) This Rynek favourite offers a welcome, simple menu of meat dishes made from chicken, pork and beef, with sides of rice, potatoes or buckwheat groats.

Café Bar Kordegarda CAFE
(☑602 102 225; Rynek 12; ☉9.30am-11.30pm; 🖤) This trendy cafe and restaurant offers drinks on the terrace overlooking the Rynek, plus a mix of salads and light food options. Service can be hit or miss, so feel free to take your order to the bar. Summer evenings, the terrace is the place to be for drinks and people watching.

Iluzjon Art Cafe CAFE
(☑883 121 416; www.iluzjoncafe.pl; Rynek 25/26; ☉8am-11pm Mon-Thu, 10am-midnight Sat & Sun; 🖤) This cafe on the Rynek serves excellent homemade lemonade, as well as coffees and teas, and an enticing range of cakes and ice

WORTH A TRIP

CRAZY KRZYŻTOPÓR CASTLE

The small village of Ujazd (oo-yahst), around 30km west of Sandomierz, is home to arguably Poland's most bizarre ruin. **Krzyżtopór Castle** (☑15 860 1133; www.krzyztopor. org.pl; Ujazd 73; adult/concession 10/6zł; ⊙8am-8pm Apr-Oct, to 4pm Nov-Mar) was commissioned by eccentric governor Krzysztof Ossoliński and built according to his fantastic imagination, incorporating his love of magic and astrology, among other things. These days visitors are free to walk the grounds, climb the turrets, and marvel at what must have been one enormous manor.

The architect commissioned to create Ossoliński's dream was Italian Lorenzo Muretto (known in Poland as Wawrzyniec Senes), who worked on the mammoth project between 1631 and 1644.

History and legend offer zany accounts of the castle. It was designed to embody a calendar, with four towers representing the four seasons, 12 halls for the 12 months of the year, 52 rooms for the 52 weeks, and 365 windows for 365 days – plus one to be used only during leap years. Some cellars were used as stables for Ossoliński's 370 white stallions, and are adorned with mirrors and black marble. The crystal ceiling of the great dining hall is believed to have been the base of an enormous aquarium.

Perhaps the most enchanting report is the one concerning the tunnel that ran under the manor, linking it to the castle of Ossoliński's brother. The 15km tunnel to Ossolin was believed to have been covered with sugar so the two brothers could visit each other on horse-drawn sledges, pretending they were travelling on snow.

Sadly, Ossoliński was barely able to enjoy a full calendar year in his playground; he died in 1645, only a year after the castle was completed.

After damage done by the Swedes in the 1650s and the abandonment of the castle by its subsequent owners in 1770, this dreamland fell to ruin. Since WWII, talk of converting the castle into a military school or hotel has petered out, leaving Krzyżtopór Castle as a landscape for the daydreams of its visitors.

cream sundaes. The retro interior is about as trendy as it gets in sleepy Sandomierz.

❶ Information

➸ The **Tourist Information Centre** (Centrum Informacja Turystyczne; ☑15 644 6105; www. sandomierz.travel; Rynek 20; ⊙9am-6pm Mon-Fri, 10am-4pm Sat & Sun May-Sep, 9am-4pm Mon-Fri Oct-Apr) is a gold mine of helpful information and offers a free simple map of the Old Town.

➸ There is a *kantor* in the **post office** (Rynek 10). The PKO Bank Polski a couple doors away has an ATM. There are also *kantors* on ul Mickiewicza close to the corner of ul 11 Listopada, about 1km northwest of the Old Town.

❶ Getting There & Away

BUS

➸ The **PKS bus terminal** (☑15 833 2614; www. pks.tarnobrzeg.pl; ul Listopada 22) is 1.5km northwest of the Old Town.

➸ There are a dozen fast buses daily to Warsaw (40zł, four hours), and regular buses to Kielce (18zł, two hours) and Lublin (20zł, two hours).

➸ There are regional buses to Tarnobrzeg (4zł, 30 minutes, every half-hour), which is a good

hub for more distant coach services. For Ujazd, change at Opatów (7zł, 45 minutes, hourly, 30km) or Klimontów.

THE RADOM PLAIN

The Radom Plain (Równina Radomska) extends between Małopolska to the south and Mazovia in the north. This gentle area is seldom visited by tourists, but Radom city is a pleasant enough place to decamp for the night, and one of the most expansive skansens (open-air museums of traditional architecture) in Małopolska is just outside the city.

Radom

POP 217,200

Radom is a large industrial city that offers few traditional attractions for visitors. That said, its main pedestrian thoroughfare, ul Żeromskiego, is unexpectedly charming and a lovely place for lunch and a stroll. Radom lies astride one of the country's most important rail connections, linking Kraków and Warsaw, and as such is a convenient stopover point.

⊙ Sights

Church of St John the Baptist CHURCH
(Kościół Świętego Jana Chrzciciela; ☑ 48 362 3806; www.fara.radom.pl; Rwańska 6; ⊙8am-6pm) The main parish church, the Church of St John the Baptist, was founded by Kazimierz III Wielki in 1360 and altered by numerous people up to the present. The church is located just near the Rynek.

St Wenceslaus Church CHURCH
(Kościół Świętego Wacława; ☑ 48 362 6851; www.waclaw.radom.pl; Plac Stare Miasto 13; ⊙8am-6pm) The most significant relic of Radom's earliest years is St Wenceslaus Church in what was once Radom's Old Town Square. Built originally in the 13th century from wood, it was the first parish church of Old Radom. It was used for various purposes (such as a military hospital and psychiatric ward) and completely restored in the 1970s – sadly stripping away any sense of the church's history. It's located southwest of the Rynek.

Radom Village Museum MUSEUM
(Muzeum Wsi Radomskiej; ☑ 48 332 9281; www.muzeum-radom.pl; ul Szydłowiecka 30; adult/concession 10/6zł; ⊙9am-5pm Tue-Fri, 10am-8pm Sat & Sun) One of the most popular outings is the short hop to this outdoor folklore museum about 8km from the centre. Furnished interiors showcase styles from the whole region. City bus 14 or 17 will get you within a few hundred metres of the entrance. Returning to Radom, turn left back onto the highway; the bus stop is in a small side street 20m or so past a turn-off.

⊨ Sleeping

There's not much in the way of budget accommodation in Radom, but there are ample moderately priced hotels not far from the train and bus stations.

Rynek 6 Hostel & Retro Pub GUESTHOUSE €
(☑ 693 602 482; www.rynek6.radom.pl; Rynek 6; s/d/tr 100/120/160zł; P🤶) Not a hostel in a traditional sense – though one room has bunk beds – the Rynek 6 is more akin to a guesthouse or even boutique hotel, given the attention to cleanliness, the stylish, traditional room decor and the high-thread-count cottons on the beds. The property is located in one of the few renovated buildings on Radom's gritty, but gentrifying, Rynek.

Hotel Iskra HOTEL €
(☑ 48 363 8745; www.hoteliskra.radom.pl; ul Planty 4; s/d 100/150zł; P🤶) Just a couple of minutes' walk from the train station, the Iskra is a revitalised former-communist-era structure that offers bright, well-maintained rooms big enough to stretch out in.

Hotel Gromada HOTEL €€
(☑ 48 368 9100; www.gromada.pl; ul Narutowicza 9; s/d 160/200zł, apt 260-300zł; P@🤶) This generic business hotel has spacious rooms and an on-site restaurant and bar. Apartments are reasonable value given their terrace and kitchen annex. Another branch is located 2.5km west of the town centre.

✕ Eating

Pleasant eateries line ul Żeromskiego. One of Poland's best **zapiekanka** (☑ 48 366 9517; ul Moniuszki 16; sandwiches 6zł; ⊙10am-8pm) stands, specialising in oven-baked, open-faced baguettes, is located nearby.

★ Pivovaria PUB FOOD €€
(☑ 48 384 8878; www.pivovaria.pl; ul Moniuszki 26; mains 20-40zł; ⊙11am-midnight; 🤶) Don't be put off by the 'pub food' label – this is Radom's best restaurant, and it even brews its own (very good) beer on the premises. The menu tends toward simple grilled meats, pastas, salads and a few Polish treats, such as *pierogi* (stuffed dumplings), and most items are cooked with uncommon care. The cellar dining room is clean and bright.

Teatralna ITALIAN €€
(☑ 48 363 7763; www.teatralna.radom.pl; ul Żeromskiego 55; mains 20-40zł; ⊙noon-10pm Sun-Thu, to 11pm Fri & Sat) This handsome restaurant has something for everyone. The cooking leans toward Mediterranean, but in addition to the usual offerings of pizza and pasta, you'll find fish, duck, and our favourite: braised pork loin served in mushroom sauce with a side of spinach and pine nuts.

Olivio ITALIAN €€
(☑ 48 363 6300; www.restauracjaolivio.pl; ul Żeromskiego 17; mains 20-35zł; ⊙noon-10pm Sun-Thu, to 11pm Fri & Sat) This ambitious Italian cafe/restaurant on the main drag offers creative takes on traditional dishes in a casual yet upscale setting. Start with fried chicken livers in a raspberry sauce, and then move on to pasta or beefsteak. Eat on the streetside terrace in summer.

JEWISH RADOM

Radom was a significant Jewish settlement, and the Jewish community here numbered around 30,000 just before WWII (about a quarter of the population). Unfortunately, few Jews survived the war and little of that heritage remains. Most Jews lived in the area around the (now very dilapidated) Rynek. Near here, you'll find four stones and a small memorial that mark where the main **synagogue** (cnr uls Bóżnicza & Podwalna) once stood.

About 4km east of the city centre is what remains of the former Jewish **cemetery** (ul Towarowa). The Germans destroyed the cemetery and used the grave markers as paving stones, but in the past decade some of the tombstones have been returned. The gate is usually locked and there's not much to see, but the tourist office may be able to arrange a viewing.

ⓘ Information

There are plenty of *kantors* and ATMs along ul Żeromskiego.

Post Office (☑ 48 362 7347; www.radom. poczta-online.com/ul-jacka-malczewskiego-5; ul Jacka Malczewskiego 5; ⊙ 8am-8pm Mon-Fri, to 2pm Sat)

Tourist Office (☑ 48 360 0610; www.cit. radom.pl; ul Traugutta 3; ⊙ 10am-5pm Mon-Fri, 11am-1pm Sat) Situated in a kiosk, three minutes by foot from the train station. Look for the free booklet *A Walk Around Radom* in English.

ⓘ Getting There & Away

The train and bus stations are next to each other, 2km south of ul Żeromskiego.

BUS

There's a small minibus lot in front of the train station, with frequent minibus service to Warsaw (20zł, 2½ hours). Most big buses bound for Warsaw and Kraków (25zł to 30zł, three hours, 175km) depart in the afternoon. There are five buses leaving for Łódź (20zł, 3½ hours, 135km) between 6am and 6.30pm, as well as a couple of daily buses to Lublin (15zł, 2½ hours) and Puławy (10zł, 1½ hours).

TRAIN

Radom lies on a major north–south train line. Around a dozen trains go to Warsaw daily (25zł, 2½ hours, 100km), and six or so to Kraków (35zł, 3½ hours, 175km). Kraków-bound trains stop in Kielce (25zł, 1½ hours, 85km). Two trains head to Lublin daily (1½ hours), and at least one to Wrocław (four hours). For more information, ask at the information counter (6am to 10pm) in the train station.

THE LUBLIN UPLAND

Stretching east of the Vistula and San Rivers up to the Ukrainian border is the Lublin Upland (Wyżyna Lubelska). Lublin, its biggest city, still bears the scars of WWII, but carries itself with dignity. The area also boasts Kazimierz Dolny, a quaint town on the banks of the Vistula that attracts weekenders looking to escape the city – and the 21st century. Also worth visiting is the town of Zamość and the nearby village of Zwierzyniec, both built on the Renaissance dreams of nobleman Jan Zamoyski.

Lublin

POP 341,700

Lublin is the largest city in southeastern Poland, with a thriving cultural and academic scene. It offers the usual amenities of any city this size, including decent hotels, restaurants and nightlife. It's also a main transport hub, with excellent road and rail connections to all parts of Poland.

That said, it's not a looker. Lublin was ravaged during WWII and the forced industrialisation of the communist period added insult to injury. Nevertheless, the city's historic core, the Rynek, is slowly being gentrified, and trendy clubs and restaurants are giving new lustre to the centre's impressive stock of Renaissance and Baroque town houses.

Lublin is of special interest to travellers seeking Poland's Jewish past. For centuries the city was a leading centre of Jewish scholarship, giving rise to Lublin's nickname the 'Jewish Oxford'. That heritage came to a brutal end in WWII, but here and there you can still find traces.

History

Though Lublin feels a little marginalised these days, located in the extreme east of the country, for centuries it played a central role in Polish history. On three separate occasions it was Poland's de facto capital, at least temporarily.

In 1569 it was here in Lublin that the union between the Polish and Lithuanian

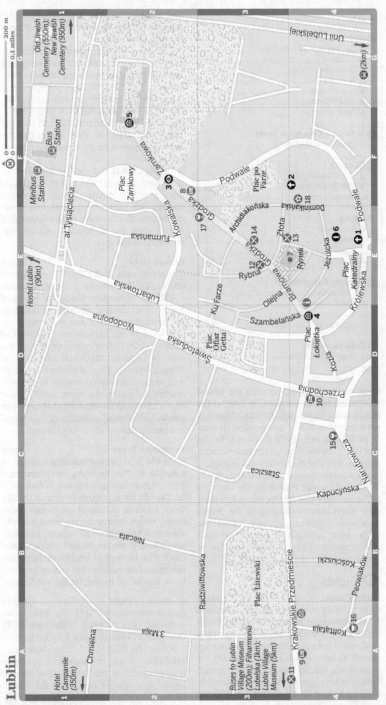

Lublin

MAŁOPOLSKA

0 — 200 m
0 — 0.1 miles

Hotel Campanile (350m)

Chmielna

Old Jewish Cemetery (550m);
New Jewish Cemetery (950m)

Unii Lubelskiej

(2km)

Bus Station

Minibus Station

al. Tysiąclecia

Plac Zamkowy

Zamkowa

Furmańska

Kowalska

Grodzka

Podwale

Plac po Farze

Dominikańska

18

2

Archidiakońska

17

8

Złota

14

13

6

1

Hostel Lublin (90m)

Lubartowska

Wodopojna

Świętoduska

Plac Ofiar Getta

Ku Farze

Rybna

Grodzka

Bramowa

7

Rynek

Jezuicka

Plac Katedralny

Królewska

Podwale

Olejna

Szambelańska

Plac Łokietka

4

Przechodnia

Kozia

10

Staszica

15

Narutowicza

Kapucyńska

Niecała

Radziwiłłowska

Plac Litewski

Buses to Lublin
Village Museum (200m); Filharmonia
Lubelska (1km);
Lublin Village
Museum (5km)

3 Maja

Krakowskie Przedmieście

Kołłątaja

16

Peowiaków

Kościuszki

9

11

Lublin

kingdoms was signed, creating the largest state in Europe at the time. In 1918, at the end of WWI, Lublin was the site of the first government of newly independent Poland. In 1944, at the end of WWII, it was in Lublin that the first provisional communist government installed by the Soviets was housed.

On a more sombre note, in 1941, during WWII, Lublin was chosen by the Germans as the headquarters for Operation Reinhard, their secret plan to exterminate the Jewish population of German-occupied Poland. Two of the most infamous Operation Reinhard extermination camps, Sobibór and Bełżec (p182), lie within an hour's drive of Lublin.

◉ Sights

Lublin Castle MUSEUM
(☏81 532 5001; www.zamek-lublin.pl; ul Zamkowa 9; adult/concession museum 6.50/4.50zł, chapel 6.50/4.50zł; ☺10am-5pm Tue-Sun) Lublin's royal castle dates from the 12th and 13th centuries, though it's been rebuilt many times over the years. It was here in 1569 that the union with Lithuania was signed. The castle is home to both the **Lublin Museum** and the surviving

Gothic Chapel of the Holy Trinity, which dates from the 14th century. Each requires a separate entry ticket.

The museum's permanent collection features mainly art, folk art and weaponry. The 14th-century chapel is considered a masterpiece of the Middle Ages, with Russian-Byzantine-inspired frescos. Painted in 1418, only to be later plastered over, they were rediscovered in 1897 and painstakingly restored over a 100-year period. These are possibly the finest examples of medieval wall paintings in the country.

During WWII the occupying German army used the castle as a prison, holding as many as 40,000 inmates. The darkest day of the war here came in July 1944, just ahead of the prison's liberation by the Soviet Red Army, when the Germans executed 300 prisoners on the spot.

Kraków Gate MUSEUM
(Brama Krakowska; ☏81 532 6001; www.muzeumlubelskie.pl; Plac Łokietka 3; adult/concession 5.50/4.50zł; ☺9am-4pm Wed-Sat, to 5pm Sun) The only significant surviving remnant of the fortified walls that once surrounded the Old Town is the 14th-century Gothic-style Kraków Gate. It was conceived during the reign of Kazimierz III Wielki following the Mongol attack in 1341. It received its octagonal Renaissance superstructure in the 16th century, and its Baroque crown in 1782. These days it's home to the **Historical Museum of Lublin** and its small collection of documents and photographs of the town's history.

Trinitarian Tower TOWER
(☏81 444 7450; www.archidiecezjalubelska.pl; ul Królewska 10, Plac Katedralny; adult/concession 7/5zł; ☺10am-5pm daily Mar-Nov, to 5pm Sat & Sun Dec-Feb) For an expansive view of the Old Town, climb to the top of Trinitarian Tower (1819), which houses the underrated **Archdiocesan Museum**. The chaotic layout of artworks in hidden nooks and crannies, combined with the lack of English explanations, means that you can discover ancient artefacts in the haphazard manner of Indiana Jones.

Dominican Priory CHURCH
(Kościół Dominikanów; ☏81 532 8990; www.domikikanie.lub.pl; ul Złota 9; ☺9am-4pm) FREE Originally a Gothic complex founded by King Kazimierz III Wielki in 1342, the Dominican Priority was rebuilt in Renaissance style after it was ravaged by fire in 1575. Two historic highlights inside the church are the Chapel of the Firlej Family (1615), containing family

members' tombstones, and the Tyszkiewicz Chapel (1645–59), with impressive Renaissance stuccowork.

For an insight into 18th-century Lublin, note the large historical painting *The Fire of Lublin*, which depicts a devastating fire of 1719, which destroyed much of the city (in the Szaniawski family chapel to your right as you enter the church).

Cathedral of St John the Baptist CHURCH
(www.diecezja.lublin.pl; Plac Katedralny; ⊙dawn-sunset, treasury 10am-2pm & 3-5pm Tue-Sun) FREE
This former Jesuit church dates from the 16th century and is the largest in Lublin. There are many impressive details to behold, including the Baroque trompe l'oeil frescos (the work of Moravian artist Józef Majer) and the 17th-century altar made from a black Lebanese pear tree. The acoustic vestry (so called for its ability to project whispers) and the treasury *(skarbiec)*, behind the chapel, also merit attention.

The painting of the *Black Madonna* is said to have shed tears in 1945, making it a source of much reverence for local devotees.

◉ Outside the Centre

Lublin Village Museum MUSEUM
(Muzeum Wsi Lubelskiej; ☑81 533 8513; www.skansen.lublin.pl; ul Warszawska 96; adult/concession 10/5zł; ⊙9am-6pm May-Sep, to 5pm Apr & Oct, to 3pm Nov-Mar) The well-designed skansen, 5km west of the centre on the Warsaw road, covers an undulating terrain of 25 hectares. Appearing as a traditional village of numerous buildings with fully equipped interiors, there is a fine manor house, a windmill, an Orthodox church and a carved timber gate (1903) designed by Stanisław Witkiewicz. The skansen hosts various temporary displays and cultural events. To get there from the centre, take bus 18, 20 or 5 from al Racławickie.

Majdanek HISTORIC SITE
(Państwowe Muzeum na Majdanku; ☑81 710 2833; www.majdanek.pl; Droga Męczenników Majdanka 67; admission free; ⊙9am-6pm Apr-Oct, to 4pm Nov-Mar) Four kilometres southeast of the centre of Lublin is the German-Nazi Majdanek extermination camp, where tens of thousands of people, mainly Jews, were murdered during WWII. The Germans went to no effort to conceal Majdanek, as they did at other extermination camps. A 5km walk starts at the visitors centre, passes the foreboding Monument of Fight & Martyrdom, goes through parts of the barracks and finishes at the mausoleum. The camp is accessible by public transport: from the Krakowska Gate, take bus 23.

Coming from the main road, the sudden appearance of time-frozen guard towers and barbed-wire fences interrupting the sprawl of suburbia is disquieting. The details are even more confronting; gas chambers are open to visitors, and many of the prisoners' possessions are on display. Children under 14 are not permitted.

🏃 Activities

One of the most popular activities is a stroll underground below the Rynek, If you'd rather walk above ground, check out one of the city's five self-guided **walking routes** outlined in free brochures available from the tourist office.

Underground Route WALKING TOUR
(☑tour bookings 81 534 6570; Rynek 1; adult/concession 9/7zł; ⊙10am-4pm Tue-Fri, noon-5pm Sat & Sun) This 280m trail winds its way through connected cellars beneath the Old Town, with historical exhibitions along the way. Entry is from the neoclassical Old Town Hall in the centre of the pleasant Market Sq (Rynek) at approximately two-hourly intervals; check with the tourist office for exact times.

🎉 Festivals & Events

As the largest city in eastern Poland, Lublin has an active cultural calendar, with something big (usually related to music or theatre) nearly every month of the year. Check in with the tourist information office.

Codes Festival of Traditional and Avant-Garde Music MUSIC
(www.codes-festival.com; ⊙May) Dedicated to fusing archaic and new strains of music.

Festival of European Neighbours THEATRE
(Festiwal Teatrów Europy Środkowej Sąsiedzi; www.festiwal-sasiedzi.pl; ⊙Jun) Popular theatre fest involving troupes from neighbouring countries.

International Dance Theatres Festival DANCE
(Międzynarodowe Spotkania Teatrów Tańca; www.dancefestival.lublin.pl; ⊙Nov) Attracts modern dance troupes from around Europe.

International Folk Music Festival MUSIC
(Mikołajki Folkowe; www.mikolajki.folk.pl; ⊙Dec) Draws folk musicians from around the world.

THE 'JERUSALEM' OF POLAND

For centuries Lublin served as a centre of European Jewish culture, earning the nickname the 'Jerusalem' of the Polish kingdom. The first mention of Jews living here dates from the 14th century; around the same period they were granted rights by the king to settle in the area below the castle. Jewish historians look back on the 16th and 17th centuries as the high points for the community. The first census in 1550 shows 840 Jews lived in Lublin; 200 years later Lublin had the third-largest Jewish population in Poland. By the time WWII broke out, around a third of the city's 120,000 residents were Jewish.

For centuries, the city's Jews lived in area surrounding Lublin Castle. These days, the area is mostly parking lots and parkland stretching all the way to the bus station. It's hard to imagine that before the German occupation this was a densely populated community filled with streets, shops and houses. The **Grodzka Gate** (Brama Grodzka; ul Grodzka 21) that links the Old Town and the castle area was once called the 'Jewish Gate', as it effectively marked the end of 'Christian' Lublin and the start of the Jewish quarter.

This centuries-old division came to an end with the Nazi occupation of the city on 18 September 1939. The Germans initially moved the Jews into a restricted ghetto made up of part of the traditional Jewish quarter and a relatively small piece of territory marked by today's ul Kowalska and ul Lubartowska. The ghetto was liquidated in 1942, with most of the residents sent to their deaths at the extermination camps at **Bełżec and Sobibór** (p182), and the **Majdanek** (p179) labour camp. Of the approximately 40,000 Jewish Lubliners, only a few hundred survived the Holocaust.

Memories of the Holocaust languished during the communist period, but since 1989, the city has made strides in recognising the contributions of the city's Jews. The tourist office has marked out an extensive tourist route, 'The Heritage Trail of the Lublin Jews'. To appreciate the size of the lost Jewish community, take a walk to the area northeast of the bus station to see both the **Old Jewish Cemetery** (Cmentarz żydowski; cnr uls Kalinowszczyzna & Sienna; ☺ by appointment) and the **New Jewish Cemetery** (ul Walecznych). The old cemetery is surrounded by a high brick wall and the gate is usually locked. Stop by the **tourist office** (p182) to arrange a visit.

The new cemetery was founded in 1829 and is the resting place of 52,000 Jews; Jews were buried here until 1942. The cemetery was destroyed by the Nazis during WWII (who used tombstones in the construction of parts of Majdanek extermination camp). It is still in the process of being restored.

🛏 Sleeping

Hostel Lublin　　　　　　　　　　HOSTEL **€**
(☎792 888 632; www.hostellublin.pl; ul Lubartowska 60; dm/r 40/100zł; ☎) The city's first modern hostel is situated within a former apartment building and contains neat, tidy dorms, a basic kitchenette and a cosy lounge. Take trolleybus 156 or 160 north from the Old Town; after you cross busy al Tysiąclecia, exit at the second stop.

Vanilla Hotel　　　　　　　　　　HOTEL **€€**
(☎81 536 6720; www.vanilla-hotel.pl; ul Krakowskie Przedmieście 12; s 265-330zł, d 315-390zł; P@☎) The name must be tongue-in-cheek. This beautiful boutique, just off the main pedestrian corso, is anything but vanilla. The rooms are filled with inspired, even bold, styling: vibrant colours, big headboards behind the beds, and stylish, retro lamps and furniture. There's lots of attention to detail here, which continues into the chic restaurant and coffee bar. Lower prices on weekends.

Hotel Campanile　　　　　　　　HOTEL **€€**
(☎81 531 8400; www.campanile.com; ul Lubomelska 14/16; s/d 189/249zł; P✳@☎) The clean, quiet rooms at this business-oriented chain are on the dull side, but are good value for money, with niceties such as air-conditioning and a reliable wi-fi connection tossed in at no extra cost. The location, about 1.5km west of the Old Town and a good 15-minute walk away, is a potential drawback. Breakfast costs 35zł. Rates drop on the weekend and big discounts can be found on the hotel website.

Hotel Waksman　　　　　　　　HOTEL **€€**
(☎81 532 5454; www.waksman.pl; ul Grodzka 19; s/d 210/230zł, apt from 290zł; P@☎) Hotel Waksman deserves a blue ribbon for many reasons, not least of which is the atmospher-

ic Old Town location. Each standard room (named 'yellow', 'blue', 'green' or 'red' for its decor) has individual character. The two apartments on top are special; they offer ample space for lounging or working, and views over the Old Town and castle.

IBB Grand Hotel
HOTEL €€€

(☑ 81 446 6100; www.lublinianka.com; ul Krakowskie Przedmieście 56; d/ste from 420/600zł; P❄@🌐🏊) What was the Commercial Chamber of Lublin 100 years ago is now the grandest place to stay in Lublin. The classic foyer of this four-star hotel isn't at all overbearing and the same stylish minimalism translates to the calming pastel rooms. Marble bathrooms in suites include bathtubs, but even the economy guest is entitled to use the Turkish bath and sauna.

✖ Eating

For fine dining in the Old Town, see what's cooking around the Rynek. If you're in a more modern mood, take a walk along ul Krakowskie Przedmieście.

★Kardamon
INTERNATIONAL €€

(☑ 81 448 0257; www.kardamon.eu; ul Krakowskie Przedmiescie 41; mains 30-55zł; ⊙ 11am-10pm; 🌐) By many accounts, Lublin's best restaurant is this lush, cellar affair on the main street. The menu is a mix of international staples such as grilled pork tenderloin, along with Polish favourites such as duck served in cranberry sauce, and some rarer regional specialities. We can't resist the 'gooseneck', a regional dish served with liver stuffing and buckwheat groats.

Złoty Osioł
POLISH €€

(☑ 81 532 9042; ul Grodzka 5a; mains 20-35zł; ⊙ 3pm-midnight; 🌐) Złoty Osioł offers traditional ambience and extraordinarily good-value traditional meals. There are delicious fish dishes, slightly bizarre drink selections (like hot dry wine with jelly), and daily meal sets for the indecisive. The restaurant is set in a candlelit cellar with a cosy, annexed green courtyard. Folk music concerts are occasionally held here.

Mandragora
JEWISH €€

(☑ 81 536 2020; www.mandragora.lublin.pl; Rynek 9; mains 20-40zł; ⊙ noon-10pm; 🌐) There's good kitsch and there's bad kitsch, and at Mandragora, it's all good. Sure they're going for the *Fiddler on the Roof* effect with the lace tablecloths, knick-knacks and photos of old Lublin, but in the romantic Rynek locale,

it works wonderfully. The food is a hearty mix of Polish and Jewish, featuring mains such as goose and duck.

Magia
INTERNATIONAL €€

(☑ 502 598 418; www.magia.lublin.pl; ul Grodzka 2; mains 20-45zł; ⊙ noon-midnight; 🌐) Magia's atmosphere is eclectic; there are numerous vibes to choose from throughout the warren of dining rooms and large outdoor courtyard, with each area decorated with a touch of magic. The chef uses only fresh ingredients to create dishes ranging from tiger shrimps and snails to deer and duck, with every sort of pizza, pasta and pancake in between.

🍷 Drinking & Nightlife

Szklarnia
CAFE

(Centrum Kultury w Lublinie; ☑ 81 466 6140; www.ck.lublin.pl; ul Peowiaków 12; ⊙ 10am-11pm Mon-Fri, noon-midnight Sat & Sun; 🌐) It's not easy finding good coffee in Lublin. This sleek cafe in the recently refurbished Lublin Cultural Centre has great coffee as well as a daily selection of cakes. There's live entertainment some nights, and a nice terrace at the back in warm weather.

Czarna Owca
PUB

(☑ 81 532 4130; www.czarnaowca.lublin.pl; ul Narutowicza 9; ⊙ noon-midnight Sun-Tue, to 5am Wed-Sat) The 'Black Sheep' is a legendary Lublin watering hole, going strong until the wee morning hours from Wednesday to Saturday. In addition to beers and shots of vodka chasers, it has decent pub food, pizzas and toasts to munch on.

U Szewca
IRISH PUB

(Pub; ☑ 81 532 8284; www.uszewca.pl; ul Grodzka 18; mains 19-42zł; ⊙ 9.30am-1am; 🌐) Fun, faux-Irish pub that's right on the Rynek and popular with local Lubliners and visitors alike. Most people come for the extensive beer list, but there's also a decent list of pub food: pizzas, salads and snacks, and Irish-sounding things such as beef stew, Angus steaks, and beefburgers.

Klub Czekolada
CLUB

(☑ 727 507 905; www.klubczekolada.pl; ul Narutowicza 9; ⊙ noon-late; 🌐) This is a conventional lounge and dance club that attracts well-groomed night owls.

☆ Entertainment

Filharmonia Lubelska
CLASSICAL MUSIC

(Filharmonia im H Wieniawskiego w Lublinie; ☑ 81 531 5112; www.filharmonialubelska.pl; ul Obrońców

FORGOTTEN HOLOCAUST: SOBIBÓR & BEŁŻEC

When it comes to the Holocaust, much of the world's attention has gone to the atrocities of the Auschwitz-Birkenau extermination camp. In the far east of Poland are two camps – **Sobibór** and **Bełżec** – that are less well known, but that certainly merit a visit in order to better understand the breadth of the Germans' extermination policy. At these camps, there was no 'selection' process, very little chance for the prisoners to work, and crucially no chance for them to survive. In most instances, the victims were simply transported to the camps, off-loaded, undressed and gassed.

Both camps were formed under the Germans' 'Operation Reinhard', their secret plan to murder the Jewish population of occupied Poland, and both operated from early-1942 to 1943. It was at these camps that the Germans perfected their mass-killing techniques, such as using gas, which they would later apply at other extermination centres, including Auschwitz-Birkenau. Though the exact numbers of casualties is impossible to verify, the consensus is that around 170,000 people were murdered at Sobibór and 400,000 to 600,000 at Bełżec. There were only three known survivors from Bełżec.

Though these camps attract a tiny fraction of the number of visitors to Auschwitz-Birkenau, both Sobibór and Bełżec have small, thoughtful memorials (Bełżec also has a small museum) where you can learn more about these lesser-known killing camps. Sobibór, which lies about 80km east of Lublin, 50km north of Chełm, and 10km south of the modern Polish village of Sobibór, is the harder of the two to reach; there's only one daily train from Chełm. Inquire at the **LOIT offices** in Lublin about arranging a tour with a guide. At the time of research, the small museum at Sobibór was closed, but the grounds of the former camp were open to the public and signposted in English.

Bełżec, which lies about 100km south of Lublin, is accessible by regular minibuses from Zamość, or inquire at the LOIT offices in Lublin for tour information. At Bełżec there's a small **museum** (☑84 665 2510; www.belzec.eu; ul Ofiar obozu 4, Bełżec; parking 5zł; admission free; ⊙9am-5pm May-Oct, to 4pm Nov-Apr) with photos and text.

Pokoju 2; ⊙box office 9am-4pm Mon, noon-5pm Tue-Fri, 6-7pm Sat & Sun) This large auditorium stages classical and contemporary music concerts. It's located about 2km southwest of the Old Town. Buy tickets at the venue box office during the day or two hours before the show starts on the day of the performance.

Teatr Im H Ch Andersena PUPPET THEATRE
(☑81 532 3225; www.teatrandersena.pl; ul Dominikańska 1; tickets around 20zł; ⊙box office 9am-4pm Tue-Fri) Performances are in Polish, but the puppets of Hans Christian Andersen can be enjoyed in any language. Check the website for show times. Buy tickets at the venue box office during the day, or two hours before the performance on the day of the show.

ℹ Information

Plenty of *kantors* and ATMs line ul Krakowskie Przedmieście and adjacent streets.

Bank Pekao (ul Krakowskie Przedmieście 64; ⊙8am-6pm Mon-Fri, 10am-2pm Sat) Convenient bank and ATM on the main pedestrian thoroughfare.

Post Office (ul Krakowskie Przedmieście 50; ⊙9am-5pm)

Tourist Information Centre (LOITiK; ☑81 532 4412; www.lublin.eu; ul Jezuicka 1/3; ⊙9am-7pm Mon-Fri, 10am-7pm Sat & Sun May-Oct, 9am-5pm Mon-Fri, 10am-5pm Sat & Sun Nov-Apr) Extremely helpful English-speaking staff. There are souvenirs for sale and lots of brochures, including handy maps of the most popular walking tours in Lublin. There's also a computer on hand for short-term web-surfing.

ℹ Getting There & Away

BUS

PKS buses run from the bus station (p183) to major cities throughout Poland, and depart from opposite the castle. From here, Polski Bus (www.polskibus.com) also heads to Warsaw (25zł, three hours, five daily). Private minibuses run to various destinations, including Zamość (15zł, two hours, hourly), from a minibus station (p183) north of the bus terminal.

Minibuses to Kazimierz Dolny (8zł, one hour, every 30 minutes, 60km) are more efficient than normal buses (20zł, 2½ hours, every 30 minutes). Normal buses to Puławy pass through Kazimierz Dolny.

Bus Station (📞 703 402 622; lublin.pks.bus-portal.pl; ul Hutnicza 1, cross al Tysiąclecia) The sprawling and dilapidated main bus terminal is just north of the Old Town, across a busy road from the castle. There's an information booth here. This is also where Polski Bus (www.polskibus.com) long-haul coaches arrive at and depart from.

Minibus Station (ul Nadstawna)

TRAIN

The train station is 2km south of the Old Town. Useful direct train connections include Kraków (62zł, four hours, two daily), Warsaw (37zł, 2¾ hours, five daily) and Zamość (22zł, two hours, four daily).

Kazimierz Dolny

POP 2600

For more than a century, the ancient river port of Kazimierz Dolny has been an artist colony and a haven for free thinkers. In more recent times, it's evolved into a hugely popular weekend getaway for Warsaw and Lublin residents.

Once you arrive, you'll see why. Kazimierz Dolny is picturesquely perched along the banks of the Vistula. Its ramshackle main square, the Rynek, lined with historic buildings, is charming. The little lanes that radiate from the square are filled with quaint galleries, shops, and, naturally, endless places to grab a beer or an ice-cream cone.

One caveat: because of its popularity, this is one place for which you'll need to plan your arrival carefully. Try to avoid turning up in town on a Friday afternoon, when traffic can stretch back kilometres and Kazimierz Dolny–bound buses are filled to bursting. This is doubly true on holiday weekends. Instead, aim for an early weekday arrival. Museums are closed on Mondays, but on the bright side, you'll have this lovely place all to yourself.

History

Earliest accounts of settlement in the region refer to a wooden cloister along the Vistula in 1181. The town was formally founded in the 14th century by King Kazimierz III Wielki, who built a castle and gave the town its municipal charter. The town was called Dolny (lower), to distinguish it from the town of Kazimierz, upriver, which is today part of Kraków.

Kazimierz Dolny became a thriving trade centre, with grain, salt, wood and oxen being shipped to Gdańsk and further on for export. The 16th and early-17th centuries were particularly prosperous, and a number of splendid mansions and granaries were constructed. By 1630 Kazimierz Dolny's population had risen above 2500 (about where it is now).

The high times came to an end with the Swedish wars of the mid-17th century, various epidemics, and the slow displacement of the Vistula bed toward the west, which allowed Puławy to overshadow it in the 19th century as the trade and cultural centre of the region.

At the end of the 19th century attempts were made to revive Kazimierz Dolny as a tourist centre, but the two world wars caused serious damage to the town. WWII was particularly tragic. Before the war, the Jews comprised around 50% of the population; by the end of 1942, Nazi Germany had systematically rounded up and deported the entire community to the death camp at Bełżec.

Since the end of WWII preservation efforts have gone a long way toward restoring the historical character of Kazimierz Dolny.

◉ Sights

Most of the main sights, galleries and attractions are on or near the town's pretty Rynek. At the centre of the square is a wooden well, which still functions. Fine buildings line the square on all sides, a testament to the town's former prosperity. From an architectural standpoint, the best are probably the two connecting **Houses of the Przybyła Brothers** (Kamienice Przybyłów; Rynek 12), built in 1615 by brothers Mikołaj and Krzysztof, with rich Renaissance mannerist facades. Decorations depict the brothers' patron saints, St Nicholas (guardian of traders) and St Christopher (guardian of travellers). Also on the Rynek are the Baroque-style **Gdańsk House** (Kamienica Gdańska; Rynek 16) from 1795 and several characteristic arcaded houses with wooden-tiled roofs from the 18th and 19th centuries.

House of the Celej Family   MUSEUM

(Kamienica Celejowska; 📞 81 881 0288; www.mnkd.pl; ul Senatorska 11/13; adult/concession 10/5zł; ⊙10am-5pm Sun-Thu, to 6pm Fri & Sat) The town's main museum is housed in a 17th-century town house (built around 1635) for the Celej family. Though it's billed as a general museum, it's actually an art museum, with several rooms on the upper floor dedicated to the considerable output of artists who have called Kazimierz Dolny home. Some of the works are fantastic, some merely interesting,

MAŁOPOLSKA KAZIMIERZ DOLNY

Kazimierz Dolny

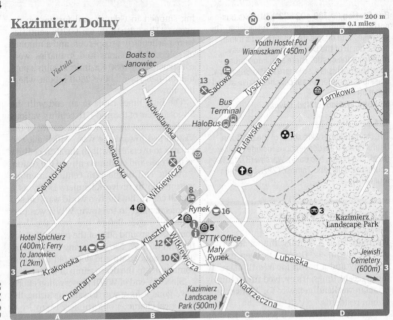

but the collection amply demonstrates the town's role in Poland's artistic history.

Parish Church
CHURCH

(Kościół Farny p w św Jana Chrzciciela i św Bartłomieja Apostoła; ☎81 881 0870; www.kazimierz-fara.pl; ul Zamkowa 6; ⏰8am-6pm) The Gothic parish church presiding over the Rynek was built in the mid-14th century, and remodelled when Renaissance styles swept Poland in the 16th century. The ornate wooden organ from 1620 sounds as lavish as it looks; organ recitals are often held here. Note the Renaissance choir stalls in the chancel and the stucco decoration of the nave's vault, a classic example of Lublin-Renaissance style and typical of the region. Be sure to raise an eyebrow at the stag-antler chandelier.

Hill of Three Crosses
VIEWPOINT

(Góra Trzech Krzyży; ul Zamkowa) Uphill from the parish church, a path to the right leads to the Hill of Three Crosses, where three large crosses stand to commemorate victims of the plagues that swept through the town in the 18th century. There's some historical debate about the relationship between the crosses and the epidemics, as some historians believe the site was referred to as 'hill of crosses' long before the plagues. Whatever the origin of the name, the hill affords sensational views.

Castle
RUIN

(Zamek; ul Zamkowa; admission 5zł; ⏰10am-6pm May-Oct) Above the parish church along ul Zamkowa is what's left of Kazimierz Dolny's castle. Originally built in 1341 as a stronghold against the Tatar incursion, the castle was extended in the 16th century and embellished further during the Renaissance. The castle fell into ruin after its partial destruction by the Swedes; the remaining fragments offer a pleasant view over the town and the Vistula.

Watchtower
HISTORIC BUILDING

(ul Zamkowa; admission 5zł; ⏰10am-6pm May-Oct) The watchtower, 100m uphill from the castle, dates from the end of the 13th century and is one of the oldest defensive structures of its kind in the country. The building's primary purpose was as a watchtower to protect an important river crossing in this area. These days, you can climb to the top to take in sweeping views of the river and valley.

Jewish Cemetery
CEMETERY

(Cmentarz Żydowski; ul Czerniawy; ⏰24hr) Over the centuries, Kazimierz Dolny had a significant Jewish population, and in the decades leading up to WWII as much as half the population was Jewish. While few traces of this community can be seen today, the Jewish Cemetery, outside of the centre, is moving

Kazimierz Dolny

and highly recommended. At the front of the cemetery is a monument to the community assembled in 1984 from several hundred tombstone fragments. It's located 2km from the Rynek on the road to Opole Lubelskie.

🏃 Activities

In 1979 the area around Kazimierz was decreed the **Kazimierz Landscape Park** (Kazimierski Park Krajobrazowy). Many **walking** trails have been traced in its 150 sq km, winding through the distinct gorges of the region.

There are three easy short trails known as *szlaki spacerowe* (walking routes) signposted in yellow, green and red, and three significantly longer treks called *szlaki turystyczne* (tourist routes) marked in blue, green and red. Almost all these routes originate in the Rynek. The tourist information centre sells maps of the park and its trails.

Many of these same trails are also suited to **cycling**. Most area hiking maps also show bike trails. Bicycles can be hired at most pensions and places around town, including at Kawiarnia Rynkowa (p187) for 10zł per hour.

⚜ Festivals & Events

Festival of Folk Bands & Singers WORLD MUSIC
(Festiwal Kapel i Śpiewaków Ludowych; www.kazimierzdolny.pl; ⊙ Jun) This highly acclaimed folk festival takes place in the last week of June. For more than 30 years, performers from the region have gathered at Mały Rynek in traditional garb to perform folk music from eras (and tastes) gone by.

Film & Art Festival FILM
(Festiwal Dwa Brzegi; www.dwabrzegi.pl; ⊙ Aug) Lasts around a week in early August and consists of musical concerts, art exhibitions, and indoor and outdoor screenings of foreign and national films.

🛏 Sleeping

There are options aplenty in Kazimierz, but advanced bookings are essential on weekends in spring and summer. The most common accommodation is rooms in private houses (50zł to 90zł), some of which are run like small hotels.

The PTTK office (p187) just off the Rynek can help find private rooms, or wander through town looking for '*pokoje*' (rooms) or '*noclegi*' (accommodation) signs. Two good streets on which to hunt for rooms are ul Krakowska and ul Sadowa.

Youth Hostel Pod Wianuszkami HOSTEL €
(⌨ 81 881 0327; www.schroniskakazimierzdolny.pl; ul Puławska 80; dm/d 40/120zł) Large and relatively pretty for a Polish youth hostel, but 1.5km northeast of town; located in an old granary.

★ Eger Pensjonat BOUTIQUE HOTEL €€
(⌨ 601 500 855; www.pensjonateger.pl; ul Czerniawy 53b; s/d 240/300zł) This elegant pension/boutique hotel is situated 2.5km out of the centre on the road to Opole Lubelskie and offers sleek, stylish rooms in trendy muffled chocolates and greys. Many rooms have balconies and everything is as fresh and clean as if it opened a week ago. The in-house restaurant serves Hungarian food that's a cut above the Kazimierz Dolny average.

Dom Architekta HOTEL €€
(⌨ 81 883 5544; www.domarchitektasarp.pl; Rynek 20; d from 220zł; P 🖥) This refurbished 17th-century town house occupies prime real estate on the Rynek, but despite the history and location – and the beautifully tiled and arcaded lobby, the hardwood floors, and the mock Renaissance garden out back – it

MAŁOPOLSKA KAZIMIERZ DOLNY

COCK-A-DOODLE-DOUGH

Spend any time in Kazimierz Dolny and you will soon wonder why its townspeople have such a proclivity for rooster-shaped bread. After seeing enough signs around for *koguty* (roosters), you will find yourself wanting to try some. When you do, you will discover that bread tastes like bread no matter how it's shaped, and promptly return to your initial question: Why?

Though its taste may be as bland as, well, bread, the rooster has an interesting history in Kazimierz. Many years ago, a rooster is believed to have averted certain disaster by warning the townsfolk of an approaching devil. This, combined with local bread-weaving traditions, resulted in the rooster's heroic portrayal in dough.

After a long golden era, when rooster-shaped bread was baked all over town, tensions suddenly surfaced. In 1996 **Piekarnia Sarzyński** bakery, convinced that its many years promoting the product and winning awards for its rooster renditions entitled it to exclusive rights, registered the rooster as a company trademark. The other bakers in town were outraged and demanded that the courts reinstate the rooster's status as the cultural (culinary?) property of the Kazimierz public.

Eight years later, the court released the rooster back into the public domain. But patent or not, no one can bake a bird like Sarzyński's.

remains delightfully relaxed and unstuffy. The rooms are on the plain side and not all the furniture works, but it somehow all comes together.

Hotel Dwa Księżyce   HOTEL €€
(☑ 81 881 0833; www.dwaksiezyce.com.pl; ul Sadowa 15; s/d/ste 240/280/420zł; P@☎) The 'Two Moons' is a pretty inn on a quiet street where you can immerse yourself in the pace of Kazimierz Dolny. Some rooms are bigger than others in the same price category (with separate sitting areas), while apartment rooms in the main building have private balconies.

✖ Eating

Kazimierz has no shortage of restaurants; most are in the centre but not all are on the Rynek.

Bar Galeria   POLISH €
(ul Plebanka 7a; mains 10-15zł; ☺11am-7pm) This little hole-in-the-wall away from the tourist throng promises '*pierogi domowe*' (homemade dumplings) and that's exactly what you get. They come seven pieces to an order in five varieties, including the usual meat and cabbage, all served by the same woman who cooked them.

Restauracja Kwadrans   POLISH €€
(☑ 81 882 1111; www.kwadrans.kazimierzdolny.pl; ul Sadowa 7a; mains 20-40zł; ☺11am-10pm) The Kwadrans is a surprisingly elegant space, with high ceilings, shiny parquet flooring, and antique clocks on the walls. The menu

is standard fare for these parts, with baked duck, pork chops and relative rarities such as venison sharing space on the menu with *pierogi* and pasta. Dine on the terrace in fine weather.

Knajpa U Fryzjera   JEWISH €€
(☑ 81 888 5513; www.restauracja-ufryzjera.pl; ul Witkiewicza 2; mains 18-38zł; ☺9am-midnight) Knajpa u Fryzjera is a likeable, kitschy restaurant that serves heaping plates of traditional Jewish–Central European mains – veal tongue, goose, beef brisket, stuffed peppers – in a welcoming, tourist-friendly environment. It opens early for breakfast.

Piekarnia Sarzyński   POLISH €€€
(☑ 605 330 335; www.restauracja.sarzynski.com.pl; ul Nadrzeczna 6; mains 25-50zł; ☺1-9pm Mon-Fri, noon-10pm Sat, noon-8pm Sun) The Sarzyński bakery and restaurant complex has something for everyone. Get in line to buy a fresh-baked bread-dough rooster (p186) or some ice cream, or wander into the fancier restaurant for very skillfully prepared grilled pork, schnitzels and baked duck, among other popular main dishes.

🍷 Drinking & Nightlife

Most of the drinking in Kazimierz Dolny happens around the Rynek, particularly on the southern side of the square, which is lined with generic cafes that morph magically into bars around the cocktail hour. Two worth seeking out are on picturesque ul Krakowska, not far from the Rynek.

Kawiarnia Rynkowa CAFE
(☑ 505 544 965; Rynek 7; ☺ 10am-midnight)
Popular Rynek cafe with the typical range
of hot and cold beverages, including a very
welcome beer on a hot day. It has one computer inside for customers to surf the web
(per hour 5zł). It also rents bikes in season
(per hour around 10zł).

Galeria Herbaciarnia U Dziwisza TEAHOUSE
(☑ 502 628 220; www.herbaciarniaudziwisza.pl; ul
Krakowska 6; teas from 6zł; ☺ 11am-10pm; ☏) A
civilised taste of an era when tea was a pastime; it boasts more than 100 varieties of tea
leaf and an appealing range of calorie-rich
accompaniments. Note this place doesn't
open until 11am.

Café Faktoria CAFE
(☑ 81 881 0057; www.cafefaktoria.pl; ul Krakowska
6b; coffee 6zł; ☺ 10am-8pm; ☏) Café Faktoria
is a veritable temple to coffee and its loyal
companion, chocolate; thrilling concoctions
of both brew in various pots on the stove.

ℹ Information

Useful amenities are at or near the Rynek. There's
a *kantor* in the **post office** (☑ 81 881 0500; ul
Tyszkiewicza 2; ☺ 9am-7pm Mon-Fri, to 3pm
Sat) and an ATM in the back wall of the same
building. There is also an ATM diagonally opposite
the PTTK Office (at the Houses of the Przybyła
Brothers) and another on the wall of Piekarnia
Sarzyński.

PTTK Office (☑ 81 881 0046; Rynek 27; ☺ 8am-
5.30pm Mon-Fri & 10am-5.30pm Sat May-Sep,
8am-4pm Mon-Fri & 10am-2.30pm Sat Oct-Apr)
This local branch of the national PTTK organisation is situated just off the Rynek, behind the
city's tourist information centre. Like the information centre (with which it has no connection),
it's generally not much use, but it may be able to
help find accommodation in private rooms (50zł
to 90zł), and it sells hiking and cycling maps.

Tourist Information Centre (☑ 81 881 0709;
www.kazimierz-dolny.pl; Rynek 15; ☺ 9am-6pm
Mon-Fri & 10am-5pm Sat & Sun Apr-Oct, 10am-
5pm daily Nov-Apr) The city's tourist information centre is conveniently located on the main
square, but it is firmly oriented toward Poles,
and aside from a free city map it has relatively
little information in English. There are regional
hiking and cycling maps for sale. The English-
language speaking ability of staff depends very
much on who is sitting behind the desk.

ℹ Getting There & Around

Kazimierz can be conveniently visited as a stop
on your Lublin–Warsaw route, or as a day trip

from Lublin. There's no railway in Kazimierz but
there's a decent bus service.

BOAT

In summer, pleasure boats run to Janowiec (one
in the style of a Viking ship, minus oars and
whips) on the opposite side of the Vistula – ask at
the **wharf** at the end of ul Nadwiślańska.

There's also a **car and passenger ferry**
(PROM; ☑ 602 858 898; ul Krakowska; adult/
concession/car 6/4/9zł; ☺ 8am-8pm Mon-Fri,
to 9pm Sat & Sun May-Sep), which takes five
minutes to cross over to Janowiec and departs
from a small landing at the very end of ul
Krakowska, 1km west of Hotel Spichlerz.

BUS

The town's tiny PKS **bus and minibus terminal**
(PKS; ul Tyszkiewicza 10) is 100m north of the
Rynek. There are normal buses to Puławy (4zł,
45 minutes, every half-hour).

There are a dozen minibuses per day to Lublin
(10zł, 1½ hours, roughly every hour) between
6.20am and 5pm; and some to Zamość (15zł,
1¼ hours).

HaloBus (☑ 602 664 419; www.halobus.com.
pl; ul Tyszkiewicza 10) runs several daily fast
buses to Warsaw (30zł, three hours), or change
for the train in Puławy. Check the timetable
posted at the PKS bus terminal.

Chełm

POP 64,850

Chełm (pronounced khelm) isn't experiencing the same sort of facelift as other towns
in the region. While there are a couple of
decent places to stay, Chełm is best explored
as a day trip from Zamość. Visitors come
to experience its proudest asset – the chalk
tunnels. The centre is compact and easy to
explore on foot.

Chełm is about 70km east of Lublin, 25km
from the Ukrainian border. Interestingly, the
town sits on an 800m-thick layer of almost
pure chalk, a natural phenomenon that has
both wreaked havoc and been the source of
the town's economic development. It has
since been tamed into a tourist attraction.
There is also a cathedral sanctuary, which is
a pleasant place for a stroll.

Though Chełm's Jewish population was
lost during WWII, the Jewish community
has left its legacy in various ways. Curiously,
the people of Chełm once played the role of
the good-natured hick in the rich tradition
of Eastern European Jewish humour. Back
in the day, many a joke sure to end in lots of

WORTH A TRIP

THE CASTLE AT JANOWIEC

The village of Janowiec (yah-*no*-vyets) and its castle make for a popular day trip from Kazimierz Dolny. You can get there by bus, but a more scenic journey involves taking a ferry (p187) and combining that with either a bike ride or a short hike.

The castle was built in the first half of the 16th century by Italian architect Santi Gucci Fiorentino at the request of Mikołaj Firlej. Through many years and owners (including the Tarło, Lubomirski and Osławski families), the castle grew to more than 100 rooms and became one of the most splendid in Poland. The Swedes began the process of ruination and two world wars completed the castle's demise. Under communism, it was the only private castle in Poland; it was finally handed over to the state in 1975 by its last owner, Leon Kozłowski.

The castle is still in ruins, but intense renovations have restored some rooms and revived external painted decorations. Upon entering the castle, note the red-and-white striped walls. This is not the work of a prankster graffiti artist; it is, apparently, how the castle was originally dressed.

The castle houses the **Janowiec Museum** (☑ 81 881 0288; www.mnkd.pl; ul Lubelska 20; adult/concession 12/8zł; ⊙ 10am-5pm Tue-Sun May-Sep, 9am-4pm Tue-Sun Oct-Apr). Inside the grounds, visitors can climb a few levels to viewing platforms offering a wide perspective of the castle and the surrounding countryside. Various rooms show exhibitions and contemporary art. In the park beside the castle is a **manor house** from the 1760s (another part of the museum), which offers insights into how Polish nobility lived.

It's also worth going down to Janowiec village at the foot of the castle to see its mid-14th-century Gothic **parish church**, extensively rebuilt in Renaissance style in the 1530s. Inside is the tomb of the Firlej family, carved in the workshop of Santi Gucci from 1586 to 1587.

From the ferry on the Janowiec side, the most straightforward way to the castle is to walk the flat 2.5km to the Rynek. Return the same way, following the signs to the 'Prom'.

laughter would start out 'there once was a rabbi from Chełm...'.

History

Chełm was founded in the 10th century and, like most towns along the eastern border, shifted between the Polish Piast crown and the Kyivan duchy on various occasions. King Kazimierz III Wielki eventually got hold of the area in 1366 and King Władysław II Jagiełło established a bishopric here some 50 years later.

Around this time Jews began to settle in the town, and swiftly grew in number. By the end of the 18th century, 60% of the town's population was Jewish.

As happened elsewhere in the country, Chełm's golden era ended in the war-torn 17th century. Later came the Polish Partitions, and the town fell under Austrian and later Russian occupation. It wasn't until WWI that Chełm began to recover as part of independent Poland, only to be cast down again by the horrors of WWII two decades later. This included the mass execution of the town's 17,000 Jews by the Germans.

◉ Sights

Chełm Chalk Tunnels TUNNEL
(Chełmskie Podziemia Kredowe; ☑ 82 565 2530; www.podziemiakredowe.pl; ul Lubelska 55a; adult/concession 12/9zł; ⊙ 9am-5pm Mon-Fri, 10am-6pm Sat & Sun) The city's star attraction is an array of chalk passages hewn by hand 12m below ground. The chalk mine began in medieval times. By the 16th century the chalk extracted was renowned throughout the country. Visits are by guided-tour (in Polish only); tours depart at 11am, 1pm and 4pm daily and take less than an hour. The temperature underground is 9°C year-round, so come prepared. A friendly and endearing ghost haunts the tunnels and is a highlight of the tour.

Over the years the tunnels expanded in size and complexity, and by 1939 a multilevel labyrinth of corridors had grown to 15km. During WWII some of the shafts served as a shelter for the town's Jews, but they were eventually discovered by the Germans.

St Mary's Basilica CHURCH
(Bazylika Mariacka; ☑ 82 565 2475; www.bazylika.net; ul Lubelska 2; ⊙ 9.30am-4pm Mon-Sat, 2-4pm Sun) The hill in the middle of Chełm is

crowned with the white St Mary's Basilica and a complex of religious buildings that were once a bishop's palace and a monastery. The late-Baroque basilica was rebuilt in the mid-18th century on the site of the 13th-century church that originally stood here. The sober interior lacks much decoration, except for the silver antependium (hanging) at the high altar depicting Polish knights paying homage to Our Lady of Chełm.

The icon of the Madonna overlooking the altar is a replica; the original was removed by the Russians during WWI and is now in Ukraine. The free-standing 40m-high belfry, originally built in the 19th century in the Orthodox style, was later given a partial neoclassical makeover.

Chełm Museum   MUSEUM
(Muzeum Chełmskie; ☑ 82 565 2693; www.mzch.pl; ul Lubelska 55; adult/concession 8/4zł; ☺ 10am-4pm Tue-Fri, noon-4pm Sat & Sun) This former monastery houses a museum containing modern Polish paintings, natural history displays and temporary exhibitions. Other outlets of the museum are open during the same hours and charge the same admission. The **Ethnography and Archaeology branch** (ul Lubelska 56a) displays archaeological finds dating from the Stone Age. The **Department of History branch** (ul Lubelska 57) houses documents relating to Chełm's past. The third one, **St Nicholas' Chapel branch** (ul Św Mikołaja 4), showcases religious art.

🛌 Sleeping

Chełm's meagre accommodation options provide a strong argument for not staying overnight; it's better to make a day trip from Lublin or Zamość.

PTSM Youth Hostel   HOSTEL €
(☑ 661 946 249; ul Czarnieckiego 8; dm 40zł) This hostel has seen better days, but is pleasantly situated in a welcome patch of greenery. It's well signed by the green triangle symbol, but not well staffed; reception is only open from 5pm to 10pm. Outside those hours, the Chełm Tourist Information Centre may be able to contact someone to welcome you.

Hotel Kamena   HOTEL €€
(☑ 82 565 6401; www.hotelkamena.pl; ul Armii Krajowej 50; s 130-150zł, d 170-190zł, apt 300zł; ℗🛜) The Kamena has received a facelift, and many of the rooms a needed makeover, transforming what was once a drab '60s-style communist pile into an acceptable overnight option. Rooms are divided into economy and lux, with the only difference being the latter have updated baths. Breakfast is not included and costs 15zł.

🍴 Eating

⭐**Restauracja Gęsia Sprawki**   POLISH €€
(☑ 82 565 2321; ul Lubelska 27; mains 20-30zł; ☺ 11am-11pm) This is the only spot in town for excellent Polish food and home cooking in the best sense of the term. *Golonka* (pork knee) is a house favourite, served with sides of mustard and horseradish, and a big plate of pickles. The cellar location is comfortable and romantic, especially when the jukebox belts out a string of French *chansons*.

McKenzee Saloon   POLISH €€
(☑ 82 565 6464; ul Kopernika 8; mains 18-25zł; ☺ 11am-midnight; 🛜) This popular and fun Western-style saloon is oddly housed in the town's former synagogue. There's ample bar food, decent Polish cooking, and lots of beer, all served under the tarp of a wagon. This is the place to come to at night as well, as the 'saloon' morphs into a club with occasional live music.

ⓘ Information

Kantors and ATMs are in reasonable supply; try along ul Lwowska and ul Lubelska.

Bank Pekao (ul Lubelska 65) Convenient ATM, just next to the tourist office.

Chełm Tourist Information Centre (Chełmski Ośrodek Informacji Turystycznej; ☑ 82 565 3667; www.itchelm.pl; ☺ 8am-4pm Mon-Fri, 9am-2pm Sat & Sun) Excellent source of local information, offering a number of very useful brochures.

Main Post Office (☑ 82 565 2236; ul Sienkiewicza 3; ☺ 10am-5pm Mon-Fri, 9.30am-2pm Sat) The main post office is north of Plac Łuczkowskiego. There is a smaller branch on the square itself.

ⓘ Getting There & Away

BUS

The bus terminal is on ul Lwowska, 300m south of Plac Łuczkowskiego. There are PKS buses to Lublin (14zł, 1½ hours, every 1½hours), and more frequent private minibuses (13zł, one hour, every hour) departing from just outside the terminal. Half a dozen buses a day run from Zamość (14zł, 1½ hours), plus several private minibuses (12zł, 70 minutes) from 8am onwards. The last minibus back to Zamość leaves Chełm at around 6pm.

There are a couple of daily fast buses to Warsaw (35zł, four hours, 229km).

TRAIN

The town has two train stations: Chełm Miasto 1km west of the Old Town, and Chełm Główny 2km to the northeast. Most trains stop at both stations, and both are served by the municipal buses. Trains to Lublin (15zł, 1½ hours, 70km) run every hour or two.

Zamość

POP 65,055

The town of Zamość (*zah*-moshch) is unique in Poland as a nearly perfectly preserved example of Renaissance town planning, as practised in the 16th century. Zamość was added to the Unesco World Heritage List in 1992, and an inflow of redevelopment funds since has rejuvenated the town's postcard-ready main square and the impressive fortification bastions that surround the centre in all directions.

The town owes its origins to a wealthy Polish nobleman, Jan Zamoyski (1542–1605), who came up with the idea to put a town here in the first place, and to the Paduan architect he hired to realise his dream, Bernando Morando. Zamość wears its Renaissance roots on its sleeve, embracing not one, but two grandiose nicknames: the 'Pearl of the Renaissance' and the 'Padua of the North'. Take your pick.

History

Zamość began as something of a Renaissance-era housing estate. When Zamoyski, the country's chancellor and commander-in-chief at the time, decided to build his 'perfect' city, he looked to Italy rather than neighbouring Russia for artistic inspiration. Morando was hired to build Zamoyski's dream, and in doing so created a model city showcasing leading Italian theories of urban design. The project began in 1580, and within 11 years, some 217 houses had been built, with public buildings following soon afterwards.

By the end of the 16th century, the town's beauty – and its location on the crossroads of the Lublin–Lviv and Kraków–Kyiv trading routes – attracted international settlers, including Armenians, Jews, Hungarians, Greeks, Germans, Scots and Italians. Many of the original Jewish settlers here were descendants of Sephardic Jews, fleeing persecution in Spain at the end of the 15th century.

The fortifications, which are now completely restored, were built to protect the city and its inhabitants. They were tested many times but never fell to the enemy. The Cossack raid of 1648 proved little match for the strength of Zamość. Its impregnability was confirmed again in 1656, when Zamość, along with Częstochowa and Gdańsk, boldly withstood the Swedish siege.

Zamość was a key target of Hitler's plan for eastward expansion; German occupiers intended that some 60,000 ethnic Germans would be resettled here before the end of 1943 (former German president Horst Köhler was born near Zamość). Due to fierce resistance by the Polish Underground, the determination of the people of Zamość, and eventually the arrival of the Red Army, the number of Germans to relocate to the town barely reached 10,000. However, the Jewish population was brutally expelled from the town and the surrounding areas.

⊙ Sights

◉ Rynek Wielki

The Old Town is 600m long, 400m wide and surrounds a main square (Rynek Wielki) of exactly 100m by 100m. Look out for plaques on key buildings around Rynek Wielki, which offer succinct information about the buildings' former use. The Italianate Renaissance Rynek is lined with arcaded burghers' houses (arcades were made compulsory by Jan Zamoyski himself). Each side of the Rynek (bar the northern side, which is dominated by the lofty pinkish town hall) has eight houses bisected by two main axes of town; one runs west–east from the palace to the bastion, and the other joins the three market squares north to south.

Town Hall   HISTORIC BUILDING
(Rynek Wielki) The town hall was built between 1639 and 1651, and features were added and extended over the years: its curving stairway came in 1768. Zamoyski didn't want the town hall to overshadow the palace or interrupt the view, and so unusually placed it on the northern side of the square rather than in the centre. In summer, a bugle is played at noon from the 52m-high clock tower. The building and tower are not open to the general public.

Museum of Zamość   MUSEUM
(Muzeum Zamojskie; ☑84 638 6494; www.muzeum-zamojskie.pl; ul Ormiańska 30; adult/concession 10/5zł; ⊙9am-5pm Tue-Sun) Two Armenian houses shelter the Zamość museum, with intriguing displays such as a scale mod-

Zamość

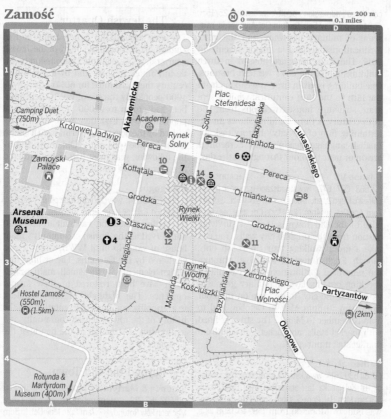

Zamość

el of the 16th-century town and a letter to Jan Zamoyski from his architect, Bernardo Morando, with a hand-drawn plan of the square and names of the first occupants of each building. Also on display are archaeological finds, such as Gothic treasures from cemeteries in the Hrubieszów Valley.

Originally, all of the houses in the square were topped with decorative parapets, but these were removed in the 1820s; only those on the northern side have been (and still are being) restored. As these houses once belonged to Armenian merchants, you will find some distinctive motifs on their facades.

◉ Around the Rynek

★ Arsenal Museum
MUSEUM

(Muzeum Fortyfikacji i Broni Arsenał; ☎84 638 4076; www.muzeum-zamojskie.pl; ul Zamkowa 2;

combined admission adult/concession 25/15zł; ⊘ 9am-5pm May-Sep, to 4pm Oct-Apr) This museum of military hardware and the city's fortifications received a major facelift in 2015. The collections are housed in three buildings along the city's western bastions. One building is given over to weapons from the 15th to the 19th centuries, while a separate structure houses weapons from the 20th century. A third building shows an entertaining film of the city's history (ask for English-language headphones). Screenings are on or near the hour throughout the day.

Bastion VII
FORTIFICATION

(☑ 663 077 677; www.nadszaniec.zamosc.pl; ul Łukasińskiego 2; adult/concession 8.50/5zł; ⊘ 9am-7pm Apr-Oct, to 4pm Nov-Mar) On the eastern edge of the Old Town is the best surviving bastion from the original city walls. You can take a group walking tour (in Polish only, though English text is available) through the renovated fortifications and casemates, checking out displays of military gear and views over the city. Tours leave on the hour from 9am to 6pm May to October, and to 3pm November to March. The street is lined with market stalls, and tickets are sold from market stall number 28.

Cathedral
CHURCH

(☑ 84 639 2614; www.katedra.zamojskolubaczowska. pl; ul Kolegiacka 1a; admission free; ⊘ 9.30am-5.30pm Mon-Sat, 2pm-5.30pm Sun) The cathedral was built by Morando from 1587 to 1598 as a votive offering and mausoleum for the Zamoyskis. The exterior changed dramatically in the 19th century, but the interior has maintained many original features. Note the authentic Lublin Renaissance–style vault, the stone and stuccowork, and the unusual arcaded organ loft. In the high altar is the Rococo silver tabernacle of 1745. Jan Zamoyski's tomb is under the black marble in the chapel, at the head of the right-hand aisle.

Bell Tower
TOWER

(☑ 846392614; www.katedra.zamojskolubaczowska. pl; ul Kolegiacka 1a; admission 3zł; ⊘ 10am-9pm Mon-Sat, 1-10pm Sun May-Sep) You can climb this free-standing bell tower, though the terrace is not high enough to offer a bird's-eye view of the Old Town. The present tower was built from 1755 to 1775 after the original timber tower went up in flames. It contains three bells: Wawrzyniec (170kg), Tomasz (1200kg) and the largest, Jan (4300kg).

◉ The Jewish Quarter

The area around the Rynek Solny and ul Zamenhofa was once the heart of the Jewish quarter. Jews were granted permission to settle in Zamość in 1588, and by the mid-19th century they accounted for 60% of the town's 4000 people. By the eve of WWII their numbers had grown to 12,000 (45% of the total population). In 1941 they were forcibly removed by the occupying Germans to a ghetto formed to the west of the Old Town, and by the following year most had been murdered in extermination camps.

Synagogue
SYNAGOGUE

(☑ 84 639 0054; www.zamosc.fodz.pl; ul Pereca 14; admission 6zł; ⊘ 10am-6pm Tue-Sun) The city's fascinating synagogue was built around 1620 and served as the Jewish community's main house of worship until WWII, when it was shuttered by the Germans. The ceilings and design elements in the small main prayer room have been restored to their former opulence. The highlight of the exhibition is a gripping computer presentation on the history of the town's Jewish community and its eventual destruction at the hands of the Germans.

◉ Beyond the Old Town

Rotunda & Martyrdom Museum
MUSEUM

(☑ 692 162 219; www.muzeum-zamojskie.pl; Droga Męczenników Rotundy; ⊘ 7am-8pm May-Oct, to 3pm Mon-Fri Nov-Apr) **FREE** About 500m southwest of the Old Town is the Rotunda – a ring-shaped fort 54m in diameter surrounding a circular yard. The rotunda was built in the 1820s as part of the defensive infrastructure of the town, but during WWII the German SS converted it into an interrogation centre. Some 8000 people from the Zamość area are believed to have been murdered here and their bodies burnt in the courtyard.

The graveyard surrounding the rotunda is the resting place of people who were killed here, including Polish soldiers and members of the Polish underground. Walking through the various cells (particularly by yourself) can be a disturbing and desolate experience.

✪ Festivals & Events

Jazz on the Borderlands
MUSIC

(www.kosz.zam.pl; ⊘ May) Zamość is rich in jazz and blues festivals, including Jazz on the Borderlands.

Zamość Theatre Summer THEATRE
(www.zdk.zamosc.pl; ☉ mid-Jun–mid-Aug) The Zamość Theatre Summer, organised by **Zamojski Dom Kultury** (☎ 84 639 2021; www.zdk.zamosc.pl; ul Partyzantów 13), takes place from mid-June to mid-August, with dramatic open-air performances on the Rynek in front of the town hall.

Summer Film Festival FILM
(www.stylowy.net; ☉ Aug) Film screenings on the Rynek and at the town's art cinema, **Kino 'Stylowy'** (☎ 84 639 2313; www.stylowy.net; ul Odrodzenia 9).

International Meeting of Jazz Singers MUSIC
(www.kosz.zam.pl; ☉ Aug-Sep) Performances and competitions between jazz singers from the region and far beyond.

🛌 Sleeping

Hostel Zamość HOSTEL €
(☎ 724 968 902; www.hostelzamosc.pl; ul Szczebrzeska 9; dm/s/d 60/90/135zł; P @ 🛜) Clean, family-friendly guesthouse about 1km southwest of the main square and adjacent to the train station. There are dorm beds, and also private singles and doubles. Nothing overly fancy but everything is well-run and secure. There's a serene garden at the side where kids can play, and anyone can relax.

Camping Duet CAMPGROUND €
(☎ 84 639 2499; www.duet.virgo.com.pl; ul Królowej Jadwigi 14; s/d 80/95zł, per tent/person 15zł/10zł; 🛜) This conveniently located camping ground, about 1.5km west of the Old Town, has bungalows for up to six people, tennis courts, a restaurant, a sauna and a Jacuzzi. In summer it can be crowded with families.

★Hotel Korunny HOTEL €€
(☎ 84 677 7100; www.hotel-koronny.pl; ul Koszary 7; s/d 180/270zł; P ✱ @ 🛜) This affordable four-star hotel makes for a perfect splurge. The designers wanted to create a modern take on Renaissance Zamość, meaning overly plush carpets and curtains, chandeliers, and oversize rooms – in short, exactly what a holiday hotel should be. The breakfast buffet is ample and there's a terrace out back on which to take morning coffee.

Hotel Senator HOTEL €€
(☎ 84 638 9990; www.senatorhotel.pl; ul Rynek Solny 4; s/d/ste 220/250/360zł; ✱ @ 🛜) The Senator offers impressive value and more charm than its chain-hotel competition. Rooms have a tasteful aesthetic and even standard rooms offer impressive space. The on-site restaurant, with its own fireplace, aims for medieval mellow (and looks just a bit like a medieval theatre set). Weekend discounts add to the ambience.

Mercure Zamojski HOTEL €€
(☎ 84 639 2516; www.mercure-zamosc-staremiasto.com; ul Kołłątaja 2/4/6; s/d/ste from 230/290/400zł; P ✱ @ 🛜) Occupying three interconnected, historic houses, the Mercure is a reliable choice offering conventional professionalism. Some rooms are bigger than others, some have more reliable internet access, and some offer better views. The hotel's downfall is that the old-world charm of its exterior has not always been matched with modernised interiors.

Hotel Renesans HOTEL €€
(☎ 84 639 2001; www.hotelrenesans.pl; ul Grecka 6; s/d/apt 160/200/230zł; P ✱ @ 🛜) OK, Jan Zamoyski would not be a fan of the scruffy '60s exterior, but the rooms themselves have had a major makeover, complete with big comfy beds, thick carpets, and large, stylish baths. In short, it's excellent value for money, and just a block from the Rynek. Skip the restaurant, though, there's better food to be found elsewhere.

🍴 Eating & Drinking

For summer drinking, a table on the Rynek is the place to be, from early afternoon until the wee hours of the morning.

Bar Asia POLISH €
(☎ 84 639 2304; ul Staszica 6; mains from 15zł; ☉ 8am-5pm Mon-Fri, to 4pm Sat) For fast and filling soup/dumplings/cabbage-style food, head to this old-style, self-serve milk bar.

★Restauracja Muzealna ARMENIAN €€
(www.muzealna.com.pl; ul Ormiańska 30; mains 20-50zł; ☉ 11am-midnight Mon-Fri, 10am-midnight Sat & Sun) This is a cut above the typical Rynek offerings in terms of presentation, creating the impression it takes its food seriously here, and it does. There's an elegant cellar restaurant, or eat upstairs on the main square in summer. The menu is a mix of Polish and Armenian cooking, with spicy kebabs sharing menu space with pork cutlets and duck.

Bohema POLISH €€
(☎ 84 627 1443; www.bohemazamosc.pl; ul Staszica 29; mains 19-50zł; ☉ 10am-11pm; 🛜) The Rynek is brimming with choice when it comes to pizzas, coffees and square-side

dining. Bohema is one of the better options, with good home-cooked Polish food (try the 'mixed *pierogi* set, with 12 dumplings, including sauces). Poetry could be written about the unsurpassable hot chocolate with chilli (possibly the best 9zł you'll spend in Poland).

Corner Pub POLISH €€

(☑ 84 627 0694; www.cornerpub.pl; ul Żeromskiego 6; mains 22-50zł; ⊙ 10am-10pm; 🐾) This cosy Irish pub is the place to head in the evening for excellent regional Polish cooking, plus treats such as Irish sausages, and fish and chips (as well several types of pizza). There are a few garden tables in summer.

ℹ Information

Most banks and internet facilities are located around the Rynek or not far from it.

Bank Pekao (ul Grodzka 2) Changes cash and gives advances on Visa and MasterCard.

Ksero Internet (Rynek Wielki 10; per hr 3zł; ⊙ 7.30am-5pm Mon-Fri, 10am-2pm Sat) Handy internet access right on the main square.

Tourist Office (☑ 84 639 2292; www.travel.zamosc.pl; Rynek Wielki 13; ⊙ 8am-6pm Mon-Fri, 10am-5pm Sat & Sun May-Sep, 8am-5pm Mon-Fri, 9am-3pm Sat & Sun Oct-Apr) Helpful tourist service in the town hall with maps, brochures and souvenirs. Staff can arrange walking tours of the town in various languages. There is also a computer for respectful gratis internet use, and a handy timetable of travel options in and out of town. The tourist office also rents bikes (per hour 5zł).

ℹ Getting There & Away

BUS

➡ The **bus terminal** (PKS; ☑ 84 638 5877; www.ppks-zamosc.com.pl; ul Hrubieszowska 9) is 2km east of the Old Town. The tourist information office maintains up-to-date timetables for buses, minibuses, and trains to popular destinations.

➡ Private minibuses are often faster and cheaper than larger buses. They leave from a stand right opposite the main bus terminal; check the timetable for details of departures.

➡ Buses to Lublin (14zł, two hours, every half-hour) run roughly between 5am and 6pm. There are also plenty of minibuses (15zł, two hours, hourly). There is sporadic daily service to Kraków (35zł, four to five hours), and a few buses daily to Warsaw (35zł, five hours).

➡ There are frequent normal buses and minibuses to Zwierzyniec (5zł, 40 minutes, 32km), the entry point for Roztocze National Park.

➡ Several minibuses daily travel to Bełżec, dropping you not far from the former extermination

camp and museum (15zł, one hour). Contact the tourist information office or call the Tomaszów minibus line (☑ 84 664 1539).

TRAIN

The **train station** (PKP; ☑ information 19 757; www.pkp.pl; ul Szczebrzeska 11) is about 1km southwest of the Old Town; walk or take the city bus. Note that train service to Zamość has been scaled back in recent years, though trains are still useful for Chełm (15zł, two hours, 50km) and Lublin (22zł, two hours, 80km).

Zwierzyniec & Roztocze National Park

POP 3800

The town of Zwierzyniec (zvyeh-*zhi*-nyets) is 32km southwest of Zamość; like Zamość, it was created by Jan Zamoyski, but on a more modest scale. In the 16th century the Polish nobleman built a summer palace and residential complex here, and tossed in an enormous game reserve for his recreational enjoyment. While the family's once-grand summer palace was pulled down in the 19th century (all that's left is a tiny chapel), the game reserve survives to this day and forms the core of the modern-day Roztocze National Park.

Zwierzyniec itself is no great shakes. It's little more than a forlorn-looking square surrounded by a few shops selling cheap clothing. Still, it's the gateway to an enchanting national park, with hundreds of kilometres of unspoiled hiking and biking trails.

◉ Sights & Activities

Roztocze National Park PARK

(Roztoczański Park Narodowy; ☑ 84 687 2286; www.roztoczanskipn.pl; ul Plażowa 2, Zwierzyniec) The park, which covers an area of 79 sq km and lies to the south and east of Zwierzyniec, was a nature reserve for more than 350 years as part of the Zamoyski family estate. Today, it's home to a diverse range of flora and fauna, and is popular for its hiking and cycling opportunities.

The symbol of the park is the Polish pony – a descendent of a wild horse known as the tarpan that died out in the 19th century. The horse was reintroduced to the park in 1982 and there's a small pony refuge near Echo Ponds.

The normal starting point for walks is the **Education and Museum Centre**, where you can buy booklets and park maps. For a Roztocze sampler, take the Bukowa Mount didactic path (2.6km) south from the museum to the top of Bukowa Góra (Beech

Mountain, 306m) along a former palace park lane. If you want to visit the pony reserve near Echo Ponds, there is a short route (1.2km) from the museum.

Longer walks generally weave from Zwierzyniec through forest terrain to neighbouring villages (such as Florianka, known for its Polish pony breeding). Intersecting paths enable you to return by a different route or cut to another path.

Education and Museum Centre MUSEUM
(Ośrodek Edukacyjno-Muzealny; ☎84 687 2286; www.roztoczanskipn.pl; ul Plażowa 3; adult/concession 10/6zł; ⏲9am-5pm Tue-Sun Apr-Oct, to 4pm Tue-Sun Nov-Mar) Located near the entrance to Roztocze National Park, this centre has interesting displays of local flora and fauna, but the primary interest is the small bookshop, where you can pick up maps and other hiking info. There's a small car park on-site, and many of the best hikes set out from around here.

Chapel on the Water CHAPEL
(Kościółek na wodzie) Just near the Roztocze National Park's Educational and Museum Centre is this small chapel, the only significant structure remaining from the Zamoyski's residential complex. The small Baroque church sits on one of four tiny islets on the small lake of Staw Kościelny (Church Pond), which was allegedly dug by Turkish and Tatar prisoners in the 1740s.

Zwierzyniec Brewery BREWERY
(☎669 611 981; www.zwierzyniec.pl; Browarna 7; ⏲10am-4pm Fri-Sun May-Sep) The local brewery is now producing beer again after being bought by national giant Perła and standing idle for a few years. It makes popular Zwierzyniec pale lager and has announced it will begin guided brewery tours during the summer; ask at the brewery during your trip.

Letnisko BICYCLE RENTAL
(Wypożyczalnia rowerów; ☎601 507 306; www.zwierzyniec-rowery.pl; ul 1-go Maja 22; per hr/day 10/25zł) Reputable bike rental outfit, not far from the entrance to Roztocze National Park, where you can buy cycling and hiking maps.

Sleeping & Eating

The tourist office can help find agroturist accommodation, well-equipped holiday centres and local rooms in and around town. In most, longer stays bring the rates down.

Relaks PENSION €
(☎607 938 211; www.noclegizwierzyniec.pl; ul 2 Lutego 12a; s/d 60/100zł; P 📶) This well-mannered stucco chalet is a little hard to find, hidden along a small street behind the main square, but it's worth the effort. Inside you'll find eight spotless rooms done out in cheerful colours. Some have full baths, others only showers. One has a balcony, and several overlook a grill in the back garden.

Karczma Młyn PENSION €
(☎84 687 2527; www.karczma-mlyn.pl; ul Wachniewskiej 1a; s/d 80/110zł; P) This cheery inn with a postcard-perfect view of the Baroque Chapel on the Water offers clean accommodation at reasonable prices, as well as the best meals in town. Eat in the back garden.

Camping Echo CAMPGROUND €
(☎84 687 2314; www.echozwierzyniec.pl; ul Biłgorajska 3; camp sites per person 12zł, cabins with bathrooms/basins per person 30/25zł, cars 3zł; ⏲May-Sep; P) This is a pleasant family-oriented camping ground not far from the bus station. Offers spots to pitch a tent as well as comfy bungalows for three to six people.

Information

The small **tourist office** (☎84 687 2660; www.zwierzyniec.info.pl; ul Słowackiego 2; ⏲8am-4pm daily Apr-Sep, to 4pm Mon-Fri Oct-Mar) outside the centre of town sells hiking maps and advises on places to stay. Alternatively, ask at the tourist office (p194) in Zamość. To find tourist information, go right from the bus station to a busy roundabout and then make a left. The tiny office is just behind a small shopping centre.

Getting There & Away

The bus station is on ul Zamojska, just north of the lake (if you're facing the road with your back to the bus station, follow the road left to get to the lake). Buses to Zamość (5zł, 40 minutes, 32km) pass every half-hour.

Carpathian Mountains

POP 3.8 MILLION

Why Go?

When thinking about Poland, mountains are not usually the first thing to spring to mind. In fact, the country's southern border is defined by the beautiful and dramatic Carpathian (Karpaty) chain, the highest mountain range in Central Europe.

The wooded hills and peaks here are a beacon for hikers, cyclists and skiers in season. And because of the region's remoteness, this 'forgotten corner' has been able to preserve its traditional folkways better than other parts of the country.

The centre is the resort of Zakopane in the heart of the Tatra Mountains (Tatry), the highest section of the Polish Carpathians, but the prettiest hills are arguably in the Pieniny or Bieszczady ranges. Elsewhere, a mosaic of modest towns provide jumping-off points for a half-dozen national parks. Historic regional towns such as Przemyśl, Tarnów and Sanok offer insights into the past.

Best Places to Eat

➡ Café Helenka (p234)
➡ U Becza (p227)
➡ Cuda Wianki (p213)
➡ Stary Kredens (p217)
➡ Kryjówka (p209)

Best Places to Stay

➡ Małopolanka (p231)
➡ Hotel GAL (p205)
➡ Miasteczko Galicyjskie (p229)
➡ Grand Hotel (p209)

When to Go
Zakopane

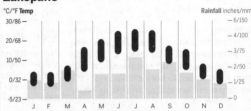

Jan–Mar Zakopane is *the* place for skiing and snowboarding in a season that lasts through March.

Apr–Jun Welcome the arrival of spring in the Bieszczady, Poland's remotest mountain range.

Jul & Aug There's no better place on a sunny summer afternoon than aboard a raft on the Dunajec River.

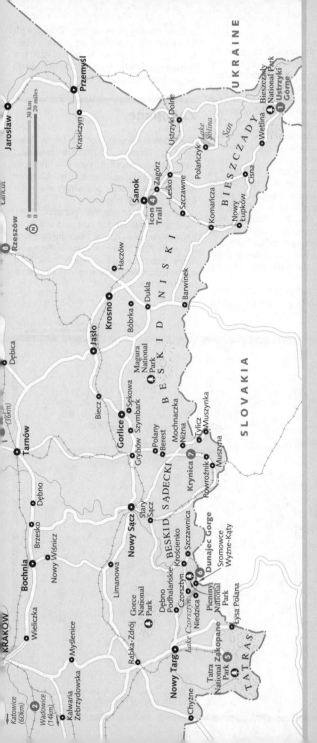

Carpathian Mountains Highlights

1 Viewing the natural beauty of the Bieszczady up close in **Ustrzyki Górne** (p220).

2 Enjoying a papal cream cake in **Wadowice** (p202).

3 Marvelling at the colours and patterns of the painted houses of **Zalipie** (p206).

4 Following the **Icon Trail** (p216) from Sanok and visiting the region's charming timber churches.

5 Hiking or skiing in the Tatra Mountains above the fashionable resort of **Zakopane** (p198).

6 Relaxing on a raft down the **Dunajec Gorge** (p235).

7 Taking to the waters for a spa treatment in **Krynica** (p230).

8 Hitting the town after dark in lively, studenty **Rzeszów** (p207).

TATRAS

The Tatras form the highest range of the Carpathians, with towering peaks and steep rocky sides dropping hundreds of metres to icy lakes. There are no glaciers in the Tatras, but patches of snow remain all year.

This is prime terrain for hiking in summer and skiing in winter, with most of the action centred on Zakopane. The town and region are easily accessible via a two-hour bus ride from Kraków.

The Tatra range, roughly 900 sq km, stretches for 60km across the Polish–Slovakian border and is 15km at its widest point. About a quarter of it is Polish territory and forms the Tatra National Park (Tatrzański Park Narodowy), encompassing 211 sq km and headquartered in Zakopane. The Polish Tatras boast two dozen peaks exceeding 2000m, the highest of which is **Mt Rysy** (2499m).

At the northern foot of the Tatras lies the Podhale region, which extends from Zako-pane to the city of Nowy Targ. Dotted with small villages populated by *górale* ('high-landers'), the Podhale is one of the few Polish regions where old folk traditions still form a part of everyday life.

Zakopane

POP 27,300

Nestled in the foothills of the Tatras, Zako-pane is Poland's best-known mountain resort. It's an excellent base for hiking in summer and skiing in winter, though at the height of the summer and winter seasons it can get positively overrun.

In addition to outdoor pursuits, Zako-pane is known for the size and beauty of its wooden villas, dating from the late 19th and early 20th centuries. Some of these now house museums, while others have been converted into hotels or pensions, or remain in private hands.

Zakopane

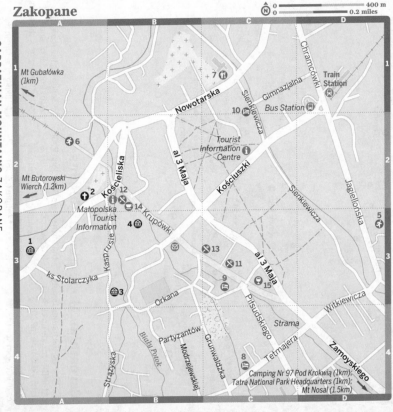

The father of this craze for all things wooden was the architect Stanisław Witkiewicz (1851–1915), and the first of several magnificent wooden villas that he built in the area, the Willa Koliba, now houses the Museum of Zakopane Style.

Witkiewicz's creations in the early 20th century helped to establish Zakopane as a haven for painters, poets, writers and composers. Two of the town's most famous former residents include Witkiewicz's son, the writer and painter Stanisław Ignacy Witkiewicz (better known as 'Witkacy'), and the composer Karol Szymanowski.

◉ Sights

◉ In the Centre

Most of Zakopane's cultural sights draw on the town's unique wooden architecture and its history as an artistic haven in the 19th and early 20th centuries.

Museum of Zakopane Style MUSEUM
(Willa Koliba; ☑18 201 3602; www.muzeum tatrzanskie.pl; ul Kościeliska 18; adult/concession 7/5.50zł; ☺10am-6pm Tue-Sat, 9am-3pm Sun Jul & Aug, 9am-5pm Wed-Sat, 9am-3pm Sun Sep-Jun) Housed in the Willa Koliba, this was the first of several grand wooden villas designed by the noted Polish painter and architect Stanisław Witkiewicz in his 'Zakopane

Style' (similar to the Arts and Crafts movement that swept the US and Britain at the turn of the 20th century). The interior has been restored to its original state, complete with highlander furnishings and textiles, all designed for the villa.

Old Church & Cemetery CHURCH
(Stary Kościół, Pęksowy Brzyzek National Cemetery; ul Kościeliska; ☺dawn-dusk) **FREE** This small wooden church and adjoining atmospheric cemetery date from the mid-19th century. The Old Church has charming carved wooden decorations and pews, and the Stations of the Cross painted on glass on the windows. Just behind, the old cemetery is certainly one of the country's most beautiful, with a number of amazing wood-carved headstones, some resembling giant chess pieces. The noted Polish painter and creator of the Zakopane Style, Stanisław Witkiewicz, is buried here beneath a modest wooden grave marker.

Tatra Museum MUSEUM
(☑18 201 5205; www.muzeumtatrzanskie.pl; ul Krupówki 10; adult/concession 7/5.50zł; Sun free; ☺10am-6pm Tue-Sat, 9am-3pm Sun Jul & Aug, 9am-5pm Wed-Sat, 9am-3pm Sun Sep-Jun) This is the main branch of the Tatra Museum, with sections on regional and natural history, ethnography and geology. The presentations are on the dry side, but it's nevertheless a good introduction to the flora and fauna of the region. Though the address is listed as ul Krupówki, it's set back away from the main street.

Szymanowski Museum MUSEUM
(☑18 202 0040; www.muzeum.krakow.pl; ul Kasprusie 19; adult/concession 9/5zł; Sun free; ☺10am-5pm Tue-Sun) About 500m south of the centre, the Szymanowski Museum highlights the life and work of the early-modern Polish composer Karol Szymanowski (1882–1937). Though he's practically unknown outside Poland, Szymanowski is considered the country's second-greatest composer after Chopin. The setting is the wooden Willa Atma, where Szymanowski lived for several years at the end of his life. The museum also hosts regular piano recitals of Szymanowski's music.

◉ Outside the Centre

Morskie Oko LAKE
(☑18 202 3300; www.tpn.pl; park 5zł) The most popular outing near Zakopane is to this emerald-green mountain lake, about 20km

southeast of the centre. Buses regularly depart from ul Kościuszki, across from the main bus station, for Polana Palenica (45 minutes), from where a 9km-long road continues uphill to the lake. Cars, bikes and buses are not allowed, so you'll have to walk (about two hours each way). Travel agencies organise day trips.

🏃 Activities

Skiing

Zakopane is Poland's capital of winter sports. The town's environs have a number of ski areas, ranging from flat surfaces for cross-country touring to steep slopes – suitable for everyone from beginners to advanced – served by 50 ski lifts and tows in all.

Mt Kasprowy Wierch (1985m) offers some of the most challenging ski slopes in the area, as well as the best conditions, with the spring skiing season sometimes extending as late as early May. You can get to the top in 20 minutes by **cable car** (☑ 18 201 5356; www.pkl.pl; Kuźnice; adult/concession return 63/48zł; ⊙ 7.30am-4pm Jan-Mar, 7.30am-6pm Apr-Jun, Sep & Oct, 7am-9pm Jul & Aug, 9am-4pm Nov-Dec), then stay in the mountains and use the two chairlifts, in the Goryczkowa and Gąsienicowa Valleys, on both sides of Mt Kasprowy. The view from the top is spectacular (clouds permitting) and you can stand with one foot in Poland and the other in Slovakia.

Mt Gubałówka is another popular skiing area and it, too, offers some pistes and good conditions. It's easily accessible from central Zakopane by **funicular** (☑ 18 201 5356; www.pkl.pl; adult/concession return 20/16zł, adult/concession one way 14/12zł, day pass 65zł; ⊙ 9am-8pm Jan-Sep, to 7pm Oct, to 6pm Nov & Dec), covering the 1298m-long route in 3½ minutes and climbing 300m from the lower station just north of ul Krupówki.

Some 2km to the west is **Mt Butorowski Wierch**, with its 1.6km-long chairlift. One more major ski area is at **Mt Nosal**, on the southeastern outskirts of Zakopane. Facilities include a chairlift and a dozen T-bars.

Ski-equipment hire is available from outlets throughout Zakopane. Try **Sukces** (☑ 502 681 170; www.ski-sukces.zakopane.pl; ul Nowotarska 39). Complete kits for skiing/snowboarding average 45/50zł a day.

Other Activities

An excellent place to cool off on a warm summer's day is **Aqua Park** (☑ 18 200 1122; www.aquapark.zakopane.pl; ul Jagiellońska 31; per hr/day adult 20/60zł, child 3-16yr 13/45zł; ⊙ 9am-10pm; 🚗), with indoor and outdoor pools, slides, various saunas and, incongruously, bowling.

In summer, Mt Nosal is a popular spot for **hang-gliding** and **paragliding**. For information, stop by one of the tourist offices or check out www.paraglidingmap.com, which has a good section on paragliding sites in Poland.

🎊 Festivals & Events

Throughout summer, the Willa Atma hosts a series of **chamber music concerts** (usually 35zł) to highlight the music of Karol Szymanowski and other composers.

International Festival of Mountain Folklore   MUSIC

(Międzynarodowy Festiwal Folkloru Ziem Górskich; www.mffzg.pl; ⊙ Aug) The town's leading cultural event is this annual late-summer festival featuring folk music and dance groups from around the world.

🛏 Sleeping

Zakopane has no shortage of places to stay and, except for occasional peaks, finding a bed is no problem. Even if the hotels and hostels are full, there will always be private rooms, which provide some of the most reasonable and best-value accommodation in town. Check at the tourist office for details (rooms should cost around 50zł per person) or look for signs reading '*pokoje*', '*noclegi*' or '*zimmer frei*' outside private homes.

Good Bye Lenin Hostel   HOSTEL €

(☑ 18 200 1330; www.zakopane.goodbyelenin.pl; ul Chłabówka 44; dm 35-50zł, d/tr 120/150zł; 🅿@🛜) This five-room place with 30 beds in a century-old farmhouse is as chilled as you'll find. The only downside, or maybe an upside if you've come to get away from things, is location: the hostel is 2.5km southeast of the centre. The hostel will pick you up from the bus or train station, or take minibus 73 to the 'Jaszczurowka' stop.

Target Hostel   HOSTEL €

(☑ 730 955 730, 18 207 4596; www.targethostel.pl; ul Sienkiewicza 3b; dm 37-52zł; @🛜) This private, well-run hostel is within easy walking distance of the bus station, which is convenient if you're arriving from Kraków. Accommodation is in four- to 10-bed dorms, with the smaller rooms priced slightly higher. Dorms are classic light wood, with wooden floors. There's a common room and collective kitchen, as well as niceties such as free wi-fi and computers to check email.

Camping Nr 97
Pod Krokwią
CAMPGROUND €

(☑ 18 201 2256; www.podkrokwia.pl; ul Żeromskiego 34; camping per person/tent 15/14zł; beds in bungalows 45zł; P) The camping ground has large heated bungalows, each containing several double and triple rooms. They are often full in the July and August period. To get here from the bus or train stations, take any bus heading south and get off at the roundabout.

Czarny Potok
HOTEL €€

(☑ 18 202 2760; www.czarnypotok.pl; ul Tetmajera 20; s/d from 200/280zł; P @ 🛜 🏊) The 'Black Stream', set upon a pretty brook amid lovely gardens, is a 44-room pension-like hostelry along a quiet street just south of the pedestrian mall. It has a great fitness centre with two saunas.

Hotel Litwor
HOTEL €€€

(☑ 18 202 4200; www.litwor.pl; ul Krupówki 40; s/d 450/600, ste 625-840zł; P @ 🛜 🏊) This is a sumptuous four-star place, with large, restful rooms and all the usual top-end facilities, including a gym and sauna. It has an excellent restaurant serving traditional Polish dishes and is just a short stroll away from the main pedestrian area.

Eating

Ul Krupówki is lined end to end with faux highlander-style rustic taverns, all featuring pretty much the same *jadło karpackie* (Carpathian cuisine), accompanied by hokey mountain music performed by a *kapela góralska* (folk-music ensemble). Still, there are a few diamonds in the rough.

HIKING IN THE TATRA MOUNTAINS

With a huge variety of some 300km of trails, the Tatras are ideal for walking. No other area of Poland is so densely criss-crossed with hiking paths, and nowhere else will you find such a diversity of landscapes.

Although marked trails go all across the region, the most popular area for hiking is the **Tatra National Park** (Tatrzański Park Narodowy; ☑ 18 200 0308; www.tpn.pl; ul Chałubińskiego 42; adult/concession 5/2.50zł; ⊙ office 9am-4pm Mon-Fri), which begins just south of Zakopane. Geographically, the Tatras are divided into three parts: the West Tatras (Tatry Zachodnie), the High Tatras (Tatry Wysokie) to the east and the adjoining Belianske Tatras (Tatry Bielskie). All the areas are attractive, though they offer quite different scenery. In general the West Tatras are lower, gentler, easier to walk and safer. The High Tatras and Belianske Tatras are completely different: a land of bare granite peaks with alpine lakes at their bases. Hikers will face more challenges here but will also enjoy more dramatic scenery.

If you just want to go for a short walk, there are several picturesque and densely forested valleys south of Zakopane, of which **Dolina Strążyska** is the most attractive. It's long been a popular walking and picnic area for locals, and for reasonably fit walkers it should take no longer than 50 minutes to walk all of it by the red trail up to Polana Strążyska. From there you can come back the same way or transfer by the black trail to either of the neighbouring valleys, the **Dolina Białego** to the east being the usual way. It takes around an hour to get to this charming valley and another hour to go all the way down to Zakopane.

The most popular mountaintop climbed in the Tatras is **Mt Giewont** (1894m), the very symbol of Zakopane. You can reach it via the red trail in about 3½ hours from Zakopane. A reasonable level of fitness is required to attempt this climb.

Before you do any walking or climbing, you should get hold of the 1:25,000-scale *Tatrzański Park Narodowy* map (15zł), published by Sygnatura. It shows all the trails in the area, complete with walking times both uphill and downhill. Another option is the 1:20,000-scale *Tatry Polskie* (Polish Tatras) map (14zł), which is divided into two sheets.

Camping is not allowed in the park, but there are several basic PTTK mountain hostels dotted around the slopes and mountaintops. The tourist office in Zakopane has a list and details.

Pstrąg Górski
SEAFOOD €€

(📞 512 351 746; ul Krupówki 6a; mains 20-40zł; ⏱10am-10pm; 🖥) This fish restaurant, done up in traditional style and overlooking a narrow stream, serves some of the freshest trout, salmon and sea fish in town. Trout is priced at 5zł and up per 100g (whole fish), bringing the price of a standard fish dinner to around 30zł, not including sides.

Karczma Zapiecek
POLISH €€

(📞 18 201 5699; www.karczmazapiecek.pl; ul Krupówki 43; mains 15-25zł; ⏱10am-11pm) One of the better choices among a group of similar highlander-style restaurants along ul Krupówki, with great food, an old stove and a terrace.

Stek Chałupa
POLISH €€

(📞 18 201 5918; www.stekchalupa.pl; ul Krupówki 33; mains 20-40zł; ⏱9am-midnight) This atmospheric highlander outfit is good for grilled sausages and steaks in all their guises.

🍸 Drinking & Nightlife

Cafe Piano
BAR

(📞 18 201 2108; www.cafepianozakopane.net; ul Krupówki 63; ⏱3pm-midnight) This secretive bar, situated down a back alley with a beautiful garden out back, is something of an insider's secret: located close to the throngs piling down ul Krupówki yet far away in atmosphere. The clientele tends toward local with an artistic bent.

Appendix
CAFE

(📞 18 200 0220; ul Krupówki 6; ⏱1pm-midnight; 🖥) A mellow venue for an alcoholic or caffeine-laden drink, hidden away above a mineral shop with an ambient old-meets-new decor. It occasionally hosts live jazz.

ℹ Information

Bank Pekao (📞 18 202 2850; al 3 Maja 5; ⏱9am-6pm Mon-Fri, 9am-1pm Sat) Centrally located bank and ATM.

Małopolska Tourist Information (Małopolski System Informacji Turystycznej; 📞 18 201 2004; www.visitmalopolska.pl; ul Kościeliska 7; ⏱9am-5pm Mon-Sat) The regional tourist information office has lots of info on the Tatras, as well as loads of brochures on neighbouring towns and cities, including Kraków, depending on where you're planning to go.

Post Office (📞 18 201 2277; ul Krupówki 20; ⏱7am-7.30pm Mon-Fri)

Tourist Information Centre (📞 18 201 2211; www.zakopane.pl; ul Kościuszki 17; ⏱9am-5pm Mar-Aug, 9am-5pm Mon-Fri Sep-Feb) Small but helpful municipal tourist office just south of the bus station on the walk toward the centre. It has free city maps and sells more-detailed hiking maps.

ℹ Getting There & Away

Bus is far and away the best transport option for reaching Zakopane, though there are a few |trains that still use the town's small **train station** (PKP; 📞 information 19 757; www.pkp.pl; ul Chramcówki 35).

BUS

Szwagropol (📞 12 271 3550; www.szwagropol. pl) operates hourly bus services to Kraków (16zł, 1¾ hours), departing from the **bus station** (PKS; 📞 666 396 090; www.zdazakopane.pl; ul Kościuszki 23). Here you'll find at least two daily buses to Nowy Sącz (20zł, three hours), Przemyśl (40zł, 4½ hours) and Rzeszów (40zł, 4½ hours). **Strama** (📞 602 501 415; www.strama. eu) offers regular coach service between Zakopane and Poprad, Slovakia (22zł, two hours), with stops at major points on the Slovak side of the High Tatras.

TRAIN

A few trains throughout the day go to Kraków (25zł, 3½ hours), but buses are faster and more frequent.

CARPATHIAN FOOTHILLS

The Carpathian Foothills (Przedgórze Karpackie) form a green and hilly belt sloping from the Vistula and San River valleys in the north to the true mountains in the south. Except for Wadowice and Kalwaria Zebrzydowska, which are usually visited from Kraków, most sights in the region are located along the Kraków–Tarnów–Rzeszów–Przemyśl road.

Wadowice
POP 19,200

The birthplace of one Karol Wojtyła (better known to the world as Pope John Paul II), Wadowice (vah-do-*vee*-tsah) has evolved into a popular pilgrimage destination in its own right. People come to walk the pretty cobblestones, pay their respects to the Wojtyła family home and, maybe most importantly, have a slice of the town's legendary cream cake, *kremówka*. The former pope himself was a big fan.

The **tourist office** (📞 33 873 2365; www. it.wadowice.pl; ul Kościelna 4; ⏱9am-8pm Mon-

A PILGRIMAGE TO KALWARIA ZEBRZYDOWSKA

Fourteen kilometres east of Wadowice (35km southwest of Kraków) is Kalwaria Zebrzy-dowska (kahl-vah-ryah zeb-zhi-dof-skah), Poland's second-most-important pilgrimage site after Jasna Góra in Częstochowa.

The town owes its existence and fame to the squire of Kraków, Mikołaj Zebrzydowski, who commissioned the church and monastery for the Bernardine order in 1600. Having noticed a resemblance in the area to the topography of Jerusalem, he set about creating a place of worship similar to the Via Dolorosa in the Holy City. By 1617, 24 chapels were built over the surrounding hills, some of which looked as though they'd been brought directly from the mother city. As the place attracted growing numbers of pilgrims, more chapels were erected, eventually totalling 42. In 1999 Kalwaria Zebrzydowska was added to Unesco's list of World Heritage sites.

The original hilltop church north of the centre was gradually enlarged and today is the massive **Basilica of Our Lady of the Angels** (Bazylika Matki Bożej Anielskiej). The holiest image in the church is the icon of Mary in the **Zebrzydowska Chapel** (Kaplica Zebrzydowska) to the left of the high altar. Tradition has it that the eyes shed tears of blood in 1641, and from that time miracles occurred. Pilgrims come to Kalwaria year-round but especially on Marian feast days, when processions along the **Calvary Trails** (Dróżki Kalwaryjskie) linking the chapels take place. The basilica is flanked to the north by the huge **Bernardine Monastery** (Klasztor Bernardynów; ☑ 33 876 6304; www.kalwaria. eu; ul Bernardyńska 46; ☉ 7am-7pm), which contains impressive 16th- and 17th-century paintings in its cloister.

Kalwaria is also known for its **Passion plays**, a blend of religious ceremony and popular theatre re-enacting the final days of Christ's life and held here since the 17th century. They are performed by locals, including Bernardine monks, during a two-day procession starting in the early afternoon of Maundy (Holy) Thursday during the Holy Week of Easter.

Fri, 10am-4pm Sat & Sun May-Oct, 8am-4pm Mon-Fri, 10am-4pm Sat Nov-Mar) can provide all the information you need, including a free booklet entitled *Karol Wojtyła's Foot Trail*, which marks out the most important pope-related sights in town.

◉ Sights

Family Home of John Paul II   MUSEUM

(Dom Rodzinny Jana Pawła II; ☑ 33 823 2662, reservations 33 823 3565; www.domjp2.pl; ul Kościelna 7; adult/concession incl Polish guide 18/10zł, incl English guide 27/25zł; ☉ 9am-7pm May-Sep, shorter hours rest of year) The home where Karol Wojtyła was born on 18 May 1920 and spent his childhood is now a popular museum, fitted out as a replica of how the rooms once looked.

The Wojtyła family lived in this small 1st-floor apartment, with just two rooms and a kitchen, from 1919 to 1938. Entry is by guided tour, with English-speaking guides available. Order tickets by phone or online, or buy them at a special ticketing office at Plac Jana Pawła II 5.

Town Museum   MUSEUM

(Muzeum Miejskie; ☑ 33 873 8100; www.muzeum. wadowice.pl; ul Kościelna 4; adult/concession 5/3zł; ☉ 9am-5pm Mon-Fri, 10am-4pm Sat & Sun May-Sep, 9am-4pm Mon-Fri, 10am-4pm Sat Oct-Apr) Located inside the same building as the tourist office, the Town Museum features an interactive multimedia exhibition on the pope's life and Wadowice at the time of his childhood.

⛉ Drinking

Kawiarna Mieszczańska   CAFE

(☑ 500 636 842; ul Kościelna 6; cream cakes 5zł; ☉ 9am-7pm Apr-Oct, to 5pm Nov-Mar) Wadow-ice is famous in Poland for its *kremówka*, a calorific pastry of cream, eggs, sugar and a dash of brandy. Everyone claims to serve the real McCoy, but we think the best is here at Kawiarna Mieszczańska, next to the tourist office.

ⓘ Getting There & Away

There are hourly buses to Kraków (11zł, 1¼ hours), some of which go via Kalwaria Zebrzy-dowska (6zł, 30 minutes). A half-dozen daily buses go to Katowice (15zł, two hours).

Tarnów

POP 111.370

Though you probably wouldn't guess it while strolling about its pleasant, finely restored Old Town, Tarnów (*tar*-noof) is an important regional industrial centre and transport hub. With just the right number of attractions and of a manageable size, it's the perfect place to stay put for a while.

History

The town layout – an oval centre with a large square in its middle – is unusual, suggesting the town was planned in medieval times. Tarnów is indeed an old city: its municipal charter was granted in 1330. Developing as a trade centre on the busy Kraków–Kyiv route, the town enjoyed good times in the Renaissance period. But a fire in the 15th century completely destroyed the medieval city, which was not rebuilt for almost 200 years.

Tarnów traditionally had a sizable Jewish community, which by the 19th century accounted for half the city's population. Of the 25,000 Jews living here in 1939, only a handful survived WWII. To remind itself and others of its past, Tarnów uses a stylised yellow Star of David in its tourist-office logo.

The city is also one of the major centres for Poland's small Roma population and the museum here has one of Europe's few exhibitions of Roma history. The museum includes a small section on the Roma Holocaust, in which hundreds of Roma from around the Tarnów region were rounded up by the Germans and killed.

◎ Sights

Town Hall   MUSEUM

(Muzeum Okręgowe w Tarnowie/Ratusz; ☑14 621 2149; www.muzeum.tarnow.pl; Rynek 1; adult/concession 8/5zł, Sun free; ◎9am-5pm Tue-Fri, 10am-4pm Sat & Sun) The dramatic city hall, at the centre of the Rynek, began as a Gothic building in the 15th century. It was given a Renaissance makeover and renovated again in the 19th century. The clock dates from the 16th century and is one of the country's oldest. The building holds a branch of the regional museum, where you can see the grand interiors and admire the extensive holdings of silver, art and glass of the noble family that once controlled the town.

Ethnographic Museum   MUSEUM

(Muzeum Etnograficzne; ☑14 622 0625; www.muzeum.tarnow.pl; ul Krakowska 10; adult/concession 8/5zł, Sun free; ◎9am-5pm Tue & Thu, 9am-3pm Wed & Fri, 10am-4pm Sat & Sun) This branch of the city's regional museum has Europe's only permanent collection relating to Roma culture. In the backyard there's an open-air exhibition of original Roma horse carriages, and visitors to the museum, on request, can take part in a traditional fire ring with dancing. The museum is housed in an old inn dating from at least the 18th century, featuring exterior walls with floral motifs from Zalipie.

Cathedral   CHURCH

(☑14 621 4501; www.katedra.tarnow.opoka.org.pl; Plac Katedralny; ◎9am-noon & 1-5.30pm Mon-Sat) Tarnów's cathedral dates from the 14th century but was remodelled at the end of the 19th century in neo-Gothic style. The interior shelters several Renaissance and Baroque tombs, of which two in the chancel are among the largest in the country. Also of interest are the 15th-century oak stalls under the choir loft, a pair of ornately carved pulpits facing one another and two early-16th-century stone portals at the western and southern porches.

Diocesan Museum   MUSEUM

(Muzeum Diecezjalne; ☑14 621 9993; www.muzeum.diecezja.tarnow.pl; Plac Katedralny 6; ◎10am-noon & 1-3pm Tue-Sat, 9am-noon & 1-2pm Sun) FREE This museum has a very good collection of Gothic sacred art, including some marvelous Madonnas and altarpieces, and an extensive display of folk and religious painting on glass.

Former Synagogue   HISTORIC SITE

(ul Żydowska) The area east of the Rynek was traditionally inhabited by Jews, but little of the original architecture survived the German occupation in WWII. Of the 17th-century former synagogue off ul Żydowska, destroyed by the Germans in 1939, only the brick bimah (from where the Torah was read) and a few pieces of mortar still stand.

Jewish Cemetery   CEMETERY

(Cmentarz Żydowski-Kirkut; ul Szpitalna) This former Jewish burial ground is the largest of its kind in southern Poland; it lies 1km north of the centre. The cemetery dates from the 16th century and has about 4000 tombstones in various states of decay and disarray. It was ravaged by the Germans

Tarnów

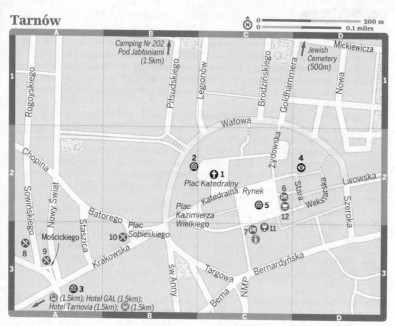

during WWII and the cemetery served as a place of mass slaughter in 1942 and 1943. The gates are often open; ask at the tourist-information centre if you will need a key.

🛏 Sleeping

Tourist Information Centre   GUESTHOUSE €
(☑14 688 9090; www.it.tarnow.pl; Rynek 7; s/d 90/120zł; 🛜) Tarnów's tourist-information centre offers one of the best sleeping deals in town, letting out rooms above its office on the Rynek. Don't expect luxury: this is as basic as it gets – just a bed and bath. But you can't beat it for value. No breakfast, but several cafes are nearby. Call or email to reserve a room.

Camping Nr 202 Pod Jabłoniami   CAMPGROUND €
(☑502 562 005; www.camping.tarnow.pl; ul Piłsudskiego 28a; per person/tent/caravan 17/10/20zł, d/tr/q 110/130/160zł; ⊙Apr-Oct; 🅿) About 1km due north of the Old Town, this camping ground also has 18 simple bungalows with shared facilities.

★Hotel GAL   HOTEL €€
(☑14 688 9930; www.hotel.tarnovia.pl; ul Dworcowa 5; s/d/tr 180/220/240zł; 🅿@🛜) Every Polish city should be so lucky as to have such an attractive hotel so close to the train

and bus stations. This Art Nouveau hotel, dating from 1904, got a total makeover in 2014. The rooms are done out in contemporary style and are large, light and airy. There's free parking on site and the staff is friendly and helpful.

Hotel U Jana   HOTEL €€
(☑14 626 0564; www.hotelujana.pl; Rynek 14; s/d/tr 160/220/280zł; 🛜) This all-suite hotel

Tarnów

PAINTED HOUSES OF ZALIPIE

The village of Zalipie, 36km northwest of Tarnów, has been known as a centre for folk painting for more than a century, ever since its inhabitants started to decorate both the inside and outside of their houses with colourful floral designs. Today about 20 such houses can be seen in Zalipie, with another dozen or so in the neighbouring villages of Kuzie, Niwka and Kłyż.

The best-known painter was Felicja Curyłowa (1904–74), and since her death her three-room farmhouse has been opened to the public as the **Felicja Curyłowa Farmstead Museum** (Muzeum Zagroda Felicji Curyłowej; ☑14 641 1912; www.muzeum.tarnow. pl; Zalipie 135, Olesno; adult/concession 6/4zł; ☺10am-6pm Tue-Sun). Every flat surface is painted with colourful flowers, and on display are painted dishes, icons and costumes.

In order to help maintain the tradition, the Painted Cottage (Malowana Chata) contest for the best-decorated house has been held annually since 1948, during the weekend following Corpus Christi (late May or June).

At the **House of Painters** (Dom Malarek; ☑14 641 1938; www.dommalarek.pl; Zalipie 128a; ☺8am-6pm Mon-Fri, 11am-6pm Sat & Sun Jun-Aug, 8am-4pm Mon-Fri Sep-May), which serves as a centre for the village's artists, you can watch the women painters at work.

There are only a few buses daily from Tarnów, making a trip here more practical if you have your own wheels. The Tarnów tourist-information centre can help sort out bus timetables.

is the classiest and most central place to stay in the Old Town, conveniently located on the Rynek. The 10 apartments have decent artwork on the walls, the beds are huge and the bathrooms are up to date. Breakfast is 15zł extra.

✖ Eating

Bar Mleczny Łasuch POLISH €
(☑14 627 7123; ul Sowińskiego 4; mains 7-12zł; ☺8am-7pm Mon-Fri, 9am-3pm Sat) Inexpensive milk bar serving low-priced but very good Polish staples like *bigos* (cabbage and meat stew) and stuffed cabbage rolls, located 200m southwest of the Rynek.

★ Kawiarnia Tatrzańska POLISH €€
(☑14 622 4636; www.kudelski.pl; ul Krakowska 1; mains 15-30zł; ☺9am-10pm; ☎) This atmospheric restaurant-cafe sports an eclectic menu, with a starters list that includes *żurek* (traditional sour rye soup), carpaccio and spinach pancakes. Mains revert more or less to the mean, with items such as pork tenderloin and fried trout. The traditional 19th-century cafe setting is elegant without being stuffy. It's a good stop for coffee, cake and ice cream as well.

Bombay Music INDIAN €€
(☑14 627 0760; www.bombay.pl; ul Krakowska 11a; mains 15-30zł; ☺10am-10pm; ☑) The Bombay serves up somewhat less-than-authentic Indian dishes (plus a few European ones) in elegant surrounds, with the occasional live-music set in the evenings. The restaurant is a little hard to find; it's not right on ul Krakowska as the address indicates but in a modern-looking building entered from ul Mościckiego (a small side street 200m south of the Rynek).

☐ Drinking & Nightlife

Kawiarnia Pod Arkadami CAFE
(☑14 688 9050; ul Wekslarska 2; ☺noon-midnight Mon-Fri, from 3pm Sat & Sun) Popular cafe on the southeastern corner of the Rynek. Has a local reputation for drawing actors and the arts crowd.

Alert Pub BAR
(☑14 676 0614; Rynek 9; ☺10am-late; ☎) Set in beautifully decorated cellars, this studenty place offers plenty of drinks, a few budget dishes and dance music on some weekends. In summer it has tables on the Rynek.

ⓘ Information

Bank Pekao (☑14 631 8204; ul Wałowa 10; ☺8am-6pm Mon-Fri) Centrally located bank and 24-hour ATM.

PTTK Office (☑14 655 4352; www.tarnow. pttk.pl; ul Żydowska 20; ☺noon-7.30pm Mon & Thu, 9am-3.30pm Tue, Wed & Fri) The local branch of Poland's nationwide Tourist & Sightseeing Society is weak on Tarnów, but it's a good source of information if you're planning to do any mountain hikes or need information on staying at PTTK-run mountain huts. It also sells hiking and cycling maps.

Tourist Information Centre (☑14 688 9090; www.it.tarnow.pl; Rynek 7; ⊗8am-8pm Mon-Fri, 9am-5pm Sat & Sun May-Oct, shorter hours rest of year; ☎) One of the best tourist-information offices in the country, offering a wealth of useful brochures, as well as free internet access, bike rental and low-cost accommodation above the office.

❶ Getting There & Away

Unlike many train stations in Poland, Tarnów's **station** (PKP; ☑ information 19 757; www.pkp.pl; Plac Dworcowy 1) is worth seeking out in its own right. The grand Art Nouveau structure was completed in 1910 and lovingly restored in 2010. It's located next to the bus terminal, 1km southwest of the Rynek, and is an easy 15-minute walk following ul Krakowska.

Trains to Kraków (17zł, 1½ hours) and Rzeszów (17zł, 1½ hours) run every hour or so. There are departures every other hour to Nowy Sącz (18zł, two hours). Two or three trains go daily to Warsaw (90zł, 4½ hours), usually through Kraków.

The **bus station** (PKS; ☑14 688 0755; www.pkstarnow.pl; ul Braci Saków 5; ⊗info desk 8am-4pm Mon-Fri) is not far from the train station, and also about 1km southwest of the Rynek. There are hourly buses west to Kraków (16zł, two hours) and east to Rzeszów (17zł, two hours), as well as south to mountain jumping-off points like Nowy Sącz (14zł, one hour) and Sanok (30zł, four hours).

Rzeszów

POP 157,800

The chief administrative and industrial centre of southeastern Poland, Rzeszów is a surprisingly elegant medium-sized city boasting a handsome square lined with some great clubs, restaurants and hotels, all enlivened by a large student population. It's a highly recommended sojourn if you're looking for some more urbanised fun to balance out your treks in the mountains. It's also a transport hub, meaning you're likely to pass through in any event. As far as stopovers go, this is the most promising around.

Rzeszów started life in the 13th century as a remote Ruthenian settlement. It grew rapidly in the 16th century when Mikołaj Spytek Ligęza, the local ruler, commissioned a church and a fortified castle. It later fell into the hands of the powerful Lubomirski clan, but this couldn't save the town from subsequent decline.

◉ Sights

Rzeszów's main square is a festive spot lined with some lovely Art Nouveau townhouses. In the centre is a monument to Tadeusz Kościuszko, honoured by Poles and Americans alike. In the southwest corner, the 16th-century **town hall** was wholly remodelled a century ago in neo-Gothic style.

★**Underground Tourist Route** CELLARS
(Podziemna Trasa Turystyczna; ☑ reservations 17 875 4774; www.trasa-podziemna.erzeszow.pl; Rynek 26; adult/concession 6.50/4.50zł; ⊗10am-7pm Tue-Fri, 11am-6pm Sat & Sat) Rzeszów's prime attraction is this 369m-long route that links 25 old cellars; it took 17 years to complete. The cellars date from the 15th to the 20th centuries and are on different levels (the deepest is nearly 10m below the Rynek). Visits are by guided tour and last about 45 minutes. Three English-language tours depart daily through the week (11.50am, 2.50pm, 4.50pm) and two on weekends (12.50pm and

(sidebar running vertically) CARPATHIAN MOUNTAINS RZESZÓW

RZESZÓW'S JEWISH HERITAGE

As a regional hub, Rzeszów was traditionally home to a large number of Jews. The pre-WWII Jewish population numbered around 18,000, or about one-third of the city's total. Most of this community perished in 1942 at the German-run extermination camp at Bełżec (p000), near Lublin. Not much trace of this once-vibrant community remains, with the exception of two impressive synagogues northeast of the Rynek. The 18th-century **New Town Synagogue** (Synagoga Nowomiejska; ul Sobieskiego 18) FREE dates originally from the early 18th century and was built in a fusion of Renaissance and Baroque styles. It was used by the Germans as a warehouse during WWII, and after the war fell into ruin. It now houses a contemporary-art gallery. Note the gate on the 1st floor – made of wrought iron and clay, it's the work of the contemporary sculptor Marian Kruczek. The smaller 17th-century **Old Town Synagogue** (Synagoga Staromiejska; ul Bożnicza 4) is the older of the two. The style here is Renaissance. It was partly destroyed by the Germans during WWII and now holds the city's archives. It's closed to the public.

Rzeszów

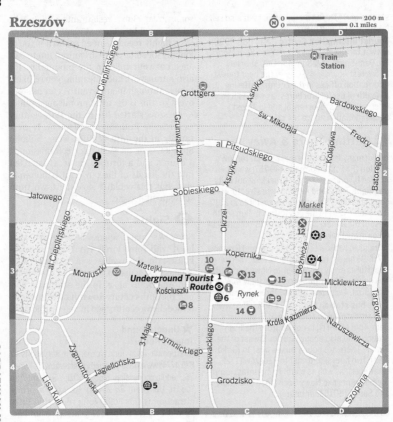

2.50pm). Buy tickets from the tourist-information centre in the same building.

Rzeszów Regional Museum MUSEUM
(Muzeum Okręgowe w Rzeszowie; ☑ 178535278; www.muzeum.rzeszow.pl; ul 3 Maja 19; adult/concession 7/5zł; ◷ 9am-3.30pm Mon-Thu, 10am-5.30pm Fri, 3pm-8pm Sun) Housed in a one-time Piarist monastery, complete with frescoed vaulting from the 17th century, the Rzeszów Regional Museum contains Polish paintings from the 18th to the 20th centuries and European art from the 16th to the 19th centuries.

Communist Monument MONUMENT
(al Cieplińskiego) Rzeszów's overblown *Monument of the Revolutionary Deed* is impressive indeed and was dedicated to the fight against Nazi Germany. It was designed and erected in the 1970s and has withstood frequent calls over the years to pull it down.

🛏 Sleeping

Alko Hostel HOSTEL €
(☑ 17 853 4430; www.ptsm-alko.pl; Rynek 25; dm 40zł, d/tr from 90/150zł) We're not so sure it's a good idea to call a hostel 'alko', but this is a fairly laid-back affair. There are no amenities to speak of aside from a hard bed, but the Rynek location could hardly be better and the price is definitely right.

Hotel Pod Ratuszem HOTEL €
(☑ 17 852 9770; www.hotelpodratuszem.rzeszow.pl; ul Matejki 8; s/d/apt 115/140/170zł; ☏) This modern, perfectly central hotel is not the fanciest place in town – it's only rated at two stars – but it might just represent the best value, given the clean rooms and excellent location just off the Rynek. One drawback if you're bringing a car is the lack of convenient parking spaces.

Rzeszów

★**Grand Hotel** HOTEL €€
(☑17 250 0000; www.grand-hotel.pl; ul Dymnickiego 1a, ul Kościuszki; s 210-230zł, d 290-320zł; P❄@🛜🏊) All we can say is 'wow'. This boutique, a block from the Rynek, is one of the swankiest hotels we've seen in Poland. Postmodern touches – such as throw pillows in trendy earth tones scattered around the lobby – adorn this sensitively restored townhouse. The edgy contemporary look of the rooms is straight out of *Wallpaper** magazine. Rates drop 10% on weekends.

Hotel Ambasadorski Rzeszów HOTEL €€
(☑17 250 2444; www.ambasadorski.com; Rynek 13/14; s/d 300/380zł; P❄🛜) This smart four-star hotel occupies a beautifully renovated 17th-century townhouse at the back of the Rynek. The rooms are not quite eye-catchingly modern, but are plush, comfortable and quiet just the same. The hotel's coffee shop, Cukiernia Wiedeńska, at Rynek 14, offers very good ice cream and cake confections.

🍴 **Eating**

★**Kryjówka** POLISH €
(☑17 853 2717; www.kryjowka.eu; ul Mickiewicza 19; mains 10-15zł; ☺9am-10pm Mon-Fri, 10am-10pm Sat) One of the few addresses in the centre for high-quality, good-value Polish cooking.

It's set up like a typical milk bar, where you go to the steam table and pick out your meal from among classics like *bigos* (cabbage and meat stew), pork cutlets, potato pancakes and more, but the standard is higher.

Restauracja Saigon ASIAN €
(☑17 853 3593; www.saigon.rzeszow.pl; ul Sobieskiego 14; mains 14-20zł; ☺11am-10.30pm; ☑) Though this is nominally a Vietnamese restaurant, the food is more reminiscent of old-school Chinese, c 1985. Think sweet-and-sour pork and egg-drop soup. That said, they have added a few Vietnamese dishes to the menu, including a very good *pho* (beef noodle soup), and the food does make for welcome relief from *pierogi* and pizza.

Stary Browar Rzeszowski INTERNATIONAL €€
(☑17 250 0015; www.browar-rzeszow.pl; Rynek 20-23; mains 25-40zł; 🛜) Big, handsome brew-pub on the main square that serves oversized plates of steaks, ribs, and grilled meats, plus (as a nod to Poland) dishes of housemade *pierogi* and an enormous *golonka* (oven-baked pork knuckle), here placed on a bed of coleslaw with a side of mashed potatoes. Dine on the Rynek when weather permits.

🍷 **Drinking & Nightlife**

For pubs and clubs or just hanging out in the sunshine, head for the Rynek.

★**Graciarnia u Plastików** BAR
(☑17 862 5647; www.graty.itl.pl; Rynek 10; ☺10am-2am Sun-Thu, to 4am Fri & Sat) Popular student bar beneath and behind the Rynek that defies easy description. Walk down a flight of steep stairs to find thrift-shop furnishings, old lamps, plaster-of-paris sculptures, caricatures on the wall and a very laid-back vibe.

Życie jest Pękne CAFE
(☑17 862 5647; www.zyciejestpiekne.freehost.pl; Rynek 10; ☺9am-midnight Sun-Thu, to 2am Fri & Sat; 🛜) Charming cafe located on the southeastern corner of the main square. It's got a funky thrift-shop decor and a relaxed, student-friendly atmosphere.

Hola Lola CAFE
(☑730 119 180; ul Mickiewicza 3; ☺9am-2am Mon-Fri, 10am-2am Sat, noon-midnight Sun; 🛜) Industrial decor, big collaborative tables, third-gen coffees to order – yep, this is where Rzeszów's hipsters cool their heels. In addition to coffee, there are lots of beers and

ŁAŃCUT: HOW THE OTHER HALF LIVED

Just 24km east of Rzeszów, Łańcut (*wine*-tsoot) has Poland's largest and richest aristocratic home. The building started life in the 15th century, but it was Stanisław Lubomirski, 100 years later, who turned it into both a mighty fortress and a great residence when he redesigned the building in 1641.

Over the years, the residence has been reshaped and remodelled, gaining Rococo and neoclassical elements. The final important alteration, at the end of the 19th century, gave the building its neo-Baroque facades.

The last private owner, Alfred Potocki, one of the richest men in pre-WWII Poland, accumulated a fabulous collection of art during his tenancy. Shortly before the arrival of the Red Army in July 1944, he loaded 11 railway carriages with the most valuable objects and fled with the collection to Liechtenstein.

Just after WWII, the 300-room castle was taken over by the state and opened as the **Castle Museum** (Muzeum Zamek; ☑ 17 225 2008; www.zamek-lancut.pl; ul Zamkowa 1; adult/concession incl entry to castle, stables & coach house with audioguide 34/26zł, castle only 27/22zł; ☺ 11.45am-3pm Mon-Fri, 9.45am-5pm Sat & Sun). Visits are by guided tour only. Among the highlights are the 17th-century Grand Hall (Wielka Sień), the Renaissance-style Eastern Corridor (Korytarz Wschodni) and the Rococo Corner Room (Pokój Narożny). You'll be shown the Orangery (Oranżeria), with palms and parrots, and Potocki's collection of 55 carriages and sleighs in the Coach House (Wozownia), 300m south of the castle. The Stables (Stajnie), north of the Coach House, have a fine collection of more than 1000 icons from the 15th century onwards.

Just outside the large park surrounding the castle is the former **synagogue** (☑ 22 436 6000; www.fodz.pl; Plac Sobieskiego 16; admission 6zł; ☺ 11am-6pm Mon-Wed, Fri & Sat, to 4pm Thu, 2-6pm Sun), built in the 1760s. It has retained much of its original Rococo decoration and some liturgical items are on display.

There are several places to stay. The most atmospheric is the **Hotel Zamkowy** (☑ 17 225 2671; www.zamkowa-lancut.pl; ul Zamkowa 1; s/d/apt 130/200/320zł; ⓟ ⓢ), within the castle complex, though the rooms fall a little short of the overall opulence of the place. There's also a pretty castle **restaurant** (☑ 17 225 2805; www.zamkowa-lancut.pl; ul Zamkowa 1; mains 20-30zł), but try to book ahead, especially on weekends, when the restaurant tends to close down for wedding parties.

lemonades to choose from. Good wi-fi and big tables make it the perfect spot to open up a laptop and write your latest blog post or upload photos to Instagram.

ⓘ Information

Bank PKO (☑ 17 875 2800; ul 3 Maja 21; ☺ 8am-6pm Mon-Fri) Currency exchange and ATM located in a lovely neoclassical building.

Hard Drive Café (☑ 17 852 6147; ul Grunwaldzka 7; per hour 4.50zł; ☺ 8am-11pm Mon-Sat, 10am-10pm Sun) Copy shop with internet access.

Post Office (☑ 17 852 0813; ul Moniuszki 1; ☺ 7am-9pm Mon-Fri, 8am-2pm Sat)

Tourist Information Centre (☑ 17 875 4774; www.podkarpackie.travel; Rynek 26; ☺ 9am-5pm Mon, 10am-6pm Tue-Fri, 11am-6pm Sat & Sun) Cheerful tourist-information office situated on the western end of the Rynek and sharing space with the city's Underground Tourist Route.

ⓘ Getting There & Around

BUS

The **bus station** (PKS; ☑ information 17 852 3435; ul Grottgera 1) is about 500m north of the Rynek. Buses depart roughly every hour for Tarnów (16zł, 1½ hours), Sanok (14zł, 1½ hours), Krosno (12zł, 1½ hours), Przemyśl (15zł, two hours) and Lublin (30zł, 3½ hours). Buses also go to Ustrzyki Dolne (18zł, 2½ hours, five daily) and Ustrzyki Górne (26zł, 3½ hours, three daily). Buses to Łańcut (8zł, 30 minutes) run roughly every half-hour or so and are more convenient than trains, as they stop near the palace.

TRAIN

The train station is north of the centre, about 100m east of the bus station. Trains depart almost hourly for Przemyśl (22zł to 42zł, 1½ hours) and Tarnów (15zł, one hour). A dozen or so daily trains leave for Kraków (25zł, 2½ hours); several go to Warsaw (90zł, five hours).

Przemyśl

POP 66,600

A sleepy town with an impossible name, Przemyśl (*psheh*-mishl) is close to the Ukrainian border and off the usual tourist route. Przemyśl has an attractive main square and some beautiful churches and worthwhile museums to explore.

History

Founded in the 10th century on terrain long fought over by Poland and Ruthenia (today's Ukraine), Przemyśl changed hands several times before being annexed by the Polish crown in 1340. It experienced its golden period in the 16th century but declined afterwards. During the Partitions it fell under Austrian administration in the early 19th century.

Around 1850, the Austrians began to fortify Przemyśl. This work continued until the outbreak of WWI and resulted in one of the largest fortresses in Europe. It consisted of a double ring of earth ramparts, including a 15km-long inner circle and an outer girdle three times longer, with more than 60 forts placed at strategic points.

This formidable system played an important role in the early months of WWI and saw intense fighting between the Austro-Hungarian empire and tsarist Russia. The Austrian garrison eventually surrendered to the Russians in 1915 due to a lack of provisions.

Przemyśl had the bad luck to end up in the crosshairs in WWII as well. The town marked the border between Nazi Germany and Stalin's Russia from 1939 to 1941, when the two countries were allied. The actual border followed the San River, meaning Przemyśl's southern half went to Russia and the northern half to Germany. After the Germans attacked the Russians in 1941, Przemyśl endured weeks of heavy shelling and fighting before eventually falling to the Germans that same year.

⊙ Sights

Perched on a hillside and dominated by several mighty churches, Przemyśl's Old Town is a picturesque place. The sloping **Rynek** has preserved some of its old arcaded houses, mostly on its north and south sides. Many houses bear plaques in English giving the history of the place. Look especially at **Nos 16** and **17**. The former sports a beautifully restored Mannerist facade, while the latter boasts a Renaissance portal from 1560.

Przemyśl Cathedral CATHEDRAL
(☑16 678 2792; www.katedra-przemysl.pl; Plac Katedralny; church and crypts by donation, tower free; ⊙ church 8am-6pm, crypts 9am-4pm Tue-Sun, tower 8.30am-4.30 Tue-Sun) Przemyśl's cathedral, particularly its 71m-high freestanding **bell tower**, lords over the upper (southern) end of the Rynek. There's been a church up here since at least the 12th and 13th centuries. The interior is impressive, but be

PRZEMYŚL'S JEWISH HERITAGE

Przemyśl was an important Jewish settlement for centuries leading up to WWII. At the outbreak of the war, the Jewish community numbered around 22,000, one-third of the city's population. The initial situation for Przemyśl's Jews during WWII was different from that in other Polish cities, owing to Przemyśl's easterly position. For the first two years of the war (when Germany and the Soviet Union were allies and had carved up Poland between them), the frontier ran straight down the middle of Przemyśl. Most Jews found themselves in the Soviet occupation zone and were comparatively better off than their brethren in the Nazi-occupied areas. The situation deteriorated in 1941 after the Germans invaded the Soviet Union and quickly occupied the entire town. Most Jews were eventually sent to their deaths at the German-run Bełżec extermination camp near Lublin in 1942.

The only significant relics of the Jewish legacy are two synagogues (of four that existed before WWII), both dating from the end of the 19th century. The most important surviving **synagogue** (ul Słowackiego 13) is behind the building at ul Słowackiego 13, east of the Rynek. It functioned as a branch of the public library until 2015 but now stands vacant. The former **Jewish cemetery** (Cmentarz Żydowski; ☑16 678 3194; ul Słowackiego; ⊙8am-6pm) FREE can also be visited. It's at the far southern end of ul Słowackiego.

sure to visit the **crypts** in the basement for a fascinating exhibit on burial customs, some actual crypts and the exposed wall of the original 12th-century rotunda. You can climb the bell tower, though unfortunately the windows are closed at the top.

Franciscan Church of St Mary Magdalene
CHURCH

(Kościół Franciszkański Św Marii Magdaleny; ☑16 678 2460; www.przemysl.franciszkanie.pl; ul Franciszkańska 2a; ◉8am-6pm) This beautifully evocative church, with its enormous pillars dwarfing the three Baroque statues at the front, was built between 1754 and 1778 in late-Baroque and classical style. The church has a beautiful Rococo interior with a vaulted and frescoed nave.

Castle
RUIN

(al 25 Polskiej Drużyny Strzeleckiej 1) A short walk along ul Zamkowa brings you to what is left of this 14th-century castle. Built by King Kazimierz III Wielki (Casimir III the Great) in the 1340s to guard the kingdom's once eastern flank, it mutated into a Renaissance building two centuries later when it acquired its four loopholed towers, two of which have been restored. A local theatre and a cultural centre now occupy the restored rooms.

National Museum of Przemyśl
MUSEUM

(Muzeum Narodowe Ziemi Przemyskiej; ☑16 670 3000; www.muzeum.przemysl.pl; Plac Joselewicza 1; adult/concession 10/5zł; ◉10.30am-5.30pm Tue & Fri, 10am-3pm Wed, 9am-3pm Thu, 9am-4pm Sat, 11am-3pm Sun) This work in progress is slated to be the most important museum of history and artefacts in this part of Poland when it's eventually finished in the coming years. There's currently a splendid collection of Ruthenian icons and other religious art dating back to the 15th century and an exhibition on Przemyśl's role as a fortress town.

Museum of Bells & Pipes
MUSEUM

(Muzeum Dzwonów i Fajek; www.muzeum. przemysl.pl; ul Władycze 3; adult/concession 10/5zł, Wed free; ◉10.30am-5.30pm Tue, Thu & Fri, 10am-2pm Wed, 9am-3pm Thu, 9am-4pm Sat, 11am-3pm Sun) This curious museum, housed in an 18th-century Baroque clock tower, contains vintage bells as well as elaborately carved wooden and meerschaum pipes and cigar cutters (items that Przemyśl has long been famous for manufacturing). The rooftop affords a panoramic view of the town.

Przemyśl Fortress
FORTRESS

(Twierdza Przemyśl) Military buffs will want to see the remnants of Austria-Hungary's Przemyśl Fortress (Twierdza Przemyśl) surrounding the town. As these were mostly earth ramparts, however, they are now overgrown and resemble natural rather than artificial bulwarks. Among the best examples are **Fort I** (Salis Soglio) in Sieliska, **Fort VIII** (Łętownia) in Kuńkowce and **Fort XIII** (San Rideau) in Bolestraszyce. The tourist office can provide information about the sites and transport details.

Literature fans may be interested in knowing that Czech author Jaroslav Hašek set part of his classic WWI novel *The Good Soldier Švejk* in Przemyśl, and in fact Hašek's hapless anti-hero, Švejk, even spent some time behind bars here. Town fathers have made a virtue of this dubious connection to world literature and you'll see Czech artist Josef Lada's famous comical illustration of Švejk on signs around town. There's even a little **statue** of Švejk on the Rynek, where you can pose with him for a photo.

Caponier 8813
BUNKER

(☑505 077 838; www.projekt8813.pl; ul Piłsudskiego, next to Hotel Accademia; admission by donation; ◉2-6pm Sat, noon-6pm Sun, other times by appointment) This scary-looking cement bunker was built by the Russians in 1939 to fortify their then-border with Nazi Germany. It saw intense fighting in 1941, after the Germans attacked their former allies and later overran Przemyśl (and much of Eastern Europe).

🛏 Sleeping

Schronisko Młodzieżowe PTSM Matecznik
HOSTEL €

(☑16 670 6145; www.ptsm-matecznik.pl; ul Lelewela 6; dm from 25zł, s/d 50/90zł; @🛜) Rooms are basic with big iron bunks, but everything is clean and the staff is helpful. There are tables and wardrobes in the rooms, as well as a common kitchen and library. The hostel is located on the northern side of the San River and is about 20 minutes on foot from the train station. Note there's a 10am to 5pm lockout.

Hotel Europejski
HOTEL €

(☑16 675 7100; www.hotel-europejski.pl; ul Sowińskiego 4; s/d/tr 110/140/170zł; 🛜) Housed in a renovated building facing the neoclassic train station (1895), this old-school but well-maintained place has 29 bright rooms with high ceilings and modern bathrooms.

FAIRYTALE CASTLE OF KRASICZYN

The **castle** (☑16 671 8312; www.krasiczyn.com.pl; Krasiczyn ; adult/concession incl guided tour 14/7zł, park only 5/3zł; ☺9am-5pm) in the village of Krasiczyn (krah-*shee*-chin), about 11km southwest of Przemyśl, is right out of a fairy tale, with its formal rectilinear shape and turreted towers on the corners. The good news is that you can stay the night here, in what is one of Poland's most lavish accommodation options.

The castle was designed in Renaissance style by Italian architect Galeazzo Appiani and built between 1592 and 1618 for the wealthy Krasicki family. The design features a spacious, partly arcaded courtyard.

The cylindrical towers were meant to reflect the social order of the period and were named (clockwise from the southeastern corner) after God, the pope, the king and the nobility. The **God Tower** (Baszta Boska), topped with a dome, houses a chapel. The **King Tower** (Baszta Królewska), with its conical roof and little turrets, would make a lovely home for Rapunzel of long-haired fame. On the courtyard side of the castle walls are Renaissance sgraffiti decorations of biblical scenes and Polish nobility.

The **hotel** (☑16 671 8321; www.krasiczyn.com.pl; Krasiczyn 179; s/d/tr/ste from 160/220/320/500zł; [P][☎]) offers several different types of rooms, ranging from relatively modest, good-value single and double rooms in the coach house (separate from the castle) to more opulent doubles and suites (260/500zł) in the castle itself. There's even a luxurious five-bed Hunter's Pavilion (600zł), which has its own kitchen and garden. Within the grounds is a **restaurant** (☑16 671 8321; www.krasiczyn.com.pl; Krasiczyn; mains 20-40zł; ☺2-10pm Mon, 10am-10pm Tue-Sun; [P][☎]) that serves mostly Polish dishes in traditional surrounds.

The castle is an easy trip from Przemyśl (4zł, 20 minutes) on one of the frequent PKS buses. From Krasiczyn you can also reach Sanok (14zł, one hour, four daily) by bus.

Hotel Accademia HOTEL €€
(☑16 676 1111; www.hotelaccademia.pl; ul Piłsudskiego 4; s/d/ste 140/180/290zł; [☎]) Admittedly, the Accademia is one of those soulless modern hotels with a whiff of lingering neglect about it, but it wins points for good value, a decent breakfast buffet and a good location, 10 minutes on foot west of the Rynek. Many of the rooms boast tranquil views out over the river, but they are in varying states of repair.

Eating

Bar Rubin POLISH €
(☑16 678 2578; www.barrubin.pl; ul Kazimierza Wielkiego 19; mains 12-22zł; ☺9am-8pm) This popular 1970s-style diner serves delicious traditional Polish food at reasonable prices. With its red laminate walls and chrome chairs, the interior has a milk-bar feel. One welcome touch, at least on the hot summer day we stopped by, was air-conditioning. The address is misleading. Walk east from the Rynek along ul Kazimierza Wielkiego and you'll find it.

Fiore Cafe ICE CREAM €
(☑16 675 1222; www.cukierniafiore.pl; ul Kazimierza Wielkiego 17b; ☺10am-8pm) If you're looking for ice cream or a slice of something sweet, this retro, diner-style cafe on a pedestrian street just east of the Rynek should be your destination.

★**Cuda Wianki** INTERNATIONAL €€
(☑533 090 999; Rynek 5; mains 25-40zł; ☺10am-10pm; [☎]) It's been a long wait, but Przemyśl finally has a destination restaurant on the main square. The warm interior of white brick walls, light woods, and flowers on the table hint at the quality on the menu. You'll find inventive soups and salads, grilled seafood, creative meat courses and a liberal use of fresh basil. Good-value lunch specials.

Dominikańska POLISH €€
(☑16 678 2075; www.dominikanska.com.pl; Plac Dominikańska 3; mains 20-30zł; ☺11am-10pm) You'll find excellent Polish cooking at this upscale restaurant on a small square on the western end of the Rynek. We're a big fan of the home-style *żurek* soup and the beef roulade stuffed with buckwheat groats.

Drinking & Nightlife

Absynt CAFE
(☑16 675 1755; Plac Dominikańska 4; ☺11am-11pm; [☎]) Some of the city's best coffee and

espresso-based drinks – but not much absinthe – at this secluded spot on the far western end of the Rynek.

Kawiarnia Libera CAFE
(☑16 676 0520; Rynek 26; ☺10am-11pm; 🛜)
This offbeat student cafe is connected to a bookstore of the same name; it's on the northwestern side of the Rynek. Walk through a small metal gate to find what feels like a secret student meeting place inside.

ⓘ Information

The main commercial artery, ul Jagiellońska, which runs north and east of the Rynek, is a good place to look for ATMs.

Bank Pekao (☑16 678 3459; ul Jagiellońska 7; ☺9am-5pm Mon-Fri) Currency exchange and ATM.

Main Post Office (☑16 678 3270; ul Mickiewicza 13; ☺7.30am-8pm Mon-Fri, 8am-2pm Sat) Post office close to the train station.

Tourist Information Office (☑16 675 2163; www.visit.przemysl.pl; ul Grodzka 1; ☺9am-5pm Mon-Fri, 10am-6pm Sat & Sun Apr-Oct, 9am-5pm Mon-Fri, 10am-2pm Sat Nov-Mar; 🛜) Przemyśl's tiny but helpful tourist-information office is located just above the Rynek on the southern side of the square. It has free city maps, several useful brochures in English and a computer on hand to check email.

ⓘ Getting There & Away

The train and bus stations are next to each other on the northeastern edge of the town centre, about 600m from the Rynek.

Up to four buses a day depart for Sanok (12zł, 1½ hours), and there are also departures for Ustrzyki Dolne (14zł, two hours, three to four daily) and Rzeszów (10zł, two hours, 10 daily). Buses to Krasiczyn (4zł, 20 minutes) run as often as twice an hour.

Trains to Rzeszów (24zł, 1½ hours) depart regularly throughout the day. There are half a dozen fast trains and two express trains a day to Kraków (50zł, 4½ hours). One express and several fast trains go daily to Warsaw (120zł, seven hours), and one relatively fast train runs to Lublin (30zł, four hours).

BIESZCZADY

The region around the Bieszczady (byesh-*chah*-di), in the far southeastern corner of Poland and sandwiched between Ukraine and Slovakia, is one of thick forests and open meadows. Scantily populated and unspoilt, it's one of the most attractive areas of the country. As tourist facilities are modest, roads sparse and public transport limited, the Bieszczady region retains its relative isolation and makes for an off-the-beaten-track destination. It's popular with nature-lovers and hikers.

The range's eastern end, the highest and most spectacular part, has been decreed the Bieszczady National Park (Bieszczadzki Park Narodowy), with its headquarters in Ustrzyki Górne. At 292 sq km, it's Poland's third-largest national park after Biebrza and Kampinos. Its highest peak is Mt Tarnica (1346m).

Sanok

POP 38,818

Sanok, nestled in a picturesque valley in the Bieszczady Foothills, is the largest city in the region and a logical base for starting your exploration of the Bieszczady. It has been subjected to Ruthenian, Hungarian, Austrian, Russian, German and Polish rule in its eventful history. Although it contains an important industrial zone (where Autosan, the bus used in intercity and urban transport throughout Poland, is produced), it is a picturesque city, with an attractive town square and a few worthy sights of its own. It's also the springboard for several fascinating theme-based hiking trails, including the Icon Trail, which takes in the surrounding countryside's wealth of wooden churches.

⊙ Sights

Castle HISTORIC BUILDING
(Zamek; ul Zamkowa 2) The 16th-century building you see today in Renaissance style is simply a makeover of a Gothic castle that's been on this site since at least the 13th century. The high position overlooking the San River was prized for its defensive capability. Today the building houses the Historical Museum.

Historical Museum MUSEUM
(Muzeum Historyczne; ☑13 463 0609; www.muzeum.sanok.pl; ul Zamkowa 2; adult/concession 11/7zł; ☺8am-noon Mon, 9am-5pm Tue-Sun) Housed in the Renaissance-style castle, the museum is best known for its 700-piece collection of Ruthenian icons. The selection consists of about 260 large pieces dating from the 15th to the 18th centuries, most acquired after WWII from

abandoned Uniat churches. The museum's other treasure is the collection of paintings by Zdzisław Beksiński (1929–2005) on the top floor. Beksiński, who was born in Sanok, was one of Poland's most remarkable contemporary painters, with a fantastical style all his own.

Museum of Folk Architecture MUSEUM
(🖉 13 493 0177; www.skansen.mblsanok.pl; ul Rybickiego 3; adult/concession 14/8zł; ☉ 8am-6pm May-Sep, 9am-2pm Oct-Apr) Sanok's Museum of Folk Architecture is Poland's largest skansen (open-air museum of traditional architecture). You'll find around 120 historic buildings here and gain insight into the cultures of the Boyks and Lemks. Among the highlights are four timber churches, an inn, a school and even a fire station. To reach the skansen, walk north from the town centre for around 1km along ul Mickiewicza and ul Białogórska, cross the bridge over the San and turn right.

The museum is laid out loosely according to geography, with each region having its own ethnic identity and style. The interiors of many cottages are furnished and decorated as they once were, while some buildings house exhibitions; one of these features a collection of 200 icons.

**Franciscan Church
of the Holy Cross** CHURCH
(Kościół Franciszkanów Św Krzyża; 🖉 13 463 2352; www.franciszkanie.esanok.pl; ul Franciszkanska 7; ☉ 8am-6pm) At the southeast corner of the Rynek is the Franciscan Church of the Holy Cross, the town's oldest. The interior and exterior are in Baroque style and date to the mid-17th century, though recent

---

BOYKS & LEMKS: A TALE OF TWO PEOPLES

The Bieszczady, along with the Beskid Niski and Beskid Sądecki further west, were settled from around the 13th century by various nomadic Slavic groups migrating northwards from the south and east. Most notable among them were the Wołosi from the Balkans and the Rusini from Ruthenia. Though they lived in the same areas and even intermarried for centuries, they maintained distinct ethnic identities, which came to be known as Bojkowie and Łemkowie.

The Bojkowie (Boyks) inhabited the eastern part of the Bieszczady, east of Cisna, while the Łemkowie (Lemks) populated the mountainous regions stretching from the western Bieszczady up to the Beskid Sądecki. The two groups had much in common culturally, including a shared Orthodox faith that was similar to that of their Ukrainian neighbours.

After the Union of Brest in 1596, in which some western Orthodox faiths broke with the Patriarch in Constantinople, most Lemks and Boyks turned to the Uniat Church, which accepted the supremacy of Rome but retained the old Eastern liturgy. This lasted until the end of the 19th century, when the Catholic Church began to impose the Latin rite. In response, many Lemks and Boyks chose to revert to the more familiar traditions of the Orthodox Church. By WWII, the total population of Lemks and Boyks was estimated at around 200,000 to 300,000. Ethnic Poles were a minority in these areas.

The situation changed dramatically in the aftermath of WWII, when the borders of Poland and the Soviet Union were redrawn. Not everyone was satisfied with the new status quo, particularly a band of Ukrainian nationalists known as the Ukrainian Resistance Army, who were unhappy at finding themselves inside a newly reconstituted Poland. Civil war continued in the region for almost two years after Germany surrendered.

In a bid to rid the region of rebels, the postwar Polish government launched Operation Vistula (Akcja Wisła) in 1947 to expel the inhabitants of the region. Most residents were either deported to the Soviet Union or resettled in the western regions of Poland that had been recently regained from Germany. Ironically, the largest groups to be deported were the Boyks and the Lemks, who had little to do with the conflict. Only 20,000 Lemks, and very few Boyks, were left in the region.

Today, the most visible reminders of their legacy are the wooden Orthodox or Uniat churches dotting the countryside, many dilapidated but others still in decent condition. When hiking on remote trails, especially along the Ukrainian border in the Bieszczady, you'll find traces of destroyed villages, including ruined houses, orchards, churches and cemeteries.

Sanok

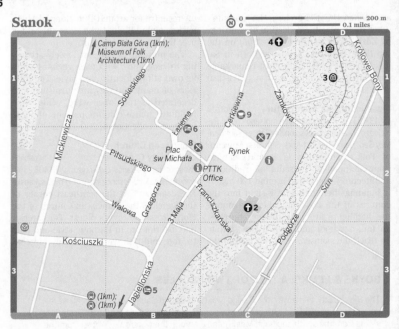

Camp Biała Góra (1km);
Museum of Folk
Architecture (1km)

Plac
św Michała

Rynek

PTTK
Office

Kościuszki

(1km);
(1km)

---

archeological discoveries indicate there was a church here going back much longer. The walls of the interior have a lacy, folksy feel. Look for the city's most famous piece of art: *The Miraculous Painting of the Virgin Mary in Consolation.*

**Orthodox Cathedral
of the Holy Trinity**　　　　CATHEDRAL
(Cerkiew Św Trójcy; ☏13 463 0681; ul Zamkowa 16; ◷8am-6pm) The neoclassical Orthodox Church of the Holy Trinity was built in 1784 and initially served the Uniat congregation. The main door behind the grill is left open for you to admire the modern iconostasis.

🏃 Activities

Sanok is an excellent base for **hiking** and the starting point (or at least en route) for several long-distance thematic hikes. The best known of these is the **Icon Trail** (Szlak Ikon), which takes you past tiny villages and their old Orthodox or Uniat churches. The most popular stretch is a 70km-long loop that begins and ends in Sanok and wends along the San River valley north of the city. The net walking time is about 15 hours.

Another fascinating long-distance trail that passes through Sanok is sure to appeal to literature fans. The **Švejk Trail**, usually marked on maps in yellow, passes through town as it traces the comical journey across several countries of the 'Good Soldier Švejk' in Czech writer Jaroslav Hašek's WWI novel of the same name.

Both trails, as well as several others, are designated on hiking maps of the Bieszczady available for purchase at the tourist information or PTTK offices. The tourist-information office also hands out a free photocopied, simplified trail map (though not detailed enough to hike with), showing the main villages and churches.

Sanok is a good base for **cycling**, both for mountain biking in the hills and for less strenuous, though still rewarding rides along the San River. The better hiking maps usually also designate cycling trails. The helpful staff of the Sanok tourist-information centre can help plan out a ride. To get started, buy a copy of the *Atlas Szlaków Rowerowych Podkarpackie* from the tourist office (50zł), which has all of the paths marked out.

Bicycles can be hired from Camp Biała Góra for 8/35zł per hour/day.

🛏 Sleeping

Camp Biała Góra　　　　CAMPGROUND €
(☏13 463 2818; www.campsanok.pl; ul Rybickiego 1, Biała Góra; camping per person/tent 15/15zł,

Sanok

◎ Sights
1 Castle...D1
2 Franciscan Church of the Holy
   Cross...C2
3 Historical Museum...............................D1
4 Orthodox Cathedral of the Holy
   Trinity...C1

◎ Sleeping
5 Hotel Pod Trzema Różami.................B3
6 Hotel Sanvit.......................................B2

◎ Eating
7 Karczma Jadło Karpackie...................C2
8 Stary Kredens....................................B2

◎ Drinking & Nightlife
9 Coś Słodkiego Cafe.............................C1

beds in bungalows per person 35zł; **P**) With not much room for caravans and only modest ground to pitch a tent, Biała Góra has mainly two- and four-person bungalows. There are communal cooking facilities and clean bathrooms, though the property itself is run-down. Located 1km north of the Rynek, on the other side of the river from town.

Hotel Pod Trzema Różami   HOTEL €
(☑13 464 1243; www.podtrzemarozami.pl; ul Jagiellońska 13; standard s/d/tr 90/120/140zł, luxury r 150zł; **P 🤝**) About 200m south of the main square, 'Under Three Roses' offers both standard and 'lux' rooms, the latter with full bathrooms and updated decor. Both types of room are clean and adequate for a short stay.

★ Hotel Sanvit   HOTEL €€
(☑13 465 5088; www.sanvit.sanok.pl; ul Łazienna 1; s/d/tr 140/190/240zł; **P 🤝**) Clean, reasonably priced and central, just west of the Rynek, the Sanvit is our top choice in Sanok. The 31 rooms are bright and modern, with shiny bathrooms. There's a restaurant and cafe, as well as a wellness centre with sauna, gym and salt cave.

✕ Eating & Drinking

Karczma Jadło Karpackie   POLISH €€
(☑13 464 6700; www.karczmasanok.pl; Rynek 12; mains 15-30zł; ⊗10am-11.30pm) This amenable, folksy bar and restaurant on the main square serves up unusual Carpathian dishes, including *hreczanyky* (a local dish made with minced pork and buckwheat groats) and *ogórki małosolne* (lightly salted pickles). Enjoy the terrace in nice weather.

★ Stary Kredens   POLISH €€€
(☑797 317 279; www.starykredens.com; Plac Świętego Michała 4; mains 25-50zł; ⊗11am-10pm; 🤝) Drawing on the inspiration of Polish TV-star chef Magda Gessler, the 'Old Wardrobe' has high culinary ambitions, and delivers. From creative appetisers like tart with herring and red beets to pan-fried trout and baked lamb, the chefs are clearly reaching for a more sublime side of Polish cooking. The setting – lace tablecloths and antiques – is refined but not stuffy.

Coś Słodkiego Cafe   CAFE
(☑507 671 191; ul Cerkiewna 2; ⊗10am-8pm) Easily the best ice-cream and coffee joint within walk of Sanok's Rynek. The ice cream is homemade and the espressos prepared with an eye for quality. There are also homemade lemonades and cakes and pastries. Take away or enjoy your treats in the back garden.

ℹ Information

Bank Pekao (☑13 465 6840; ul Kościuszki 4; ⊗9am-6pm Mon-Fri, to 1pm Sat) Centrally located bank and 24-hour ATM.

Post Office (☑13 464 4935; ul Kościuszki 26; ⊗7am-8pm Mon-Fri, 8am-3pm Sat)

PTTK Office (☑508 066 679; www.pttk. sanok.pl; ul 3 Maja 2; ⊗8am-5pm Mon-Fri) Convenient port of call for buying hiking maps and obtaining the latest information. The PTTK office organises hikes in the mountains and can help advise on planning routes and overnights in mountain cabins.

Tourist Information Centre (☑13 463 6060; www.sanok.pl; Rynek 14; ⊗9am-5pm Mon-Fri, to 1pm Sat & Sun) You'll come out of this convenient tourist-info centre on the main square clutching handfuls of free maps and other information on what to see and do in Sanok. There's a computer on hand for short-term web surfing. Also sells hiking and cycling maps.

Turizmusan (☑509 539 947; www.turizmusan. pl; ul Rybickiego 1, Biała Góra; bikes per hour/day 8/35zł; ⊗9am-5pm Mon-Fri) Travel agency focus on adventure tourism. It rents bikes and organises cycling and kayaking trips from the Biała Góra camping ground. Best to contact them in advance by phone or email in advance.

ℹ Getting There & Away

The train and bus stations are next to each other, connected via a pedestrian overpass, about 1.2km southeast of the Rynek.

There's hourly bus transport to Rzeszów (12zł, 1½ hours). Buses also run to Ustrzyki Dolne (10zł, one hour, 12 daily) and Ustrzyki Górne

(15zł, 1½ to 2½ hours, seven daily). Five to six buses run to Cisna (9zł, one hour) and Wetlina (13zł, 1½ to two hours), with additional departures in summer. Several fast buses go directly to Kraków (40zł, three hours), and a smaller number to Warsaw (60zł, four to five hours).

Passenger train service has been scaled back and trains now serve only a handful of destinations, including Rzeszów (22zł, four hours) and Krosno (9zł, 1½ hours), but these are better served by bus.

Lesko

POP 5639

Founded in 1470 on the banks of the San River, Lesko had a mixed Polish-Ruthenian population for centuries, a reflection of the region's history. From the 16th century, many Jews arrived from Spain, fleeing the Inquisition. Their migration continued and by the 18th century Jews made up nearly two-thirds of the town's population.

WWII and the years that followed changed the ethnic picture altogether. The Jews were slaughtered by the Nazis, the Ukrainians were defeated by the Polish military and the Lemks (p215) were deported. The town was rebuilt and, without having developed any significant industry, is now a small tourist centre. While it may not be the 'Gateway to the Bieszczady' as it likes to call itself – that distinction really goes to Sanok – it is a pleasant stopover on the way south.

Sights

Synagogue   SYNAGOGUE
(ul Joselewicza; adult/concession 4/2zł; ⊙10am-5pm May-Oct) This impressive former synagogue is the only one of five synagogues to survive WWII. It's located about 100m north of the Rynek. It was built in the Mannerist style in the mid-18th century and has an attached tower – a dead giveaway that it was once part of the town's fortifications. Little of the temple's original decoration has survived. The interior houses an art gallery (Galeria Sztuki Synagoga), which is supposed to showcase artists from the Bieszczady.

In the entryway is a list of towns and shtetls in the region with Jewish populations of more than 100, a poignant reminder of what the make-up of the region was before the German murderers arrived.

Jewish Cemetery   CEMETERY
(Kirkut w Lesku; ☑695 652 364; ul Moniuszki; adult/concession 7/5zł) Before WWII, Jews accounted for two-thirds of Lesko's population. This moving cemetery, dating back to the mid-16th century, has more than 2000 gravestones and gives a tiny hint of the size and importance of the community. To find the entrance, follow ul Moniuszki north (downhill) from the synagogue for 100m. The stairs on the right lead up to the cemetery. The gate is sometimes locked. If so, call the telephone number listed and someone will come to let you in.

WHEN GOD WAS ON VACATION

Based on the number of day-tours to Auschwitz-Birkenau on offer, especially out of Kraków, you would be forgiven for thinking the nightmare of the Holocaust, the time 'when God was on vacation' as some put it, was played out solely in the German-run extermination camps at Oświęcim in Silesia. But even a cursory trip around Galicia, the Austro-Hungarian province that was heavily Jewish and included many towns and cities in the south and east of modern-day Poland, will dispel that notion. As dozens of plaques, memorials and crude markers point out, hundreds of thousands of Polish Jews – in fact, a quarter of the three million Polish Jews annihilated – were murdered in their fields and forests at the hands of the Germans. And in some respects it is even more horrible to imagine such crimes committed in the idyllic surrounds of a country town or village.

And the cemeteries… You may have wondered why they are so overgrown, their broken stones pitched this way and that. The answer is simple: there are no relatives left. Brothers, mothers, husbands, lovers, nephews and granddaughters – none survived the Holocaust.

When a Jew dies, a prayer called the Mourner's Kaddish is recited for them. The kaddish is repeated at Yahrzeit, the first anniversary of the death, and annually after that. But virtually no Jews lying in cemeteries such as the one at Lesko have anyone to say this prayer for them.

Parish Church of Our Lady

CHURCH

(Kościół Parafialny Najświętszej Marii Panny; ☑13 469 6533; www.lesko.przemyska.pl; ul Kościuszki 10; ☺8am-6pm) Lesko's very pretty parish church stands west of the synagogue. It was built in 1539 and its exterior retains many Gothic features, including the eastern portal. The freestanding Baroque bell tower was added in the mid-18th century.

🛏 Sleeping & Eating

Stare Lisko

HOTEL €

(☑13 469 8632; www.starelisko.pl; Rynek 12, enter from ul Parkowa; s/d/tr 70/100/130zł; ℗) The Stare Lisko is the only hotel in Lesko that's right on the Rynek. That said, it's a modest, family-run affair, with eight small and rather plain rooms up under the eaves of its restaurant (mains 10zł to 25zł, open 9am to 9pm), which serves Polish favourites.

Pensjonat Zamek

HOTEL €€

(☑13 469 6268; www.zamek.bieszczady.pl; ul Piłsudskiego 7; s/d/tr 110/150/195zł; ℗🛜) From the exterior, Lesko's aging *zamek* (castle) looks none too inviting. Prospects change once you walk through the door to discover a well-run, atmospheric inn and the best place in town to stay. The public areas have retained some of the castle's 16th-century heritage. Alas, the rooms are unadorned, but they're comfortable. The location is a short walk from the Rynek.

ℹ Information

Bank Pekao (☑13 469 7051; ul Przemysłowa 11; ☺9am-4pm Mon-Fri)

Main Post Office (ul Parkowa 8; ☺7am-8pm Mon-Fri, 8am-3pm Sat) Central post office, situated just southwest of the Rynek.

Tourist Office (☑13 469 6695; www.lesko.pl; Rynek 1; ☺9am-5pm Mon-Fri) Helpful tourist office in a kiosk in the centre of the Rynek.

ℹ Getting There & Away

The bus station is on ul Piłsudskiego – the road to Sanok – about 1km west of the Rynek. There are plenty of buses to Sanok (6zł, 20 minutes), about 11 of which continue to Krosno (12zł, one hour). A dozen daily buses run to Rzeszów (14zł, two hours) and four express buses go directly to Kraków (46zł, three hours).

For the Bieszczady, three daily buses go to Cisna (8zł, one hour), and some wind up as far as Wetlina (10zł, 1½ hours). As many as 10 buses serve Ustrzyki Górne (12zł, two hours), half of which go via Ustrzyki Dolne.

Ustrzyki Dolne

POP 9600

An unprepossessing town in the southeastern corner of Poland, Ustrzyki Dolne (oost-*shi*-kee *dol*-neh) is only really worth a stop for those heading south into the Bieszczady. If you plan on trekking in the mountains independently, Ustrzyki Dolne is the last reliable place to exchange money and stock up on a decent range of provisions.

◉ Sights & Activities

There are several colour-coded hiking trails that begin around the centre, including the red-marked loop trail that starts at the bus station and takes in some of the surrounding peaks (4½ hours). The trails, as well as some recommended cycling routes, can be found in the English-language 'Town and Commune Guide' available for free at the tourist-information office.

Natural History Museum

MUSEUM

(Muzeum Przyrodnicze; ☑13 461 1091; www.bdpn.pl; ul Bełska 7; adult/concession 7/5zł; ☺8am-4pm Tue-Fri, 9am-5pm Sat) This modest museum, on a quiet street just a few metres north of the Rynek, is a good introduction to the geology, flora and fauna of the Bieszczady. The staff can advise on what to see and do in the Bieszczady National Park.

🛏 Sleeping & Eating

Hotel Laworta

HOTEL €

(☑13 468 9000; www.laworta.pl; ul Nadgórna 107; s/d/tr 100/160/200zł; ℗🛜) This isolated modern high-rise hotel is a good 1.5km walk uphill from the Rynek and the main bus station. Nevertheless, it offers clean rooms and good facilities, including tennis courts and a sauna. Call or book in advance to make sure someone is at the reception desk on your arrival.

Gościniec Dębowa Gazdówka

GUESTHOUSE €€

(☑13 461 3081; www.debowagazdowka.pl; ul Łodyna 43, Łodyna; s/d/tr 120/160/195zł) This rustic wooden farmhouse in a village 5km north of Ustrzyki Dolne is far better than anything in town. In addition to comfy, basic rooms of exposed wooden walls and floors, you get big, sweeping views of the mountains and a good, country-style restaurant. You'll need a lift from town, so work out transport in advance.

Orlik   PIZZA €

(☑13 471 1900; www.pizzeria-orlik.pl; Rynek 4a; pizza 12-17zł; ☉10am-10pm) This modest pizzeria, on the southern side of the Rynek, is the best of a slim range of dining options in town. Expect big, satisfying pizzas, plus surprisingly good espresso coffee, served on the terrace in good weather.

ℹ Information

Bank PKO (ul Belska 10; ☉8.30am-4pm Mon-Fri) Bank and 24hr ATM across the street from the museum.

Eko-Karpaty (☑570 631 315; www.eko-karpaty.com; Rynek 19; bikes per hr/day 8/35zł; ☉9am-8pm Mon-Fri, noon-5pm Sat) Rents bikes and organises rides and excursions in the Bieszczady and neighbouring countries.

Tourist Information Office (Bieszczadzkie Centrum Informacji i Promocji; ☑13 471 1130; www.cit.ustrzyki-dolne.pl; Rynek 16; ☉10am-6pm Mon-Fri, 10am-4pm Sat) Hands out a city map and the English-language *Town and Commune Guide*, both free. Also sells hiking and cycling maps of the Bieszczady area.

ℹ Getting There & Away

The train and bus stations are in one building. You won't get far by train, but the bus service is reasonably good. Two dozen daily buses run to Sanok (10zł, one hour), some passing through Lesko (5zł, 30 minutes) on the way. Up to seven buses (several more in summer) go daily to Ustrzyki Górne (9zł, 1½ hours). Destinations further afield include Przemyśl (14zł, two hours, four daily), Rzeszów (20zł, 2½ hours, seven daily) and Kraków (50zł, four hours).

Ustrzyki Górne

POP 120

Less a village than a string of houses scattered along the main road, Ustrzyki Górne is the Bieszczady's premier hiking base.

Since the Bieszczady loop road opened in 1962, the mountains have become more accessible. But this is still remote country and Ustrzyki Górne is a good example: it has a few mostly basic places to stay and eat, a little bit of life around the bus station and car park as you enter the village, and not much else. The village springs to life in summer, then sinks into a deep sleep for most of the rest of the year, stirring only a little in winter when the cross-country skiers arrive.

You can buy hiking maps and some general info from the reception desk at the Hotel Górski. A decent hiking map, with information in English, is ExpressMap's widely available 1:65,000 *Bieszczady* (15zł). The Bieszczady National Park has a small information centre near the bus stop. There's a store at the camping ground and a few small shops around the bus stop to buy provisions.

🏃 Activities

The number-one activity here, at least in summer, is **hiking**. Ustrzyki Górne is the most popular base for hiking the **Bieszczady National Park**, and several great walks along colour-coded trails start out from here (most from near the camping ground or the bus station and car park).

You'll find several longer and shorter routes marked out on hiking maps, but one popular loop to get you started begins in the village of Wołosate (take the regular bus from Ustrzyki Górne, about 3zł, 15 minutes). From here, follow the blue path (two hours) to the region's highest peak at Tarnica (1346m) and then back to Ustrzyki Górne along the red path (two to three hours).

The park is full of fascinating sights and sounds: the remnants of villages abandoned or destroyed during Operation Vistula (p215), ancient cemeteries, peat reserves (complete with quicksand) and the cry of a lone wolf in the distance.

🛏 Sleeping

Addresses in Ustrzyki Górne don't typically use street names, but the general directions in the hotel reviews should get you to where you're going.

Schronisko PTTK Kremenaros   HOSTEL €

(☑13 461 0605; www.kremenaros.com.pl; Ustrzyki Górne; dm 25-35zł; ☉Apr-Oct; ℗) This hostel is in the last house of the village, on the western side of the road heading towards Wetlina and opposite a huge border station. It's old and basic, but the staff is friendly and the atmosphere good. Rooms have between two and 10 beds. The restaurant has a very short menu, but the food is inexpensive and acceptable.

Camping Nr 150 PTTK   CAMPGROUND €

(☑13 461 0604; www.hotel-pttk.pl; Ustrzyki Górne; per person/tent 10/7zł, cabins with/without bathroom 40/35zł; ☉May-Sep; ℗) The pleasant camping ground next door to the well-marked Hotel Górski has some old triple cabins without bathrooms and newer double cabins with en suites.

HIKING IN THE BIESZCZADY

The Bieszczady is one of the best places in Poland to go hiking. The region is beautiful and easy to walk around, and you don't need a tent or cooking equipment as mountain hostels are a day's walk apart and provide food. The main area for trekking is the national park, with Ustrzyki Górne and Wetlina being the most popular starting points, followed by Cisna.

Bieszczady National Park counts about a dozen well-marked hiking trails, with a total length of 130km. All three jumping-off points have PTTK hostels, with helpful staff who can provide information, and all have boards outlining the trails, complete with walking times, both uphill and downhill. Ascending **Mt Tarnica** (the region's highest peak at 1346m) from Wołosate, southeast of Ustrzyki Górne, will take two to three hours. At least one of the trails reaches (but does not cross) the Ukrainian border at one point. Be sure to carry your passport when hiking in this area.

Mountain hostels will try their best to put you up for the night and feed you regardless of how crowded they get, but bear in mind that in July and August the floor will most likely be your bed, as these places are pretty small. Take a sleeping bag with you.

Get a copy of ExpressMap's 1:65,000-scale *Bieszczady* map (15zł), which covers the entire region. You can buy it and similar maps at the Hotel Górski in Ustrzyki Górne or at tourist-information offices in towns throughout the Bieszczady area.

Hotel Górski   HOTEL €€
(☑13 461 0604; www.hotel-pttk.pl; Ustrzyki Górne; s 95-125zł, d 170-200zł, apt 253-270zł; P@⊠) At the northern end of the village on the road to Ustrzyki Dolne and bedecked with flower baskets, this PTTK-run hotel is significantly better than anything else around. With 63 clean, comfortable and modern rooms, all with their own bathrooms, it's also the biggest place in town. The hotel has a gym and sauna, and its own reasonably priced restaurant.

✗ Eating & Drinking

Zajazd Pod Caryńską   POLISH €€
(☑511 311 552; www.carynska.pl; Ustrzyki Górne; mains 20-35zł; ⊙May-Oct; P) This handsome traditional wooden lodge and restaurant, 50m from the bus station in the direction of Ustrzyki Dolne, has the best cooking in the immediate vicinity. Big plates of pork and potato pancakes, goulash, baked pork knuckle and lots of soups are on the menu. Order at the counter and wait for your number. Live country music some nights.

Bieszczadzka Legenda   CAFE
(☑530 978 287; Ustrzyki Górne; ⊙10am-midnight May-Sep) Counter-culture comes to the Bieszczady in the form of this chilled-out, welcoming cafe and lunch bar, situated 60m from the bus station toward Ustrzyki Dolne. Grab a coffee or beer, scout out a lounge chair and kick back to some

electronica in the open air. There's light food, including some vegan and vegetarian options, served throughout the day.

ℹ Information

Bieszczady National Park Information Centre (Ośrodek Informacji i Edukacji Turystycznej BdPN; ☑13 461 0350; www.bdpn.pl; Lutowiska 2; park admission 6zł; ⊙7am-3pm Mon-Fri May-Oct) The national park's information centre is located about 200m into the park, along an unmarked road due east of the bus station and car park. Note the office is closed on weekends.

ℹ Getting There & Away

There are up to six buses daily to Ustrzyki Dolne (9zł, 1½ hours), two to Krosno (18zł to 19.50zł, three hours), three to Rzeszów (25zł, 3½ hours) and as many as seven to Lesko (12zł, two hours) and Sanok (15zł, 2½ hours). The frequency increases in July and August, while several buses and minibuses go to Wetlina (5zł, 30 minutes) and up to six to Cisna (7zł, 45 minutes).

Wetlina
POP 300

Wetlina is another popular jumping-off spot for hiking in the Bieszczady. Like Ustrzyki Górne, it stretches along one main road (in this case Hwy 897) and has a limited choice of simple places to sleep and eat.

BEACH BREAK AT SOLINA LAKE

About 30km southwest of Ustrzyki Dolne and accessible by bus is Solina Lake (Jezioro Solińskie), a reservoir 27km long and 60m deep, created in 1968 when the San River was dammed. Today it is the Bieszczady region's most important centre for water sports and recreation.

Polańczyk, the attractive town on the irregularly shaped lake's western shore, offers visitors everything from sailing and windsurfing to fishing and beaches. The **tourist office** (☑13 470 3028; www.esolina.pl; ul Wiejska 2, Polańczyk; ⊗8am-6pm Mon-Fri, 10am-5pm Sat), just off Hwy 894 on the way to Lesko, can supply you with all the details.

Ul Zdrojowa, which starts just east of the tourist office, is lined with hotels and sanatoriums offering any number of treatments. Many are huge, soulless blocks; instead head for **Pensjonat Korona** (☑13 469 2201; www.pensjonatkorona.pl; ul Zdrojowa 29; s/d 100/150zł), a pleasant guesthouse with 40 beds and its own restaurant just over 1km south down the peninsula.

🛏 Sleeping & Eating

Dom Wycieczkowy PTTK HOSTEL €
(☑13 468 4615; www.wetlinapttk.pl; Wetlina; dm 26zł, d 50-70zł; ℗) This simple hostel offers beds year-round in doubles and five-bed dorms. In summer you can also stay in cabins (30zł per person) or pitch your tent (11zł) on the grounds. The rustic restaurant here has rough pine tables and is decorated with carved wooden figures.

Camping Górna Wetlinka CAMPGROUND, HOSTEL €
(☑13 461 0830; www.bieszczadywetlinka.pl; Szlak Pieszy Czarny; per person/tent/car 8/7/10zł, family cabins 200zł; ⊗May-Oct; ℗) This excellent and very friendly camping ground also serves as an information point for Bieszczady National Park. Several hiking trails start from here and the staff can organise horse riding (30zł per hour). The home cooking at the on-site restaurant is excellent. Look for a turnoff heading north from Hwy 897 about 2km east of Wetlina.

★ **W Starym Siole** POLISH €€
(☑503 124 654; www.staresiolo.com; Wetlina 71; mains 25-50zł; ⊗11am-11pm; ℗ 🐾) On the Cisna (western) side of Wetlina, this is possibly the best restaurant in this part of Poland. They pay keen attention to detail, from the custom woodworking in the dining room to the wine list and the quality of the cooking. Mains range from fish cooked over a fire to grilled meats, *pierogi* and other simple foods done well.

ℹ Getting There & Away

Up to 10 buses a day go to Sanok (11zł, two hours) via Lesko (9zł, 1½ hours). Count on up to nine buses a day to Ustrzyki Górne (5zł, 30 minutes) to the east and Cisna (5zł, 30 minutes) to the west.

Cisna

POP 460

Cisna sits on the borderland between territories once inhabited by the Boyks to the east and Lemks to the west (p215). The region was densely populated before WWII, but today it counts fewer than 500 inhabitants – yet Cisna is still the largest village in the central part of the Bieszczady. Though not especially attractive in itself, the village has a decent choice of accommodation and is a good base for hiking. It is also the place to board the narrow-gauge tourist train.

🏃 Activities

Bieszczady Forest Railway MOUNTAIN RAILWAY
(Bieszczadzka Kolejka Leśna; ☑13 468 6335; www.kolejka.bieszczady.pl; Majdan 17; to Przysłup adult/child one way 19/14zł, return 23/17zł, to Balnica adult/child one way 17/13zł, return 20/16zł; ⊗departures 10am Mon-Fri, 10am & 1.30pm Sat & Sun Jul & Aug; 🚼) This narrow-gauge train, the Bieszczady Forest Railway, was built at the end of the 19th century to transport timber. Some tracks were in use as recently as the 1990s, but the line has since been turned into a tourist attraction and is particularly popular with families.

Based in Majdan, 2km west of Cisna, two runs are on offer: a longer, higher 12km stretch that goes to Przysłup (one hour), and a flatter 9km stretch that runs to Balnica (45 minutes).

🛏 Sleeping & Eating

Cisna has plenty of places to stay, though most of these are in tiny pensions or mountain hostels. The tourist office is happy to help find rooms.

Ośrodek Wczasowy Perełka   BUNGALOW €
(☑ 13 468 6325; perelka@naturatour.pl; Cisna 105; s/d 70/100zł, cabins per person 50zł; P 🐾) The first house on the left as you enter Cisna from the west, this comfortable holiday home has 34 beds in singles and doubles, plus another 54 in seasonal A-frame cabins. Also rents bikes.

Bacówka PTTK Pod Honem   HOSTEL €
(☑ 503 137 279; www.podhonem.home.pl; dm 25zł, d/tr/q 60/90/120zł; P) The 40-bed PTTK mountain hostel is 668m up on a slope at the eastern end of Cisna; it's about 1km up the hill behind the Wołosan, along a steep dirt track. It's simple and friendly and serves uncomplicated meals.

OSW Wołosan   GUESTHOUSE €€
(☑ 13 468 6373; www.wolosan.pl; Cisna 87; s/d 100/160zł; P 🛜) By far the classiest place in this part of the Bieszczady, the 27-room Wołosan at the eastern end of Cisna is geared towards hunters (thus the trophies and taxidermied animals throughout) but can organise any number of activities – from quad bikes and snowmobile excursions to off-road 4WD safaris.

Bar Siekierezada   POLISH €
(☑ 606 313 330; www.siekierezada.pl; Cisna 92; mains 12-25zł; ⊙ 9am-midnight) This is a combination bar, art gallery and club that also happens to serve Cisna's best simple cooking, like sausages, *pierogi*, grilled meats and other local favourites. It's across a small road from the car park and can be a little tricky to find. Ask for directions.

ℹ Information

Dzikie-Bieszczady (☑ 697 718 163; www.dzikie-bieszczady.pl; Cisna 23; bikes per hour/day 8/30zł; ⊙ 8am-4pm Mon-Fri) Adventure-travel agency renting bikes and planning outings to the Bieszczady mountains, as well as longer excursions to neighbouring countries. Located in the same office as the tourist-information centre.

Tourist Information Centre (☑ 13 468 6465; www.cisna.pl; Cisna 23; ⊙ 8am-8pm Mon-Fri, 9am-5pm Sat May-Aug, 8am-4pm Mon-Fri Sep-Apr) The tourist office is in the county cultural centre in the middle of the village, just behind the car park.

ℹ Getting There & Away

Half a dozen buses run daily to Sanok (8zł, one hour) and Wetlina (5zł, 30 minutes). There are more seasonal buses in summer, including up to six to Ustrzyki Górne (8zł, 45 minutes).

BESKID NISKI

The Beskid Niski (Lower Beskid) is a forest-covered mountain range with gentle slopes that runs for about 85km west to east along the Slovakian frontier. It's bordered on the west by the Beskid Sądecki and on the east by the Bieszczady. As its name suggests, it is not a high outcrop: its tallest peak does not exceed 1000m and the range is made for easy walks. The Beskid Niski offers less spectacular vistas than the neighbouring Bieszczady, but its dozens of small Orthodox and Uniat churches, especially in the western half of the region, are a strong draw.

Krosno

POP 46,930

Founded in the 14th century and prosperous during the Renaissance – even nicknamed 'little Kraków' for a time – Krosno slid into decay from the 18th century onwards. It revived with the trade of linen and Hungarian wine, and, in the mid-19th century, with the development of the oil industry. It is known throughout Poland for its ornamental and commercial glassworks.

There's enough here to see and do to occupy a half-day, and there are a few very good lodging options, making this a sensible choice for an overnight stay.

👁 Sights

👁 Centre

The Old Town's spacious **Rynek** has retained some of its Renaissance appearance, notably in the houses fronted by wide arcaded passageways that line the southern and northeastern parts of the square. The best example is the **Wójtowska Townhouse** (Kamienica Wójtowska; Rynek 7).

★**Centre of Glass Heritage**   MUSEUM
(Centrum Dziedzictwa Szkła; ☑ 13 444 0031; www.miastoszkla.pl; ul Blich 2; adult/concession 18/15zł; ⊙ 10am-7pm Mon-Sat, 11am-7pm Sun Jul & Aug, 9am-5pm Mon-Fri, 11am-7pm Sat, to 5pm

HIKING IN THE BESKID NISKI

Two main trails cover the entire length of the Beskid Niski range. The trail marked in blue originates in Grybów, goes southeast to the border and then eastwards along the frontier to eventually bring you to Nowy Łupków near Komańcza. The red trail begins in Krynica, crosses the blue trail around Hańczowa, continues east along the northern slopes of the Beskid, and arrives at Komańcza. Both of these trails head further east into the Bieszczady.

You need four to six days to do the whole of the Beskid Niski on either of these routes, but other trails, as well as a number of rough roads, link the two main trails.

A dozen hostels scattered in small villages throughout the region provide shelter, but most are open only in high summer (July and August). There are also a number of agrotourist farms; these are open for a longer season and sometimes year-round. If you plan on more ambitious trekking, camping gear may be useful. You can buy some basic supplies in the villages you pass, but you're better off stocking up on essentials before you set out.

The major starting points for the Beskid Niski are Krynica, Grybów and Gorlice from the west; Komańcza and Sanok from the east; and Krosno and Dukla in the centre.

The 1:50,000 *Beskid Niski* map (12zł) from Compass will give you all the basic information you need for hiking. You can find this map, or similar versions from other companies, at tourist offices in Nowy Sącz, Krynica and Krosno.

Sun Sep-Jun; 🖳) Krosno's newest attraction is this exhibition centre that highlights the town's important role as Poland's glass-working capital. The family-friendly attraction, signposted in English, tells the story of a century of glass-making in Krosno. Visitors are invited to try a bit of glass-fashioning and glass-blowing on their own. The exhibition trail leads underground, below the Rynek. The entrance is located on the northeastern corner of the Rynek.

Franciscan Church of the Holy Cross CHURCH
(Kościół Franciszkanów Św Krzyża; ☎13 436 8088; www.krosno.franciszkanie.pl; ul Franciszkańska 5; ⊙8am-6pm) A few steps southeast of the Rynek is the large 15th-century Franciscan church, today filled with neo-Gothic furnishings. The showpiece here is the **Oświęcim Family Chapel** (Kaplica Oświęcimów), just to the left as you enter the church. Built in 1647 by Italian architect Vincenti Petroni, and embellished with magnificent stucco work by another Italian master, Jan Falconi, this is considered one of the finest early-Baroque chapels in Poland.

Subcarpathian Museum MUSEUM
(Muzeum Podkarpackie; ☎13 432 1376; www.muzeum.krosno.pl; ul Piłsudskiego 16; adult/concession 10/5zł, Sun free; ⊙9am-5pm Tue-Fri, 10am-3pm Sat & Sun May-Oct, shorter hours rest of year) Just opposite the Craft Museum and around 200m north of the Rynek is this regional-history museum, housed in the 15th-century former Bishops' Palace. The museum has interesting historical, archaeological and art sections on this mountainous region. The highlight, however, is the extensive collection of decorative old kerosene lamps, reputedly the largest in Europe.

Craft Museum MUSEUM
(Muzeum Rzemiosła; ☎13 432 4188; www.muzeumrzemiosla.pl; ul Piłsudskiego 19; adult/concession 5/3zł, Sat & Sun free; ⊙8am-6pm Mon-Fri, 10am-4pm Sat & Sun May-Sep, shorter hours rest of year) Directly opposite the Subcarpathian Museum, about 200m north of the Rynek, is the Craft Museum, featuring ethnographic displays related to such local crafts and trades as clockmaking, weaving, saddlery and even hairdressing. The Art Nouveau–style building, dating from the turn of the 20th century, is interesting in its own right and served as the headquarters of a company that made tower clocks.

⊙ Outside Krosno

Church of the Assumption of Mary CHURCH
(Kościół Wniebowzięcia Najświętszej Maryi Panny w Haczowie; ☎13 439 1012; www.parafiahaczow.pl; Haczów 605; ⊙8am-6pm) Located in the village of Haczów (*hah*-choof), 16km east of Krosno and accessible by bus, this is considered the largest timber Gothic church

in Europe and is a Unesco World Heritage site. The church was built in the mid-15th century on the site of a previous church founded by Władysław Jagiełło in 1388. The walls and coffered ceiling inside are covered in naive paintings dating from the late 15th century and restored in the 1990s.

Museum of the Oil & Gas Industry MUSEUM
(Muzeum Przemysłu Naftowego i Gazowniczego; ☑ 13 433 3478; www.bobrka.pl; 38-458 Chorkówa; adult/concession 10/6zł; ☺ 9am-5pm Tue-Sun May-Sep, 7am-3pm Tue-Sun Oct-Apr) The village of Bóbrka, 17km southwest of Krosno, is the cradle of the Polish oil industry. It was here in 1854 that the world's first oil well was sunk by Ignacy Łukasiewicz, inventor of the paraffin lamp. These days, the site is a curious open-air museum. From Krosno several buses go daily to Bóbrka village (4zł, 30 minutes), though fewer depart at weekends. The site is at Chorkówa, about 2km north of where the bus will let you off.

Among the early wells and derricks on display is the world's oldest surviving hand-dug oil shaft, named Franek and dating back to 1860.

Sleeping

Hotel Śnieżka HOTEL €€
(☑ 13 432 3449; www.hotelsniezka.pl; ul Lewakowskiego 22; s/d 160/210zł; P※@☎) For atmosphere and charm, this attractive brick-red Victorian townhouse is hard to beat. You'll find 14 cosy rooms, all sparklingly modern, with polished wood floors and big bathrooms. The in-house restaurant is pretty stylish too. The location is within comfortable walking distance of the bus and train stations, but is about 2km west of the Rynek.

Pensjonacik Buda PENSION €€
(☑ 13 432 0053; www.budahotel.pl; ul Jagiellońska 4; d/tr/ste 150/200/250 zł; P☎) Despite sitting next to the railway tracks, this B&B is a long 2km walk from the train station and about 1km southwest of the Rynek. Still, it boasts the best restaurant in town and the rooms are clean and comfortable (but not always quiet, owing to the occasional train whistle).

Hotel Krosno Nafta HOTEL €€
(☑ 13 436 6212; www.hotel.nafta.pl; ul Lwowska 21; s/d/tr 170/240/350zł; P@☎) In the modern-convenience camp, this is the city's first choice for business clients, but its rates are low enough to appeal to private travellers as well. There are 41 big, comfortable rooms on offer and a decent upmarket restaurant. The hotel is 1km southeast of the centre on the Sanok road. Prices drop 20% at the weekend.

Eating & Drinking

★Restauracja Buda POLISH €€
(☑ 13 432 0053; www.budahotel.pl; ul Jagiellońska 4; mains 20-35zł; ☺ 10am-11pm; ☎) This family-run restaurant, 2km southwest of the Rynek, is easily the best restaurant in Krosno. Excellent traditional Polish cooking with a modern touch – such as roast pork with plum sauce and walnuts – in a refined but not stuffy atmosphere. From the centre, follow ul Czajkowskiego southwest about 1km from Plac Konstytucji 3 Maja and take a left on ul Jagiellońska.

Posmaky POLISH €€
(☑ 13 436 5055; www.posmakujkrosno.pl; Rynek 24; mains 20-40zł; ☺ noon-10pm; ☎) The best of several similarly nondescript Polish and pizza joints that line the Rynek. The kitchen is more ambitious here, adding a few steaks and even a serious attempt at a hamburger (23zł). Dine on the terrace in warm weather or in the renovated Gothic cellar space.

Klubokawiarnia Ferment CAFE
(☑ 13 420 3242; ul Portiusa 4; ☺ 10am-midnight Mon-Sat, noon-midnight Sun) A little hipster haunt on a small side street just off the northwestern corner of the Rynek. Great coffee, Hungarian wines, cocktails and small snacks, all served up in a colourful, airy, modern space that occasionally does double duty as a club and gallery.

Shopping

Glass Studio Habrat GLASS
(☑ 13 431 7239; www.glassstudiohabrat.com; Rynek 28; ☺ 9am-5pm Mon-Fri, 10am-2pm Sat) Colourful plates, glasses, vases and decorative glassware, reflecting the often-playful, absurd and abstract styles pioneered at the Krosno glassworks.

Information

Bank PKO (☑ 13 432 1761; ul Słowackiego 4; ☺ 8.30am-4pm Mon-Fri) Convenient bank northeast of the Rynek.

Post Office (Poczta Polska; ☑ 13 432 0591; Podwale 38; ☺ 7am-8pm Mon-Fri, 8am-3.30pm Sat) The closest post office to the centre of town, about 100m west of the Rynek.

Tourist Information Centre (☑13 432 7707; www.krosno.pl; Rynek 5; ☺9am-6pm Mon-Fri, 10am-4pm Sat & Sun) At the southeast corner of the main square, the cheerful staff dispense maps and brochures. There's a small gift shop here as well as a free computer for surfing the web.

❶ Getting There & Away

The train and bus stations sit eyeballing one another 1.5km west of the Rynek.

A dozen or so daily buses head eastwards for Sanok (10zł, 1½ hours), up to four of which continue to Ustrzyki Dolne (18zł, two hours) and two to Ustrzyki Górne (20zł, three hours). Several fast buses depart daily for Kraków (30zł, three hours), and hourly buses go to Rzeszów (12zł, 1½ hours). There are frequent buses south to Dukla (5zł, 45 minutes) and regular buses to Bóbrka (4zł, 30 minutes). For Haczów (3zł, 40 minutes), count on up to six buses a day, most of which terminate at Brzozów.

Krosno has lost a lot of its passenger rail service in recent years. Currently, there are three departures daily to Sanok (10zł, 1½ hours) and three to Rzeszów (18zł, three hours), but nearly everyone takes the bus to these destinations.

Biecz

POP 4600

One of the oldest settlements in Poland, Biecz (pronounced bee-ech) was a busy commercial centre from at least the 13th century. It benefited from the wine-trading route heading south over the Carpathians to Hungary, and some 30 crafts developed here. In the 17th century Biecz began to see its prosperity wane when the plague struck and new trade routes bypassed the town. The sleepy atmosphere seems to have remained to this day, though some important historic monuments and a good museum make the town worth a stop.

◉ Sights

Start your exploration at the spacious Rynek, which covers no less than an eighth of Biecz's entire area (making it Poland's largest town square in relation to the size of the town). The main sights, including some impressive remnants of the old **town walls**, can be found west of the Rynek, along ul Węgierska.

Tower   TOWER
(☑13 447 1113; www.biecz.pl; Rynek 1; adult/concession 5/2.50zł; ☺9am-5pm Apr-Oct, 8am-4pm Mon-Fri Nov-Mar) Biecz's town tower

looks a lot like a lighthouse, and because of its surprising height, 56m, it's visible for miles around. It was built between 1569 and 1581, except for the top, which is a Baroque addition. Its original Renaissance decoration and the unusual 24-hour clock face on its eastern side have been restored in recent years.

Corpus Christi Parish Church   CHURCH
(Kościół Parafialny Bożego Ciała; ☑13 447 1617; www.fara.biecz.pl; ul Kromera 16a; ☺10am-1pm) The town's monumental parish church is located 100m west of the Rynek. This mighty Gothic brick structure, evidence of the town's erstwhile affluence, dates from the 15th century. Inside, the chancel (the area surrounding the altar) holds most of the church's treasures, notably the late-Renaissance high altar and massive stalls, all from the early 17th century. Note the impressive crucifix from 1639.

House with a Tower   MUSEUM
(Dom z Basztą; ☑13 447 1950; www.muzeum.biecz.pl; ul Węgierska 1; adult/concession 8/4zł; ☺8am-5pm Mon-Fri, 9am-5pm Sat & Sun) This branch of the Biecz Regional Museum occupies what's called the 'House with a Tower', a 16th-century structure with, yes, an impressive tower. Take a peek inside to the complete contents of an ancient pharmacy, including a laboratory, as well as musical instruments, traditional household utensils, equipment from old craft workshops and a cellar for storing Hungarian wine.

Kromer Townhouse   MUSEUM
(Kamienica Kromerówka; ☑13 447 1950; www.muzeum.biecz.pl; ul Kromera 3; adult/concession 4/2zł; ☺8am-5pm Mon-Fri, 9am-5pm Sat & Sun) A second branch of the Biecz Regional Museum is found at the Kromer Townhouse, a 16th-century building 100m west of the Rynek and directly in front of the parish church. Here, you'll find exhibits relating to the history of the town, plus archaeological and numismatic collections and Biecz's famous 600-year-old 'Urban' bell.

🍴 Sleeping & Eating

Hotel Restauracja Grodzka   HOTEL €
(☑13 447 1121; www.restauracjagrodzka.pl; ul Kazimierza Wielkiego 35; s/d/apt 65/80/100zł; restaurant mains 10zł to 20zł; ☺restaurant 8am-10pm Mon-Sat, 10am-10pm Sun; ℗) The best of a slim range of acceptable lodging options is this 16-room budget hotel, located

along the main road about 300m east of the Rynek. The rooms are plain but clean. The restaurant is good value, with a big plate of potato pancakes covered in goulash for 15zł.

★U Becza   POLISH €€

(☑733 612 616; www.restauracjaubecza.pl; Rynek 2; mains 12-25zł; ☺10am-10pm) This handsome cafe and restaurant occupies a historic townhouse on the main square. It's completely unassuming from outside, so the period interior with wood-beamed ceilings and lace tablecloths comes as a total surprise. The specialities are the potato pancakes, but the herring is excellent as well and the pizzas are big, fresh and popular. It also has cakes and coffee.

❶ Information

Bank Pekao (☑134 471 809; Rynek 17; ☺8am-3pm Mon-Fri) Convenient bank and 24-hour ATM on the main square.

Tourist Information Office (☑13 447 1114; www.biecz.pl; Rynek 1; ☺9am-5pm Apr-Oct, 8am-4pm Mon-Fri Nov-Mar) A small, helpful tourist-information office is at the centre of the Rynek, below the tower. It has a computer terminal on hand if you want to check your email.

❶ Getting There & Away

All buses pass through and stop on the northeast and southwest sides of the Rynek. Buses to Jasło (5zł, 35 minutes) run regularly, but only a few buses continue to Krosno (12zł, one hour). There are a couple of daily departures to Nowy Sącz (12zł, 1½ hours).

BESKID SĄDECKI

Fanning out to the south of Nowy Sącz, the Beskid Sądecki (bes-keed son-dets-kee) is yet another attractive mountain range where you can hike, sightsee or simply have a rest at a mountain spa such as Krynica or Muszyna. The mountains are easily accessible from Nowy Sącz by two roads (Hwy 87 and Hwy 75) that head south along the river valleys, joining up with Hwy 971 to form a convenient loop; public transport is good along this route.

The Beskid Sądecki consists of two ranges, the Pasmo Jaworzyny and the Pasmo Radziejowej, which are separated by the Poprad River valley. There are a number of peaks over 1000m, the highest being Mt Radziejowa (1261m).

The Beskid Sądecki was the westernmost territory populated by the Lemks (p215), and a dozen of their charming rustic churches survive, particularly around Krynica and Muszyna. Beskid Sądecki maps (scale 1:50,000; 15zł) published by two different firms (WiT and Demart) are helpful for both hikers and cerkiew (wooden church) peepers.

Nowy Sącz

POP 84,600

Nowy Sącz (no-vi sonch), the economic and cultural centre of the Sącz region, is a laidback town with a large main square and a few decent attractions, most notably its large skansen. It can also be a good base for further exploration of the surrounding countryside.

Founded in 1292 and fortified in the middle of the following century by King Kazimierz III Wielki (Casimir III the Great), Nowy Sącz developed rapidly until the 16th century, thanks to its strategic position on trading crossroads. As elsewhere, decline in the 17th century gave way to a partial revival at the close of the 19th century. Nowy Sącz grew considerably after WWII, and its historic district has been largely restored over recent years.

⊙ Sights

Measuring 160m by 120m, Nowy Sącz's Rynek is the second largest in Poland (after Kraków's) and is lined by a harmonious collection of historic houses. The **town hall**, erected in the middle in 1897, incorporates a number of architectural styles, including Art Nouveau.

⊙ City Centre

Gothic House   MUSEUM

(Dom Gotycki; ☑18 443 7708; www.muzeum. sacz.pl; ul Lwowska 3; adult/concession 8/5zł, Sat free; ☺10am-3pm Tue-Thu, to 5.30pm Fri, 9am-2.30pm Sat & Sun) The 15th-century Gothic building houses the district museum. This museum is dedicated to religious art, with naive religious paintings and folk-art woodcarvings collected from rural churches and roadside chapels throughout the region. The collection of Ruthenian Orthodox icons, which includes a splendid iconostasis of the 17th century, is especially fine.

COBBLESTONES OF STARY SĄCZ

Stary Sącz (*stah*-ri sonch) is the older and smaller sister of Nowy Sącz, with a pretty, cobblestoned main square and some fetching churches. There's also an excellent restaurant in the centre, making it an ideal day trip planned around lunch.

The town owes its existence to 13th-century Duchess Kinga, wife of King Bolesław Wstydliwy (Bolesław the Shy), who in the 1270s founded the convent of the Poor Clares here. After the king's death, Kinga entered the convent, where she lived for the last 13 years of her life, becoming its first abbess.

Though there's a small regional museum here, the main sights are two historic churches. The **Church of the Poor Clares** (Kościół SS Klarysek; www.klaryski.sacz.pl; Plac Św Kingi 1; ⊙8am-6pm) was where the town was born. It was originally Gothic in style and completed in 1332, though it was later given opulent Baroque fittings. The traces of its creator, Kinga, are clearly visible: the Baroque frescoes in the nave depict scenes from her life, and her chapel on the south side boasts a 1470 statue of her on the altar. The pulpit (1671) on the opposite wall is an extraordinary piece of art.

The nearby **Parish Church of St Elizabeth of Hungary** (Kościół Parafialny Św Elżbiety Węgierskiej; www.parafia.stary.sacz.pl; ul Kazimierza Wielkiego; ⊙8am-6pm), two blocks south of the Rynek, dates from the town's 13th-century beginnings but was changed considerably in the 17th and 18th centuries. It's now a textbook example of unbridled Baroque, with five large, florid altars.

For lunch or dinner, look no further than **Restauracja Marysieńka** (☑18 446 0072; Rynek 12; mains 12-25zł; ⊙10am-10pm). It's nothing fancy – just good Polish food served in a friendly, welcoming atmosphere.

Collegiate Church of St Margaret
CHURCH

(Kościół Kolegiacki Św Małgorzaty; ☑18 443 6198; www.bazylika.org.pl; Plac Kolegiacki 1; ⊙9am-6pm) This church, a block east of the Rynek, dates back to the 14th century but has undergone many changes since then. The small 15th-century image of Christ on the Renaissance main altar suggests a Byzantine influence. Note the remnants of a medieval fresco of the Last Supper on the column to the left as you enter.

Synagogue
MUSEUM

(Galeria Dawna Synagoga w Nowym Sączu; ☑18 444 2370; www.muzeum.sacz.pl; ul Joselewicza 12; adult/concession 6/3zł; Sat free; ⊙10am-3pm Wed & Thu, 10am-5.30pm Fri, 9am-2.30pm Sat & Sun) For centuries Jews lived in the area north of the Rynek. This is also the area where the Germans built their wartime Jewish ghetto, before shipping 25,000 residents to extermination camps in 1942. Not much of the community or the ghetto remains, with the exception of a beautiful 18th-century synagogue. Miraculously, it survived the war and holds a small but interesting gallery of black-and-white photos from the community as well as a small display of Judaica.

⊙ Outside the Centre

Sącz Ethnographic Park
MUSEUM

(Sądecki Park Etnograficzny; ☑18 444 3570; www.muzeum.sacz.pl; ul Lwowska 226; adult/concession 14/8zł, Sat free; ⊙10am-6pm Tue-Sun May-Sep, to 3pm Oct-Apr) About 3.5km southeast of the centre, Sącz Ethnographic Park is one of the largest and best skansens in the country. Houses and other buildings typical of several ethnic cultures from the Carpathian Mountains and foothills are displayed. Visits are in groups guided in Polish; follow along with *The Sącz Ethnographic Park* by Magdalena Kroh, available in English from the skansen shop. There are around 70 buildings and other structures, including a farmhouse, forge and windmill.

Jewish Cemetery
CEMETERY

(Cmentarz Żydowski; ☑18 441 9381; ul Rybacka) Around 500m north of the Old Town on the other side of the Kamienica River is the former Jewish cemetery. It contains a couple of hundred derelict headstones amid overgrown grass. During WWII it was the site of mass executions; there is a monument to the several hundred Jews taken from the Nowy Sącz wartime ghetto and shot here.

🛏 Sleeping

Dom Turysty PTTK HOSTEL, CAMPGROUND €
(☑18 441 5012; ul Nadbrzeżna 40; s/d/tr 85/95/130zł, camping per person/tent 13/7zł; ☺campground May-Sep; P 🛜) This year-round PTTK hostel has 21 spartan but spick-and-span rooms. It also operates a camping ground next door. The hostel is situated outside the centre, about 2km southeast of the Rynek, in the direction of the Sącz Eth-nographic Park.

★ Miasteczko Galicyjskie HISTORIC HOTEL €€
(☑18 441 6390; www.miasteczkogalicyjskie.pl; ul Lwowska 226; s/d/tr 140/220/290zł; P 🛜) This modern hotel is located within the grounds of the Sącz Ethnographic Park, 3.5km southeast of the Rynek. It's a pleasing mix of modern and traditional. The rooms have updated baths but are furnished with big, period wooden chests and wardrobes. The buffet breakfast is one of the best around, with lots of smoked meats, and eggs cooked to order.

Hotel Panorama HOTEL €€
(☑18 443 7110; www.hotelpanoramanowysacz. pl; ul Romanowskiego 4a; s/d/tr 150/190/220zł; P @ 🛜) The clean, modern Panorama, just off the Rynek, boasts the best location of all the city's hotels. The 32 large rooms are unimaginatively furnished but are well maintained and offer all modern conveni-ences. Ask for a room looking west towards the Dunajec River.

🍴 Eating & Drinking

Restauracja Ratuszowa POLISH €€
(☑18 443 5615; Rynek 1; mains 15-30zł; ☺10am-11pm) This restaurant below the Town Hall specialises in *pierogi* and has an impres-sive range indeed, including some stuffed with nettles, buckwheat groats and black pudding for the especially daring. Eat out-doors behind the Town Hall or downstairs, where you can admire the collection of communist-era propaganda posters on the wall.

Trattoria Da Sandro ITALIAN €€
(☑530 222 227; www.trattoriadasandro.pl; ul Wa-zów 8; mains 25-40zł; ☺11am-10pm) A narrow alleyway south of the Rynek hides a beauti-ful, modern Italian restaurant, tucked away in a brightly lit cellar space. Serves up the city's best pizzas, along with a full range of pasta dishes, grilled meats, fish and salads. Great wine selection and the prices are good value.

Strauss Café CAFE
(☑600 883 311; Rynek 16; ☺9am-1am) Beauti-ful throwback cafe on the Rynek harks back to the 19th century and the Austrian occu-pation, complete with sepia-tone photos of Emperor Franz Joseph on the walls and lavish neoclassical interior elements, chan-deliers and period furnishings. Very good coffee drinks, as well as breakfast, light food items and wine and beer.

ℹ Information

There are plenty of ATMs, banks and *kantors* (exchange offices) around the Rynek and along the main pedestrian street that trails south from the Rynek, ul Jagiellońska.

Bank PKO (☑18 448 3500; al Wolności 16; ☺8am-6pm Mon-Fri) Bank and 24-hour ATM several blocks south of the Rynek.

Post Office (☑18 443 5513; ul Dunajewskiego 10; ☺7am-7pm Mon-Fri, 8am-2pm Sat) Just off the southwest corner of the Rynek.

PTTK Office (☑18 443 7457; www.beskid. pttk.pl; Rynek 9; ☺7am-3pm Mon, Wed & Thu, 11am-7pm Tue & Fri) Less helpful than the city's tourist-information centre, the PTTK office on the Rynek is a good place to source hiking information, buy maps and find out about possible overnight stays in PTTK-run mountain huts.

Tourist Information Centre (☑18 444 2422; www.nowysacz.pl; ul Szwedzka 2; ☺8am-6pm Mon-Fri, 9am-2pm Sat) Standard tourist office with limited information in English. There's a computer available for visitors to check email.

ℹ Getting There & Away

BUS

The bus station is midway between the city cen-tre and the train station. Buses to Kraków (18zł, 2½ hours) and Krynica (6zł, 1½ hours) depart every half-hour or so and are much faster than the train. There's an hourly service to Szczawni-ca (10zł, two hours), and up to nine departures to Zakopane (18zł, three hours). There's a handy online timetable at www.pks.pl.

TRAIN

The main train station is 2km south of the Old Town, but city buses run frequently between the two. A few trains go to Kraków (30zł, four hours), but buses are more useful for this route. Trains run regularly throughout the day to Krynica (12zł, 1½ hours) and pass Stary Sącz (5.50zł, 10 minutes) on their way. There's a reasonable service to Tarnów (22zł, two hours), with trains departing every couple of hours.

Krynica

POP 12,200

Set in attractive countryside amid the wooded hills of the Beskid Sądecki, Krynica (kri-*nee*-tsah), often known as Krynica-Zdrój (Krynica Spa), is Poland's largest spa and mountain health resort.

Much of the year, patients repair here to drink from around a dozen local mineral springs, each one prescribed for a different ailment, and to relax in the mountain air. In midsummer, though, you can banish any notion about this being a laid-back spa for quiet convalescence amid the pines. It's a full-on summer holiday retreat, chock-a-block with families, long queues at ice-cream stands and impromptu rock concerts on the promenade featuring local knock-offs of Axl Rose and Lady Gaga.

It wasn't always this way. In the early decades of the 20th century, Krynica was a fashionable hangout for the artistic and intellectual elite and continued to be so right up until WWII. Splendid villas and pensions were constructed during that period, blending into the wooded landscape.

◉ Sights & Activities

As with many Polish towns, the main activity in Krynica is drinking. In this case it's not beer or vodka but rather the bitter water that flows from one of around a dozen medicinal mineral springs.

Main Pump Room   MINERAL SPRINGS
(Pijalnia Główna; ☎18 477 7432; www.krynica. pl; ul Nowotorskiego 9-3; per glass/10 samples 1.70/13zł; ⊙10am-9pm) This modern structure on the main promenade (ul Nowotarskiego) looks more like a retro-futuristic

airport terminal than a spa colonnade. Still, it's the main game in town when it comes to taking the cure. Select from a menu of eight different mineral springs, with each spring purporting to cure a different ailment. The website has a list of the springs in English. Sip from a plastic cup or buy a ceramic tankard with a porcelain straw for 12.50zł.

You can choose from a number of different waters, and displays list the chemical composition of each. By far the heaviest is Zuber, which has over 21g of soluble solid components per litre – a record for all liquids of that type in Europe. It's a sulphurous brew that won't be to everyone's taste. Local practice is to drink the water slowly while walking up and down the promenade.

Góra Parkowa Funicular   FUNICULAR RAILWAY
(Kolej Linowa na Górę Parkową; ☎18 471 2262; www.pkl.pl; ul Nowotarskiego 1; adult/concession return 16/13zł, one way 11/8zł; ⊙10am-7pm May-Sep, 10am-6pm Oct-Apr; ⊕) The Góra Parkowa funicular railway is a fun family outing. The bottom station is near the northern end of the promenade in Park Zdrojowy. Cars depart every 15 minutes; the ascent of 142m takes less than three minutes. At the top, you'll find pretty views in all directions, as well as a giant slide and a tubing run for kids. If it's a nice day, buy a one-way ticket and hike back down through the park to town.

Mt Jaworzyna Cable Car   CABLE CAR
(Kolej Gondolowa na Jaworzynę; ☎18 473 6624; www.jaworzynakrynicka.pl; ul Czarny Potok 75; adult/concession return 26/21zł, one way 19/15zł; ⊙9am-5pm; ⊕) A little bit out of the centre

---

HIKING IN THE BESKID SĄDECKI

Krynica is an excellent springboard for hiking in the Beskid Sądecki. Two marked trails, green and red, head westwards from Krynica up to the top of **Mt Jaworzyna**. It takes three hours to walk there by either trail (or you can get there faster via the Mt Jaworzyna cable car). At the top you'll have good views and you may even be able to spot the Tatras on clear days.

Continue on the red trail northwest to **Hala Łabowska** (1038m), another three hours' walk from Mt Jaworzyna. The red trail carries on northwest to **Rytro** (four hours' walk). This route, leading mostly through the forest along the ridge of the main chain of the Beskid Sądecki, is spectacular and easy. From Rytro, you can go back to Krynica by train or bus.

There are several PTTK mountain hostels along these trails, where you can usually find something to eat and bed down for the night. Before setting out, visit the **PTTK office** in Krynica or Nowy Sącz to pick up maps and reserve space in the hostels.

but more exciting than the funicular, this cable-car system consists of 55 six-person cars that run from the bottom station in the Czarny Potok Valley, about 6km west of the centre of Krynica, to the top of Mt Jaworzyna (1113m). The route is 2210m long and the cable car climbs 465m in seven minutes.

Sleeping

Krynica has a slew of hotels, pensions and holiday homes. Many places – particularly holiday homes – will offer half or full board, which can be convenient. There are also plenty of private rooms welcoming guests. The tourist office can arrange private accommodation for around 40/50zł per person without/with private bathroom. Remember that in high season (July and August, January and February) few owners will be interested in travellers staying just a night or two.

★ Małopolanka   HOTEL €€
(☑18 471 5896; www.malopolanka.eu; ul Bulwary Dietla 13; s/d/apt 140/220/290zł; P @ 🛜) Old-fashioned, 20-room pension and spa just off the promenade that dates from the 1930s and could be a setting for an Agatha Christie mystery. There's a lively bar and coffee shop on the ground floor, from where creaky wooden steps lead up to well-appointed, eclectic rooms, furnished in period style. There's also a spa with sauna, massage and various treatments.

Stefania   HOTEL €€
(☑18 472 5110; www.hotelstefania.pl; ul Piłsudskiego 13; s/d 150/250zł; P @ 🛜) The snazzy dark-and-lime-green Stefania opened its doors in a renovated historic spa building in 2009 and retains the feel of a brand-new hotel. The snug rooms have parquet floors and walls painted a creamy yellow – as warm and inviting as a slice of cream cake. The hotel is on the main drag, not far from where the bus drops you from Nowy Sącz.

Pensjonat Witoldówka   PENSION €€
(☑18 471 5577; www.witoldowka-krynica.pl; ul Bulwary Dietla 10; d/apt 160/190zł; P @) Looking like a grand Gothic lodge from the outside, this big, wooden hotel is in a great central location, set along the narrow Kryniczanka River and close to the main pump room. The 40 upgraded rooms are comfortable and spacious; there's also a bar and restaurant.

✕ Eating

Pod Zieloną Górką   POLISH €€
(☑18 471 2177; www.zielonagorka.pl; Nowotarskiego 5; mains 25-40zł; ⊘10am-11pm) This atmospheric old-style pub is divided into two sections: an informal family-friendly part with picnic tables at one end, and a slightly more upscale dining area with wood-beamed ceilings, lace tablecloths and beautiful porcelain chandeliers on the other. There's also a park-side terrace in fine weather. The menu features Polish favourites, including pork knuckle cooked in beer, and Czech Pilsner Urquell beer on tap.

Czekolada i Zdroj   CAFE €
(☑18 471 5031; ul Nowotarskiego 2; coffee 9zł; cakes 12zł; ⊘9.30am-10pm; 🛜) This great spot for coffee and cakes also offers a free and reliable wi-fi connection. It's just opposite the Main Pump Room at the northern end of the Old Spa House (Stary Dom Zdrojowy).

ℹ Information

Bank PKO (ul Zdrojowa 1; ⊘9am-5pm Mon-Fri) Bank and 24-hour ATM at the northern end of the main promenade.

Post Office (☑18 471 5404; ul Zdrojowa 28; ⊘7am-7pm Mon-Fri, 8am-2pm Sat)

PTTK Office (☑18 471 5576; www.krynica.pttk.pl; ul Zdrojowa 32; ⊘7.30am-5pm Mon-Fri, 9am-11am Sat) Good spot to purchase hiking and cycling maps of the surrounding area, as well as obtain information on treks and overnighting in PTTK-maintained mountain cottages. It's located on a ridge above the main promenade, just across the street from the tourist-information centre.

Tourist Information Point (☑18 472 5577; www.krynica.pl; ul Zdrojowa 4/2; ⊘9am-5pm Mon-Fri, to 1pm Sat; 🛜) Clean, modern tourist-information office, situated on a rise above the main spa area. Good English, as well as heaps of maps and brochures. There's a computer terminal in the office for checking email.

ℹ Getting There & Away

The train and bus stations are next to one another on ul Dr Henryka Ebersa in the southern part of town, about 1.2km from the centre.

Buses to Nowy Sącz (6zł, 1½ hours) run every 30 to 60 minutes. Buses to Grybów (8zł, 50 minutes, six daily) pass through Berest and Polany. There are plenty of buses south to Muszyna (3zł, 25 minutes) via Powroźnik, and a fairly regular service to Mochnaczka and Tylicz (3zł).

Regular trains serve Nowy Sącz (12zł, 1½ hours) via a roundabout but pleasant route,

WOODEN CHURCHES AROUND KRYNICA

The countryside surrounding Krynica, with its beautiful wooded valleys, hills and charming small villages, is worth exploring, particularly for its wealth of old wooden churches. An essential aid for exploring the region is one of the *Beskid Sądecki* maps, readily available in these parts. Most of the churches – all originally Uniat and Lemk (p215) – are accessible by bus, though it's better to travel with your own car or bicycle.

To the north of Krynica, 13km and 16km respectively on the road to Grybów, are good *cerkwie* (the plural of *cerkiew* or wooden church) in **Berest** (1842) and **Polany** (1820). Both retain some of the old interior fittings, including iconostases and wall paintings. Buses ply this route regularly, so you shouldn't have problems getting back to Krynica or continuing on to Grybów, from where there's frequent transport west to Nowy Sącz.

The 24km loop via Mochnaczka, Tylicz and Powroźnik to the east and south of Krynica is another interesting trip. Along the route, the village of **Tylicz** boasts two churches, a Catholic one and an Uniat *cerkiew* dating from 1743. The latter is used only for funerals. If you have your own transport, head due east for 3km to **Muszynka**, which is almost at the border with Slovakia. The striking *cerkiew* here dates from 1689.

From Tylicz, a quiet back road skirts the Muszyna River valley for 8km to **Powroźnik**, which features yet another *cerkiew*. This one is the oldest in the region (1606) and the best known. The exterior is beautiful, and inside is an 18th-century iconostasis and several older icons on the side walls.

passing through Muszyna and Stary Sącz. Half a dozen daily trains go to Tarnów (20zł, 3½ hours).

Muszyna

POP 5000

Much smaller than Krynica, Muszyna (moo-*shin*-na), 11km to the southwest, is another spa town that exploits its mineral springs for tourism, and there are a number of old-fashioned sanatoriums in the area.

◉ Sights & Activities

Most people come to Muszyna to relax and walk the hills and woods around town. Two popular **hiking trails** originate in Muszyna and wend their way northwards up the mountains. The green trail takes you to **Mt Jaworzyna** (1113m), while the yellow one goes to the summit of **Mt Pusta Wielka** (1061m). You can get to either in around four hours, then continue on to Krynica. Any one of the *Beskid Sądecki* maps has all the details. For a shorter walk, there's also a pretty promenade along the Poprad River, about 300m beyond the Rynek. To find it, follow ul Kity from the Rynek out of town about 200m and cross the railway tracks.

⏿ Sleeping

Sanatorium Uzdrowiskowe Korona　　　　　　　HOTEL **€€**
(☑18　477　7960; www.sanatoriumkorona.pl; ul Mściwujewskiego 2; s/d/tr 105/170/220zł;

P 🛜 🌊) Perched above the Poprad River 1km southwest of the Rynek, this modern hotel–hydrotherapy centre has 120 beds in bright, well-maintained rooms and a good choice of spa treatments. The sanatorium offers a popular weekend package that includes a two-night stay with breakfast, a massage and use of the sauna and Jacuzzi from around 600zł per person.

Hotel Klimek Spa　　　　　　　HOTEL **€€€**
(☑18　477　8222; www.hotel-klimek.com.pl; Złockie 107; s/d/tr/ste 400/500/800/1000zł; P ❄ 🛜 🌊) In Złockie, about 3km northwest of the centre of Muszyna, this 53-room spa hotel is one of the best (and most expensive) places around, with a long list of hydrotherapy programs and treatments on offer, plus a sauna, steam room and small water park. There's also a good restaurant and bar.

✖ Eating & Drinking

Pizzera & Restauracja Rzym　　ITALIAN **€€**
(☑18 440 8370; www.restauracjarzym.pl; Rynek 25; mains 25-35zł; ⊙10am-10pm; 🛜) What looks like an unassuming pizzeria on the outside is actually a pretty good all-around restaurant, with Polish dishes like *pierogi* and potato pancakes, as well as more demanding chicken, beef and fish dishes. Muszyna's Rynek is, unfortunately, devoid of truly good restaurants and this is probably the best lunch or dinner option in the vicinity.

Szarlotka   CAFE
([☑]18 471 4013; Rynek 14a; ⊙9am-9pm) Old-fashioned cafe and ice-cream parlour that's been going strong since 1963. It has fabulous ice-cream sundaes, homemade pies and cookies, as well asblocks of white and dark chocolate. The dining area has a faintly retro '60s throwback feel and the patio, surrounded by a garden, has a pretty view out over the northern end of the Rynek.

ℹ Information

Bank PKO (ul Kity 1; ⊙9am-4pm Mon-Fri) Handy bank and 24-hour ATM on the south-western end of the Rynek.

Post Office (Rynek 24; ⊙7am-7pm Mon-Fri, 8am-2pm Sat)

Vector Travel Agency ([☑]18 471 8003; www. btvector.com; ul Kity 24; ⊙10am-5pm Mon-Fri, to 1pm Sat) Muszyna doesn't have a public tourist-information office, though this private travel agency, 200m southwest of the Rynek, can provide basic information, help with accommodation and organise tours and outings.

ℹ Getting There & Away

Buses to Krynica (3zł, 25 minutes) run frequently, and there's also an adequate service to Nowy Sącz (10zł, 1½ hours). Muszyna is on the rail line linking Krynica (4zł, 20 minutes) and Nowy Sącz (14zł, 1¼ hours), and trains run regularly to both destinations.

PIENINY

A startlingly beautiful mountain range between the Beskid Sądecki and the Tatras, the Pieniny is famous for the raft trip down the spectacular Dunajec Gorge, which has become one of Poland's major tourist highlights. Yet there's much more to see and do here. Walkers won't be disappointed with the hiking paths, which offer more dramatic vistas than the Beskid Sądecki or Bieszczady, while lovers of architecture will find some amazing old wooden churches here. There's also a picturesque castle in Niedzica, or you can just take it easy in the pleasant spa resort of Szczawnica.

The Pieniny consists of three separate ranges divided by the Dunajec River, the whole chain stretching east–west for about 35km. The highest and most popular is the central range topped by Mt Trzy Korony (Three Crowns; 981m), overlooking the Dunajec Gorge. Almost all of this area is now the Pieniny National Park (Pieniński Park Narodowy), whose headquarters is at Krościenko. To the east, behind the Dunajec River and south of Szczawnica, lies the Małe Pieniny (Small Pieniny), while to the west extends the Pieniny Spiskie. The latter outcrop, south of Czorsztyn Lake and including Niedzica, is the lowest and least spectacular, though the region around it, known as the Spisz, has an interesting blend of Polish and Slovakian cultures.

Szczawnica

POP 7350

Picturesquely located along the Grajcarek River, Szczawnica (shchahv-*nee*-tsah) has developed into a popular summer resort, while its mineral springs have made it an important spa. It's also the disembarkation point for Dunajec Gorge raft trips.

The town spreads out for 4km along the main road, ul Główna, and is divided into two sections, Szczawnica Niżna (Szczawnica Lower) to the west and Szczawnica Wyżna (Szczawnica Upper) to the east, with the bus station more or less in between. Most of the tourist and spa facilities are in the upper section, which also boasts most of the fine old timber houses.

◉ Sights & Activities

Szczawnica is a good starting point for **hiking** in both the Pieniny and the Beskid Sądecki ranges. Three trails originate in town and two more begin at Jaworki, 8km to the southeast.

It's also an excellent centre for **biking**, with some demanding mountain-bike trails in the hills, and a stunningly beautiful, family-friendly run that skirts the Dunajec Gorge for most of its length. The Dunajec Gorge cycling trail starts at the base of the Palenica chairlift and runs 15km along the Dunajec River to the Slovak town of Červený Kláštor. There are several rental outfits around town, including **Pod Koleją** ([☑]18 262 2724; ul Głowna 7; 4/20zł per hour/day; ⊙9am-7pm May-Sep) at the base of the chairlift.

Szczawnica Spa   MINERAL SPRINGS
(Uzdrowisko Szczawnica; [☑]18 540 0438; www. uzdrowiskoszczawnica.pl; ul Zdrojowa 28/Plac Dietla; tastings 1.30zł; ⊙7.30am-6pm Mon-Sat, 9am-5pm Sun) Walk uphill from the centre along ul Zdrojowa about 300m to find this handsome spa and mineral springs. On tap

CARPATHIAN MOUNTAINS SZCZAWNICA

HIKING IN THE PIENINY

Almost all hiking concentrates on the central Pieniny range, a compact area of 40 sq km that now encompasses Pieniny National Park. Trails are well marked and short, and no trekking equipment is necessary. There are three starting points on the outskirts of the park, all providing accommodation and food. The most popular is Krościenko at the northern edge, then Szczawnica on the eastern rim and Sromowce Niżne to the south. Arm yourself with the 1:50,000 *Gorce i Pieniny, Pieniński Park Narodowy* map, which includes a 1:125,000 map of the park showing all hiking routes.

Many walkers start from the Rynek in Krościenko. Follow the yellow trail as far as the **Przełęcz Szopka** pass, then switch to the blue trail branching off to the left and head up to the top of **Mt Trzy Korony** (981m), the highest summit of the central range. If the weather is clear, the reward for this two-hour walk is a breathtaking panorama that includes the Tatras, 35km to the southwest. You are now about 520m above the level of the Dunajec River.

Another excellent view is from **Mt Sokolica** (747m), 2km east as the crow flies from Mt Trzy Korony, or a 1½-hour walk along the blue trail. From Mt Sokolica, you can go back down to Krościenko by the green trail in about 1¼ hours, or to Szczawnica by the blue one in less than an hour.

are waters from six different springs. The local favourite water is 'Helena', said to help cure a range of maladies. There's a list of the springs in English on the wall of the spa, including a list of the ailments the waters are supposed to treat.

Palenica Chairlift
CHAIRLIFT

(Kolej Krzesełkowa Palenica; www.pkl.pl; ul Główna 7; adult/concession return 17/14zł, one way 12/9zł; ⊙9am-8pm) The chairlift near the centre of town makes the ride up to the nearby hill, Palenica (719m), in a few minutes. In winter, this is a popular snowboard run. In summer, it's a great start to several mountain hikes.

🛏 Sleeping

Most of the better places to stay are located in the upper part of the town; follow ul Zdrojowa uphill for 200m to 300m. Plenty of locals also rent out rooms: look for signs along ul Główna and the side streets. Expect to pay from 50zł to 60zł per person for a room with a bathroom.

Hotel Batory
HOTEL €€

(☑18 262 0207; www.batory-hotel.pl; Park Górny 13; r 240zł; P 🛜) A well-run, welcoming hotel with clean rooms and a peaceful park location high above Szczawnica. From the outside, it looks like a typically timbered mountain lodge; the rooms are on the ordinary side but fitted out with quality wooden furnishings. Prices have risen in recent

years but are still good value. To find it, follow ul Zdrojowa uphill 300m.

Solar Spa Centrum
HOTEL €€

(☑18 262 0810; www.solarspa.pl; ul Zdrojowa 4; s/d incl entry to water park 230/440zł high season; P @ 🛜 ≋) This huge hotel and spa complex has 103 plainly furnished, spotless rooms in four separate buildings. The list of spa treatments goes on forever. Best of all is the **water park complex** (Park Wodny; adult/concession 18/15zł; ⊙10am-9pm), which has indoor pools and slides and is open to non-guests.

🍴 Eating & Drinking

★ Café Helenka
INTERNATIONAL €€

(☑18 540 0402; www.cafe-helenka.pl; Plac Dietla 1; mains 20-25zł; ⊙10.30am-10pm Mon-Thu, to 10.30pm Fri, 10am-10.30pm Sat, 10am-10pm Sun; 🖉) Café Helenka is an unexpected delight: an upmarket cafe that offers an eclectic menu featuring rarities such as pumpkin soup, quiches and inspired local dishes such as grilled sheep's cheese served with cranberry jam. The coffee drinks are excellent too. The cafe is next to the main spa room, 200m uphill from the centre along ul Zdrojowa.

Eglander Caffe
CAFE

(☑664 564 201; ul Zdrojowa 2; coffee 8zł; ⊙9am-8pm) Keep this tiny cafe in mind for late-afternoon refreshment. Located at the bottom of ul Zdrojowa, it also does coffee to go.

ℹ Information

Bank Spółdzielczy (ul Główna 1; ⊘8am-6pm Mon-Fri, 7.30am-1pm Sat) Next to the well-marked Pieniny Tourist Centre (PTTK office) in the dead centre of town; has an ATM.

Pieniny Tourist Centre (Pienińskie Centrum Turystyki; ☑18 262 2332; www.pieninskie centrumturystyki.pl; ul Główna 1; ⊘8am-5pm Mon-Sat) Helpful local branch of the PTTK. Offers several excursions, including Dunajec rafting trips at 10am and 1.30pm, as well as a decent selection of hiking maps for sale. The office is situated in the heart of the centre at the intersection of ul Główna and ul Zdrojowa.

Szewczyk Travel (☑600 202 636; www. szewczyktravel.pl; ul Zdrojowa 2a; ⊘8am-8pm Mon-Sat, to 7pm Sun) De facto tourist office in the centre of town; organises excursions, including day trips over the border to Slovakia, and daily Dunajec rafting trips.

ℹ Getting There & Away

Regular buses run to Nowy Sącz (8zł, two hours) via Stary Sącz (7zł, 1½ hours). Up to eight fast buses go daily to Kraków (18zł, 2½ hours). Buses to Krościenko (2.50zł, 15 minutes) depart frequently.

For the Dunajec Gorge, take a bus (up to four daily in high season) to Sromowce Wyżne-Kąty (8zł, 30 to 40 minutes) – the driver will set you down at the right place. There are also private minibuses that depart when full.

Dunajec Gorge

Dunajec Gorge (Przełom Dunajca) is a spectacular stretch of the Dunajec (doo-*nah*-yets) River, which snakes from Czorsztyn Lake (Jezioro Czorsztyńskie) west for about 8km through steep cliffs, some of which are over 300m high. The river is narrow, in one instance funnelling through a 12m-wide bottleneck, and changes incessantly from majestically quiet, deep stretches to shallow mountain rapids. Be advised, however, that this is not a white-water experience but a leisurely pleasure trip.

The gorge has been a tourist attraction since the mid-19th century, when primitive rafts ferried guests of the Szczawnica spa on a day out. Today, the raft trip through the gorge attracts thousands of people every year, not counting do-it-yourselfers in their own kayaks. The raft itself is a set of five narrow, 6m-long, coffinlike canoes lashed together with rope. Holding 10 to 12 passengers, it is steered by two people, each decked

out in embroidered folk costume and armed with a long navigating pole.

The raft trip begins in the small village of Sromowce Wyżne-Kąty, at the **Raft Landing Place** (Przystań Flisacka; ☑18 262 9721; www.flisacy.com.pl; ul Kąty 14, Sromowce Wyżne; ⊘8.30am-5pm May-Aug, 9am-4pm Apr & Sep, to 3pm Oct, closed Nov-Mar). You'll take an 18km-long trip and disembark in Szczawnica. The journey takes about 2¼ hours, depending on the level of the river. Some rafts go further downstream to Krościenko (23km, 2¾ hours), but there's not very much to see on that stretch of the river.

The trip to Szczawnica costs 49/25zł adult/concession, while the one to Krościenko is 59/30zł. Return bus tickets cost an additional 9/7zł.

All of the private travel agencies in Kraków, Zakopane and Nowy Targ offer rafting package tours, including transport, equipment and guides. Prices vary, but trips from Zakopane start at around 90zł and from Kraków at around 270zł. The tour sponsored by Szewczyk Travel in Szczawnica is around 65zł, including transport.

ℹ Getting There & Away

Sromowce Wyżne-Kąty is serviced by several buses daily from Nowy Targ (10zł, 45 minutes) and, in season, four from Szczawnica (7zł, 30 minutes). Another way of getting to Sromowce Wyżne-Kąty is to hike from Krościenko or Szczawnica.

If you have private transport, you'll have to either leave your vehicle in Sromowce Wyżne-Kąty and come back for it after completing the raft trip in Szczawnica, or drive to Szczawnica and leave your vehicle there, so you'll have it as soon as you complete the trip. There are car parks in both Sromowce Wyżne-Kąty and Szczawnica, and the raft operator provides a bus service between the two locations.

Niedzica

POP 3000

Five kilometres northwest of Sromowce Wyżne-Kąty, Niedzica (signposted as 'Niedzica Zamek') is known for its castle. Perched on a rocky hill above the southeastern end of Czorsztyn Lake, the castle was built in the early 14th century to protect the Hungarian frontier, as this region marked the northern border of the Hungarian kingdom. It remained in Hungarian hands until the end of WWII. It was partially restored in the 1920s

WORTH A TRIP

ABANDONED BEAUTY OF CZORSZTYN

The village of Czorsztyn (*chor*-shtin), across the lake from Niedzica, boasts romantic **castle ruins** (☑ 18 262 5602; ul Zamkowa; adult/concession 5/2.50zł; ⊙ 9am-6pm daily May-Sep, 10am-3pm Tue-Sun Oct-Apr) dating from the second half of the 13th century. The fortress was built as the Polish counterpart to the Hungarian stronghold opposite at Niedzica. You see a 15th-century gatehouse, courtyards and the remains of an old kitchen. Best of all are the excellent views over the lake, the Dunajec River valley and the distant Tatras. There's also a small exhibition on the Pieniny region.

The village is just off the Krośnica–Sromowce Wyżne-Kąty road, accessible via the same bus you take for the Dunajec raft trip at Sromowce Wyżne-Kąty, or you can sail over for an hour from the Niedzica side.

and again 50 years later, but it essentially looks the same as it did in the 17th century, managing to retain a graceful Renaissance shape.

⊙ Sights & Activities

Niedzica Castle Museum   MUSEUM
(Muzeum Zamkowy w Niedzicy; ☑ 18 262 9480; www.shs.pl; ul Zamkowa 1; adult/concession 12/9zł; ⊙ 9am-6.30pm daily May-Sep, 9am-4pm Tue-Sun Oct-Apr) The castle is home to a museum on the building's and region's history. There's not a tremendous amount to see – some period costumes, furnishings, hunting trophies, a chapel from the late 14th century and collections on the archaeology and history of the Spisz region – but there are fine views over the lake and surrounding area. Everything is signposted in English.

Granary   MUSEUM
(Spichlerz; ☑ 18 262 9480; www.shs.pl; ul Zamkowa 1; admission 4zł; ⊙ 9am-6.30pm daily May-Sep) A separate ethnographic section of the Niedzica Castle Museum is located in an old timber granary, 150m from the castle. The exhibits focus on Spisz folk art. You can also walk over to the nearby Coach House (Powozownia).

Harnaś   BOAT TOUR
(☑ 18 275 0121; www.turystyka.wolski.pl; Niedzica; adult/concession 14/12zł) The pleasure boat *Harnaś* plies the waters of Czorsztyn Lake daily in July and August and at the weekend in May and June. Boats leave the pier at the Harnaś Café beneath the castle to the northwest between 9am and 6pm for a 50-minute cruise. A simple ferry to Czorsztyn village on the other side of the lake costs 6/5zł adult/concession each way.

🛏 Sleeping & Eating

Zespół Zamkowy   HOTEL €€
(☑ 18 262 9489; www.shs.pl; ul Zamkowa 1; s/d/tr 200/250/400zł, Celnica r 200zł; 🅿 🛜) Part of the Niedzica Castle has been turned into a hotel, providing 39 beds in 13 rooms, some of which occupy the historic chambers and are decorated with antique furniture. There are also a couple of cheaper rooms without a private bathroom in a timber house, called the Celnica, about 200m from the castle. Contact by email or telephone.

Hotel Lokis   HOTEL €€
(☑ 18 262 8540; www.lokis.com.pl; ul Cisowa 4; d/tr/apt 260/320/500zł; 🅿 🛜) In a wonderful spot overlooking the lake, about 500m from the castle on the road to Nowy Targ, the Lokis is a modern hotel and one of the more attractive places to stay in the Spisz region. It has 23 rooms and a sauna, and there's a balcony with lake views. Guests can rent bicycles for around 25zł a day.

Karczma Hajduk   POLISH €€
(☑ 18 262 9507; www.karczmahajduk.pl; Zamkowa 1; mains 15-25zł; ⊙ 9am-10pm) This inn, whose name recalls the castle's Hungarian links (*hajduks* were Hungarian mercenaries who fought against the Habsburgs in the 17th and 18th centuries), serves basic Polish dishes, such as *pierogi* and grilled meats, next door to the castle. Sit outside if weather permits.

❶ Getting There & Away

There are several buses a day from Nowy Targ (6zł, 30 to 40 minutes) to Niedzica village; some but not all stop at Niedzica Castle. A few minibuses a day link the castle to Szczawnica (8zł, 25 minutes).

Silesia

POP 9.5 MILLION

Best Places to Eat

➡ Steinhaus (p248)
➡ Bernard (p247)
➡ Madame (p270)
➡ Tatiana (p276)
➡ Frykówka (p279)

Best Places to Stay

➡ Hotel Piast (p245)
➡ Villa Navigator (p269)
➡ Hotel Fado (p254)
➡ Hotel Fenix Strauss (p257)
➡ Hotel Diament (p275)

Why Go?

Occupying the whole of southwestern Poland, Silesia (Śląsk, pronounced 'shlonsk', in Polish), is a diverse collection of attractive cities, industrial centres and mountain scenery.

Wrocław is a historical gem and well worth a visit, while inviting smaller centres such as Nysa and Jelenia Góra offer distinctive sights and activities. A natural attraction is presented by the Sudetes Mountains; stretching along the Czech border, the mountains are home to scenic beauty and idyllic resort towns, popular with hikers, bikers and spa fans alike. The rich history of the region underpins its charm, with architecture ranging from medieval fortresses to Baroque cathedrals. Silesia also contains the Auschwitz-Birkenau extermination camp complex set up by Nazi Germany, now a grim but moving memorial.

From tumultuous history to modern-day cities and countryside, Silesia affords plenty of opportunities for relaxation, and for immersion in the story of this once-turbulent corner of Europe.

When to Go
Wrocław

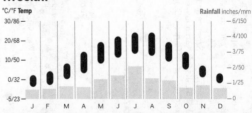

Apr Spring's vitality is a good match for the Jazz on the Odra festival in Wrocław.

Jun–Aug Summer is the season to enjoy hiking in the Sudetes Mountains.

Sep In autumn Polish wine is celebrated at Zielona Góra's Wine Festival.

238

Silesia Highlights

① Marvelling at the enormous Panorama of Racławice in **Wrocław** (p239).

② Eyeballing bony remains at the macabre **Chapel of Skulls** (p265) near Kudowa-Zdrój.

③ Contemplating the infinite within the tranquil Church of Peace in **Świdnica** (p253).

④ Hiking between Mt Szrenica and Mt Śnieżka in **Karkonosze National Park** (p259).

⑤ Learning the lessons of history at the former German extermination camp at **Auschwitz-Birkenau Memorial & Museum** (p279) in Oświęcim.

⑥ Visiting the impressive **Ksiaż Castle** (p255) near Świdnica.

⑦ Exploring the mighty fortress at **Kłodzko** (p263).

⑧ Enjoying the peaceful atmosphere of spa town Cieplice Śląskie-Zdrój (p260) in the outskirts of **Jelenia Góra**.

⑨ Spotting dwarf statues in **Wrocław's Old Town** (p241).

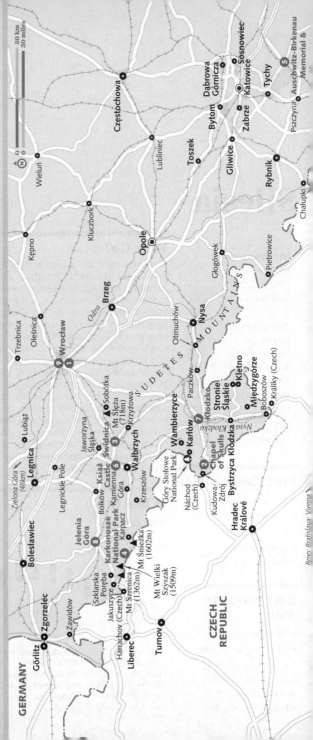

Rmo: Bratislava, Vienna

WROCŁAW

POP 635,000

Everyone loves Wrocław (*vrots*-wahf) and it's easy to see why. Though in some ways it's a more manageable version of Kraków, with all the cultural attributes and entertainment of that popular destination, the capital of Lower Silesia also has an appealing character all its own. Having absorbed Bohemian, Austrian and Prussian influences, the city has a unique architectural and cultural make-up, symbolised by its magnificent market square (Rynek). Wrocław's location on the Odra River, with its 12 islands, 130 bridges and riverside parks, is idyllic, and the beautifully preserved Cathedral Island is a treat for lovers of Gothic architecture.

But Wrocław is not just a pretty face. It is Poland's fourth-largest city and the major industrial, commercial and educational centre for the region; virtually everything in southwestern Poland starts, finishes or is taking place in Wrocław. At the same time it's a lively cultural centre, with several theatres, major festivals, rampant nightlife and a large student community.

History

Wrocław was originally founded on Cathedral Island (Ostrów Tumski), and the first recorded Polish ruler, Duke Mieszko I, brought the town, together with most of Silesia, into the Polish state. It must have been a fair-sized settlement by the turn of the first millennium, as it was chosen, along with Kraków and Kołobrzeg, as one of Piast Poland's three bishoprics.

During the period of division in the 12th and 13th centuries, Wrocław was the capital of one of the principalities of the Silesian Piasts. Like most settlements in southern Poland, Wrocław was burnt down by the Tatars. The town centre was then moved to the river's left bank.

Wrocław continued to grow under Bohemian administration (1335–1526), reaching the height of its prosperity in the 15th century and maintaining trade and cultural links with the Polish crown. New fortifications were constructed at the beginning of the 16th century, and the remains of the Fosa Miejska (City Moat) show where they were once positioned.

The Habsburgs, who ruled the city for the next two centuries, were less tolerant of the Polish and Czech communities, and things got even worse for the Slavic populations after 1741, when Wrocław fell to Prussia. For the next two centuries the city was increasingly Germanised and became known as Breslau.

As one of the major eastern outposts of the Third Reich, Breslau was given a key defensive role in the last stages of WWII, with the whole city converted into a fortified compound, 'Fortress Breslau'. Besieged by the Red Army in February 1945, the Germans defended their last bastion until May, executing anyone who refused to fight. During the battle, 75% of the city was razed to the ground.

Of the prewar population of more than 600,000, an estimated 30% died, mostly as a result of the fighting and the botched evacuation that preceded it. The handful of Germans who remained were expelled to Germany, and the ruined city was resettled with people from Poland's prewar eastern regions, mostly from Lviv (Lwów in Polish), which had been ceded to the Soviet Union.

The difficult reconstruction of Wrocław continued well into the 1980s, when the city surpassed its prewar population level for the first time.

Since the fall of communism, the city has had some success in attracting new investment, including the presence of LG Electronics in nearby Kobierzyce. Wrocław has also established itself as a centre of finance and tourism, and was designated a 2016 European Capital of Culture by the EU.

◎ Sights

◉ Old Town

Wrocław's extensive Old Town is so full of historic buildings that you could wander round for weeks and still feel like you hadn't seen everything. It's the kind of area that well repays a wander through its backstreets after you've visited the vibrant central square.

★ Old Town Hall   HISTORIC BUILDING

(Stary Ratusz; Rynek) This grand edifice took almost two centuries (1327–1504) to complete, and work on the 66m-high tower and decoration continued for another century.

The eastern facade reflects three distinct stages of the town hall's development. The segment to the right, with its austere early-Gothic features, is the oldest, while the delicate carving in the section to the left shows elements of the early Renaissance style. The central 16th-century section is topped by an ornamented triangular roof adorned with pinnacles.

SILESIA WROCŁAW

Wrocław

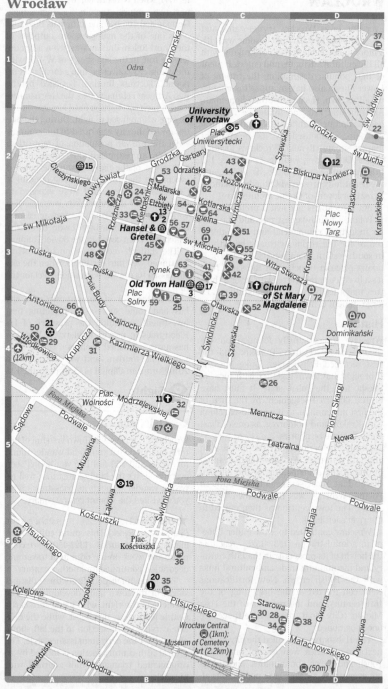

The astronomical clock, made of larch wood and showing the time and the phases of the moon, was built in 1580.

The southern facade, dating from the early 16th century, is the most elaborate, with three projections, a pair of ornate bay windows and carved stone figures.

The western elevation is the most austere, apart from the early-Baroque portal (1615) leading to the **Museum of Bourgeois Art** (Muzeum Sztuki Mieszczańskiej; www.muzeum.miejskie.wroclaw.pl; Stary Ratusz, Rynek; permanent exhibitions free, temporary exhibitions adult/concession 10/7zł; ☉10am-5pm Wed-Sat, to 6pm Sun) **FREE**. The museum's Gothic interiors are every bit as magnificent as the building's exterior, particularly the Great Hall (Sala Wielka) on the 1st floor, with carved decorations from the second half of the 15th century. Adjoining it is the Princes' Room (Sala Książęca), which was built as a chapel in the mid-14th century. The historic rooms house several exhibitions, including the Wrocław Treasury (Wrocławski Skarb) of gold- and silverware from the 16th to 19th centuries.

★**Hansel & Gretel** HISTORIC BUILDING
(Jaś i Małgosia; ul Odrzańska 39/40) Set in the northwestern corner of the Rynek are two charming houses named after Jaś i Małgosia, who English and German speakers know better as Hansel and Gretel. They're linked by a Baroque archway from 1728, which once led to the church cemetery (the inscription in Latin reads 'Death is the gateway to life').

Dwarves of Wrocław STATUE
(Wrocławskie Krasnale; www.krasnale.pl) See if you can spot the diminutive statue of a resting dwarf at ground level, just to the west of the Hansel and Gretel houses off Wrocław's main square. A few metres away you'll spot firemen dwarves, rushing to put out a blaze. These figures are part of a collection of over 300 scattered through the city. Though whimsical, they're also a reference to the symbol of the Orange Alternative (p245), a communist-era dissident group that used ridicule as a weapon.

They're sometimes identified in English as gnomes, as the Polish folkloric character they're based on (the leprechaun-like *krasnoludek*) resembles a cross between a dwarf and a gnome. Buy a 'dwarf map' (6zł) from the tourist office and go dwarf-spotting.

Church of St Elizabeth CHURCH
(Kościół Św Elżbiety; www.kosciolgarnizon.wroclaw.pl; ul Św Elżbiety 1; tower admission 5zł; ☉10am-7pm)

Wrocław

This monumental Gothic brick church features an 83m-high tower. Climb the 300-plus steps in the narrow stairwell for a great view of Wrocław.

★ **Church of St Mary Magdalene** CHURCH
(ul Łaciarska; tower adult/concession 4/3zł; ⊙ tower 10am-6pm Apr-Oct) One block east of the Rynek is this mighty Gothic redbrick building dating from the 14th century. Its showpiece is a copy of a Romanesque portal from around 1280 on the south wall, which originally adorned the

Benedictine Abbey in Ołbin but was moved here in 1546 after the abbey was demolished. You can climb the 72m-high tower and cross the so-called Penance Footbridge.

◎ University Quarter

★ **University of Wrocław** UNIVERSITY
(Uniwersytet Wrocławski; www.uni.wroc.pl; Plac Uniwersytecki 1) The main edifice of the University of Wrocław was built between 1728 and 1742. Enter through the grand blue

and gold Rococo gate at the western end to start exploring. The university sits within the university quarter, which occupies the northernmost part of the Old Town, between the riverfront and ul Uniwersytecka.

➡ **Church of the Holy Name of Jesus**

(Kościół Najświętszego Imienia Jezus; Plac Uniwersytecki) The Baroque-Rococo university church, arguably the city's most beautiful, was built in the 1690s on the site of the former Piast castle. Its spectacular interior is crammed with ornate fittings and adorned with fine illusionist frescoes of the life of Jesus.

➡ **Aula Leopoldinum**

(Plac Uniwersytecki; adult/concession 12/8zł; ⊙10am-3.30pm Thu-Tue) Found on the 1st floor of the main edifice of the University of Wrocław. Embellished with elaborate stuccowork, sculptures, paintings and a trompe l'oeil ceiling fresco, it's the city's best Baroque interior. The more modest Oratorium Marianum, on the ground floor, is included in the admission fee, as is the Mathematical Tower, topped with a sphere and decorated with allegorical figures.

➡ **Church of SS Vincent and James**

(Kościół Św Wincentego i Św Jakuba; Plac Biskupa Nankiera 15a) The Gothic Church of SS Vincent and James was originally a Romanesque basilica founded in the early 13th century. The largest church in the city, it's now used by the Uniat (Eastern Rite Catholic) faithful.

◉ East of the Old Town

★**Panorama of Racławice**　　MUSEUM

(Panorama Racławicka; www.panoramaraclawicka.pl; ul Purkyniego 11; adult/concession 25/18zł; ⊙9am-5pm May-Sep, to 4pm Tue-Sun Oct-Apr) Wrocław's pride and joy is this giant painting of the battle for Polish independence fought at Racławice on 4 April 1794, between the Polish army led by Tadeusz Kościuszko and Russian troops under General Alexander Tormasov. The Poles won, but it was all for naught: months later the nationwide insurrection was crushed by the tsarist army. The canvas measures 15m by 114m, and is wrapped around the internal walls of a rotunda.

Visits are by guided tour, departing every half-hour. You move around the balcony, inspecting each scene in turn, while an audioguide provides recorded commentary. The small rotunda behind the ticket office features a model of the battlefield and the uniforms of forces engaged in the battle.

The painting came into being when, a century after the battle, a group of patriots in Lviv (then the Polish city of Lwów) commissioned the panorama. The two main artists, Jan Styka and Wojciech Kossak, were helped by seven other painters who did the background scenes and details. They completed the monumental canvas in just over nine months, using 750kg of paint.

After WWII the painting was sent to Wrocław, but since it depicted a defeat of the Russians (Poland's then official friend and liberator), the communist authorities were reluctant to put it on display. The pavilion built for the panorama in 1967 sat empty until 1985, when the canvas was shown for the first time in more than four decades.

National Museum　　MUSEUM

(Muzeum Narodowe; www.mnwr.art.pl; Plac Powstańców Warszawy 5; adult/concession 15/10zł; ⊙10am-5pm Tue-Sun) A treasure trove of fine art, 200m east of the Panorama of Racławice. Medieval stone sculpture is displayed on the ground floor; exhibits include the Romanesque tympanum from the portal of the Church of St Mary Magdalene, depicting the Assumption of the Virgin Mary, and 14th-century sarcophagi from the Church of SS Vincent and James. There are also collections of Silesian paintings, ceramics, silverware and furnishings from the 16th to 19th centuries.

The 2nd floor holds Polish art, mainly paintings, from the 17th century to the present. The collection covers most of Poland's big names, including Jacek Malczewski, Stanisław Wyspiański, Witkacy (Stanisław Ignacy Witkiewicz) and Jan Matejko; be prepared for moody portraits and massive battle scenes. Among the modern painters, Władysław Hasior, Eugeniusz Stankiewicz-Get and Tadeusz Makowski are names to look out for, especially for their humorous takes on war and religion.

Museum of Architecture　　MUSEUM

(Muzeum Architektury; www.ma.wroc.pl; ul Bernardyńska 5; adult/concession 15/8zł; ⊙11am-5pm) A 16th-century former Bernardine church and monastery houses this collection featuring stone sculptures and stained-glass windows from various historic buildings of the region. The oldest exhibit, a Romanesque tympanum on the ground floor, dates from 1165. The museum also has a 12th-century Jewish tombstone, a 1:500 scale model of Wrocław (1740), and a delightful cloister garden.

⊙ Cathedral Island

The erstwhile Cathedral Island (Ostrów Tumski) – it was connected to the mainland in the 19th century – was the cradle of Wrocław. It was here that the Ślężanie, a tribe of West Slavs who gave their name to the region, constructed their stronghold in the 7th or 8th century. After the town was incorporated into the Polish state and a bishopric established in 1000, Wrocław's first church was built here. Over time a number of churches, monasteries and other religious buildings were constructed, giving a distinctive, markedly ecclesiastical character to the district.

Cathedral of St John the Baptist   CHURCH
(Archikatedra Św Jana Chrzciciela; www.katedra. archidiecezja.wroc.pl; Plac Katedralny 18; tower adult/concession 5/4zł; ⊙ tower 10am-4.30pm Mon-Sat, 2-4pm Sun) The centrepiece of Cathedral Island, this three-aisled Gothic basilica was built between 1244 and 1590. Seriously damaged during WWII, it was reconstructed in its previous Gothic form, complete with dragon guttering. The high altar boasts a gold and silver triptych from 1522 attributed to the school of Veit Stoss, and the western portico is a medieval gem. For once you don't need strong legs to climb the 91m-high tower, as there is a lift.

Church of Our Lady on the Sand   CHURCH
(Kościół Najświętszej Marii Panny na Piasku; ul Św Jadwigi) This lofty 14th-century building dominates the tiny islet known as Sand Island (Wyspa Piasek). Almost all the fittings were destroyed during WWII and the half-dozen old triptychs you see inside were collected from other Silesian churches. The wonderful Romanesque tympanum in the south aisle is the only remnant of the original 12th-century church that once stood here. There's a mechanised *szopka* (nativity scene) in the first chapel to the right; make a small donation when an assistant turns it on.

Church of St Giles   CHURCH
(Kościół Św Idziego; Plac Św Idziego) In contrast to the enormous neighbouring cathedral, the Church of St Giles is barely a cupboard. Built between 1218 and 1230, this is the oldest surviving church in Wrocław, and has an original Romanesque portal.

Archdiocesan Museum   MUSEUM
(Muzeum Archidiecezjalne; www.muzeum. archidiecezja.wroc.pl; Plac Katedralny 16; adult/concession 4/3zł; ⊙ 9am-3pm Tue-Sat) A few steps east of the Church of St Giles is the Wrocław Archdiocesan Museum, with a large collection of sacred art.

Botanical Gardens   GARDENS
(Ogród Botaniczny; www.ogrodbotaniczny. wroclaw.pl; ul Sienkiewicza 23; adult/concession 15/5zł; ⊙ 8am-6pm Apr-Oct) Cathedral Island contains the city's Botanical Gardens, a charming patch of greenery with palm houses. They make a nice change of pace when you've had enough of bricks and mortar – sacred or otherwise.

⊙ West & South of the Old Town

Military Museum   MUSEUM
(Muzeum Militariów; www.muzeum.miejskie. wroclaw.pl; ul Cieszyńskiego 9; ⊙ 10am-5pm Tue-Sun) **FREE** Just outside the ring road encircling the Old Town, this collection of militaria is housed within the squat brick Arsenal (Arsenał). With two towers and an enormous courtyard, the building is the most significant remnant of the city's 15th-century fortifications. This is also the home of the **Archaeological Museum**, which opens the same hours and also offers free admission.

White Stork Synagogue   SYNAGOGUE
(Synagoga Pod Białym Bocianem; ul Włodkowica 7) The restored White Stork Synagogue, built in 1829, is a reminder that this city was once home to more than 20,000 Jews.

New Synagogue Memorial   MEMORIAL
(Pomnik Nowej Synagogi; ul Łąkowa) This memorial marks the site of the New Synagogue, built in 1872. It was the country's second-largest synagogue until it was torched on Kristallnacht (9 November 1938).

Museum of Cemetery Art   CEMETERY
(Muzeum Sztuki Cmentarnej; www.mmw.pl; ul Ślężna 37/39; adult/concession 7/5zł; ⊙ 10am-6pm) This museum incorporates the Old Jewish Cemetery, founded in 1856, which is located about 1.5km south of the train and bus stations. Take tram 9 or 15.

Church of SS Stanislaus, Wenceslas and Dorothy   CHURCH
(Kościół Franciszkanów Św Stanisława, Wacława i Doroty; Plac Franciszkanski) Founded in 1351, this massive Gothic affair just south of the Old Town commemorates the meeting between Polish King Kazimierz III Wielki (Casimir III the Great) and his Bohemian counterpart, Charles IV, at which they agreed to leave Silesia in Bohemia's hands. Note the sizeable Rococo tomb at the start of the south aisle.

Passage SCULPTURE

(Przejście; cnr uls Świdnicka & Piłsudskiego) Fascinating sculpture depicting a group of seven bronze pedestrians being swallowed into the pavement, only to re-emerge on the other side of the street. It was created by Jerzy Kalina and was unveiled in 2005 to mark the 24th anniversary of the declaration of martial law. Look for it 500m west of the train station.

Tours

Wrocław Sightseeing Tours TOUR

(698 900 123; www.wroclawsightseeingtours. com; ul Wita Stwosza 3; 10am-5pm Mon-Sat) Operates guided walking tours (85zł) and bus tours (160zł) of the city, as well as day trips further afield in Lower Silesia (290zł) and the Sudetes (310zł).

Gucio CRUISE

(www.statekpasazerski.pl; Bulwar Piotra Włostowica; 10am-6pm Mar-Nov) In the warmer months this boat runs 50-minute cruises (15zł) on the Odra departing hourly from the southern end of Sand Island. Hour-long sailings (25zł) depart at 8pm and 9pm on Friday, Saturday and Sunday.

Festivals & Events

Musica Polonica Nova MUSIC

(www.musicapolonicanova.pl; Apr) Festival of contemporary music held in early April.

Jazz on the Odra JAZZ

(Jazz nad Odrą; www.jazznadodra.pl; Apr) One of Poland's foremost jazz festivals.

Arsenal Nights MUSIC

(www.wieczorywarsenale.pl; Jun-Jul) Chambermusic festival at the Arsenal building.

Wratislavia Cantans MUSIC

(www.wratislaviacantans.pl; Sep) Top international classical-music festival.

Wrocław Marathon SPORTS

(www.wroclawmaraton.pl; Sep) Running event in September.

Sleeping

★**Hotel Piast** HOTEL €

(71 343 0033; www.piastwroclaw.pl; ul Piłsudskiego 98; s/d from 130/140zł;) Known as the *Kronprinz* (Crown Prince) in German times, this former hostel has recently been upgraded to a neat and tidy two-star hotel. Its renovated rooms are clean and light, great value for the price and very handy for the train station. There's a restaurant on the premises, and breakfast costs an additional 20zł.

Hostel Mleczarnia HOSTEL €

(71 787 7570; www.mleczarniahostel.pl; ul Włodkowica 5; dm from 40zł, r 220zł;) On a quiet road not far from the Rynek, this hostel has bags of charm, having been decorated in a deliberately old-fashioned style within a former

---

THE DWARVES ARE REVOLTING

How do unarmed civilians take on a totalitarian regime? For Wrocław University art-history graduate Waldemar Fydrych, nicknamed 'Major', the answer was obvious – by ridiculing it.

In the early 1980s Fydrych set up the Orange Alternative (Pomarańczowa Alternatywa), a group that intended to place banana skins beneath the feet of Poland's humourless communist government. It initially painted pictures of dwarves on areas where the authorities had already painted over antigovernment graffiti – neatly drawing attention to the critical sentiments that had once been on display there.

In the second half of the decade the Alternative upped the ante by organising actions intended to both embarrass the regime and encourage independent thought. Members handed out items in short supply such as toilet paper and feminine-hygiene products; overdressed in red on the anniversary of Russia's communist revolution; and marched to demand the release of Father Christmas. The high point was a demonstration in 1988 in support of dwarves, in which thousands marched while wearing floppy orange hats.

Nowadays the communists are long gone and the dwarves have taken over the streets, in the form of **small statues** (p241) that are said to be a tribute to the icon of the Orange Alternative. 'Major' Fydrych has continued to campaign for change via silliness; in addition to continuing the Alternative's actions, he's twice run for election as Mayor of Warsaw under the slogan 'Merrier and more competent'. Though he didn't win the election, in 2012 Fydrych received his PhD from the capital's Academy of Fine Arts.

You can read more about the Orange Alternative's history and current activities at its website, www.pomaranczowa-alternatywa.org.

residential building. There's a women-only dorm available, along with a kitchen and free laundry facilities. Downstairs is the excellent Mleczarnia cafe-bar.

The One
HOSTEL €

(☏71 337 2402; www.onehostel.pl; Rynek 30; dm 44-75zł, r 140-170zł; ☏) The best-located hostel in Wrocław, perched above the southeast corner of the main square. Dorms are modern and bright, and there's the option of Japanese-style capsule beds.

Hostel Babel
HOSTEL €

(☏71 342 0250; www.babelhostel.pl; ul Kołłątaja 16/3; dm from 45zł, r 140zł; ☏) A tatty old staircase leads up to pleasant budget accommodation just 100m from the train station. Dorms are set in renovated apartment rooms with ornate lamps and decorative ceilings. Bathrooms are shiny clean, and guests have access to a kitchen. There's a DVD player for rainy days.

Cinnamon Hostel
HOSTEL €

(☏71 344 5858; www.facebook.com/cinnamon hostel.wroclaw; ul Kazimierza Wielkiego 67; dm 29-55zł, r 130zł; ☏) Right on the ring road and within spitting distance of pedestrianised ul Świdnicka, this charming and upbeat place has rooms (with two to 12 beds) named for spices and herbs, along with a kitchen, laundry and comfortable common room.

MDK Kopernik Hostel
HOSTEL €

(☏71 343 8857; www.mdk.wroclaw.pl; ul Kołłątaja 20; dm 39-42zł, d 96zł; ☏) A mere 100m from the train station, this is a basic old-style hostel, located in a grand mustard-coloured building. Some dorms are huge and beds are packed close together. There's a kitchen and bike storage, and prices are cheaper after the first night.

Hotel Patio
HOTEL €€

(☏71 375 0417; www.hotelpatio.pl; ul Kiełbaśnicza 24; s/d from 300/340zł; P❄☏) The Patio offers pleasant lodgings a short hop from the main square, within two buildings linked by a covered, sunlit courtyard. Rooms are clean and light, sometimes small but with reasonably high ceilings, and there's a spectacular breakfast spread.

Dwór Polski
HOTEL €€

(☏71 372 3415; www.dworpolski.wroclaw.pl; ul Kiełbaśnicza 2; s/d 280/360zł; P☏) You couldn't ask for more character than this: a restored 16th-century house, complete with idiosyncratic rooms, some original dark wood fittings and fixtures, and a popular restaurant (enter from Rynek 5). The atmospheric internal courtyard is a plus.

Art Hotel
HOTEL €€

(☏71 787 7400; www.arthotel.pl; ul Kiełbaśnicza 20; r 310-500zł; P❄☏) An elegant splurge candidate in a renovated apartment building, with tastefully restrained decor, quality fittings and gleaming bathrooms. There's a top-notch Polish-French restaurant, and a fitness room for working off any extra weight gained therein. There's also a massage studio on site. Breakfast is a hefty 50zł per person.

AS Apartments
APARTMENT €€

(☏79 341 8759; www.asapart.com; Rynek 18/4; apt from 200zł; ☏) Company offering a choice of apartments in the Old Town, many of them with a view of the Rynek itself. The fixtures and fittings can be old-fashioned (think sofa beds and hand-held shower heads), but the locations are fabulous for the price. Most apartments come with a kitchen and washing machine, along with free wi-fi access.

Hotel Tumski
HOTEL €€

(☏71 322 6099; www.hotel-tumski.com.pl; Wyspa Słodowa 10; s/d from 240/345zł; ☏) Located on an islet in the Odra, about 300m north of the river along ul Św Jadwigi, this neat hotel has a riverside setting and is set back from a busy road. There's an attractive rustic-style restaurant serving both Polish and international cuisine.

Hotel Europeum
HOTEL €€

(☏71 371 4500; www.europeum.pl; ul Kazimierza Wielkiego 27a; s/d from 305/360zł; P❄☏) Business-oriented Hotel Europeum has stylish rooms in a good location not far from the Rynek. Rates drop dramatically at weekends, generally by 20%.

Hotel Europejski
HOTEL €€

(☏71 772 1000; www.silfor.pl; ul Piłsudskiego 88; s/d from 200/250zł; P❄☏) Smart business hotel with clean, agreeable rooms, located just 200m west of the train station. There's a restaurant on the premises, along with an airy cafe that receives plenty of natural light.

Hotel Savoy
HOTEL €€

(☏71 344 3071; www.savoy-wroclaw.pl; Plac Kościuszki 19; s 135zł, d 159-185zł; ☏) It may not look like much, but the downbeat Savoy is one of your best shots at a bargain. Pot plants, half-decent furniture and little balconies liven up the best rooms. It's 700m south of the Rynek along ul Świdnicka. Breakfast is an extra 14zł.

Hotel Polonia
HOTEL €€

(📞71 343 1021; www.poloniawroclaw.pl; ul Piłsudskiego 66; s 105-180zł, d 130-200zł; 🛜) There's little that is spectacular about this large hotel 400m west of the train station, but it's close to transport, and occasional special promotions make it even better value. Room prices depend on size, and quality of decoration.

Hotel Monopol
HOTEL €€€

(📞71 772 3777; www.monopolwroclaw.hotel.com.pl; ul Modrzejewskiej 2; s/d 600/650zł; ✻🛜⊠) In its heyday the elegant Monopol hosted such luminaries as Pablo Picasso and Marlene Dietrich (along with unsavoury characters such as Adolf Hitler). It's opposite the opera house, 350m south of the Rynek off ul Świdnicka. It boasts restaurants, bars, a cafe, a spa and boutiques, so you won't be short of pampering options – though you might soon be short of cash.

🍴 Eating

The market square and its central buildings are jam-packed with eateries, but it's worth checking out the quieter streets for less tourist-happy establishments.

For self-catering supplies, visit **Eko Supermarket** (ul Kuźnica 48; ⏲6.30am-10pm Mon-Sat, 9am-8pm Sun), Hala Targowa (p249) or the supermarket at Galeria Dominikańska (p249).

Bar Wegetariański Vega
VEGETARIAN €

(Rynek 1/2; mains 6-8zł; ⏲8am-7pm Mon-Thu, 9am-9pm Fri & Sat, 9am-7pm Sun; 🥄) Cheap, meat-free cafeteria on two floors in the centre of the Rynek, offering vegetarian and vegan dishes in a light green space. There's a good choice of soups and crêpes. Set-menu options run from 10zł to 22zł.

STP
CAFETERIA €

(ul Kuźnica 10; dishes per 100g 2.59zł; ⏲10am-9pm) Short for 'Szybko, Tanio, Pysznie', the name says it all: 'Fast, Cheap, Delicious'. This cafeteria sells its food by weight and it's surprisingly good. Just grab a plate, pile it up and it'll be weighed when you reach the cashier. Choices include *naleśniki* (crêpes), *pierogi* (dumplings), pasta dishes, and healthy options such as salmon with curried rice and vegetables.

Bernard
CZECH, INTERNATIONAL €€

(Rynek 35; mains 29-83zł; ⏲10.30am-11pm; 🛜) This lively split-level bar-restaurant is in-

SILESIA WROCŁAW

spired by the Czech beer of the same name, and the menu features some Czech dishes such as rabbit and pork knee. There's upmarket comfort food including burgers, steak and fish dishes, as well as plenty of beer. The stylish interior is conducive to a quiet evening or group outing. Breakfast is served from 10.30am to noon.

Masala
INDIAN €€

(ul Kuźnica 3; mains 30-62zł; ⏲11am-11pm; 🥄) Indian restaurant just off the Rynek with contemporary interior design, its silver wallpaper contrasting with brightly coloured place mats. Masala offers fairly authentic subcontinental cuisine, with a few twists for Polish palates.

Darea
JAPANESE, KOREAN €€

(ul Kuźnica 43/45; mains 26-50zł; ⏲noon-11pm) Over time the menu at this place has become steadily more Japanese, but you'll still find authentic Korean dishes such as bibimbap and bulgogi on the list. It's all good Asian food in atmospheric surrounds.

Karczma Lwowska
POLISH €€

(Rynek 4; mains 30-70zł; ⏲noon-midnight) Karczma Lwowska serves up tasty Polish standards in a rustic, rural space; try the beer served in big ceramic mugs. Some dishes hail from the former eastern Poland (now western Ukraine).

Szpilka
INTERNATIONAL €€

(ul Szewska 8; mains 18-65zł; ⏲9am-8pm Mon-Fri, 11am-8pm Sat & Sun) This friendly informal eatery combines the owner's love of food and fashion in its decor. The long and diverse menu includes pasta, pizzas, steaks and salads, along with more exotic dishes such as tandoori chicken. Breakfast is available until 11.30am.

Amalfi
ITALIAN €€

(ul Więzienna 21; mains 16-86zł; ⏲noon-midnight) Just north of the Rynek is this pizzeria with a wood-burning stove and a pleasant long terrace. It's the best option for decent Italian cuisine on a street with plenty of Mediterranean offerings.

Mexico Bar MEXICAN €€

(ul Rzeźnicza 34; mains 15-45zł; ⊙noon-11pm) Compact, warmly lit Mexico Bar features sombreros and backlit masks on the walls, and serves all the Mexican favourites. There's a small bar to lean on while waiting for a table.

La Scala ITALIAN €€

(Rynek 38; mains 19-60zł; ⊙10am-midnight) Authentic but relatively pricey Italian food; the cheaper trattoria at ground level serves good pizza and pasta in an atmospheric interior of checked tablecloths and timber tables.

★Steinhaus POLISH €€€

(☑512 931 071; ul Włodkowica 11; mains 40-70zł; ⊙11am-11pm; 🐾) Old-fashioned Polish and Jewish cooking in an elegant but unfussy setting. The goose in cranberry sauce can't be topped, though the grilled duck breast comes close. Be sure to reserve on weekends, as this place is justifiably popular.

Restauracja Jadka POLISH €€€

(☑71 343 6461; ul Rzeźnicza 24/25; mains 54-89zł; ⊙1-11pm) Well-regarded fine-dining option presenting impeccable modern versions of Polish classics and silver-service table settings (candles, crystal, linen) in delightful Gothic surrounds. Bookings are recommended.

Akropolis GREEK €€€

(Rynek 16/17; mains 20-75zł; ⊙noon-11pm) This restaurant serves excellent Greek food with a view onto the market square, defying the usual rule that restaurants in such a prominent position aren't worth bothering with. The baked lamb in lemon sauce is superb.

🍸 Drinking & Nightlife

There are two areas to head for if you fancy a big night out: the Rynek, and Pasaż Niepolda, off ul Ruska, west of the Old Town, which offers a bit more variety.

★Vinyl Cafe CAFE, BAR

(ul Kotlarska 35/36; ⊙10am-late; 🐾) Hitting the retro button hard, this cool cafe-bar is a jumble of mismatched furniture, old framed photos and stacks of vinyl records. It's a great place to grab a drink, both day and night.

Mleczarnia CAFE, BAR

(ul Włodkowica 5; ⊙8am-4am; 🐾) Hidden away in an area that was once the city's main Jewish neighbourhood, this atmospheric place is stuffed with chipped old wooden tables bearing lace doilies and candlesticks. It turns out good coffee and light meals, including breakfast. At night the cellar opens, adding another moody dimension. There's a beautiful back garden in summer.

PRL BAR, CLUB

(Rynek-Ratusz 10; ⊙noon-late) The dictatorship of the proletariat is alive and well in this tongue-in-cheek venue inspired by communist nostalgia. Disco lights play over a bust of Lenin, propaganda posters line the walls, and red-menace memorabilia is scattered through the maze of rooms. Descend to the basement – beneath the portraits of Stalin and Mao – if you'd like to hit the dance floor.

Papa Bar BAR

(ul Rzeźnicza 32/33; ⊙noon-late Mon-Fri, 4pm-late Sat & Sun; 🐾) This spacious bar is a cut above the rest, with its designer decor, huge rectangular bar and fine cocktails. Try the Wrocław Sling, a mix of vodka and citrus juices. There's also a menu of light meals.

Pub Więzienna PUB

(ul Więzienna 6; ⊙11am-late) Housed in what was a prison in the Middle Ages, and located below a well-concealed courtyard, this atmospheric bar with timber furniture serves Polish and Czech beer, and wine from around the world.

Cafe Artzat CAFE

(ul Malarska 30; 🐾) Low-key Cafe Artzat is just north of the landmark Church of St Elizabeth. It's one of the best places in town to recharge your batteries over coffee or tea (or a beer) and a good book.

Frankie's JUICE BAR

(ul Wita Stwosza 57; ⊙7am-11pm; 🐾) Contemporary-themed juice bar, mixing a delicious array of creatively named drinks from the 'Copenhagen' to the 'Life Cure', and offering a selection of salads and sandwiches too.

Spiż BREWERY

(Rynek-Ratusz 2; ⊙10am-late) This popular microbrewery bar-restaurant is buried in a basement under the town hall. Bustling staff scurry around the copper vats to serve the voracious clientele.

Literatka CAFE, BAR

(Rynek 56/57; ⊙10am-late) As the name suggests, this cafe next to a library will suit the literary minded. The interior is a cosy blend of wood panelling, faded carpet and old books.

Czekoladziarnia CAFE
(ul Więzienna 30; ☺10am-10pm) Little corner cafe selling its own shop-made chocolate in both solid and liquid forms.

Bezsenność CLUB
(ul Ruska 51; ☺7pm-late) With its alternative/ rock/dance line-up and distressed decor, 'Insomnia' attracts a high-end clientele and is one of the most popular clubs in town. It's located in the Pasaż Niepolda, home to a group of bars, clubs and restaurants, just off ul Ruska.

Jazzda BAR, CLUB
(Rynek 60; ☺5pm-late Mon-Fri, noon-late Sat & Sun) Looking for a John Travolta kind of evening? This central bar and club, with a lit-up, multicoloured dance floor and strobe lights, will fit the bill.

Novocaina BAR, CLUB
(Rynek 16; ☺1pm-late) A Rynek cafe-restaurant that dons its party duds late in the evening, this neo-Gothic space with intimate nooks and crannies attracts a fashion-conscious crowd.

Metropolis CLUB
(ul Ruska 51; ☺8pm-3am) Enormous Metropolis has two dance floors over three levels. Music ranges from dance and techno to hits from recent decades.

☆ Entertainment

Wrocław is an important cultural and nightlife centre, and there's a lot of stuff going on all year round. The monthly freebie *Aktivist* (www.aktivist.pl/wroclaw) has listings in Polish; you can pick up a copy of the English-language *The Visitor* (www.thevisitor.pl) from the tourist office. For a more detailed rundown of clubs, bars and the like, seek out the reliably forthright *Wrocław in Your Pocket* (www.inyourpocket.com/poland/wroclaw) or consult the useful *Wrocław Life* website (www.local-life.com/wroclaw).

Kino Nowe Horyzonty CINEMA
(www.kinonh.pl; ul Kazimierza Wielkiego 19a) Arthouse cinema screening movies from around the world, including English-language films.

Filharmonia CLASSICAL MUSIC
(Philharmonic Hall; ☑tickets 71 792 1000; www. filharmonia.wroclaw.pl; ul Piłsudskiego 19) Hear classical music at this venue, located 800m southwest of the Rynek.

Opera House OPERA, BALLET
(Opera Wrocławska; ☑71 344 5779; www.opera. wroclaw.pl; ul Świdnicka 35; ☺box office noon-7pm Mon-Sat, 11am-5pm Sun) This venerable building is the traditional venue for opera and ballet performances.

Wrocławski Teatr Współczesny THEATRE
(Wrocław Contemporary Theatre; ☑71 358 8922; www.wteatrw.pl; ul Rzeźnicza 12; ☺box office noon-7pm Mon-Fri) Near the centre of town, this theatre stages productions from modern Polish and international playwrights.

🛍 Shopping

Księgarnia Podróżnika BOOKS
(ul Wita Stwosza 19/20; ☺10am-6pm Mon-Fri, to 3pm Sat) Travel specialist, selling maps and guidebooks.

Empik BOOKS
(Rynek 50; ☺9am-9pm Mon-Sat, 11am-9pm Sun) Big range of books and maps on the Rynek.

Hala Targowa FOOD, GIFTS
(ul Pisarska 17; ☺8am-7pm Mon-Fri, 9am-3pm Sat) Lively historic market hall selling food, souvenirs and an endless variety of knick-knacks.

Galeria Dominikańska MALL
(www.galeria-dominikanska.pl; Plac Dominikański 3; ☺9.30am-9pm Mon-Sat, 10am-8pm Sun) Shopping mall with a supermarket and hundreds of shops selling everything under the sun.

ℹ Information

Intermax (ul Psie Budy 10/11; per hour 4zł; ☺9am-11pm) Internet access. Enter from ul Kazimierza Wielkiego.

Post Office (Rynek 28; ☺24hr)

PTTK (☑71 343 0344; www.pttk.wroclaw.pl; 1st fl, Rynek-Ratusz 11/12; ☺8am-5pm Mon-Fri) Agency offering adventurous tours to the Polish countryside.

Tourist Office (☑71 344 3111; www.wroclaw-info.pl; Rynek 14; ☺10am-8pm) Provides advice and assistance to visitors to Wrocław. There's another branch (☑71 344 3111; www. wroclaw-info.pl; Rynek-Ratusz 24; ☺10am-8pm) within the nearby complex next to the town hall.

ℹ Getting There & Away

AIR

Wrocław Airport (☑71 358 1381; www.airport. wroclaw.pl; ul Graniczna 190) is in Strachowice, 13km west of the city centre. There are direct connections via LOT to Warsaw (six times daily). International links:

Dublin Ryanair, daily

Frankfurt Lufthansa, three daily

London Wizz Air and Ryanair, three daily

Munich Lufthansa, three daily

Paris Ryanair, four weekly; Wizz Air, twice weekly

LOT (☑ 71 342 5151; ul Piłsudskiego 36; ☺ 9am-5pm Mon-Fri) has an office near the train station.

BUS

The **bus station** (Dworzec Centralny PKS; ul Sucha 1/11) is 1.3km south of the Rynek, behind the train station. At the time of research the old bus station had been demolished, to be rebuilt as part of a shopping complex planned to open in 2017. In the meantime a temporary bus station has been set up just to the east of the site, a little further along ul Sucha.

Regional buses run at least hourly to Trzebnica (7zł, 40 minutes), Sobótka (7zł, 55 minutes) and Świdnica (15zł, 1½ hours). They also serve Kudowa-Zdrój (28zł, 2¾ hours, eight daily), Nysa (18zł, 1½ hours, four daily) and Zielona Góra (40zł, 3½ hours, 10 daily).

Trains are generally more convenient for more distant destinations, though private company Polski Bus (www.polskibus.com) operates some useful services. Fares vary from day to day; book online ahead of time for the best deals.

DESTINATION	TIME (HR)	FREQUENCY
Berlin	4½	2 daily
Gdańsk	7	4 daily
Katowice	2½	8 daily
Kraków	3	hourly
Łódź	3¼	hourly
Poznań	3¾	4 daily
Prague	5	4 daily
Rzeszów	5¾	7 daily
Szczecin	7½	3 daily
Warsaw	5	hourly

There are other international buses departing from Wrocław to destinations including Berlin (from 140zł, five hours, daily).

TRAIN

Trains depart from the impressive mock castle that is **Wrocław Główny station** (ul Piłsudskiego 105), 1.2km south of the Rynek. Built in 1857 by the Kingdom of Prussia and recently extensively renovated, it's worth visiting to admire its architecture even if you're not catching a train. While there, check out the extravagantly decorated ceilings within the chain restaurants inside the ticket hall. Trains to Katowice (30zł, three hours, 11 daily) usually pass through Opole (26zł, 55 minutes) on the way. Most continue to Kraków (40zł, 3½ hours, eight daily). There are seven daily services to Warsaw, mostly via fast Express InterCity trains (150zł, 3¾ hours).

Wrocław also has regular train links to a range of other Polish destinations.

DESTINATION	FARE (ZŁ)	TIME (HR)	FREQUENCY
Gniezno	50	3½	6 daily
Jelenia Góra	24	2¾	hourly
Kłodzko	20	2	10 daily
Łódź	35	4	6 daily
Poznań	34	2¾	at least hourly
Wałbrzych	20	1½	hourly
Zielona Góra	26	3	8 daily

❶ Getting Around

TO/FROM THE AIRPORT

The airport can be reached on bus 406 from the main train station (3.20zł, 30 minutes, every 20 to 40 minutes), or via infrequent night bus 249. A taxi to the airport costs about 50zł.

CAR & MOTORCYCLE

Micar (☑ 71 325 1949; www.micar.pl; ul Zmigrodzka 75a; ☺ 8am-6pm Mon-Fri, to 2pm Sat) has cars with unlimited kilometres starting from 70zł per day.

PUBLIC TRANSPORT

Wrocław has an efficient network of trams and buses covering the city centre and suburbs. Journeys within the centre cost 3zł; longer trips, fast buses and night buses (numbered over 200) are 3.20zł.

TAXI

Some of the better-known companies include **Domino Taxi** (☑ 71 19625), **Radio Taxi** (☑ 71 19622) and **Super Taxi** (☑ 71 19663).

AROUND WROCŁAW

Trzebnica

POP 13,000

A small town 25km north of Wrocław, Trzebnica (tsheb-*nee*-tsah) is noted for its former Cistercian abbey. It's an impressive site and a pleasant half-day trip from Wrocław. Buses to and from Wrocław (7zł, 40 minutes) run at least hourly.

◉ Sights

Abbey Church   CHURCH

(Kościół Św Jadwigi; ul Jana Pawła II 3) The abbey church is thought to be one of the first brick buildings erected in Poland. Though rebuilt in the 18th century, it's preserved much of its original Romanesque shape and boasts two original portals. The one next to the main entrance, partly hidden behind the Baroque tower (1780s), is particularly fine; on the tympanum (1220s), you can make out King David on his throne playing the harp to Queen Bathsheba.

The church's showpiece is St Hedwig's Chapel (Kaplica Św Jadwigi), to the right of the chancel.

The chapel was built soon after the canonisation of the princess, and the graceful, ribbed Gothic vaulting has been preserved unchanged. Its central feature is the saint's Gothic sarcophagus, an elaborate work in black marble and alabaster created in stages between 1680 and 1750. To the left of the tomb is the entrance to the three-nave crypt, the oldest part of the church.

The rest of the chapel is full of gilded and marbled altars; in the nave are 18 scenes from the saint's life. The beautiful black organ is striking against the white walls and pastel colours of the ornamentation.

Sobótka & Mt Ślęża

POP 7000

Some 34km southwest of Wrocław, the solitary forested cone of Mt Ślęża rises to 718m above the surrounding open plain. Mt Ślęża was one of the holy places of an ancient pagan tribe that set up cult sites in the area from at least the 5th century BC until the 11th century AD, when Christianity put a halt to it. The summit was circled by a stone wall marking off the sanctuary where rituals were held, and the remains of these ramparts survive to this day. Mysterious votive statues were carved crudely out of granite, and several of them are scattered over the mountain's slopes.

The Ślęża massif is surrounded by the 156sq-km Ślęża Landscape Park (Ślężański Park Krajobrazowy; www.dzpk.pl). At the northern foot of Mt Ślęża is the small town of Sobótka, the starting point for a hike to the top. The red route will lead you up the mountain, a hike that should take about two hours. You'll find two statues called the Bear (Miś) and the Fish (Ryba) on the way, plus a tall TV mast and a 19th-century church at the top.

Coming down, you can take the steeper but faster (1¼ hours) yellow route directly to the PTTK hostel, about 800m west of your starting point. On the road back into town

you'll pass another stone statue, called the Monk (Mnich) but resembling an urn to our untrained eyes.

Sobótka is easily accessible by bus from Wrocław (7zł, 55 minutes, at least hourly) and Świdnica (6zł, 30 minutes, six daily).

LOWER SILESIA

A fertile lowland extending along the upper and middle course of the Odra River, Lower Silesia (Dolny Śląsk) was settled relatively early on and is full of interesting old towns and villages. Architecture buffs will have a field day with the wide assortment of castles and churches, and the area's larger towns have more than enough to tempt those with entertainment on their minds.

Zielona Góra

POP 119,000

The pretty western town Zielona Góra (Green Mountain) lives up to at least half its name – there's little that's mountainous about it, but there's much leafy greenness courtesy of the trees shading its pedestrian streets.

The presence of nature is also a reminder that Zielona Góra (zhyeh-lo-na goo-rah) stands out as Poland's only wine producer. It's a tradition running all the way back to the 14th century, though the climate is less than ideal and viticulture was never a very profitable endeavour here. Though the output today is merely symbolic, the wine association is reflected in the city's attractions.

Like the majority of other towns in the region, Zielona Góra was founded by the Silesian Piasts. It was part of the Głogów Duchy, one of numerous regional principalities, before it passed to the Habsburgs in the 16th century and to Prussia two centuries later. Unlike many other Silesian towns, however, Zielona Góra came through WWII with minimal damage, so prewar architecture is well represented here.

◉ Sights

Lubuski Regional Museum   MUSEUM
(Muzeum Ziemi Lubuskiej; www.mzl.zgora.pl; al Niepodległości 15; adult/concession 6/3zł; ⊙ 11am-5pm Wed-Fri, 10am-3pm Sat & Sun) The regional museum houses a collection of Silesian religious art from the 14th to 18th centuries, a fascinating clock gallery and a permanent exhibition of artwork by Marian Kruczek (1927–83). Kruczek used everyday objects –

anything from buttons to spark plugs – to create striking assemblages, and this is the largest collection of his work in Poland. In the same building (and included in the ticket price) is the Wine Museum, illustrating the history of local winemaking, and the Museum of Torture.

The charming torture submuseum holds Poland's largest exhibition on the history of criminal law, the penalty system and torture methods employed from the Middle Ages until the 18th century.

Palm House
GARDENS

(Palmiarnia; www.palmiarnia.zgora.pl; ul Wrocławska 12a; ⊙noon-8pm Tue-Sun) FREE Located within the handsome Wine Park (Park Winny), this building is an extravagant home to various species of palm, as well as cacti, and fish housed within aquaria. A restaurant and cafe is threaded through the building, allowing diners to enjoy the greenery from vantage points high and low.

Stary Rynek
SQUARE

(Old Market Square) Lined with brightly painted houses, the renovated old market square is a pleasant and harmonious rectangular space at the end of the long pedestrian stretch along al Niepodległości and ul Żeromskiego. The 18th-century town hall, complete with a slim 54m tower, is a stately landmark.

Ethnographic Museum
MUSEUM

(Muzeum Etnograficzne; www.muzeumochla. pl; ul Muzealna 5, Ochla; adult/concession 8/6zł; ⊙10am-5pm Tue-Sun) This outdoor museum is in Ochla, 7km south of the city, and is served by bus 27. Over 60 traditional buildings – many of them residential – have been reassembled over 13 hectares of land.

🎎 Festivals & Events

Wine Festival
WINE

(Winobranie; www.winobranie.zgora.pl; ⊙Sep) Celebration of the grape held in mid-September each year, including concerts, feasts and a parade. The tourist office can inform you about specific events.

🛏 Sleeping

★ Hotel Śródmiejski
HOTEL €€

(☑68 415 2415; www.hotel-srodmiejski.pl; ul Żeromskiego 23; s 218zł, d 270-350zł; P 🛜) Offers pleasant rooms of contemporary design, and the location is as central as you could want. Weekend discounts are available.

Hotelik Senator
HOTEL €€

(☑68 324 0436; www.senator.zgora.pl; ul Chopina 23a; s/d 180/220zł; P 🛜) Bright Hotelik Senator has friendly service and simple, comfortable rooms. There's a restaurant on the premises, and it's in a good location for both the train and bus stations and the eating strip along al Niepodległości. Enter from ul Jana Keplera.

B&B Pokoje Gościnne
HOTEL €€

(☑609 058 862; www.pokoje-hotelowe.zgora.pl; Plac Pocztowy 10; s/d 140/210zł; P 🛜) Centrally located and affordable, these lodgings are only a stone's throw from the Stary Rynek. Rooms are modern and comfortable, and a great deal for the price. For longer stays, rates are negotiable.

Apartamenty Betti
HOTEL, APARTMENT €€

(☑509 246 205; www.apartamentybetti.pl; ul Drzewna 1; s 140-160zł, d 180-200zł, apt 300-400zł; P 🛜) Has an attractive selection of rooms, which are spread through connected historic buildings near the main square. The three apartments allow self-catering and more elbow room than the hotel accommodation. Breakfast costs 20zł more.

🍴 Eating & Drinking

Pizzeria Gioconda
PIZZA €

(ul Mariacka 5; mains 10-24zł; ⊙noon-10pm) Tuck into the fastest Italian food on the Stary Rynek under the inscrutable gaze of Mona Lisa. It's a simple place in a quiet corner of the square, and serves up decent pizzas.

Winnica
POLISH €€

(Plac Poztowy 17; mains 15-40zł; ⊙9am-11pm) In an elegant building overlooking compact Plac Pocztowy, this attractive eatery offers outdoor tables dotted among potted plants and grapevines. The menu features Polish classics and pizza; breakfast is also available.

Essenza
INTERNATIONAL €€

(al Niepodległości 11; mains 22-80zł; ⊙11am-11pm) Essenza creates tasty 'fusion cuisine' – essentially dishes with a Mediterranean flavour and some Polish influence. The terrace is a pleasant place from which to watch the strolling crowds.

Haust
PUB, BREWERY

(Plac Pocztowy 9; ⊙noon-11pm; 🛜) Lively pub and microbrewery near the Stary Rynek. Serves multiple variants of its own beer, including seasonal specials, from pilsner to porter.

ℹ Information

Post Office (ul Bohaterów Westerplatte 21; ⊘ 7am-8pm Mon-Fri, 9am-3pm Sat)

Tourist Office (📋 68 323 2222; www.cit. zielona-gora.pl; Stary Rynek 1; ⊘ 9am-5pm Mon-Fri, 10am-2pm Sat; 🛜) In the town hall. Offers free wireless internet access too.

ℹ Getting There & Away

The **bus station** (www.pks.zgora.pl; ul Dworcowa 27) is about 1km northeast of the city centre, and the **train station** (Plac Kolejarza) is just along ul Dworcowa from the bus station. Major destinations by bus include Poznań (35zł, three hours, five daily), Wrocław (40zł, 3½ hours, 10 daily) and Jelenia Góra (35zł, 3½ hours, five daily).

There are eight daily trains to Wrocław (26zł, three hours), three to Jelenia Góra (30zł, four hours), eight to Poznań (24zł, two hours), three to Szczecin (32zł, four hours) and three to Warsaw (65zł to 134zł, four to five hours).

Świdnica

POP 59,000

One of the wealthiest towns in Silesia in the Middle Ages, Świdnica (shfeed-*nee*-tsah) escaped major damage in WWII and has retained some important historic buildings, including its distinctive wooden Church of Peace. It's an agreeable place for a stopover, and a convenient springboard for the impressive castle at Książ.

Świdnica was founded in the 12th century, and in 1290 became the capital of the Duchy of Świdnica-Jawor. This was one of myriad Silesian Piast principalities but among the most powerful, thanks to its two gifted rulers: Bolko I, who founded it, and his grandson Bolko II, who extended it significantly.

The capital itself was a flourishing commercial centre, well known for its beer, which ended up on the tables of Kraków, Prague and Buda. Until the Thirteen Years' War (1454–66) it was one of the largest Polish towns, with some 6000 inhabitants. By 1648, however, the population had dropped to 200, and Świdnica has ever since been dwarfed by its former rival, Wrocław.

◉ Sights

★ **Church of Peace**   CHURCH
(Kościół Pokoju; www.kosciolpokoju.pl; Plac Pokoju 6; adult/concession 10/5zł; ⊘ 9am-6pm Mon-Sat, 11.30am-6pm Sun) This magnificent timber church was erected between 1656 and 1657, in just 10 months. The builders were not trying to set any records; the Peace of

Westphalia of 1648 allowed the Protestants of Silesia to build three churches as long as they went up in less than a year, had no belfry, and used only clay, sand and wood as building materials. The churches at Świdnica and Jawor remain; the one at Głogów burnt down in 1758.

The church is 400m northeast of the Rynek; enter via the arched gateway off ul Kościelna.

The Świdnica church is a shingled structure laid out in the form of a cross and contains not a single nail. The interior is a beautiful, peaceful place to sit in contemplation for a few minutes; the timber structure seems to possess an intimate inclusiveness that big stone churches sometimes lack. The Baroque decoration, with paintings covering the walls and coffered ceiling, has been preserved intact. Along the walls, two storeys of galleries and several small balconies were installed, allowing some 3500 seated worshippers and 4000 standees. The church was added to Unesco's World Heritage List in 2001.

Rynek   SQUARE
(Market Square) The Old Town's market square contains a bit of every architectural style, from Baroque to postwar concrete structures, the cumulative effect of rebuilding after successive fires and the damage caused by Austrian, Prussian and Napoleonic sieges.

The bright yellow **town hall** (Ratusz; www.wieza.swidnica.pl; Rynek 37; ⊘ 10am-8pm May-Sep, to 6pm Oct-Apr) **FREE** dates from the 1710s, though its white tower only dates from 2012. The original collapsed in 1967, and it took over four decades to find the funds and will to rebuild it. You can walk the 223 steps to the top for free city views, or save your feet and take the lift.

The town hall also contains the **Old Trades Museum** (Muzeum Dawnego Kupiectwa; www.muzeum-kupiectwa.pl; Rynek 37; adult/concession 5.50/3.50zł, Fri free; ⊘ 10am-3pm Tue-Fri, 11am-5pm Sat & Sun), with reconstructions of an old tavern, a pharmacy and a shop, and a collection of historic scales and balances.

A bugle call sounds from the townhall tower at 10am, noon, 2pm and 4pm. Alas, however, this is not the live *hejnał* of Kraków but a recording.

**Church of SS Stanislaus
and Wenceslas**   CHURCH
(Kościół Św Stanisława i Wacława; Plac Jana Pawła II 1) East of the Rynek, this massive Gothic stone building has a facade adorned with four elegant 15th-century doorways and an

18m-high window (the stained glass is not original). The tower, completed in 1565, is 103m high, making it Poland's tallest historic church tower after that of the basilica in Częstochowa (106m). The spacious interior has a Gothic structure and ornate Baroque decoration and furnishings.

The original church was accidentally burnt down in 1532 by the town's *burmistrz* (mayor), Franz Glogisch. He fled Świdnica pursued by angry townsfolk, who beat him to death in Nysa.

🛏 Sleeping

Dom Rekolekcyjny HOTEL €
(☑74 853 5260; www.dom-rekolekcyjny.pl; ul Muzealna 1; s 70zł, d 90-150zł; P 🕸) Conveniently positioned just one block west of the Rynek (enter from ul Zamkowa), this pleasant accommodation run by the Pentecostal Church is excellent value and nowhere near as monastic as you might expect. Breakfast is not available, but there is a communal kitchen on the premises.

Youth Hostel HOSTEL €
(Szkolne Schronisko Młodzieżowe; ☑74 852 2645; www.ssm.swidnica.pl; ul Kanonierska 3; dm 25zł, r 85-145zł; P 🕸) Friendly hostel 700m north of the Rynek. Offers basic, comfortable accommodation in dorm rooms with three to five beds, as well as private rooms with bathrooms.

★ Hotel Fado HOTEL €€
(☑74 666 6370; www.hotelfado.eu; ul Konopnickiej 6; s/d 220/270zł; P ❄ 🕸 🏊) Shiny new, central Hotel Fado has elegantly appointed rooms, illuminated by plenty of natural light. There's a bar and restaurant within the premises, and a beer garden out front. Facilities include swimming pool, sauna, and massage centre. A classy place to spend a night or two.

Hotel Piast-Roman HOTEL €€
(☑74 852 1393; www.hotel-piast-roman.pl; ul Kotlarska 11; s/d 140/180zł; P 🕸) This conveniently placed hotel, just off the Rynek, isn't as swish as the ground-floor restaurant might lead you to believe, but it's a reasonable three-star choice. The rooms are spick and span, and you can't top the location. Breakfast consists of a choice of set menus rather than the usual buffet spread.

🍴 Eating & Drinking

Pierogarnia Pod Filarami POLISH €
(ul Trybunalska 2; mains 9-28zł; ⊙10am-6pm Mon-Sat) Cosy eatery just east of the market square, dishing up *pierogi* (dumplings) in a variety of tasty flavour combinations. There's a breakfast menu too.

Rynek 43 POLISH €€
(Rynek 43; mains 15-49zł; ⊙11am-11pm) The interior of this restaurant on the western side of the town-hall complex is a little gloomy, but there's no criticising its beautiful courtyard hidden away from the square through an arched passage. The friendly staff serve up a range of tasty Polish dishes, including regional specialities such as wild-boar stew.

Da Grasso PIZZA €€
(ul Zamkowa 9; mains 10-35zł; ⊙11am-11pm; 🕸) Just another pizzeria, you might think, but this colourful place 200m west of the Rynek is a slice or two above the usual. The colourful retro decor, with its bright-red banquettes, make it a cool place to refuel.

Baroc CAFE
(Plac Pokoju 7; ⊙10am-8pm) This cafe occupying the gatehouse at the entry to the Church of Peace (p253) is an enticing place for a quiet drink.

ℹ Information

Library (Biblioteka; ul Franciszkańska 18; ⊙10am-6pm Mon-Fri, to 2pm Sat) Free internet access in the public library; walk up the stairs to room 202 on the 1st floor.

Post Office (Plac Grunwaldzki 1; ⊙7am-7pm Mon-Fri, 8am-2pm Sat) Opposite the train station.

Tourist Office (☑74 852 0290; www.um.swidnica.pl; ul Wewnętrzna 2; ⊙10am-8pm May-Sep, to 6pm Oct-Apr) On the north face of the town-hall complex.

ℹ Getting There & Away

Świdnica Miasto train station (ul Dworcowa) is a convenient five-minute walk southwest from the Rynek, with the **bus station** (www.pks.swidnica.pl; ul Kolejowa 1) behind it.

Hourly buses run to Wrocław (15zł, 1½ hours), while three buses a day head to Jelenia Góra (22zł, 1½ hours). Private minibuses to Wrocław and Wałbrzych also depart from the bus station.

There's just one daily train service to Kłodzko (17zł, 1½ hours), departing at 7.32am. For other rail connections, travel one station to Jaworzyna Śląska, where you can change for destinations such as Wrocław and Jelenia Góra. The conductor on board the local trains can sell you a through ticket from Świdnica to your final stop.

Książ

Located within a pretty forested area, Książ (pronounced 'kshonzh') is home to a magnificent castle, and makes for an easy day trip from Świdnica.

◉ Sights

Książ Castle CASTLE
(Zamek Książ; www.ksiaz.walbrzych.pl; ul Piastów Śląskich 1; adult/concession 30/20zł; ⊙10am-5pm Apr-Sep, to 3pm Oct-Mar) With 415 rooms, this castle is the largest in Silesia, majestically perched on a steep hill amid lush woods at Książ. It was built in the late 13th century by the Silesian Piast Duke Bolko I, acquired by the aristocratic von Hoberg (later Hochberg) family in 1509, and continuously enlarged and remodelled until well into the 20th century. It's thus an amalgam of styles from Romanesque onwards; the central portion, with three massive arcades, is the oldest.

The eastern part (to the right) is an 18th-century Baroque addition, while the western segment was built between 1908 and 1923 in a neo-Renaissance style.

During WWII, under Hitler's direct orders, the German authorities confiscated the castle and began construction of a mysterious underground complex (p256) beneath the building and surrounding areas. The Soviet military then used it as a barracks until 1946, after which it was pretty much abandoned for a decade and started falling into ruin.

Luckily, restoration work began in 1974, and the lavish interiors can now be visited. Approaching the castle from the car park, you pass through a large decorative free-standing gateway and get your first view of the castle, standing at the end of a beautifully landscaped garden.

Thankfully, this is one Polish stately home that you can visit without having to accompany a Polish-language tour or wear shower caps over your shoes. As an individual visitor, you follow a prescribed (and rather convoluted) route through the castle, seeing a selection of rooms. The showpiece is Maximilian Hall, built in the first half of the 18th century. It's the largest room in the castle and completely restored to its original lavish form, including the ceiling (1733) painted with mythological scenes. The identical fireplaces on either side of the room are sublime.

Along with the main rooms, including 'themed' salons (Baroque, Chinese, white etc) on the 1st floor, you'll encounter various temporary exhibits and galleries en route, sometimes with objets d'art for sale. There's also an exhibition on the various dukes up to the castle's last owners, Prince Hans Heinrich XV and his wife, Princess Daisy, who was born in Wales.

There are several restaurants and cafes dotted about the complex, including a grill and beer garden with leafy views on a terrace within the castle itself.

National Stallion Depot HISTORIC BUILDING
(Stado Ogierów Skarbu Państwa; ☏74 840 5860; www.stadoksiaz.pl; ul Jeździecka 3; adult/concession 8/5zł; ⊙10am-6pm) A five-minute walk east of Książ castle is the National Stallion Depot, housed in what were once the castle's stables. It offers 45-minute horse-riding sessions for 60zł on Monday, Tuesday, Wednesday and Thursday evenings, and on weekend afternoons. It's best to book ahead.

🛏 Sleeping

Hotel Przy Oślej Bramie HOTEL €€
(☏74 664 9270; www.mirjan.pl; ul Piastów Śląskich 1; s/d 165/220zł; P🛜) 'Before the Donkey Gate' has rooms contained in four pretty little stone buildings to the right before you pass through the gateway to Książ castle. Just the thing for dyed-in-the-wool romantics.

Hotel Książ HOTEL €€
(☏74 664 3890; www.ksiaz.walbrzych.pl; ul Piastów Śląskich 1; s 140-160zł, d 230-250zł, apt 480-500zł; P@) This hotel occupies several outbuildings just past the gateway of the Książ Castle complex, with varied standards and facilities. Reception is to the left as you walk up the main path.

ℹ Getting There & Away

The castle is 7.5km from Wałbrzych; you can reach it from a bus stop near Wałbrzych Miasto train station via city bus 8 (2.80zł, 30 minutes), which runs about every 45 minutes. From Świdnica, 14km to the east, catch a regular route 31 minibus in the direction of Wałbrzych (6zł, 30 minutes, every 20 minutes) and ask the driver to let you off on the main-road turn-off to the castle (zamek). From here the castle is an easy 20-minute walk along a paved footpath. Be careful alighting from the minibus and waiting for a later return bus, as it's a busy major road.

SUDETES MOUNTAINS

The Sudetes Mountains run for more than 250km along the Czech–Polish border. The

THE ENIGMATIC GIANT

In 1941 the Nazi government of Germany confiscated Schloss Fürstenstein, now **Książ Castle** (p255), from the aristocratic Hochbergs, its owners for over four centuries. It soon formed its own plan for the property, known as **Project Riese** ('riese' is the German word for 'giant'). As the name suggests, it was of mind-boggling proportions.

From 1943 construction began on a series of sprawling underground complexes beneath the castle and the Eulengebirge (now Góry Sowie) mountain range, part of the Sudetes. It was an enormous undertaking involving the creation of tunnels and chambers using explosives, concrete and steel. In addition to mining specialists, the project used forced labour from both prisoner-of-war and concentration camps.

The sheer scale of the work was a drain on the Nazi regime's resources. Hitler's armaments minister Albert Speer later admitted in his memoirs that the construction of the complex used more concrete than was available for building air-raid shelters across Germany in 1944.

What's most fascinating about Project Riese is that no one is quite sure what its vast subterranean chambers were for, as they were never completed and key witnesses and documents were lost in the postwar turmoil. Speer referred to a bunker complex, other references were made to bombproof underground factories, and many have assumed that Hitler intended to move his headquarters there. The wildest theories suggest that stolen treasures were hidden in the complex, or that the regime was undertaking an atomic-bomb program within its depths.

Whatever the truth, Project 'Giant' retains its giant-sized air of intrigue. For more details on the project and its aftermath, visit www.riese.krzyzowa.org.pl.

highest part of this old and eroded chain of mountains is the Karkonosze, reaching 1602m at Mt Śnieżka. Though the Sudetes don't offer much alpine scenery, they're amazingly varied and heavily covered in forest, with spectacular geological formations such as those at the Góry Stołowe.

To the north, the Sudetes gradually decline into a belt of gently rolling foothills known as the Sudetes Foothills (Przedgórze Sudeckie). This area is more densely populated, and many of the towns and villages in the region still boast some of their centuries-old timber buildings. Combining visits to these historic settlements with hikes into the mountains and the surrounding countryside is the best way to explore the region.

Jelenia Góra

POP 81,000

Jelenia Góra (yeh-*len*-yah goo-rah) is set in a beautiful valley surrounded by the Western Sudetes. The city has a relaxed feel and an attractive appearance, and it makes a great base for trips into the Karkonosze Mountains.

Jelenia Góra was founded in 1108 by King Bolesław Krzywousty (Bolesław the Wry-Mouthed) – legend has it that the monarch had been following a wounded deer and was so taken by the beauty of the place that he named it 'Deer Mountain'. The border stronghold later came under the rule of the powerful Duchy of Świdnica-Jawor. Gold mining in the region gave way to glass production around the 15th century, but weaving gave the town a solid economic base, and its high-quality linen was exported all over Europe.

◎ Sights

Church of the Holy Cross   CHURCH
(Kościół Św Krzyża; ul 1 Maja 45) Jelenia Góra's main attraction is this massive church; it was built in 1718 for a Lutheran congregation, though it's served a Catholic one since 1947. The three-storey galleries plus the dark, densely packed ground floor can accommodate 4000 people. The ceiling is embellished with illusionist Baroque paintings of scenes from the Old and New Testaments, while the magnificent organ over the high altar dates from 1729.

Karkonosze Museum   MUSEUM
(Karkonoskie Muzeum Okręgowe; www.muzeum karkonoskie.pl; ul Matejki 28; adult/concession 7/4zł, Sun free; ⊙9am-5pm Tue-Sun) Karkonosze Museum, 650m south of the Rynek, is renowned for its extensive collection of glass dating from medieval times to the present; the Art Nouveau pieces are wonderful. On the museum grounds is a small *skansen* (open-air museum of traditional architec-

ture) featuring traditional mountain huts typical of the Karkonosze Mountains.

Rynek
SQUARE

(Market Square; Plac Ratuszowy) The elongated market square, also called Plac Ratuszowy, is lined with a harmonious group of 17th- and 18th-century houses. Much of their charm is due to their porticoes and ground-floor arcades, which provide a covered passageway all around the square. The town hall was built in 1749, after its predecessor collapsed.

Church of SS Erasmus and Pancras
CHURCH

(Kościół Św Erazma i Pankracego; Plac Kościelny 1) This place of worship, northeast of the Rynek, was erected in the 15th century; note the Gothic doorway in the southern entrance portraying Mary and St John at the foot of the cross. The interior, with its theatrical 22m-high Rococo main altar crafted from brick-red marble, boasts mostly Baroque furnishings, including a richly decorated organ.

🛏 Sleeping

Youth Hostel Bartek
HOSTEL €

(Szkolne Schronisko Młodzieżowe Bartek; ☑ 517 930 050; www.ssm.bartek.e-meteor.pl; ul Bartka Zwycięzcy 10; dm 12-24zł, d 48zł; ⓟ ⓐ) Modest, pleasant and housed in a cabinlike wooden building, this hostel southeast of the Old Town has dorm rooms with between four and 10 beds, as well as a few doubles. From al Wojska Polskiego, turn onto ul Nowowiejska, then left onto ul Bartka Zwycięzcy.

★ Hotel Fenix Strauss
HOTEL €€

(☑ 75 641 6600; www.hotel-fenix.pl; ul 1 Maja 88; s/d from 145/175zł; ⓟ ⓢ) More convenient for the train station than the centre, the town's flashest hotel offers businesslike modern rooms, and a spa and wellness centre. Even if you're not staying here, it's worth dropping into its excellent restaurant, which serves upmarket Polish dishes. Great value for the price.

Hotel Jelonek
HOTEL €€

(☑ 75 764 6541; www.hotel-jelonek.com.pl; ul 1 Maja 5; s 150zł, d 210-320zł; ⓟ ⓢ) Situated in a fine 18th-century burgher's house, this appealing set of lodgings is the nicest in Jelenia Góra. Concentrate on the old prints and antiques in the public areas, and turn a blind eye to the Pizza Hut downstairs with its separate entrance. The rooms are stylishly modern, and the more expensive 'lux' rooms are ideal for self-pampering.

Hotel Europa
HOTEL €€

(☑ 75 649 5500; www.ptkarkonosze.pl; ul 1 Maja 16/18; s/d 115/180zł; ⓟ ⓢ) This accommodation in a large block east of the Rynek isn't particularly atmospheric, but the rooms are huge and there's a budget restaurant on site (open breakfast and lunch only). Rates are 20% lower at weekends; rear rooms look over the car park.

🍴 Eating

Metafora
POLISH, ITALIAN €€

(Plac Ratuszowy 49; mains 14-30zł; ⓢ 10am-late Mon-Sat, noon-late Sun; ⓢ) It's unclear what the metaphor actually is, but the moody interior of this versatile restaurant-cafe-bar is a lovely place to dine. It serves mostly Polish cuisine, with a dash of Italian in the menu, and there are breakfast options too. There's a long drinks list if you just want to sip.

Mała Arkadia
POLISH €€

(Plac Ratuszowy 25/26; mains 20-60zł; ⓢ 9am-late) Within a cosy interior that resembles a living room due to its floral wallpaper, this attractive restaurant on the main square presents quality Polish dishes. Choices range from pasta to steak, with a surprising number of fish options.

Restauracja Pokusa
POLISH €€

(Plac Ratuszowy 12; mains 18-25zł; ⓢ 11am-11pm) With outdoor tables in the arcaded passageway encircling the Rynek, Pokusa is a very agreeable place, with upbeat decor and a repertoire of mostly Polish food.

Pizzeria Tokaj
PIZZA €€

(ul Pocztowa 8; mains 12-46zł; ⓢ noon-10pm Mon-Thu, 1pm-midnight Fri-Sun) An inexpensive option, Tokaj is a cafe-bar serving a dizzying array of pizzas. There's a good selection of pasta and salads as well.

🍸 Drinking & Nightlife

Pożegnanie z Afryką
CAFE

(Plac Ratuszowy 4; ⓢ 10am-6pm Mon-Fri, 10am-5pm Sat, 11am-5pm Sun) This inviting branch of the cafe chain 'Out of Africa' sells any number of imported beans within its dim and character-packed premises and, of course, serves great coffee. Sip and savour.

Kurna Chata
CAFE, BAR

(Plac Ratuszowy 23/24; ⓢ 10am-late) Small, cosy cafe-bar with a pub feel and folksy decor (think mountain hut and bales of hay); a good place on the Rynek for a drink and a snack.

SILESIA

Jelenia Góra

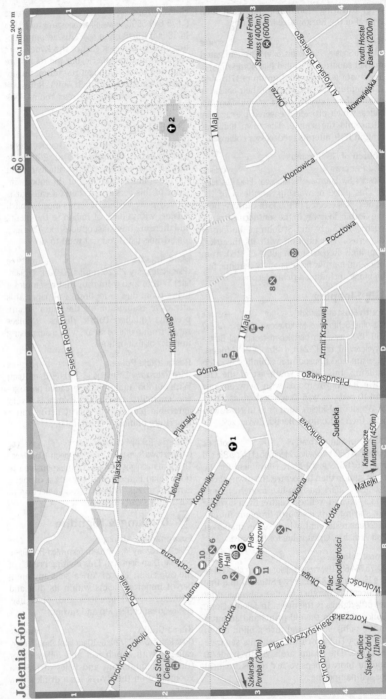

200 m
0.1 miles

Hotel Fenix
Strauss (400m);
(600m)

Youth Hostel
Bartek (200m)

Nowowiejska

1 Maja

Klonowica

Pocztowa

Al Wojska Polskiego

Okrzei

Osiedle Robotnicze

Kilińskiego

1 Maja
4

5

Górna

Armii Krajowej

8

Piłsudskiego

Pijarska

Pijarska

Jelenia

Kopernika

Forteczna

Bankowa

Sudecka

Matejki

Karkonosze
Museum (450m)

1

Szkolna

Krótka

Forteczna

6
10
9
Town
Hall
3
11

7

Plac
Ratuszowy

Plac
Niepodległości

Jasna

Grodzka

Długa

Wolności

Korczaka

Plac Wyszyńskiego

Chrobrego

Cieplice
Śląskie-Zdrój
(11km)

Podwale

Obrońców Pokoju

Bus Stop for
Cieplice

Szklarska Poręba (20km)

Jelenia Góra

ⓘ Information

Amigos (☑ 75 753 2601; Plac Ratuszowy 56;
◔ 9am-5pm Mon-Fri, 10am-2pm Sat) Travel
agency; enquire here for international bus
tickets.

Main Post Office (ul Pocztowa 9/10;
◔ 7am-9pm Mon-Fri, 9am-3pm Sat)

Tourist Office (☑ 519 509 343; www.
jeleniagora.pl; Plac Ratuszowy 6/7; ◔ 9am-
6pm Mon-Fri, 8am-8pm Sat & Sun; 🛜)
Provides information to travellers, and is
happy to let you use its wi-fi for free.

ⓘ Getting There & Away

➡ The **train station** (ul 1 Maja 77) is about
1.5km east of the Rynek, while the **bus station**
(www.pks.jgora.pl; ul Obrońców Pokoju 1b) is on
the opposite side of town, just northwest of the
ring road.

➡ Hourly buses run to Karpacz (6zł, 45 minutes),
including some minibuses, which leave from the
train station rather than the bus station. Regular
services also head to Szklarska Poręba (7zł, 55
minutes, hourly). There are also useful bus links
to Świdnica (22zł, 1½ hours, three daily) and
Zielona Góra (35zł, 3½ hours, five daily).

➡ Trains service Szklarska Poręba (10zł, 50
minutes, eight daily), Wrocław (24zł, 2¾ hours,
hourly), Zielona Góra (30zł, four hours, three
daily) and Warsaw (67zł, 9½ hours, twice daily).
For Świdnica, buy a through ticket with a change
at Jaworzyna Śląska.

Karkonosze National Park

Karkonosze National Park (Karkonoski Park
Narodowy; www.kpnmab.pl; ul Chałubińskiego 23,
Jelenia Góra; adult/concession 6/3zł) is a 56-sq-

km belt that runs along the Polish–Czech
border for some 25km. The two main settlements here are the resort towns of Szklarska
Poręba and Karpacz.

The range is divided by the Karkonosze
Pass (Przełęcz Karkonoska; 1198m). The
highest summit of the eastern section is Mt
Śnieżka (1602m), while the western portion
is topped by Mt Wielki Szyszak (1509m).
The park is predominantly spruce forest up
to an altitude of about 1250m.

The characteristic features of the
Karkonosze landscape are *kotły* (cirques),
huge hollows carved by glaciers during
the Ice Age and bordered with steep cliffs.
There are six cirques on the Polish side of
the range, the most spectacular being Kocioł Małego Stawu and Kocioł Wielkiego
Stawu near Mt Śnieżka, and Śnieżne Kotły
at the foot of Mt Wielki Szyszak.

The Karkonosze range is known for its
harsh climate, with heavy rainfall (snow
in winter) and highly variable weather,
including strong winds and mists at any
time of year. Statistically, the best chances
of good weather are in January, February,
May and September.

The national park is the most popular hiking territory in the Sudetes and
boasts 33 trails covering 100km. The
two main gateways are Szklarska Poręba
and Karpacz, from where most tourists
ascend Mt Szrenica and Mt Śnieżka respectively. For longer walks, the red trail
runs right along the ridge between the
two peaks, with excellent views on both
sides. The trail also passes along the upper edges of the *kotły*. You can walk the
whole stretch in six to seven hours. If you
start early enough, it's possible to do the
Karpacz–Szklarska Poręba (or vice versa)
trip within a day, preferably by using the
chairlift to Mt Szrenica or Mt Kopa to
speed up the initial ascent.

You can break the walk by taking any
of the trails that branch off from the main
route, or by stopping at one of the half-
dozen mountain hostels.

The national park also has 19 mountain-
bike trails totalling some 450km, and the
tourist offices in Szklarska Poręba and
Karpacz can supply you with an excellent
free map of them.

Whatever you're into, take warm, water-
proof clothes to deal with the unpredictable
weather and get a detailed map of the area.
The best one is the 1:25,000 *Karkonosze i
Góry Izerskie* (7zł), which also includes the

WORTH A TRIP

CIEPLICE ŚLĄSKIE-ZDRÓJ

In the suburbs of Jelenia Góra, Cieplice (cheh-plee-tseh) is the oldest spa in the region, and an easy day trip. Its sulphurous hot springs have been used for a millennium, and the first spa house here was established as early as the late 13th century. The supposedly curative properties of the springs, which come out of the ground at a scalding 90°C, became popular in the late 18th century. This paved the way for the building of the resort and spa town.

Sights

Spa Park (Park Zdrojowy; ul Cervi) This large park makes up the town's core, and holds an embarrassment of lovely fin-de-siècle pavilions and buildings, including the domed Spa Theatre (Teatr Zdrojowy) and the wooden open-air Concert Shell (Muszla Koncertowa).

Church of St John the Baptist (Kościół Św Jana Chrzciciela; ul Cieplicka 9) At the western end of pedestrian Plac Piastowski is this 18th-century church, which contains an altarpiece painted by famed Baroque artist Michael Willmann. Should you wish to sample the local waters, the statue-topped automatic pump in a small square near St John's dispenses free water from Cieplice's springs into whatever container you provide.

Natural History Museum (Muzeum Przyrodnicze; www.muzeum-cieplice.pl; ul Cieplicka 11a; adult/concession 5/4zł, Sat free; ⊙9am-5pm Tue-Sun) South of the town's Spa Park is the timbered Norwegian Pavilion (Pawilon Norweski), which houses the Natural History Museum. Its display of birds and butterflies from all over the world stems from the collection of the prominent Schaffgotsch family, local nobles who established the museum in 1876.

Getting There & Away

Cieplice Śląskie-Zdrój lies 11km south of Jelenia Góra's centre, and can be reached by suburban bus 17 (3zł, 20 minutes), which departs from a stop near the bus station on ul Podwale. If you're staying closer to the train station, catch bus 9 or 14 from there instead. Buy your bus ticket from a street-side kiosk, then validate on board.

Izera Mountains of the Western Sudetes, to the northeast of Szklarska Poręba.

🛏 Sleeping

Odrodzenie Hostel HOSTEL €
(Schronisko Odrodzenie; ☑75 752 2546; www.schroniskoodrodzenie.com; ul Karkonoska 1, Przesieka; dm 39-42zł, s 49zł, d 81-101zł) The sizeable Odrodzenie Hostel is roughly halfway between Mt Szrenica and Mt Śnieżka. Book in advance.

Samotnia Hostel HOSTEL €
(Schronisko Samotnia; ☑75 761 9376; www.samotnia.com.pl; ul Na Śnieżkę 16; dm 40-45zł, s/d 50/92zł) The hostel at Kocioł Małego Stawu has the best views in the park. Book in advance.

Szklarska Poręba

POP 6800

At the foot of Mt Szrenica (1362m) at the western end of Karkonosze National Park, Szklarska Poręba (shklahr-skah po-rem-bah) is usually a lively little place, full of

walkers, skiers and souvenir cudgels (mini-tomahawks). This major health resort and ski centre, 21km southwest of Jelenia Góra, makes a good base for the region's many outdoor activities. Along its main street, ul Jedności Narodowej, skirting the Kamienna River, lie the bus station at the south end and the train station at the north end.

⊙ Sights & Activities

The **Mt Szrenica chairlift** (☑75 717 2118; www.sudetylift.com.pl; ul Turystyczna 25a; one way/return 31.50/34.50zł; ⊙9am-4.30pm) rises 603m in two stages and deposits you at the top in about 25 minutes; it's used by skiers and snowboarders to reach five trails and two slopes in season, and by hikers the rest of the year. The lower station is 1km south of the centre, uphill along ul Turystyczna. During the ski season there's also a second lift in operation, with greater capacity.

There are some attractions within easy walking distance of town. The road to Jelenia Góra winds east in a beautiful valley along the Kamienna River. Some 3km down the road (or along the green trail on the right bank of the river) is the 13m-high Szklarka Waterfall (Wodospad Szklarki). From here the blue trail heads to the mountains and you can follow it to Mt Szrenica in two to three hours.

The road that heads west 4km to the Czech border at Jakuszyce passes rocky cliffs called Ravens' Rocks (Krucze Skały). About 500m further on, a red trail branches to the left. It's a 1.5km walk along this trail to Kamieńczyk Waterfall (Wodospad Kamieńczyka), the highest (843m) in the Polish part of the Sudetes. Continue for about 1½ hours along the same trail to get to Mt Szrenica. It's possible to hike across the border and join the yellow trail heading south to Vosecká in the Czech Republic.

Ask at the tourist office for a list of businesses hiring out bikes and snow-sports gear, as these fluctuate from season to season.

Sleeping

Hotel Kryształ
HOTEL €€
(☏75 717 4930; www.hotelkrysztal.pl; ul 1 Maja 19; s/d from 190/290zł; P✳☎☂) Classy resort-style accommodation in a convenient location. Rooms are decorated in earthy tones, with elegant furniture; book the deluxe version for extra space. On the premises you'll find a cafe, bar and restaurant, along with a swimming pool, a spa, a sauna and massage treatments.

Fantazja
HOTEL €€
(☏75 717 2907; www.fantazja.com.pl; ul Jedności Narodowej 14; s/d 160/260zł; P☎) Very central accommodation offering comfortable rooms, a solarium, massage services and a popular restaurant serving international dishes. There's also a pleasant cafe.

Mauritius
HOTEL €€
(☏75 717 2083; www.mauritius.karkonosz.pl; ul Dworcowa 6; s/d 95/170zł; P☎) At the northern end of town next to the train station, this exotically named place is a basic holiday home run by the post office. Rooms with balconies and a cafe-bar add to the attraction. A spacious terrace provides a great view of the mountains, and there's a dartboard and a pool table for indoor amusement.

Apartamenty Carmen
APARTMENT €€
(☏75 717 2558; www.apartamentycarmen.pl; ul Jedności Narodowej 16; apt 160-280zł; P☎) These apartments provide a spacious, modern alternative to hotel rooms, with the bonus of enabling guests to self-cater. They're located in the middle of town, and the largest apartment can house up to four people.

✕ Eating

Restauracja Młyn Łukasza
POLISH €€
(ul 1 Maja 16; mains 19-49zł; ☉11am-11pm) Its interior has been given the full-on rustic treatment, but this restaurant's outdoor seating alongside a babbling brook is what makes it special. The reasonably priced menu features *pierogi* (dumplings), soups and a range of meat dishes. It's across the river from the bus station.

Kaprys
POLISH, ITALIAN €€
(ul Jedności Narodowej 12; mains 19-69zł; ☉noon-late) Roomy but mellow restaurant on the main drag, with comfy couch seating and potted plants enlivening the decor. The menu is evenly split between pizzas and pasta, and Polish dishes.

Metafora
POLISH, PIZZA €€
(ul Objazdowa 1; mains 18-42zł; ☉11am-10pm; ☎) Relaxed venue with a timber interior and a big outdoor area, opposite the bus station across the river. Metafora serves pizzas along with good Polish cuisine, and has a breakfast menu. It's also a fine place to have a drink.

ⓘ Information

Biuro Turystyki WNW (☏75 717 2100; ul Wzgórze Paderewskiego 4) Travel agency, useful for local accommodation.

Post Office (ul Jedności Narodowej 8; ☉8am-6pm Mon-Fri, to 2.30pm Sat)

Tourist Office (☏75 754 7740; www.szklarskaporeba.pl; ul Jedności Narodowej 1a; ☉8am-6pm Mon-Fri, 9am-5pm Sat & Sun)

ⓘ Getting There & Away

Szklarska Poręba Górna train station (ul Dworcowa 10) is 350m north of the post office, up a steep hill. The **bus station** (Plac PKS) is on the other side of the centre, about 450m southeast of the post office between ul Jedności Narodowej and the Kamienna River.

Buses to Jelenia Góra depart at least hourly (7zł, 55 minutes), and there are three daily buses to Wrocław (32zł, three hours). In July and August there are four daily buses to Karpacz (8zł, 55 minutes).

Eight daily trains go to Jelenia Góra (10zł, 50 minutes), while seven trains head to Wrocław (26zł, 3¾ hours); two of these continue to Warsaw (66zł, 10½ hours). Szklarska Poręba also has an international rail connection, with four trains a day crossing the Czech border to Harrachov (6zł, 25 minutes). They then continue to Kořenov, but for this leg you must pay on the train in Czech currency (15Kč, six minutes).

Karpacz

POP 4900

Karpacz (*kar*-pach), 22km south of Jelenia Góra on the slopes of Mt Śnieżka, is one of the most popular mountain resorts in Poland, for skiing in winter and hiking the rest of the year. This small town is a fun place to visit and has some fine wooden buildings.

Karpacz is essentially a village spread over 3km along winding ul Konstytucji 3 Maja, without any obvious centre. The eastern part, known as Karpacz Dolny (Lower Karpacz), has most of the places to stay and eat. The western part, Karpacz Górny (Upper Karpacz), is largely a collection of holiday homes. In the middle of the two districts is the landmark Hotel Biały Jar. About 1km uphill from here is the lower station of the chairlift to Mt Kopa (1377m).

💿 Sights

Wang Church   CHURCH
(Kościół Wang; www.wang.com.pl; ul Na Śnieżkę 8; adult/concession 8/5zł; ⊙9am-6pm) Karpacz has a curious architectural gem – the Wang Church, the only Nordic Romanesque building in Poland. This remarkable wooden structure in Upper Karpacz was one of about 400 such chapels built at the turn of the 12th century on the bank of Lake Vang in southern Norway; only 28 of these 'stave churches' survive there today. King Friedrich Wilhelm IV of Prussia bought it in 1841, and had it dismantled piece by piece and then transported to Karpacz via Berlin.

Not only is it the oldest church in the Sudetes, it's also the highest situated (886m).

The church is made of hard Norwegian pine and has been constructed without a single nail. It's surrounded by a cloister that helps to protect it from the mountain wind. Part of the woodcarving is original and in excellent shape, particularly the doorways and the capitals of the pillars. The free-standing stone belfry was built when the church was reconstructed here.

🏃 Activities

Bordered to the south by Karkonosze National Park, Karpacz is an ideal starting point for hiking. Most tourists aim for Mt Śnieżka, and there are half a dozen different trails leading there. The most popular routes originate from the landmark **Hotel Biały Jar** (ul Konstytucji 3 Maja 79) and will take you to the top in three to four hours. When planning a trip to Mt Śnieżka, try to include in your route two picturesque postglacial lakes, Wielki Staw and Mały Staw, both bordered by rocky cliffs. A couple of trails pass near the lakes.

Mt Kopa Chairlift   SNOW SPORTS, HIKING
(ul Turystyczna 4; one way/return 25/30zł; ⊙8.30am-5pm) If you prefer not to walk up Mt Kopa, this chairlift, which caters for skiers and snowboarders in winter, will take you up 528m in 17 minutes. From Mt Kopa, you can get to the top of Mt Śnieżka in less than an hour via the black trail.

Summer Sleigh Track   SLEIGHING
(www.kolorowa.pl; ul Parkowa 10; 1/2/5/10 rides 9/16/35/55zł; ⊙9am-late) On Kolorowa Hill in the centre of Karpacz, this summer sleigh track is more than 1km long and allows for speeds of up to 30km/h.

🛏 Sleeping

The tourist office can provide an extensive list of accommodation, including private rooms.

Camping Pod Lipami   CAMPGROUND €
(☑504 231 039; www.pod-lipami.pl; ul Konstytucji 3 Maja 8; per person/tent/caravan 14/12/19zł; 🅿🏊) Camping ground close to the bus station, with its own outdoor pool.

★**Hotel Rezydencja**   HOTEL €€
(☑75 761 8020; www.hotelrezydencja.pl; ul Parkowa 6; s 200-240zł, d 240-270zł; 🅿🛜) The tastefully decorated rooms of this stunner of a hotel, housed in an 18th-century hilltop villa overlooking the centre of Lower Karpacz, are among the most desirable in town. There's a spa, restaurant and cafe-bar on site, and massage treatments can be arranged.

Hotel Vivaldi   HOTEL €€
(☑75 761 9933; www.vivaldi.pl; ul Olimpijska 4; s 180zł, d 230-500zł; 🅿🛜🏊) A pale-yellow building in the midst of the trees, the Vivaldi is a classy proposition on the winding road up to the chairlift and national-park entrance. It contains smart, modern rooms and a well-equipped spa with saunas and a whirlpool spa. There's also a swimming pool.

Hotel Kolorowa   HOTEL €€
(☑75 761 9503; www.hotel-kolorowa.pl; ul Konstytucji 3 Maja 58; s/d 90/160zł; 🅿🛜) This affordable hotel opposite the summer sleigh track in Lower Karpacz offers good standards, the all-important sweets on pillows and some rooms with restful hillside views. Restaurant and bar on-site.

✖ Eating

Central Bar 49
POLISH €

(ul Konstytucji 3 Maja 49; mains 5-39zł; ⊘9am-10pm) An atmospheric cross between a bar and a restaurant, serving up simple but better-than-average Polish dishes such as beetroot soup with croquette and grilled *kiełbasa* (Polish sausage).

Bistro Aurora
RUSSIAN €€

(ul Konstytucji 3 Maja 45; mains 17-29zł; ⊘11am-11pm) Cosy Russian restaurant and bar that bills itself as a 'minimuseum of Socialist Realism', as the decor features large portraits of communist bigwigs as well as red banners and posters from the era. The slightly mad menu includes such gems as Revolutionary Blintzes and Brezhnev Pork Knuckle.

Pizzeria Verde
PIZZA €€

(ul Konstytucji 3 Maja 48; mains 19-29zł; ⊘1-9pm Tue-Sun) This eatery in modern premises is an improvement on the average pizzeria, and also offers some decent pasta and meat dishes, along with salads.

❶ Information

Biuro Turystyczne Karpacz (ul Konstytucji 3 Maja 50; ⊘10am-6pm Mon-Sat, noon-4pm Sun) Travel agency.

Post Office (ul Konstytucji 3 Maja 23; ⊘8am-6pm Mon-Fri, to 2.30pm Sat)

Tourist Office (☑75 761 8605; www.karpacz.pl; ul Kolejowa 1; ⊘9am-5pm Mon-Sat) In the former train-station building; can advise about bicycle hire, as well as skiing and snowboarding options in season.

❶ Getting There & Away

Buses and minibuses run regularly to Jelenia Góra (6zł, 45 minutes, hourly), some of which terminate at the Jelenia Góra train station rather than its bus station. They go along Karpacz's main road, and you can pick them up at at least half a dozen points, though fewer go all the way to the Upper Karpacz stop. In July and August there are four daily buses to Szklarska Poręba (8zł, 55 minutes).

Kłodzko

POP 28,000

Kłodzko's strategic position over the centuries is responsible for its big attraction: a monstrously huge brick fortress, begun by the Austrians in 1662 and only completed two centuries later by the Prussians. It's the dominant, somewhat apocalyptic, landmark of the town and the best reason to pay a visit, though the Old Town sits on a hillside and its steep, winding streets have a charm of their own.

One of the oldest settlements in Silesia, Kłodzko (*kwots*-koh) started out as a major trade centre thanks to its location on the Nysa Kłodzka River, a tributary of the Odra. Like most settlements in the region, it changed hands every century or so, with Bohemia, Austria and Prussia all having a crack; only after WWII did the town revert to Poland.

⊙ Sights

★Kłodzko Fortress
FORTRESS

(Twierdza Kłodzka; www.twierdza.klodzko.pl; ul Grodzisko 1; adult/concession 18/14zł; ⊘9am-6pm May-Oct, to 3pm Nov-Apr) This mighty fortification, begun under Austrian rule in the mid-17th century, was extended, modernised and modified over the following 200 years. Today it covers 17 hectares, making it the largest and best-preserved fortification of its kind in Poland. The walls in the lower parts measure up to 11m thick, and even at the top they are never narrower than 4m.

The entrance is up the hill north of the town's central Rynek.

On entering, you can wander around various pathways and chambers and go to the top of the fortress for a bird's-eye view of town. There are several exhibitions in the grounds, including a lapidarium containing old stone sculptures (mostly tombstones) collected from historic buildings around the region.

However, the real attraction here is the extensive network of defensive tunnels. Guided 40-minute tours of this so-called labyrinth begin on the hour, taking you on a 1km circuit including some passageways that are so low you have to bend over. The average temperature is about 8°C and the humidity is very high.

Altogether 40km of tunnels were drilled around the fortress; they served two purposes. Those under the fortifications were principally for communication, shelter and storage, while the others, running up to 500m away from the fortress, were designed to attack and destroy enemy artillery. The tunnels were divided into sectors and stuffed with gunpowder; when the enemy happened to move their guns into a particular sector, the relevant chamber could be blown up. This bizarre minefield was initiated in 1743 by a Dutch engineer, and by 1807 an immense labyrinth of tunnels had been built. The system was never actually used – at least not here.

Underground Tourist Route TUNNEL

(Podziemna Trasa Turystyczna; www.podziemia. klodzko.pl; ul Zawiszy Czarnego 3; adult/concession 12/9zł; ⊙9am-6pm May-Oct, to 3pm Nov-Apr) Near the parish church is the entrance to this interesting set of tunnels. The 600m route, enlivened by audiovisual exhibits, uses some of the medieval storage cellars that were hollowed out under the Old Town. You can walk the whole length in 15 minutes, exiting near the Kłodzko Fortress.

Rynek SQUARE

(Market Square; Plac Bolesława Chrobrego) Below the town's fortress is the market square, officially titled Plac Bolesława Chrobrego. Several pastel-coloured houses on its southern side have preserved their original Renaissance and Baroque decor. The town hall was built in 1890 after its predecessor was destroyed by fire; only the 17th-century Renaissance tower survived.

Parish Church CHURCH

(Kościół Parafialny; Plac Kościelny) This church, southwest of the Rynek and dedicated to Our Lady of the Assumption, is the most imposing religious building in town. It took almost 150 years before the massive Gothic structure was eventually completed in 1490. Inside, the altars, pulpit, pews, organ and carved confessionals all blaze with florid Baroque ornamentation, and even the Gothic vaulting, usually left plain, has been sumptuously decorated with plasterwork.

Kłodzko Regional Museum MUSEUM

(Muzeum Ziemi Kłodzkie; www.muzeum.klodzko. pl; ul Łukasiewicza 4; adult/concession 8/6zł; ⊙10am-4pm Tue-Fri, 11am-5pm Sat & Sun) Kłodzko museum, 50m west of the parish church, has displays relating to the history of the town and the region, and a collection of contemporary glass by local artists (the region is noted for its glass production).

St John's Bridge BRIDGE

(Most Św Jana; ul Stwosza) Southeast of the Rynek, this Gothic stone bridge (1390) spans the narrow Młynówka River. With half a dozen Baroque statues flanking the sides, it's Kłodko's scaled-down answer to the Charles Bridge in Prague.

🏃 Activities

The helpful and well-informed tourist office has information on activities as wide-ranging as rock climbing, hiking, cy-

cling, horseback riding, skiing and taking to the waters.

If you're a snow-sports fan, the **Czarna Góra ski centre** (Czarna Góra Osrodek Narciarski; ☑74 884 3401; www.czarnagora.pl; ul Sienna 11, Stronie Śląskie) is easily accessible from Kłodzko, about 35km south by road.

🛏 Sleeping

Hotel Marhaba HOTEL €

(☑74 865 9933; www.marhaba.ng.pl; ul Daszyńskiego 16; s/d 90/110zł; P🕸) Basic rooms with shower or full en suite are the choices at this unfussy two-star establishment on the south side of town, backing onto the Młynówka River. Rooms without a bathroom are slightly cheaper, and breakfast is 16zł extra per person.

Nad Kanalem HOSTEL €

(☑74 813 6722; www.nad-kanalem.dobrynocleg.pl; ul Nad Kanalem 9; dm 35-60zł; P🕸) Tiny hostel in a convenient spot near St John's Bridge, with only eight beds available. There's access to a kitchen and a bar. If you want to book the whole place out, it'll cost 200zł per night.

★ Casa D'Oro HOTEL €€

(☑74 867 0216; www.casadoro.com.pl; ul Grottgera 7; s 100-120zł, d 180zł; 🕸) Located between the Rynek and the bus and train stations, this small, attractive hotel is the handiest accommodation you'll find in Kłodzko. Its pleasantly appointed restaurant is worth dropping into for its menu of *pierogi* (dumplings), *naleśniki* (crêpes) and other Polish dishes.

Hotel Korona HOTEL €€

(☑74 867 3737; www.hotel-korona.pl; ul Noworudzka 1; s/d 125/150zł; P🕸) Located in the far-northwestern part of town, this modern establishment is a comfortable option if you're just transiting through Kłodzko for the night. It has a colourful rustic-style restaurant.

🍴 Eating

Bar Małgosia CAFETERIA €

(ul Połabska 2; mains 6-10zł; ⊙7am-7pm Mon-Fri, 8am-6pm Sat, 9am-5pm Sun; ☑) An old-fashioned joint, Małgosia is basically a simple self-service bar that serves hearty Polish dishes at crazily low prices in a soothing green interior. Just east of the train and bus stations.

Secesja
POLISH, ITALIAN €€

(ul Daszyńskiego 10; mains 20-45zł; ☺10am-10pm)
Distinctively decorated restaurant opposite
the monumental Franciscan church on the
south side of the Młynówka River. It serves
a number of Polish dishes, but our money is
on the pizza and pasta choices. There's also
an inexpensive breakfast menu.

Restauracja w Ratuszu
POLISH €€

(Plac Bolesława Chrobrego 3; mains 20-65zł;
☺10am-9pm) Kłodko's most formal restaurant
is housed within the town hall. It has a good
range of regional dishes, and a tree-shaded
terrace opens in the warmer months.

☆ Entertainment

Kłodzko Cultural Centre
CINEMA

(Kłodzko Centrum Kultury; ☑74 867 3364; www.
centrum.klodzko.pl; Plac Jagiełły 1) Gives information on cultural events, and screens art-
house films.

❶ Information

Main Post Office (Plac Jagiełły 2; ☺7.30am-
7.30pm Mon-Fri, 8am-3pm Sat)

PTTK Office (www.klodzko.pttk.pl; ul Wita
Stwosza 1; ☺8am-3pm Mon-Fri) Travel agency
just off the Rynek.

Tourist Office (☑74 865 4689; www.klodzko.
pl; Plac Bolesława Chrobrego 1; ☺8am-4pm
Mon-Fri, 10am-4pm Sat, 10am-2pm Sun) In the
town hall.

❶ Getting There & Away

BUS

The **bus station** (www.pks-klodzko.pl; Plac Jedności 1) is the transport hub of the region. Buses
run hourly to Kudowa-Zdrój (8zł, 50 minutes),
Bystrzyca Kłodzka (7zł, 25 minutes) and Wrocław
(19zł, 1¾ hours). There are five daily buses to
Nysa (15zł, one hour), passing through Paczków
(12zł, 40 minutes); and four buses to Opole (25zł,
2½ hours).

    You can also travel to the Czech Republic from
Kłodzko. One daily bus runs across the border
from Kłodzko to Náchod (12zł, 1¼ hours), leaving
at 8am and travelling via Kudowa-Zdrój. Alternatively, take the daily 6am bus from Kłodzko to
Boboszów (12zł, 1½ hours) and walk 2km across
the border to Králíky.

TRAIN

Kłodzko has two useful train stations. The
centrally located **Kłodzko Miasto station** (Plac
Jedności), next to the bus station, has trains to
Bystrzyca Kłodzka (7zł, 17 minutes, 10 daily),
Kudowa-Zdrój (7zł, 1¼ hours, seven daily),
Wrocław (20zł, two hours, 10 daily) and Świd-
nica (17zł, 1½ hours, one daily). There are more
long-distance trains from the main station,
Kłodzko Główne (ul Dworcowa 1), 2km north.

Kudowa-Zdrój
POP 10,300

Kudowa-Zdrój (koo-*do*-va zdruy) is an appealing spa town 37km west of Kłodzko,
favoured by a mild climate and several
mineral springs. Renowned since the 18th
century, it's one of the oldest spas in Europe, with well-preserved architecture and
a pleasant park off the single main road.

    It's the ideal place for recharging before
or after enjoying the more strenuous activities the region has to offer, and is the
ideal jumping-off point for the marvellous
Góry Stołowe National Park.

❂ Sights & Activities

★ Chapel of Skulls
CHURCH

(Kaplica Czaszek; www.czermna.pl; ul Moniuszki 8; adult/concession 5/2.50zł; ☺10am-5pm)
You can't miss this macabre chapel in the
Church of St Bartholomew's grounds at
Czermna, 1km north of Kudowa's town centre. The length of its walls and ceiling are
covered with human skulls and bones –
about 3000 of them, with another 20,000 to
30,000 filling the crypt below (p266). The
overall effect is stunning and will certainly
offer you a reality check.

Frog Museum
MUSEUM

(Muzeum Żaby; ul Słoneczna 31; ☺8am-3pm Mon-
Fri) **FREE** Hop on over to the Góry Stołowe
National Park headquarters and check out
Poland's only frog museum, which holds
thousands of everyday objects with an am-
phibian theme. The national park was the
first in Poland to build tunnels under roads to
allow frogs to return to their ponds to spawn
without injury. The aim of the museum is to
raise awareness of frog-conservation issues.

Toy Museum
MUSEUM

(Muzeum Zabawek; www.muzeum-zabawek.pl; ul
Zdrojowa 46b; adult/concession 11/8zł; ☺9am-
5pm) Opposite the spa park and back from
the main street, this small museum with
interesting displays of historic toys is a good
place to while away a wet afternoon.

Spa Park
HEALTH & FITNESS

(Park Zdrojowy) Kudowa has an attractive
17-hectare Spa Park, but most treatments
on offer involve room and board at one of

HEAD CASES

The **Chapel of Skulls** (p265) in Czermna, north of Kudowa-Zdrój, was built in 1776 and looks pretty modest from the outside. Inside, however, it's a different story: thousands of neatly arranged skulls and bones decorate the walls, with more suspended from the ceiling. It's the only chapel of its kind in Poland and one of just three in Europe.

The creator of this unusual 'Sanctuary of Silence' was one Václav Tomášek, a Czech parish priest (Czermna belonged to the Prague Archdiocese at that time). He and the local gravedigger spent two decades collecting human skeletons, which they then cleaned and conserved. The 'decoration' of the chapel wasn't completed until 1804. Skulls and bones that didn't fit on the walls and ceiling were deposited in a 4m-deep crypt.

Since the region was the borderland of the Polish, Czech and German cultures, and of Catholic, Hussite and Protestant traditions, many of the bones belonged to victims of nationalist and religious conflicts. The skeletons came mostly from numerous mass graves, the result of two Silesian wars (1740–42 and 1744–45) and the Seven Years' War (1756–63). The cholera epidemic that plagued the region also contributed to such an impressive quantity of raw material.

Several anatomically interesting skulls are displayed on the main altar, including those of a Tatar warrior, a giant and a victim of syphilis. Alongside them are the skulls of the mastermind of the enterprise – the priest and the gravedigger – at one with their work for all eternity.

the sanatoriums (p266). If you want (literally) a taste of what the park has to offer, the **Pump Room** (Pijalnia; Park Zdrojowy; adult/concession 1.50/0.80zł; ☺ 7am-7pm Mon-Fri, 9am-7pm Sat & Sun) in the southeastern corner serves up two of the local mineral waters.

The **Galos Salt Caves** (Jaskinie Solno Galos; www.galos.pl; Park Zdrojowy; ☺ 9am-9pm) establishment to the west claims to relieve all your ills via remarkable artificial sea-salt chambers, as does its rival **Solana Salt Grotto** (Grota Solna Solana; www.solana.pl; ul Zdrojowa 41; ☺ noon-6pm), near the tourist office. The prices of their treatments vary with the different packages available, so enquire at each venue.

The **Water World Aqua Park** (Aqua Park Wodny Świat; www.basen.eurograf.pl; ul Moniuszki 2a; adult/concession 14/12zł; ☺ 9am-9pm), on the southern edge of the park opposite where the buses stop, offers more-active watery fun.

🛌 Sleeping

Willa Sanssouci   HOTEL €€
(☎ 74 866 1350; www.sanssouci.info.pl; ul Buczka 3; s/d 120/160zł; P 🖥) Located in a lovely villa dating back to 1894, the Sanssouci has comfortable, ample rooms and good service. If you're feeling lucky, give the wishing well in the garden a go.

Willa Sudety   HOTEL €€
(☎ 74 866 1223; www.kudowa.net.pl; ul Zdrojowa 32; s 105zł, d 160-208zł; P 🖥) Well-placed hotel and recreation centre offering affordable accommodation in an attractive building.

There's table tennis on the premises, and management can arrange activities and excursions including hiking and cycling.

Pensjonat Akacja   HOTEL €€
(☎ 74 866 2712; www.akacja.info.pl; ul Kombatantów 5; s/d 120/160zł; P 🖥) This modernised villa is a family-run business providing excellent accommodation in a quiet spot with plenty of space. Some of the rooms on the upper floors have balconies.

Uzdrowiska Kłodzkie   VILLA €€
(☎ 74 868 0401; www.zuk-sa.pl; ul Moniuszki 2; s/d 199/318zł; P 🖥) The Kłodzko Spa Company administers two fine old villa sanatoriums in the centre of town, providing an unparalleled variety of rooms. The emphasis is on medical treatment, but it will accept casual guests. Reception is housed within the elegant Polonia sanatorium.

🍴 Eating

Cudova Bistro   POLISH, PIZZA €€
(ul Zdrojowa 44; mains 16-33zł; ☺ 10am-10pm; 🖥) Overlooking the spa park, this bright contemporary eatery serves a tasty selection of Polish dishes and pizzas. There's a cosy back room for more intimacy. Breakfast is available too.

Zdrojowa   CZECH €€
(ul Słoneczna 1; mains 18-52zł; ☺ noon-10pm) Homely but spacious restaurant near the main bus stand serving Czech cuisine, a nod to the neighbours across the mountains.

Dishes range from filling soups to tasty schnitzels.

Café Domek
PIZZA **€€**

(ul Zdrojowa 36; mains 15-39zł; ☺noon-10pm; 🛜) Large pizzeria with a huge, leafy terrace out front, ideal for relaxing in after a day of hiking in the Góry Stołowe National Park. It's a good place to sip a quiet beer.

ⓘ Information

Post Office (ul 1 Maja 12; ☺8am-6.30pm Mon-Fri, to 1.45pm Sat)

Tourist Office (☎74 866 1387; www.kudowa. pl; ul Zdrojowa 44; ☺8am-4pm Mon-Fri, 9am-2pm Sat)

ⓘ Getting There & Away

Buses depart from a **stand** (ul 1 Maja) in the town centre, on ul 1 Maja between the intersections of ul Poznańska and ul Lubelska. There are hourly departures for Kłodzko (8zł, 50 minutes) and eight buses a day to Wrocław (28zł, 2¾ hours).

There are also 11 buses each day to Náchod in the Czech Republic (5zł, 20 minutes). Alternatively, go to the border (3km) and cross it on foot to Náchod, 2km beyond the frontier, from where there are onward buses and trains.

It's possible to arrive and depart from Kudowa-Zdrój by rail, though the **train station** (ul Główna 23) is an inconvenient 1.7km south of the Spa Park along ul Zdrojowa and ul Główna. Each day there are seven trains to Kłodzko (7zł, 1¼ hours), and two to Wrocław (36zł, 3½ hours); one of these continues to Warsaw (61zł, 10½ hours).

Bystrzyca Kłodzka

POP 10,400

Bystrzyca Kłodzka (bist-*shi*-tsah *kwots*-kah), perched on a hilltop above the Nysa Kłodzka River, is a sleepy, atmospheric old town that has retained much of its medieval architecture and layout. Though there aren't that many specific attractions, the squares and narrow streets of the Old Town have an appealing character.

Since the 13th century, when it was founded, the town has been destroyed and rebuilt several times, though ironically it survived WWII virtually unmolested.

⊙ Sights

In the 14th century the town was granted municipal status and surrounded by fortified city walls, some elements of which are still in place. The most substantial structures include the **Water Gate** (Brama Wodna; ul Podmiejska), just south of the Rynek, and the **Kłodzko Tower** (Baszta Kłodzka; ul Okrzei; adult/concession 3/2zł; ☺10am-4pm Mon-Sat), which you can climb, on the north side of the Old Town.

Rynek
SQUARE

(Market Square; Plac Wolności) The buildings lining the Rynek, officially known as Plac Wolności, are a pleasing blend of architectural styles. The octagonal Renaissance tower (1567) of the Italianate town hall in the centre gives the square an almost southern European feel. Next to the town hall is an elaborate Baroque plague pillar (1737) dedicated to the Holy Trinity.

Phillumenistic Museum
MUSEUM

(Muzeum Filumenistyczne; www.muzeum. filumenistyka.pl; Mały Rynek 1; adult/concession 6/4.50zł; ☺8am-4pm Tue-Sat, 10am-3pm Sun) East of the Rynek, the Knights' Tower (Baszta Rycerska) was reshaped in the 19th century and turned into the belfry of a Protestant church that had been built alongside it. After WWII the church was occupied by this rather esoteric museum, which displays lighters, matchbox labels and other paraphernalia related to fire lighting. On the small square outside the museum stands the old whipping post from 1566; the Latin inscription on its top reads 'God punishes the impious'.

Parish Church of St Michael the Archangel
CHURCH

(Kościół Parafialny Św Michała Archanioła; Plac Skłodowskiej 3) This Gothic place of worship sits at the highest point of the Old Town, two blocks northwest of the Rynek. It has a nave and just one aisle with a row of six Gothic columns running right across the middle.

🛏 Sleeping

★Hotel Castle
HOTEL **€€**

(☎74 812 0560; www.hotelcastle.pl; ul Okrzei 26; s/d 130/210zł; 🅿🛜) Housed in an attractive old building fancifully resembling a castle, this hotel offers Bystrzyca Kłodzka's best lodgings. Rooms are tastefully decorated, and there's a good restaurant decked out in baronial splendour. It's 200m north of the tourist office; turn right when leaving the train station.

Hotel Abis
HOTEL **€€**

(☎74 811 0645; www.hotelabis.pl; ul Strażacka 28; s/d 110/170zł; 🅿🛜) Inexpensive lodgings about 1.5km northwest of the Rynek. Clean, simple rooms are good value, and there's an in-house restaurant serving Polish favourites.

SILESIA BYSTRZYCA KŁODZKA

WORTH A TRIP

GÓRY STOŁOWE

Góry Stołowe (goo-ri sto-wo-veh; Table Mountains) is among the most spectacular range of the Sudetes, as it's topped by a plateau punctuated by fantastic rock formations.

One of the highlights of the 63-sq-km **park** (Park Narodowy Gór Stołowych; www.pngs. com.pl; adult/concession 7/3zł) is Szczeliniec Wielki, its highest outcrop. Both German poet Goethe and the USA's sixth president, John Quincy Adams, walked here and admired the dramatic scenery. From a distance, the plateau looks like a high ridge adorned with pinnacles, rising abruptly from the surrounding fields.

From just beyond Karłów, a small village about 1km south of the plateau, you ascend 682 stone steps, which takes about 40 minutes. From there, the one-hour trail around the summit gives excellent views of both the mountain scenery and the rock formations, before arriving back at its starting point. About 4km to the west, the Błędne Skały are another impressive sight, comprising hundreds of gigantic boulders deposited by glaciers in vaguely geometric shapes, forming a vast stone labyrinth. A sometimes very narrow trail runs between the rocks.

Located 650m southeast of the tourist office in Kudowa-Zdrój, the **Góry Stołowe National Park Headquarters** (Dyrekcja PNGS; ☑ 74 866 1436; www.pngs.com.pl; ul Słoneczna 31; ☉ 7.30am-3.30pm Mon-Fri) can tell you everything you need to know about the park, and sells maps and English-language guides.

Getting There & Away

To get to Karłów, catch a privately run minibus from Kudowa-Zdrój (6zł, 20 minutes). Alternatively, take one of the frequent buses from Kudowa-Zdrój to Polanica-Zdrój (8zł, 35 minutes, half-hourly), from where there are three daily buses to Karłów (9zł, 50 minutes).

✖ Eating & Drinking

La Salle ITALIAN €€
(Plac Wolności 1; mains 14-49zł; ☉ noon-10pm; ☜) Atmospheric restaurant within the town hall's cellar, turning out a good range of pasta dishes and pizzas.

Malibu CAFE, BAR
(Plac Wolności 4; ☉ 11am-11pm) Cosy establishment right on the market square, with a close-up view of the town hall. The outdoor seating is a good place from which to take in the town's unhurried street life.

ⓘ Information

Tourist Office (☑ 74 811 3731; www.bystrzyca klodzka.pl; Mały Rynek 2/1; ☉ 8am-5pm Mon-Fri, 10am-4pm Sat) On the small square near the Knights' Tower.

ⓘ Getting There & Away

➡ The **bus station** (ul Sienkiewicza 5), on ul Sienkiewicza 200m north of the parish church, has services to Kłodzko (7zł, 25 minutes) at least once every two hours. There are also bus connections to Boboszów (10zł, one hour, twice daily) near the Czech border.

➡ The **train station** (ul Międzyleśna) is just east of the tourist office. From here trains connect with Kłodzko Miasto (7zł, 17 minutes, 10 daily) and Wrocław (22zł, two hours, eight daily).

UPPER SILESIA

This part of Silesia presents extreme contrasts. Heavily developed and industrialised, Upper Silesia (Górny Śląsk) occupies just 2% of Poland's territory, yet it's home to a full 9% of the population. Thanks to large deposits of coal, it's traditionally been the nation's centre of heavy industry and the most densely urbanised area in Central Europe. Under socialism this region was the 'reddest' in Poland and relatively well treated as a result. However, despite the urban sprawl centred on Katowice, the region has its share of attractive cities and towns worth a visit. At the other end of the emotional scale is the Auschwitz-Birkenau extermination camp complex, tragic but unmissable. Upper Silesia is also an easy port of call if you're heading to Kraków or the Czech Republic.

Nysa

POP 45,000

It has to be admitted that Nysa doesn't boast the harmonious architecture of many other Silesian towns. Around 80% of its buildings were destroyed during fierce battles between German and Soviet forces in 1945, and some of the postwar reconstruction leaves a lot to be desired in aesthetic terms. Still, the mishmash of old and new is intriguing in its own way, especially the juxtaposition of Nysa's dramatic cathedral with other historic remnants scattered around its central square.

For centuries Nysa (*ni-*sah) was one of the most important religious centres in Silesia. In the 17th century it became a seat of the Catholic bishops, who were in flight from newly 'Reformed' Wrocław. The bishops soon made Nysa a bastion of the Counter-Reformation; so strong was their hold that the town came to be known as the Silesian Rome.

◉ Sights

Cathedral of SS James and Agnes
CHURCH

(Katedra Św Jakuba i Agnieszki; www.bazylika-nysa.pl; Plac Katedralny 7) There's no overlooking Nysa's mighty cathedral on the Rynek, with its imposing blackened bulk and fine stone double portal. Built in 1430, it was remodelled after a fire in 1542 but hasn't changed much since then. The cathedral's 4000-sq-m roof, supported by 18 brick columns inside, is one of the steepest church roofs in Europe. The vast interior, much of it dating from the late 19th century, looks distinctly sober and noble, its loftiness being the most arresting feature.

On closer inspection, you'll see that its side chapels (a total of 18) boast wonderful stained glass and a wealth of tombstones, funeral monuments and epitaphs, making up the largest collection of funerary sculpture in any Silesian church.

The free-standing block next to the cathedral is the bell tower, which was begun 50 years after the church was built and was originally intended to be over 100m high. Despite 40 years' work it reached only half that height, and consequently looks truncated and oddly proportioned, especially with the tiny turret tacked onto it.

Nysa Museum
MUSEUM

(Muzeum w Nysie; www.muzeum.nysa.pl; ul Jarosława 11; adult/concession 10/7zł, Wed free; ⊙9am-3pm Tue-Fri, 10am-3pm Sat & Sun) This museum is located within the 17th-century Bishops' Palace, a spacious double-fronted former episcopal residence. Exhibits range from archaeological finds to photos documenting war damage, plus a model of the town in its heyday. A more stimulating section deals with witches of the region. The museum also features European paintings from the 15th to the 19th centuries, mostly from the Flemish and Dutch schools.

Rynek
SQUARE

(Market Square) Diverse architecture within Nysa's vast market square suggests the extent of damage done in WWII. Only the southern side retains anything like its historic appearance, with restored houses dating from the 16th century. The detached building facing them, the 1604 **Town Weighing House** (Dom Wagi Miejskiej; Rynek), retains fragments of 19th-century painting on a side wall. Just round the corner, on ul Bracka, are more historic houses and a 1701 copy of the Baroque Triton Fountain by Bernini in Rome.

Just past the fountain is the twin-towered **Church of SS Peter and Paul** (Kościół Św Piotra i Pawła; www.piotripawel.nysa.pl; ul Bracka 18), built in 1727 for the Hospitallers of the Holy Sepulchre. It has one of Silesia's best Baroque interiors, complete with an opulent high altar, organ and trompe l'oeil wall paintings.

◉ Fortifications

There are several interesting remains of fortifications around Nysa. The restored 17th-century **St Hedwig's Bastion** (Bastion Św Jadwigi; ul Piastowska 19), two blocks northwest of the Rynek, was once home to a Prussian garrison. It's now a cultural centre that also houses the tourist office and a restaurant.

The only significant traces of the medieval defences are two 14th-century brick towers: the **Ziębice Tower** (Wieża Ziębicka; ul Krzywoustego), west of the Rynek, with unusual turrets and dragon guttering; and the white-plastered **Wrocław Tower** (Wieża Wrocławska; ul Wrocławska), 200m northeast towards the train station.

🛏 Sleeping

Pod Ziębickim Lwem Hostel
HOSTEL €

(☑77 433 3731; www.kadett.d.pl/nysa; ul Krakiecka 28; dm 25zł; ℗⏢) About 2km south of the Old Town, this 48-bed hostel has small but smart dorms of two to four beds, providing a little more privacy than many other hostels. A common kitchen is available to guests.

★Villa Navigator
HOTEL €€

(☑77 433 4170; www.villanavigator.pl; ul Wyspiańskiego 11; s 80-110zł, d 110-160zł; ℗⏢) Charming establishment about 400m west of the Rynek. It's exactly what a family-run hotel should be, from the antique furniture, oil paintings and potted plants to the sociable breakfasts in the

WORTH A TRIP

THE WALLS OF PACZKÓW

If you're staying in Nysa or Kłodzko, sleepy Paczków (*patch*-koof) makes a good day trip. It may be small, but the town has one of the most complete sets of medieval fortifications in Poland.

The oval ring of Paczków's defensive walls was built around 1350 and was surrounded by a moat. Remarkably, these walls remained in place over the centuries and, as the town escaped major destruction during WWII, they still encircle the historic quarter. They were initially about 9m high for the whole of their 1200m length and had a wooden gallery for sentries below the top.

Four gateways were built, complete with towers (all of which still stand) and drawbridges, and there were two dozen semicircular towers built into the walls themselves (19 have survived, though most are incomplete). The most interesting is the round **Kłodzko Gate Tower** (Wieża Bramy Kłodzkiej; ul Narutowicza), with its irregular loopholes; the oldest is the 14th-century **Wrocław Gate Tower** (Wieża Bramy Wrocławskiej; ul Wrocławska; ⊙6am-6pm Mon-Sat, 9am-4pm Sun) FREE, which can be climbed. Ask for the key at the nearby 'Ruch' kiosk on ul Armii Krajowej.

There are six daily buses to Paczków from Nysa (10zł, 30 minutes) and five from Kłodzko (12zł, 40 minutes).

If there's time to kill before your return service, duck into the surprisingly interesting **Gas Industry Museum** (Muzeum Gazownictwa; www.muzeumgazownictwa.pl; ul Pocztowa 6; admission 4/2zł; ⊙9am-5pm Mon-Fri), a short walk north of the Rynek in an old redbrick gasworks that operated from 1902 to 1977. Among its varied gas-related exhibits, it contains an extensive collection of gas meters.

family parlour. Rooms on the 3rd floor are simpler but still thoroughly serviceable. For a visual treat, ask for the Danzig room (number 4) or the Secessionist room (number 3).

Hotel Fryderyk   HOTEL €€
(🖉77 421 0426; www.hotel.nysa.pl; ul Szopena 12; s 190zł, d 250-300zł; P❄🐾) New central hotel within a historic building, with comfortable rooms outfitted in a classic style. There's an accomplished Polish restaurant on the premises, and guests have the option of a 'prestige' double room with more space.

✖ Eating

Bar Popularny   CAFETERIA €
(Rynek 23/24; mains 4-14zł; ⊙8am-6pm Mon-Fri, to 4pm Sat; 🖉) This unreformed milk-bar cafeteria on the main square looks drab and basic, but the food is tasty. The set meals provide an even better bargain.

★Madame   POLISH €€
(Rynek 24/25; mains 15-48zł; ⊙9am-11pm) Celebrity chef Magda Gessler has given this classy restaurant a makeover. Elegant decor in pink and green tones is complemented by a menu of reimagined Polish dishes alongside classics. It's the best place in Nysa in which to dine in style.

Pizzeria Piec   PIZZA €€
(Rynek 39; mains 16-26zł; ⊙11am-11pm) Drinkers and diners alike congregate in this den of pasta and pizza attached to the Town Weighing House. The interior is done out in timber and dark-green tones, making it a soothing place for a break.

ℹ Information

Post Office (ul Krzywoustego 21; ⊙8am-7pm Mon-Fri, to 2pm Sat)

PTTK Office (🖉77 433 4171; ul Bracka 4; ⊙9am-5pm Mon-Fri) Centrally located travel agency.

Tourist Office (🖉77 433 4971; www.informacja-turystyczna.nysa.pl; ul Piastowska 19; ⊙8am-4pm) Inside St Hedwig's Bastion.

ℹ Getting There & Away

➡ The **bus station** (www.pksnysa.pl; ul Racławicka 1) and **train station** (ul Racławicka) face one another, about 500m northeast of the Rynek.

➡ By bus, there are services to Paczków (10zł, 30 minutes, six daily), Kłodzko (15zł, one hour, five daily), Opole (10zł, 1¼ hours, 12 daily) and Wrocław (18zł, 1½ hours, four daily).

➡ Trains are less frequent but may be useful when travelling to Opole (14zł, 1¼ hours, eight daily). To travel by rail to Wrocław, buy a through ticket at the station with a change at Brzeg.

Opole

POP 120,000

Opole is best known within Poland for the National Festival of Polish Song, which has taken place annually in June since 1963 and is broadcast nationwide on TV. Though it's a fairly large regional industrial centre, Opole also has an attractive Old Town with pleasant waterside views along the Młynówka Canal, which flows through the historic centre.

Lying on the border of Upper and Lower Silesia, the city is the capital of its own voivodeship (province) called Opolskie. The region is known for an active German minority, one of the few communities of its kind to survive the war. They number about 100,000 and are represented in local government.

The first Slav stronghold was built here in the 9th century. In the 13th century Opole became the capital of its principality and was ruled by a line of Silesian Piasts until 1532, even though it was part of Bohemia from 1327. Later, Opole fell to Austria, then to Prussia, and after significant destruction in WWII returned to Poland in 1945.

Sights

Rynek SQUARE

(Market Square) Though badly damaged during WWII, Opole's central market square was rebuilt after the conflict. It's lined with handsome sand-coloured Baroque and Rococo houses, and populated with pubs and bars. The 64m-high tower of the oversized town hall in the middle was modelled after the Palazzo Vecchio in Florence and looks a little overly grand here. The original, dating from 1864, collapsed in 1934, but it was rebuilt in the same style.

**★ Franciscan Church
of the Holy Trinity** CHURCH

(Kościół Franciszkanów Św Trójcy; Plac Wolności 2) This church off the southern corner of the Rynek was built of brick around 1330. It boasts an ornate high altar, an 18th-century organ, and a domed Renaissance chapel in the left-hand aisle, separated by a fine, late-16th-century wrought-iron grille. A highlight is the Chapel of St Anne, accessible from the right-hand aisle through a doorway with a tympanum. The Gothic-vaulted chapel houses a pair of massive double tombs (where the local dukes were interred) carved in sandstone in the 1380s.

Opole Silesian Museum MUSEUM

(Muzeum Śląska Opolskiego; www.muzeum.opole.pl; Mały Rynek 7; adult/concession 5/3zł, Sat free; ⊙9am-4pm Tue-Fri, 11am-5pm Sat & Sun) Two blocks east of the market square, this museum is housed in a former Jesuit college (1698). The permanent display features the prehistory and history of the city and the surrounding area, and there are always temporary exhibitions. Enter from ul Muzealna.

Holy Cross Cathedral CHURCH

(Katedra Św Krzyża; ul Katedralna 2) Gothic cathedral a short walk north of the Rynek, featuring 73m-high towers and mostly Baroque interior furnishing. The lovely bronze gate at the western entrance was erected in 1995 to mark the church's 700th year.

★ Piast Tower TOWER

(Wieża Piastowska; ul Piastowska 14; adult/concession 10/6zł; ⊙10am-6pm Mon-Fri, to 3pm Sat & Sun) The only vestige of the castle that once housed Opole's dukes is this 33m-tall sturdy watchtower, with walls 3m thick and foundations 6m deep. Built in the 14th century, the castle was pulled down in the 1920s to make room for office buildings. You can climb the 163 steps to the top for a panoramic view over the city.

Sleeping

Szara Willa HOTEL €€

(☑77 441 4570; www.szarawilla.pl; ul Oleska 11; s 269-309zł, d 319-339zł; P 🗟) The 'Grey Villa' has a crisp modern feel, and design elements with an Asian influence. Its rooms are generously sized, with high ceilings, and four rooms in front look onto a large terrace. A plus is the attached fitness centre.

Hotel Piast HOTEL €€

(☑77 454 9710; www.hotel-piast.com; ul Piastowska 1; s 310-399zł, d 369-460zł; P ❋ 🗟) Commanding the best location of Opole's accommodation, the Piast sits on the northern tip of Pasieka Island, a short trot away from the Old Town. Its rooms are classy and comfortable, and there's a bar on the premises.

Hotel Kamienica HOTEL €€

(☑77 546 6196; www.hotelkamienica.com.pl; Plac Kopernika 14; s 165-190zł, d 240zł; 🗟) Neat and tidy three-star hotel behind the Old Town, opposite a modern shopping mall. Rooms are simple but comfortable, and there's an on-site restaurant serving Polish cuisine and pasta.

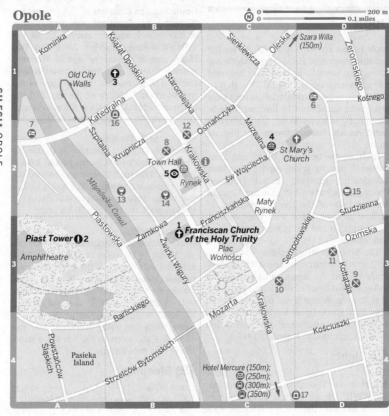

Opole

◎ Top Sights
1 Franciscan Church of the Holy Trinity	B3
2 Piast Tower	A3

◎ Sights
3 Holy Cross Cathedral	B1
4 Opole Silesian Museum	C2
5 Rynek	B2

🛏 Sleeping
6 Hotel Kamienica	D1
7 Hotel Piast	A2

⊗ Eating
8 Delikatesy Piast	B2
9 Hamburg	D3
10 Kaiseki	C3
11 Restauracja U Mnicha	D3
12 Smaki Świata	B2

🍷 Drinking & Nightlife
13 Highlander Klub	B2
14 Maska	B2
15 Pauza	D2

🛍 Shopping
16 Cepelia	B1
17 Empik	D4

Hotel Mercure   HOTEL **€€**
(☎ 77 451 8100; www.mercure.com; ul Krakowska 57; r from 205zł; 🅿 🛜) A cookie-cutter offering from the international chain, but there's no denying its handy location near the bus and train stations. It has a bar and restaurant, and you can score a rate up to 50% cheaper by booking online. Breakfast is an extra 35zł per person.

✖ Eating

The majority of eateries are gathered around the market square. For self-catering supplies, drop into the central **Delikatesy Piast** (Rynek 13; ⊕7am-10pm Mon-Fri, 8am-11pm Sat, 10am-8pm Sun).

Hamburg   BURGERS €
(ul Kołłątaja 16a; burgers 11-15zł; ⊕11am-8pm Mon-Sat; ☑) Cool, contemporary fast-food joint serving quality burgers made from fresh ingredients. In addition to the standard hamburger, there are Greek, Italian and Balkan variants, and three types of vegetarian burger. Soup and salads are also on the menu.

Smaki Świata   INTERNATIONAL €
(ul Książąt Opolskich 2/6; dishes per 100g 3.09zł; ⊕11am-8pm) 'Tastes of the World' is true to its name, serving Polish, Hungarian, Italian and Chinese cuisine in a cheerful cafeteria. All food is charged at a flat rate by weight.

Restauracja U Mnicha   POLISH €€
(ul Ozimska 10; mains 12-30zł; ⊕11am-10pm) Modern, monk-themed basement U Mnicha creates sandwiches, pizzas and hefty salads. It also holds regular summer barbecues in its small garden area. Enter from ul Kołłątaja.

Kaiseki   JAPANESE €€
(ul Ozimska 4; dishes 12-39zł; ⊕noon-10pm Mon-Sat, to 9pm Sun) This very stylish and very Japanese eatery, upstairs in a modern shopping mall, serves sushi as well as more substantial mains such as tempura.

⚑ Drinking & Nightlife

Pauza   CAFE
(ul Ozimska 19b; ⊕9am-9pm Mon-Fri, noon-8pm Sat & Sun) A relaxed split-level cafe tucked away in a backstreet, this is the perfect place for coffee and cake after a hard day's sightseeing. There's a smattering of outdoor seating too. Enter from ul Podgórna.

Maska   PUB
(Rynek 4-6; ⊕11am-late) Long-lived atmospheric pub, right on the main square. Also serves filling Polish food.

Highlander Klub   PUB, CLUB
(ul Szpitalna 3; ⊕11am-late) A good place for a beer and dance, this friendly (but not very Scottish) venue hosts DJs playing anything from house to Latin.

🛍 Shopping

Cepelia   ARTS, CRAFTS
(ul Koraszewskiego 25) Opole is famed for its porcelain hand-painted with fine floral motifs, and this is where you'll find the widest selection.

Empik   BOOKS
(ul Krakowska 45/47; ⊕9am-8pm Mon-Fri, 10-4pm Sat & Sun) Sells books, maps and magazines.

ℹ Information

Main Post Office (ul Krakowska 46; ⊕24hr)

PTTK Office (☑77 454 5113; www.opole.pttk. pl; ul Krakowska 15; ⊕10am-4.30pm Mon-Fri) Travel agency.

Tourist Office (☑77 451 1987; www.mosir. opole.pl; Rynek 23; ⊕10am-6pm Mon-Fri, to 3pm Sat & Sun; 🖧) Provides assistance to travellers, and offers free wi-fi access.

ℹ Getting There & Away

➔ The **train station** (Opole Główne; ul Krakowska 48) and **bus station** (www.pks.opole. pl; ul 1 Maja 4) face each other at the end of ul Krakowska, south of the Old Town.

➔ Useful buses head to Nysa (10zł, 1¼ hours, 12 daily) and Kłodzko (25zł, 2½ hours, four daily).

➔ Opole is on the main rail line between Katowice (24zł, 1½ hours, at least hourly) and Wrocław (26zł, 55 minutes, at least hourly). Eight daily trains head to Kraków (40zł, 2¾ hours), and 11 to Częstochowa (25zł to 44zł, one hour). To Warsaw there's one TLK train (59zł, 5½ hours) and five fast Express InterCity trains (123zł, three hours).

Katowice

POP 302,000

Katowice (kah-to-*vee*-tseh) is at the centre of the so-called Upper Silesian Industrial District (Górnośląski Okręg Przemysłowy, or GOP). The GOP contains 14 cities and a number of neighbouring towns, forming one vast conurbation with a population of well over three million.

Historically, Katowice is a product of the 19th-century industrial boom, but it only became a city in the interwar period. After WWII, at the height of the Stalinist cult craze, the city was renamed Stalinogród, but it reverted to its old name soon after Comrade Joe died in 1953. Katowice has few significant historical monuments, but it's a major commercial and cultural centre and holds sufficient attractions to make it worth a stopover.

WORTH A TRIP

PASS THE CROWBAR, JEEVES

The small town of Toszek is worth a side trip simply to look around its impressive Gothic **castle** (Zamek w Toszku; www.zamektoszek.eu; ul Zamkowa; ⊙8am-10pm) FREE, dating from 1222, but on the other side of town there's a literary footnote awaiting book lovers.

In May 1940 popular British novelist PG Wodehouse, creator of the masterful valet Jeeves and his hapless employer Bertie Wooster, was captured by the German army at his home in France. In September he was moved to a civilian internment camp in German Tost, now Toszek.

The prison was set up within the grounds of the **psychiatric hospital** (Szpital Psychiatryczny; ul Gliwicka 5), and its sinister story didn't end with the Germans – after the war it operated as a political prison of the Soviet Union's feared NKVD secret police. Though you can't enter, you can get a good view of its grim redbrick exterior from the dishevelled park across the road. Within the complex are grounds that were used as an exercise yard for the prisoners, beyond which was their dining hall and hospital.

Wodehouse, then 58, coped well with the privations of camp life but was unimpressed with what he could see of Toszek through the barred windows, writing: 'If this is Upper Silesia, what must Lower Silesia be like?'

The internationally famous author was treated well by his captors, being allowed to work on a rented typewriter. Then, in 1941, he was invited by the German authorities to make a series of radio broadcasts to reassure his readers in still-neutral America of his good health. Naively, Wodehouse agreed, unaware of the defiant mood in the UK after the Blitz and the Battle of Britain. The broadcasts caused an outpouring of indignation and accusations of collaboration.

Although after the war British intelligence secretly cleared Wodehouse of any wrongdoing, the incident left its mark. The author never returned to Britain, living out his days on Long Island, New York.

Sir Pelham Grenville Wodehouse died in 1975, aged 93, just six weeks after receiving a belated knighthood from his homeland. He is survived by almost 100 books, including the one he completed while a prisoner in Toszek – *Money in the Bank*.

If you're interested in visiting Toszek, there are 10 trains a day from Opole (14zł, 50 minutes). From the **train station** (ul Dworcowa), turn left and take a 20-minute walk along ul Dworcowa to the town centre.

⊙ Sights

Rynek SQUARE
(Market Square) The city's central market square is not lined with historic burghers' houses as you'd find elsewhere in Silesia, but instead is encircled by drab postwar blocks. It's a showpiece of the 'early Gierek style' – the term Poles sarcastically give to architecture spawned during the fleeting period of apparent prosperity in the early 1970s, when Edward Gierek's communist government took out hefty loans from the West with the fanciful aim of making Poland a 'second Japan'.

At the time of research, however, the Rynek was undergoing a major makeover that should produce a more pleasant public space once completed – the colourful planter boxes and timber benches are a good start.

Silesian Museum MUSEUM
(Muzeum Śląskie; www.muzeumslaskie.pl; al Korfantego 3; adult/concession 12/7zł, Sat free; ⊙10am-5pm Tue-Fri, 11am-5pm Sat) North of the Rynek, this museum features Polish paintings from 1800 to 1939, as well as various temporary displays from its vast collections (fine art, archaeology, ethnography, and local history and culture). A new section, opened in mid-2015, is partly underground, housed within a former coal mine.

Cathedral of Christ the King CHURCH
(Katedra Chrystusa Króla; www.katedra.katowice.opoka.org.pl; ul Plebiscytowa 49a) Some 800m south of the Rynek is Poland's largest cathedral, its base measuring 89m by 53m. The massive sandstone structure was erected between 1927 and 1955. The spacious interior is topped with a large dome that rises 59m from the floor, but apart from colourful stained-glass windows and an unusual 'wheel' crucifix, it's fairly plain. Behind it, the **Archdiocesan Museum** (ul Jordana 39; ⊙2-6pm Tue-Thu, 11am-3pm Sat) FREE has a collection of sacred art from the late 14th

century, including beautiful Gothic altarpieces. Enter from ul Wita Stwosza.

Skyscraper
ARCHITECTURE

(Drapacz Chmur; ul Żwirki i Wigury 15) This blocky, 14-storey, 60m-tall structure was Poland's tallest building from 1934 until 1955. It's considered the best example of functionalism in Poland.

Garrison Church of St Casimir
CHURCH

(Parafia Wojskowa Św Kazimierza; ul Skłodowskiej-Curie 20) The Garrison Church of St Casimir, with lovely Art Deco interiors, opened in 1933 – just a year before the functionalist skyscraper opposite.

★Museum of Katowice
History at Nikiszowiec
MUSEUM

(Muzeum Historii Katowic w Nikiszowcu; www.mhk.katowice.pl; ul Rymarska 4; adult/concession 8/4zł; ⊙10am-6pm Tue-Fri, 11am-3pm Sat & Sun; ▣30) The city's museum has a branch in the distinctive suburb of Nikiszowiec, 5km southeast of the city centre. The district is a unique estate created for miners (and their families) who worked at a nearby shaft between 1908 and 1924. Built of attractive redbrick, with a network of streets between, the nine blocks are interconnected by gateways. The complex was designed to be self-sufficient, with shops, restaurants, a swimming pool, a hospital, a school and a detention centre. The museum adds context to this interesting architectural gem.

Upper Silesian
Ethnographic Park
MUSEUM

(Górnośląski Park Etnograficzny; www.muzeumgpe-chorzow.pl; ul Parkowa 25, Chorzów; adult/concession 8/6zł; ⊙9am-7pm; ▣0, 6, 11, 19, 23) This sprawling open-air museum contains scores of traditional wooden buildings spread over 20 hectares. It's situated within the even bigger Provincial Park of Culture and Recreation, which also houses a stadium, a zoo, amusement grounds and a planetarium. The park is about 3km northwest of the centre.

🛏 Sleeping

Jopi Hostel
HOSTEL €

(☑32 204 3432; www.jopihostel.pl; ul Plebiscytowa 23; dm 41-51zł, s/d 101/107zł; ☜) Modern hostel south of the train station, with a well-equipped kitchen and a comfortable lounge/dining area. Rooms are painted a cheery orange-yellow shade, lending a touch of brightness to the interior.

Pokoje Gościnne Zacisze
HOTEL €

(☑32 205 0935; www.noclegizacisze.pl; ul Słowackiego 15; r from 100zł; ☜) Don't let the creaky old staircase put you off – this accommodation offers pleasantly appointed rooms in an old building near the bus station. Not much English is spoken, however, and there's no breakfast available, though guests have access to a kitchen. Note that the cheaper rooms have shared bathrooms.

★Hotel Diament
HOTEL €€

(☑32 253 9041; www.hoteldiament.pl; ul Dworcowa 9; s/d from 255/300zł; ▣❄☜) Business-friendly Diament is a member of a Silesian hotel chain. It's comfortable, convenient and reliable, with a good restaurant downstairs. It's great value for the comfort level, and booking online usually secures a lower rate.

Hotel Katowice
HOTEL €€

(☑32 258 8281; www.hotel-katowice.com.pl; al Korfantego 9; s/d from 120/180zł; ▣☜) Only a Soviet central planner could admire the exterior of this communist-era relic, but the rooms have been renovated and the city centre's a light stroll away. Amenities include a bar and restaurant.

Hotel Monopol
HOTEL €€€

(☑32 782 8282; www.monopolkatowice.hotel.com.pl; ul Dworcowa 5; s/d 490/580zł; ▣❄☜▨) A tasteful reincarnation of Katowice's most celebrated prewar hotel, with friendly, helpful staff. Rooms are full of stylish walnut and chrome surfaces, and bathrooms feature huge shower heads. There are also two restaurants, a fitness centre with two saunas, and a swimming pool. Check out the fabulous 19th-century floor mosaic under glass in the foyer.

🍴 Eating

The new **Galeria Katowicka shopping mall** (www.galeriakatowicka.eu; ul 3 Maja 30; ⊙9am-9pm Mon-Sat, 10am-8pm Sun), attached to the train station, has plenty of snack bars and unfussy restaurants, as well as a supermarket. The areas around ul Staromiejska and ul Wawelska, northeast of the station, are a bit more cosmopolitan and upmarket.

Złoty Osioł
VEGETARIAN €

(ul Mariacka 1; mains 12zł; ⊙10am-10pm Mon-Sat, noon-10pm Sun; ☜▨) A cheerful, popular vegetarian cafe, the 'Golden Donkey' has cool hippy decor (think psychedelic walls and distressed furniture) and a tasty range of meat-free dishes, including some vegan options.

Katowice

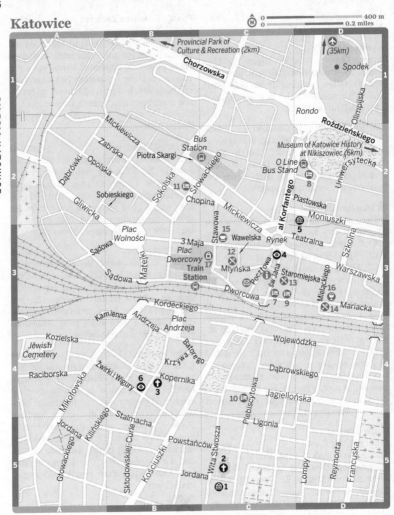

★Tatiana
POLISH €€

(ul Staromiejska 5; mains 18-89zł; ⊘11am-11pm)
Serves a range of contemporary Polish dishes in an elegant interior with lots of timber touches. Choices range from homemade dumplings with spinach and walnuts to leg of rabbit in a mustard sauce. A classy place to kick back of an evening.

Restauracja A Dong
ASIAN €€

(ul Wawelska 3; mains 30-45zł; ⊘11am-11pm; 🖥)
This is the place to find authentic Asian food in Katowice. Dishes include Sichuan squid, Malaysian shrimps, Vietnamese octopus and lobster Saigon-style.

🍷 Drinking & Nightlife

Kofeina Bistro
CAFE

(ul 3 Maja 13; ⊘8am-8pm Mon-Sat, 11am-8pm Sun; 🖥) Bright, modern cafe creating Katowice's best coffee, along with a selection of cakes and light meals. Breakfast is on offer, including omelettes and pancakes.

Komitet PRL
CLUB

(ul Mariacka 4; ⊘4pm-late Wed-Sat) Nightclub with a sense of humour and a weakness for nostalgia. Dance the night away to disco hits from the 1970s to the 1990s.

Katowice

◉ Sights

▣ Sleeping

✕ Eating

● Drinking & Nightlife

⌂ Shopping

❶ Information

Cafe Kontakt (ul Stawowa 3; per hour 5zł; ⊙8am-11pm Mon-Sat, 10am-10pm Sun) Internet access.

Post Office (ul Pocztowa 9; ⊙24hr)

Tourist Office (✆32 259 3808; www.katowice. eu; Rynek 13; ⊙9am-5pm Mon-Fri, to 4pm Sat) If you're interested in finding out more about Katowice's distinctive interwar architecture, ask here for the architectural walking trail brochure.

❶ Getting There & Away

AIR

Katowice Airport (✆32 392 7000; www. katowice-airport.com; ul Wolności 90) is in Pyrzowice, 35km north of the city. There are domestic flights to Warsaw (three daily), and international services to numerous European cities:

Dublin Ryanair, three weekly

Frankfurt Lufthansa and Wizz Air, four daily

London Ryanair and Wizz Air, three daily

Paris Wizz Air, three weekly

You can transfer between the airport and Katowice train station via shuttle services offered by Matuszek (✆32 236 1111; www.matuszek. com.pl; single/return to Katowice 20/40zł, to Kraków 44/88zł). Buying on the bus rather than booking online incurs an extra 5zł fee each way. The company also runs services from Katowice Airport to Kraków.

BUS

The **bus station** (www.katowicedworzec.pl; ul Piotr Skargi 1), some 500m north of the train station, handles most regional, long-distance and international services. Other short-haul regional buses depart from the new underground bus station integrated with the train station in the city centre.

For most journeys the train will be a better option, though private firm **Polski Bus** (www. polskibus.com) operates a number of useful bus services. Book online in advance; fares vary dramatically from day to day.

DESTINATION	TIME (HR)	FREQUENCY
Berlin	7½	2 daily
Bratislava	5¾	2 daily
Częstochowa	1½	4 daily
Vienna	7¾	2 daily
Warsaw	4½	9 daily
Wrocław	2½	every 2 hr
Zakopane	3¾	3 daily

The three daily PKS buses to Oświęcim (12zł, one hour) may also be useful. However, the best bus option to Oświęcim is the special **'O Line' bus** (ul Korfantego; 8zł, 55 minutes), which departs for the Auschwitz-Birkenau Museum four times a day from Monday to Saturday between 6am and 4.30pm, from a stop in front of the Hotel Katowice on ul Korfantego. The last return is at 6.30pm.

TRAIN

Trains are the main means of transport in the region and beyond. The busy, modern **train station** (Plac Szewczyka 1) is in the city centre.

Domestic Services

DESTINATION	FARE (ZŁ)	TIME (HR)	FREQUENCY
Częstochowa	24	1½	at least hourly
Kraków	21	2	at least hourly
Opole	24	1½	at least hourly
Oświęcim	11	1	9 daily
Poznań	56	5½	7 daily
Pszczyna	12	40min	at least hourly
Warsaw	60-117	2¾	hourly
Wrocław	30	3	11 daily

International Services

DESTINATION	TIME (HR)	FREQUENCY
Bratislava	5½	1 daily
Budapest	8½	1 daily
Prague	5½	1 daily
Vienna	5	2 daily

Pszczyna

POP 26,000

One of the oldest towns in Silesia (its origins go back to the 11th century), Pszczyna (*pshchi*-nah), the 'pearl of Silesia', is an attractive burg with an impressively palatial castle.

The town was home for centuries to the Piast dynasty. In 1847, after centuries of changing ownership, it became the property of the powerful Hochberg family of Prussia.

In the last months of WWI Pszczyna was the flashpoint of the first of three consecutive Silesian uprisings in which Polish peasants took up arms and demanded that the region be incorporated into Poland. Their wishes were granted in 1921, following a plebiscite held by the League of Nations.

◉ Sights

Castle Museum
MUSEUM

(Muzeum Zamkowe; www.zamek-pszczyna.pl; ul Brama Wybrańców 1; museum adult/concession 14.50/8.50zł, library adult/concession 5/3zł, Cabinet of Miniatures adult/concession 3/2zł; ⏱ 11am-3pm Mon-Tue, 10am-4pm Wed-Sun) This grandiose former residence (which looks more like a palace) dates back to the 12th century, when the Opole dukes built a hunting lodge here. It has been enlarged and redesigned several times, most recently in 1870. Today the palace houses the Castle Museum, with about a dozen rooms open over three floors. Those wanting more detailed information should pick up a copy of the English-language guidebook *The Castle Museum in Pszczyna* (22zł) from the ticket office or tourist office.

The Hochbergs, who owned the Pszczyna Castle (Zamek w Pszczynie) until 1945, furnished their home according to their status – they were among the richest families in Europe, ruling vast swathes of land from their Silesian family seat, the castle at Książ. Priceless works of art completed the scene, but most were lost during WWII.

The castle's interiors feature bedchambers, drawing rooms and salons filled with tapestries, ceramics, paintings and hunting trophies. Unforgettable are the library, panelled entirely in walnut, and the stunning Mirror Chamber, which hosts occasional chamber-music concerts. Some of the palace's rooms also contain themed exhibitions, including a collection of armour in the basement and one of minuscule portraits in the Cabinet of Miniatures on the 3rd floor. Behind the castle is the extensive English-style Castle Park along the Pszczynka River.

Rynek
SQUARE

(Market Square) Pszczyna's elongated and leafy market square is lined with old burghers' houses dating mostly from the 18th and 19th centuries. On its northern side is the Protestant church and, next to it at number 2, the town hall, both remodelled last century. Behind the town hall is the 14th-century parish church, extensively rebuilt over the years, with a typically lavish interior featuring a ceiling painting of the Ascension. To the west of the square sits Pszczyna Castle, now a museum.

Pszczyna Farm Village
MUSEUM

(Zagroda Wsi Pszczyńskiej; www.skansen.pszczyna. pl; ul Parkowa; adult/concession 6/4zł; ⏱ 9am-6pm Mar-Sep, to 4pm Oct-Feb) A five-minute walk east of Pszczyna's Rynek is this small but interesting open-air museum, with half a dozen 200-year-old timber houses – including a mill, a smithy and a barn – collected from the region.

⌁ Sleeping

Hotel PTTK
HOTEL €

(☑ 32 210 3833; www.pttk-pszczyna.slask.pl; ul Bogedaina 16; s 45-75zł, d 66-99zł; ⓟ ⭑) Budget hotel 500m south of the Rynek, and 500m west of the train station. It's charmingly situated in a former redbrick prison – the last inmate left in 1975. There's nothing cell-like about the rooms now, though the cheaper rooms share facilities. Breakfast is not included, but there's a kitchen for guest use.

Pensonjat Piano Nobile
HOTEL €€

(☑ 32 447 7882; www.pianonobile.com.pl; Rynek 16; s 170zł, d 220-280zł; ⭑) Small hotel within an impressively renovated 200-year-old residence in a convenient location right on the market square. Provides comfortably appointed rooms and an atmospheric restaurant.

Hotel U Michalika
HOTEL €€

(☑ 32 210 1355; www.umichalika.com.pl; ul Dworcowa 11; s/d 110/165zł; ⓟ ⭑) This hotel is owned and operated by the family of local chef-turned-entrepreneur Stefan Michalika, and it offers 21 modern and upbeat rooms. There's also a gym for guest use.

✖ Eating & Drinking

Café U Telemanna
CAFE €

(ul Brama Wybrańców 1; dishes 5-16zł; ⏱ 10am-8pm Mon-Thu, 9am-9pm Fri & Sat, 10am-8pm Sun) Located in the courtyard of Pszczyna Castle, this is a good pit stop for a drink or a snack after viewing the building. The cafe is named after composer Georg Philip Telemann (1681–1767), who lived here for four years in the early 18th century.

★ **Frykówka**   POLISH, PIZZA €€
(Rynek 3; mains 15-69zł; ⊙11am-10pm; 🛜) Elegant award-winning restaurant on the main square, with an atmospheric timber-lined interior. Serves a range of regional dishes, plus pizza for variety.

Bednarska 3   PUB, CLUB
(ul Bednarska 3; ⊙11am-late) This pub and club is a bit more relaxed than the places on the square, and makes a good spot for a leisurely beer.

❶ Information

Post Office (ul Batorego 1; ⊙7am-7.30pm Mon-Fri, to 1pm Sat)
Tourist Office (🗹 32 212 9999; ul Brama Wybrańców 1; ⊙8am-4pm Mon-Fri, 10am-6pm Sat & Sun) Just inside Pszczyna Castle gate.

❶ Getting There & Away

The attractively restored **train station** (Plac Dworcowy) is to the east of the centre, with buses leaving from stands next to the station along ul Sokoła. Trains are the best option; services to Katowice (12zł, 40 minutes) run at least hourly, and the train to Vienna (4½ hours) stops here twice a day.

Oświęcim
POP 39,500

Oświęcim (osh-*fyen*-cheem) is a quiet, medium-sized industrial city on the border between Silesia and Małopolska, about 30km southeast of Katowice and about 40km west of Kraków. The Polish place name may be unfamiliar to most foreigners, but the German version, Auschwitz, is not. This was the scene of the largest attempt at genocide in human history. Though visiting it is a grim experience, it's an essential element in understanding the full evil of the Holocaust.

⊙ Sights

Auschwitz-Birkenau
Memorial & Museum   HISTORIC SITE
(Auschwitz-Birkenau Miejsce Pamięci i Muzeum; 🗹guides 33 844 8100; www.auschwitz.org; ul Wieźniów Oświęcimia 20; tours adult/concession 40/30zł; ⊙8am-7pm Jun-Aug, to 6pm Apr-May, to 5pm Mar & Sep, to 4pm Feb & Oct, to 3pm Jan & Nov, to 2pm Dec) **FREE** Auschwitz-Birkenau

is synonymous with genocide and the Holocaust. More than a million Jews, and many Poles and Roma, were murdered here by the German occupiers during WWII. Both sections of the camp, base camp Auschwitz I and a much larger outlying camp at Birkenau (Auschwitz II), have been preserved and are open for visitors. It's essential to visit both to appreciate the extent and horror of the place.

From April to October it's compulsory to join a tour if you arrive between 10am and 3pm; book well ahead either via www.visit. auschwitz.org, or by phoning.

English-language tours leave at numerous times throughout the day, generally most frequently between 11.30am and 1.30pm, when they operate half-hourly. All tours include a short documentary film about the liberation of the camp by Soviet troops in January 1945 (not recommended for children under 14).

The Auschwitz extermination camp was established in April 1940 by the German occupiers in prewar Polish army barracks on the outskirts of Oświęcim. Auschwitz was originally intended for Polish political prisoners, but the camp was then adapted for the wholesale extermination of the Jews of Europe in fulfilment of Nazi ideology. For this purpose, the much larger camp at Birkenau (Brzezinka) was built 2km west of the original site in 1941 and 1942, followed by another one in Monowitz (Monowice), several kilometres to the west.

The museum's visitor centre is at the entrance to the Auschwitz site. Photography and filming are permitted throughout the camp without the use of a flash or stands. There's a self-service snack bar by the entrance as well as a *kantor* (private currency-exchange office), free left-luggage room and bookshops with publications about the place.

If not on a tour, get a copy of the museum-produced *Auschwitz Birkenau Guidebook* (5zł). It has plans of both camps and gets you round the grounds.

➡ **Auschwitz**

Auschwitz was only partially destroyed by the fleeing Germans, and many of the original brick buildings stand to this day as a bleak testament to the camp's history. Some 13 of the 30 surviving prison blocks now house museum exhibitions – either general, or dedicated to victims from particular countries or ethnic groups that lost people at Auschwitz.

From the visitor centre in the entrance building, you enter the barbed-wire encampment through the infamous gate, displaying the grimly cynical message in German: 'Arbeit Macht Frei' (Work Brings Freedom). The sign is in fact a replica, which replaced the original when it was stolen in late 2009. Though it was recovered within a few days, it had been cut into pieces by the thieves and took 17 months to restore. The replica has remained in place, with the original sign now on display within the museum.

➡ **Birkenau**

It was actually at Birkenau, not Auschwitz, that most of the killing took place. Massive (175 hectares) and purpose-built for efficiency, the camp had more than 300 prison barracks – they were actually stables built for horses, but they housed 300 people each. Birkenau had four huge gas chambers, complete with crematoria. Each could asphyxiate 2000 people at one time, and there were electric lifts to raise the bodies to the ovens.

Though much of Birkenau was destroyed by the retreating Germans, the size of the place, fenced off with long lines of barbed wire and watchtowers stretching almost as far as your eye can see, will give you some idea of the scale of the crime; climb the tower at the entrance gate to get the full effect. Some of the surviving barracks are open to visitors for viewing, silent contemplation and prayer. If you're not part of a tour, make sure to leave enough time (at least an hour) to walk around the camp.

Jewish Museum MUSEUM
(Muzeum Żydowskie; www.ajcf.pl; Plac Skarbka 5; adult/concession 10/6zł; ☺10am-6pm Sun-Fri Apr-Sep, to 5pm Sun-Fri Oct-Mar) In the centre of the town of Oświęcim, this institution has permanent exhibitions about Oświęcim's thriving Jewish community in the years before WWII. Within the restored synagogue (1913) are photos and Judaica found beneath the town's Great Synagogue in 2004. It's hard to forget you're looking at the last remnants of Polish Jewry, an all but exterminated culture.

🍴 Sleeping & Eating

Hotel Olecki HOTEL €€
(☑33 847 5000; www.hotelolecki.pl; ul Leszczyńskiej 12; s/d 180/210zł; 🅿🛜) This hotel near the entrance to Auschwitz is the most comfortable and conveniently located accommodation in Oświęcim. Its restaurant serves both Polish and international cuisine, and has a beer garden.

Centre for Dialogue and Prayer HOTEL, CAMPGROUND €€
(Centrum Dialogu i Modlitwy; ☑33 843 1000; www.cdim.pl; ul Kolbego 1; sites per person 40zł, s/d 130/260zł; 🅿🛜) Catholic facility located 500m southwest of the tourist office, providing comfortable and quiet accommodation in rooms of two to six beds (most with en suite) and a restaurant. Full board is available.

❶ Information

Tourist Office (☑33 843 0091; www.it.oswiecim.pl; ul Leszczyńskiej 12; ☺8am-6pm Mon-Fri, to 4pm Sat & Sun) Near the Auschwitz site.

❶ Getting There & Away

FROM KRAKÓW

For most tourists, the jumping-off point for Oświęcim is Kraków.

Bus Buses (12zł, 1½ hours, hourly) can be a more convenient option than trains, as they generally drop you off in the parking lot opposite the entrance to Auschwitz. There are also numerous minibuses to Oświęcim from the minibus stands off ul Pawia, next to Galeria Krakowska.

Train The alternative is catching a train from Kraków (14zł, 1½ hours, hourly) to Oświęcim train station, then walking 1.5km to the museum entrance. If you don't fancy walking, take any southbound city bus (2.70zł).

FROM KATOWICE

There are nine daily trains (11zł, one hour) and three buses (12zł, one hour) from Katowice to Oświęcim. The best option, however, is the dedicated 'O Line' bus (8zł, 55 minutes), which heads directly to the museum from Monday to Saturday. It operates between 6am and 4.30pm from a stop in front of the Hotel Katowice on ul Korfantego. The last return from Oświęcim is at 6.30pm.

❶ Getting Around

A free shuttle bus links Auschwitz with Birkenau, departing at 15-minute intervals from April to October, then half-hourly from November to March. Alternatively, it's an easy 2km walk between the two sites.

Most travel agencies in Kraków offer organised tours of Auschwitz (including Birkenau), from 130zł per person. Check with the operator for exactly how much time the tour allows you at Auschwitz, as some run to a very tight schedule.

Wielkopolska

POP 3.5 MILLION

Best Places to Eat

➡ Drukarnia (p293)

➡ Papierówka (p293)

➡ Ludwiku do
Rondla (p292)

➡ Bajeczny (p303)

➡ Antonio (p303)

Best Places to Stay

➡ Hotel Stare
Miasto (p291)

➡ Rezydencja
Solei (p290)

➡ Frolic Goats
Hostel (p290)

➡ Hotel Europa (p303)

➡ Hotel Atelier (p300)

Why Go?

If you want to distil the essence of Poland's eventful history, head for Wielkopolska. The region's name means Greater Poland, and this is where the Polish state was founded in the Middle Ages. Centuries later, the local population has an understandable pride in its long history.

Though Poznań is a city focused on commerce, it exudes a lively character and has plenty of sights. Beyond, the Wielkopolska countryside offers a selection of charming towns and rural scenery. Among the region's attractions are castles, steam trains, palaces, churches, nature reserves and a memorable Iron Age settlement. And at the heart of it all is the great cathedral of Gniezno, the birthplace of Catholic Poland.

It's an impressive menu, but Wielkopolska is also a great place to strike out on your own. Wherever you end up, you'll be sure to find something of historic interest: it's that kind of place.

When to Go
Poznań

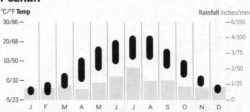

Mar–May Welcome spring by hiking through Wielkopolska National Park near Poznań.

Jun Summer is the time for alternative theatre and other arts at Poznań's Malta Festival.

Sep Iron Age culture is commemorated in autumn at the archaeological festival in Biskupin.

Wielkopolska Highlights

1 Learning about Poland's earliest history on the **Poznań** island Ostrów Tumski (p289) and at the Porta Posnania Interactive Heritage Centre.

2 Travelling back to the Iron Age at the fortified village of **Biskupin** (p301).

3 Exploring the monumental historic cathedral at **Gniezno** (p297).

4 Visiting the small, distinctive castle at **Kórnik** (p295).

5 Encountering meteorite craters at **Morasko** (p297).

6 Viewing the intriguing 1920s architecture of central **Kalisz** (p301).

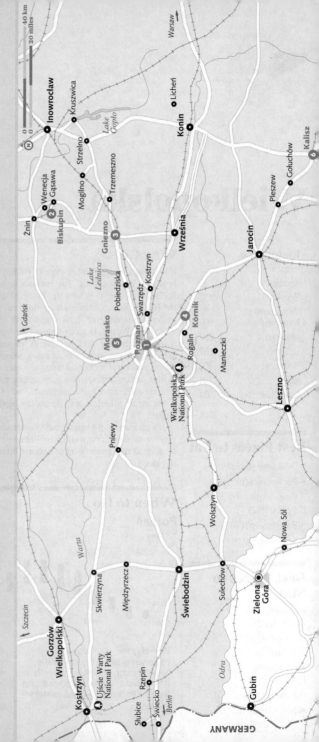

POZNAŃ

POP 546,000

Stroll into Poznań's central market square on any evening and you'll receive an instant introduction to the characteristic energy of Wielkopolska's capital. The city's Old Town district is buzzing at any time of the day, and positively jumping by night, full of people heading to its many restaurants, pubs and clubs. The combination of international business travellers attending its numerous trade fairs and the city's huge student population has created a distinctive vibe quite independent of tourism.

In addition to its energetic personality, Poznań offers many historical attractions in its centre, particularly museums, and its plentiful transport links make it a great base from which to explore the quieter surrounding countryside.

History

The history of Poznań and the history of Poland were much the same thing in the nation's earliest days. The city was founded as a 9th-century settlement on the easily defensible island of Ostrów Tumski, during the reign of Poland's first ruler, Duke Mieszko I. Some historians even claim that it was here, not in Gniezno, that the duke's baptism took place in 966.

Mieszko's son, the first Polish king, Bolesław Chrobry, further strengthened the island, and the troops of the Holy Roman Empire that conquered the region in 1005 didn't even bother to lay siege to it. The Bohemian prince Bratislav (Brzetysław), however, liked a challenge and damaged the town considerably in 1038. This marked the end for Poznań as the royal seat (though kings were buried here until 1296), as subsequent rulers chose Kraków as their capital.

Poznań continued to develop as a commercial centre – in 1253 a new town centre was laid out on the left bank of the Warta River. Soon afterwards a castle was built and the town was encircled with defensive walls. Poznań's trade flourished during the Renaissance period, and by the end of the 16th century the population had passed the 20,000 mark.

But into every city's life a little rain must fall. From the mid-17th century on, Swedish, Prussian and Russian invasions, together with a series of natural disasters, battered the city. In the Second Partition of 1793, Poznań fell under Prussian occupation and was renamed Posen, later becoming part of Germany and experiencing steady industrial growth up to the outbreak of WWI.

The Wielkopolska Uprising, which broke out against Germany in Poznań in December 1918, led to the city's addition to the newly recreated Polish state. Poznań's long trading traditions were then revived with the establishment of regular trade fairs in 1921.

The city fell into German hands once more during WWII, and was incorporated into Hitler's Third Reich. In 1945 the battle for its liberation took a month and did a huge amount of damage.

In the postwar era, Poznań was one of the first cities to feel the forceful hand of the communist regime, during a massive workers' strike in June 1956. The spontaneous demonstration, cruelly crushed by tanks, turned out to be the first of a wave of popular protests on the long and painful road to overcoming communist rule.

Since the return of democracy, Poznań has taken advantage of its business traditions and favourable location near Germany to develop its role as an important educational and industrial centre.

⊙ Sights

◎ Old Town

The historic heart of the city is centred on the lively and attractive Stary Rynek (Old Market Square). It was laid out in 1253 and contains a vibrant mix of sights, restaurants and entertainment outlets.

Town Hall   HISTORIC BUILDING

(Ratusz; Map p286; Stary Rynek 1) Poznań's Renaissance town hall, topped with a 61m-high tower, instantly attracts attention. Its graceful form replaced a 13th-century Gothic structure, which burned down in the early 16th century. Every day at noon two metal goats appear through a pair of small doors above the clock and butt their horns together 12 times, in deference to an old legend. These days, the town hall is home to the city's Historical Museum.

The building was designed by Italian architect Giovanni Battista Quadro and built from 1550 to 1560; only the tower is a later addition, built in the 1780s after its predecessor collapsed. The crowned eagle on top of the spire, with an impressive wingspan of 2m, adds some Polish symbolism.

WIELKOPOLSKA POZNAŃ

WIELKOPOLSKA

Greater Poznań

See Poznań Map (p286)

1 km
0.5 miles

Cybina River

Warta River

Porta Posnania Interactive Heritage Centre 2

ŚRÓDKA

Panny Marii

Poznań Cathedral 3

4

Bydgoska

Wyszyńskiego

Ostrów Tumski Island

Camping Malta (1.7km)

Rondo Śródka

Malta Park Railway 7

Lake Malta

11

Szelągowska

Poznań Garbary Train Station

Północna

Estkowskiego

Grobla

6 Mostowa

Garbary

Kazimierza Wielkiego

Kórnik (20km); Rogalin (32km)

13

al. Armii Poznań

5

9

10

8 św. Wojciech

Plac Wielkopolski

Małe Garbary

18

Strzelecka

Przepadek

Solna

Kościuszki

Wieniawskiego

Młyńska

Nowowiejskiego

św. Marcin

Półwiejska

Rybaki

16

Stary Browar

Kościuszki

12

17

Morasko (8.5km)

Piaskiego

Park Moniuszki

Roosevelta

Pułaskiego

al. Niepodległości

City Information Centre

Poznań Główny Train Station

Słowackiego

Składowa

19

Rondo Kaponiera

Dąbrowskiego

Dworcowa

Głogowska

Poznańska

Park Wieniawskiego

14

Bukowska

Fairgrounds

Wielkopolska

Patucka

Grudzieniec

Wieniawskiego

Zoological Gardens

Wielkopolska National Park (21km)

15

(5km); LOT Office (5km)

Palm House 1

Greater Poznań

WIELKOPOLSKA POZNAŃ

Concerning the legend of the goats: apparently two goats intended for a banquet escaped and ended up clashing horns above the about-to-be-unveiled clock, much to the amusement of the assembled dignitaries. The clockmaker was duly ordered to add the errant animals' images to his piece.

★**Historical Museum of Poznań**   MUSEUM
(Muzeum Historii Miasta Poznania; Map p286; www.mnp.art.pl; Stary Rynek 1; adult/concession 7/5zł, Sat free; ⊙11am-5pm Tue-Thu, noon-9pm Fri, 11am-6pm Sat & Sun) Inside the town hall, this museum displays an interesting and well-presented exhibition on the town's history, and the building's original interiors are worth the entry price on their own. The Gothic vaulted cellars are the only remains of the first town hall. They were initially used for trade but later became a jail. The 1st floor is home to three splendid rooms. The largest, the richly ornamented Renaissance Hall, is a real gem, with its original stucco work and paintings from 1555. The 2nd floor contains artefacts from the Prussian/German period, documents illustrating city life in the 1920s and '30s, and a collection of interesting memorabilia from the past two centuries.

In front of the building, near the main entrance, is the *pręgierz* (whipping post), once the site of public floggings, and of more serious penalties. The original miniature model executioner that accompanied the post, dating from 1535, is on display in the museum.

Fish Sellers' Houses   HISTORIC BUILDINGS
(Domki Budnicze; Map p286) South of the town hall is this endearing row of small arcaded buildings. They were built in the 16th century on the site of fish stalls and later reconstructed after major WWII damage.

Wielkopolska Military Museum   MUSEUM
(Wielkopolskie Muzeum Wojskowe; Map p286; www.mnp.art.pl; Stary Rynek 9; adult/concession 7/5zł, Sat free; ⊙11am-5pm Tue-Thu, noon-9pm Fri, 11am-6pm Sat & Sun) Showcases arms from Poland's many conflicts, dating from the 11th century to the present. Among its exhibits is a rare 16th-century rapier from Milan.

Museum of Musical Instruments   MUSEUM
(Muzeum Instrumentów Muzycznych; Map p286; www.mnp.art.pl; Stary Rynek 45; adult/concession 7/5zł, Sat free; ⊙11am-5pm Tue-Thu, noon-9pm Fri, 11am-6pm Sat & Sun) Institution housing hundreds of instruments, from whistles to concert pianos. It includes intriguing musical devices such as a typewriter for musician notation and a polyphon, the precursor of the record player.

Croissant Museum   MUSEUM
(Rogalowe Muzeum; Map p286; ☑690 077 800; www.rogalowemuzeum.pl; Stary Rynek 41; adult/concession 14/12zł; ⊙11.10am-3pm) Located in a historic townhouse on the main square, this institution is devoted to the sweet St Martin's croissants peculiar to Poznań. In four sessions each day (at 11.10am, 12.30pm, 1.45pm and 3pm) visitors are told about the croissant's history, and can take part in making a batch. Note the 1.45pm session is the only one usually translated into English, so bookings are advisable. Enter from ul Klasztorna 23, one block east of the Rynek.

Archaeological Museum   MUSEUM
(Muzeum Archeologiczne; Map p286; www.muzarp.poznan.pl; ul Wodna 27; adult/concession

WIELKOPOLSKA

Poznań

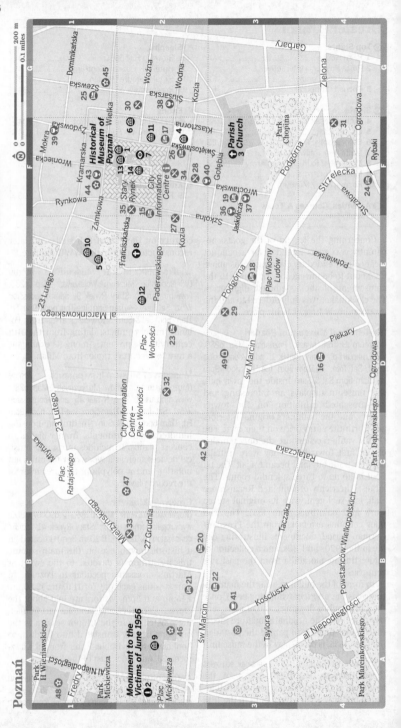

0 — 200 m
0 — 0.1 miles

Park
H Wieniawskiego

Park
Mickiewicza

Plac
Ratajskiego

Plac
Wolności

City Information
Centre –
Plac Wolności

Monument to the
Victims of June 1956

Historical
Museum of
Poznań

Parish
Church

City Information
Centre

Park Chopina

Park Dąbrowskiego

Park Marcinkowskiego

Poznań

8/4zł, Sat free; ☺9am-4pm Tue-Fri, 10am-5pm Sat, noon-4pm Sun) Located off the southeastern corner of the Rynek, inside the 16th-century **Górka Palace** (Map p286). Before going in, stop and have a look at the fine Renaissance doorway on the building's eastern facade. The museum presents the prehistory of the region, from the Stone Age to the early medieval period, as well as housing an extensive Egyptian collection.

Franciscan Church CHURCH
(Kościół Franciszkanów; Map p286; ul Franciszkańska 2) Just west of the Rynek is this richly decorated baroque church. Its chapel in the left transept has a carved oak altar and a tiny, reputedly miraculous image of St Mary.

★**Parish Church** CHURCH
(Kościół Farny; Map p286; ul Gołębia) Two blocks south of the Rynek, this church was originally built for the Jesuits by architects from Italy, and completed only after more than 80 years of work (1651–1732). The impressive baroque structure has an ornamented facade, and a lofty interior supported on massive columns that is crammed with monumental altars.

Museum of Applied Arts MUSEUM
(Muzeum Sztuk Użytkowych; Map p286; www.mnp.art.pl; Góra Przemysława 1) Housed within Poznań's **castle** (Map p286) – which looks more like a palace – this museum's collection includes furniture, gold and silverware, glass, ceramics, weapons, clocks, watches and sundials from Europe and the Far East. At the time of research it was undergoing major renovations, but it is scheduled to reopen in 2017. Check with the tourist office for more information.

Ethnographic Museum MUSEUM
(Muzeum Etnograficzne; Map p284; www.mnp.art.pl; ul Grobla 25; adult/concession 7/5zł, Sat free; ☺11am-5pm Tue-Thu, noon-9pm Fri, 11am-6pm Sat & Sun) Southeast of the Rynek is this collection of folk woodcarving and traditional costumes of the region. Of particular note are the large roadside posts and crosses on display.

West of the Old Town

Stretching west from Plac Wolności to the trade-fair buildings and the train station is this area of broad thoroughfares and grand buildings from the 19th and 20th centuries.

National Museum   MUSEUM
(Muzeum Narodowe; Map p286; www.mnp.art. pl; al Marcinkowskiego 9; adult/concession 12/8zł, Sat free; ◷ 11am-5pm Tue-Thu, noon-9pm Fri, 11am-6pm Sat & Sun) Extensive collection of Polish and European art displayed in numerous rooms. Polish painting of the last two centuries is represented by almost all the big names, including Jan Matejko, Stanisław Wyspiański and Jacek Malczewski. Look out for the distinctive work of Tadeusz Makowski, a 20th-century artist who created curious human figures from basic geometric shapes. An older, noteworthy curiosity is the museum's collection of coffin portraits.

★ Monument to the
Victims of June 1956   MONUMENT
(Pomnik Ofiar Czerwca 1956; Map p286; Plac Mickiewicza) On Plac Mickiewicza you'll find one of Poznań's most significant memorials, which commemorates the ill-fated workers' protest of 1956 (p288). The monument,

consisting of two 20m-tall crosses bound together, was unveiled on 28 June 1981, the 25th anniversary of the strike, at a ceremony attended by more than 100,000 people. It's a huge, evocative landmark, similar to Gdańsk's Monument to the Shipyard Workers (p318).

★ Palm House   GREENHOUSE
(Palmiarnia; Map p284; www.palmiarnia.poznan. pl; ul Matejki 18; adult/concession 7/5zł; ◷ 9am-5pm Tue-Sat, 9am-6pm Sun) A short walk from the main train station along ul Głogowska, Park Wilsona contains one of the biggest greenhouses in Europe. Constructed in 1910, it houses thousands of species of tropical and subtropical plants, including the continent's largest cactus collection and its tallest bamboo trees.

North of the Old Town

Monument to the Poznań Army   MONUMENT
(Pomnik Armii Poznań; Map p284; Plac Niepodległości) Stark modern monument 500m north of the Old Town, dedicated to the local armed force that resisted the German invasion of 1939 for almost two weeks. It's just opposite the sloping Cemetery of the Meritorious, the oldest existing graveyard in the city (1810).

STRIKING OUT

The June 1956 industrial strike in Poznań was the first mass protest in the Soviet bloc, breaking out just three years after Stalin's death.

It originated in the city's largest industrial plant, the Cegielski metalworks (then named after Stalin), which produced railway stock. When the workers demanded the refund of an unfairly charged tax, the factory management refused and simply threw the workers' delegates out of the meeting room. This sparked a spontaneous strike the next day, in which the metalworkers, joined by workers from other local industrial plants, headed for Plac Mickiewicza (then named Plac Stalina).

The 100,000-strong crowd that gathered (a quarter of the city's total population) demanded 'bread and freedom', insisting that changes had to be introduced to improve working conditions, and requested that authorities come and discuss the issue. The demonstration was disregarded by city officials.

Matters soon got out of hand. The angry crowd stormed police headquarters and the Communist Party building, releasing 257 prisoners from jail after disarming the guards. Shortly afterwards, a battle for the secret-police headquarters broke out; it was there that the bloodshed began when police started firing at people surrounding the building. Tanks were introduced to the action, while troops were hastily brought from Wrocław and told they were there to pacify a German riot. Fierce street battles continued for the whole night and part of the next day, resulting in a total of at least 76 dead and 900 wounded. More than 300 people were arrested, 58 of whom were indicted.

These figures make the protest the most tragic in communist Poland, yet it was underreported and for a long time overlooked. The historic importance of the revolt has only recently been recognised and given the status it deserves, an event on par with the internationally famous shipyard strikes in Gdańsk.

Citadel Park
PARK

(Map p284; Wzgórze Cytadela) This large park is laid out on what was once a massive Prussian fortress. The fortress was involved in one major battle, when the Germans defended themselves for four weeks in 1945; as a result it was destroyed, apart from a few fragments.

Today Citadel Park incorporates two museums: the **Museum of Armaments** (Muzeum Uzbrojenia; Map p284; www.muzeumniepodleglosci. poznan.pl; Park Cytadela; adult/concession 6/3zł, Fri free; ☺9am-4pm Tue-Sat, 10am-4pm Sun) and the **Poznań Army Museum** (Muzeum Armii Poznań; Map p284; www.muzeumniepodleglosci. poznan.pl; Park Cytadela; adult/concession 6/3zł, Fri free; ☺9am-4pm Tue-Sat, 10am-4pm Sun). There are also cemeteries for Polish, Soviet, British and Commonwealth soldiers, all on the southern slopes of the hill.

◎ Ostrów Tumski

To the east of the Old Town, over the Warta River, is the island of Ostrów Tumski (Cathedral Island). You're walking through deep history here, the place where Poznań was founded, and with it the Polish state. The original 9th-century settlement was gradually transformed into an oval stronghold surrounded by wood-and-earth ramparts, with an early stone palace. Mieszko I added a cathedral and further fortifications, and by the end of the 10th century Poznań was the most powerful stronghold in the country.

In the 13th century, when Poznań had spread beyond the island and the newly designed town was laid out, Ostrów Tumski lost its trade and administrative importance but remained the residence of the Church authorities.

★Poznań Cathedral
CHURCH

(Katedra Poznańska; Map p284; www.katedra. archpoznan.pl; ul Ostrów Tumski 17; crypt adult/ concession 3.50/2.50zł; ☺9am-4pm) Ostrów Tumski is dominated by this monumental double-towered cathedral. Basically Gothic with additions from later periods, most notably the Baroque tops of the towers, the cathedral was damaged in 1945 and took 11 years to rebuild. The aisles and the ambulatory are ringed by a dozen chapels containing numerous tombstones. The most famous is the Golden Chapel behind the high altar, which houses the remains of the first two Polish rulers: Mieszko I and Bolesław Chrobry.

The rulers' original burial site was the crypt, accessible from the back of the left-hand aisle. Apart from the fragments of what are thought to have been their tombs, you can see the relics of the first pre-Romanesque cathedral dating from 968 and of the subsequent Romanesque building from the second half of the 11th century, along with dozens of coins tossed in by more recent Polish visitors.

Archdiocesan Museum
MUSEUM

(Muzeum Archidiecezjalne; Map p284; www. muzeum.poznan.pl; ul Lubrańskiego 1; adult/ concession 8/5zł; ☺10am-5pm Tue-Fri, 9am-3pm Sat) North of the cathedral, this museum is located within the former Lubrański Academy, the first high school in Poznań (1518). Within its walls you'll find a collection of sacred art from the 12th century onwards.

★Porta Posnania
Interactive Heritage Centre
MUSEUM

(Brama Poznania ICHOT; Map p284; www. bramapoznania.pl; ul Gdańska 2; adult/concession 15/9zł, audioguide 5/3zł; ☺9am-6pm Tue-Fri, 10am-7pm Sat & Sun) Cutting-edge multimedia museum that opened in 2014, telling the tale of the island's eventful history and the birth of the Polish nation via interactive displays and other technological gadgetry. It's located opposite the island's eastern shore and is linked to the cathedral area by footbridge. The exhibitions are multilingual, but opt for an audioguide to help put everything together. To reach the museum from the city centre, take tram 8 eastward to the Rondo Śródka stop.

◎ Lake Malta

Malta Park Railway
TOURIST RAILWAY

(Kolejka Parkowa Maltanka; Map p284; www. mpk.poznan.pl/maltanka; ul Jana Pawła II; adult/ concession 6/4zł; ☺10am-6.30pm Apr-Oct) East of Ostrów Tumski on the far bank of the river, beyond the Rondo Śródka intersection, you'll find the western terminus of this tourist railway. It runs miniature trains along the shoreline of the 70-hectare artificial Lake Malta (Jezioro Maltańskie), a favourite summer spot for families, picnickers and boating enthusiasts. The railway terminates at the New Zoo.

New Zoo
ZOO

(Nowe Zoo; www.zoo.poznan.pl; ul Krańcowa 81; adult/ concession 20/10zł; ☺9am-7pm Apr-Sep, 9am-4pm Oct-Mar) This sprawling institution covers 116 hectares at the eastern end of Lake Malta. It houses diverse species, including Baltic grey seals, in a leafy pine-forest environment.

🏃 Activities

If you're challenged for time in Poznań, a good way to get a quick feel for the city's history is to follow one or more of the six self-guided walking routes outlined in free brochures from the tourist office. A more ambitious stroll is the Royal-Imperial Rte, mapped out in another free brochure, which takes you from the shores of Lake Malta to the city's west, passing dozens of sights along the way.

Poznań's flat terrain is also good for cycling. Ask the tourist office for both the Poznań cycling map (9zł) and the free brochure *Cycle Trails in Wielkopolska*.

Malta Bike　　　　　　　BICYCLE RENTAL
(Map p284; www.maltabike.pl; ul Baraniaka; 9/50zł per hour/day; ⊗10am-9pm Apr-Oct) Bicycles can be hired from this outfit at the southern side of the western end of Lake Malta. Prices are cheaper on weekdays.

🎊 Festivals & Events

Poznań's trade fairs are its pride and joy, though few are of interest to casual visitors. The main ones take place in January, June, September and October, with dozens of other trade shows of varying size throughout the year. July, August and December are almost free of fairs.

St John's Fair　　　　　　　CULTURAL
(Jarmark Świętojański; www.jarmarkswietojanski. poznan.pl; ⊗mid- to late Jun) Take in street-artist performances and buy craft items and local foods from the stalls on the Stary Rynek.

**Malta International
Theatre Festival**　　　　　　THEATRE
(www.malta-festival.pl; ⊗Jun) Fringe and alternative theatre. This unconventional celebration of the arts takes place across the city, often in squares and streets, as well as on the shores of Lake Malta.

Old Jazz Festival　　　　　　JAZZ
(www.oldjazzfestival.pl; ⊗late Sep) A range of local and international jazz performers strut their stuff at various venues.

St Martin's Day　　　　　　PARADE
(⊗11 Nov) Parades and festivities descend on the town, but the highlight is the baking and eating of St Martin's sweet croissants.

🛏 Sleeping

Try not to arrive in Poznań during one of the city's numerous trade fairs – they wreak havoc on the city's accommodation range, doubling prices and reducing available beds. You can check the dates of the fairs online at www.mtp.pl.

Outside trade-fair periods, room prices drop significantly on weekends. Prices given here are standard weekday rates for 'off-fair' periods. The tourist offices are knowledgeable about lodging options and can help you find a bed. In addition, the private agency **Przemysław** (Map p284; 🕿61 641 7884; www.przemyslaw. com.pl; ul Śniadeckich 28; ⊗9am-3pm Mon-Fri), located not far from the train station, can organise accommodation in private rooms.

🏚 Old Town

Frolic Goats Hostel　　　　　HOSTEL €
(Map p286; 🕿61 852 4411; www.frolicgoatshostel. com; ul Wrocławska 16/6; dm 30-50zł, r 100-150zł; 🕿) Named after the feisty goats who fight above the town-hall clock, this popular hostel is aimed squarely at the international backpacker. The pleasant lounge complements tidy, reasonably uncrowded dorms, there's a washing machine, and bike hire is available for 50zł per day. Enter from ul Jaskółcza.

Tey Hostel　　　　　　　HOSTEL €
(Map p286; 🕿61 639 3497; www.tey-hostel. pl; ul Świętosławska 12; dm 25-40zł, s 69-95zł, d 99-139zł; 🕿) Centrally located hostel offering budget accommodation within a contemporary interior, decorated in pale green and pink tones. There's a spacious kitchen and lounge, and all beds have reading lamps and lockers. The cheaper private rooms have shared bathrooms.

Rezydencja Solei　　　　　HOTEL €€
(Map p286; 🕿61 855 7351; www.hotel-solei.pl; ul Szewska 2; s/d from 149/239zł, ste 330zł; 🕿) Temptingly close to the Rynek, this tiny hotel offers small but cosy rooms in an old-fashioned residential style, with wallpaper and timber furniture striking a homey note. The attic suite is amazingly large and can accommodate up to four people.

Brovaria　　　　　　　HOTEL €€
(Map p286; 🕿61 858 6868; www.brovaria. pl; Stary Rynek 73/74; s 250-290zł, d 290-330zł; @🕿) This multi-faceted hotel also operates as a restaurant and bar. Most impressive of all is its in-house boutique brewery, whose operations you can view within the building.

The elegant rooms have tasteful dark-timber tones, and some have views onto the Rynek.

Dom Polonii
ROOM €€

(Map p286; ☑ 61 852 7121; pozhan@swp.org.pl; Stary Rynek 51; s/d 140/230zł) Dating from 1488, this accommodation belonging to a community association is tucked into a corner of the market square, offering just two double rooms to anyone who's organised enough to book sufficiently in advance. The only way you could get more central would be by tunnelling under the town hall. No breakfast.

West of the Old Town

Fusion Hostel
HOSTEL €

(Map p286; ☑ 61 852 1230; www.fusionhostel. pl; ul Św Marcin 66/72; dm 49-55zł, s/d 119/195zł; ☎) Hostel with a view, perched on the 7th floor of a scuffed commercial building. The decor is modern and bright, and guests have access to a lounge, a kitchen and a washing machine. There's dorm accommodation in four- and six-bunk rooms, as well as private singles and doubles. The lift is hidden behind the security booth in the foyer.

Hotel Royal
HOTEL €€

(Map p286; ☑ 61 858 2300; www.hotel-royal. com.pl; ul Św Marcin 71; s 220-285zł, d 260-320zł, ste 400-500zł; ❄☎) Tasteful terracotta tones predominate in this smart, refined hotel, situated on the main road leading into the city centre. Opt for a spacious suite for extra elbow room, or just hang around the lobby perusing the photos of famous Polish TV stars who've laid their heads here.

Hotel Rzymski
HOTEL €€

(Map p286; ☑ 61 852 8121; www.hotelrzymski.pl; al Marcinkowskiego 22; s 275zł, d 344-380zł; ☎) If walls could talk, this hotel would have a story worth listening to. It began life as the German-owned Hotel de Rome, changed to Polish ownership, was used in WWII as a hotel for the German military, then became Polish owned once more, with the same name (Rzym is Rome in Polish). The rooms are comfortable and the multilingual staff helpful.

Hotel Lech
HOTEL €€

(Map p286; ☑ 61 853 0151; www.hotel-lech. poznan.pl; ul Św Marcin 74; s/d 140/215zł; ☎) Comfortable choice, with basic fittings and high ceilings. It's located midway between the train station and the Old Town, and staff are used to dealing with tourists. Flash your ISIC student card for a substantial discount.

Hotel Mercure Poznań
HOTEL €€€

(Map p284; ☑ 61 855 8000; www.mercure.com; ul Roosevelta 20; s/d from 380/475zł; ❄❄☎) In a gigantic modern building off a busy main road 500m west of the Kaiserhaus, this hotel offers all the expected facilities for business travellers, including a gym, a restaurant and a bar. The location is handy for the train station and near the airport bus stop, but it's a bit of a walk to the Old Town. Breakfast is an additional 35zł.

South of the Old Town

★Hotel Stare Miasto
HOTEL €€

(Map p286; ☑ 61 663 6242; www.hotelstaremiasto. pl; ul Rybaki 36; s 224zł, d 270-319zł; ❄❄☎) Stylish value-for-money hotel with a tasteful foyer and spacious breakfast room. Rooms can be small but are clean and bright with lovely starched white sheets. Some upper rooms have skylights in place of windows.

Don Prestige Residence
HOTEL €€

(Map p286; ☑ 61 859 0590; www.donprestige. com; ul Św Marcin 2; s/d 300/362zł; ❄❄☎) While some hotels try to make you feel like you're at home, the Don Prestige makes you wish your home was a bit more like this. Its rooms are outfitted with stylish contemporary furniture and fittings, including parquet floors and air-conditioning. There's a classy restaurant on the premises.

Capital Apartments
APARTMENTS €€

(Map p286; ☑ 61 852 5300; www.capitalapart.pl; ul Piekary 16; apt 150-360zł; ☎) This company maintains a number of modern apartments dotted around the city centre, all within walking distance of the Stary Rynek. They're a good-value option if you're tired of hotel breakfasts and want to prepare your own food, or if the lack of laundrettes in Poland has you desperate for a washing machine.

Hotel Ibis Poznań Centrum
HOTEL €€

(Map p284; ☑ 61 858 4400; www.ibishotel.com; ul Kazimierza Wielkiego 23; r from 250zł; ❄❄☎) A typical hotel in this reliable business chain, the local Ibis offers a multitude of predictably well-maintained rooms, an easy 700m walk southeast of the Rynek. If you don't like surprises, this is a good place to hang your hat.

Blow Up Hall 5050
HOTEL €€€

(Map p284; ☑ 61 657 9980; www.blowuphall5050. com; ul Kościuszki 42; s/d from 490/530zł; ❄❄☎) Wild art hotel housed within the solid ex-brewery walls of the Stary Browar shopping mall, 750m south of the Rynek.

Each room has an individual hyper-modern design whose colour scheme can range from dazzling white to gleaming black, with shiny angular furniture and fittings. The restaurant and bar are equally impressive.

Lake Malta

Camping Malta CAMPGROUND €
(☑ 61 876 6203; www.campingmalta.poznan.pl; ul Krańcowa 98; camping per person 20zł, per tent 10zł, s 170, d 230-270zł; P ＠) Malta is the best of Poznań's camping grounds and the closest to the centre – it's on the northeastern shore of Lake Malta, 3km east of the Old Town. Heated bungalows provide good all-year shelter.

Eating

Poznań's sophisticated dining scene centres on the Old Town, whose narrow streets contain eateries offering every cuisine imaginable. For self-catering, there's a supermarket within the central **Galeria MM shopping mall** (Map p286; www.galeriamm.poznan.pl; ul Św Marcin 24; ⊗ 9am-9pm Mon-Fri, 10am-7pm Sat & Sun).

Old Town

Apetyt CAFETERIA €
(Map p286; ul Szkolna 4; mains 3-10zł; ⊗ 9am-8pm Mon-Sat, 11am-10pm Sun; ✎) This late-closing *bar mleczny* (milk bar) enjoys a central location. The Polish cafeteria food is exactly what you'd expect – cheap serves of unfussy, filling food such as *pierogi* (dumplings) and *zupy* (soups), with *naleśniki* (crêpe) choices galore. Includes several good vegetarian items.

Ludwiku do Rondla JEWISH, POLISH €€
(Map p286; ul Woźna 2/3; mains 26-38zł; ⊗ 1-10pm) Small, cosy place east of the main square, specialising in both Jewish and Polish cooking – particularly where the two intertwine. Menu items are helpfully marked if an item is Polish or Jewish in origin, and include such items as herring in oil (Polish/Jewish) and stuffed meat roulade with buckwheat (Polish). The lunchtime set menu is top value at 22zł.

Wiejskie Jadło POLISH €€
(Map p286; Stary Rynek 77; mains 21-52zł; ⊗ 10am-11pm) Compact Polish restaurant hidden a short distance back from the Rynek along ul Franciszkańska. It offers a range of filling dishes including *pierogi* (dumplings), soups and pork in all its varied possibilities, served in a rustic space with flowers on the tables.

Tapas Bar SPANISH €€
(Map p286; Stary Rynek 60; mains 12-88zł; ⊗ 9am-midnight) Atmospheric place dishing up authentic tapas and Spanish wine in a room lined with intriguing bric-a-brac, including jars of stuffed olives, Mediterranean-themed artwork and bright red candles. Tapas dishes cost about 25zł, so forget the mains and share with friends. There's a breakfast menu too.

Donatello ITALIAN €€
(Map p286; ul Wrocławska 7; mains 15-63zł; ⊗ 1-11pm; ✎) Referencing the Renaissance sculptor rather than the mutant-ninja-turtle character, this smooth restaurant serves a wide variety of pizza, pasta and other Italian specialities, well suited to a glass of vino. Look for the sax player stationed above the street.

West of the Old Town

Shivaz INDIAN €€
(Map p286; ul Mielzynskiego 16/3a; mains 20-38zł; ⊗ 11am-10pm ; ✎) Dark, modern space, generally acclaimed as the city's best Indian restaurant. The menu includes all the favourites and can be spiced to suit individual palates. The daily lunch special comes in two variants: vegetarian (18zl) and meat (24zl). Enter from the back on ul Grudnia 27.

Restauracja Delicja FRENCH, ITALIAN €€€
(Map p286; Plac Wolności 5; mains 51-66zł; ⊗ 1-10pm) One of Poznań's top restaurants, Delicja is tucked away off Plac Wolności, with its own miniature courtyard and an illustrious reputation for top-notch French and Italian cuisine.

South of the Old Town

Stary Browar Food Court INTERNATIONAL €
(Map p284; ul Półwiejska 42; mains 10-15zł; ⊗ 9am-9pm) The dining section of this gigantic shopping mall 750m south of the Rynek offers decent food in chic surrounds, including Chinese, Italian and seafood dishes. There are also cafes scattered through the complex, and the building's spectacular old-meets-new architecture is worth a visit in its own right.

Bar Wegetariański Chwirot VEGETARIAN €
(Map p284; ul Rybaki 10; mains 11-17zł; ⊗ 11am-7pm Mon-Fri, noon-5pm Sat; ✎) Cheap eatery 500m south of the Rynek offers tasty meat-free dishes, including its signature wholemeal crêpes stuffed with mushrooms and cabbage. It's in a homely little space, with dishes prepared in a domestic-style open kitchen behind the counter.

★ **Drukarnia** INTERNATIONAL €€
(Map p286; ul Podgórna 6; mains 10-79zł; ⊘7am-11pm Mon-Fri, 11am-11pm Sat & Sun) Some Polish restaurants are finally opening for breakfast, and this sleek eatery with exposed beams above concrete floors is a top choice for first meal of the day. Choices include a full English breakfast with sausage, bacon, eggs and beans, and a more adventurous pasta with smoked mackerel. Later on there's a menu featuring steaks and burgers, as well as a long wine list. A historical footnote: inter-war German president Paul von Hindenburg was born in this building in 1847.

Papierówka POLISH €€
(Map p286; ul Zielona 8; mains 20-40zł; ⊘9am-10pm; 🐾) No-frills slow-food restaurant offering some of the best cooking in town. Order at the counter and watch a team of chefs prepare your meal in the open kitchen. There are a half-dozen daily options, reflecting what's in season. The speciality is duck, though expect a couple of pork and fish choices. The wine list is tiny but impeccable.

🍷 Drinking & Nightlife

Once you've done the rounds of the beer gardens on the Rynek, there are plenty of places elsewhere in town worth seeking out for a drink or a dance.

★ **Stragan** CAFE
(Map p286; ul Ratajczaka 31; ⊘8am-10pm Mon-Fri, 11am-10pm Sat, 11am-7pm Sun; 🐾) Cool, contemporary cafe in which even the most bearded hipster would feel at home. Coffee ranges from Chemex brews to flat whites, complemented by excellent cakes and light meals. Also serves breakfast.

Ptasie Radio CAFE, BAR
(Map p286; ul Kościuszki 74; ⊘8am-midnight Mon-Fri, 10am-midnight Sat & Sun; 🐾) A funky drinking hole, 'Bird Radio' is a retro riot of chipped wooden tables, potted plants and bird images everywhere along its shelves and walls (the name comes from a famous Polish poem). It's a mellow place for a coffee or something stronger. There's also a breakfast menu.

La Rambla WINE BAR
(Map p286; ul Wodna 5/6; ⊘1-11pm; 🐾) Ambient wine bar serving only the Spanish drop, with up to 70 bottles in stock. A simple menu of tapas dishes is available to complement the vino.

Proletaryat BAR
(Map p286; ul Wrocławska 9; ⊘3pm-late; 🐾) Bright-red communist-nostalgia bar with an array of socialist-era gear on the walls, including military insignia, portraits of Brezhnev and Marx, and the obligatory bust of Lenin in the window. Play 'spot the communist leader' while sipping a boutique beer from the Czarnków Brewery.

Chmielnik BAR
(Map p284; ul Żydowska 27; ⊘2pm-late) Ideal place to sample the output of the booming Polish craft-beer scene, with more than 150 beers in stock. Lounge and sip in the pleasant wood-lined interior or in the ambient beer garden out the back.

PRL BAR
(Map p286; ul Żydowska 11; ⊘4pm-late) Not easy to find even with a map and compass, this tiny subterranean bar is decorated with communist-era memorabilia, from uniforms to chunky appliances. It's grungy but fun. Enter through the narrow door on ul Mokra.

Czarna Owca BAR, CLUB
(Map p286; ul Jaskółcza 13; ⊘6pm-late Thu-Sat) Calling your bar the 'Black Sheep' hardly encourages good behaviour, so sipping a quiet pint is seldom on the agenda here. When you've finished boozing in the dark, intimate bar, join the herd on the downstairs dance floor for DJs playing house, pop, rock, Latin or retro sounds, depending on the night.

Van Diesel Music Club CLUB
(Map p286; Stary Rynek 88; ⊘9pm-5am Fri & Sat) Happening venue on the main square, with DJs varying their offerings between pop, house, R&B, soul and dance. Given the variety, you're sure to find a night that will get you on the dance floor.

Czekolada CLUB
(Map p286; ul Wrocławska 18; ⊘9pm-late) If you feel like dressing up and dancing, this super-smooth venue is what you're looking for. Chandeliers and good cocktails add touches of class.

☆ Entertainment

Poznań's comprehensive monthly *iks* (4.10zł) contains listings of everything from museums to outdoor activities, with a short summary of the most important events in English. It's available from the tourist offices.

WORTH A TRIP

ALL STEAMED UP

Almost everywhere in Europe, the grand age of steam is over. The steam-powered trains that still operate are confined to picturesque tourist railways, functioning as museum pieces on wheels. But not in the town of Wolsztyn, 65km southwest of Poznań.

Thanks partly to the enthusiasm of British trainspotters, steam-train services still run along Poland's regular lines from Wolsztyn. Eager customers sign up for the **Wolsztyn Experience** (☑ +44 1842 860436; www.thewolsztynexperience.org; courses from £400), a steam-train course that instructs would-be drivers and gives them a chance to actually operate a train on cross-country routes.

In the past, the course has included operating a daily regularly scheduled steam-train service from Wolsztyn to Poznań Główny station. Though these services have recently been suspended, they're likely to return at some point. In the meantime, trainee drivers get to operate their steam-powered vehicles on special one-off routes as far as Wrocław and Kołobrzeg. It's also possible to drive narrow-gauge steam trains on lines at Żnin and Gniezno.

On the first Saturday in May, Wolsztyn is also home to the Steam Parade, a festival featuring steam locomotives from across Europe. And if too much steam is never enough, the town also offers the **Wolsztyn Roundhouse steam train museum** (Parowozownia Wolsztyn; www.parowozowniawolsztyn.pl; ul Fabryczna 1; adult/concession 5/3zł; ⊘ 8am-3pm Mon-Fri), within its working steam-engine depot south of the town's train station.

Live Music

Alligator　　　　　　　　　　LIVE MUSIC
(Map p286; Stary Rynek 86; ⊘ noon-late) Simultaneously happening and laid-back, this venue is in a prime position on the Rynek. Friendly crowds sit drinking and eating in the dimly lit interior, and the bar serves decent cocktails. There's live music every night, largely rock and blues.

BaRock　　　　　　　　　　　LIVE MUSIC
(Map p286; ul Wielka 9; ⊘ 6pm-late) Smooth basement venue that hosts regular live-music gigs and stand-up comedy acts.

Blue Note Jazz Club　　　　　　　　JAZZ
(Map p286; www.bluenote.poznan.pl; ul Kościuszki 79) Major live-jazz spot and occasional dance club within the Kaiserhaus. It hosts regular concerts and jam sessions by local groups, as well as the occasional big name. It's only open for gigs, so check the online program first.

Classical Music, Opera & Theatre

Centrum Kultury Zamek　　　CONCERT VENUE
(Castle Cultural Centre; Map p286; ☑ 61 646 5260; www.zamek.poznan.pl; ul Św Marcin 80/82; ⓢ) Within the grand neo-Romanesque **Kaiserhaus** (Map p286), built from 1904 to 1910 for German emperor Wilhelm II, this active cultural hub hosts cinema, art and music events.

Filharmonia　　　　　　CLASSICAL MUSIC
(Philharmonic Hall; Map p284; ☑ 61 853 6935; www.filharmoniapoznanska.pl; ul Św Marcin 81; ⊘ box office 1-6pm) This musical institution holds concerts at least weekly by the house symphony orchestra. Poznań also has Poland's best boys' choir, the Poznańskie Słowiki (Poznań Nightingales), who can be heard here. Buy tickets at the box office or one hour before performances.

Teatr Wielki　　　　　　OPERA, BALLET
(Map p286; ☑ 61 659 0231; www.opera.poznan. pl; ul Fredry 9) Usual stage for opera, ballet and various visiting performances.

Teatr Polski　　　　　　　THEATRE
(Map p286; ☑ 61 852 5628; www.teatr-polski. pl; ul 27 Grudnia 8/10) The Polish Theatre is Poznań's main repertory stage.

ⓘ Information

INTERNET ACCESS

Salon Gier (ul Dworcowa 1; per hour 5zł; ⊘ 24hr) In the platform tunnel leading from the main train-station concourse.

POST

Main Post Office (Map p286; ul Kościuszki 77; ⊘ 7am-8pm Mon-Fri, 8am-3pm Sat)

TOURIST INFORMATION

The Poznań City Card (one day, 35zł) is available at all city information centres (www.poznan. travel). It provides free entry to major museums, sizeable discounts at restaurants and recreational activities, and unlimited public-transport use.

City Information Centre (Map p286; ☑ 61 852 6156; Stary Rynek 59/60; ☺10am-8pm Mon-Sat, 10am-6pm Sun May-Sep, 10am-5pm Oct-Apr) Located conveniently on the main square.

City Information Centre – Plac Wolności (Map p286; ☑ 61 851 9645; ul Ratajczaka 44; ☺10am-7pm Mon-Fri, 10am-5pm Sat) Branch office located near Plac Wolności.

City Information Centre – Train Station (Map p284; ☑ 61 633 1016; ul Dworcowa 2; ☺8am-9pm Mon-Fri, 10am-5pm Sat & Sun) Branch office located at Poznań Główny train station.

City Information Centre – Airport (☑ 61 849 2140; ul Bukowska 285; ☺8am-9pm Mon-Fri, 10am-5pm Sat & Sun) Branch office at Ławica Airport.

TRAVEL AGENCIES

Almatur (☑ 61 855 7633; ul Ratajczaka 26; ☺10am-6pm Mon-Fri, 10am-2pm Sat)

Glob-Tour FB (☑ 61 866 0667; www.globtourfb. poznan.pl; ul Głogowska 15; ☺24hr) Travel agency in the Dworzec Zachodni station, connected by tunnel to the main train station.

ℹ Getting There & Away

AIR

Poznań Airport (☑ 61 849 2343; www.airport-poznan.com.pl; ul Bukowska 285) Poznań's airport is in the suburb of Ławica, 7km west of the centre. There are flights from Poznań to Warsaw (four daily) via LOT. London is served by Ryanair (once daily) and Wizz Air (twice daily); Ryanair also connects to Dublin (twice daily). For other destinations, check the airport's website.

BUS

The **bus station** (Dworzec PKS; Map p284; www.pks.poznan.pl; ul Dworcowa 1) is beneath the main train station. Buses run at least hourly to Kórnik (13zł, 25 minutes). On longer routes, buses head to Kalisz (29zł, 2½ hours, hourly) and Zielona Góra (35zł, three hours, five daily).

Private company **Polski Bus** (www.polskibus. com) runs buses to Wrocław (3½ hours, three daily), Warsaw (four to 5½ hours, seven daily), Szczecin (3¾ hours, three daily), Gdańsk (five hours, four daily), Berlin (four hours, twice daily) and Prague (nine hours, twice daily). Fares vary from day to day; book online in advance for the best price.

TRAIN

Poznań is a busy railway hub. From **Poznań Główny train station** (ul Dworcowa 1) there are hourly trains to Warsaw, including eight TLK trains (60zł, 3½ hours) and eight Express InterCity trains (129zł, 2¾ hours). Equally frequent services run to Wrocław (34zł, 2½ hours), Szczecin (40zł, 2¾ hours) and Kraków (67zł, six hours).

Trains to Gdańsk (60zł, 3¾ hours, eight daily) and Toruń (26zł, 2½ hours, nine daily) all pass through Gniezno (14zł, 45 minutes, hourly). Eight trains depart for Zielona Góra daily (24zł, two hours). There are also seven daily trains to Wolsztyn (18zł, 1½ hours).

Five international trains run to Berlin daily (168zł, 2¾ hours). There's also one direct train to Cologne daily (9¾ hours).

ℹ Getting Around

TO/FROM THE AIRPORT

Poznań's airport is accessible by express bus L from the main train station (4.60zł, 20 minutes), which travels via the Bałtyk stop near Rondo Kaponiera. Buses 48 and 59 and night bus 242 also head to the airport from the Bałtyk stop (4.60zł, 25 minutes). A taxi should cost 20zł to 30zł (20 minutes).

PUBLIC TRANSPORT

Tickets for the city's trams and buses cost 3zł for a 15-minute ride, and 4.60zł for a ride of up to 40 minutes. Approximate journey times are posted at stops. A day ticket costs 13.60zł.

AROUND POZNAŃ

Kórnik

POP 7600

The town of Kórnik, 20km southeast of Poznań, is proof that mad German kings didn't have a monopoly on eccentric castle design. Its unconventional castle was built by the powerful Górka family in the 15th century. Nowadays it's more like a mansion than a castle; anyone who's visited a stately home in the English countryside will experience déjà vu (it even has tasteful tea rooms outside the main gate).

◉ Sights

Castle Museum MUSEUM
(www.bkpan.poznan.pl; ul Zamkowa 5; adult/ concession 12/7zł; ☺10am-4pm Tue-Sun Feb-Nov) Kórnik Castle's present-day appearance dates from the mid-19th century, when its owner, Tytus Działyński, gave the castle an outlandish mock-Gothic character, partly based on a design by German architect Karl Friedrich Schinkel. The building now looks as though two halves of completely different castles were spliced together and provides interesting photos from varying angles.

Part of it is now open as a museum. You can wander through its 19th-century interiors, dotted with items collected by the family. The collection was expanded by Działyński's son Jan and his nephew Władysław Zamoyski; the latter donated the castle and its contents to the state in 1924.

Its treasures are well presented in a surprisingly light-filled space, and include some intriguing pieces like elaborately designed furniture, medieval weaponry and centuries-old books, including a copy of Copernicus' masterwork, *De Revolutionibus Orbium Coelestium* (On the Revolutions of the Heavenly Spheres).

On the 1st floor a spectacular Moorish hall (clearly influenced by the Alhambra in Granada) was created as a memorable setting for the display of armour and military accessories.

Some of the castle's outbuildings are also used for exhibitions. Galeria Klaudynówka, a servants' house from 1791, displays contemporary paintings, while the coach house on the opposite side of the road holds three London coaches, brought from Paris by Jan Działyński in 1856.

Kórnik Arboretum   GARDENS

(Arboretum Kórnickie; www.idpan.poznan.pl; ul Parkowa 5; adult/concession 6/4zł; ⊙10am-5pm) Behind Kórnik's castle is this large, English-style park known as the Arboretum, which was laid out during the castle's reconstruction and stocked with exotic species of trees and shrubs from Europe's leading nurseries. Today the Arboretum is run by a scientific research institute and has some 3000 plant species and varieties; the best times to visit are May to June and September to October, when the greatest number of specimens come into flower.

❶ Getting There & Away

There's frequent bus transport from Poznań to Kórnik (13zł, 25 minutes), which deposits you at the Rynek in Kórnik, a three-minute walk from the castle. Follow the road as it veers to the right past the town hall and becomes ul Zamkowa.

Rogalin

POP 700

The tiny village of Rogalin, 12km west of Kórnik, was the seat of yet another Polish aristocratic clan, the Raczyński family, who built a palace here in the closing decades of the 18th century, and lived in it until WWII. Plundered but not damaged during the war, the palace was taken over by the state. In 1991, Count Edward Raczyński, who had been Polish ambassador to Britain at the outbreak of WWII and a leading figure of the Polish government in exile, confirmed its use as a National Museum branch.

◉ Sights

Palace Museum   MUSEUM

(Muzeum Pałac; www.mnp.art.pl; ul Arciszewskiego 2; adult/concession 10/7zł, Wed free; ⊙9.30am-4pm Tue-Sat, 10am-6pm Sun) Less visited than Kórnik's castle and much more Germanic in its appearance, the Rogalin palace consists of a massive, two-storey Baroque central structure and two modest symmetrical wings linked to the main body by curving galleries, forming a giant horseshoe around a vast forecourt. Entry to the main building involves a compulsory tour; English-language tour guides can be organised in advance for 85zł.

Within the main house you can peruse an exhibition on the history of the palace and the Raczyński family, and see a replica of the London study of Count Raczyński.

Just beyond the left wing is the Gallery of Painting (Galeria Obrazów), an adapted greenhouse displaying Polish and European canvases from the 19th and early 20th centuries. The Polish collection includes some first-class work, with Jacek Malczewski best represented. The dominant work, though, is Jan Matejko's *Joan of Arc*.

In the coach house, near the front courtyard, are a dozen coaches, including Poznań's last horse-drawn cab, and a restaurant.

Opposite the main house is a small French garden, which leads into the larger English landscaped park, originally laid out in primeval oak forest. Not much of the park's design can be deciphered today, but the ancient oak trees are still here, some of them centuries old. The three most imposing specimens have been fenced off and baptised with the names Lech, Czech and Rus, after the legendary founders of the Polish, Czech and Russian nations.

One more place to see is the **chapel** (📋61 813 8345; ⊙noon-5pm Sat & Sun Apr-Oct) FREE, on the eastern outskirts of the village, built in the 1820s to serve as a mausoleum for the Raczyński family. It's a replica of the Roman temple known as the Maison Carrée in Nîmes, southern France. It lies 300m east of the entrance to the palace grounds. If you'd like to visit outside of regular opening hours, book ahead.

ⓘ Getting There & Away

There are two buses each day from Poznań to Rogalin (11zł, 40 minutes), but they're both in the afternoon. The alternative is to first catch a morning bus to Śrem (13zł, one hour, hourly), then on to Rogalin from there (8zł, 30 minutes, three daily).

Wielkopolska National Park

Just a few kilometres southwest of Poznań's administrative boundaries is the 76-sq-km **Wielkopolska National Park** (Wielkopolski Park Narodowy; www.wielkopolskipn.pl) `FREE`. About 80% of the park is forest – pine and oak being the dominant species – and its postglacial lakes give it a certain charm.

Hiking is the main attraction here, and a good point to start your stroll is the town of Mosina (21km from Poznań), which is served regularly by both train and bus from Poznań.

From Mosina, follow the blue-marked trail heading northwest to Osowa Góra (3km). Once you reach small Lake Kociołek, switch to the red trail, which winds south-westwards. After passing another miniature lake, the trail reaches Lake Góreckie, the most beautiful body of water in the park. The trail then skirts the eastern part of the lake and turns northeast to bring you to the town of Puszczykowo, from where trains and buses can take you back to Poznań. It's about a 17km walk altogether through the most attractive area of the park.

If you want to do more walking, there are four more trails to choose from. Get a copy of the *TopMapa Wielkopolski Park Narodowy* map (scale 1:35,000), which has all the details.

The two towns sit conveniently on the eastern edge of the park, just 4km apart on the Poznań–Wrocław railway line. There are regular slow trains from Poznań Główny to Puszczykowo (6zł, 16 minutes, hourly) and Mosina (7zł, 25 minutes, hourly).

Morasko

Great balls of fire! Just 10km from the centre of Poznań is the **Morasko Meteorite Reserve** (Reserwat Meteoryt Morasko; ul Meteorytowa) `FREE`, one of just two registered meteorite impact sites in Europe. The idea of flaming space rock crash-landing in the peaceful forest here may seem bizarre, but that's exactly what happened roughly 10,000 years ago, and eight craters are still clearly visible, some filled with water.

The largest crater is more than 100m across and 13m in depth, and while it's over-grown enough not to look like the surface of the moon, the extent of the dent is still pretty impressive.

To get to the reserve you can catch tram 12 or 14 from the train station to the Osledle Sobieskiego tram terminus and follow the 4km walking trail, or change to bus 902 (roughly hourly), which stops at the reserve.

EASTERN WIELKOPOLSKA

Gniezno

POP 69,000

Appearances can be deceptive: at first glance, you'd never guess that relaxed Gniezno (*gnyez*-no) played a huge part in the founding of Poland. Its Old Town, attractively renovated in 2000 for the millennial anniversary of the establishment of the city's historic bishopric, is a charming collection of winding streets and colourful, slope-roofed buildings centred on a pleasant cobblestone square and the city's famous cathedral. Its historic cathedral is well worth a visit and is also a great place to catch your breath after the hustle of Poznań.

It may be slow-paced now, but in its day Gniezno served as both a royal and a reli-gious seat. It is also considered to be the cra-dle of the Polish state, as it was here that the various tribes of the region were first united as Poles in the 10th century. In a key devel-opment, Duke Mieszko I is thought to have been baptised here in 966, thus raising the autonomous region of Wielkopolska from obscurity to the rank of Christianised na-tions. Later, in 1025, Bolesław Chrobry was crowned in the local cathedral as the first Polish king.

The town has retained its status as the seat of the Church of Poland and is still the formal ecclesiastical capital, despite the fact that the archbishops are only occasion-al guests these days.

◎ Sights

★**Cathedral**　　　　　　　　　　CHURCH
(Katedra Gnieźnieńska; ul Łaskiego 9; tower adult/concession 3/2zł; ⊙9am-5pm Mon-Sat, 1-6pm

Gniezno

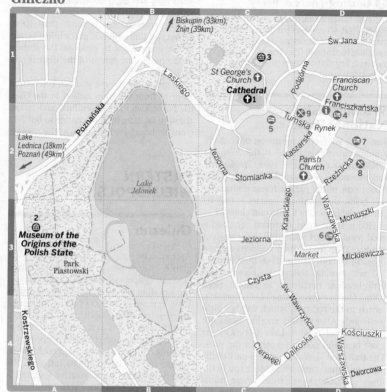

Sun, tower 9.30am-5pm Mon-Sat, 1-5.45pm Sun) Gniezno's history and character are inextricably intertwined with its cathedral, an imposing, double-towered brick Gothic structure. The present church was constructed after the Teutonic Knights destroyed the previous Romanesque cathedral in 1331. It has changed significantly over the centuries: chapels sprouted up around it, and the interior was redecorated in successive styles. After considerable damage in WWII, it was rebuilt according to the original Gothic design.

You can climb the tower for city views.

Its focal point is the elaborate silver sarcophagus of St Adalbert, which is in the chancel. The Baroque coffin was the work of Peter van der Rennen and was made in 1662 in Gdańsk. It's topped with a semi-reclining figure of the saint, who looks remarkably lively considering his unfortunate demise.

Adalbert was a Bohemian bishop who passed through Gniezno in 997, on a missionary trip to convert the Prussians, a heathen Baltic tribe inhabiting what is now Masuria in northeastern Poland. The pagans were less than enthusiastic about accepting the new faith and terminated the bishop's efforts by cutting off his head. Bolesław Chrobry recovered the bishop's body, paying its weight in gold, then buried it in Gniezno's cathedral in 999. In the same year, Pope Sylvester canonised the martyr. This contributed to Gniezno's elevation to an archbishopric a year later, and also led to the placing of several important memorials to the saint in the church.

One example is the pair of Romanesque bronze doors from around 1175, in the back of the right-hand (southern) aisle, at the entrance from the porch. Undeniably one of the best examples of Romanesque art in Europe, the doors depict, in bas-relief, 18 scenes from the life of St Adalbert.

Framing the doors is the exquisite 15th-century Gothic portal with the scene of the Last Judgement in its tympanum. In

Gniezno

⊚ **Top Sights**
1 Cathedral C1
2 Museum of the Origins of the
   Polish State A3

⊚ **Sights**
3 Archdiocesan Museum C1

🛏 **Sleeping**
4 City Hotel D2
5 Hotel Atelier C2
6 Hotel Awo D3
7 Hotel Pietrak D2

✖ **Eating**
8 Restauracja Ratuszowa D2
9 Trattoria Cechowa D2

17 screens in all, ranging in style from Gothic and Renaissance to Baroque, and constituting one of the most beautiful collections of its kind to be gathered in a single church in Poland. Inside the chapels are some fine tombstones, altarpieces, paintings and wall decorations – well worth a closer look.

One interesting modern artwork sits in the body of the church: a statue of Cardinal Stefan Wyszyński, the Polish primate credited with persuading the Soviets to relax their anti-religious stance during the communist era. The panelled piece shows various scenes from the cardinal's eventful life and career.

the opposite porch, right across the nave, is another elaborate Gothic portal, dating from the same period, this one with the scene of the Crucifixion in its tympanum.

The nearby entrance in the back wall of the church leads downstairs to the basement, where the relics of the previous Romanesque cathedral can be seen, along with the Gothic tombstones of the bishops.

Also on this back wall are two carved tombstones. To the left is the red-marble tomb of Primate Zbigniew Oleśnicki, attributed to Veit Stoss, and to the right is the late-15th-century bronze tomb of Archbishop Jakub from Sienna. Also note an expressive wooden crucifix from around 1440, placed high on the rood beam at the entrance to the chancel.

All along the aisles and the ambulatory are chapels, built from the 15th to 18th centuries, and separated from the aisles by decorative wrought-iron screens. There are

★**Museum of the Origins of the Polish State**   MUSEUM
(Muzeum Początków Państwa Polskiego; www.mppp.pl; ul Kostrzewskiego 1; adult/concession 10/6zł; ⊙9am-6pm Tue-Sun) On the far side of Lake Jelonek, this museum illustrates Gniezno's pivotal role in Polish history. The permanent collection contains archaeological finds and works of art related to the development of the Polish nation, from pre-Slavic times to the end of the Piast dynasty. The museum also runs an audiovisual presentation about Poland under the Piasts.

Archdiocesan Museum   MUSEUM
(Muzeum Archidiecezji Gnieźnieńskiej; www.muzeumag.com; ul Kolegiaty 2; adult/concession 6/4zł; ⊙9am-5pm Mon-Sat, 9am-4pm Sun) North of the cathedral, behind St George's Church, this museum holds a collection of sacred sculptures and paintings, liturgical fabrics, coffin portraits and votive offerings.

WORTH A TRIP

THE PIAST TRAIL

The Piast Trail (Szlak Piastowski) is a tourist trail weaving together a selection of sites related to Poland's early history. Dozens of attractions are strung out in a giant figure eight stretching from Poznań in the west to Inowrocław in the east, with Gniezno at the centre. The trail provides good inspiration for a driving holiday through Wielkopolska. If pressed for time, you could do a simple loop from Poznań through Gniezno and back, or use Gniezno as a base for day trips along the trail in all directions. For more details, drop into the Gniezno tourist office and ask for the free Szlak Piastowski brochure.

Highlights along the route include the following:

➡ **Lake Lednica** A postglacial lake containing the island of Ostrów Lednicki, a 10th-century stronghold. Museums here exhibit archaeological remains and 19th-century rural architecture.

➡ **Gniezno** Where Poland's connection with the Catholic faith began.

➡ **Biskupin** Much older than the Piasts with its reconstructed Iron Age town site.

➡ **Strzelno** Boasts two of the best Romanesque churches in the region.

➡ **Kruszwica** With its Mouse Tower, the only remainder of a 14th-century castle built by King Kazimierz III Wielki.

🛏 Sleeping

City Hotel HOTEL €
(☑ 61 425 3535; www.hotelgniezno.com; Rynek 15; s/d from 80/100zł; 🛜) This hotel doesn't make much effort to live up to its prestigious position on the Rynek – rooms contain fairly basic furnishings. But the price is right, and the rooms and the cafe look out onto the square. Enter via the kebab shop downstairs.

★ **Hotel Atelier** HOTEL €€
(☑ 61 424 8550; www.hotelatelier.pl; ul Tumska 5; s 210zł, d 240-280zł; 🅿 ❄ 🛜) Classy four-star hotel within a residential building that once housed a photographer's studio, or atelier. The tastefully appointed green-hued rooms contain elegant timber furniture, and there's a restaurant and cafe-bar.

Hotel Pietrak HOTEL €€
(☑ 61 426 1497; www.pietrak.pl; ul Bolesława Chrobrego 3; s/d 180/210zł; 🅿 🛜) Located in two 18th-century burghers' houses just shy of the Rynek, the Pietrak provides good facilities, including a fitness centre with a spa. The restaurant serves up quality food and operates a colourful beer garden in the street during summer.

Hotel Awo HOTEL €€
(☑ 61 426 1197; www.hotel-awo.pl; ul Warszawska 32; s/d 160/210zł; 🅿 🛜) Midrange place with neat, clean rooms, a pleasant courtyard with a beer garden, and a restaurant on the premises. Note that it's right by the city market, making it potentially noisy for south-facing rooms.

🍴 Eating

Restauracja Ratuszowa POLISH €€
(ul Bolesława Chrobrego 41; mains 18-65zł) Restaurant with an elegantly old-fashioned interior within the town-hall building and a spacious deck on the street in the warmer months. There are plenty of meaty options on the menu, along with fish and pasta dishes.

Trattoria Cechowa POLISH, ITALIAN €€
(ul Tumska 15; mains 12-25zł; ⊙ 11am-11pm) Attractive eatery with a great view of the cathedral from its outdoor tables. The menu is a blend of Polish and Italian, from pizza to local favourites.

ℹ Information

Post Office (ul Bolesława Chrobrego 36; ⊙ 8am-8pm Mon-Fri, 8am-2pm Sat)

Tourist Office (☑ 61 428 4100; www.szlakpiastowski.com.pl; Rynek 14; ⊙ 9am-5pm Mon-Fri, 10am-2pm Sat & Sun; 🛜) Also provides free internet access.

ℹ Getting There & Away

The **bus station** (www.pks.gniezno.pl; ul Poczto-wa) and **train station** (ul Dworcowa) are next to each other, about 800m south of the Rynek.

There are eight daily buses running to Żnin (13zł, one hour), where you can change for the narrow-gauge train to Biskupin.

Trains run regularly throughout the day to Poznań (14zł, 45 minutes, hourly). There are also departures to Toruń (20zł, 1½ hours, nine daily), Gdańsk (51zł, three hours, eight daily) and Wrocław (40zł, three hours, six daily).

Biskupin

Forget static museum displays in dimly lit rooms – Biskupin's re-created Iron Age town site, with its wooden palisades, thatched roofs and costumed historical re-enactors, is a stimulating way to learn about the distant pre-Polish past.

The fortified lake town was built about 2700 years ago by a tribe of the Lusatian culture, then accidentally rediscovered in 1933 by a school teacher who noticed some wooden stakes poking out of the lake. The town's remnants were then unearthed from beneath a thick layer of turf. It is the only known surviving Iron Age town in Poland, and proves that the region was already inhabited by well-organised social groups more than 1600 years before the Polish state was born.

◎ Sights & Activities

Archaeological Reserve　　　HISTORIC SITE
(Rezerwat Archeologiczny; ☑52 302 5055; www. biskupin.pl; adult/concession 10/8zł; ◎8am-6pm) The Iron Age town is situated within the Archaeological Reserve. You can either wander through the grounds on your own or organise an English-speaking guide in advance for 150zł. The ticket office sells publications about the site in English.

Once past the gate, follow the path to the museum, which presents finds excavated on and around the island, together with background information. There's also a model of the town as it once looked.

The Iron Age town lies further along, on the peninsula in the northern end of the park. The gateway, a fragment of the defensive wall and two rows of houses have been reconstructed to give some idea of what the town once looked like. The interiors of a few houses have been fitted out as they may have been 2700 years ago. Within the thatched structures you'll find various stalls selling handcrafted arrows, jewellery and replica coins, and a man in period garb giving hatchet-throwing demonstrations out the front.

Diabeł Wenecki　　　BOAT TOUR
(Venetian Devil; trips 7zł) The pleasure boat *Diabeł Wenecki* departs several times a day for a short trip around the lake from the wharf near the Archaeological Reserve gateway.

⚔ Festivals

Archaeological Festival　　　CULTURAL
(Festyn Archeologiczny; adult/concession 15/12zł; ◎Sep) In addition to demonstrations of ancient cultures including dance, handicrafts and food, this festival is an annual excuse to stage rousing re-enactments of battles between Germanic and Slavic tribes, providing a colourful (and photogenic) spectacle.

❶ Getting There & Away

BUS
From the bus stop at the entrance to the Archaeological Reserve, buses run every hour or two north to Żnin (7zł, 20 minutes, Monday to Friday) and south to Gąsawa (4zł, five minutes, Monday to Friday). From either of these places, regular buses go to Gniezno (11zł, one hour). If you miss your bus, Gąsawa is an easy 2km walk away.

TRAIN
A narrow-gauge tourist train operates from May to September, from Żnin to Gąsawa, passing Biskupin on the way (7zł to 10zł, 40 minutes). The Biskupin station is right by the entrance to the reserve. In Żnin, the station is 150m east of the bus station; in Gąsawa it's 700m southwest of the Rynek on the Gniezno road.

SOUTHEASTERN WIELKOPOLSKA

Kalisz

POP 103,000

Given how little the average traveller knows about Kalisz (*kah*-leesh), its centre comes as a pleasant surprise, revealing a charming collection of city parks, gently curving streets and simple but harmonious architecture.

Kalisz has the longest documented history of any town in Poland: it was mentioned by Claudius Ptolemy in his renowned *Geography* of the 2nd century AD as Calisia, a trading settlement on the Amber Route between the Roman Empire and the Baltic Sea.

In more modern times, Kalisz was razed to the ground by the invading Germans in the first days of WWI. Within a month, the population dropped from 70,000 to 5000 and most buildings were reduced to ruins. The town was rebuilt on the old street plan, but in a new architectural style. Luckily, given the circumstances, most of the new buildings survived WWII without much damage.

◎ Sights

The Old Town sits in the angle between the Prosna and Bernardynka Rivers, with a

WORTH A TRIP

ŻNIN DISTRICT RAILWAY

For an entertaining day trip on narrow rails, step aboard a train running along the **Żnin District Railway** (Żnińska Kolej Powiatowa; www.smkznin.eu; ul Potockiego 4, Żnin; one way/return 12/20zł; ☉1hr). This narrow-gauge line was opened in 1894 to carry sugar beets to the local sugar factory, and also functioned as public transport. The passenger service was cancelled in 1962, but the line lives on as a tourist attraction.

Once the train leaves the dinky narrow-gauge station at Żnin (east of the town's bus station), it trundles very slowly through a succession of low green hills covered with crops, pausing briefly at a stop serving the village of Wenecja before reaching the **Wenecja Narrow Gauge Railway Museum** (Muzeum Kolei Wąskotorowej w Wenecji; www.muzeumznin.pl; adult/concession 10/8zł; ☉9am-4pm), a showcase of narrow little engines, carriages and their associated memorabilia. Across the rails from the museum are the ruins of a 14th-century castle.

The next stop on the line is the Archaeological Reserve at Biskupin, a major attraction; then the train finally reaches the village of Gąsawa. The main sight of interest here is **St Nicholas' Church** (Kościół Św Mikołaja; ul Żnińska 1, Gąsawa), a 17th-century wooden structure with an unusual mix of architectural styles: Gothic, baroque, neoclassical and more modern additions. When the church was renovated in 1999, the workers discovered original frescoes that had been covered up by a mixture of reeds and plaster. The paintings depict saints and other biblical figures, and have been revealed by careful 'excavation'.

If you take an early train from Żnin, it's possible to stop off at the railway museum, Biskupin and Gąsawa, then return to Żnin on the last train of the day. Five trains depart from Żnin daily from May to August between 9am and 1.50pm (in July and August there's an extra departure at 3.35pm), then make the return journey from Gąsawa.

dozen small bridges and the City Park (Park Miejski) stretching to the southeast.

Główny Rynek
SQUARE

(Main Market Square) Start your sightseeing with the **Town Hall tower** (Wieża Ratuszowa; Główny Rynek 20; ☉1-5pm Sat & Sun) **FREE** in the low-key but attractive Main Market Square. There are fine views from the top and an exhibition of the history of Kalisz.

Kalisz Regional Museum
MUSEUM

(Muzeum Okręgowe Ziemi Kaliskiej; www.muzeum. kalisz.pl; ul Kościuszki 12; adult/concession 5/3zł; Sun free; ☉10am-3pm Tue, Thu, Sat & Sun, 11am-5.30pm Wed & Fri) Presenting an in-depth examination of the city's story, this museum features archaeological and historical exhibits from Kalisz and surrounding areas. It's 500m southwest of the Rynek, across the Prosna River.

Centre of Drawing & Graphic Arts
GALLERY

(Centrum Rysunki i Grafiki; ul Kolegialna 4; adult/concession 5/3zł, Sun free; ☉10am-3pm Tue-Sun) Displays temporary exhibits of drawings and graphic arts, including works by Tadeusz Kulisiewicz (1899–1988), a Kalisz-born artist known mainly for his drawings. Enter from ul Łazienna.

Zawodzie Archaeological Reserve
MUSEUM

(Rezerwat Archeologiczny Zawodzie; www.muzeum. kalisz.pl; ul Pobożnego 87; adult/concession 5/3zł; ☉10am-3pm Tue-Fri, 10am-6pm Sat & Sun) Located upon the site of a 10,000-year-old village, this attraction includes full-size facsimiles of timber structures of the era, along with authentic archaeological remains. To take a pleasant 30-minute walk there from the vicinity of the Hotel Europa, head east along al Wolności, following it to the right past the theatre as it becomes ul Częstochowska. Once across the Prosna River, turn left and follow the riverbank as far as ul Zawodzie. This street takes you to the reserve.

St Nicholas' Church
CHURCH

(Kościół Św Mikołaja; ul Kanonicka 5) Dating from the 13th century, this church was originally Gothic but has been modernised several times. The painting *Descent from the Cross* over the high altar is a copy. The original, painted in Rubens' workshop around 1617 and donated to the church, was burnt or stolen during a mysterious fire in 1973.

Bernardine Church
CHURCH

(Kościół Pobernardyński; ul Stawiszyńska 2) The 1607 former Bernardine Church, now owned by the Jesuits, has a spectacular interior. It is unprepossessing from the outside, but its wide nave glows with sumptuous baroque decoration. The altars and the wall paintings on the vault date from around the mid-18th century.

Collegiate Church CHURCH
(Bazylika Kolegiacka Wniebowzięcia; Plac Jana Pawła II 3) Typical example of a lavish Catholic church, first constructed in 1353 and rebuilt in the 18th century. It boasts a baroque interior flooded with gilt and glitter and is a popular pilgrimage site thanks to an allegedly miraculous picture of the Holy Family, dating from the 17th century.

🛏 Sleeping

Baba Hostel HOSTEL €
(☑ 887 081 887; www.babahostel.pl; ul Babina 19; dm 40zł, s/d 80/90zł; 🛜) Bright new hostel not far from the centre of town, with comfortable contemporary-styled rooms. Bathrooms are shared, and there's a washing machine and kitchen for guest use. Breakfast costs an extra 8zł.

★ Hotel Europa HOTEL €€
(☑ 62 767 2032; www.hotel-europa.pl; al Wolności 5; s 185zł, d 230-295zł, ste 420-590zł; 🅿🌡🛜) If you've schlepped through numerous three-star hotels in a hot Polish summer, you'll weep with joy on encountering this excellent hotel's deluxe doubles with air-conditioning, kettles and gleaming bathrooms. Go crazy and shell out for the Egyptian-themed suite. You'll find it just south of the Old Town across the Prosna River.

Hotel Roma HOTEL €€
(☑ 62 501 7555; www.restauracje-kalisz-turek.pl; ul Chopina 9; s/d from 160/220zł; 🅿🛜) A nice surprise in a shabbier part of town, this white villa-style accommodation 500m northwest of the Rynek offers just seven spacious rooms with skylights, above the in-house Italian restaurant with a garden courtyard.

Hotel Calisia HOTEL €€
(☑ 62 767 9100; www.hotel-calisia.pl; ul Nowy Świat 1; s/d 170/220zł; 🅿🛜) This hotel's corridors are boxy and the rooms are a touch faded, but the service is good and the staff will even cook you up an omelette at breakfast. There's a restaurant and bar on the premises, which are located 750m south of the main square.

🍴 Eating & Drinking

There are plenty of eating options on the Rynek and the surrounding streets.

★ Bajeczny CAFETERIA €
(ul Złota 8; mains 5-12zł; ⊘ 8am-6pm Mon-Fri, noon-4pm Sat & Sun; 🎵) This renovated *bar mleczny* sweeps aside the communist-era reputation of milk bars as drab and functional. Sit within its fresh, bright interior decked out with white furniture, potted plants and zany lightshades, and enjoy all the Polish classics from *pierogi* (dumplings) to *naleśniki* (crêpes).

Antonio ITALIAN €€
(ul Śródmiejska 21; mains 16-45zł; ⊘ 11am-11pm) If you're not hungry after smelling the garlic aroma drifting up to the street from this cellar restaurant just southwest of the Rynek, you must have just eaten. The dining area features red-checked tablecloths, candlelight, roses, Renaissance-inspired artwork and quality Italian food.

Mamma Mia PIZZA €€
(Główny Rynek 3; mains 10-31zł; ⊘ noon-10pm; 🛜🎵) A wide array of pizzas are served up within this cosy eatery off the Rynek, with a decent number of vegetarian choices. Enter off ul Piskorzewska.

Złoty Róg PUB, BREWERY
(al Wolności 3; ⊘ 10am-11pm Mon-Fri, 1-11pm Sat & Sun; 🛜) Good place for a drink, right next to the Hotel Europa. Sample one of the four boutique beers brewed out the back, and recuperate from sightseeing within the cool timber interior.

☆ Entertainment

Centre of Culture & Arts CINEMA
(Centrum Kultury i Sztuki; www.ckis.kalisz.pl; ul Łazienna 6) This cultural institution a block southeast of the Rynek hosts a variety of events, including screenings of arthouse movies.

❶ Information

Cafe Calisia (al Wolności 6; per hour 5zł; ⊘ 8am-10pm Mon-Fri, 11am-9pm Sat & Sun) Internet access east of the Hotel Europa.

Post Office (ul Zamkowa 18/20; ⊘ 8am-8pm Mon-Fri, 8am-3pm Sat)

Tourist Office (☑ 62 598 2731; www.cit.kalisz. pl; ul Chodyńskiego 3; ⊘ 9am-5pm Mon-Fri, 10am-2pm Sat & Sun; 🛜) Offers helpful advice and internet access. Enter from ul Zamkowa.

❶ Getting There & Around

The **bus station** (www.pks.kalisz.pl; ul Podmiejska 2a) and **train station** (ul Dworcowa 1) are close to each other, about 2km southwest of the Old Town. To get to the centre, take a city-bound local bus (2.70zł) from the stop on ul Górnośląska on the far side of the Galeria Amber mall next to the bus station.

BUS

There are 13 buses to Poznań daily (29zł, 2½ hours), most of which travel via Gołuchów (5zł, 20 minutes). There are also nine buses to Wrocław (32zł, 2¾ hours) and four to Toruń (43zł, four hours). The half-hourly suburban bus A to Pleszew also passes through Gołuchów (5zł, 40 minutes); it picks up from Plac Jana Pawła II in central Kalisz.

TRAIN

Trains to Łódź (22zł, two hours) run about every two hours throughout the day. There are also trains to Warsaw (49zł, four hours, four daily), Wrocław (35zł, two hours, six daily) and Poznań (24zł, 2½ hours, three daily).

Gołuchów

POP 2200

This small village near Kalisz is unremarkable save for its attractive castle, which provides sufficient reason for a day trip.

◎ Sights

Castle Museum   MUSEUM
(Muzeum Zamek; www.mnp.art.pl; ul Działyńskich 2; adult/concession 10/7zł, Tue free; ◎10am-4pm Tue-Sat, 10am-6pm Sun) Gołuchów's castle began life around 1560 as a small fortified mansion with octagonal towers at its corners, built by the Leszczyński family. Some 50 years later it was enlarged and reshaped into a palatial residence in the late Renaissance style. Abandoned at the end of the 17th century, it gradually fell into ruins until the Działyński family, the owners of Kórnik castle, bought it in 1856. It was completely rebuilt between 1872 and 1885, when it acquired its French appearance.

The castle's stylistic mutation was essentially the brainchild of Izabela Czartoryska, daughter of Prince Adam Czartoryski and wife of Jan Działyński. She commissioned the French architect Eugène Viollet-le-Duc to reinvent the residence; under his supervision many architectural bits and pieces were brought from abroad, mainly from France and Italy, and incorporated into the building.

Having acquired large numbers of works of art, Izabela crammed them into her new palace, which became one of the largest private museums in Europe. During WWII the Nazis stole the art, but the building itself survived relatively undamaged. Part of the collection was recovered and is now once more on display in its rightful home.

On exhibition inside the building is a wealth of furniture, paintings, sculptures, weapons, tapestries, rugs and the like. One of the highlights is a collection of Greek vases from the 5th century BC. You enter the castle through a decorative 17th-century doorway, which leads into a graceful arcaded courtyard. Admission is strictly limited, with tours running for a set number of visitors every half-hour.

Museum of Forestry   MUSEUM
(Muzeum Leśnictwa; www.okl.lasy.gov.pl; ul Działyńskich 2; adult/concession 7/4zł; ◎10am-4pm Tue-Sun) To the south of Gołuchów's castle, this museum is housed in a former distillery which was considerably extended in 1874. It contains displays on the history of Polish forestry and the timber industry, along with a collection of contemporary art.

Entry includes the museum's annexe, east of the castle, displaying ecological exhibits in an old coach house. The collection includes *księgi drzewne*, boxes shaped like books, which were used to collect seeds and other plant matter.

Another outpost you can visit as part of the same entry fee is a former farm which is now home to an exhibition of forestry techniques, 750m beyond the castle in the far north of the park. It contains tools and machinery used in forestry.

Several bison live relatively freely in a large, fenced-off **bison enclosure** (◎7am-sunset), west of the park, 500m beyond the forestry techniques exhibition (follow the Żubry signs).

ⓘ Getting There & Away

Suburban bus A goes roughly half-hourly to/from Kalisz (5zł, 40 minutes). Get off at the bus stand next to the cemetery, cross the main road and walk around the church to find the park entrance. About 10 PKS buses each day run both to Poznań (26zł, 2¼ hours) and Kalisz (5zł, 20 minutes).

Gdańsk & Pomerania

POP 6.5 MILLION

Best Places to Eat

➡ Velevetka (p322)

➡ Bulaj (p330)

➡ Gothic (p347)

➡ Atmosphere (p356)

➡ Dym na Wodzie (p357)

Best Places to Stay

➡ Hotel Apollo (p358)

➡ Kamienica Gotyk (p320)

➡ Hotel Podewils (p321)

➡ Hotel Neptun (p352)

➡ Sand Hotel (p360)

Why Go?

Cream-hued beaches shelving smoothly into the nippy Baltic Sea, wind-crafted dunes vivid against leaden skies, stern red-brick churches and castles erected by a medieval order of pious knights, and silenced shipyards that once seethed with anti-communist tumult – this is Pomerania, Poland's north, a land with many faces.

The epicentre of Pomerania is Gdańsk, northern Poland's metropolis, a forward-looking city with a photogenic historical centre. Like most of the region, Gdańsk has changed hands many times over the centuries, each invader and overseer bequeathing a layer of architecture and culture for today's tourists to ogle.

Away from the beaches and Gdańsk's miracles in red brick you'll discover Kashubia, a region that keeps the traditional fires burning, including its own language – the perfect place to slow down and escape Poland's beaten tracks.

When to Go
Gdańsk

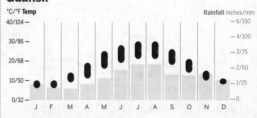

Apr Go amber hunting after spring's high tides along Pomerania's white-sand beaches.

Aug Enjoy a spot of bric-a-brac browsing and local culture during Gdańsk's Dominican Fair.

Dec Explore the deserted dunes and lakes of the Słowiński National Park.

BALTIC SEA

Bay of Pomerania

Szczecin Lagoon

GERMANY

← Berlin

Ustka

Darłowo

Sławno
Korzyb

Koszalin

Kołobrzeg

Gościno

Karlino

Trzebiatów

Białogard

Wolin National Park

Międzyzdroje

Pomorski Kamień

Wolin Island

Świnoujście

Sławoborze

Płoty

Resko

Świdwin

Połczyn Zdrój

Szczecinek

Nowogard

Łobez

Szczecin Airport

Goleniów

Dobra

Złocieniec

Czaplinek

Jastrowie

Maszewo

Drawsko Pomorskie

Chociwel

Szczecin

Stargard Szczeciński

Kołbaskowo

Kalisz Pomorski

Wałcz

Pyrzyce

Choszczno

Drawa National Park

Piła

Barlinek

Dobiegniew

Noteć

Gorzów Wielkopolski

Strzelce Krajeńskie

Gdańsk & Pomerania Highlights

1 Admiring the architecture of **Gdańsk**'s Długi Targ (p311), one of Poland's grandest thoroughfares.

2 Boogying on the beach at one of **Sopot**'s many nightclubs (p330).

3 Wandering the halls, corridors and chapels of the castle at **Malbork** (p345), Europe's biggest medieval fortress.

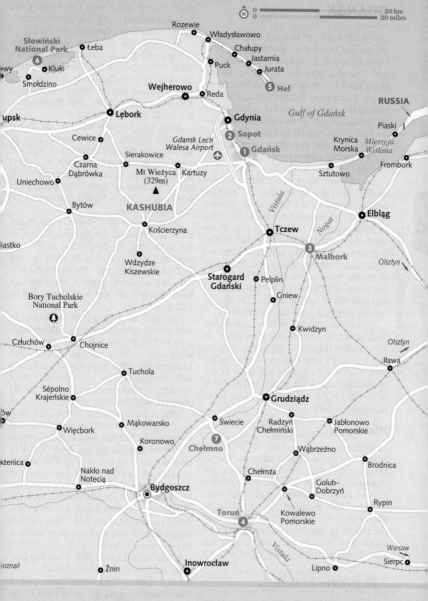

0 ────── 50 km
0 ────── 30 miles

Rozewie
Władysławowo
Chałupy
Jastarnia
Puck
Jurata
5 Hel

Słowiński
National Park
6
Kluki Łeba
Smołdzino
wy

upsk

Wejherowo
Reda

RUSSIA

Gdynia
2 Sopot
1 Gdańsk

Gulf of Gdańsk

Piaski

Lębork

Cewice
Sierakowice
Gdansk Lech
Walesa Airport
Krynica
Morska
*Mierzeja
Wiślana*

Czarna
Dąbrówka
Mt Wieżyca
(329m)
Kartuzy
Sztutowo
Frombork

Uniechowo

KASHUBIA

Bytów

iastko

Kościerzyna
Tczew
Elbląg

Vistula

Nogat

3 Malbork
Olsztyn

Wdzydze
Kiszewskie

Bory Tucholskie
National Park

**Starogard
Gdański**
Pelplin

Gniew

Człuchów
Chojnice

Kwidzyn
Olsztyn

Iława

Tuchola

Sépolno
Krajeńskie

Grudziądz

Więcbork
Mąkowarsko
Świecie
Radzyń
Chełmiński
Jabłonowo
Pomorskie

Koronowo
7
Chełmno
Wąbrzeźno

Brodnica

Nakło nad
Notecią
Chełmża
Golub-
Dobrzyń

Bydgoszcz
Rypin

Toruń
Kowalewo
Pomorskie

4

Vistula

Warsaw

Inowrocław
Sierpc
Lipno

oznań
Żnin

4 Marvelling at the Gothic
masterpieces that make **Toruń**
(p334) one of Poland's most
intriguing destinations.

5 Going to **Hel** (p332) and
back to see the seals.

6 Doing a spot of dune
surfing in the intriguing
Słowiński National Park
(p353).

7 Revelling in the off-beat
ambience of the walled town
of **Chełmno** (p341), a real
blast from the Polish past.

GDAŃSK

POP 460,000

Like a mini-state all to itself, Gdańsk has a unique feel that sets it apart from the other cities in Poland. Centuries of maritime ebb and flow as a port city; streets of distinctively un-Polish architecture influenced by a united nations of wealthy merchants who shaped the city's past; the to-ing and fro-ing of Danzig/Gdańsk between Teutonic Prussia and Slavic Poland; and the destruction of WWII have all bequeathed this grand old dame a special atmosphere that millions of tourists now come to enjoy.

And those visitors are coming in ever greater numbers to wander the narrow, cobbled streets of the Main Town, to gaze in wonder at monster red-brick churches, to scatter along its historical thoroughfares lined with grand, elegantly slender buildings and to wander in and out of characterful cafes, amber shops and intriguing museums. Tourism hasn't turned its back on the water, with pleasure-boat cruises upriver and a wealth of maritime history to view in between brews at dockside beer gardens.

Though an old city with a tumultuous past, and the historic scars to prove it, 21st-century Gdańsk is an energetic place and one that's investing in its tourism future. With the best transport links in the north, it's also an ideal launch pad for much of the Polish Baltic coast and many other inland attractions.

History

Describing Gdańsk's past as 'eventful' would be a major understatement. The official history of the much fought-over city is counted from the year 997, when the Bohemian Bishop Adalbert arrived here from Gniezno and baptised the inhabitants. The settlement developed as a port over the following centuries, expanding northwards into what is today the Old Town. The German community then arrived from Lübeck in the early 13th century, the first in a succession of migrants that crafted the town's cosmopolitan character.

In 1308 the Teutonic order seized Gdańsk and quickly turned it into a major trade centre, joining the Hanseatic League in 1361. In 1454 the locals decided on a spot of regime change, razing the Teutonic Knights' castle and pledging allegiance to the Polish monarch instead.

From here, the only way was up: by the mid-16th century, the successful port of 40,000 was Poland's largest city and the most important centre of trade in Central Europe. Legions of international merchants joined the local German-Polish population, adding their own cultural influences to the city's unique blend.

Gdańsk was one of the very few Polish cities to withstand the Swedish Deluge of the 1650s, but the devastation of the surrounding area weakened its position, and in 1793 Prussia annexed the shrinking city. Just 14 years later, however, the Prussians were ousted by the Napoleonic army and its Polish allies.

It turned out to be a brief interlude – in 1815 the Congress of Vienna gave Gdańsk back to Prussia, which became part of Germany later in the century. In the years that followed, the Polish minority was systematically Germanised, the city's defences were reinforced and there was gradual but steady economic and industrial growth.

After Germany's defeat in WWI, the Treaty of Versailles granted the newly reformed Polish nation the so-called Polish Corridor, a strip of land stretching from Toruń to Gdańsk, providing the country with an outlet to the sea. Gdańsk itself was excluded and designated the Free City of Danzig, under the protection of the League of Nations. With the city having a German majority, however, the Polish population never had much political influence, and once Hitler came to power it was effectively a German port.

WWII started in Gdańsk when the German battleship *Schleswig-Holstein* fired the first shots at the Polish military post at Westerplatte. During the occupation of the city, Nazi Germany continued to use the local shipyards for building warships, with Poles used as forced labour. The Red Army pitched up in March 1945; during the fierce battle that ensued the city centre virtually ceased to exist. The German residents either fled or died in the conflict. Their place

---

ⓘ THE THREE CITIES

In and around Gdańsk, you're sure to come across the term Tri-City (Trójmiasto in Polish) on everything from tourist brochures to bus timetables. The three cities in question are tourist magnets Gdańsk and Sopot, along with the less-visited port of Gdynia.

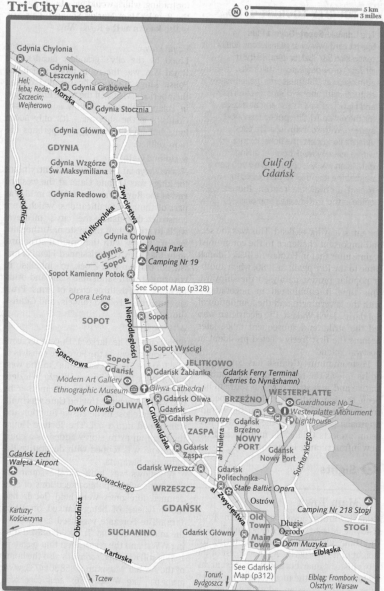

Gdynia Chylonia

Gdynia
Leszczynki

Hel;
Łeba; Reda;   Gdynia Grabówek
Szczecin;
Wejherowo   Gdynia Stocznia

Gdynia Główna

GDYNIA

Gdynia Wzgórze
Św Maksymiliana

Gdynia Redłowo

Gulf of
Gdańsk

Morska
al Zwycięstwa
Wielkopolska
Obwodnica

Gdynia Orłowo

Aqua Park

Camping Nr 19

Sopot Kamienny Potok

Gdynia
Sopot

See Sopot Map (p328)

Opera Leśna

SOPOT

Sopot

al Niepodległości

Sopot Wyścigi

Sopot
Gdańsk

JELITKOWO

Spacerowa

Gdańsk Żabianka

Gdańsk Ferry Terminal
(Ferries to Nynäshamn)

Modern Art Gallery

Ethnographic Museum

Oliwa Cathedral

Gdańsk Oliwa

WESTERPLATTE

BRZEŹNO

Guardhouse No 1

Westerplatte Monument

Dwór Oliwski

OLIWA

Gdańsk

al Grunwaldzka

Gdańsk Przymorze

Gdańsk
Brzeźno

Lighthouse

ZASPA

NOWY
PORT

Gdańsk
Nowy Port

Sucharskiego

Gdańsk
Zaspa

al Hallera

Gdańsk Lech
Wałęsa Airport

Gdańsk Wrzeszcz

Gdańsk
Politechnika

Słowackiego

State Baltic Opera

WRZESZCZ

al Zwycięstwa

Ostrów

GDAŃSK

Kartuzy;
Kościerzyna

Obwodnica

Camping Nr 218 Stogi

Old
Town

Długie
Ogrody

STOGI

SUCHANINO

Gdańsk Główny

Main
Town

Dom Muzyka

Kartuska

Elbląska

Tczew

Toruń;
Bydgoszcz

See Gdańsk
Map (p312)

Elbląg; Frombork;
Olsztyn; Warsaw

was eventually taken by Polish newcomers, mainly from the territories lost to the Soviet Union in the east.

The complex reconstruction of the Main Town took more than 20 years from 1949, though work on some interiors continued well into the 1990s. Nowhere else in Europe was such a large area of a historic city reconstructed from the ground up.

In December 1970 a huge workers' strike broke out in the shipyard and was 'pacified' by authorities as soon as the workers left

ⓘ TRI-CITY TOURIST CARD

The **Gdańsk–Sopot–Gdynia Plus tourist card** (www.visitgdansk.com; adult/concession 58/38zł for 24hr, 88/58zł for 72hr) provides discounts or free admission at 154 museums, galleries, cultural institutions, hotels, restaurants and clubs, as well as serving as a pass for the entire Tri-City public transport system. With so many service providers taking part, the ticket comes with a usefully thick booklet giving details on every location where you can unsheathe it and what discounts to expect. It's available from any tourist office in the Tri-City area and online.

the gates, leaving 44 dead. This was the second important challenge to the communist regime after that in Poznań in 1956. Gdańsk came to the fore again in 1980, when another popular protest paralysed the shipyard. This time it culminated in negotiations with the government and the foundation of Solidarity. Lech Wałęsa, the electrician who led the strike and subsequent talks, later became the first freely elected president in postwar Poland.

Postcommunist Gdańsk has consolidated its role as the region's leading administrative and industrial city, but tourism has been the big and and rather unexpected success story. The city's optimistic, vibrant approach is reflected in the large new museum projects Gdańsk is funding and the new infrastructure being installed.

◉ Sights

◉ Main Town

Gdańsk's crown jewel is the Main Town (Główne Miasto), which looks much as it did some 300 to 400 years ago, during the height of its prosperity. As the largest of the city's historic quarters and the richest architecturally, it was the most carefully restored after WWII. Prussian additions from the Partition period were airbrushed out of this remarkably impressive re-creation, so the result is a snapshot of Gdańsk up to the end of the 18th century.

The town was originally laid out in the mid-14th century along a central axis consisting of ul Długa (Long Street) and Długi Targ (Long Market). The latter was designed

for trading, which would have taken place in the Rynek (Main Market Square). This axis is also known as the Royal Way.

Royal Way   HISTORIC SITE

Lined by the city's grandest facades, the Royal Way was the route along which the Polish kings traditionally paraded during their periodic visits. Of the three Royal Ways in Poland (Warsaw, Kraków and Gdańsk), Gdańsk's is the shortest – it's only 500m long, but architecturally it is perhaps the most refined.

➡ **Upland Gate**

(Brama Wyżynna) The traditional entry point for kings was Upland Gate, at the western end of the Royal Way. It was built in 1574 as part of the new fortifications, which were constructed outside the city's medieval walls to strengthen the system. Authorities weren't happy with the original structure, so in 1586 they commissioned Flemish artist, Willem van den Block, to embellish it, covering it with sandstone slabs and ornamenting it with three coats of arms: Prussia (unicorns), Poland (angels) and Gdańsk (lions).

➡ **Foregate**

(Przedbramie) The large 15th-century construction known as the Foregate consists of the Torture House (Katownia) to the west and a high Prison Tower (Wieża Więzienna) to the east, linked to one another by two walls. When the Upland Gate was built, the Foregate lost its defensive function and was turned into a jail. The Torture House then had an extra storey added as a court room and was topped with decorative Renaissance parapets.

A gallows was built on the square to the north, where public executions of condemned foreigners were held (locals had the 'privilege' of being hanged on Długi Targ). The Foregate was used as a jail till the mid-19th century. It was damaged during WWII and the restoration that began in 1951 is still ongoing; today it's also the home of the **Amber Museum** (✆ 58 301 4733; www.mhmg.pl; Targ Węglowy 26; adult/concession 10/5zł; ☺10am-1pm Mon, to 4pm Tue-Sat, 11am-4pm Sun), where kilograms of 'Baltic gold' radiate a prehistoric glow.

➡ **Golden Gate**

(Złota Brama) Built in 1612, the Golden Gate was designed by Abraham van den Block, son of the man behind the decoration of the Upland Gate. It's a sort of triumphal arch ornamented with a double-storey colonnade and topped with eight allegorical statues.

The four figures on the side of the Prison Tower represent Peace, Liberty, Wealth and Fame, for which Gdańsk was always struggling to achieve in spite of foreign powers (sometimes including the Polish kings). The sculptures on the opposite side symbolise the burghers' virtues: Wisdom, Piety, Justice and Concord. Today's figures are postwar copies of the 1648 originals.

Once you pass the Golden Gate, you are on the gently curving ulica Długa, one of the loveliest streets in Poland, which, despite its name (meaning 'Long Street'), is only 300m in length. In 1945 it was just a heap of smoking rubble. Stop at the **Uphagens' House** (Dom Uphagena; www.mhmg.gda.pl; ul Długa 12; adult/concession 10/5zł, Mon free; ⊘11am-3pm Mon, 10am-7pm Tue-Sat, 11am-7pm Sun) to see the restored historic interior, a collection of sumptuously decorated rooms with period furniture from the 18th century.

➤ **Długi Targ**

Długi Targ (Long Market) was once the main city market and is now the major focus for visitors. Things have got a bit touristy here over the last decade (dubious amber stalls, restaurant touts), but look up from the crowds to appreciate the period architecture, all of which is a very selective postwar rebuild, of course.

According to local legend, the **Neptune Fountain** (Fontana Neptuna) `FREE` next to the Town Hall once gushed forth with the trademark Gdańsk liqueur, Goldwasser. As the story goes, it spurted out of the trident one merry night and Neptune found himself endangered by crowds of drunken locals who couldn't believe their luck. Perhaps that's why, in 1634, the fountain was fenced off with a wrought-iron barrier. The bronze statue itself was the work of Flemish artist Peter Husen; made between 1606 and 1613, it is the oldest secular monument in Poland. A menagerie of stone sea creatures was added in the 1750s during the restoration of the fountain.

The nearby 1618 **Golden House** (Złota Kamienica), designed by Johan Voigt, has the richest facade in the city. In the friezes between storeys are 12 elaborately carved

GDAŃSK & POMERANIA GDAŃSK

IN A LEAGUE OF ITS OWN

It wasn't easy being a merchant in the Middle Ages. There were no chambers of commerce or Rotary Clubs, and traders received very little respect from the ruling classes. Local lords saw travelling salesmen as easy pickings, requiring them to pay heavy tolls as they moved from province to province in Central Europe. Taking to the sea wasn't much better, as pirates preyed upon merchants' slow-moving boats.

The answer to their problems was to band together in the Hanseatic League, a group of trading ports that formed in the late 13th century and wielded unprecedented economic power. The Hansa (from the German for 'association') was based in Germany, making good use of its central location, with members also scattered throughout Scandinavia, across the Baltic to Russia and west to the Netherlands. The League also had trading posts in cities like London and Venice. As a result, it could trade wax from Russia with items from English or Dutch manufacturers, or Swedish minerals with fruit from the Mediterranean.

The League took a far more muscular approach than that of today's business councils. It bribed rulers, built lighthouses and led expeditions against pirates and, on one memorable occasion, raised an armed force that defeated the Danish military in 1368.

At its height the League had over a hundred members, including major cities now within Poland such as Danzig (Gdańsk), Stettin (Szczecin), Thorn (Toruń) and Elbing (Elbląg).

But it was all downhill from there. With no standing army and no government beyond irregular assemblies of city representatives, the League was unable to withstand the rise of the new nation-states of the 15th century and the shift of trade to Atlantic ports after the discovery of the New World. The assembly met for the last time in 1669, and by the time of its eventual disintegration in 1863 its membership had been reduced to the core cities of Hamburg, Bremen and Lübeck.

The memory of the League lives on, however, in the New Hanse (www.hanse.org), founded in 1980 and bringing together the former Hansa member cities in a body promoting cultural cooperation and tourism.

Gdańsk

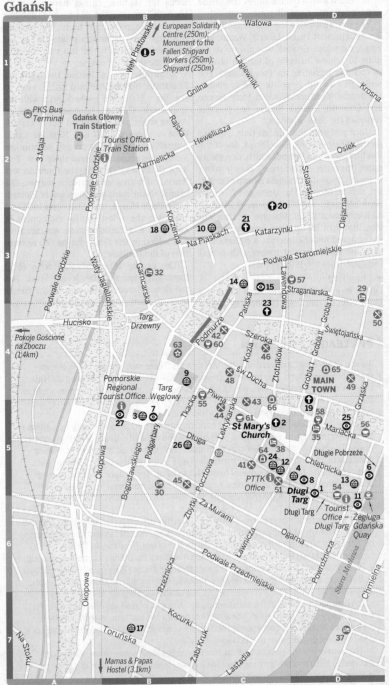

European Solidarity Centre (250m); Monument to the Fallen Shipyard Workers (250m); Shipyard (250m)

Wałowa

Wały Piastowskie

5

Łagiewniki

Gnilna

Krosna

PKS Bus Terminal

Gdańsk Główny Train Station

Rajska

Heweliusza

Osiek

Tourist Office - Train Station

3 Maja

Karmelicka

Stolarska

Olejarna

Podwale Grodzkie

47

20

21

Katarzynki

18

Korzenna

10

Na Piaskach

Podwale Staromiejskie

Wały Jagiellońskie

Garncarska

32

Lawendowa

57

Straganiarska

29

Podwale Grodzkie

14

15

Pańska

Grobla II

23

Świętojańska

Hucisko

Targ Drzewny

Podmurze

60

42

Grobla II

50

Pokoje Gościnne na Zboczu (1/4km)

63

Szeroka

46

Kozia

Grobla I

Złotników

65

MAIN TOWN

49

Grząska

Pomorskie Regional Tourist Office

9

Targ Węglowy

św. Ducha

48

19

58

25

56

Mariacka

Okopowa

Bogusławskiego

Podgarbary

3 **7**

27

Tkacka

Piwna

55

Lektykarska

44

43

61

66

35

St Mary's Church

2

Długa

26

64

38

24

12

Chlebnicka

Długie Pobrzeże

6

Pocztowa

41

4

8

13

54

Zbytki

Za Murami

45

30

PTTK Office

51

Długi Targ

1

11

Długi Targ

Tourist Office - Długi Targ

Żegluga Gdańska Quay

Ogarna

Ławnicza

Powroźnicza

Stara Motława

Podwale Przedmiejskie

Rzeźnicka

Chmielna

Na Stoku

Okopowa

Kocurki

17

Toruńska

Żabi Kruk

Lastadia

37

Mamas & Papas Hostel (3.1km)

scenes interspersed with busts of famous historical figures, including two Polish kings.

The Long Market is flanked from the east by the Green Gate, marking the river end of the Royal Way. It was built in the 1560s on the site of a medieval defensive gate and was supposed to be the residence of the kings. Today it houses an art gallery.

➡ **Green Gate**

(Zielona Brama) Długi Targ (p311) is flanked from the east by the Green Gate, marking the end of the Royal Way. It was built in the 1560s on the site of a medieval defensive gate and was supposed to be the residence of the kings. But they never stayed in what turned out to be a cold and uncomfortable lodge; they preferred the houses nearby, particularly those opposite the Artus Court (p315).

Historical Museum of Gdańsk MUSEUM
(Town Hall; www.mhmg.pl; Długa 46/47; adult/concession 12/6zł, tower 5zł, Mon or Tue free; ⊙9am-1pm Mon, to 4pm Tue-Thu & Sun, 10am-6pm Fri & Sat) This museum is located in the historic **town hall**, which claims Gdańsk's highest tower at 81.5m. The showpiece is the Red Room (Sala Czerwona), done up in Dutch Mannerist style from the end of the 16th century. The 2nd floor houses exhibitions related to Gdańsk's history, including mock-ups of old Gdańsk interiors. From here you can access the tower for great views across the city.

The Red Room's interior is not an imitation but the real deal; it was dismantled in 1942 and hidden outside the city until the end of the bombing. The richly carved fireplace (1593) and the marvellous portal (1596) all attract the eye, but the centre of attention is the ornamented ceiling – 25 paintings dominated by an oval centrepiece entitled *The Glorification of the Unity of Gdańsk with Poland*. Other striking rooms include the Winter Hall with its portraits of Gdańsk's mayors up to the 17th century and the Great Council Chamber with its huge oils of Polish kings.

⭐**St Mary's Church** CHURCH
(www.bazylikamariacka.pl; ul Podkramarska 5; adult/concession 4/2 zł, tower 6/3zł; ⊙8.30am-6pm, except during services) Dominating the heart of the Main Town, St Mary's is often cited as the largest brick church in the world. Some 105m long and 66m wide at the transept, its massive squat tower climbs 78m high into the Gdańsk cityscape. Begun

Gdańsk

in 1343, St Mary's didn't reach its present proportions until 1502. Don't miss the 15th-century astronomical clock, placed in the northern transept, and the church tower (405 steps above the city).

On first sight, the brightly whitewashed building looks almost empty, but walk around its 30-odd chapels to discover how many outstanding works of art have been accumulated. In the floor alone, there are about 300 tombstones. In the chapel at the back of the left (northern) aisle is a replica of Memling's *The Last Judgment* – the original is in the National Museum's Department of Early Art. The extraordinary

Baroque organ manages enough puff to fill the space with its tones.

The church's elephantine size is arresting and you feel even more antlike when you enter the building. Illuminated with natural light passing through 37 large windows (the biggest is 127 sq metres), the three-naved interior, topped by an intricate Gothic vault, is bright and spacious. It was originally covered with frescos, the sparse remains of which are visible in the far right corner.

The high altar boasts a Gothic polyptych from the 1510s, with the Coronation of the Virgin depicted in its central panel. Large as it is, it's a miniature in this vast space. The same applies to the 4m crucifix high up on the rood beam.

Artus Court Museum MUSEUM

(www.mhmg.gda.pl; ul Długi Targ 43/44; adult/concession 10/5zł, Mon free; ⊘9am-1pm Mon, to 4pm Tue-Thu, 10am-6pm Fri & Sat, to 4pm Sun) Rising in all its embellished grandeur behind the Neptune Fountain, the Artus Court is perhaps the single best-known house in Gdańsk. The court has been an essential stop for passing luminaries ever since its earliest days, and a photo display in the entrance shows an enviable selection of famous visitors, from King Henry IV of England to a host of contemporary presidents. It was comprehensively destroyed during WWII but was painstakingly restored from old photographs and historical records.

Built in the middle of the 14th century, the court was given its monumental facade by Abraham van den Block in the 1610s. Inside, there's a huge hall topped by a Gothic vault supported on four slim granite columns, decorated with hunting murals and dominated by a vast painting depicting the Battle of Grunwald. Wealthy local merchants used the building as a communal guildhall, holding meetings, banquets and general revelries in the lavishly decorated interior.

The plainly renovated upper floors hold a selection of historical exhibits, including a photographic 'simulacrum' of how the great hall would have looked at its peak, a breathtaking spectacle.

One unique feature of the interior is its giant Renaissance tiled stove, standing in the corner of the hall and almost touching the ceiling. It's reputedly the highest stove of its kind in Europe containing 520 tiles, 437 of which are originals.

Ulica Mariacka STREET

(ul Mariacka) The most atmospheric of all Gdańsk's streets and one of Poland's most photogenic lanes is this length of cobbles between the waterfront St Mary's Gate (Brama Mariacka) and the red-brick hulk of St Mary's Church. Almost completely recreated after WWII (mostly on the basis of old documents, photographs and illustrations) every ornamental detail unearthed from the debris, including countless scary gargoyles, was incorporated.

It's the only street with a complete row of terraces, which lends the scene enormous charm. In recent years things have really come to life, with several artisan amber jewellery shops, some great cafes and bars, and one of northern Poland's best hotels (Kamienica Gotyk). Some of the best stalls are set up here during the Dominican Fair.

Żuraw CRANE

(Crane; www.nmm.pl; ul Szeroka 67/68; adult/concession 8/5zł; ⊘10am-6pm daily) Part of the National Maritime Museum, the oh-so conspicuous Gdańsk Crane (Żuraw) rises above the waterfront. Built in the mid-15th century as the biggest double-towered gate on the shoreline, it also served to shift heavy cargo directly onto vessels docked at the quay. Incredibly, this people-powered device could hoist loads of up to 2000kg, making it the largest crane in medieval Europe. Early-17th-century wheels were added higher up for installing masts.

Blasted to pieces in 1945, everything was carefully put back together in the postwar decades, making it the only fully restored relic of its kind in the world. Inside you'll find exhibits relating to the history of shipping, plus a collection of shells, coral and other marine life; English notes are available on laminated sheets. You can also climb up into the section overlooking the water and have a closer look at the hoisting gear (but sadly not a go on the wheel).

National Maritime Museum MUSEUM

(Narodowe Muzeum Morskie w Gdańsku; ✒Maritime Cultural Centre 58 329 8700, information 58 301 8611; www.nmm.pl; ul Ołowianka 9-13; all sites adult/concession 18/10zł; ⊘10am-6pm daily) This is a sprawling exhibition of maritime history and Gdańsk's role through the centuries as a Baltic seaport. Headquarters is the multimillion-euro Maritime Cultural Centre, with a permanent interactive exhibition 'People-Ships-Ports'. Other exhibitions include the MS *Sołdek*, the first vessel to be built at the Gdańsk shipyard in the postwar years, and the Żuraw, a 15th-century loading crane that was the biggest in its day. The granaries across the river house more displays, which are highly recommended.

These exhibits on Ołowianka Island in the Motława River illustrate the history of Polish seafaring from the earliest times to the present. They include models of old sailing warships and ports, a 9th-century dugout, navigation instruments, ships' artillery, flags and the like.

Another interesting exhibit here is a collection of salvaged items from the *General*

MUSEUM OF WWII

Slated to open in 2016, the **Museum of WWII** (Muzeum II Wojny Światowej; www.muzeum1939.pl) is a bold addition to a plot of land at the northern end of the Gdańsk waterfront wasteland. This major project is intended to rejuvenate a long forgotten part of the city centre where the Kanał Raduni meets the River Motława. Set to become one of the city's must-sees, it traces the fate of Poland during the world's greatest conflict with interactive exhibits taken from private collections and museums across Poland.

Carleton, a British ship that mysteriously disappeared in the Baltic in 1785.

The museum's ferry service (per trip 1.50zł, free with ticket for all sites), shuttles between the crane and the island.

Great Arsenal HISTORIC BUILDING
(Wielka Zbrojownia; ul Tkacka) Ul Piwna terminates at the Great Arsenal, an architectural gem. The work of Antonius van Opbergen, it was built at the beginning of the 17th century and, like most of Gdańsk's architecture, clearly shows the influence of the Low Countries. The main eastern facade, framed within two side towers, is floridly decorated and guarded by figures of soldiers on the top. Military motifs predominate, and the city's coat of arms guards the doorways.

Royal Chapel CHURCH
(Kaplica Królewska; ul Świętego Ducha) Squeezed between two houses just to the north of St Mary's Church, and completely overshadowed by its massive neighbour, the small Royal Chapel is the only Baroque church in old Gdańsk. It was built between 1678 and 1681 to fulfil the last will of the primate of Poland at the time, Andrzej Olszowski. The chapel was designed by famous royal architect Tylman van Gameren, with the facade its most attractive feature.

St Nicholas' Church CHURCH
(Bazylika Św Mikołaja; ul Świętojańska; ⊘ 7.30am-8pm, to 10pm Sun) Erected by the Dominican order on its arrival from Kraków in 1227, this is one of Gdańsk's oldest places of Christian worship and it certainly feels that way inside. Amazingly, it was the only central church to escape damage in WWII – according to one story, the attacking Soviet troops deliberately avoided shelling it, due to the high regard for St Nicholas in the Orthodox tradition.

Unlike most of the other Gothic churches in the city, the musty interior of St Nick's is very richly decorated with black-and-gold Baroque altars and ornately carved, winged pews lining the nave. The magnificent Late Renaissance high altar of 1647 first catches the eye, followed by the imposing Baroque organ made a century later.

**National Museum's
Department of Early Art** MUSEUM
(Muzeum Narodowe Oddział Sztuki Dawnej; www.mng.gda.pl; ul Toruńska 1; adult/concession 10/6zł, free Fri; ⊘ 10am-5pm Tue-Sun May-Sep, 9am-4pm Mon-Fri, 10am-5pm Sat & Sun Oct-Apr) Located just outside the Main Town, the National Museum's Department of Early Art is housed in the vaulted interiors of a former Franciscan monastery. It covers the broad spectrum of Polish and international art and crafts, boasting extensive collections of paintings, woodcarvings, gold and silverware, embroidery, fabrics, porcelain, faience, wrought iron and furniture.

Some of the highlights include the original figure of St George from the spire of the defunct Court of the Fraternity of St George, an assortment of huge, elaborately carved Danzig-style wardrobes (typical of the city, from where they were sent all over the country), and several beautiful ceramic tiled stoves.

The 1st floor is given over to paintings, with a section devoted to Dutch and Flemish work. The jewel of the collection is Hans Memling's (1435–94) triptych of *The Last Judgment*, one of the earlier works of the artist, dating from 1472 to 1473. You'll also find works by the younger Brueghel and Van Dyck, and the beautifully macabre *Hell* by Jacob Swanenburgh, who was the master of the young Rembrandt.

Market Hall MARKET
(Hala Targowa; Plac Dominikański; ⊘ 9am-6pm Mon-Fri, to 5pm Sat) Built on the site of a Dominican monastery, the late-19th-century Market Hall is more interesting for its wrought-iron railway-station architecture than for the procession of butchers, bakers and wedding-dress makers inside.

Hyacinthus' Tower HISTORIC BUILDING
(Baszta Jacek; Plac Dominikański) The tall octagonal tower rising in front of the market hall is a remnant of the medieval fortifications

and dates from around 1400. Today it houses a photo shop.

Old Town

Despite its name, Gdańsk's Old Town (Stare Miasto) was not the cradle of the city. The earliest inhabited site, according to archaeologists, was in what is now the Main Town area. Nonetheless, a settlement existed in the Old Town from the late 10th century and developed parallel to the Main Town.

Under the Teutonic order, the two parts merged into a single urban entity, but the Old Town was always poorer and had no defensive system of its own. One other difference was that the Main Town was more 'German' while the Old Town had a larger Polish population. During WWII it suffered as much as its wealthier cousin but, apart from a handful of buildings (mainly churches), it was not rebuilt.

St Bridget's Church   CHURCH
(Kościół Św Brygidy; ul Profesorska 17; adult/concession 2/1zł; ⊙7am-7pm) Founded over 700 years ago, St Bridget's was reduced to medieval brick dust in 1945, and until 1970 only the outer walls were left standing. Very little of the prewar furnishings survived, but if you've taken a fancy to amber you're sure to appreciate the spectacular 174cm-high amber monstrance depicting the tree of life and the monumental high altar. This recent construction is the highlight of the interior and contains a record-breaking 6500kg of polished prehistoric tree resin.

Lech Wałęsa attended Mass here when he was an unknown electrician in the nearby shipyard. With the wave of strikes in 1980 the church became a strong supporter of the dockyard workers, and its priest, Henryk Jankowski, took every opportunity to express their views in his sermons. The church remains a record of the Solidarity period, with several contemporary works related to the trade union and to modern Polish history in general. You'll find the tombstone of murdered priest Jerzy Popiełuszko, the Katyń epitaph, a collection of crosses from the 1980 and '88 strikes, and a door covered with bas-reliefs of scenes from Solidarity's history – all in the right-hand (northern) aisle.

St Catherine's Church   CHURCH
(Kościół Św Katarzyny; ul Profesorska 3) FREE The largest monument of the Old Town is St Catherine's Church, Gdańsk's oldest, which was begun in the 1220s. It was the parish church for the entire town until St Mary's was completed. As is common, the church evolved over centuries and only reached its final shape in the mid-15th century (save for the Baroque top to the tower, added in 1634).

Unfortunately, a major fire in May 2006 caused the roof to collapse and resulted in considerable damage to the interior. Much was restored, but the walls remain unrendered and some work is still ongoing – it will obviously be a long time before this wonderful church returns to its former glory. There's a small exhibition on the fire, including TV news footage.

Great Mill   HISTORIC BUILDING
(Wielki Młyn; ul Na Piaskach) Standing conspicuously opposite St Catherine's Church, the Great Mill certainly lives up to its name. Created by the Teutonic Knights in northern Poland's typical red brick around 1350, it was medieval Europe's largest mill at over 40m long and 26m high. With a set of 18 monster millstones (now gone), each 5m in diameter, the mill produced 200 tonnes of flour per day right up until 1945.

No longer serving the purpose for which it was built, the mill has become a mall, containing a convenient supermarket and several low-grade eateries.

Old Town Hall   HISTORIC BUILDING
(Ratusz Staromiejski; ul Korzenna 33) The Old Town Hall was once the seat of the Old Town council. A well-proportioned Renaissance building crowned with a high central tower typical of its Flemish provenance, it was designed at the end of the 16th century by Antonius van Opbergen, the architect later responsible for the Great Arsenal. The brick structure is delicately ornamented in stone, including the central doorway and a frieze with the shields of Poland, Prussia and Gdańsk.

The building now houses the Baltic Sea Culture Centre and an exhibition hall. Go upstairs to see the foyer, notable for its rich decoration, which was partly assembled from old burghers' houses. Note the arcaded stone wall (1560) with three Roman gods in bas-relief. This composition, older than the town hall itself, was moved here from one of the houses in the Main Town. One of the doors leads to the Great Hall, which can also be visited. Concerts are held here; check the program for details.

GDAŃSK & POMERANIA GDAŃSK

Shipyard Area

★ European Solidarity Centre   MUSEUM

(Europejskie Centrum Solidarności; ☎58 772 4112; www.ecs.gda.pl; Plac Solidarności 1; admission 17zł; ⊘10am-8pm Jun-Sep, to 6pm Oct-May) Housed in a mind-boggling ugly, oh-so 21st-century hulk of architecture, the exhibition in this unmarked centre (finding the entrance will be your first task) has quickly become one of Gdańsk's unmissables since it opened in 2014. Audioguide clamped to ears, the seven halls examine Poland's postwar fight for freedom, from the strikes of the 1970s to the round-table negotiations of the late 1980s and beyond. The displays are a blend of state-of-the-art multimedia experiences and real artefacts. Allow at least two hours.

Each hall is lettered and the exhibition runs chronologically from A to G. Hall A takes you to the 1970s shipyard, with yellow docker helmets lining the ceiling and a battered electric truck, the type Lech Wałęsa once worked on as an electrician, almost blocking your way. Footage includes the negotiations between dockers and the communist regime and the signing of the 1980 agreements (the crazy pen Wałęsa used to sign is sadly missing).

Hall B is all communist-era interiors, a fascinating retro experience that takes you to a prison cell, interrogation room and typical family living room. Solidarity and martial law are the themes of halls C and D, while hall E is a large mock-up of the famous round table complete with TV cameras and name badges. An interesting section on the various revolutions across Eastern Europe follows in hall F, while hall G is a spartan affair dedicated to Pope John Paul II.

The special hall opposite the ticket desk hosts Polish-themed exhibitions, which are usually free.

Gdańsk Shipyard   SHIPYARD

(Stocznia Gdańska) Gdańsk's former Lenin Shipyard is a key fragment of 20th-century European history. It was here that the first major cracks in Eastern Europe's commu-

nist wall appeared when discontent with the regime boiled over into strikes and dissent, brutally stamped out by armed force in 1970. A decade later an electrician named Lech Wałęsa emerged to rouse crowds of strikers here, leading to the formation of the Solidarity movement and ultimately to democracy for Poland and most of the Eastern bloc.

However, since the giddy years of the Wałęsa presidency, the yard has largely lost its hallowed status and at one time the vast area was even slated for redevelopment and general gentrification. Nothing ever came of this and there has even been a minor revival in the shipbuilding industry, though nothing like the scale of the postwar years.

Monument to the
Fallen Shipyard Workers   MONUMENT

(Plac Solidarności) Just in front of the shipyard gates, the striking Monument to the Fallen Shipyard Workers commemorates the workers killed in the riots of 1970. Unveiled on 16 December 1980, 10 years after the massacre, the monument is a set of three 42m-tall steel crosses, with a series of bronze bas-reliefs in their bases. The first monument in a communist country to commemorate the regime's victims, it became an instant symbol and remains so today.

Westerplatte & Nowy Port

Westerplatte is a long peninsula at the entrance to the harbour, 7km north of the historical centre. When Gdańsk became a free city after WWI, Poland was permitted to maintain a post at this location, at the tip of the port zone. It served both trading and military purposes and had a garrison to protect it.

Buses 106, 606 and 138 shuttle between Westerplatte and the main train station. It's also accessible via infrequent boat services from Gdańsk waterfront. The lighthouse in Nowy Port can be reached by tram 10 from outside Gdańsk Główny train station.

Lighthouse   HISTORIC BUILDING

(Latarnia Morska; www.latarnia.gda.pl; ul Przemysłowa 6a; adult/concession 10/6zł; ⊘10am-7pm daily May-Aug, to 5pm Sat & Sun Sep) The first Polish bullets of WWII were fired from the windows of the Nowy Port Lighthouse. Today there are incredible views across the Bay of Gdańsk, including the Hel Peninsula, from the top.

WALL OF SOLIDARITY

At the entrance to the now defunct Roads to Freedom exhibition stands a lonely piece of the **Berlin Wall** (Wały Piastowskie). The mammoth building next to it is Solidarity's headquarters.

GDAŃSK WATERFRONT

Lining the Motława River is Gdańsk's waterfront, once a busy quay crowded with hundreds of sailing ships loading and unloading their cargo, which was stored either in the cellars of the burghers' houses in town or in the granaries on the other side of the river, on Spichlerze Island. Today it's an enjoyable promenade lined with cafes, small art galleries and souvenir emporia.

In medieval times, the parallel east–west streets of the Main Town all had defensive gates at their riverfront ends. Some of them still exist, though most were altered in later periods. Walking north along Długie Pobrzeże (literally, Long Waterfront), you first reach the **Bread Gate** (Brama Chlebnicka), at the end of ul Chlebnicka. It was built around 1450, still under the Teutonic order, as shown by the original city coat of arms consisting of two crosses. The crown was added by King Kazimierz Jagiellończyk in 1457, when Gdańsk was incorporated into the kingdom.

Enter the gate and walk a few steps to see the palatial **House Under the Angels** (Dom Pod Aniołami), which is also known as the English House (Dom Angielski) after the nationality of the merchants who owned it in the 17th century when it was the largest burgher's house in Gdańsk.

Guardhouse No 1
HISTORIC BUILDING

(Map p309; Wartownia Nr 1; ul Sucharskiego; adult/concession 4/2zł; ⊙9am-6pm mid-May–mid-Sep) The Westerplatte area is famous for one thing: it was here, at 4.45am on 1 September 1939, that the first shots of WWII were fired during the German invasion of Poland. The German battleship *Schleswig-Holstein* began shelling the Polish guard post. The garrison of just 182 men held out for seven days before surrendering. The site is now a memorial, with some of the ruins left as they were after the bombardment, plus a massive monument put up in memory of the defenders. The surviving Guardhouse No 1 houses a small exhibition related to the event.

⊙ Oliwa

A gentrified suburb about 9km from the historic centre, Oliwa boasts a fine cathedral set in a quiet park and provides an enjoyable half-day break from the dense attractions of the Main Town. To get here, take the commuter train from central Gdańsk and get off at Gdańsk Oliwa station, from where it's a 10-minute walk.

Oliwa Cathedral
CHURCH

(Map p309; ul Nowickiego 5; ⊙9am-5pm) The first surprise as you approach the cathedral is the facade, a striking composition of two slim octagonal Gothic towers with a central Baroque portion wedged between them. The interior looks extraordinarily long, mainly because of the unusual proportions of the building – the nave and chancel together

are 90m long but only 8.3m wide. At the far end of this 'tunnel' is a Baroque high altar (1688); the marble tombstone of the Pomeranian dukes (1613) is in the right transept.

The showpiece of the church is the organ (www.gdanskie-organy.com). This glorious instrument, begun in 1763 and completed 30 years later, is renowned for its fine tone and the mechanised angels that blow trumpets and ring bells when the organ is in action. In July and August, recitals take place on Tuesday and Friday evenings, but 20-minute performances are held six times a day (in the afternoon only on Sunday). Check the schedule with the tourist offices before setting off.

Modern Art Gallery
GALLERY

(Map p309; ul Cystersów 18; adult/concession 10/6zł; ⊙10am-5pm Tue-Sun May-Aug, shorter hours Sep-Apr) This 18th-century abbots' palace is now home to the Polish modern art branch of the National Museum of Gdańsk.

Ethnographic Museum
MUSEUM

(Map p309; www.mng.gda.pl; ul Cystersów 19; adult/concession 8/4zł, Fri free; ⊙10am-5pm Tue-Sun) Installed in a granary, this small collection is more interesting for those with a passion for 19th- and early-20th-century fishing and agricultural paraphernalia.

⚜ Festivals & Events

The Dominican Fair (p320) is the year's biggest event.

Open'er Festival
MUSIC

(www.opener.pl; ⊙July) One of Poland's biggest rock and pop music festivals featuring big international acts. Held at Gdynia-Kosakowa Airport.

International Festival of Open-Air & Street Theatre
THEATRE

(FETA; www.feta.pl; ☺ Jul) Street theatre festival.

International Organ Music Festival
MUSIC

(www.gdanskie-organy.com; ☺ mid-June–Aug) Organ recitals held in the Oliwa Cathedral.

International Shakespeare Festival
THEATRE

(www.shakespearefestival.pl; ul Bogusławskiego 1; ☺ Aug) Performances take place at the Shakespeare Theatre.

Sounds of the North Festival
MUSIC

(www.nck.org.pl; ☺ Aug) Held every two years in August (next in 2016 and 2018), featuring traditional folk music from the Baltic region.

🛏 Sleeping

At the bottom end of the market, the city has some long-established hostels; at the top end look out for discounted rates at weekends and off season (October to April). On the rare occasion when Gdańsk is fully booked, consider staying in Sopot and using the cheap SKM train to commute into the city centre. Almost all hotels in Gdańsk are located in the city centre.

★ Mamas & Papas Hostel
HOSTEL €

(☑ 58 717 5564; www.mamas-papas.pl; ul Nowiny 19; dm/tw 40/140zł) The location south of the

---

DON'T MISS

DOMINICAN FAIR

Gdańsk's biggest bash of the year is the **Dominican Fair** (www.jarmarkdominika. pl; ☺ Jul & Aug), held in the city since 1260. Launched by Dominican monks on Plac Dominikański as a feast day, the fun has spread to many streets and lasts for three weeks from the last Saturday of July. Amid the stalls selling cheap Chinese charms, dubious antiques, general bric-a-brac and craft items, interesting events take place on four stages and various other venues around the city centre. It's a great time to be in Gdańsk, but accommodation can be madly expensive and unfilled beds rare during the festivities.

---

city centre may not be the most convenient (take bus 151, 189, 200 or 205 to Gościnna), but this family-run hostel offers the best welcome in the Tri-City. It's a cosy affair with just 28 beds, a common room and kitchen, but its the owners who make this place, often inviting guests to eat or drink with them.

It's more like a homestay than a modern hostel.

Dom Harcerza
HOSTEL €

(☑ 58 301 3621; www.domharcerza.pl; ul Za Murami 2/10; dm/s/d from 25/60/100zł; ☎) Though occupying a former cinema, the 75-bed 'Scouts' House' has a decidedly un-Hollywood feel. There's dirt-cheap student-oriented dorm accommodation and rooms for one to three people with and without bath. The simple, snug rooms are nothing fancy, but they're clean and tidy. The location near ul Długa is a winner.

Camping Nr 218 Stogi
CAMPGROUND €

(Map p309; ☑ 58 307 3915; www.kemping-gdansk. pl; ul Wydmy 9; site per person/tent 15/7zł, cabins 70-150zł; ☺ May-Sep) Located in a pine forest in the suburb of Stogi, about 5.5km northeast of the centre, this is the most convenient of Gdańsk's three camping grounds. Just 200m away is one of the city's best beaches, with the cleanest water you'll find for miles. Tram 8 from the main train station passes here (25 minutes).

★ Staying Inn
HOTEL €€

(☑ 58 354 1543; www.stayinngdansk.com; ul Piwna 28/31; dm 70zł, d 250-350zł; ❄ ☎) Still a hostel, but slowly converting to a hotel, this is the city centre's best deal with up-to-the-second decor and gadgets, guest kitchen, common room, the city's fastest wi-fi, two rooms with disabled access and a heart-of-the-action location. There aren't many hotels with both dorms and conference facilities making this a superb option for both business people and backpackers.

Kamienica Gotyk
HOTEL €€

(☑ 58 301 8567; www.gotykhouse.eu; ul Mariacka 1; s/d 280/310zł; P ☎) Wonderfully located at the St Mary's Church end of ul Mariacka, Gdańsk's oldest house is filled by this neat, clean, Gothic-themed guesthouse. The seven rooms have Gothic touches such as broken-arched doorways and hefty drapery, though most are thoroughly modern creations and bathrooms are definitely of the third millennium. Breakfast is served in your room.

APARTMENTS

As across Poland's north, a good way to save a bagful of złoty is to rent a room or a flat. The following agencies have a good selection of short-term rentals:

Grand-Tourist (☎58 301 2634; www.gt.com.pl; ul Garncarska 29) This efficient agency handles private rooms and apartments for up to six people. There are some city centre places on their books, but if you're banished to the suburbs, find out how close the place is to the SKM commuter train. Prices start at 126zł for a studio flat. Not all choices have kitchens or wi-fi.

Patio Apartments (☎535 773 997; www.patioapartamenty.pl) This small agency has 12 trendy apartments all in the historical centre (there are even two in ul Mariacka). Prices start from around 200zł per room. All have kitchens and wi-fi.

Villa Pica Paca HOTEL €€
(☎58 320 2070; www.picapaca.com; ul Spichrzowa 20; s/d from 250/300zł; 🖧) One of a cluster of small design hotels to have sprung up on Spichlerze Island's ul Spichrzowa, the Pica Paca won't quite do it for seasoned boutique hotel dwellers, but it's an attention-grabbing place to tarry nonetheless. The eight cosy rooms and seven suites are all named after famous personalities, though some are better known than others (Nina Soentgerath room, anyone?).

The celebrity-obsessed theme continues in the Germanic minimalist breakfast room.

Dom Aktora HOTEL €€
(☎58 301 5901; www.domaktora.pl; ul Straganiarska 55/56; r from 210zł, apt from 310zł; P🖧) The no-nonsense apartments at this former thespians' dorm are affordable and have simply equipped kitchens, making this a prime target for self-caterers. Bathrooms throughout are 21st-century conceptions, but otherwise not much has changed here decor-wise since the mid-1990s. The breakfast is a buffet affair.

Dom Muzyka HOTEL €€
(Map p309; ☎58 326 0600; www.dommuzyka.pl; ul Łąkowa 1/2; r from 300zł; ❀🖧) During the day, this understated hotel within a music college has a background soundtrack of random sounds and tuneful melodies. Its light-filled rooms hoist elegantly high ceilings and are discreetly decorated with old prints. Sparkling bathrooms complete the graceful look, and there's a classy restaurant and bar off the foyer. It's located about ten minutes' walk from the waterfront, across the river.

Willa Litarion HOTEL €€
(☎58 320 2553; www.litarion.pl; ul Spichrzowa 18; s/d from 170/250zł; 🖧) On Spichlerze Island, the 13 stylishly furnished, light-flooded rooms here are bedecked in browns, creams and golds with the odd splash of other hues, and bathrooms are crisp. More often than not this place is booked up, so be sure to reserve ahead.

Pokoje Gościnne na Zboczu GUESTHOUSE €€
(☎509 984 939; www.noclegi-gdansk.eu; ul Na Zboczu; r 140-200zł; P🖧) A fair way out of the city centre west along ul Kartuska, these guest rooms are spacious, clean and there's a well-equipped kitchen. Take tram 12 to Ciasna.

Ołowianka B&B GUESTHOUSE €€
(☎534 407 040; www.olowianka.eu; ul Ołowianka 3a; s/d from 200/250zł; P🖧) Located on Ołowianka Island across from the Main Town, these cheap, basic digs are within ambling distance of all the sights and some rooms have pretty river views. There's a no-frills bar-restaurant downstairs. Breakfast is extra.

★Hotel Podewils HOTEL €€€
(☎58 300 9560; www.podewils.pl; ul Szafarnia 2; s/d 480/570zł; P🖧) The view from the Podewils across the river to the Main Town can't be beaten, though the owners probably wish they could take its cheery Baroque facade and move it away from the incongruously soulless riverside development that's sprouted next door. Guestrooms are a confection of elegantly curved timber furniture, classic prints and distinctive wallpaper.

Hotel Królewski HOTEL €€€
(☎58 326 1111; www.hotelkrolewski.pl; ul Ołowianka 1; s 380zł, d 470-520zł; P🖧) This stylish hotel marries its historical granary-building exterior with a 21st-century interior and top-notch service. The waterside location, just a hop across the Motława to the Main

Town, makes this an outstanding base if you've got the cash to splash.

Qubus Hotel
HOTEL €€€

(58 752 2100; www.qubushotel.com; ul Chmielna 47/52; r from 450zł; P❄@🕏) The only Pomeranian branch of the Polish Qubus chain, this 110-room mammoth in the city centre's southern reaches caters to both business clients and tourists. Inoffensively decorated rooms are generously proportioned and bathrooms pristine, but breakfast is extra. The hotel's boat takes guests to the city centre (from 10am to 4pm).

🍴 Eating

Plenty of eateries throughout the city centre cater to every budget. Variety is also on the increase with everything from milk-bar basics to molecular fusion on the menu.

Bar Mleczny Neptun
CAFETERIA €

(www.barneptun.pl; ul Długa 33/34; mains 4-9zł; ⊘7.30am-7pm Mon-Fri, 10am-7pm Sat & Sun; 🕏) It's surprising just where some of Poland's communist-era *bar mleczny* (milk bars) have survived and this one, right on the tourist drag, is no exception. However, the Neptun is a cut above your run-of-the-mill *bar mleczny,* with potted plants, decorative tiling and free wi-fi. Popular with foreigners on a budget, it even has an English menu of Polish favourites such as *naleśniki* (crêpes) and *gołąbki* (cabbage rolls).

Bar Turystyczny
CAFETERIA €

(www.barturystyczny.pl; cnr uls Szeroka & Węglarska; mains 4-10zł; ⊘8am-6pm Mon-Fri, 9am-5pm Sat & Sun) Gdańsk's most clean-cut milk bar may have 'since 1956' on the door, but inside it's received a post-millennium makeover. Though the interior may not be gritty enough for the average *bar mleczny* connoisseur, the food is authentically basic, filling and tasty.

Pellowski Bakery
CAFE €

(ul Rajska 5; cakes & snacks from 2zł; ⊘6.30am-7.30pm Mon-Sat, 7am-7pm Sun) The bakeries belonging to this chain are located throughout the city centre and are great for a coffee-and-pastry breakfast.

Vegebar
VEGETARIAN €

(ul Długa 11; mains around 14zł; ⊘11am-7pm; 🖉) Simple vegetarian milk bar with a central location and a menu of curries and lentil dishes as well as *szarlotka* (apple cake) and juices.

★ Tawerna Mestwin
POLISH €€

(📁58 301 7882; ul Straganiarska 20/23; mains 20-40zł; ⊘11am-10pm Tue-Sun, to 6pm Mon; 🕏) The specialty here is Kashubian regional cooking from the northwest of Poland, and dishes like potato dumplings and stuffed cabbage rolls have a pronounced homemade quality. There's usually a fish soup and fried fish as well. The interior is done out like a traditional cottage and the exposed beams and dark-green walls lend a special atmosphere.

Velevetka
POLISH €€

(www.velevetka.pl; ul Długa 45; mains 26-49zł; ⊘noon-11pm daily) Go Kashubian at this delightful eatery opposite the Town Hall, which manages to evoke a rural theme without a single ancient agricultural knick-knack or trussed waitress in sight. Admire the crisp interior of heavy wooden furniture decorated with stylised Kashubian motifs and soothing scenes of the countryside, while sampling finely prepared regional dishes.

The traditional duck with apple and *slivovitz* sauce (plum brandy) comes highly recommended.

Kresowa
EASTERN EUROPEAN €€

(ul Ogarna 12; mains 19-45zł; ⊘noon-10pm) Take your tastebuds to Poland's long-lost east and beyond at this two-level, 19th-century period restaurant with the mood of an Imperial-era Chekhovian parlour. Start with Ukrainian borscht, order a main of Hutsul lamb and finish with a piece of Polish cheesecake while sipping homemade *kvas* (partially fermented bread and water). There's even bison goulash for those who dare to ask.

Czerwone Drzwi
POLISH €€

(www.reddoor.gd.pl; ul Piwna 52/53; mains 10-35zł; ⊘10am-10pm) Step through the Red Door into a relaxed, refined cafe atmosphere, for a small but interesting seasonal menu of Polish and international meals.

Kos
INTERNATIONAL €€

(www.restauracjakos.pl; ul Piwna 9/10; mains 25-35zł; ⊘9am-midnight; 🕏) If you're travelling with the family in tow, this internationally minded, kid-friendly place is an excellent choice. The crowd-pleasing menu is a pizza-pasta affair, plus Polish chops, sandwiches and hefty breakfasts. There's a playroom where the kids can rampage while parents monitor them upstairs via CCTV. Decor is all whites and greys, with splashes of strategic colour.

SONS OF DANZIG

As a lively cultural and intellectual centre, Gdańsk has spawned some famous personalities over the years. Here are the biggest names:

➜ **Johannes Hevelius** (1611–87) Astronomer who produced one of the first detailed maps of the moon's surface.

➜ **Gabriel Daniel Fahrenheit** (1686–1736) Inventor of the mercury thermometer.

➜ **Arthur Schopenhauer** (1788–1860) Philosopher who felt that irrational human behaviour was driven by a force he called the 'will to live'.

➜ **Günter Grass** (1927-2015) German author, Nobel laureate and perhaps Gdańsk's most famous son. Best known for his first novel *The Tin Drum*.

➜ **Lech Wałęsa** (b 1943) Former Gdańsk dockyard electrician, Solidarity leader and Polish president.

➜ **Jacek Kaczmarski** (1957–2004) Poet and singer-songwriter whose fierce opposition to the communist regime led to his exile in the 1980s.

➜ **Donald Tusk** (b 1957) Poland's best-known politician, former prime minister and current president of the European Council.

Restauracja Gdańska POLISH €€€
(☑58 305 7671; www.gdanska.pl; ul Św Ducha 16; mains 28-65zł; ⊙noon-midnight) Dining in any of the five banqueting rooms and salons here is a bit like eating out in a well-stocked museum, with surroundings of antique furniture, oil paintings, model ships and random objets d'art. The upper-end traditional menu of herring, white Gdańsk-style *żurek* (traditional sour rye soup), duck and slabs of cheesecake is as heavy as the sumptuous drapery.

Restauracja Pod Łososiem POLISH €€€
(☑58 301 7652; www.podlososiem.com.pl; ul Szeroka 52/54; mains 65-110zł; ⊙noon-11pm) Founded in 1598 and famous for salmon, this is one of Gdańsk's most highly regarded restaurants. Red leather seats, brass chandeliers and a gathering of gas lamps fill out the rather sober interior, illuminated by the specialty drink – Goldwasser. This gooey, sweet liqueur with flakes of gold was produced in its cellars from the 16th century until WWII.

Metamorfoza POMERANIAN €€€
(☑58 320 3030; www.restauracjametamorfoza.pl; ul Szeroka 22/23; set menu 90-270zł; ⊙1pm-last customer) Pomeranian fare is hardly ever given the gourmet treatment, but if refined seasonal dishes are what you seek, Metamorfoza is the place. Enjoy dishes prepared with only the finest local ingredients from the region's farms, forests, rivers and offshore waters in an interior that blends crystal chandeliers and Chesterfield sofas with ultra-modern display cases and the odd antique.

Filharmonia FUSION €€€
(www.restauracjagdansk.pl; ul Ołwianka 1; mains 45-105zł; ⊙noon-midnight) Occupying a red-brick corner of the Philharmonia building facing the Targ Rybny across the river, the cooks here dabble in Heston Blumenthal–style molecular cuisine to admirable effect. If you came to Pomerania to glut out on braised flesh and ale, then the pernickety creations here will disappoint with their finesse, attention to detail and obsessive focus on taste.

🍷 Drinking & Nightlife

Getting a dose of Arabica, a jug of ale or something a lot, lot stronger is pretty easy in central Gdańsk, with cafes and bars assembling anywhere tourists do. More characterful nooks can be found in ul Mariacka and ul Piwna. As anyone in town will concede, Sopot (p330) is the place to go for a serious night out.

★ **Józef K** BAR
(ul Piwna 1/2; ⊙10am-last customer; 🔊) Is it a bar or a junk shop? You decide as you relax with a cocktail or a glass of excellent Polish perry on one of the battered sofas, illuminated by an old theatre spotlight. Downstairs is an open area where the party kicks off at weekends; upstairs is more intimate with lots of soft seating and well-stocked bookcases.

Brovarnia MICROBREWERY
(www.brovarnia.pl; ul Szafarnia 9; ⊙1-11pm) Northern Poland's best microbrewery cooks

up award-winning dark, wheat and lager beers in polished copper vats amid sepia photos of old Gdańsk. Tables are tightly packed but this place lacks a beer-hall feel, possibly as it's squeezed into vacant granary space in the posh Hotel Gdańsk.

Lamus
BAR

(Lawendowa 8, enter from Straganiarska; ☺ noon-1am Mon-Fri, to 3am Sat, to midnight Sun) This fun retro-drink halt has a random scattering 1970s furniture, big-print wallpaper from the same period, and a menu of Polish craft beers, cider and coffee. There's also a spillover bar for the Saturday night crowd.

Literacka
WINE BAR

(www.literacka.gda.pl; ul Mariacka 52; ☺ noon-last customer) This intimate, two-level wine bar stocks reds and whites from all over the world, including – wait for it – Poland! Staff know their Dornfelder from their Douce noir and there are inexpensive pasta dishes, sandwiches and soups to accompany your wine of choice.

Cafe Absinthe
CAFE

(www.cafeabsinthe.pl; ul Św Ducha 2; ☺ 10am-4am Mon-Fri, until 6am Sat) By day this unassuming bar occupying an inconspicuous corner of the Teatr Wybrzeże building is the haunt of a few coffee-cradling newspaper readers. But when darkness falls, the inebriated debauchery starts – when there's no dance floor, use the tables.

Degustatornia Dom Piwa
PUB

(ul Grodzka 16; ☺ 3pm-midnight Mon-Thu, to 1am Fri & Sat, to 10pm Sun) If beer brings you cheer, then the 180 types of ale, lager, porter and myriad other hop-based concoctions at this pub will have you ecstatic. Some 80 Polish bottled beers are poured alongside such gems as Czech Radegast, Kentish Spitfire, dark Erdinger wheat beer, Belgian strawberry ale and cloudy Ukrainian Chernihivske.

Goldwasser
CAFE

(Długie Pobrzeże 22; ☺ 10am-8pm) Experience the spirit of the interwar Free City of Danzig at the home of three tasty local tipples – Goldwasser, Kurfüsten and locally produced Machandel vodka. A quiet oasis with a leathery upmarket feel. Enter from Długi Targ.

Pi Kawa
CAFE

(ul Piwna 5/6; ☺ 10am-11pm; 🛜) One of the early post-communist originals, this aromatic coffeehouse is still worth a shot for the expertly barristered brews and the huge blown-up images of Gdańsk on the walls.

Kamienica
CAFE, BAR

(ul Mariacka 37/39) The pick of the bunch on ul Mariacka is this excellent two-level cafe with a calm, sophisticated atmosphere and the best patio on the block. As popular for a daytime caffeine-and-cake halt as it is for a sociable evening bevvy.

Miasto Aniołów
CLUB

(www.miastoaniolow.com.pl; ul Chmielna 26) The City of Angels covers all the bases – late-night revellers can hit the spacious dance floor, crash in the chill-out area or hang around the atmospheric deck overlooking the Motława River. Nightly DJs play disco and other dance-oriented sounds.

Parlament
CLUB

(www.parlament.com.pl; ul Św Ducha 2; ☺ 8pm-late Thu-Sat; 🛜) Popular mainstream club with strutting nights devoted to the hits of yesteryear, pop, dance, R'n'B and hip-hop.

☆ Entertainment

Check the local press for up-to-date cultural and entertainment listings.

Baltic Philharmonic Hall
CLASSICAL MUSIC

(☑ 58 320 6262; www.filharmonia.gda.pl; ul Ołowianka 1) The usual home of chamber music concerts also organises many of the major music festivals throughout the year.

State Baltic Opera Theatre
OPERA

(Map p000; ☑ 58 763 4906; www.operabaltycka.pl; Al Zwycięstwa 15) Founded in 1950, Gdańsk's premier opera company resides in this opera house in the Wrzeszcz district, next to the Gdańsk Politechnika train station. It also stages regular ballets. Symphonic concerts are also held here.

Teatr Wybrzeże
THEATRE

(☑ 58 301 1328; www.teatrwybrzeze.pl; Targ Węglowy 1) Top productions of Polish and foreign classics next to the Great Arsenal in the Main Town.

🔒 Shopping

Gdańsk shopping isn't all about amber – Goldwasser makes an unusual take-home item and pretty Kashubian handicrafts (p333) are also worth considering.

Galeria Sztuki Kaszubskiej
HANDICRAFTS

(ul Św Ducha; ☺ 11am-6pm Mon-Sat Jul-Aug, shorter hours Sep-Jun) For genuine handmade

Kashubian handicrafts, look no further than this small shop near St Mary's Church. Porcelain and embroidery dominate the range, much of which is designed and produced by the owner.

Cepelia ARTS & CRAFTS
(ul Długa 47; ⏰10am-6pm Mon-Fri, to 2pm Sat) A branch of the national chain and hence the most obvious place to head for Kashubian trinkets.

Galeria SAS ARTS
(www.galeriab.pl; ul Szeroka 18/19; ⏰10.30am-5pm Mon-Fri, to 4pm Sat) The quality oil paintings at this commercial gallery make unique and interesting souvenirs. All are by local artists and the owner is very knowledgeable about her collection.

Information

INTERNET RESOURCES
http://guide.trojmiasto.pl Detailed Tri-City tourist guide.
www.gdansk4u.pl Gdańsk's official tourist website.
www.gdansk.pl Excellent city information site.
www.lonelyplanet.com/poland/pomerania/gdansk For planning advice, author recommendations, traveller reviews and insider tips.

POST
Post Office (ul Długa 23/28; ⏰24hr) The main post office with its old interior under a glass roof is worth a look even if you aren't sending anything. ATM and currency exchange window.

TOURIST INFORMATION
Tourist Office Train station (☎58 721 3277; www.gdansk4u.pl; ul Podwale Grodzkie 8; ⏰9am-7pm May-Sep, to 5pm Oct-Apr); Main

Town (☎58 301 4355; www.gdansk4u.pl; Długi Targ 28/29; ⏰9am-7pm May-Sep, 9am-5pm Oct-Apr); Airport (☎58 348 1368; www.gdansk4u.pl; ul Słowackiego 210, Gdańsk Lech Wałęsa Airport; ⏰24hr) Relatively efficient but occasionally visitor-weary info points. The train station branch is hidden in the underpass leading to the city centre.

Pomorskie Regional Tourist Office (☎58 732 7041; www.pomorskie.travel; Brama Wyżynna, Wały Jagiellońskie 2A; ⏰9am-8pm daily) Housed in the Upland Gate, this friendly regional tourist office has info on Gdańsk and the surrounding area.

PTTK Office (☎58 301 6096; www.pttk-gdansk.pl; ul Długa 45; ⏰10am-6pm) Arranges foreign-language tours, excursions and accommodation.

TRAVEL AGENCIES
JoyTrip (☎58 320 6169; www.pl.joytrip.eu) Specialises in group and corporate events. Whatever you want to do in the Tri-City, these guys can help you do it.

Travel Plus (☎58 346 3118; www.travel-plus.eu; ul Długi Targ 1-7) Gdańsk and Pomerania-wide tours.

Getting There & Away

AIR
Lech Wałęsa airport (☎801 066 808, 52 567 3531; www.airport.gdansk.pl; ul Słowackiego 210) is in Rębiechowo, 14km west of Gdańsk. There are domestic flights to Warsaw with LOT (every two hours). To reach any other destination in Poland you must travel via Warsaw. The exception to this Kraków, which is served by **Ryanair** (www.ryanair.com).

International flights to many European capitals and regional destinations in the UK and across Europe are operated by budget airlines

AMBER GAMBLER

For some visitors, one of the main reasons to come to Gdańsk is to source jewellery made of Baltic gold – fossilised tree resin found on the Baltic shores of Poland and Russia, commonly known as amber.

But beware: at some smaller, less-reputable stalls, you may not be getting the real deal, with some pieces containing well-crafted chunks of Russian or Chinese plastic.

Here are three ways locals recommend you can tell if the amber you are being offered is bona fide prehistoric sap. Not all shopkeepers will be happy to see you testing their wares in these ways, for obvious reasons.

➡ Take a lighter and put amber into the heat – it should give off a characteristic smell, like incense.

➡ Amber floats in 20% salt water, while plastic or synthetic amber won't.

➡ Rub amber against cloth and the static electricity produced attracts tiny pieces of paper.

Ryanair and Hungarian low-cost carrier **Wizz Air** (www.wizzair.com).

BOAT

Polferries (p428) operates car ferries from Gdańsk Nowy Port to Nynäshamn in Sweden (19 hours, up to 15 departures a month in high season).

BUS

Gdańsk's **bus terminal** is right behind the central train station, linked by an underground passageway. Buses are handy for regional destinations, which have little or no train service.

Elbląg 16zł, 1½ hours, at least hourly

Frombork 20zł, two hours, three daily

Kartuzy 8.50zł, one hour, half-hourly (Gryf bus)

Kościerzyna 16.50zł, 1½ hours, hourly

Lidzbark Warmiński 30zł, three to 3½ hours, six daily

Olsztyn 33zł, 3½ hours, hourly

Warsaw 50zł, 4½ to six hours, at least hourly

There are plenty of connections from Gdańsk to Western European cities plus daily services east to Kaliningrad (60zł, five hours), and Vilnius (160zł, 16 hours) via Olsztyn.

TRAIN

The grand main train station, **Gdańsk Główny** (Map p309), is on the western outskirts of the Old Town and handles all services.

Almost all long-distance trains to/from the south originate and terminate in Gdynia, while many trains running along the coast to western destinations start in Gdańsk and stop at Gdynia (and Sopot) en route.

Gdańsk has the following rail connections:

Lębork (for Łeba) 12zł, 1¾ hours, hourly (SKM)

Malbork 13.50zł, 50 minutes, frequent

Olsztyn 39zł, 2¾ hours, six daily

Poznań 60zł, 3½ hours, eight daily

Szczecin 60zł, five to six hours, four daily (or change in Słupsk)

A THOUSAND AND ONE KNIGHTS

It's impossible to travel anywhere in Pomerania without encountering the ghosts of the Teutonic Knights, the military monks who ended up ruling great swathes of modern-day Germany and Poland. Their rise is a spectacular tale worthy of mega-budget Hollywood treatment, involving foreign origins, holy war, conquest, defeat and an unexpected sideline in charitable works.

The Order of the Hospitallers of Saint Mary of the Teutons in Jerusalem, as it was formally known, was founded in Palestine in 1190, as a medical body to treat Germanic knights fighting in the Crusades.

In this religion-infused landscape, the order attracted many fighters wanting to take holy orders. From this potent military and spiritual mix emerged the Teutonic Knights, warrior monks who wore a distinctive white habit with a black cross.

Back in Europe, their big break came when the Polish Duke Konrad I of Mazovia needed help subduing the pagan Prussians of the Lower Vistula. By the end of the 13th century, the Teutonic Knights had conquered all of Prussia. They then set about consolidating their rule by building castles, importing German peasants to build up the population and developing trade. Towns such as Thorn (Toruń) and Elbing (Elbląg) became important Teutonic centres, and the castle at Marienburg (Malbork) was a potent symbol of the order's might.

Inevitably, territorial tensions arose with the neighbouring and newly resurgent Kingdom of Poland. After a century of friction, the Knights fell to combined Polish and Lithuanian forces at the Battle of Grunwald (1410). But their greatest defeat at Polish hands was yet to come – the Thirteen Years' War saw the order's own subjects turn against it, and the Treaty of Toruń in 1466 forced it to give up much of Pomerania, Warmia and the banks of the Vistula.

The Teutonic Knights were on the way out. In 1525 the order's Grand Master Albert transformed Prussia into a secular state, ending the knights' rule and naming himself duke. Then, after centuries of decline, Napoleon declared the Teutonic order dissolved in 1809.

Curiously though, the order refused to die. In 1834 the Austrian Emperor Franz I re-established the Teutonic order as a religious body, restricted to charitable and nursing activities – neatly returning the body to its medieval roots. Nowadays the Grand Master holds office at Singerstrasse 7 in Vienna, where the Teutonic order operates a museum and archive. It even has a website: www.deutscher-orden.at (in German).

Toruń 40zł, three hours, nine daily

Warsaw 60zł to 119zł, three to six hours, hourly (two overnight services)

Wrocław 61zł, six to seven hours, three daily (or change in Warsaw or Poznań)

ℹ️ Getting Around

TO/FROM THE AIRPORT

Bus 210 leaves from the Brama Wyżynna (Upland Gate) every 30 minutes from 5.21am to 10.20pm, hourly on Saturday and Sunday.

BOAT

Żegluga Gdańska (www.zegluga.pl; adult/concession 35/25zł) From May until September, Żegluga Gdańska runs pleasure boats and hydrofoils from Gdańsk's wharf, near the Green Gate, to Hel.

Ustka-Tour (www.rejsyturystyczne.pl; adult/concession return 40/25zł; ⊘ hourly) Operates cruises to Westerplatte aboard the *Galeon Lew* and the *Perła*, replica 17th-century galleons.

TRAIN

A commuter train, known as the SKM (Szybka Kolej Miejska; Fast City Train), runs constantly between Gdańsk Główny and Gdynia Główna (35 minutes), stopping at a dozen intermediate stations, including Sopot. The trains run every five to 10 minutes at peak times and every hour or so late at night. You buy tickets at the stations and validate them in the machines at the platform entrance (not in the train itself), or purchase them prevalidated from vending machines on the platform.

TRAM & BUS

These are a slower means of transport than the SKM but cover more ground, running from 5am until around 11pm, when a handful of night lines take over. Tickets cost 3zł for any one way journey, and 3.60zł for one hour's travel. A day ticket valid for a 24-hour period costs 12zł. Remember to validate your ticket in the vehicle, so it is stamped with the date and time.

AROUND GDAŃSK

Sopot

POP 38,140

The junior partner in the Tri-City set-up (along with Gdańsk and Gdynia), Sopot is a kind of Incongruity-on-Sea, a mix of elegant villas and marauding clubbers, an over-developed 21st-century seafront just streets away from typically Polish soot-cracked facades. Like the British seaside towns of Brighton and Eastbourne rolled into one, Sopot is about moneyed Poles flashing their cash in ritzy eateries standing alongside old Polish literary-themed cafes, a strutting club scene illuminating pensioners taking to the waters while kids on the beach build sandcastles. Whatever Sopot has become, it certainly remains popular, with international visitors mingling with the Slavic waffle-and-ice-cream crowds on hot summer days then getting down at the beachside clubs of a balmy Baltic eve.

Sopot's incarnation as a fashionable resort arose in 1823 when Jean Georges Haffner, a former doctor in Napoleon's army, popularised sea-bathing here. The settlement, originally established in the 13th century as a fishing village, rapidly became the beach destination of the rich and famous, particularly after WWI when it was included in the territory of the Free City of Danzig. Since 1990 it's once again become the playground of wealthy entrepreneurs and A-list celebrities, and remains unrivalled among the Baltic's resorts for glitz and pretentiousness.

◉ Sights & Activities

Ulica Bohaterów Monte Cassino STREET

(ul Bohaterów) Sopot's unavoidable spine is 'Heroes of Monte Cassino' Street, an attractive and invariably crowded mall stretching from the railway line to the pier. Many of Sopot's eateries and places of entertainment line its pedestrianised length, some of which can be found in the unmissable **Crooked House** (Krzywy Domek; www.krzywydomek.info; ul Bohaterów Monte Cassino 53).

Sopot Museum MUSEUM

(www.muzeumsopotu.pl; ul Poniatowskiego 8; adult/concession 5/3zł, Thu free; ⊘10am-4pm Tue & Wed, 11am-5pm Thu-Sun) At the southern end of the beachfront in a grand old villa, the Sopot Museum showcases 19th-century furniture and fittings, including some enormous, ornately carved wardrobes. Other displays include old sepia photos and maps of German Zoppot and other Baltic resorts. The building, an early-20th-century holiday home of a wealthy merchant, is worth a look in itself.

Pier PIER

(Molo; www.molo.sopot.pl; Seafront; admission 7.50zł May-Sep) At the end of Monte Cassino, beyond Plac Zdrojowy, is the famous Molo, Europe's longest wooden pier, built in 1928 and jutting 515m out into the Bay of

Sopot

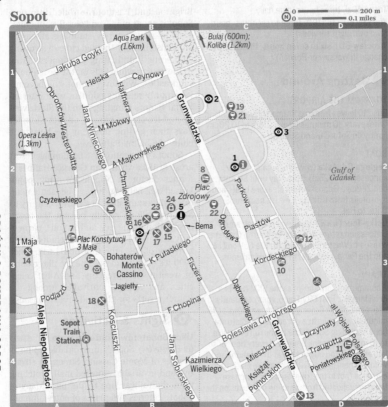

Sopot

◎ Sights

Art Gallery	(see 1)
1	Dom Zdrojowy	C2
2	Grand Hotel	C1
3	Pier	C2
4	Sopot Museum	D4
5	Tightrope Walker Statue	B2
6	Ulica Bohaterów Monte Cassino	B3

🛏 Sleeping

7	Central Hostel Sopot	A3
8	Hotel Bayjonn	C2
9	Hotel Rezydent	A3
10	Pensjonat Eden	C3
11	Pensjonat Wanda	D4
12	Zhong Hua Hotel	D3

🍴 Eating

13	Bar Bursztyn	D4
14	Bar Mleczny Trendy	A3
15	Błękitny Pudel	B3
16	Green Way	B3
17	Kebabistan	B3
18	Pub Kinski	A3

🍸 Drinking & Nightlife

19	Klub Atelier	C1
20	Młody Byron	B2
21	Scena	C1
22	Spatif	C2
23	Zaścianek	B2

🛍 Shopping

24	Crooked House	B2

Gdańsk. Various attractions along its length come and go with the seasons. The cheeky summer admission charge puts few off.

Opera Leśna THEATRE
(Forest Opera; Map p309; ☎58 555 8400; www.operalesna.sopot.pl; ul Moniuszki 12) In a wooded hilly area of the town stands the

Opera Leśna, an amphitheatre that seats 5000 people and is host to the prestigious August International Sopot Festival, a Eurovision-style song contest and festival famous across Central and Eastern Europe. Check the website for the summer programme.

Aqua Park
AMUSEMENT PARK

(Map p309; www.aquaparksopot.pl; ul Zamkowa Góra 3/5; per hr 23zł; ⊙8am-10pm daily) This large indoor aqua park has tubes, slides, spas and a wild river ride.

Tightrope Walker Statue
STATUE

(ul Bema) FREE While ambling your way along Ulica Bohaterów Monte Cassino towards the sea, take a right into ul Bema to see one of the most unusual statues in Poland. An African fisherman carrying a net is suspended above the street on a tightrope, the piece of public art seeming to defy gravity. It's the work of Polish sculptor Jerzy Kedziora who specialises in these odd balancing spectacles.

Art Gallery
GALLERY

(Państwowa Galeria Sztuki; www.pgs.pl; Plac Zdrojowy 2; adult/concession 10/7zł; ⊙11am-7pm Tue-Sun) Funded by the town of Sopot, this glitzy art gallery within the reconstructed Dom Zdrojowy (Spa House) has changing exhibitions of mostly Polish art.

Dom Zdrojowy
MINERAL SPRING

(Plac Zdrojowy 2; ⊙10am-6pm) FREE Take the space-age glazed lift to the 3rd floor to enjoy a free sip of Sopot's natural, mineral-rich spring water.

Grand Hotel
LANDMARK

(Powstańców Warszawy 12/14) North of the pier is the landmark 1927 Grand Hotel, adjoining the long waterfront spa park that first popularised the town.

🛏 Sleeping

Central Hostel Sopot
HOSTEL €

(☑530 858 717; www.centralsopot.com; ul Bohaterów Monte Cassino 15; dm/d from 75/200zł) Spacious both horizontally and vertically, this three-storey former workers' hostel has dorms containing four to ten beds plus myriad other singles and doubles, all en suite. As there's no kitchen or common room, the place lacks atmosphere, but rooms are well-kept and the location-to-price ratio is a winner.

Camping Nr 19
CAMPGROUND €

(Map p309; ☑58 550 0445; www.kemping19.cba.pl; ul Zamkowa Góra 25; per person/tent 14/10zł) A large but often full camping ground located at the northern end of town near the beach (a five-minute walk from the Sopot Kamienny Potok train station).

Pensjonat Eden
HOTEL €€

(☑58 551 1503; www.hotel-eden.pl; ul Kordeckiego 4/6; s 160-270zł, d 210-380zł) The crumbly facade of this early-20th-century villa doesn't promise much, but once inside this family-run guesthouse you'll receive a friendly welcome before being shown up to one of the 26 well-kept rooms, flaunting stylishly high ceilings and lots of fun-and-fusty furniture straight from granny's parlour.

Pensjonat Wanda
GUESTHOUSE €€

(☑58 550 3037; www.bws-hotele.pl; ul Poniatowskiego 7; s/d 200/260zł; 🅿🛜) A traditional, 25-room guesthouse with en-suite rooms, some with balconies overlooking the sea and sand. There's a reasonably priced restaurant on the premises.

★ Hotel Bayjonn
HOTEL €€€

(☑58 664 6883; www.bayjonnhotel.pl; ul Powstańców Warszawy 7; s 475-599zł, d 550-699zł; 🅿🛜) Occupying an architecturally striking corner of the Haffner Centre, this design hotel is all retro stripes and faux '70s browns, but with stunningly contemporary bathrooms and little nods to the past in the shape of old German-era maps of Zoppot. Facilities are kept shiny, staff are friendly enough and the location is superb.

Facilities include a fitness and centre and sauna. Buffet breakfast is a whopping 39zł extra.

Hotel Rezydent
HOTEL €€€

(☑58 555 5800; www.hotelrezydent.pl; Plac Konstytucji 3 Maja 3; s from 420zł, tw from 450zł; 🅿✳@🛜) The Rezydent is the most elegant hotel in town, though you'll pay for the privilege of staying here. Its rooms' tasteful tones are set off by stylish carpets, timber furniture and lustrous bathrooms. When you're done luxuriating, there's a classy restaurant and pub downstairs, along with an art gallery, a sauna and massage services.

Zhong Hua Hotel
HOTEL €€€

(☑58 550 2020; www.hotelchinski.pl; Al Wojska Polskiego 1; s/d from 470/500zł) Unique hotel housed within a 19th-century bathing pavilion right on the beach (it's Poland's only beach hotel), but one quite incongruously done out in Chinese style with lacquered furniture and lanterns. The rooms also have little Chinese touches and bathrooms with marble fittings. There's a decent restaurant on the premises and the sand comes right up to the door.

Even the receptionists have little explanation of the Chinese styling, the owners perhaps having got ready for hordes of Chinese tourists that never came.

✖ Eating

Much of Sopot's cuisine scene is seasonal, particularly in the beach area, but there's no shortage of good year-round options.

★ Bar Bursztyn CAFETERIA €
(www.barbursztyn.pl; ul Grunwaldzka 78-80, 8a; mains 6.50-20zł; ⊙8am-10pm daily; 🌐) A millennium away from the milk bars of yesteryear, this snazzy canteen with nightclub decor, polite English-speaking staff, free magazines, pagers that let you know when your order is ready, a toy corner and authentic pizzas blasts the worker's canteen concept into outer space. In fact, it has been described as *a bar mleczny* that's somehow come back from the future.

Green Way VEGETARIAN €
(ul Bohaterów Monte Cassino 47; mains 10-15zł; ⊙10am-9pm Sun-Thu, to 10pm Fri & Sat; 🖋) One of the few Green Ways to have survived, this modern, meat-free *bar mleczny* plates up generous portions of budget veggie nosh in no-frills surroundings. The menu features such exotic dishes as mousaka and kofta plus dumplings and pasta.

Bar Mleczny Trendy CAFETERIA €
(Al Niepodległości 786; mains 9-15zł; ⊙11am-6pm Mon-Sat, noon-5pm Sun) If you can get past the awful name, you'll find budget fare that is Polish, tasty and filling – plus it's the less glamorous side of the tracks so wholly tourist-free. No old-school *bar mleczny*, there's coffee and big-print monochrome prints of Sopot on the walls.

Kebabistan KEBAB €
(ul Bohaterów Monte Cassino 36; kebabs around 14zł; ⊙11am-late) Not hard to guess what this places serves up – *döner*, in a box, in bread, plus *baklava* and drinks. Great name and popular stop-off for those stumbling or crawling their way to the SKM at 3am.

★ Błękitny Pudel CAFE €€
(ul Bohaterów Monte Cassino 44; mains 21-35zł; ⊙9am-last customer; 🌐) This top pub-cafe is a real knick-knack fest with the cobbled interior bedecked in wooden tennis rackets, *balalaikas* (Russian stringed instruments), richly upholstered divans and seemingly everything in between. Choose between the cosy interior and an outdoor pew for a bit of people watching on ul BMC. Unusual menu items include black pudding in mushroom and cider sauce and Eton mess.

Pub Kinski PUB FOOD €€
(ul Kościuszki 10; mains 25-40zł; ⊙11pm-3am) The house and birthplace of legendary German actor and psychopath Klaus Kinski has been converted into an offbeat bar-restaurant, with film posters and decadent leather sofas within a cosy, candlelit setting. The man himself probably would have trashed the place, but in a loving way.

★ Bulaj SEAFOOD €€€
(📷58 551 5129; www.bulaj.pl; Al Franciszka Mamuszki 22; mains around 20-60zł; ⊙11am-11pm) One of Poland's best restaurants, foodies flock here to sample chef Artur Moroz's seafood dishes, served in a crisp but basic, pub-like environment. For those who don't like fish, there's always local rabbit and duck on the menu, but it's the zander, cod and halibut most come for, prepared in delicious but simple ways. On the beach at entrance No 12.

🍷 Drinking & Nightlife

Sopot has a vibrant club and live-music culture that's always changing; ask the locals about the current favourites or check www.sopot.klubowa.pl. The scene here is also notably gay-friendly.

Spatif BAR
(www.spatif.sopot.pl; ul Bohaterów Monte Cassino 54; ⊙4pm-1am; 🌐) Head up the steps off ul BMC to find this unmissable, avant-garde place packed with charity-shop leftovers and backstage kitsch. The crowd ranges from wannabe novelists to Warsaw party gals, and the atmosphere gets more vodka-inspired the later things get. You might have to get past face control at weekends.

Młody Byron CAFE
(ul Czyżewskiego 12; ⊙noon-11pm daily) Far from the lubricated wannabes on ul BMC, this renovated mini-palace houses a quaint little

GDAŃSK & POMERANIA SOPOT

cafe (the former U Hrabiego), where more bookish types take the cake and engage in highbrow banter.

Zaścianek CAFE
(ul Haffnera 3; ⊙11am-10pm Sun-Thu, to 11pm Fri & Sat; ☎) Delightful olde-worlde hideaway full of antique bric-a-brac, potted plants, oil paintings and intimate tables for two run by friendly owners. Popular with locals and well hidden from the holidaying mobs.

Scena CLUB
(www.scenaklub.pl; Al Franciszka Mamuszki 2) Eclectic beach club with a calendar of jazz, DJs, live music and special events. One of Sopot's best.

Klub Atelier CLUB
(www.klubatelier.pl; Al Franciszka Mamuszki 2) Classic Sopot club with beach access, a different big-name DJ every night and a cool, well-to-do Baltic feel attracting the Tri-City's beautiful people.

Koliba CLUB
(www.koliba.pl; beach entrance 5, ul Powstanców Warszawy 90; ⊙24hr) A beach hike or bike ride north along the Baltic, this traditional Tatra Mountain–style chalet is a restaurant by day, but at 9pm the tables and chairs are pushed back to create the Tri-City's most unlikely and unpretentious nightclub. Great beach access and Baltic-side terrace.

❶ Information

Post Office (ul Kościuszki 2)
Tourist Office (☑790 280 884; www.sts.sopot. pl; Plac Zdrojowy 2; ⊙10am-6pm daily) One of northern Poland's best tourist offices with free wi-fi, a left luggage facility, a cheap souvenir shop and lots of space to laze around.

❶ Getting There & Away

All trains between Gdańsk and Gdynia stop in Sopot. SKM commuter trains to Gdańsk (3.80zł) run every five to 10 minutes at peak times. The train station is around 1km from the pier.

Hel Peninsula

Located north of the Tri-City, the Hel Peninsula (Półwysep Helski) is a 34km-long, crescent-shaped sandbank arcing out into the Baltic Sea. A mere 300m wide at the base, it's no wider than 500m for most of its length, though it does expand out to

around 3km at the end to accommodate the 'capital', Hel. Reaching just 23m above sea level, much of the landscape is covered with trees – picturesque, wind-deformed pines predominate – and there are also a number of typical coastal plant varieties including sand sedge and dune thistle.

The peninsula was formed over the course of about 8000 years by sea currents and winds, which gradually formed an uninterrupted belt of sand. At the end of the 17th century, as old maps show, the sandbar was still cut by six inlets, making it a chain of islands. In the 19th century the peninsula was cut into separate pieces several times by storms. The edges have been strengthened and the movement of the sand has been reduced by vegetation, but the sandbar continues to grow.

The peninsula is bookended by two fishing ports: the aforementioned Hel at its tip and Władysławowo at its base. Between them is a third port, Jastarnia, and three villages: Chałupy, Kuźnica and Jurata. All are tourist resorts during the short summer season (July and August) and are linked by a railway line and a surprisingly good road running the peninsula's entire sandy length.

The northern shore is one long stretch of beautifully sandy beach and, except for small areas around the resorts (which are usually packed with holidaymakers), they're clean and deserted.

The Hel Peninsula is easily accessible from the Tri-City by train and bus.

Hel

POP 3900
Most English-speakers can't help cracking a smirk as they ask for their ticket to Hel. But this relaxed holiday town at the end of its long slender sandbar is far from purgatory. In fact, it's quite a pleasant getaway and feels a long way from Poland's post-communist cares. The beach is the obvious main draw when it's hot; the rest of the year the town shows few vital signs.

Throughout history, Hel benefited from its strategic location at the maritime gateway to Gdańsk. By the 14th century Hel was a prosperous fishing port and trading centre. However, it was constantly threatened by storms and the shifting coastline, and declined in importance in the 18th century before reinventing itself as a popular seaside resort.

⊙ Sights

Fokarium AQUARIUM

(www.fokarium.com; ul Morska 2; admission 5zł; ⊙9.30am-8pm) Just off the beach in the centre of town is the Fokarium, where Baltic grey seals can be seen in captivity. The three large pools are home to half a dozen of the creatures, and feeding takes place at 11am and 2pm when keepers put these incredibly obedient animals through their paces for fishy rewards. You'll need a 5zł piece to unlock the main turnstile and another 1zł if you want to visit the small museum once inside.

Museum of Fishery MUSEUM

(Muzeum Rybołówstwa; www.nmm.pl; Bulwar Nadmorski 2; adult/concession 6/4zł; ⊙10am-6pm daily Jul & Aug, shorter hours rest of year) Hel's Gothic church dates from the 1420s, making it the oldest building in town. Pews and monstrances have given way to exhibits on fishing and boat-building, a display of stuffed sea birds and a collection of old fishing boats, all part of the National Maritime Museum. The tower provides views of the peninsula and Gulf of Gdańsk. The whole caboodle was closed for much-needed renovation at the time of research.

Lighthouse LIGHTHOUSE

(ul Bałtycka 3; adult/concession 6/4zł; ⊙10am-2pm & 3-7pm Jul & Aug, shorter hours May, Jun & Sep) Through a patch of scrappy woodland at the end of ul Wiejska, the 42m-high octagonal brick lighthouse is a now radar station but houses temporary exhibitions.

Memorial MEMORIAL

(cnr uls Wiejska & Sikorskiego) A park near the train station contains a memorial to the 1939 defence of the town during the German invasion. Hel was the last place in Poland to surrender; a garrison of some 3000 Polish soldiers defended the town until 2 October. The peninsula became a battlefield once more on 5 April 1945, when about 60,000 Germans were caught in a bottleneck by the Red Army and didn't lay down their arms until 9 May, making it the last piece of Polish territory to be liberated.

Izba Kaszubska ARTS CENTRE

(ul Wiejska 78; ⊙11am-4pm daily) FREE An old 19th-century fisherman's cottage on the main street houses a small exhibition of Kashubian handicrafts and a souvenir stall. The staff also give out town maps.

🛏 Sleeping

There are beds in ample numbers during the summer months though few classic hotels or guesthouses. The best place to start if you're looking to stay over is the official Hel website (www.gohel.pl) which has lots of listings and an interactive map. Many locals rent out rooms in their homes – look out for the many official signs on gates and houses bearing a number – this means the property has been checked by the municipality.

Cassubia HOTEL €

(✆26 126 7469; www.hotelewam.pl; ul Boczna 11; d from 110zł; P🛜) Take a trip back to Poland's institutional past at this 64-bed relic with furniture from the days of martial law and wi-fi that feels like it might be, too. The location near the train station is this place's biggest plus – no dragging heavy bags into town. Another positive is that there are almost always beds free.

Duna Guesthouse GUESTHOUSE €€

(✆58 351 2063; www.duna.org.pl; ul Morska; d/tr 150/180zł) This beachside place has fresh, well-tended rooms and apartments with flat-pack furniture and modern bathrooms. Outside of the high season you can pay as little as 60zł per person.

✗ Eating

★**Kutter** POLISH €€

(www.kutter.pl; ul Wiejska 87; mains 20-40zł; ⊙9am-midnight daily) Hel's top place to eat is the beautifully done out Kutter where fishing knick-knacks of yesteryear combine with old wooden floors, colourful Kashubian motifs, an entire fishing boat and an aquarium. The restaurant's speciality is Baltic fish (price per 100g), brought to prettily laid tables by waitresses in Kashubian folk costume.

Bar Mewa SEAFOOD €€

(www.mewahel.pl; ul Morska 84; mains around 20zł; ⊙9am-10pm daily) Enjoy 12 types of fish from the Baltic in the tiny antique-packed interior or out by a set of fountains in the sea breeze at this popular spot just steps from the beach.

ⓘ Information

Post Office (ul Wiejska 55; ⊙9.30am-4.30pm Mon-Fri, 8am-2pm Sat) Has a currency exchange desk.

❶ Getting There & Away

To reach Hel by train, you'll first have to make your way to Gdynia (from Gdańsk on the SKM, 6zł, 30 minutes) and change there (17.10zł, two hours, hourly); even in low season there are fairly regular services. A couple of sleepers for southern destinations, including Kraków, originate here too. Regular buses also leave from the lighthouse end of ul Wiejska for Gdynia (14-22zł, one hour 40 minutes, 10-15 daily).

A waterborne option is the Żegluga Gdańska (p327) pleasure boat/hydrofoil from May to September from Gdańsk.

Kashubia

If you believe the legend, the region of Kashubia (Kaszuby) was created by giants, whose footprints account for the many hills and lakes that characterise the landscape. Stretching for 100km southwest of Gdańsk, it's a picturesque area noted for its small, traditional villages, and a lack of cities and industry.

In contrast to most of the other groups who gradually merged to form one big family of Poles, the Kashubians have managed to retain some of their early ethnic identity, expressed in their distinctive culture, dress, crafts, architecture and language.

The Kashubian language, still spoken in the home by some 50,000, mostly elderly locals, is the most distinct Polish dialect. It's thought to derive from the old Slavic Pomeranian language; other Poles have a hard time deciphering it.

The area between Kartuzy and Kościerzyna is the most topographically diverse part of the region, including the highest point of Kashubia, Mt Wieżyca (329m). This is also the most touristy area of Kashubia, with the most facilities. Public transport between Kartuzy and Kościerzyna is fairly regular, with buses running every hour or two.

Unless you have your own transport, you miss out on some of the region by being limited to the major routes. Public transport becomes less frequent the further off the track you go. Visiting the two regional destinations Kartuzy and Wdzydze Kiszewskie will give a taste of the culture of Kashubia, though less of its natural beauty.

Kartuzy

POP 15,000

The town of Kartuzy, 30km west of Gdańsk, owes its birth and its name to the Carthusi-

ans, a religious order that was brought here from Bohemia in 1380. Originally founded in 1084 near Grenoble (France), the order was known for its austere monastic rules – its monks passing their days in the contemplation of death, following the motto 'Memento Mori' (Remember You Must Die)

Whether you're looking to stay or move on, the **tourist office** (✆58 684 0201; ul Klasztorna 1; ☺9am-6pm Mon-Fri, to 3pm Sat & Sun) can help out. The office is also a superb source of information on Kashubian culture throughout the region.

Gryf buses (not PKS) shuttle between Gdańsk (7zł, one hour) and Kartuzy every half an hour.

◉ Sights

Church   CHURCH
(ul Klasztorna 5) When the monks arrived in Kartuzy they built a church and, beside it, 18 hermitages laid out in the shape of a horseshoe. The church seems to be a declaration of the monks' philosophy; the original Gothic brick structure was topped in the 1730s with a Baroque roof that looks like a huge coffin. On the outer wall of the chancel there's a sundial and, just beneath it, a skull with the 'Memento Mori' inscription. The adjacent cemetery continues the morbid theme.

Kashubian Museum   MUSEUM
(Muzeum Kaszubskie; www.muzeum-kaszubskie. gda.pl; ul Kościerska 1; adult/concession 10/6zł; ☺8am-6pm Tue-Fri, 9am-5pm Sat & Sun Jul & Aug, shorter hours rest of year) Slavophiles should make a beeline for this surprisingly good and delightfully old-school museum, south of the train station near the tracks. Amid the inevitable wooden farm implements and kitchen utensils there are some beautiful toffee-brown and metallic-black pottery so typical of the region, wonderfully simple textiles and hefty rural furniture. One room is given over to the Carthusians.

❶ Getting There & away

Gryf buses (not PKS) shuttle between Gdańsk (8.50zł, one hour) and Kartuzy every half-hour or so.

Wdzydze Kiszewskie

POP 200

Kashubian Ethnographic Park   MUSEUM
(Kaszubski Park Etnograficzny; www.muzeum-wdzydze.gda.pl; adult/concession 14/9zł;

⊙ 10am-6pm Tue-Sun Jul & Aug, shorter hours rest of year) Some 16km south of Kościerzyna, Wdzydze Kiszewskie is a tiny village with a big attraction, namely the Kashubian Ethnographic Park, an open-air museum displaying the typical rural architecture of Kashubia. Established in 1906 by the local schoolmaster, this was Poland's first open-air museum of traditional architecture.

Many have followed in its wake. Pleasantly positioned on the lakeside, it now contains a score of buildings rescued from central and southern Kashubia, including cottages, barns, a school, a windmill and an 18th-century church used for Sunday Mass. Some of the interiors boast authentic furnishings, implements and decorations, showing how the Kashubians lived a century or two ago.

ⓘ Getting There & Away

Reaching Wdzydze is tricky without your own wheels. A few buses a day link the village with Kościerzyna (7zł, 40 minutes), which has frequent services to/from Gdańsk (16.50zł, 1½ hours, hourly).

LOWER VISTULA

The fertile land within the valley of the Lower Vistula, bisected by the wide, slowly flowing river, was prized by invaders for centuries. Flat, open and dotted with green farms, this region developed during the 13th and 14th centuries into a thriving trade centre, via the many ports established along the Vistula's banks from Toruń to Gdańsk. The history of these towns is intertwined with that of the Teutonic order, the powerful league of Germanic knights who by then occupied much of the valley. Remnants from the order's heyday now comprise some of the most prominent sights in the region.

Though the Lower Vistula suffered much destruction in the closing months of WWII, what survived is a rich cultural inheritance of great depth and interest.

Toruń

POP 204,800

If you've spent your time so far in Poland jostling with the stag and hen crowds in Kraków and wandering Warsaw's concrete, then Toruń will come as a mini-revelation. This magnificently walled Gothic town on the Vistula should be high on every traveller's list, possibly as its delights seem low on everyone else's, leaving visitors who make it here to revel unrestricted in its wealth of red-brick buildings, Unesco-listed sites and medieval city defences, all of which WWII mercifully decided to ignore.

Beyond architecture, Toruń is also well known as the birthplace of Nicolaus Copernicus (1473–1543). His name (Mikołaj Kopernik in Polish) is all over town, and you can even buy gingerbread shaped in his image. This other Toruń icon – its *pierniki* (gingerbread) – is famous across Poland.

History

Toruń was kickstarted into prominence in 1233, when the Teutonic Knights transformed the existing 11th-century Slav settlement into one of their early outposts. The knights surrounded the town, then known as Thorn, with walls and a castle. Rapid expansion as a port meant that newly arriving merchants and craftspeople had to settle outside the city walls and soon built what became known as the New Town. In the 1280s Toruń joined the Hanseatic League, giving further impetus to its development.

Toruń later became a focal point of the conflict between Poland and the Teutonic order, and when the Thirteen Years' War finally ended in 1466, the Treaty of Toruń returned a large area of land to Poland, stretching from Toruń to Gdańsk.

The following period of prosperity ended with the Swedish wars, and the city fell under Prussian domination in 1793, later becoming part of Germany. Toruń didn't return to Poland until the nation was recreated after WWI.

After WWII, Toruń expanded significantly, with vast new suburbs and industries. Luckily, the medieval quarter was unaffected and largely retains its old appearance.

ⓘ JUST THE TICKET

If you're planning to visit all seven attractions affiliated with the Regional Museum in Toruń, why not buy a single **pass** (adult/concession 35/25zł) valid for two days, but not valid for the Town Hall Tower or the 3D Book of Toruń. A more expensive **pass** (45/30zł) includes the latter two attractions.

Toruń

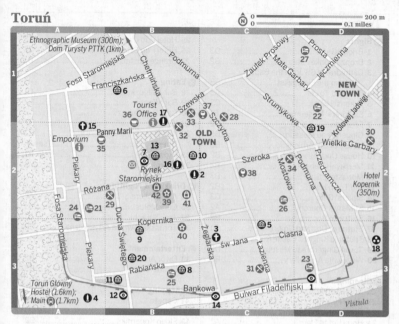

◉ Sights

Old Town Hall
MUSEUM

(Ratusz Staromiejski; www.muzeum.torun.pl; Rynek Staromiejski 1; adult/concession museum 11/7zł, tower 11/7zł, combined ticket 17/12zł; ⏱museum 10am-6pm Tue-Sun, tower 10am-8pm May-Sep, shorter hours Oct-Apr) The Old Town Hall dates from the 14th century and hasn't changed much since, though some Renaissance additions lent an ornamental touch to the sober Gothic structure. Today, it houses the main branch of the Toruń Regional Museum boasting displays of Gothic art (painting and stained glass), a display of local 17th- and 18th-century crafts and a gallery of Polish paintings from 1800 to the present, including a couple of Witkacys and Matejkos. Climb the tower for a fine panoramic view of Toruń's Gothic townscape.

Cathedral of SS John the Baptist & John the Evangelist
CHURCH

(www.katedra.diecezja.torun.pl; ul Żeglarska 16; ⏱9am-5.30pm Mon-Sat, 2-5.30pm Sun) Toruń's mammoth Gothic cathedral was begun around 1260 but only completed at the end of the 15th century. Its massive tower houses Poland's second-largest historic bell, the Tuba Dei (God's Trumpet). On the southern side of the tower, facing the Vistula, is a large 15th-century clock; its original face and single hand are still in working order. Check out the dent above the VIII – it's from a cannonball that struck the clock during the Swedish siege of 1703.

The interior is a light-filled environment with elaborate altars resting beneath the whitewashed vaulting. Its most striking murals are the monochrome paintings set high at the back of each aisle, which depict a monk and a devil or plague figure. Created by an unknown artist, the black-and-white style is highly unusual for this kind of church art.

The high altar, adorned with a Gothic triptych and topped with a crucifix, has as a background a superb stained-glass window in the best medieval style. The first aisle chapel on the right as you enter holds the oldest object in the church, the font where Copernicus was baptised. To one side is his epitaph.

House of Copernicus
MUSEUM

(www.muzeum.torun.pl; ul Kopernika 15/17; museum adult/concession 11/8zł, audiovisual presentation 13/8zł; ⏱10am-6pm Tue-Sun May-Sep, to 4pm Oct-Apr) While it's not clear if Copernicus was actually born here, this branch of the regional museum is dedicated to the famed astronomer's life and

Toruń

◉ Sights

◎ Sleeping

✸ Eating

◉ Drinking & Nightlife

◉ Entertainment

◉ Shopping

works. More engaging than the exhibitions of period furniture and writing is a short audiovisual presentation regarding Copernicus' times in Toruń, with a model of the town.

Explorers' Museum MUSEUM

(Muzeum Podróżników; www.muzeum.torun.pl; ul Franciszkańska 11; adult/concession 8/5zł; ☺10am-4pm Tue-Sun Oct-Apr, to 6pm May-Sep) This is usually the last subdivision of the Regional Museum on visitors' mental itineraries, which is a shame as it tells an interesting story. It contains artefacts from the amassed collection of seasoned nomad Tony Halik (1921–98), including his battered suitcases, travel documents, souvenirs of his many journeys and a criminal number of pilfered hotel keys! One of his longest journeys was a 180,000km epic from Tierra del Fuego to Alaska.

More recent additions to the collection have been donated by his wife, Elżbieta Dzikowska, who continues to travel, most notably in Asia. There's also a room dedicated to some of history's greatest explorers (Captain Cook, Marco Polo etc) and another to famous Polish wanderers.

St Mary's Church CHURCH

(Kościół NMP; ul Panny Marii) Toruń's third great Gothic structure in the Old Town (after the Town Hall and Cathedral) is St Mary's Church, erected by the Franciscans at the end of the 13th century. Austere and plain from the outside, the highly strung interior has tall, slender, intricate stained-glass windows, painted Gothic vaulting and a prominent golden altarpiece.

Eskens' House MUSEUM

(Dom Eskenów; www.muzeum.torun.pl; ul Łazienna 16; adult/concession 11/7zł) The recently renovated Gothic House of the Esken Family, set behind the cathedral, was converted into a granary in the 19th century. It contains city history displays on the 1st floor, and a collection of medieval weaponry and archaeological exhibits from the Iron and Bronze Ages on the 2nd floor. A new feature is the Book of Toruń, a 14-minute 3D film on the city's history.

House Under the Star MUSEUM

(Kamienica Pod Gwiazdą; www.muzeum.torun.pl; Rynek Staromiejski 35; adult/concession 8/5zł; ☺10am-6pm Tue-Sun May-Sep, to 4pm Oct-Apr) The House Under the Star is a chunk of madly stuccoed architectural confectionery embellishing the Main Square. Inside you'll discover another outpost of the Regional Museum, this time a small but elegant collection of Asian art, including Japanese swords, Indian statues and Chinese pottery from the Tang dynasty.

Toruń Gingerbread Museum
MUSEUM

(Muzeum Toruńskiego Piernika; www.muzeum.torun.pl; ul Strumykowa 4; adult/concession 11/7zł; ⊙10am-6pm Tue-Sun May-Sep, to 4pm Oct-Apr) Not to be confused with the commercial Gingerbread Museum across town, this branch of the Toruń Regional Museum is housed in a former gingerbread factory and looks at the 600-year-long history of the city's favourite sweet.

Ethnographic Museum
MUSEUM

(Muzeum Etnograficzne; www.etnomuzeum.pl; Wały Sikorskiego 19; adult/concession 9/6zł; ⊙9am-4pm Wed & Fri, to 5pm Tue & Thu, 10am-6pm Sat & Sun) The thatched cottages in parkland to the north of the city centre aren't relics from some former age, but belong to this undervisited museum of rural life.

Gingerbread Museum
MUSEUM

(Muzeum Piernika; www.muzeumpiernika.pl; ul Rabiańska 9; adult/concession 12/9.50zł; ⊙9am-6pm, tours every hour, on the hour) Learn about gingerbread's history and create a spicy concoction of your own under the enlightened instruction of a mock-medieval gingerbread master. All of it takes place in a renovated 16th-century gingerbread factory.

Wozownia Art Gallery
GALLERY

(www.wozownia.pl; ul Rabiańska 20; admission varies, Tue & Sun free; ⊙noon-8pm Tue, 11am-6pm Wed-Sun) This small art gallery has changing displays of contemporary art, providing some contrast to the Gothic frenzy outside.

✯ Festivals & Events

Jazz Odnowa
JAZZ

(www.jazz.umk.pl; ⊙Feb) One of Poland's top jazz festivals.

Polish Speedway Grand Prix
SPORTS

(www.speedway.torun.pl; ⊙Oct) Held at Europe's largest speedway stadium.

Probaltica Music & Art Festival of Baltic States
MUSIC

(www.probaltica.art.pl; ⊙May) Classical music and opera festival.

Toruń Days
CARNIVAL

(www.torun.pl; ⊙24 Jun) City festival.

🛏 Sleeping

Toruń has plenty of central places to stay and finding a bed outside of July and August is easy. During the summer, booking ahead is recommended.

Toruń Główny Hostel
HOSTEL €

(www.hosteltg.com; Toruń Główny train station; dm/d 39/70zł; 🖷) This 56-bed hostel opened in 2015 and is housed in the old post office building right on the platform at Toruń's recently renovated main train station. The six- and eight-bed dorms are spacious with suitcase-size lockers and reading lamps; free breakfast is taken in the basement kitchen. There are attractive wall frescoes of Toruń's old town and, surprisingly, no train noise to keep you awake at night.

CITY DEFENCES

Lost count of the museum's myriad branches? Teeth aching from too much gingerbread? Could be time to take a break and stroll the remnants of the town's original medieval fortifications, a popular activity with no admission to pay. Take a picnic if the weather's good.

To the east, in a triangle squeezed between the Old and New Towns, are the **ruins of the castle** (ul Przedzamcze; adult/concession 8/5zł, Mon free; ⊙10am-6pm), built by the Teutonic Knights. It was destroyed by the town's inhabitants in 1454 as a protest against the order's economic restrictions (they must have been really miffed – those Teutonic castles were quite sturdy).

Following the old city walls west from the castle, you'll come to the first of three surviving city gates, the **Bridge Gate** (Brama Mostowa). A 700m-long bridge was built here between 1497 and 1500 and survived for over three centuries. Continue along the walls to find the other two gates: the **Sailors' Gate** (Brama Żeglarska) and the **Monastery Gate** (Brama Klasztorna). At the far western end are a few gentrified **medieval granaries** and the **Crooked Tower** (Krzywa Wieża).

STRANGE STATUARY

Toruń's main square is furnished with a number of interesting pieces of statuary, but relatively few locals know the stories behind them.

Starting a few steps from the Old Town Hall entrance, the **statue of Copernicus** is one of the oldest monuments dedicated to the stargazer and a regular feature in holiday snaps.

West of the Town Hall, opposite the post office, is an intriguing small **fountain** dating from 1914. Bronze-cast frogs sit on its rim, admiring a statue of a violin-playing boy known as Janko Muzykant, Toruń's very own answer to the Pied Piper. Legend has it that a witch once came to the town, but wasn't welcomed by the locals. In revenge, she invoked a curse, and the town was invaded by frogs. The mayor offered a sackful of gold and his daughter to anyone who would rescue the town. A humble peasant boy then appeared and began to play his rustic fiddle and the frogs, enchanted by the melody, followed him to the woods and the town was saved.

On the opposite side of the Rynek, at the corner of ul Chełmińska, you'll find another curious critter-related statue at knee-level, depicting **a dog and an umbrella**. The pooch's name is Filuś; he starred in a famous long-running Polish comic strip as the pet of brolly-wielding Professor Filutek.

The **bronze donkey** in the southeast corner (dubbed the 'brass ass' by some Americans) has a much more sinister story attached. Few tourists straddling its back are aware that this is actually a copy of a wooden donkey that stood here in medieval times, to which criminals were strapped and flogged.

Orange Hostel
HOSTEL €

(☑ 56 652 0033; www.hostelorange.pl; ul Prosta 19; dm/s/d 35/65/110zł; ☞) Modern, friendly base with a range of dorm accommodation in 12-, three- or two-bed rooms, plus some private rooms, a guest kitchen and clean washing facilities. There's a second branch at ul Jęczmienna.

Fort IV
HOSTEL €

(☑ 56 655 8236; www.fort.torun.pl; ul Chrobrego 86; dm 30-45zł, s/d from 30/60zł) Toruń is encircled by the ruins of 19th-century forts, but this is the only one to put up guests for the night in basic rooms. Rooms come with and without bathrooms; there's also a guest kitchen. Take bus 14 to the end of the line.

Dom Turysty PTTK
HOSTEL €

(☑ 56 622 3855; www.pttk.torun.pl; ul Legionów 24; s/d 70/84zł) The 65-bed PTTK hostel is in a residential house, a 10-minute walk north of the Old Town with 24-hour reception and a snack bar. Rooms are simple but clean and functional.

★ Hotel Petite Fleur
HOTEL €€

(☑ 56 621 5100; www.petitefleur.pl; ul Piekary 25; s/d from 180/230zł; ☞) One of the better midrange options in Toruń has understated rooms containing slickly polished timber furnishings and elegant prints, though the singles can be a touch small. The French brick-cellar restaurant is one of Toruń's better hotel dining options and the buffet breakfast is one of the best in the north.

Hotel Karczma Spichrz
HOTEL €€

(☑ 56 657 1140; www.spichrz.pl; ul Mostowa 1; s/d 250/310zł; ❋ ☞) Wonderfully situated within a historic waterfront granary, this hotel's 19 rooms are laden with personality, featuring massive exposed beams above characterful timber furniture and contemporary bathrooms. The location by the river is within walking distance of the sights but away from the crowds. Good restaurant next door.

Hotel Gotyk
HOTEL €€

(☑ 56 658 4000; www.hotel-gotyk.com.pl; ul Piekary 20; s/d 180/220zł; ☞) This beautifully restored townhouse hotel is a good choice for those who like a little historical character. Passing the suit of armour in the foyer, head up green carpeted stairs to find individually decorated rooms, some with heavy classic antique furniture. Some rooms could do with a bit of an update, but all in all a great place to stay.

B&B
HOTEL €€

(☑ 56 621 8100; www.hotelbb.pl; ul Szumana 8; r from 135zł; P ❋ ☞) The first in the B&B chain to open in Poland, this purpose-built cube near the bus station north of town has 93 spartan, easily-maintainable rooms providing the basics every 21st-century traveller needs. Despite its location just metres from the busy ring road, absolutely no traffic din will disturb your sleep. Breakfast is an extra 22zł.

Hotel Kopernik
HOTEL €€

(📞56 659 7333; www.hotelewam.pl; ul Wola Zamkowa 16; r 80-200zł; P🐾🛜) This former army hostel has long been a favourite among travellers to Toruń and continues to offer a great deal on the eastern edge of the Old Town. Rooms are basic with pine furniture and cheap carpets, and bathrooms are standard-issue, but staff are superb and the no-frills breakfast taken in the basement provides a filling set-up for the day.

Hotel Heban
HOTEL €€

(📞56 652 1555; www.hotel-heban.com.pl; ul Małe Garbary 7; s/d 165/240zł; P🛜) Atmospherically billeted in a prettily gabled townhouse in quiet ul Małe Garbary, the Heban has a floral-themed restaurant, a relaxingly stylish lounge in olive green and 22 light and airy rooms.

Hotel Pod Orłem
HOTEL €€

(📞56 622 5025; www.hotel.torun.pl; ul Mostowa 17; s/d 130/170zł; P) The Pod Orłem is one of Toruń's oldest hotels, with a history going back more than a century. Leather-padded doors open onto some pretty spacious rooms; the cheaper ones are strangely like staying in your grandma's spare room. Buffet breakfast is an extra 19zł.

Hotel Pod Czarną Różą
HOTEL €€

(📞56 621 9637; www.hotelczarnaroza.pl; ul Rabiańska 11; s/d 180/220zł; 🛜) 'Under the Black Rose' fills out both a historic inn and a newer wing facing the river, though its interiors present a uniformly clean, up-to-date look with the odd antique reproduction. Buffet breakfast included.

✖ Eating

Bar Małgośka
CAFETERIA €

(ul Szczytna 10; mains 5-11zł; ⊙9am-7pm Mon-Fri, to 4pm Sat) Large, cheap and popular milk bar where all of Poland's filling staples are present, correct and ladled out by grumpy dinner ladies. Always a free table, even when invaded by three huge school groups at once.

Karotka
VEGETARIAN €

(Łazienna 9; mains 5-12zł; ⊙noon-7pm Mon-Sat, to 5pm Sun; 🖊) Enjoy tasty vegetarian dishes under a large wall mural of painted carrots

crossed in meat-free defiance at this small vegetarian milk bar.

Bar Mleczny
CAFETERIA €

(ul Różana 1; mains 5-15zł; ⊙9am-7pm Mon-Fri, 10am-5pm Sat & Sun) This very popular milk bar offers substantial Polish stodge for a fistful of złoty amid token gentrification. The outdoor window serves up waffles, ice cream and *zapiekanki* (Polish pizza).

Oberża
POLISH €

(ul Rabiańska 9; mains 8-16zł; ⊙11am-10pm Mon-Thu, to 11pm Fri & Sat, to 9pm Sun; 🛜) This large self-service canteen stacks 'em high and sells 'em cheap for a hungry crowd of locals and tourists. Find your very own thatched mini-cottage or intimate hideout lost amid stained-glass windows, cartwheels, bridles and other rural knick-knacks of yesteryear to enjoy 11 types of *pierogi* (dumplings), soups, salads and classic Polish mains from a menu tuned to low-cost belly-packing.

Cafe Lenkiewicz
CAFE €

(Wielkie Barbary 14; ⊙8am-6pm Mon-Fri, to 4pm Sat, 9am-4pm Sun) Toruń's top ice cream and gateau halt, best in summer when things spill out onto the pedestrianised street.

Prowansja
FRENCH €€

(ul Szewska 19; mains 15-30zł; ⊙noon-9pm Mon & Sun, to 10pm Tue-Thu, to 11pm Fri & Sat) This charming little place does a reasonable impression of a French restaurant. In fact the quiche, crêpes and salads might make you think you were in Normandy, but only if you've never been there. Pretty good wine list and some Polish fare on the menu.

Kuranty
BURGERS, POLISH €€

(Rynek Staromiejski 29; mains 8-30zł; ⊙11am-1am; 🛜) With leathery seating and lots of exposed wood, this place resembles a Victorian British boozer but with flat-screen TVs hanging from the bar. Big burgers, Polish mains and a list of *pierogi* filled with all types of foodstuffs populate the menu.

★ Szeroka 9
INTERNATIONAL €€€

(📞56 622 8424; www.szeroka9.pl; ul Szeroka 9; mains 29-69zł; ⊙10am-11pm daily) Arguably Toruń's top restaurant offers a changing menu of seasonal gourmet-style fare with everything from rabbit in apple and cream sauce to house tagliatelle. The dessert to plump for is local gingerbread in plum sauce. The decor is contemporary urban and the staff is friendly and knowledgeable about what's on the plate. Reservations are recommended for dinner.

Drinking & Nightlife

Atmosphera
CAFE

(ul Panny Marii 3; ⊘ 11am-9pm Sun-Thu, to 10pm Fri & Sat) Try a gingerbread-flavoured coffee *(kawa po Toruńsku)* and a hefty wedge of cheesecake at this unassuming and very aromatic caffeine stop littered with odd tables and a jumble of chairs. More than 100 different kinds of tea, plus a global wine list.

Jan Olbracht
BREWERY

(www.browar-olbracht.pl; ul Szczytna 15; ⊘ 10am-11pm) Take a seat in an egg-shaped indoor booth or at the street-side mini beer garden to sip some of this microbrewery's unusual beers. These include pils, wheat beer, a special ale and, this being Toruń, gingerbread beer, all brewed in the huge copper vats at the front of the huge building.

Cafe Molus
CAFE

(www.cafemolus.pl; Rynek Staromiejski 19; ⊘ 8am-last customer) This stylish cafe fulfils the desires of the sweet-toothed and caffeine-cravers under broken Gothic arches, painted ceilings and some of the chunkiest beamery you've ever seen. The highlight here is the secluded Renaissance-style courtyard out back where you can leave the city behind as you take cake.

Toruńska Piwnica Artystyczna
CLUB

(www.tpart.pl; ul Łazienna 30; 🛜) Multitasking bar-cafe where you can enjoy live football, DJ parties, jam sessions, 30+ dance nights or just an afternoon beer and pizza.

☆ Entertainment

Dwór Artusa
CLASSICAL MUSIC

(🖳 56 655 4929; www.artus.torun.pl; Rynek Staromiejski 6) The Artus Court, one of the most impressive mansions on the main square, is now a major cultural centre and has an auditorium hosting musical events, including concerts and recitals.

Lizard King
LIVE MUSIC

(www.lizardking-torun.pl; ul Kopernika 3; ⊘ 6pm-late; 🛜) Live-music venue with gigs ranging from local tribute bands to major rock acts from Eastern and Central Europe.

🔒 Shopping

Gingerbread is Toruń's signature souvenir, but it's so scrumptious it's doubtful much of it actually makes it out of the country. The two stores listed here are traditional gingerbread emporia, but the delicacy can be found in many other gift shops and even local supermarkets.

Pierniczek
FOOD

(ul Żeglarska 25; ⊘ 9am-8pm) Small shop selling gingerbread creations straight from the factory.

Sklep Kopernik
FOOD

(Rynek Staromiejski 6; ⊘ 9am-8pm Mon-Fri, 10am-7pm Sat & Sun) *The* place to purchase Toruń's favourite gingerbread, housed in the Artus Court on the southern side of the main square.

Cepelia
HANDICRAFTS

(ul Żeglarska 27; ⊘ 10am-6pm Jul & Aug, shorter hours rest of year) Small branch of the national chain selling all kinds of genuine handicrafts as well as mass-produced fridge magnets and the like.

ℹ️ Information

Emporium (🖳 56 657 6108; www.emporium. torun.com.pl; ul Piekary 28; ⊘ 10am-6pm Mon-Fri, to 4pm Sat year-round, to 4pm Sun Jul & Aug) Great little souvenir shop offering cycle hire (per hour/day 5/25zł), handy luggage storage (per hour 1zł) and city maps.

Main Post Office (Rynek Staromiejski; ⊘ 24hr)

Tourist Office (🖳 56 621 0930; www.torun.pl; Rynek Staromiejski 25; ⊘ 9am-6pm Mon-Fri, to 4pm Sat & Sun; 🛜) Free wi-fi access, heaps of info and professional staff who know their city.

ℹ️ Getting There & Away

BUS

The PKS terminal, close to the northern edge of the Old Town, handles services to the following:

Chełmno 8.80zł, one hour 20 minutes, frequent

Golub-Dobrzyń 8.80zł, one hour, frequent

Gdańsk 23zł to 44zł, 2½ hours, hourly

Warsaw 28zł to 57zł, three to four hours, at least hourly

TRAIN

Toruń has two stations: **Toruń Główny** is about 2km south of the Old Town, on the opposite side of the Vistula, while the more convenient **Toruń Miasto** is located on the Old Town's eastern edge. Not all services stop at both stations.

Trains head to:

Gdańsk 45zł, three hours, nine daily or change in Iława or Bydgoszcz

Grudziądz 9.30zł, 1½ hours, nine daily or change in Jabłonowo Pomorskie

Kraków 65zł, six to nine hours, three daily
Malbork 25zł, three to four hours, at least hourly, change in Tczew or Iława
Olsztyn 27 to 36zł, 2½ hours, seven daily
Warsaw 45zł, 2¾ hours, eight daily

ℹ Getting Around

Buses 22 and 27 (2.80zł) shuttle between Toruń Główny and the plac Rapackiego stop on Aleja Jana Pawła II, just to the west of the historical centre.

Golub-Dobrzyń

POP 13,000

Golub-Dobrzyń might sound like a minor character in *The Lord of the Rings,* but in fact it's a town about 40km east of Toruń. Dobrzyń, on the southern bank of the Drwęca River, is a boxy, uninteresting place, but Golub was founded in the 13th century as a border outpost of the Teutonic Knights, who left behind one of their typically impressive castles. If Toruń hasn't quite satisfied your appetite for Gothic-era red-brick structures, then an easy half-day excursion to G-D may do the trick.

◉ Sights

Golub Castle   CASTLE
(Zamek Golubski; www.zamekgolub.pl; adult/concession 10/8zł; ⊙9am-6pm May-Sep, to 3pm Oct-Apr) Golub's square-set castle overlooks the town from a hill, the prominent structure consisting of a massive Gothic brick base topped with a slightly more refined Renaissance cornice. The original 14th-century castle was converted into a Renaissance palace in the early 17th century during the tenureship of its most famous resident, Princess Anna Waza, sister of Polish King Zygmunt III Waza.

Somewhat bizarrely, the only way to see the castle's rather bare interiors is on an hour-long guided tour. Tagging along with a Polish group, the visit starts with an excruciatingly dull film then progresses into the various austere rooms housing modest ethnographical and archaeological exhibits. However, the Gothic architecture is pretty impressive, as are the views out across the town and the forests beyond.

⌷ Sleeping & Eating

Dom Wycieczkowy PTTK   HOSTEL, HOTEL €€
(☑56 683 2455; hostel dm/d 30/80zł; hotel s/d 160/230zł; P⊛) The castle's upper floor

houses some of the cheapest fortification accommodation in Poland. There are two standards on offer: one a basic PTTK hostel with dorm beds and simple doubles, the other consisting of hotel-type rooms. There's a restaurant and cafe downstairs.

ℹ Getting There & Away

Buses run regularly to/from Toruń (8.80zł, one hour) and many other towns and cities in the region. When coming from Toruń alight at the bus stop at the foot of the castle. On your way back, wait at the stop on the other side of the road as it's a long hike to Dobrzyń bus station.

Chełmno

POP 20,400

The most worthwhile day trip from Toruń, Chełmno (*heum*-no) is one of those enjoyably forgotten places that seems to lead a provincial life all of its own, with only occasional intrusions from the outside world. Its chipped and faded facades, sooty air and old red-brick institutions belong to the Poland of two decades ago, its churches and impressively beefy ring of defensive walls originating from a medieval golden era.

Like Toruń, Chełmno was once an important settlement in the swathe of northern Poland controlled by the Teutonic Knights. Though it had been Polish since the late 10th century, the Teutonic Knights earmarked it as a potential capital when they arrived in the late 1220s. Their castle was completed by 1265, bolstering Chełmno's profitable position on the Vistula trade route and its lucrative affiliation to the Hanseatic League.

After the Treaty of Toruń, Chełmno was returned to Poland, but a devastating plague and a series of wars rendered the town a forgotten backwater by the time it was annexed by Prussia in 1772. It was returned to Poland in 1920 and survived WWII without major damage.

◉ Sights & Activities

Regional Museum   MUSEUM
(Muzeum Ziemi Chełmińskiej; www.muzeum chelmno.pl; Rynek 28; adult/concession 4/2zł; ⊙10am-4pm Tue-Sat, 11am-3pm Sun) The epicentre of Chełmno's chessboard of streets is the Rynek, in the middle of which stands the compact Renaissance Town Hall, built around 1570 on the site of the previous Gothic structure. It now houses the Regional Museum, whose collection traces the

GDAŃSK & POMERANIA GOLUB-DOBRZYŃ

town's history, though the building's interior, including a spectacular courtroom, is equally distracting.

Outside, affixed on the rear wall of the Town Hall is the old Chełmno measure, the 4.35m-long *pręt chełmiński*. The entire town was laid out according to this measure, setting all the streets exactly the same width apart. It is divided into 'feet' a little smaller than an English foot. This unique system was used until the 19th century; the town also had its own weights.

Parish Church   CHURCH

(ul Szkolna; viewing terrace 5zł; ⊘ viewing terrace 9am-5.30pm Mon-Sat, 2-5pm Sun) Just off the Rynek, this massive, Gothic church was commissioned by the Teutonic Knights in the late 13th century. The magnificent interior is crammed with ornate Baroque and Rococo furnishings, and also holds some supposed relics of St Valentine, patron saint of lovers, locked within the right-hand pillar as you face the altar (this has inevitably spawned an entire miniature tourist industry and a raft of marketing campaigns). The church tower can be climbed for views of Chełmno's grid of streets.

City Walls   HISTORIC SITE

Chełmno is encircled by 2.2km of defensive walls, which have survived almost in their entirety. Alas, it's not possible to walk around the entire circumference as various gardens and buildings block the way. Walking along ul Dworcowa from the bus terminal, you'll enter the Old Town through the Grudziądz Gate (Brama Grudziądzka), the only surviving medieval gateway in the town's defences.

Church of SS John the
Baptist & John the Evangelist   CHURCH

(Kościół Św Jana Chrzciciela i Jana Ewangelisty; ul Dominikańska) At the far western tip of the Old Town, this church was built between 1266 and 1325 and has a richly gilded high altar with an ornate organ to the side. Underneath the organ is a black-marble tombstone from 1275, one of the oldest in the region. The church is part of the renovated Dominican and Benedictine convent – the nuns have returned, walking through the vista-rich garden behind the church with their rosaries in hand.

Church of SS Peter & Paul   CHURCH

(ul Wodna) Occupying the town's northern corner, the impressive red-brick stepped gable of this 14th-century church fronts an interior containing doored Rococo stalls, a huge Baroque altar straddled by a star-studded globe and the tomb of the first bishop of Chełmno, Heidenreich. Sadly, it's not open to the public very often.

Miniature Castles of
the Teutonic Knights   PARK

(Park Miniatur Zamków Krzyżackich; ul Podmurna; ⊘ 10am-7pm Mon-Sat, from 11am Sun) FREE Head south from the Grudziądz Gate through the park to find this open-air exhibition of nearby Teutonic knights' castles. All nine are depicted in their full glory (not the ruins they are today) with Toruń, Grudziądz and Malbork as well as six minor piles all recreated in medieval miniature.

🛏 Sleeping & Eating

Sleepy Chełmno has just a handful of places to stay and very few restaurants. From around Easter to September a few beer gardens sprout on the Rynek, which also has a couple of bakery cafes.

Hotelik   HOTEL €

(✓ 56 676 2030; www.hotelik.info; ul Podmurna 3; s/d 100/140zł; ⑳) Located 60m to the right of the Grudziądz Gate as you enter the Old Town, this well-maintained half-timbered mini-hotel offers a jumble of good-value en-suite rooms, some small and cosy, others more spacious with antique elements.

Karczma Chełmińska   HOTEL €€

(✓ 56 679 0605; www.karczmachelminska.pl; ul 22 Stycznia 1b; s/d 190/220zł; P ⑳) This tourist-friendly courtyard hotel, in the southwestern corner of the Old Town, offers neat rooms with great stone-effect bathrooms. The courtyard restaurant, with waiters in traditional garb, serves up tasty fare including interesting seasonal specials.

Gościniec pod Różą   B&B €€

(www.gosciniec-pod-roza.pl; ul Prosta 3; s/tw 105/165zł) When all else fails, this 16-room guesthouse around 10-minutes' walk from the bus station is an acceptable option for one night. It's cheaply furnished, but clean and inexpensive. It's located in a residential location with a supermarket nearby.

Rabar Bar   CAFETERIA €

(Rynek 20; mains 7-8zł; ⊘ 11am-6pm Mon-Sat, from noon Sun) This new self-service canteen on the main square is a welcome addition to the town's eating scene, with US diner-style leatherette seats and a blackboard menu of basic Polish favourites.

Restauracja Spichlerz POLISH €€
(ul Biskupia 3; mains 8-30zł; ⊙10am-10pm Mon-Sat, from 11am Sun) Ask anyone in Chełmno where to head when it's feeding time and they'll point you in the direction of this pub-restaurant just off the Rynek. The fare is mostly Polish and hearty, the crowd a mix of vodka-swigging old-timers and beer-caressing youths.

❶ Information

Tourist Office (📷 56 686 2104; www.chelmno. pl; Ratusz, Rynek; ⊙8am-3pm Mon, to 4pm Tue-Fri, 10am-3pm Sat, 11am-2pm Sun) In the museum entrance within the Town Hall.

❶ Getting There & Away

Chełmno is located 40km north of Toruń. Buses depart roughly hourly to/from Toruń (8.80zł, 1½ hours) and Grudziądz (8.20zł, one hour).

Grudziądz

POP 98,200

Grudziądz (*groo*-jonts), located some 30km down the Vistula River from Chełmno, probably doesn't have enough to warrant a special trip, but could be a minor diversion on the way between Toruń and Malbork. Some post-WWII renovation of the Old Town has been attempted and trams still trundle through the now pretty main square, lending it atmosphere. The remainder of Grudziądz is made up of thundering motorways, communist-era blocks and scrappy streets of 19th-century tenements.

The town may not be too focused on appearances, but its history is certainly colourful. It started life as an early Piast settlement, came under the rule of the Teutonic Knights as Graudenz in the 1230s, then returned to the Polish crown in 1466. The city was caught up in the 17th-century wars with Sweden – it was burnt down while being liberated by Polish troops in 1659. In the First Partition of 1772, Grudziądz was swallowed by Prussia, developing as an industrial centre before returning to Poland in the aftermath of WWI.

Grudziądz was severely damaged in 1945 but was rebuilt and developed into a bustling, if fairly unremarkable, urban centre.

◉ Sights

Regional Museum MUSEUM
(www.muzeum.grudziadz.pl; ul Wodna 3/5; adult/concession 7.50/3.50zł, Tue free; ⊙10am-6pm Tue & Fri, to 4pm Wed & Thu, to 3pm Sat & Sun May-Sep, shorter hours Oct-Apr) Based in a former Benedictine convent and several granaries at the southern end of the old quarter, the Regional Museum is worth a perusal. It provides a general overview of the town's history and also highlights several interesting themes. Allow at least 90 minutes for your visit – you will be handed from one curator to the next during your visit; the ticket is valid for all five sites.

The main building houses contemporary paintings from the region and other historical exhibitions, with further sections in the old granaries on local archaeology, the local Stomil rubber factory, cavalry uniforms and local sports hero, Olympic gold medalist Bronisław Malinowski (steeplechase; Moscow 1980), who died in a car accident on the bridge over the Vistula in 1981. His gold medal and the silver he won in Montreal in 1976 are on display and there's a film about his career.

Castle Hill HILL
(Góra Zamkowa; ⊙tower 9am-8pm Tue-Sun Apr-Sep) FREE Grudziądz once had a 13th-century castle that stood sentinel high above the Vistula. The remains of this, essentially the 30m Klimek Tower and the results of an archaeological dig, have become the town's latest attraction following extensive renovation work. Climb to the top of the tower for stupendous views of the river, the town and Poland's longest concrete bridge below.

Granaries HISTORIC BUILDINGS
(Spichrze) The extraordinary row of crumbling granaries was built along the length of the town's waterfront to provide storage and protect the town from invaders. Begun in the 14th century, they were gradually rebuilt and extended until the 18th century, and some were later turned into housing blocks by knocking through windows in the walls. These massive buttressed brick buildings – most of them six storeys high – are an impressive sight rising high above the Vistula.

Church of St Francis Xavier CHURCH
(Kościół Św Franciszka Ksawerego; ul Kościelna; ⊙8am-8pm Mon-Thu, to 5.30pm Fri-Sun) A few buildings in the centre retain their historical significance, the most impressive of

which is this early 18th-century church. Most of the narrow interior is taken up by a beautiful Baroque high altar, and the surrounding ornamentation includes some unusual chinoiserie created by a local Jesuit monk in the late 17th century.

🛏 Sleeping & Eating

Camping 134   CAMPGROUND €
(☑56 462 2581; www.moriw.pl; ul Za Basenem 2; adult/tent 5/5zł, bungalows 120-230zł; P �) Two-star camping ground on a lake 5km south of town boasting a long list of facilities. Take seasonal bus R.

★ Hotel RAD   HOTEL €€
(☑56 465 5506; www.hotelrad.pl; ul Chełmińska 144; s/d from 130/170zł; P �) One of northern Poland's best deals, the plush but incredibly cheap RAD is located on the Toruń road 2.5km south of the centre. Immaculate business-standard rooms have TV with English channels, super-fast wi-fi and desks. The restaurant attracts wedding parties and travelling salesmen alike; the breakfast buffet is as good as anything in Western Europe. Take tram 3 to the Wiejska stop.

★ Kuchnia   POLISH €
(ul Długa 2; mains 10-20zł; ⊙noon-7pm daily) With its white tiles, bar made of pallettes and painted brick walls, this trendy looking place has a simple menu of well-cooked Polish favourites as well as *kompot* (juice from cooked fruit) in jars, brain-reactivating coffee and some outdoor seating on the main square. The menu changes daily but usually includes *pierogi*, soups, *naleśniki* (crêpes) and local *kluski* (dumplings). By far the best place to eat in town.

ℹ Information

Tourist Office (☑56 461 2318; www.it.gdz. pl; Rynek 3/5; ⊙8am-5pm Mon-Fri, 10am-2pm Sat May-Sep, 10am-2pm Sun Jul & Aug, shorter hours Oct-Apr)

Post Office (cnr uls Sienkiewicza & Mickiewicza; ⊙8am-8pm Mon-Fri, 10am-3pm Sat) One of Grudziądz's most attractive red-brick edifices.

ℹ Getting There & Away

BUS
The bus station is a short walk north of the train station. Buses leave for the following:

Chełmno 8.20zł, one hour, hourly
Gdańsk 22zł, 1½ to three hours, seven daily
Toruń 11zł to 28zł, one to 2½ hours, hourly

TRAIN
The post-apocalyptic train station is about 1km southeast of the Old Town. It's a 15-minute walk or a quick trip on tram 1. Grudziądz has the following rail connections:

Kwidzyn 10.60zł, 50 minutes, four daily
Malbork 17.10zł, 1½ hours, four daily
Toruń 9.30zł, 1½ hours, nine daily or change in Jabłonowo Pomorskie

Kwidzyn

POP 37,800

Kwidzyn is a sleepy town that would be wholly unremarkable were it not for the presence of a mammoth Gothic castle and cathedral. Located 40km downriver from Grudziądz, it's yet another medieval stronghold of the Teutonic order and was formerly known as Marienwerder. Under the rule of German authorities for most of its history, the town became part of Poland after 1945.

⊙ Sights

Kwidzyn Castle   CASTLE
(Zamek w Kwidzynie; www.zamek.kwidzyn.pl; ul Katedralna 1; adult/concession 10/5zł; ⊙9am-5pm Tue-Sun May-Aug, to 4pm Tue-Fri, to 3pm Sat & Sun Sep-Apr) Kwidzyn's 14th-century castle has experienced numerous ups and downs over its lifetime, suffering the most grievous loss in 1798 when the Prussians pulled down two sides (eastern and southern) and the main tower. Unlike many of its red-brick peers, it survived WWII unscathed. Most of the building now houses the Kwidzyn Museum, which has several sections, including displays on medieval sacred art, regional folk crafts and plenty of farming implements, as well as a display in the cellar detailing the German-funded archaeological excavations around the site.

The most curious feature of the castle is the two unusual towers standing some distance away from the western and southern sides, linked to the main building by arcaded bridges. One (the smaller tower) held a well, while the other served as the *gdaniska* (knights' toilet), a long drop if ever there was one (many of the Teutonic Knights' castles had them – the origin of the name is unknown). They once stood above the river, which later changed course leaving the knights high and dry. You can visit both towers while wandering the interior, but it's also worth seeing them from the outside.

Cathedral
CHURCH

(ul Katedralna) The cathedral attached to the castle is the familiar Gothic brick blockbuster, which has a suitably defensive appearance thanks to its 19th-century tower. Look for the interesting ceramic mosaic (from around 1380) in the external wall above the southern porch.

🛏 Sleeping & Eating

Hotel Kaskada
HOTEL €

(☑703 400 440; www.hotelkaskada.emeteor.pl; ul Chopina 42; s 110-140zł, d 120-140zł; P🛜) Opposite the train station, this is an inexpensive, handy option if you decide to stay over. The restaurant is a simple affair, as are the rooms.

Hotel Centrum
HOTEL €€

(☑55 613 1366; www.centrumhotel.pl; ul Kopernika 32; s 260-320zł, d 310-370zł; P🛜) Cleancut and trendily designed for rural Poland, these new digs boast 32 en-suite rooms and some of the best facilities you're likely to find outside the big tourist centres, including a swanky restaurant.

❶ Getting There & Away

The bus and train stations are 200m apart, both around a 10-minute walk from the castle.

BUS
Kwidzyn has the following bus services:
Grudziądz 14zł, 45 minutes, two daily
Malbork 8zł, 45 to 70 minutes, nine daily

TRAIN
Trains head to the following:
Grudziądz 10.60zł, 50 minutes, four daily
Malbork 6zł, 45 minutes, eight daily
Toruń 20zł, three to four hours, five daily, change in Grudziądz

Malbork

POP 38,500

Around 30km southeast of Gdańsk, the quiet, rural town of Malbork would be bypassed by 99% of foreigners were it not for its astounding castle, one of the unmissables of any trip to Poland and a stunning spectacle both inside and out. Top dog among Polish fortifications, the magnificent Unesco-listed structure is a classic example of the medieval fortress and Europe's largest Gothic castle to boot. The fortress is an easy day trip from Gdańsk by train. It's probably not worth overnighting here as there's precious little to Malbork other than its Gothic pile.

MALBORK TRAIN STATION

Malbork's train station is worth a look, even if you aren't catching a train. Returned to its original splendour in 2011, it's a riot of wood panelling, embossed ceilings, neo-Gothic broken arches and pseudo-medieval decor. This grandeur is in stark contrast to many Polish stations that are receiving bland, 21st-century makeovers.

◉ Sights

Malbork Castle
CASTLE

(☑tickets 55 647 0978; www.zamek.malbork.pl; ul Starościńska 1; adult/concession 35/25zł; ⊙9am-7pm May-Sep, 10am-3pm Oct-Apr) Malbork's blockbuster attraction is its show-stoppingly massive castle that sits on the banks of the sluggish Nogat River, an eastern arm of the Vistula. The Marienburg (Fortress of Mary) was built by the Teutonic Knights and was the headquarters of the order for almost 150 years. Its vast bulk is an apt embodiment of its weighty history. Visits are by audio headphone, which you pick up at the ticket office. Allow at least two hours to do the place justice.

The immense castle took shape in stages. First was the so-called High Castle, the formidable central bastion that was begun around 1276. When Malbork became the capital of the order in 1309, the fortress was expanded considerably. The Middle Castle was built to the side of the high one, followed by the Lower Castle still further along. The whole complex was encircled by three rings of defensive walls and strengthened with dungeons and towers. The castle eventually spread over 21 hectares, making it the largest fortress built anywhere in the Middle Ages.

The castle was seized by the Polish army in 1457, during the Thirteen Years' War, when the military power of the knights had started to erode. Malbork then became the residence of Polish kings visiting Pomerania, but from the Swedish invasions onwards it gradually went into decline. After the First Partition in 1772, the Prussians turned it into barracks, destroying much of the decoration and dismantling sections of no military use.

In the 19th century the Marienburg was one of the first historic buildings taken under government protection, becoming a symbol of medieval German glory. Despite sustaining damage during WWII, almost the entire complex has been preserved, and the castle today looks much as it did six centuries ago, dominating the town and the surrounding countryside. The best view is from the opposite side of the river (you can get there via the footbridge), especially in the late afternoon when the brick turns an intense red-brown in the setting sun.

The entrance to the complex is from the northern side, through what used to be the only way in. The somewhat stuffy audio commentary takes you round 38 stops – accept the fact that you *will* get lost at some point. From the main gate, you walk over the drawbridge, then go through five iron-barred doors to the vast courtyard of the Middle Castle (Zamek Średni). On the western side (to your right) is the Grand Masters' Palace (Pałac Wielkich Mistrzów), which has some splendid interiors. Alongside is the Knights' Hall (Sala Rycerska), which is the largest chamber in the castle at 450 sq metres. The remarkable ceiling has its original palm vaulting preserved. The building on the opposite side of the courtyard houses a collection of armour and an excellent amber museum – the latter would be a major place of interest on its own, were it anywhere else.

The tour proceeds to the High Castle (Zamek Wysoki), over another drawbridge and through a gate (note the ornamented 1280 doorway) to a spectacular arcaded courtyard that has a reconstructed well in the middle.

One of the most striking interiors is St Mary's Church, accessed through a beautiful Gothic doorway, known as the Golden Gate. This is where the brothers would have met to pray every three hours, 24/7, but it was the part most damaged during the bombardment of 1945. Renovation work has been slow but should be finished for the summer of 2016. Underneath the church's presbytery is St Anne's Chapel, with the grand masters' crypt below its floor.

Other highlights of the tour include the *gdaniska*, the knights' loo perched high atop its own special tower and connected to the castle by a walkway. Perhaps it was one of the order who coined the phrase 'long drop' as he reached for the cabbage leaves they used for toilet paper. The knights' kitchen also sticks in the memory, fragrant with its calendar of fast days (the knights seemed to have liked two things – fasting and drinking beer). Also look out for the interesting underfloor heating system in many of the rooms and the little Gothic stucco figures pointing the way to the nearest WC.

Skwer Esperanto
PARK

(Plac Zamenhofa) If you've seen the castle and have more time to kill, walk south along the line of the river, past impressive remnants of the old city walls, to this square behind Hotel Stary Malbork. This scrappy park isn't much to look at, but around its edge are commemorative stones placed by keen international speakers of Esperanto from as far away as Korea and Congo, in honour of the world language invented by Ludwig Zamenhof.

There's a monument to the great man in the middle of the park. The explanatory signage is in Polish…and Esperanto, naturally.

🛏 Sleeping & Eating

Zajazd Karat
MOTEL €

(📞55 272 8953; www.karat.malbork.net.pl; ul Boczna 2; s/d from 126/140zł; 🅿️ ❄️ 🤶) The large well-furnished rooms at this motel on the main road heading west are Malbork's best deal. It's within walking distance of both the castle and the town centre on the other side of the river. Rooms have fridges, there's free tea and coffee, and breakfast (an extra 15zł) is served at reception.

Hotel Grot
HOTEL €€

(📞55 646 9660; www.grothotel.pl; ul Kościuszki 22d; s/d 199/289zł; 🅿️ 🤶) British and Australian travellers may crack a smirk as they check into the Grot, but there's nothing unhygienic about this place. In fact, it's pretty classy for its price range, with contemporary furniture and spotless bathrooms. On the ground floor you'll find a snazzy restaurant.

Hotel Stary Malbork
HOTEL €€

(📞55 647 2400; www.hotelstarymalbork.com.pl; ul 17 Marca 26/27; s 210-250zł, d 330-360zł; 🅿️ 🤶) This graceful if slightly over-renovated hotel has airy, relaxing rooms with high ceilings and adorned with period touches. The singles have double beds and the very spacious deluxe doubles, costing just a fraction more than an ordinary room for two, are a quantum leap up in comfort. There's a sauna, cafe and restaurant on the premises.

Przystanek Patrzałkowie
INTERNATIONAL €

(📞055 272 3991; ul Kościuszki 25; mains 10-20zł; ⏰11am-9pm daily) At the station end of town, this friendly, uncluttered cafe serves up helpings of pizza, pasta, *pierogi,* salads and

and all-day breakfast to a mixed crowd of locals and tourists. The staff speak English.

★ Gothic
POLISH €€€

(☑ 55 647 0889; www.gothic.com.pl; Malbork Castle, ul Starościńska 1; mains around 45zł; ⊙ 9am-8pm daily Apr-Dec) Malbork's blockbuster castle also contains one of Poland's best restaurants, where the medieval theme continues in commendable authenticity. Taking recipes and ingredients from the Grand Master's cookbook and shopping list (dating back to 1399–1409), chef Bogdan Gałązka re-creates dishes the brothers would have enjoyed, with ingredients mainly from the Malbork area.

Bogdan also travels the world seeking out the very ingredients listed by the Grand Master's cooks: Stilton from England, saffron from Iran and dried fruit from the Middle East feature in some dishes. Some concessions are made to modern Polish tastes (yes, some dishes include potatoes and tomatoes). There's mead and excellent local beer to drink, plus a braille and children's menu. Reservations are essential, especially if you don't have a ticket to the castle.

ℹ Information

Post Office (ul 17 Marca 38; ⊙ 8am-6pm Mon-Fri, to 2pm Sat)

Tourist Office (☑ 55 647 4747; www.visit malbork.pl; ul Kościuszki 54; ⊙ 8am-4pm Mon, to 6pm Tue-Fri, 10am-3pm Sat & Sun Apr-Oct, shorter hours rest of year; 🛜) Large welcome centre with free internet access (plus wi-fi hotspot), free left-luggage service and a library.

ℹ Getting There & Away

The train station and bus terminal are at the eastern end of the town centre, 1km from the castle. Coming from Gdańsk by train, you'll catch a splendid view of the castle; watch out to your right when crossing the river. Malbork sits on the busy Gdańsk–Warsaw railway route, and has services to the following destinations:

Elbląg 8.20zł, 30 minutes, 18 daily

Gdańsk 13.50zł, 30 to 50 minutes, two hourly

Grudziądz 17.10zł, 1½ hours, four daily

Kwidzyn 6zł, 45 minutes, eight daily

Olsztyn 23.60zł, two hours, six daily

Warsaw 55 to 110zł, 2½ to three hours, at least hourly

Elbląg
POP 124,000

Few used to linger longer than a night in Elbląg (*el*-blonk), at one end of the Elbląg–Ostróda Canal, as boats moored up long after it was possible to get anywhere else. However, in the 1990s the authorities decided to give canal navigators a reason to stay on by rebuilding the Old Town, levelled by the Red Army in 1945.

But instead of a painstakingly precise, budget-bustingly expensive rebuild, the new structures are computer-generated versions of what stood here before the shells began to fall. While full marks should be awarded for effort, the old-new streets are a touch sterile and lifeless, leaving visitors with the impression that Elbląg is happening elsewhere (don't worry, it isn't). It's all still a work in progress and might work out yet; amid the stylised medieval gables in metal tubing and period-faithful plastic windows, a few reminders of a more glorious red-brick past do survive.

Centuries before WWII turned its historical centre into landfill, Elbląg was a stronghold and port of the Teutonic Knights. In the 13th century, the Vistula Lagoon (Zalew Wiślany) extended further south than it does today, allowing the town to develop as a maritime centre and a member of the Hanseatic League. When Elbląg came under Polish rule after the Treaty of Toruń, it was a major gateway to the sea. Later, Swedish invasions and the gradual silting up of the waterway capsized the town's prosperity, though a partial revival came with industrial development in the late 19th century.

◉ Sights & Activities

St Nicholas' Church
CHURCH

(Kościół Św Mikołaja; Stary Rynek; ⊙ tower 10am-5pm Tue-Fri, 10am-2pm Sat, 2-5pm Sun) One blast from the past amid the evolving rebuild of the Old Town is this sturdy, red-brick island of true oldness, noted for its 95m-high, carefully reconstructed and now ascendable tower. Within, you'll find some of the original woodcarving, including several triptychs, which escaped war damage. On summer mornings the beautiful stained-glass windows speckle the marble floors with ecclesiastical disco light.

Elbląg Museum
MUSEUM

(www.muzeum.elblag.pl; Bulwar Zygmunta Augusta 11; adult/concession 10/5zł, Sun free Sep-Jun, Wed Jul & Aug free; ⊙ 11am-7pm Tue-Sun Jul & Aug, 8am-4pm Tue-Sun Sep-Jun) A five-minute walk south along the riverbank is the Elbląg Museum. Occupying two large buildings, the museum has sections on archaeology and the town's history, plus a photographic record of Elbląg from the 19th century to WWII.

Galeria El
GALLERY

(www.galeria-el.pl; ul Kuśnierska 6; admission varies; ☺10am-6pm Tue-Sat, to 5pm Sun) Some 200m to the north of the Market Gate is the Galeria El, formerly St Mary's Church. Another massive Gothic brick structure, the original church was gutted and now houses a gallery of contemporary art, with occasional concerts and events. It's worth a visit just to see the imposing interior and the large modern-art objects dotting the grounds, including a monster supermarket trolley and some bashed cubes of XXL proportions.

Market Gate
HISTORIC BUILDING

(Brama Targowa; Stary Rynek) FREE The northern entrance to the Old Town was once through the Market Gate, the only surviving gate from the medieval fortifications. In front of it is a statue of a baker who legendarily saved the town in the 16th century when he spotted the approaching Teutonic Knights, bent on invasion, and cut the ropes that held the gates open. The tower houses a seasonal tourist office and is worth the climb to the top for views across the town.

🛏 Sleeping

Camping Nr 61
CAMPIROUND €

(☎55 641 8666; www.camping61.com.pl; ul Panieńska 14; per person/tent 14/6zł, cabins 50-120zł; ☺May-Sep) Elbląg's pleasantly shaded camping ground occupies an unusually convenient spot on the Elbląg River, close to the Old Town.

Hotel Pod Lwem
HOTEL €€

(☎55 641 3100; www.hotelpodlwem.pl; ul Kowalska 10; s/d 250/330zł; 🅿❄🛜) Occupying one of Elbląg's old-new reconstructions, this design hotel is a stylish place to sleep prior to, or following, a trip on the canal. Room decor unites cream leather, dark wood and flurries of white punctuated with exclamations of colour, and the dominance of light tones makes some rooms feel bigger than they are. Buffet breakfast is taken in the smart cellar restaurant.

Hotel Sowa
HOTEL €€

(☎55 233 7422; www.sowa.elblag.biz.pl; ul Grunwaldzka 49; s/d 135/170zł; 🛜) This 75-bed option opposite the train and bus stations is handy and inexpensive. There's a restaurant on the premises and buffet breakfast is included.

Eating

Cafe Carillon
CAFE €

(ul Mostowa 22; mains 9-18zł; ☺10am-10pm) Elbląg's best cafe with Art Deco–style stained glass and a view of St Nicholas' Church.

Dom Królów
INTERNATIONAL €€

(☎55 611 6695; www.hotelelblag.eu; Stary Rynek 54-59; mains 24-60zł; ☺7am-11pm daily; ❄🛜) Within the new luxury Hotel Elbląg, the town's finest restaurant is overseen by chef Jacek Faltyn who cooks up Polish favourites as well as Argentine steak, Italian pastas and Indian curries to please the hotel's international business clientele. There's an expansive wine list and the inoffensive interior is Elbląg's most contemporary, all metal, greys and blacks with strategic splashes of colour.

Złota Arka
SEAFOOD €€

(ul Wigilijna 12; mains 15-40zł; ☺11.30am-11.30pm) Characterfully stuccoed three-level eatery with a menu of fish and *pierogi*, an antiques roadshow of furniture, period wallpaper and stylish light fittings. Attractively secluded walled garden out back.

Cztery Pory Roku
ITALIAN €€

(ul Wieżowa 15; mains 17-40zł; ☺noon-10pm) Modern pizzeria and cafe also serving pasta, soup and fish dishes within its brown-and-white pseudo-Mediterranean interior. Multilingual service.

❶ Information

Post Office (Plac Słowiański 1; ☺8am-7pm Mon-Fri)

Tourist Office (☎55 239 3377; www.ielblag. eu; Stary Rynek 25; ☺10am-6pm daily Jun-Sep, 9am-5pm Mon-Fri Oct-May) Inconspicuous office buried deep in the town hall.

❶ Getting There & Away

BOAT

Boats heading for the Elbląg–Ostróda Canal depart from the quay next to the Old Town. Information and tickets are available from **Żegluga Ostródzko-Elbląska** (☎55 232 4307; www. zegluga.com.pl; ul Wodna 1b), just back from the quay.

BUS

The bus terminal is next to the train station 1km southeast of the centre. Buses run to the following:

Gdańsk 14zł, one hour, frequent

Frombork 7zł, 40 minutes, at least twice hourly

Warsaw 50zł, 4½ to 5½ hours, hourly

TRAIN

There are services to/from the following:

Gdańsk 17.10zł, 1½ hours, 12 daily

Malbork 8.20zł, 30 minutes, 18 daily

Olsztyn 20zł, 1½ hours, 10 daily

Frombork

POP 2500

Tucked away on the northeast edge of coastal Poland, just a few kilometres shy of Russia's Kaliningrad enclave, Frombork is actually in Warmia (we won't tell if you don't) but has good transport links with Pomerania. Its impressive walled complex overlooking the tranquil town and the water beyond is what people come to see, and the town makes for an enjoyable day trip from Elbląg or even Gdańsk if you plan things right.

Alighting from the bus on the main road, what looks like a castle above you is, in fact, a cathedral, established by the Warmian bishops in the 13th century after a forced departure from nearby Braniewo, following an uprising of pagan Prussians. Later, from 1466 to 1772, Frombork was part of Poland, before it shifted to Prussian control as Frauenburg.

The town took a serious pummelling in WWII, but the cathedral miraculously survived. Frombork was repopulated by Poles exiled from territories annexed by the Soviet Union.

The complex is the main draw in Frombork, but the icing on the cake is its association with Nicolaus Copernicus. It was here that he spent the latter half of his life and conducted most of the observations and research for his heliocentric theory. Copernicus was buried in the cathedral, having survived just long enough to have the first printed copy of his great work placed in his hands – or so the legend goes.

◉ Sights

The Cathedral Hill complex (Wzgórze Katedralne) is today the Nicolaus Copernicus Museum. It covers several sights within the fortified complex, each visited on a separate ticket; the cathedral and the Old Bishop's Palace are the main two sights. The entrance is from the southern side through the massive **Main Gate** (Brama Główna), where you'll find the museum ticket office.

Old Bishops' Palace   MUSEUM

(Stary Pałac Biskupi; www.frombork.art.pl; adult/concession 6/3zł; ⊙9am-4.30pm Tue-Sun) The museum's main exhibition space can be found in the southeastern corner of the complex, though the entrance can take a bit of finding. The ground floor is taken up with objects discovered during postwar archaeological excavations, stained glass and ecclesiastical treasures while the other levels are largely devoted to the life and work of Copernicus, along with temporary displays.

The most interesting section is on the 1st floor, where modern artists' interpretations of the great man, in sculpture and oils, are presented, before you pass into the room containing books and other artefacts from his time.

Though Copernicus is essentially remembered for his astronomical achievements (supplanting the old geocentric Ptolemaic system with his revelation that the earth revolves around the sun), his interests extended across many other fields, including medicine, economics and cartography. Apart from an early edition of his famous *De Revolutionibus Orbium Coelestium* (On the Revolutions of the Celestial Spheres), there are copies displayed of his treatises and manuscripts on a range of subjects, together with astronomical instruments and other scientific bric-a-brac. The exhibits are well lit and creatively placed, but English captioning is sadly lacking.

The third floor is occupied by an easily skippable collection of religious art.

Cathedral   CHURCH

(admission 8zł, during organ recital 12zł; ⊙9.30am-4.30pm, hours vary) Filling the middle of the courtyard with its huge Gothic-brick facade and with a slim octagonal tower at each corner, this impressive building was erected between 1329 and 1388, and was the largest church ever built by the Warmian bishops. So chuffed were they with the result that it became a blueprint for most of the subsequent churches they founded across the region.

Frombork's cathedral certainly doesn't save the best till last: there it is, right in front of you as you enter the main door – the highlight of a visit for most – the tomb of Nicolaus Copernicus himself. Buried under the floor, his casket is visible through an illuminated glass panel.

The rest of the chilly, elongated main nave is cluttered with a riot of Baroque altars and

WORTH A TRIP

MIERZEJA WIŚLANA

If you long to escape the tourist hordes of Gdańsk, head east to the Mierzeja Wiślana (Vistula Spit). This long, narrow sandbar is flanked by the Gulf of Gdańsk to the north and the Zalew Wiślany (Vistula Lagoon) to the south, a vast estuary that stretches all the way to Kaliningrad in Russia. The peninsula is also part Russian, being neatly bisected by the international border.

On the route from Gdańsk to the spit is **Sztutowo**, some 30km from the city. Here you'll find **Stutthof** (www.stutthof.org; ul Muzealna 6, Sztutowo; ⊙ 8am-6pm daily May-Sep, to 3pm daily Oct-Apr) FREE, the former extermination camp in which the Nazis disposed of Polish resisters from the beginning of WWII, and which later became part of their Final Solution against Jews. Nowadays it's a sombre museum presenting exhibitions and documentaries about the German occupation of the region.

Continuing on to the Mierzeja Wiślana, there's a wealth of natural attractions, including pine forests, giant sand dunes, a cormorant reserve at Kąty Rybackie and places to hire sailboats, yachts and catamarans. **Krynica Morska** is the major town on the peninsula, with a popular swimming beach, accommodation in old-fashioned villas and a lighthouse open to visitors. You can reach Krynica Morska by bus or car from Gdańsk, or by ferry from Elbląg.

For that all-over Baltic tan, there's even a nude beach near Piaski, 12km east of Krynica Morska on the far Polish end of the spit. And while you're enjoying the Mierzeja Wiślana beaches, don't forget to have a look for fragments of amber on the shore, washed up by storms in spring.

other 18th-century embellishment. Magnificent in powder blue, gold and silver, the organ, dating from 1683, is a replacement for the one nicked by the Swedes in 1626. The instrument is noted for its rich tone, best appreciated during recitals held daily at 11.30am, 1pm and 3pm Tuesdays to Saturdays in July and August and less frequently in May, June and September.

Water Tower
TOWER

(Wieża Wodna; ul Elbląska 2; adult/concession 5/3zł; ⊙ 10am-6pm Apr-Sep) Across the main road from the cathedral, down in the town, this water tower was built in 1571 making it Europe's oldest. It was used for two centuries to provide Cathedral Hill with water through oak pipes – the pumping mechanism was made by none other than composer Handel's great grandfather! The admission fee gets you to the top and there's a cafe on the ground floor serving Frombork's best cakes.

On the way up the walls are lined with pictures of every castle and mansion in Warmia and Masuria, the jolly music of Handel piped throughout as you make your way slowly up.

Belfry
TOWER

(Dzwonnica; adult/concession 8/5zł; ⊙ 9.30am-5pm daily) The high tower at the southwestern corner of the defensive walls is the former cathedral belfry, which can be ascended for

cracking views of Cathedral Hill, the town and the Vistula Lagoon and Vistula Spit.

Planetarium
PLANETARIUM

(adult/concession 10/6zł; ⊙ 9.30am-5pm daily) Located at the base of the belfry, the planetarium presents half-hour shows in Polish up to six times daily. Get there 10 minutes before the shows start.

Hospital of the Holy Ghost
MUSEUM

(adult/concession 6/3zł; ⊙ 9.30am-5pm Tue-Sat) The 15th-century Hospital of the Holy Ghost, formerly St Anne's Chapel, contains exhibitions of religious art and medical history. It's a short and well-signposted walk east of the cathedral.

🍴 Sleeping & Eating

Several private homes around town rent rooms to visitors for around 50zł per night. Look out for the *kwatery prywatne* signs or head to ul Kapłańska 5 or ul Ogrodowa 24. There's a cheap Biedronka supermarket on the Rynek for snackers, picnickers and self-caterers.

Hotelik Dom Familijny Rheticus
HOTEL €

(🖉 55 243 7800; www.domfamilijny.pl; ul Kopernika 10; s/d 120/150zł; 🅿 🛜) This fine, family-run establishment offers nine spacious apartments with full kitchens, each sleeping up to five people, in the main building;

there's also a new annex with standard hotel doubles and singles. The internationally flavoured Don Roberto restaurant attached to the new building is Frombork's finest. Breakfast is an extra 15zł.

Camping Frombork CAMPGROUND **€**
(📞506 803 151; www.campingfrombork.pl; ul Braniewska 14; per person/tent 10/10zł, d from 60zł; ☺May-Oct) Privately owned camping ground at the eastern end of town, on the Braniewo road.

Hotel Kopernik HOTEL **€€**
(📞55 243 7285; www.hotelkopernik.com.pl; ul Kościelna 2; s/d from 140/180zł; 🅿🛜) The incongruously recent-looking Hotel Kopernik has 37 neat rooms that exude early millennial optimism – all citrus walls and cheap-but-sturdy furniture. Some rooms have cathedral views. There's a budget restaurant occupied most evenings by the mostly German residents of the hotel. The Teutonic guests also guarantee the breakfast spread is a good one. No English spoken.

Restauracja Akcent RESTAURANT **€€**
(ul Rybacka 4; mains 9-50zł; ☺10am-11pm) An alternative to the town's hotel eateries, this decent place offers an honest menu of fish sold per 100g and Polish *pierogi*. The outdoor summer marquis has views of the cathedral.

ℹ️ Information

Tourist Office (📞55 243 7500; ul Elbląska 2; ☺10am-7pm Apr-Aug) Privately run, seasonal information point within a gift shop at the base of the Water Tower.

ℹ️ Getting There & Away

Buses running between Elbląg (7zł, 40 minutes, hourly) and Braniewo stop on the main drag through town, just below the Cathedral Hill.

Just north of the station is the marina; from here pleasure boats go to Krynica Morska (return adult/concession 42/30zł, 1½ hours).

NORTHERN & WESTERN POMERANIA

Stretching northwest from Gdańsk, the Baltic coast is Poland's key summer-holiday strip. It may not be as well known as Spain's Costa del Sol, but it's an attractive coastline of dunes, woods and coastal lakes, fronted by pristine white sandy beaches.

The numerous resort towns stretching all the way from Hel to Świnoujście are engaging places to spend some time. Often blessed with historic architecture, they also contain pleasant, green parks and a good mix of restaurants, bars and other diversions. Outside the urban centres, there are also two interesting national parks on the Pomeranian coast.

As you move around, you'll notice that northern and western Pomerania is basically a rural, sparsely populated region, with compact towns and little industry. This blend of natural beauty with the delights of low-key resort towns makes it a pleasing region to explore, whatever the season.

Łeba

POP 3800

Summertime in Łeba (*weh*-bah) brings Polish and German holidaymakers by the busload, who create a relaxed, good-humoured buzz as they stroll the streets, eat out and enjoy the amusements that spring up to keep them diverted. Outside high season, this small fishing port slams the shutters and hunkers down to survive another long Baltic winter.

Most come here for the generous expanse of wide sandy beach and clean water for swimming. The town is also within day-trip distance from Gdańsk, while the attractive Słowiński National Park is within walking distance.

The sea and sand that put Łeba on the tourist map were almost its undoing in the past. In the 16th century the town moved from the western to the eastern bank of the Łeba River after a huge storm flattened the settlement, but even then, Łeba was prey to the peril of shifting sand dunes, which threatened to cover its buildings and disrupt shipping. However, at the end of the 19th century a new port was constructed and forests were planted to impede the sands.

🛏️ Sleeping

Accommodation options vary according to the season, with July and August by far the busiest months. Low-season room rates drop like a pebble in the Baltic.

Dom Turysty PTTK HOSTEL **€**
(📞59 866 1324; ul Kościuszki 66; dm 40-50zł; ☺May-Sep; 🛜) Occupying a high-ceilinged building that's been home to a hotel of

WOLIN NATIONAL PARK

Best accessed from the resort of Międzyzdroje, **Wolin National Park** (Woliński Park Narodowy; www.wolinpn.pl) occupies the central section of Wolin Island. With a total area of about 50 sq km, it's one of the smaller Polish parks, yet it's picturesque enough to warrant a day or two of walking. The park's northern edge drops sharply into the sea, forming an 11km-long sandy cliff nearly 100m high in places. Back from the coast are a number of lakes, mostly on the remote eastern edge of the park.

The most beautiful lake is the horseshoe-shaped Lake Czajcze. At the southern end of the park is Lake Turkusowe (Turquoise), named after the colour of its water, while close to the seashore is the lovely Lake Gardno, next to the Międzyzdroje–Dziwnów road. The lakes are surrounded by mixed forest, with beech, oak and pine predominating. The flora and fauna is relatively diverse, with a rich bird life. The last wild bison in Pomerania were wiped out in the 14th century, but there's a small bison reserve inside the park, 2km east of Międzyzdroje.

The best way to explore the park is by hiking, and the small area means a good walk needn't be too taxing. Three marked trails wind into the park from Międzyzdroje. The red trail leads northeast along the shore, then turns inland to Wisełka and continues through wooded hills to the small village of Kołczewo. The green trail runs east across the middle of the park, skirts the lakeland and also ends in Kołczewo. The blue trail goes to the southern end of the park, passing Lake Turquoise on the way. It then continues east to the town of Wolin.

All the trails are well marked and easy. Get a copy of the detailed *Woliński Park Narodowy* map (scale 1:30,000), and consult the park headquarters in Międzyzdroje for further information.

some kind since before WWI, this large PTTK hostel has 100 beds spread between cosy, no-frills dorms, some with en-suite facilities, others sharing tired shower rooms and toilets. Breakfast is an extra 20zł, full board 40zł.

Camping Nr 41 Ambré　CAMPIROUND €
(☑ 59 866 2472; www.ambre.leba.info; ul Nadmorska 9a; per adult/tent 15/12zł, bungalows 160-520zł) This camping ground has a handy range of rooms, a restaurant and delicatessen, and neat, cared-for grounds and facilities.

Hotel Gołąbek　HOTEL €€
(☑ 59 866 2945; www.hotel-golabek.leb.pl; ul Wybrzeże 10; s/d 240/360zł; P ⊛) It may be named after a cabbage roll (actually the owner's surname), but the Gołąbek exudes style on the edge of the wharf, with charming old fishing boats and port views. Bright, cheerful rooms, a sauna, solarium and waterfront restaurant all add up to make this a great deal. Booking ahead in summer is essential.

Villa Nautica　HOTEL €€
(☑ 792 390 000; www.nauticaleba.pl; Derdowskiego 13a; d from 199zł; ⊛) Not far from the beach, the crisp Villa Nautica has breezy rooms in light veneers, bathrooms from this side of the millennium and a better-than-average breakfast. Some rooms have balconies and the owner is always eager to help.

★ Hotel Neptun　HOTEL €€€
(☑ 59 866 1432; www.neptunhotel.pl; ul Sosnowa 1; s/d from 530/785zł; P ⊛ ⊛) One of the finest places to lay your head by the Baltic, the 32 rooms at this early-20th-century beachside villa are studies in understated elegance, all antique-style furniture, regency wall coverings and multi-pillowed beds. The cherry on the cake is the terrace pool area overlooking the beach, and a bar where sunsets and sundowners can be enjoyed simultaneously. Rates nose-dive when temperatures outside do likewise.

❶ Orientation

The train and bus stations are next to each other in the southwestern part of Łeba, two blocks west of ul Kościuszki, the main drag. This shopping street crosses the Chełst canal then runs north to the port, on a brief stretch of the Łeba River that joins Lake Łebsko to the sea. The river divides Łeba's beachfront into two sections – the east and the quieter west.

❶ Information

Post Office (ul Kościuszki 23; ⊙ 9am-6pm Mon-Fri, to 3pm Sat)

Tourist Office (☑ 59 866 2565; www.lotleba.pl; ul 11 Listopada 5a; ⊘ 9am-6pm Mon-Fri, 10am-2pm Sat Jul & Aug, 8am-4pm Mon-Fri Sep-Jun)

ⓘ Getting There & Away

The usual transit point to/from Łeba is Lębork, 29km to the south, which is well connected to the Tri-City area by SKM services. Trains to/from Lębork (5.50zł, 40 to 50 minutes) depart eight times daily in summer. Buses (10zł, 35 minutes) do the run realtively infrequently, but these are supplemented by regular minibuses (7zł, 25 minutes).

Słowiński National Park

The 186-sq-km **Słowiński National Park** (Słowiński Park Narodowy; www.slowinskipn.pl; adult/concession 6/3zł; ⊘ 7am-9pm May-Sep, 8am-4pm Oct-Apr) takes up the 33km stretch of coast between Łeba and the tourist fishing village of Rowy, complete with two large lakes, the Łebsko and the Gardno, and their surrounding belts of peat bog, meadows and woods. It's named after the Slav tribe of the Slovincians (Słowińcy), a western branch of the Kashubians whose descendants inhabited this part of the coast right up until the 19th century. In 1977 the park was placed on Unesco's list of World Biosphere Reserves.

➔ Shifting Dunes

The most unusual feature of the national park is the shifting dunes *(wydmy ruchome)*, which create a genuine desert landscape. They're on the sandbar separating the sea from Lake Łebsko, about 8km west of Łeba. Rommel's Afrika Korps trained in this desert during WWII, and the site was also a secret missile testing ground from 1940 to 1945.

The dunes are easily reached from Łeba: take the road west to the hamlet of Rąbka (2.5km), where there's a car park and the gate to the national park. Private minibuses, open-sided electric cars and motorised trains (15zł) ply this road in summer, from a stop on Al Wojska Polskiego, north of the canal. It's also an easy walk.

The sealed road continues into the park for another 3.5km to the site of the rocket launcher, now an **outdoor museum**. From here a wide path goes on through the forest for another 2km to the southern foot of the dunes, where half-buried trees jut out of the sand. As you walk round the bend from the woods, it's quite a sight – the pale, immense dunes open up in front of you like a desert dropped into the middle of a forest,

with a striking contrast at the line where the trees meet the sand. Continue up the vast dunes for a sweeping view of desert, lake, beach, sea and forest.

No cars or buses are allowed beyond the car park. You can walk to the dunes (45 minutes), buy a ticket on one of the small electric cars or rent a bicycle (per hour/day 10/40zł). Coming back, you can either retrace your steps or walk to Łeba along the beach (8km), perhaps stopping for a swim – something you certainly can't do in the Sahara.

➔ Kluki Skansen

(www.muzeumkluki.pl; Kluki 27; adult/concession 12/8zł; ⊘ 11am-3pm Mon, 10am-6pm Tue-Sun May-Aug, shorter hours Sep-Apr) Set on the southwestern shore of Lake Łebsko, the tiny isolated hamlet of Kluki was the last holdout of Slovincian culture, now showcased in the centrally located skansen, an open-air museum of traditional architecture. It's modest but authentic, comprising original in situ buildings. The long, two-family, white-washed houses are fitted with traditional furniture and decorations. Buses run to Kluki from Słupsk (10zł, one hour, five daily).

➔ Smołdzino

West of Kluki, outside the park's boundaries, Smołdzino boasts a fine **Natural History Museum** (Muzeum Przyrodnicze; adult/concession 4/2zł; ⊘ 9am-5pm May-Sep, 7.30am-3.30pm Mon-Fri Oct-Apr), which features collections of flora and fauna from the park's various habitats.

Just 1km southwest of the village is **Mt Rowokół**, the highest hill in the area at 115m above sea level. On its top is a 20m **observation tower**, providing sweeping views over the forest, the lakes and the sea. The path up the hill begins next to the petrol station; you can get to the top in 15 minutes.

Buses to/from Słupsk (8.40zł, 40 minutes) go at least hourly throughout the day.

➔ Lakes

There are four lakes in the park, two large and two small. They are shallow lagoons that started life as bays and were gradually cut off from the sea by the sandbar. With densely overgrown, almost inaccessible marshy shores, they provide a habitat for about 250 species of birds, which live here either permanently or seasonally. Large parts of the lake shores have been made into strict no-access reserves, safe from human interference.

About 16km long and 71 sq km in area, **Lake Łebsko** is the biggest in Pomerania

GDAŃSK & POMERANIA SŁOWIŃSKI NATIONAL PARK

SHIFTING SANDS

The 'walking' dunes in the Słowiński National Park are composed of sand thrown up on the beach by waves. Dried by wind and sun, the grains of sand are then blown away to form dunes that are steadily moving inland. The 'white mountain' progresses at a speed of 2m to 10m a year, burying everything it meets on its way. The main victim is the forest, which is gradually disappearing under the sand, to reappear several decades later as a field of skeletal trees.

The process started at least 5000 years ago, and so far the dunes have covered an area of about 6 sq km and reached a height of 30m to 40m, with the highest peak at 42m. They continue to spread inland over new areas, creating a kind of miniature Sahara-by-the-Sea.

and the third largest in Poland, after Śniardwy and Mamry in Masuria. It's steadily shrinking as a result of the movement of the dunes, the growth of weeds and silting.

Słupsk

POP 95,300

Sometimes it's the anonymous, unpromising names on the map that turn out to be the most charming halts, and that certainly could be said of Słupsk (pronounced 'swoopsk'). A regional service centre with a country town pace, Słupsk has everything that makes a small Polish town just that, with its milk bar, PKP, PKS, PTTK and even a branch of Cepelia all in place. Wide 19th-century avenues lined with mature trees and park benches create an easy-going feel; throw in a touch of architectural interest and you have yourself a pleasant alternative to the busier centres on the coast, as well as a handy base between Gdańsk and Szczecin for flits to the seaside resorts of Darłowo and Ustka.

Like all Pomeranian cities, Słupsk's history involves a complex list of owners: it began life in the 11th century as a Slav stronghold on the Gdańsk–Szczecin trading route, then was ruled by Gdańsk dukes from 1236, passed to the Brandenburg margraves in 1307 and later became part of the West Pomeranian Duchy.

In 1648 it reverted to the Brandenburgs and became part of Prussia, then Germany, until returning to Polish rule after WWII.

◉ Sights

★ Museum of Central Pomerania
MUSEUM

(www.muzeum.slupsk.pl; ul Dominikańska 5-9; adult/concession 12/8zł, valid for Museum & Mill; ◷ 10am-3pm Mon, to 6pm Tue-Sun) The Museum of Central Pomerania is housed within Słupsk's main attraction, a commanding 16th-century castle. Beyond its impressive blocky tower are sacral woodcarvings, historic furniture and other exhibits illustrating the town's history. A new exhibition on the ground floor looks at the town's history in drawings, photographs and old postcards from Stolp, its German name. However the real highlight is a 250-piece collection of portraits by Stanisław Ignacy Witkiewicz (1885–1939), aka Witkacy, on the second floor.

Witkacy was a controversial writer, photographer and painter who specialised in weird-and-wonderful portraits which he produced in a drugged state at his 'portrait company'. Słupsk has no connection to the artist – the museum bought 110 of the pastels from the son of Witkacy's doctor and friend from Zakopane in the 1960s. Some 40 more were added in the 1970s, this time coming mainly from the artist's dentist! Some 125 are displayed at any one time and the exhibition is changed every few months. The body of work is fascinating, Witkacy having captured the essence of his subjects, sometimes to grotesque effect.

Mill
MUSEUM

(ul Dominikańska; entrance with museum ticket; ◷ 10am-3pm Mon, to 6pm Tue-Sun) The building opposite the castle gate is the 14th-century mill, an annex to the museum. Its three floors focus on the folk customs of Pomerania with colourful costumes and chunky kitchenware galore. There's also an exhibition looking at the 1.7 million Poles who arrived in the area from the Polish-speaking territories of the east during the 20th century.

St Hyacinthus' Church
CHURCH

(Kościół Św Jacka; ul Dominikańska 3) The 15th-century St Hyacinthus' Church, aka

St Jack's as the tourist signposting would have it, is usually closed. The time to see it is during services at 8am and 6pm and on Sundays. The fine organ can be heard at regular summer concerts, held midweek in July and August.

Witches' Tower
HISTORIC BUILDING

(Baszta Czarownic; Al F Nullo 8; ⊙10am-6pm Tue-Sun) Only three remnants of the 15th-century fortified walls that once encircled the town survive: one of these is the Witches' Tower which had a sensational career as a 17th-century jail for women suspected of witchcraft; in total, 18 women were executed here up to 1714. Nowadays the tower houses temporary exhibitions for the Baltic Gallery of Contemporary Art.

St Mary's Church
CHURCH

(ul Nowobramska; ⊙6.30am-7pm daily) Fans of red brick and stained glass should check out this chunky Gothic church with its vibrantly coloured, postwar windows. Come on Sunday to see what a queue to get into a church looks like!

Town Hall
HISTORIC BUILDING

(Plac Zwycięstwa; adult/concession 3/2zł; ⊙9am-4pm Mon-Fri) The elaborate Renaissance-Gothic town hall has an impressive main tower, which can be ascended for a full Słupsk panorama.

Baltic Gallery of Contemporary Art
GALLERY

(www.baltic-gallery.art.pl; ul Partyzantów 31a; ⊙10am-6pm Mon-Fri) The main building of Słupsk's gallery specialises in short-term exhibits of Polish and international artists.

🛏 Sleeping

Hotel Mikołajek
HOTEL €

(☑59 842 2902; ul Szarych Szeregów 1; s/d 90/120zł) The only budget accommodation in town, don't be fooled by the reception's elegant darkwood panelling and curvaceously grand staircase – this is an old PTTK hotel, sorely in need of an update. The survivable, tobacco-smoke-infused rooms have rickety fittings and time-thinned duvets, but high ceilings lift the mood a tad and showers gush scalding hot. It's just across the river from the Old Town.

★ Hotel Atena
HOTEL €€

(☑59 842 8814; www.hotelatena.slupsk.pl; ul Kilińskiego 7; s/d 160/210zł; 🛜) Słupsk's best deal is this happily non-Greek-themed mid-range option with well-groomed rooms, some with balconies and large bathrooms. The superb complimentary breakfast is laid out in the restaurant, a facility which can be a godsend at the end of a long day. Superfast wi-fi, friendly staff and an atmosphere of being generally well run make this a great choice.

Hotel Staromiejski
HOTEL €€

(☑59 842 8464; www.hotel-slupsk.pl; ul Jedności Narodowej 4; s 170-220zł, d 280-310zł; 🅿🛜) A couple of blocks west of the Stary Rynek, the Staromiejski is top dog in Słupsk with renovated rooms featuring vibrant carpets and timber furniture. The fancy in-house restaurant plates up quality Polish food.

Hotel Piast
HOTEL €€

(☑59 842 5286; www.hotelpiast.slupsk.pl; ul Jedności Narodowej 3; r from 180zł; 🅿🛜) Affordable accommodation in a grand 1897 structure, with options ranging from basic guesthouse-style rooms to proper luxury suites. The corridors are a bit dull, but the staff are friendly and the rooms are pleasantly light and airy. Breakfast is an extra 25zł.

🍴 Eating & Drinking

Bar Mleczny Poranek
POLISH €

(Al Wojska Polskiego 46; mains around 5zł; ⊙7.30am-6pm Mon-Fri, 9am-5pm Sat & Sun) Grab a tray and line up for cheap, filling socialist-era fare and glasses of weak *kompot* in a semi-institutional dining room complete with obligatory potted plants and strip lighting. Unmissable.

La Venda
POLISH €€

(☑660 224 503; www.lavenda.slupsk.pl; Kilińskiego 2; mains 16-48zł; ⊙noon-last customer; 🛜) Not much to look at from the exterior and positioned at a busy junction, things get much much better once inside La Venda. An elegantly presented dining room sets

---

GDAŃSK & POMERANIA SŁUPSK

WISH YOU WERE HERE

Słupsk is the birthplace of Heinrich von Stephan (1831–97), the reputed inventor of the postcard. He was born at former Holstentorstrasse 31, approximately where today's ul Piekiełko meets ul Grodzka. Pause for a moment and pay homage to the creator an indispensable part of travel culture at the information board that marks the spot.

the scene for Polish and more exotic fare prepared with unexpected panache for rural Pomerania. Service is polite and the price is about right.

★ Atmosphere INTERNATIONAL €€€

(☑59 844 4044; www.atmosphere-slupsk.pl; ul Norwida 20; mains 40-60zł; ⊙noon-10pm Tue-Sat, to 6pm Sun; P❄🐾) That Słupsk has one of Poland's best restaurants may come as a bit of a surprise – that it's in the suburbs 2.3km west of the train station is an even bigger shock. But there it is, flash decor, impeccably-laid tables, Chesterfield-style seating and super-polite waiters. Expect an eclectic menu that combines everything from traditional seasonal Polish fare and Baltic salmon to fresh tuna and crème brûlée.

Everything zings with flavour and can be accompanied by a bottle from one of Pomerania's best stocks of wine. It's a 15-minute walk along uls Szczecińska and Piłsudskiego, a short trip on bus 8 or 9 or a 20zł taxi ride.

Caffeteria Retro CAFE

(Al Sienkiewicza 3; ⊙9am-last customer) Down a set of steps off busy al Sienkiewicza, Caffeteria Retro is one of the town's more characterful spots to grab a cuppa joe.

🛍 Shopping

Sunday Flea Market MARKET

(ul Dominikańska and around; ⊙11am-2pm Sun) Each Sunday a superb flea market takes place near the castle with everything from commie-era vinyl to Kashubian plates, Dirty Dancing videos in Polish and biographies of Piłsudski laid out on blankets and trestle tables.

ℹ Information

Post Office (ul Łukasiewicza 3; ⊙7.30am-7.30pm Mon-Fri, 8am-3pm Sat)

Tourist Office (☑59 728 5041; www.slupsk.pl; cnr uls Starzyńskiego & Tuwina; ⊙9am-6pm Mon-Fri, to 3pm Sat & Sun mid-Jun–mid-Sep, shorter hours rest of year) Can arrange tours to Słowiński National Park.

ℹ Getting There & Away

BUS

Two small bus companies – Nordexpress and Ramzes – serve Ustka (5.90zł, 20 minutes, half-hourly) from the first bus stop on the right when heading along al Wojska Polskiego from the train station. Tickets are bought from the driver.

Other destinations include the following:

Darłowo 14.30zł, 1½ hours, seven daily

Łeba 13zł, 1¾ hours, three daily

Kluki 10zł, one hour, four daily

Smołdzino 10zł, one hour, four daily

TRAIN

Słupsk has the following train connections:

Gdańsk 20zł, 2½ hours, 13 daily (some SKM – change in Gdynia)

Szczecin 31.20zł, three to 3½ hours, six daily

Warsaw 60zł to 120zł, five to eight hours, five daily (two overnight)

Ustka

POP 16,200

With a leafy, primly maintained centre and streets of graceful architecture, this fishing port is one of the Baltic's more refined resort towns. German sun-seekers certainly seem to think so; they've been flocking to Ustka's white-sand beach ever since the 19th-century when 'Iron Chancellor' Otto von Bismarck built an elaborate beach shack here. The town has ample, good-quality digs and an animated seaside promenade, at least in the summer season.

⊙ Sights

Beach BEACH

(Seafront) Ustka's main attraction is the dune-backed beach. None of the town is visible from the sand, giving it a wild feel, unless it's carpeted with holiday-makers, that is.

Bunkry Blüchera HISTORIC SITE

(www.bunkryustka.pl; ul Bohaterów Westerplatte ; adult/concession 12/8zł; ⊙9am-9pm Jul & Aug, 10am-4pm Sep-Jun) Cross the new space-age swing bridge across the Słupia River to take a tour of Ustka's extensive network of WWII bunkers, today inhabited by wax-work Nazis.

🛏 Sleeping

If you've not booked ahead in July and August, the best place to start looking for sheet space is the helpful tourist office. At quieter times you could try your luck on ul Żeromskiego, which is lined with grand old villas offering cheap rooms.

Willa Oliwia GUESTHOUSE €

(☑504 298 290; www.willaoliwia24.pl; ul Gombrowicza 1; per person 75zł; P🐾) This guesthouse is in a recently built villa 2.7km east of the bus and train stations and within walking distance of the beach. Expect gleaming white rooms with lots of personal touches and perfect contemporary bathrooms. The friendly owners serve a hearty breakfast buffet in their kitchen (20zł extra), will lend you a bike (free) and pick you up and drop you off at the stations.

Villa Red　　　　　　　　　　GUESTHOUSE €€
(📵 59 814 8000; www.villa-red.pl; ul Żeromskiego 1; s/d 290/380zł; 🅿 🛜) A grand old red-brick pile built in 1886 for Otto von Bismarck, this is one of the most characterful places to slumber on the Baltic coast. Rooms resemble well-stocked antique emporia; the theme continues in the restaurant. The building was for sale at the time of research – hopefully the new owners will make more of its historical potential.

V Starym Kinie　　　　　　　GUESTHOUSE €€
(📵 602 772 575; www.kino.ustka.pl; ul Marynarki Polskiej 82; r 120-160zł) They pack them in so tightly in Ustka that even the old cinema has been commandeered to put up guests. Each of the smartly done up, comfortable rooms is named after a Hollywood star, and there's a small kitchen.

✕ Eating

★ Dym na Wodzie　　　　　　　POLISH €€
(📵 793 432 403; www.dymnawodzie.pl; ul Chopina 9; mains around 30zł; ⊗ 11am-10pm daily May-Nov, closed Mon rest of year) One of the best places to eat on the Baltic, 'Smoke on the Water' is the creation of chef Rafał Niewiarowski. The focus is on local seasonal ingredients with the menu changing at least seven times a year; just steps from the beach, fish feature prominently. The interior is a pleasingly simple, candlelit affair.

The chunky tables and whitewashed interior contrasts with the contemporary art hung on the walls.

Tawerna Portowa　　　　　　　POLISH €€
(bul Portowa 6; mains 29-74zł; ⊗ 2pm-last customer Tue-Fri, noon-10pm Sat, to 9pm Sun) This red-brick warehouse on the waterfront, with old railway lines running past the door and fishing boats bobbing outside, now houses one of Ustka's best dining spots. The limited menu features scrumptious dishes such as salmon in almond and lemon sauce, Kashubian herring, and beef seasoned in red wine, all of which can be savoured in the dresser-strewn interior.

ℹ Information

Doma Ustka (www.doma.ustka.pl; ul Wilcza 22) Accommodation service.

Post Office (ul Marynarki Polskiej 47; ⊗ 8am-7pm Mon-Fri, 9am-3pm Sat)

Tourist Office (📵 59 814 7170; www.ustka.pl; ul Marynarki Polskiej 71; ⊗ 8am-6pm daily mid-Jun–Aug, shorter hours rest of year)

ℹ Getting There & Away

The train station is diagonally opposite the tourist office. The bus station is a five-minute walk further north along al Marynarki Polskiej. Trains to Słupsk depart every hour (8.10zł, 20 minutes) in summer, and there are several buses per hour (5.90zł, 20 minutes). Regular buses also go to Rowy (one hour), on the edge of Słowiński National Park.

Darłowo & Darłówko

POP 14,400

Inland Darłowo and little seaside sister Darłówko on the Wieprza River form an interesting pair of siblings. The former Hanseatic trading port of Darłowo still retains traces of its wealthy medieval past, contrasting starkly with hedonistic Darłówko and its seasonal fish friers, sandy beach and as-tacky-as-they-come promenade of Chinese-made souvenirs. Inevitably, it's Darłówko that is the main draw for visitors and the town has the lion's share of accommodation and places to eat. Its only 'sight' is a pedestrian drawbridge uniting the western and eastern sides of the river, which opens when boats go into or out of the bay. The two communities are linked by a river taxi and local buses that run along both sides of the river. Otherwise it's around 30 minutes on foot.

◉ Sights

Museum of Pomeranian Dukes　　MUSEUM
(Muzeum Zamku Książąt Pomorskich; www.zamek darlowo.pl; ul Zamkowa 4; adult/concession 13/10zł, tower admission 5zł; ⊗ 10am-6pm Jul & Aug, shorter hours rest of year) South of Darłowo's central Rynek is its well-preserved 14th-century castle, erected in 1352 and renovated in 1988. It was the residence of the Pomeranian dukes until the Swedes devastated it during the Thirty Years' War; the Brandenburgs then took it following the Treaty of Westphalia. The dethroned King Erik, who ruled Denmark, Norway and Sweden between 1396 and 1438, and was known as the 'last Viking of

the Baltic', lived in the castle for the last 10 years of his life.

The castle's grand halls and noble quarters are now a museum, but your self-guided tour begins in the claustrophobic brick basement where beer and prisoners were once kept. Amid the impressive interiors, old farming implements, art from the Far East and old postcards from Rügenwalde (the German name for Darłowo), what sticks in the memory is the impressive collection of antique furniture, which includes a late-Renaissance Italian four-poster and some Danzig wardrobes of truly preposterous proportions.

King Erik is believed to have hidden his enormous ill-gotten treasure somewhere in the castle. So far it remains undiscovered, so keep your eyes peeled as you wander! The castle's main tower can be climbed for stupendous views.

St Mary's Church
CHURCH

(ul Kościelna) Behind the Baroque Town Hall on Darłowo's Rynek rises this massive brick church. Originally dating from the 1320s it has preserved its Gothic shape pretty well. Worth special attention are the three tombs placed in the chapel under the tower. The one made of sandstone holds the ashes of King Erik, who died in Darłowo in 1459. Two mid-17th-century, richly decorated tin tombs standing on either side contain the remains of the last West Pomeranian duke, Jadwig, and his wife Elizabeth.

St Gertrude's Chapel
CHURCH

(Kaplica Św Gertrudy; ul Św Gertrudy; ⊘ 8am-8pm) A few hundred metres north of the Rynek stands a truly quirky piece of medieval architecture. This 12-sided chapel topped with a high, shingled central spire was once the cemetery chapel but became a church in 1997. The outside is reminiscent of a Carpathian timber church but inside the ceiling is a huge piece of Gothic star vaulting supported by six hefty octagonal columns.

🛏 Sleeping

Most places to stay are in Darłówko. Many locals rent out rooms in their homes, from around 50zł per person.

Róża Wiatrów
CAMPGROUND €

(📞 94 314 2127; www.rozawiatrow.pl; ul Muchy 2, Darłówko; site per adult/child 14/9zł; 🤶) This multifaceted holiday complex near the sea has space for 100 campers and offers plenty of other accommodation, from plain to glam.

Hotel Irena
GUESTHOUSE €€

(📞 94 314 3692; www.hotel-irena.pl; Al Wojska Polskiego 64, Darłowo; s/d 110/170zł; 🅿🤶) The best deal in either settlement is this neat little guesthouse (not a hotel) in central Darłowo, with easy access to the castle and the bus station. The owner speaks no English but can communicate that smokers should go elsewhere. The longer you stay the less you pay per night.

★ Hotel Apollo
HOTEL €€€

(📞 94 314 2453; www.hotelapollo.pl; ul Kąpielowa 11, Darłówko; s 260-390zł, d 470-659zł, apt 840zł; 🅿✳🤶) Surely one of northern Poland's best places to linger, this tasteful hotel, crafted from a palatial spa house just steps from the Baltic briny, is welcoming, spacious and crisply luxurious. The 16 contemporary rooms are all the same, just the colour schemes differ, but stumping up a bit more cash gets you one with a knock-dead sea view.

The circular beach cafe is good for a coffee in style even if you aren't a guest.

ℹ Information

Post Office (ul Kąpielowa 4; 9am-4pm Mon-Fri)
Tourist Office (📞 504 992 452; Plac Kościuszki; ⊘10am-5pm Jul & Aug only)

ℹ Getting There & Away

The bus terminal is at the southwestern end of Darłowo, a 10-minute walk from the Rynek. Two morning buses run to Ustka (12.50zł, one hour) and there are six services to/from Słupsk (15zł, one to 1½ hours).

ℹ Getting Around

Minibuses shuttle between Darłowo and Darłówko but a more interesting way to make the short trip is by **water tram** (one way 9zł; ⊘9.30am-7.30pm May-Sep), basically a boat that leaves on the hour from Darłowo and on the half-hour from Darłówko.

Kołobrzeg

POP 46,800

The biggest resort on the Polish Baltic coast, Kołobrzeg (ko-*wob*-zhek) has much more than just its share of the north's pristine white sand. This atmospheric town of seafront attractions, spa traditions, beer gardens and summer crowds of strolling Germans is big enough to offer urban distractions on top of the delights of swimming and sunbathing.

It's actually one of Poland's oldest settlements, having been founded in the 7th century when salt springs were discovered here. In 1000 it became a seat of the Polish bishopric, putting it on a par with Kraków and Wrocław.

However, the good times couldn't last and the town became a popular destination for military invaders, including Swedes, Brandenburgs, Russians and the French forces under Napoleon. Once this phase was over, Kołobrzeg reinvented itself as a sunny spa resort, only to be demolished by the two-week battle for the city in the closing months of WWII.

Almost seven decades since the destruction of 1945, Kołobrzeg still bears the scars. The town was never rebuilt and the modern 'medieval-style' architecture that now dominates the old centre (in the same ilk as Elbląg) is pretty unconvincing. However the bombs also created a lot of parkland, and along with the beach and seafront these combine to make this Baltic base a relaxing, if not particularly aesthetically pleasing, place for a couple of days' exploration.

◉ Sights & Activities

Not much remains of Kołobrzeg's old quarter, but the odd survivor of WWII can be found among the new imitations.

Cathedral
CHURCH

(ul Katedralna; tower 6zł; ⊘9am-2.30pm & 3.45-4.30pm, tower 11am-noon & 2-3pm) The 14th-century cathedral is the most important historic sight in town. Though badly damaged in 1945, it has been rebuilt close to its original form. For such a massive building, it has a surprisingly light-filled interior, illuminated by its extremely tall and narrow windows of beautifully patterned stained glass. Its colossal two conjoined towers occupy the whole width of the building, and the facade is a striking composition of windows placed haphazardly.

No, you haven't had too much vodka, those columns on the right side of the nave really are leaning. But don't worry, you don't have to rush out to avoid being crushed – they've been that way since the 16th century. Still, the impression they create is slightly unnerving.

Old fittings include three 16th-century triptychs and a unique Gothic wooden chandelier (1523) in the central nave. There are some even older objects, such as the bronze

baptismal font (1355) featuring scenes of Christ's life; a 4m-high, seven-armed candelabrum (1327); and the stalls in the chancel (1340). Outside is a striking modern monument celebrating 1000 years of Polish Catholicism; the design, a symbolic split cross joined by a peace dove, depicts influential rulers Bolesław Chrobrego and Otto III.

Despite the short opening times, you can actually wander in whenever you like. However you'll have to time your visit well to enjoy the views from the tower.

Polish Arms Museum
MUSEUM

(Muzeum Oręża Polskiego; www.muzeum. kolobrzeg.pl; ul Gierczak 5; adult/concession 15/10zł, with History Museum 25/15zł; ⊘10am-2pm Mon, 9am-5pm Tue-Sun May-Sep, shorter hours Oct-Apr) This large museum isn't as dull as you might expect and is well worth a look if you've time on your hands. The displays cover the history of weaponry across the ages, with examples of swords, armour, halberds and more modern military technology, including an outdoor display of suitably daunting weaponry. The huge display of cannonballs are calling cards left by Kołobrzeg's many invaders, and the 1945 destruction is impressively brought to life using war debris arranged against a panorama.

History Museum
MUSEUM

(www.muzeum.kolobrzeg.pl; ul Armii Krajowej 13; adult/concession 15/10zł, with Polish Arms Museum 25/15zł; ⊘10am-2pm Mon, 9am-5pm Tue-Sun May-Sep, shorter hours Oct-Apr) Housed in an Empire-style merchant's house called the Braunschweig Palace, the sister institution to the Polish Arms Museum has a neatly presented collection, with an emphasis on weights and scales (metrology). Head downstairs for an interesting audiovisual presentation (in English on request) about the city's history, using images of old postcards from Kolberg (the town's old German name).

Town Hall
HISTORIC BUILDING

(main entrance ul Armii Krajowej; ⊘modern art gallery adult/concession 5/3zł; 10am-5pm Tue-Sun) The Town Hall, just east of the cathedral, is a neo-Gothic structure designed by Karl Friedrich Schinkel and erected by Ernst Friedrich Zwirner (who also built Cologne Cathedral) in the early 1830s after the previous 14th-century building was razed to the ground by Napoleon's troops in 1807. The area in the front of the main entrance

THE BEACH

In the seaside sector, the white-sand beach itself is the top attraction, supplemented by the usual seasonal stalls, waffle kiosks, amusement arcades, novelty boat trips, buskers and other street life. At intervals along the sands you can hire a double-seater beach chair, popular among those who've enjoyed too many waffles. Kołobrzeg now boasts two piers: the old one under which a group of swans gathers on the sand, and a new, industrial-looking structure with a noisy cafe at the end. You can actually walk in the water to the end, it's so shallow. To the west, by the harbour and its newly constructed cluster of waterside apartments, stands the red-brick **lighthouse** (Latarnia Morska; admission 6zł; ⊙10am-6pm, until sunset Jul & Aug), which you can climb for panoramic views.

is populated by beer gardens in summer, providing pleasant places to sit and admire the architecture. One of its wings houses a **modern art gallery**.

Lontowa Tower HISTORIC BUILDING
(Baszta Lontowa; ul Dubois 20) Sometimes erroneously known as the 'powder tower', this tower is a 15th-century survivor from the original city walls. It's currently closed while the city authorities decide what to do with it.

🛏 Sleeping

The summer hordes make a real dent in Kołobrzeg's substantial accommodation range, though private rooms are on offer from locals loitering around the train station brandishing *wolne pokoje* (rooms free) signs, even in low season. As a foreigner you can expect to pay about 50zł per person for these rooms. Otherwise try ul Portowa for the best pickings. Owners are very reluctant to rent for just one night.

Maxymilian Hotel HOTEL €€
(☑94 354 0012; www.hotel-maxymilian.pl; ul Borzymowskiego 3-4; s/d 299/369zł; 🅿🤶🛗) The splendidly classy Maxymilian offers a quiet location and stylishly furnished rooms. The elegant building it occupies stands in stark contrast to the Sand Hotel opposite, which casts a long shadow. A spa, restaurant, sauna and very accommodating staff make this a great deal, but book ahead as this place fills up before anywhere else. Rates drop by half in the quieter months.

Hotel Centrum HOTEL €€
(☑94 354 5560; www.ckp.info.pl; ul Katedralna 12; s/d 150/240zł; 🅿@) Generously sized rooms behind an unpromising facade often have park or garden views, but it's a bit of a hike to the beach. The hotel and associated eateries are staffed by students training

to work in the hospitality industry, often a guarantee of old-world courtesy, little textbook touches not found in other places and the occasional spillage.

⭐ **Sand Hotel** HOTEL €€€
(☑94 404 0400; www.sandhotel.pl; ul Zdrojowa 3; s 429-529zł, d 499-599zł; 🗱🤶🛗) Even the economy rooms at this glass-and-steel colossus are lessons in elegantly clean-cut retro styling, and more than get you in the mood for all the pampering and pummelling available at the hotel's spa. Rooms are pretty spacious, the modern gym is awash with technology and there's not a waffle in sight at the much-lauded restaurant.

🍴 Eating & Drinking

Bar Syrena POLISH €
(ul Zwycięzców 11; mains 12-17.50zł; ⊙11-6pm Mon-Fri, to 5pm Sat & Sun) The *bar mleczny* brought almost into the 21st century, serving Polish standards in a spick-and-span tiled dining room with abstract prints on the walls. You'll forgive the plastic trees when you fork the filling fare shoved through the serving hatch behind the bar – just the ticket after a wind-blasted day by the Baltic.

Domek Kata INTERNATIONAL €€
(ul Ratuszowa 1; mains 32-59zł; ⊙10am-11pm daily) Skip the downstairs over-the-top belle époque dining space and head upstairs for a more medieval banquet hall feel centred around a huge fireplace and capped with a cassette ceiling. The menu is a mixed bag of Polish and international dishes, all cooked to a high standard and served by friendly, English-speaking staff.

Restauracja Pod Winogronami INTERNATIONAL €€
(www.winogrona.pl; ul Towarowa 16; mains 35-60zł; ⊙11am-11pm daily) Extremely popular among

the ambling crowds, 'Under the Grapes' has a slightly French air, but the meat-heavy menu draws mainly on Polish and German cookbooks. The 'grilled boar in juniper sauce' is delicious and can be followed by desserts such as pear dipped in chocolate with whipped cream or Polish cheesecake.

Pergola   INTERNATIONAL €€€
(bul Jana Szymańskiego 14; mains 34-65zł; ⊙10am-11pm) Elevated above the snaffling promenaders and serving a mildly Mediterranean and Polish menu, this is the best of the countless eateries that gather around the lighthouse. Recommended for its fish dishes and grandstand views of the Baltic.

❶ Information

Post Office (ul Armii Krajowej 1)

PTTK (☑94 352 2311; www.pttk.kolobrzeg.pl; ul Zwycięzców 5; ⊙9am-4pm Mon-Fri, 10am-2pm Sat) Can help find accommodation and has a wealth of information on Kołobrzeg and activities in the surrounding area.

Tourist Office (www.kolobrzeg.pl) train station (☑94 352 7939; train station, ul Dworcowa 1; ⊙10am-6pm Jun-Sep, 8am-4pm rest of year); city centre (☑94 354 7220; www.klimatycznykolobrzeg.pl; Plac Ratuszowy 2/1; ⊙8am-5pm Mon-Fri, 9am-4pm Sat, 10am-3pm Sun) The train station tourist office is in an unmarked building opposite the station.

❶ Getting There & Away

BOAT

Kołobrzeska Żegluga Pasażerska (☑94 352 8920; www.kzp.kolobrzeg.pl; ul Morska 7) Operates regular catamaran cruises to Nexø on Bornholm Island, Denmark. The service sails daily in July, August and September, less often from May to October.

BUS

Buses head to the following destinations:

Świnoujście 25zł to 35zł, three hours, five daily

Szczecin 18zł, three hours, three daily

Warsaw 95zł, 10 hours, three daily (more in summer)

TRAIN

Kołbrzeg has the following rail connections:

Gdańsk 36 to 101zł, four hours, four daily (or change in Białogard)

Szczecin 23.60zł, two hours, eight daily

Warsaw 65 to 130zł, 10 hours, five daily (two overnight)

Świnoujście

POP 41,500

As far northwest as you can get in Poland without leaving the country, Świnoujście (shvee-no-*ooysh*-cheh) is an attractive seaside town occupying the eastern end of Uznam Island. There's a touch of faded grandeur along its waterfront promenade, and it emanates a relaxed atmosphere despite its role as a major port and naval base. There are plenty of green parks and a choice of watery views over sea or river, something that may have inspired its famous literary residents from its 19th-century German past (when it was known as Swinemünde), including novelist and travel writer Theodor Fontane and poet Ernst Schrerenberg. Other notable visitors included Kaiser Wilhelm II and Tsar Nicholas II, who met here in 1907, sparking fruitless hopes that their friendship would avert a European war.

The town remains popular with Germans, mostly elderly day-trippers from the former GDR. Of all the Baltic's resorts, Świnoujście attracts the most sedate crowd and those looking to rave by the sea should move on quickly.

Świnoujście's location makes the city a handy entry point for travellers across the Baltic, via ferry services from Sweden and Denmark; it also has a border crossing with Germany.

❍ Sights & Activities

Świnoujście isn't big on sights, with most visitors coming to laze on the beach, one of the widest and longest (and some say the best) in Poland. Back from the sands, the resort district still retains a certain fin-de-siècle air in places, with some elegant villas. This runs down to the seafront where the tack begins in the shape of waffle stands and fluffy toy seals.

Museum of Sea Fishery   MUSEUM
(Muzeum Rybołówstwa Morskiego; ☑91 321 2426; Plac Rybaka 1; adult/concession 7/5zł; ⊙9am-5pm Tue-Sun) If you're keen on stuffed sea life, you'll be delighted by the static displays of albatrosses, sharks and seals, along with fishing paraphernalia, model boats, amber and a few fish in tanks. On the top floor you'll discover a new exhibition on the history of Świnoujście using old postcards from Swinemünde, some hefty 18th-century Pomeranian trunks and souvenirs

of yesteryear. On the ground floor is a new section that features a coral reef aquarium (8/4zł).

🛌 Sleeping

Świnoujście has plenty of places to get some shut-eye, but you may have to approach the tourist office or accommodation agency if you decide to turn up unannounced during the short summer season.

Biuro Zakwaterowań
Barton   ACCOMMODATION SERVICES €
(☑91 321 1155; www.barton.com.pl; Wybrzeże Władysława IV) For private rooms, head to this small office by the ferry landing. Rates average around 50zł to 60zł per person; note that most are in the southwestern suburbs, with almost none in the beach area.

Camping Nr 44 Relax   CAMPING GROUND €
(☑91 321 3912; www.camping-relax.com.pl; ul Słowackiego 1; site 12zł, plus per person 16.50zł) A large, popular camping ground superbly located between the beach and the spa park.

Willa Paw   GUESTHOUSE €€
(☑91 321 4325; www.willa-paw.pl; ul Żeromskiego 25; r from 200zł; P 🐾) The seven rooms here above a relaxing cafe are big enough to swing a four-pawed animal (actually the name means peacock in Polish) and are a cut above your bog-standard guesthouse with darkwood furniture and huge bathrooms.

Hotelik Belweder   HOTEL €€
(☑91 327 1677; www.hotel-belweder.pl; ul Wyspiańskiego 1; s/d 120/180zł; P 🐾) Quite different from the town's villa-based guesthouses, this purpose-built hotel in its own compound is 600m back from the beach and has bright, well-tended rooms, friendly staff and cycle hire.

Hotel Ottaviano   HOTEL €€
(☑91 321 4403; www.ottaviano.pl; ul Monte Cassino 3; s/d 200/300zł; P 🐾) Located in the very centre of town, the Ottaviano is a pretty good deal. Rooms are colourful, furnished with imagination and have warm, uncarpeted wood-effect floors. The in-house restaurant has views across the attractive paved street. It's handy for the ferry crossing.

🍴 Eating & Drinking

Kaisers Pavillon   POLISH €€
(www.des-kaisers-pavillon.pl; ul Wybrzeże Władysława IV 34a; mains 10-29zł; ⊙11am-11pm daily; 🐾) Though occupying a modern build-ing, the interior of this popular eatery serving Polish favourites has been convincingly done out as if it were a 1911 spa pavilion, all painted wood, scenes of happy German holidays on panels by the windows and lots of wicker and brass. In summer there's a sunny riverside terrace across the street.

Restauracja Jazz Club Centrala   POLISH €€
(ul Armii Krajowej 3; mains 18-44zł; ⊙10am-midnight Mon-Sat, from noon Sun; 🐾) Take a seat at this chilled-out club-restaurant to enjoy dishes such as wild boar stew in a round loaf and sirloin on a hot stone in a burnt-orange interior featuring striking tactile modernist murals.

Cafe Wieża   CAFE
(ul Paderewskiego 7; ⊙10am-9pm daily) Occupying the ground and first floor of a church tower that lost its church in WWII, this tiny cafe has just two tables downstairs and a few more in a cosy parlour upstairs. For 6zł you can climb to the top of the tower for views of commie-era blocks and Prussian-era villas.

ℹ️ Information

Post Office (ul Piłsudskiego 1; ⊙8am-8pm Mon-Fri, to 2pm Sat)

Tourist Office (☑91 322 4999; www.swinoujscie.pl; Plac Słowiański 6; ⊙9am-5pm Mon-Fri, 10am-2pm Sat & Sun high season)

ℹ️ Getting There & Away

The most convenient overland crossing to/from Germany is 2km west of town. The first town on the German side, Ahlbeck, handles transport further into the country.

BOAT
Tickets for all boat services are available at the terminals and from most travel agencies around town. All ferries depart from the ferry terminal on Wolin Island, on the right bank of the Świna River (across the river from the main town).

Adler-Schiffe (www.adler-schiffe.de) This German company runs cruises from Świnoujście to Zinnowitz via Ahlbeck, Heringsdorf and Bansin in Germany, up to four times daily. The tourist office has information on times and prices.

Polferries (www.polferries.pl) Major carrier Polferries operates regular ferries to Ystad (Sweden) and Copenhagen.

Unity Line (☑91 359 5600; www.unityline.pl) Runs daily ferries from the northwestern port of Świnoujście to Ystad, Sweden (adult 195/345zł one way/return, concession 150/276zł one way/return, seven hours). Information and tickets online.

BUS

Ostseebus 290 (one way €2.70) links the Polish and German sides of Uznam Island every 30 minutes between 9am and 6pm. A day pass costs €9. Otherwise Świnoujście has the following domestic bus and minibus connections:

Kołobrzeg 25zł to 35zł, three hours, five daily
Międzyzdroje 6zł, 15 minutes, frequent
Szczecin 18zł, 1¾ hours, frequent

CAR & MOTORCYCLE

Cars not belonging to local residents can only use the shuttle ferry between Uznam and Wolin Islands (between the railway station on one side and the town centre on the other) at weekends and between 10pm and 5am on weekdays; otherwise you'll have to head for the crossing serving Karsibór Island, 7km south of Świnoujście. Passage for both vehicles and passengers is free.

TRAIN

The bus terminal and train station are next to each other on the right bank of the Świna River. Passenger ferries shuttle constantly between the town centre and the stations (free, 10 minutes).

Świnoujście has the following rail connections:

Kraków 70zł, 11 to 13½ hours, three daily
Międzyzdroje 5.30zł, 15 minutes, hourly
Poznań 54zł, 4½ to 5½ hours, ten daily
Szczecin 17.50zł, 1½ hours, hourly
Warsaw 60zł, eight hours, three daily

Szczecin

POP 407,800

Well off any track non-German tourists trod, the western port city of Szczecin (*shcheh*-cheen) is a lively city awash with students and a muddle of architecture inherited from wildly different ages. Crumbly German-era Art Nouveau tenements and mansions, some now undergoing renovation, echo a past splendour but historical style is patchy. The authorities seem to have given up on the idea of rebuilding, choosing instead to fill the gaps in the city centre with glass-and-steel malls, sacrificing entire streets in the name of retail. Many of the main thoroughfares have been spruced up, but derelict buildings and overgrown plots are easy to find in the very heart of the city.

It's a busy working port, though you'd never know it wandering the city centre, with just enough to warrant a stopover between Berlin and Gdańsk.

History

Szczecin's beginnings go back to the 8th century, when a Slav stronghold was built here. In 967 Duke Mieszko I annexed the town for the newborn Polish state, but was unable to hold or Christianise it. It was Bolesław Krzywousty who recaptured the town in 1121 and brought the Catholic faith to the locals.

Krzywousty died in 1138 and the Polish Crown crumbled; Pomerania formally became an independent principality. Periods of allegiance to Germanic and Danish rulers followed, before Western Pomerania was unified by Duke Bogusław X in 1478, with Szczecin being chosen as the capital.

The next major shift in power came in 1630, when the Swedes conquered the city. Sweden then ceded Szczecin to Prussia in 1720, which as part of Germany held the region until WWII. Under Prussian rule, Szczecin (Stettin in German) grew considerably, becoming the main port for landlocked Berlin. By the outbreak of WWII the city had about 300,000 inhabitants.

In April 1945 the Red Army passed through on its way to Berlin, leaving 60% of the urban area in ruins. Only 6000 souls remained of the former population, most of the others having fled.

With new inhabitants, mostly drawn from territories lost by Poland to the Soviet Union, the battered city started a new life, developing into an important port and industrial centre for the postwar nation. Szczecin played a big part in the strikes which led to the formation of Solidarity; its three shipyards, including Poland's biggest, have survived the transition to capitalism.

⊙ Sights & Activities

★ **Castle of the
Pomeranian Dukes**   CASTLE
(www.zamek.szczecin.pl; ul Korsazy 34; ⊙ dawn-dusk) **FREE** The mother of all Szczecin monuments is the Castle of the Pomeranian Dukes. This vast, blocky building looms over the Old Town, but the square central courtyard and simple Renaissance-style decoration atop the walls have a certain understated grace (spot the repeated circular pattern that resembles the Yin and Yang symbol). The castle was originally built in the mid-14th century and grew into its current form by 1577, but was destroyed by Allied carpet bombing in 1944 before being extensively restored.

Szczecin

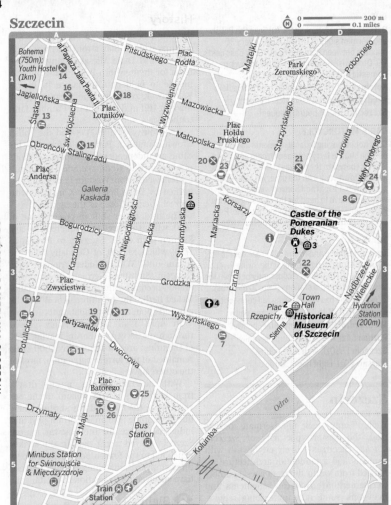

The **Castle Museum** (Muzeum Zamkowe; adult/concession 6/4zł; ⊙10am-6pm Tue-Sun) allows you to get inside the building where the star exhibits are six spectacular sarcophagi of the Pomeranian dukes. These large tin boxes are decorated with a fine engraved ornamentation and were made between 1606 and 1637 by artists from Königsberg. Following the death of the last Pomeranian duke, Bogusław XIV, the crypt was walled up until the sarcophagi were discovered during restoration work in 1946, after the castle's wartime destruction. The remains of the dukes were deposited in the cathedral, while the least-damaged sarcophagi were restored for display.

Various temporary exhibitions and displays of art take place in other rooms of the castle. In summer, concerts and opera are held in the courtyard (www.opera.szczecin. pl). The castle also houses a restaurant, a cinema and a decent gift shop.

★ Historical Museum of Szczecin

MUSEUM

(Muzeum Historii Miasta Szczecina; www.muzeum. szczecin.pl; ul Ks. Mściwoja II 8; adult/concession 10/5zł; ⊙10am-6pm Tue-Thu & Sat, to 4pm Fri &

Szczecin

Sun) Szczecin's 15th-century Gothic Town Hall, one of the most architecturally fascinating buildings in the city with its monster red-brick gable, is the only relic of the Old Town, having miraculously survived the near-total destruction of the surrounding streets in WWII. It is home to the Historical Museum, a well-curated exhibit in the light-filled interior.

The most fascinating exhibit is a medieval treasure trove unearthed in 2001 during building works elsewhere in the city, a multimillion-dollar collection of silver coins, buttons, rings and other jewellery – and the small iron pot the loot was stashed in.

★ **Szczecin Underground**   UNDERGROUND
(☑ 91 434 0801; www.schron.szczecin.pl; ul Kolumba 1; adult/concession single tour 24/19zł; ⊙ tours noon daily and 1pm Sat) This award-winning attraction near the train station is made up of a sprawling set of concrete tunnels beneath the city streets, designated as a bomb shelter in the 1940s and as a fallout shelter thereafter. Tours alternate between a WWII or Cold War theme. Buy tickets from the office at ul Kolumba 1 at least 15 minutes before the tour begins, then make your way to the entrance on Platform 3 of the newly renovated train station.

Cathedral Basilica of St James   CHURCH
(Bazylika Katedralna pw Św Jakuba Apostoła; ul Wyszyńskiego; admission 4zł; tower admission 8zł; ⊙ tower 11am-6pm Tue-Sat, from noon Sun) Head

downhill from the city centre to explore Szczecin's 12th-century cathedral, partially destroyed by Red Army shells in 1945 and reconstructed in 1972. It's the early 1970s renovation you'll notice first, an incongruously modern facade more reminiscent of a derelict factory than a place of worship. As a foreigner you'll be cherry-picked to shell out the 4zł admission, then proceed to the nave where a forest of red-brick columns provides perspective to an interior lacking atmosphere.

On the right, almost at the end of the nave, a plaque remembering those who perished in the Smolensk air disaster sits below another to the Katyń victims they were on their way to honour. Otherwise, possibly the world's tiniest crypt and some impressive stained glass are the only other distractions, except for the tower where a lift winches you up to striking views of the river.

**National Museum's
Department of Art**   MUSEUM
(Muzeum Sztuki Współczesnej; www.muzeum.szczecin.pl; ul Staromłyńska 1; adult/concession 10/5zł; ⊙10am-6pm Tue-Thu & Sat, to 4pm Fri & Sun) The National Museum's Art Gallery resides in an 18th-century palace that formerly served as the Pomeranian parliament. It displays a collection of religious art, particularly woodcarving from the 14th to 16th centuries, and you can also take a peek at the Pomeranian crown jewels.

RED TOURIST ROUTE

The Red Tourist Route, a 7km walking circuit around town, covers 42 important historic sights and buildings; pick up the explanatory map at one of the tourist offices and look for the red arrows daubed graffiti-style on the pavement. It's a great overview of Szczecin's attractions if you're pushed for time (and like walking).

🛏 Sleeping

Youth Hostel
HOSTEL €

(☎91 422 4761; www.ptsm.home.pl; ul Monte Cassino 19a; dm 17-21zł, s/d 80/120zł; 🅿@) Everything is pleasant about this place, with its simple but bright rooms, located in a leafy neighbourhood. There's a laundry for guest use, and out in the well-kept garden there are concrete table-tennis tables. It's 2km northwest of the centre; take tram 3 from the station to Plac Rodła and change for the westbound tram 1 to the 'Piotra Skargi' stop.

Hotelik Elka-Sen
HOTEL €

(☎91 433 5604; www.elkasen.szczecin.pl; Al 3 Maja 1a; s/d 120/150zł; 🛜) Sounding like the name of a cure for indigestion, these lodgings have a location almost as strange as their title. A lift acts as the front door and rooms occupy a basement space in the incredibly ugly School of Economics, itself next door to the local prison. The foyer's a little gloomy but the pine-furnished rooms receive natural light from half-moon windows, and bathrooms twinkle.

Hotelik Słowiański
HOTEL €

(☎91 812 5461; ul Potulicka 1; s 80-125zł, d 98-135zł) Formerly a police dorm, this is Szczecin's hotel of last resort offering unadorned rooms scented with that oh-so Polish aroma – second-hand, low-grade tobacco smoke. However it's clean, receptionists speak some German and the high ceilings add perspective to the smallish rooms. There's a choice of en-suite or shared bathrooms.

Camping Marina
CAMPING GROUND €

(☎91 460 1165; www.campingmarina.pl; ul Przestrzenna 23; site per adult/child 15/7zł, cabins 60-100zł; ☉May-Sep) Good camping ground with cabins on the shore of Lake Dąbie in Szczecin Dąbie, about 7km southeast of the city centre.

Hotel Focus
HOTEL €€

(☎91 433 0500; www.focushotels.pl; ul Małopolska 23; s/d from 229/269zł; 🅿🛜) If all you are looking for is a place to snooze, have breakfast and surf the web, this crisply conceived business hotel overlooking the river is the base for you. High standards throughout, cheery staff, a filling breakfast and an absence of tobacco odour earn this laudable inn glowing reviews. Rooms are standard throughout but tick all 21st-century boxes.

Hotel Campanile
HOTEL €€

(☎91 481 7700; www.campanile.com; ul Wyszyńskiego 30; r from 230zł; ✳🛜) Part of a French chain, this modern hotel is in pole position for sightseeing, as it's an easy walk from the castle, the Old Town, the train and bus stations, and the city's main drag. Rooms are compact but pristine and comfortable, with tea- and coffee-making facilities. There's a bar and restaurant off the foyer.

Hotel Rycerski
HOTEL €€

(☎91 814 6601; www.hotelewam.pl; ul Potulicka 1a; s 150-230zł, d 270-290zł; 🅿🛜) Serving a mainly weekday business clientele, this red-brick pile hides in its own walled grounds off a quiet city-centre street. Receptionists speak no English and communal spaces are a touch too utilitarian, but rooms are well sustained, very comfortable and a nifty deal at the lower end of the price scale. Rates vary at weekends.

Hotel Victoria
HOTEL €€

(☎91 434 3855; www.hotelvictoria.com.pl; Plac Batorego 2; s/d 160/220zł; 🛜) Just uphill from the bus terminal and train station, this well-mannered option, popular with German groups, has cheaply furnished but neatly kept rooms. It's in a quiet-ish location, but has an unexpected facility in the shape of the Tango Nightclub, mercifully fired up weekends only. May win the prize for Poland's grandest restaurant and breakfast room.

Sztukateria
HOTEL €€

(☎91 817 1921; www.sztuka.teria.eu; ul Śląska 4; s 135zł, d 190zł; ⊖🛜) Don't be fooled by the design-hotel reception here – rooms upstairs are rather austere affairs, though they do have good-quality furniture and pristine bathrooms. They're all pretty spacious, but need an update and the views of Szczecin's soot-streaked backyards from the windows are uninspiring. Breakfast is included and taken in the cafe on the premises.

✕ Eating

The place to head in summer for a light pasta lunch, full-blown steak dinner or a coffee and ice-cream halt (or a few beers) is the strip of al fresco eateries, interspersed with splashing fountains, which extends the entire length of al Papieża Jana Pawła II. If you prefer a roof over your food, try the following options.

Cafe Koch   BAKERY €
(ul Jagiellońska 2/1; ⊗8am-6pm Mon-Fri, 9am-5pm Sat & Sun) There aren't many small businesses here that have more than 40 years of history, but since 1972 Koch have been supplying the city with exquisite traditional cakes and pastries. Pass through the (fake) stained-glass entrance into this tiny two-table branch for a breakfast of coffee and cheesecake sold by weight.

Bar Mleczny Turysta   CAFETERIA €
(ul Obrońców Stalingradu 6; mains 3-8.50zł; ⊗8am-6pm Mon-Fri) With its chequered tile floor, tiny stools bolted down, time-warped menu boards in 1970s plastic lettering and brusque, ladle-wielding dinner ladies, this is the belly-filling milk-bar experience Szczecin style.

Rybarex   SEAFOOD €
(ul Małopolska 45; mains 7-13.50zł; ⊗9am-7pm Mon-Fri, 10am-6pm Sat; 🕿) This budget fish cafeteria has a wide range of piscine dishes to choose from, enjoyed in a clinically funky dining area.

Dom Chleba   CAFE €
(al Niepodległości 2; ⊗6am-7pm Mon-Fri, 7am-5pm Sat, 8am-3pm Sun) If your digs don't do breakfast, this place will in the form of brain-rousing coffee and monster pastries for a couple of złoty.

Restauracja Bombay   INDIAN €€
(www.india.pl; ul Partyzantów 1; mains 25-45zł; ⊗1-11pm) Possibly the last thing you might expect amid Szczecin's post-Communist cityscape: quality Indian food, including items such as thali meals, served in tasteful surrounds by waiters with impeccable English. It was established by a former Miss India (1973), and boasts an appropriately international wine list.

Bohema   INTERNATIONAL €€
(📱91 433 2230; www.bohema.szczecin.pl; ul Wojska Polskiego 67; mains 19-50zł; ⊗noon-11pm Mon-Thu, to midnight Fri, 2pm-midnight Sat, to 8pm Sun) For a blast of style in sometimes gritty Szczecin, seek out this little-touted restaurant with its romantically aristocratic decor and long menu of excellent Polish and international dishes prepped and plated by a Peruvian chef. As subscribers to the Slow Food movement, its ingredients are as seasonal as possible. The beef tenderloin with potatoes comes highly recommended.

Ukraineczka   UKRAINIAN €€
(ul Panieńska 19; mains 18-30zł; ⊗11am-10pm Mon-Thu, to 11pm Fri-Sun) Simple, small place in a new building offering authentically traditional Ukrainian and Lithuanian dishes, Ukrainian beers and Georgian wines amid photos of old Ukraine, ceremonial towels, sunflowers and other Ukrainian knickknacks.

Restauracja Chata   POLISH €€
(www.chata.szczecin.pl; Plac Hołdu Pruskiego 8; mains 22-69zł; ⊗noon-10pm Sun-Thu, to 2am Fri & Sat) Charmingly muralled place dishing up hearty Polish fare in faux-rustic timber surroundings, decked out with the odd folksy-looking item. A variety of *pierogi* and a comprehensive range of Polish soups make tasty starters; main courses consist of wild boar, beef steak and a mixed grill.

Karczma Polska Pod Kogutem   POLISH €€
(www.karczmapodkogutem.pl; Plac Lotników 3; mains 24-67zł; ⊗11am-midnight daily; 🕿) Two giant roosters guarding the entrance set the tone for this rustic barn inserted into the ground floor of a post-WWII tenement and serving traditional Polish food. Its external wooden deck is a great vantage point over the picturesque square opposite, and the menu is a veritable zoo of defunct grunters, squawkers and even rutters.

Avanti   ITALIAN €€
(al Papieża Jana Pawła II 43; mains 20-69zł; ⊗noon-10pm Sun-Thu, to 11pm Fri & Sat) The best Italian in town serves meticulously crafted Apennine fare in a refined ambience to a foodie crowd that definitely prefers pizza without pineapple. The menu is reassuringly short and changes daily.

🍷 Drinking & Entertainment

Szczecin has a sizeable student population that keeps things lively on the nightlife scene, at least in term time. For the latest club and event info pick up a copy of *Echo* or *hot* – they're both in Polish only, but listings usually need little translation.

Stara Komenda
MICROBREWERY

(www.starakomenda.pl; Plac Batorego 3; ⊘1-11pm Sun & Mon, to midnight Tue-Thu, to 1am Fri & Sat) Szczecin's very own microbrewery concocts four of its very own beers and has quickly become the city's premier elbow-bending venue for orthodox fans of the hop. First-timers can sample the entire frothy quartet for 12zł.

Christopher Columbus
BAR

(ul Wały Chrobrego 1; ⊘10am-1am Sun-Thu, to 2am Fri & Sat) Pass the large bloody-mouthed plastic shark strung up outside to discover Szczecin's best beer garden wrapped around a wooden pavilion. The place offers drinkers widescreen views of the river, there's lots of cheap food and a band occasionally strikes up in the shade of mature trees.

Brama Cafe
CAFE

(Plac Hołdu Pruskiego 1; ⊘noon-11pm Mon-Thu, to 1am Fri & Sat) Housed in the Baroque Royal Gate, another fragment of lost history, the Brama is an authentically historical place to have a drink, either in the barrel-ceiling interior or outside when the weather is good.

City Hall
CLUB

(☑91 471 1613; www.cityhall.pl; Czerwony Ratusz, ul 3 Maja 18; ⊘6pm-late) This impressive space in the basement of the massive red-brick former Town Hall just off ul Maja packs in up to 400 clubbers for some of the biggest nights in town.

Kafe Jerzy
CLUB

(www.kafejerzy.pl; ul Jagiellońska 67) Difficult to find, but worth it for the packed nights, guest DJs and easy-going crowd. Head west from al Jana Pawła II along ul Jagiellonska for seven blocks until you reach the traffic lights on al Bohaterów Warszawy. The club is across the street along an alleyway of garages on the left. Taking a taxi will save a lot of searching around.

Alter Ego Club
LIVE MUSIC

(www.alterego.art.pl; Plac Batorego 4, Czerwony Ratusz) Low-lit, red-brick live-music venue featuring local rock bands and occasional indie, jazz and reggae acts.

❶ Information

Post Office (Al Niepodległości 43; ⊘8am-6pm Mon-Fri)

Tourist Office (☑91 489 1630; www.szczecin.eu; ul Korsarzy 34 ; ⊘9am-5pm Mon-Fri, 10am-2pm Sat)

❶ Getting There & Away

AIR

The **airport** (☑91 484 7400; www.airport.com.pl) is in Goleniów, about 45km northeast of the city and is served by both Wizz Air and Ryanair from the UK and Ireland. A shuttle bus (16.90zł) operated by **Interglobus** (☑91 485 0422; www.interglobus.pl) picks up from outside the train station before every flight, and meets all arrivals. Booking a seat on the shuttle online is easy and guarantees you a spot, some reassurance if you are arriving late at night. Alternatively, a taxi should cost around 150zł.

BUS

The bus terminal is uphill from the train station and handles regular summer buses to nearby beach resorts, as well as Świnoujście (18zł, one hour 45 minutes, 15 daily). Alternatively, for Świnoujście take one of the regular minibuses operated by **Emilbus** (www.emilbus.com.pl) that depart from a special stand at the southern end of al 3 Maja.

Berlineks (www.berlineks.com) and **PKS Szczecin** (www.pksszczecin.info) both run comfortable minibuses to Berlin (three hours, frequent), the first from outside the train station, the second from the bus station. Interglobus operates similar services, as well as other trips and transfers.

TRAIN

The newly renovated main train station, Szczecin Główny, is on the bank of the Odra River, 1km south of the centre. As well as domestic connections there are also cross-border trains to Berlin (two hours, three daily) and Angermünde (one hour, hourly, change here for Berlin). The city has the following domestic rail connections:

Gdańsk 50zł, 5½ hours, three daily (or change in Słupsk)

Kołobrzeg 23.60zł, 2½ hours, seven daily

Kraków 70zł, 11 hours, six daily

Poznań 31.20zł, three hours, hourly

Słupsk 31.20zł, three to four hours, seven daily

Warsaw 65zł to 130zł, 6½ hours, seven daily

GDAŃSK & POMERANIA SZCZECIN

Warmia & Masuria

POP 4.1 MILLION

Why Go?

There's something in the water in these two northeast regions bordering the Russian enclave of Kaliningrad – mostly hundreds of sailors, windsurfers and kayakers who come to make a splash in the Great Masurian Lakes, which dominate the landscape. There's more aqua fun to be had here than in the rest of the country put together, and if water sports are your thing, this is your place.

Away from the lakes, one of the world's most intriguing canal trips – the Elbląg-Ostróda experience – and countless rivers, wetlands and swamps mean you're never far from a soaking in these parts. The Łyna and Krutynia Rivers are kayaking bliss, and Warmia even boasts a small stretch of Baltic coastline.

When you've had your fill of water fun, the region has bags of red-brick architecture left by the Warmian Bishops and is home to Hitler's wartime hideout, the Wolf's Lair – one of Europe's most significant WWII sites.

Best Places to Stay

➡ Pensjonat Mikołajki (p385)

➡ Hotel Willa Port (p375)

➡ Hotel Wileński (p372)

➡ Zajazd Pod Zamkiem (p381)

Best Lakes

➡ Lake Śniardwy (p378)

➡ Lake Niegocin (p382)

➡ Lake Łuknajno (p385)

➡ Lake Mamry (p381)

When to Go
Olsztyn

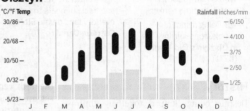

Jan Cross lakes in Masuria on a pair of skis, when the whole region turns to ice.

Aug Join the pilgrimage to Święta Lipka during the Feast of the Assumption.

Oct See the lakes reflect the fiery autumnal shades of the region's many forests.

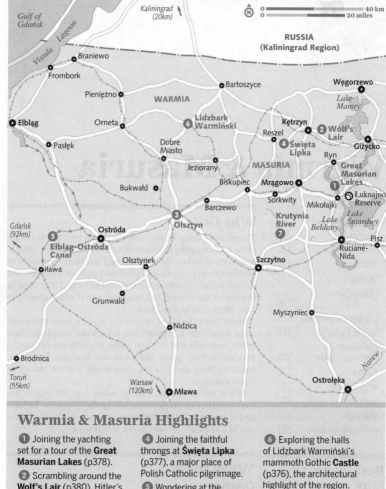

Warmia & Masuria Highlights

1 Joining the yachting set for a tour of the **Great Masurian Lakes** (p378).

2 Scrambling around the **Wolf's Lair** (p380), Hitler's secret wartime bunker.

3 Doing a spot of cobblestone-surfing in **Olsztyn's Old Town** (p371).

4 Joining the faithful throngs at **Święta Lipka** (p377), a major place of Polish Catholic pilgrimage.

5 Wondering at the spectacle of boats travelling over dry land on the **Elbląg-Ostróda Canal** (p376).

6 Exploring the halls of Lidzbark Warmiński's mammoth Gothic **Castle** (p376), the architectural highlight of the region.

7 Paddling along the **Krutynia River** (p373) in a kayak.

History

Despite being lumped together administratively today, Warmia and Masuria have always been separate entities, and their histories, though broadly similar, are largely independent.

Warmia is imaginatively named after its original inhabitants, the Warmians, who were wiped out by the Teutonic Knights in the 13th century, after which the Knights set up a Teutonic province. For more than five centuries this was largely an autonomous ecclesiastical state run by all-powerful Catholic bishops.

The Warmian diocese was the largest of four that were created by the papal bulls of 1243. Though administratively within the Teutonic state, the bishops used papal protection to achieve a far-reaching autonomy. Their bishopric extended from the north of Olsztyn up to the present-day national border, and from the Vistula Lagoon in the west to the town of Reszel in the east. Following the 1466 Treaty of Toruń, Warmia was incorporated into the kingdom of Poland, but the bishops retained much of their control over internal affairs, answering directly to the pope. When the last grand master adopted Protestantism in 1525, Warmia became a bastion of the Counter-Reformation. In 1773 the region fell under Prussian rule, along with swathes of western Poland.

In the medieval period, Masuria was dealing with its own upheavals. The Jatzvingians (Jaćwingowie), the first inhabitants, belonged to the same ethnic and linguistic family as the Prussians, Latvians and Lithuanians. For farmers they were unusually warlike, and caused plenty of headaches for the Mazovian dukes, as they ravaged the principality's northern fringes on a regular basis and even pressed as far south as Kraków. In the second half of the 13th century, however, the Teutonic Knights expanded eastwards over the region, and by the 1280s they had wiped them out too.

Both Warmia and Masuria quickly became a bone of contention between the Teutonic order and Lithuania, and remained in dispute until the 16th century. At that time the territory formally became a Polish dominion, but its colonisation was slow. Development was also hindered by the Swedish invasions of the 1650s and the catastrophic plague of 1710.

In the Third Partition of 1795, the region was swallowed up by Prussia, and in 1815 it became a part of the Congress Kingdom of Poland, only to be grabbed by Russia after the failure of the November Insurrection of 1830. After WWI Poland took over the territory, though not without resistance from Lithuania, but the region remained remote and economically unimportant. Warmia was finally restored to Poland after WWII, and the two halves became a single administrative zone.

THE OLSZTYN REGION

The Olsztyn region is principally Warmia and the land to the south of the region's capital, Olsztyn. Like Masuria, its landscape is dotted with lakes and sporadically cloaked in forest. There are several important architectural monuments here and relics of the bishops that once ruled the area. Of particular note is the castle of Lidzbark Warmiński and the church in Święta Lipka; more secular highlights include the impressive open-air museum at Olsztynek and the unique Elbląg-Ostróda Canal.

Olsztyn

POP 175,400

By far the biggest city in the region, Olsztyn (*ol*-shtin) is the natural jumping-off point and transport hub for many other towns and attractions in Warmia and Masuria. However, it's worth spending a couple of days in this bustling settlement to explore the cobblestoned Old Town and enjoy the laid-back, slightly off-the-beaten-track feel.

The town was founded in the 14th century as the southernmost outpost of Warmia, and only came under Polish control following the Treaty of Toruń in 1466. With the First Partition of Poland in 1772, Olsztyn became Prussian (renamed Allenstein) and remained so until the end of WWII.

◉ Sights

Museum of Warmia & Masuria   MUSEUM
(www.muzeum.olsztyn.pl; ul Zamkowa 2; adult/concession 10/8zł, with House of the Olsztyn Gazette 13/9zł; ⏲10am-6pm Tue-Sun Jul & Aug, slightly shorter hours rest of the year) A well-rubbed bronze of Copernicus welcomes you to Olsztyn's massive red-brick 14th-century castle, the most important historic building in town. And it's the Copernicus association that makes this the town's top sight, the astronomer as administrator of Warmia having lived in the castle from 1516 to 1520. He made some of his astronomical observations here, and you can still see the diagram he drew on the cloister wall to record the equinox and thereby calculate the exact length of the year.

The rest of the collection is an eclectic mix of rural knickknacks, dubious art and various temporary exhibitions. The tower is hardly worth the climb, though there is some interesting graffiti on the inside of the viewing platform left by visitors from down the decades.

House of the Olsztyn Gazette   MUSEUM
(Dom 'Gazety Olsztyńskiej'; www.muzeum.olsztyn.pl; Targ Rybny 1; adult/concession 7/5zł,

WARMIA & MASURIA OLSZTYN

Olsztyn

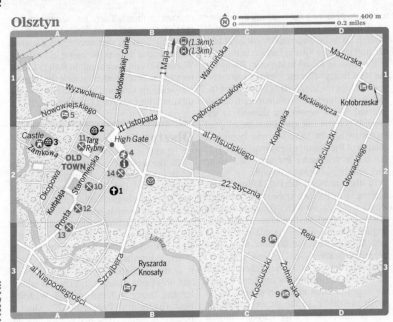

with castle 13/9zł; ⊙ 9am-5pm Tue-Sun Jul & Aug, slightly shorter hours rest of year) The Museum of Warmia & Masuria's main annexe is housed in the former *Gazeta Olsztyńska* newspaper building. The Polish paper was famed for its outspoken politics in German Allenstein, so when the Nazis marched in it was closed down and its editors sent off to Dachau. Half of the building looks at the newspaper's history from the late 19th century onwards (all sadly in Polish). The middle floor examines Olsztyn's history in a jumble sale of varied objects precious and ordinary.

The basement section deals with Polish schools between 1929 and 1939. Don't miss the political posters in the entrance, some communist era denouncing NATO, others belonging to various Solidarity campaigns.

Cathedral
CHURCH

(ul Jana Długosza) This Gothic cathedral dates from the 14th century, though its huge 60m tower was only added in 1596. As in Olsztyn's castle, the most impressive architectural feature is the webbed vaulting in the aisles, reminiscent of Gaudí's Sagrada Família in Barcelona. The nave, however, has netlike arches dating from the 17th century. Among the remarkable works of art are the 16th-century triptych at the head of

the left aisle, and a shimmering gold and silver altarpiece of the Virgin Mary.

🛏 Sleeping

PTSM Youth Hostel
HOSTEL €

(☎ 89 527 6650; www.ssmolsztyn.pl; ul Kościuszki 72/74; dm 25-35zł, s/d from 50/80zł; 🛜) This sometimes gloomy hostel has a large kitchen, bike hire and generously cut rooms that sleep up to ten. In winter you can often have the place to yourself.

★ Hotel Wileński
HOTEL €€

(☎ 89 535 0122; www.hotelwilenski.pl; ul Ryszarda Knosały 5; s 245-290zł, d 290-320zł; ❄🛜) Installed in a row of knocked-through 19th-century townhouses, this elegant hotel is a real treat. Posh corridors lead to formally furnished quarters with big-print wall coverings and imaginative bathrooms. The downside – some rooms have a view of McDonald's across the road, but bulky curtains black out the golden 'M'.

Villa Pallas
GUESTHOUSE €€

(☎ 89 535 0115; www.villapallas.pl; ul Żołnierska 4; s 170-220zł, d 200-250zł; 🅿🛜) This sophisticated villa is named after the Greek goddess Athena, whose statue makes up part of the mix 'n' match decor. Negotiate the maze of stairways to find relatively well-furnished,

Olsztyn

spotless rooms and some decent suites. A smart restaurant and small spa centre complete the picture.

Hotel Pod Zamkiem   GUESTHOUSE €€
(☑89 535 1287; www.hotel-olsztyn.com.pl; ul Nowowiejskiego 10; s/d 155/215zł; ℗ 🛜) Occupying a large early-20th-century villa, once the home of the influential Sperl family, this stylish guesthouse has character in spades. Wooden beams, murals and lots of pine provide atmosphere, and the park setting puts you right by the castle and the Old Town. It's on a busy road, so request a room at the back.

Hotel Warmiński   HOTEL €€
(☑89 522 1400; www.hotel-warminski.com.pl; ul Kołobrzeska 1; s/d from 270/300zł; 🛜) This very well-appointed hotel knows what business travellers need and provides it with a smile. Rooms are top-notch and rates fall a bit at weekends.

✖ Eating

Feniks Cafe   CAFE €
(ul Prosta 7/9; ⊙8am-10pm) A lovely little caffeine and cake stop on the main thoroughfare through the Old Town with better-than-average coffees and calorie-packed treats for the sweet-toothed such as *szarlotka* (apple cake), *sernik* (cheesecake) and that Polish favourite, *rurki z bitą śmietaną* (wafer tubes filled with whipped cream).

Greenway   VEGETARIAN €
(ul Prosta 10/11; mains 6-12zł; ⊙10am-8pm Mon-Sat, noon-8pm Sun; ✑) A branch of the popular Polish chain. Monster portions of the usual offerings, such as Mexican goulash, lasagna and spinach quiche, are great belly fillers and there's a mega-cheap lunch menu for 11zł.

★Spiżarnia Warmińska   INTERNATIONAL €€
(www.spizarniawarminska.pl; ul Lelewela 4a; mains 35-45zł; ⊙9am-11pm; ✽🛜) With its 21st-century interior, clued-up staff and occasional live music, the 'Warmian Larder' has rapidly established itself as Olsztyn's best place to eat. The mix of Polish and international dishes uses only the freshest, locally sourced ingredients and changes weekly. Though there are a few exotic additions that go into the pot such as foie gras, Madeira wine and chutney.

If you are looking for a few gastronomic souvenirs, the restaurant also sells its own bread, mustard, goat's cheese, conserves and syrups.

Česká Hospoda   CZECH €€
(Targ Rybny 14; mains 7-30zł; ⊙noon-11pm Mon-Thu, to midnight Fri & Sat, to 10pm Sun) Northern Poland's best Prague-style beer hall is a pretty authentic affair complete with three types of Bohemian lager, a menu of stodgy goulash, potato cakes and sirloin and a large outdoor terrace.

Bar Dziupla   POLISH €€
(Rynek 9/10; mains 18-29zł; ⊙8.30am-8pm) Choose between the creamy interior or out on the pretty main square to enjoy a mixed menu that pretty much covers all Polish tastes.

KAYAKING THE KRUTYNIA

The travel agency **PTTK Mazury** (p432) runs 10-day kayaking tours along the Krutynia River route (known as Szlak Kajakowy Krutyni). The 103km trip begins at Stanica Wodna PTTK in Sorkwity, 50km east of Olsztyn, and goes down the Krutynia River and Lake Bełdany to Ruciane-Nida. It's regarded as Poland's top kayak trip and few come away disappointed. Tours depart daily from May to October, and the price includes a kayak, food, insurance, lodging in cabins and a Polish-, English- or German-speaking guide.

ℹ Information

Main Post Office (ul Pieniężnego 21; ◷8am-7pm Mon-Fri, to 4pm Sat)

Tourist Office (☑89 535 3565; www.mazury. travel; ul Staromiejska 1; ◷8am-6pm Mon-Fri, 10am-3pm Sat & Sun mid-Jun–Sep, shorter hours rest of year)

ℹ Getting There & Away

The bus and train stations are both in a big, semi-derelict L-shaped building on Plac Konstytucji 3 Maja. Walk to the Old Town (15 minutes) or take one of the frequent city buses that drop off in front of the High Gate.

BUS

Buses run from Olsztyn to numerous towns:

Elbląg 24zł, 1½ to two hours, seven daily

Gdańsk 30zł, three hours, many daily

Giżycko 12zł, two hours, many

Kętrzyn 10zł to 18zł, one to two hours, many

Lidzbark Warmiński 8.50zł, one hour, ten daily

Olsztynek 5.50zł, 50 minutes, two or three hourly

Ostróda 5zł, one hour, hourly

Warsaw 30zł, three to five hours, at least hourly

TRAIN

Olsztyn has rail connections to a number of towns:

Elbląg 20zł, 1½ hours, ten daily

Gdańsk 33zł, 3½ hours, hourly

Toruń 27zł to 36zł, 2½ hours, seven daily

Warsaw 30zł, four hours, four daily (or change in Iława)

Olsztynek

POP 7600

Around 25km southwest of Olsztyn, Olsztynek is a small town with one big attraction: the Museum of Folk Architecture.

◉ Sights

On the northeastern outskirts of Olsztynek, the **Museum of Folk Architecture** (Muzeum Budownictwa Ludowego; www.muzeum olsztynek.com.pl; ul Leśna 23; adult/concession 12/7zł; ◷10am-6pm Jul & Aug, slightly shorter hours rest of the year) - a skansen or open-air ethnographic museum - features about 40 examples of regional timber architecture from Warmia and Masuria, plus a cluster of Lithuanian houses. There's a variety of peasant cottages complete with outbuild-

ings, various windmills and a thatched-roof church. A number of buildings have been furnished and decorated inside in traditional period manner and the effect is impressive.

Above the skansen's rustic restaurant is a small museum that is split in two; one half is filled with the usual collection of folk art and farming tools, while the other contains a detailed account (in Polish) of Stalag 1B Hohenstein, a POW camp located on the outskirts of the village during WWII. Some 650,000 captured soldiers passed through the camp, consisting mostly of French, Belgian, Italian and Russian nationals.

ℹ Getting There & Away

The train station is 1km northeast of the centre, close to the skansen. Hourly trains run to Olsztyn (5zł, 30 minutes).

The bus terminal is 250m south of the Rynek, but many regional buses call in at the train station. Buses and minivans run to Olsztyn (5.50zł, 50 minutes, two or three hourly).

Grunwald

Grunwald is hard to find, even on detailed maps, yet the name is known to every Pole. Here, on 15 July 1410, the combined Polish and Lithuanian forces (supported by contingents of Ruthenians and Tatars) under King Władysław II Jagiełło defeated the army of the Teutonic Knights. A crucial moment in Polish history, the 10 hours of carnage left the grand master of the Teutonic order, Ulrich von Jungingen, dead and his forces decimated. This was reputedly the largest medieval battle in Europe, involving an estimated 70,000 troops.

The battlefield is an open, gently rolling meadow adorned with three monuments. Built on the central hill is the **Museum of the Grunwald Battlefield** (Muzeum Bitwy Grunwaldzkiej; www.grunwald.warmia.mazury. pl; adult/concession 11/9zł; ◷9.30am-6.30pm Easter-Sep), which has a minuscule display of period armour, maps and battle banners. Its redeeming feature is a small cinema that plays scenes from *Bitwa pod Grunwaldem* (1931), a classic Polish flick about the battle. Five hundred metres from the museum are the ruins of a **chapel**, erected by the order a year after the battle, on the spot where the grand master is supposed to have died. All signs are in Polish, but the shop by the entrance to the battlefield sells brochures in English and German.

The best time to visit the place is in July during the **Days of Grunwald festival** (www.grunwald1410.pl; ⊙ Jul), a medieval extravaganza with heaps of stalls, tournaments, concerts and costumed characters, culminating in an epic re-enactment of the battle itself.

❶ Getting There & Away

Only three buses a day run to the battlefield from Olsztyn (15zł, 1½ hours). Other buses and minivans operate to/from Olsztynek (9zł, 30 minutes, six daily) and Ostróda (8zł, 50 minutes, 8 daily).

Ostróda

POP 33,500

Drowsy Ostróda is the southern terminus of the Elbląg-Ostróda Canal, and if you take a boat from the town you might end up spending a night here. Apparently Napoleon once ruled Europe from this quiet corner; he wouldn't look twice at it now, but Polish holidaymakers love the leisurely pace of life here, attracted by its location on placid, swan-studded **Lake Drwękie**.

🛏 Sleeping & Eating

The tourist office has lists of private rooms in and around the town; they're pasted on the door when the office is closed.

★**Hotel Willa Port**   HOTEL €€
(✆ 89 642 4600; www.willaport.pl; ul Mickiewicza 17; d from 210zł; P ✳ 🛜 🐕) Perched on the lake edge, this bold hotel is a real treat. Liberally tailored rooms are a delight of funky retro veneer; spots of audacious colour contrasting with beiges and greys, sinks like halved boiled eggs with the yokes removed and all-glass showers. Competition is high for lakeside rooms and the knock-'em-dead views from the balconies are worth the extra.

Staff fluent in English, innovative design throughout and a trendy restaurant make this one of northeast Poland's finest sleeps.

Tawerna   POLISH €€
(ul Mickiewicza 21; mains 15-30zł; ⊙ 11am-10.30pm) Tawerna occupies a lovely spot on a small lake inlet at the northern end of town. Its large wooden deck is the perfect place for an aperitif or a hearty Polish meal. Kayak hire available for burning off any excesses.

BARGING IN

The rich forests of the Ostróda region have attracted merchants from Gdańsk and Elbląg since medieval times, yet until the 19th century the only way of getting timber down to the Baltic was a long water route along the Drwęca and Vistula Rivers via Toruń. Engineers considered building a canal as a short cut but quickly found that the terrain was rugged and too steep for conventional locks.

In 1836 Prussian engineer Georg Jakob Steenke (1801–82), from Königsberg, produced a sophisticated design for an Elbląg-Ostróda Canal incorporating slipways, but Prussian authorities rejected the project as unrealistic and too costly. Steenke didn't give up, however, and eventually succeeded in getting an audience with the king of Prussia. With typical kingly shrewdness, the monarch approved the plan, not because of its technical or economic aspects but because nobody had ever constructed such a system before.

The part of the canal between Elbląg and Miłomłyn, which included all the slipways, was built between 1848 and 1860, and the remaining leg to Ostróda was completed by 1872. The canal proved to be reliable and profitable, and it cut the distance of the original route along the Drwęca and Vistula almost fivefold. Various extensions were planned, including one linking the canal with the Great Masurian Lakes, 120km to the east, but none were ever built.

The canal was damaged during the 1945 Red Army offensive but was repaired soon after liberation and opened for timber transport in 1946. A year later, the first tourist boat sailed the route. It remains the only canal of its kind in Europe and continues to operate, though the timber boats are a distant memory.

❶ Information

Tourist Office (☑ 89 642 3000; www.
mazury-zachodnie.pl; Plac 1000-lecia Państwa
Polskiego 1a; ☉ 9am-6pm Mon-Fri, 10am-4pm
Sat, to 2pm Sun Jun-Aug, shorter hours rest
of year)

❶ Getting There & Away

The train and bus stations are next to each
other, 500m west of the wharf.

BOAT

In between June and September, short cruises
run from Ostróda to Miłomłyn with boats
departing at 12.30pm.

BUS

Elbląg 17zł to 24zł, 1¼ hours, 12 daily

Olsztyn 5zł, one hour, hourly

Olsztynek 11.50zł to 16zł, 30 minutes to one
hour, 11 daily

TRAIN

Olsztyn 10.60zł, 30 to 40 minutes, hourly

Toruń 24zł to 32zł, two hours, seven daily

Warsaw 75zł, three to 4½ hours, 10 daily
(change in Iława)

Elbląg-Ostróda Canal

The 82km Elbląg-Ostróda Canal is the
longest navigable canal still in use in Poland. It's also the most unusual. The canal
deals with the 99.5m difference in water
levels by means of a unique system of **slipways**, where boats are physically dragged
across dry land on rail-mounted trolleys.

The canal follows the course of a chain
of six lakes, most of which are now protected conservation areas. The largest is **Lake
Drużno** near Elbląg. It was left behind by
the Vistula Lagoon, which once extended
deep into this region.

The five slipways are on a 10km stretch
of the northern part of the canal. Each
slipway consists of two trolleys tied to a
single looped rope, operating on the same
principle as a funicular. They are powered
by water.

🏃 Activities

Żegluga Ostródzko-Elbląska   BOAT TOUR
(www.zegluga.com.pl; ul Mickiewicza 9a, Ostróda) From June to September, Żegluga
Ostródzko-Elbląska pleasure boats sail
the most interesting parts of the canal between Ostróda and Elbląg. Sadly they no
longer do the entire route which was, you

have to admit, a rather long day. There
are two tours to choose from – Elbląg to
Buczyniec (4½ hours) which includes all
five slipways, and Ostróda to Miłomłyn
(2½ hours); both can be done in the opposite direction. Buses transfer passengers
to their starting points. For timetables
and prices see the website.

Regular services run throughout the
summer and on hot summer days it may
be an idea to book ahead. Outside this
period there are fewer services. It's worth
ringing Żegluga Ostródzko-Elbląska a couple of days in advance to find out about
the availability of tickets and the current
timetable status. Boats have snack bars on
board, which serve some basic snacks and
drinks.

Lidzbark Warmiński

POP 16,400

Lidzbark Warmiński, 46km north of Olsztyn, is a rough and ready town with a
massive Gothic castle. Its past is certainly
more glorious than its present; it was the
capital of the Warmian bishopric for over
four centuries. In 1350 the bishops chose
it as their main residence; a castle and a
church were built and the town swiftly
became an important religious and cultural centre. The astronomer Copernicus
lived here between 1503 and 1510, serving
as doctor and adviser to his uncle, Bishop
Łukasz Watzenrode.

When the Reformation arrived in the
16th century, Lidzbark, along with most of
the province, became a citadel of Catholicism, and it remained so until the First
Partition of 1772. Deprived of his office, the
last bishop, Ignacy Krasicki, turned to literature, becoming an outstanding satirist
and all-round man of letters.

Today there's little trace of the town
that was reputedly the richest and most
cultured in Warmia, but the castle alone is
enough to justify a day trip.

◎ Sights

A stocky, square-set red-brick **fortress**
(www.muzeum.olsztyn.pl; Plac Zamkowy 1; adult/
concession 9/7zł; ☉ 10am-6pm Tue & Wed, 9am-
5pm Thu-Sun mid-May–Aug, shorter hours rest
of the year), adorned with corner turrets, is
probably Warmia's most significant cultural gem. Enter from the south through
the palatial, horseshoe-shaped building

surrounding Plac Zamkowy, which was extensively rebuilt in the 18th century. A wide brick bridge runs up to the main castle gate. Most of the interior, from the cellars up to the 2nd floor, now houses a branch of the Museum of Warmia.

The castle was commissioned in the late 14th century on a square plan with a central courtyard, the whole area surrounded by a moat and fortified walls. When the bishops' era ended with the 18th-century Partitions, the castle fell into decline and served a variety of purposes, including use as barracks, a warehouse, a hospital and an orphanage. In the 1920s, restoration was undertaken and within 10 years the castle had been more or less returned to its original form. Miraculously, it came through the war unharmed, and today it is easily one of Poland's best-preserved medieval castles.

The first thing you'll notice is a beautiful courtyard with two-storey arcaded galleries all round it. It was constructed in the 1380s and has hardly been altered since then. The castle's two-storey vaulted cellar, cool on even the hottest of days, is largely empty aside from a few marble fireplaces and cannon barrels. The cannons once belonged to the bishops, who maintained their own small army.

Most of the attractions are housed on the 1st floor, which holds the main chambers; the vaulted Grand Refectory (Wielki Refektarz) is quite remarkable. The chessboard-style wall paintings, dating from the end of the 14th century, feature the names and coats of arms of bishops who once resided here. In stark contrast is an adjoining tiny room centred on a dank, dark pit, which was once used as a prison cell. Exhibitions on this floor include medieval art from the region, such as some charming Madonnas and fine silverware. The adjoining chapel was redecorated in Rococo style in the mid-18th century and is quite overbearing compared to the rest of the castle.

The top floor contains several exhibitions, including cubist and surrealist 20th-century Polish painting, a collection of icons dating from the 17th century onwards, and army uniforms and evening gowns from the early 1800s.

❶ Getting There & Away

The bus terminal occupies the defunct train station, about 500m northwest of the castle. There are 10 buses a day to Olsztyn (8.50zł, one hour), supplemented by private minibuses.

Święta Lipka

POP 200

Polish Catholics flock to this tiny hamlet for one reason only – to visit its celebrated church. The origins of Święta Lipka (*shfyen*-tah *leep*-kah), which means 'Holy Lime Tree', are linked to one of Poland's most famous miracle stories. As the tale goes, a prisoner in Kętrzyn castle was visited the night before his execution by the Virgin Mary, who presented him with a tree trunk so he could carve an effigy of her. The resulting figure was so beautiful that the judges took it to be a sign from heaven and gave the condemned man his freedom. On his way home he placed the statue on the first lime tree he encountered, which happened to be in Święta Lipka (though it obviously wasn't called that at the time).

Miracles immediately began to occur, and even sheep knelt down when passing the shrine. Pilgrims arrived in increasing numbers, including the last grand master of the Teutonic order, Albrecht von Hohenzollern, who walked here barefoot (ironically, he converted to Lutherism six years later). A timber chapel was built to protect the miraculous figure, and was later replaced with the present building. It's perhaps the most magnificent Baroque church in northern Poland, a huge attraction and still a major pilgrimage site, especially during the August **Feast of the Assumption**, which sees thousands of pious visitors descend on the village.

◉ Sights

Built between 1687 and 1693, and later surrounded by an ample rectangular cloister, the hugely popular **Church of Our Lady** (www.swlipka.org.pl; ⊙ 7am-7pm except during Mass) **FREE** was built around four identical corner towers, all housing chapels. The best artists from Warmia, Königsberg (Kaliningrad) and Vilnius were commissioned for the furnishings and decoration, which were completed by about 1740. Since then the church has hardly changed, neither inside nor out, and is regarded as one of the purest examples of a late-Baroque church in the country.

The entrance to the complex is an elaborate wrought-iron gateway. Just behind it, the two-towered cream facade holds a stone sculpture of the holy lime tree in its central niche, with a statue of the Virgin Mary on top.

Once inside (appropriate clothing is required to enter – no shorts or hats for men, covered heads for women), the visitor is enveloped in colourful and florid, but not overwhelming, Baroque ornamentation. All the frescoes are the work of Maciej Meyer of Lidzbark, and display trompe l'œil images, which were fashionable at the time. These are clearly visible both on the vault and the columns; the latter look as if they were carved. Of course Meyer also left behind his own image – you can see him in a blue waistcoat with brushes in his hand, in the corner of the vault painting over the organ.

The three-storey, 19m-high altar, covering the whole back of the chancel, is carved of walnut and painted to look like marble. Of the three paintings in the altar, the lowest one depicts the Virgin Mary of Święta Lipka with the Christ child, complete with subtle lighting for effect.

The pulpit is ornamented with paintings and sculptures. Directly opposite, across the nave, is a holy lime tree topped with the figure of the Virgin Mary, supposedly placed on the spot where the legendary tree itself once stood.

The pride of the church is its breathtaking organ, a sumptuously decorated instrument of about 5000 pipes. The work of Johann Jozue Mosengel of Königsberg, it is decorated with mechanical figures of saints and angels that dance around when the organ is played. Short demonstrations are held every hour on the half-hour from 9.30am to 5.30pm, May to September, and at 10am, noon and 2pm in October.

The cloister surrounding the church is ornamented with frescoes, also masterminded by Meyer. The artist painted the corner chapels and parts of the northern and western cloister, but died before the work was complete. It was continued in the same vein by other artists, but without the same success.

❶ Getting There & Away

Buses from Święta Lipka:

Kętrzyn 4zł, 20 minutes, half-hourly

Olsztyn 12zł, 1¾ hours, five daily (or change in Kętrzyn)

THE GREAT MASURIAN LAKES

The Great Masurian Lake district (Kraina Wielkich Jezior Mazurskich), east of Olsztyn, is a verdant land of rolling hills dotted with countless lakes, healthy little farms, scattered tracts of forest and small towns. The district is centred on **Lake Śniardwy** (114 sq km), Poland's largest lake, and **Lake Mamry** and its adjacent waters (an additional 104 sq km). Over 15% of the area is covered by water and another 30% by forest.

The lakes are well connected by rivers and canals to form an extensive system of waterways. The whole area has become a prime destination for yachtspeople and canoeists, and is also popular among anglers, hikers, bikers and nature-lovers. Any boating enthusiast worth their (freshwater) salt should make Masuria their first port of call.

The main lakeside centres are Giżycko and Mikołajki and Węgorzewo. All the lake towns lead a frenetic life in July and August, take it easy in June and September, and retire for a long snooze the rest of the year.

❶ Getting Around

Yachties can sail most of the larger lakes, all the way from Węgorzewo to Ruciane-Nida. These larger lakes are interconnected and form the district's main waterway system. Kayakers will perhaps prefer more intimate surroundings alongside rivers and smaller lakes. The best established and most popular kayak route (p432) in the area originates at Sorkwity and follows the Krutynia River and Lake Bełdany to Ruciane-Nida.

If you're not up for doing everything yourself, you can enjoy the lakes in comfort from the deck of one of the pleasure boats operated by the **Żegluga Mazurska** (www.zeglugamazurska.com.pl). Theoretically, trips run between Giżycko, Mikołajki and Ruciane-Nida daily from May to September, and to Węgorzewo from June to August. In practice, trips can be cancelled if fewer than 10 passengers turn up, so the service is most reliable from late June to late August. Schedules are clearly posted at the lake ports.

The detailed *Wielkie Jeziora Mazurskie* map (scale 1:100,000), produced by Copernicus, is a great help for anyone exploring the region by boat, kayak, bike, car or on foot. The map shows walking trails, canoeing routes, accommodation options, petrol stations and much more.

The Great Masurian Lakes

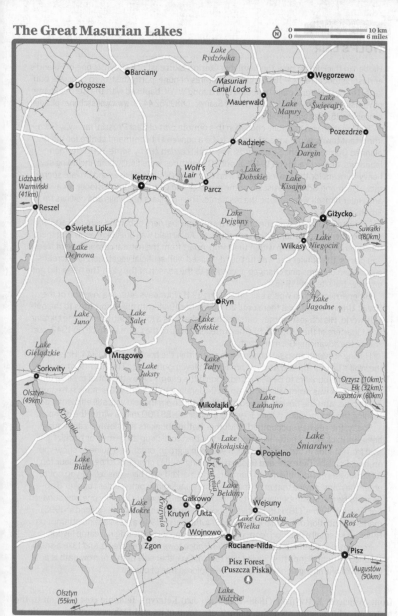

Kętrzyn

POP 28,000

Busy Kętrzyn (*kent*-shin) is the best base for daytrips to both the Wolf's Lair and Święta Lipka, though the town itself has little to offer visitors. It was founded in the 14th century by the Teutonic Knights and for most of its history was known as Rastenburg. Though partly colonised by Poles, it remained Prussian until WWII, after which it became Polish. The name derives

WOLF'S LAIR

Hidden in thick forest near the hamlet of Gierłoż, 8km east of Kętrzyn, is one of Poland's eeriest historical relics – 18 overgrown hectares of huge, partly destroyed concrete bunkers. This was Hitler's main headquarters during WWII, baptised with the German name of Wolfsschanze, or **Wolf's Lair** (Wilczy Szaniec; ☎ 89 752 4429; www.wolfsschanze.pl; adult/concession 15/10zł; ⊗ 8am-dusk).

The location was carefully chosen in this remote part of East Prussia, far away from important towns and transport routes, to be a convenient command centre for the planned German advance eastwards. The work, carried out by some 3000 German labourers, began in autumn 1940; about 80 structures were finally built, including seven heavy bunkers for the top leaders. Martin Bormann (Hitler's adviser and private secretary), Hermann Göring (Prussian prime minister and German commissioner for aviation) and Hitler himself were among the residents. Their bunkers had walls and ceilings up to 8m thick.

The whole complex was surrounded by multiple barriers of barbed wire and artillery emplacements, and a sophisticated minefield. An airfield was built 5km away and there was an emergency airstrip within the camp. Apart from the natural camouflage of trees and plants, the bunker site was further disguised with artificial vegetation-like screens suspended on wires and changed according to the season of the year. The Allies did not discover the site until 1945.

Hitler arrived at the Wolf's Lair on 26 June 1941 (four days after the invasion of the Soviet Union) and stayed there until 20 November 1944, with only short trips to the outside world. His longest journey outside the bunker was a four-month stint at the Ukraine headquarters of the Wehrmacht (the armed services of the German Reich) in 1942, overseeing the advancing German front.

Having survived an assassination attempt within the bunker in July 1944, Hitler left the Wolf's Lair as the Red Army approached a few months later. The Nazi-German army prepared the bunkers to be destroyed, should the enemy have attempted to seize them. The complex was eventually blown up on 24 January 1945 and the Germans retreated. Three days later the Soviets arrived, but the extensive minefield was still efficiently defending the empty ruins. It took 10 years to clear the 55,000 mines within the complex.

Today, the site has succumbed to Mother Nature; bunkers are slowly disappearing behind a thick wall of natural camouflage. It's best to pick up a site map or booklet sold from stands in the parking area. If you're in a group, organise a guide to show you around; English-, German- and Russian-speaking guides charge 60zł per 1½-hour tour. All structures are identified with numbers and marked with big signs telling you not to enter the ruins, advice that many people ignore, including some guides (bunker 6 appears to be the most popular one to enter). Of Hitler's bunker (13) only one wall survived, but Göring's 'home' (16) is in relatively good shape. A memorial plate (placed in 1992) marks the location of Colonel Claus von Stauffenberg's 1944 assassination attempt on Hitler and a small exhibition room houses a scale model of the original camp layout.

You can also continue 200m past the entrance towards Węgorzewo, and take a small road to the right signposted 'Kwiedzina (5km)'. On either side of this narrow path is a handful of crumbling bunkers that can be explored free of charge.

from Wojciech Kętrzyński (1838–1919), a historian who documented the history of the Polish presence in the region.

◉ Sights

Castle CASTLE
(www.muzeum.ketrzyn.pl; Plac Zamkowy 1; adult/concession 6/4zł; ⊗ 9am-6pm Tue-Fri, 10am-7pm Sat & Sun Jun-Sep, shorter hours mid-Sep–mid-Jun) Kętrzyn's Teutonic past lives on in the form of its mid-14th-century brick castle on the southern edge of the town centre. Today the building is home to the disappointingly scrappy Regional Museum, which displays exhibits tracing the town's history in very un-castlelike interiors. Highlights include a Prussian standing stone reminiscent of Central Asia's Scythian figures, old photos of Rastenburg and some beautiful old trunks.

St George's Church

CHURCH

(Bazylika Św Jerzego; www.bazylika-ketrzyn. olsztyn.opoka.org.pl; ul Zamkowa; tower adult/ concession 4/2zł; ⊙9am-5pm) With its squat, square tower, the Gothic church looks like the town's second fortress from a distance. Its interior has furnishings and decoration dating from various periods, indicating a number of alterations over time.

🍴 Sleeping & Eating

⭐Zajazd Pod Zamkiem

GUESTHOUSE €

(✆89 752 3117; www.zajazd.ketrzyn.pl; ul Struga 3; s/d 110/140zł; 🅿🛜) Sitting pretty above a superb Polish restaurant and the town's best beer garden, the four generously cut rooms (sleeping up to four) all have identical layouts but different decor and colour schemes, with antiques thrown into the mix here and there. The 19th-century villa setting, proximity to the castle and filling breakfasts make this Kętrzyn's top choice. Book ahead.

Hotel Koch

HOTEL €€

(✆89 751 1093; www.masuren2.de; ul Sportowa 1; s/d 150/200zł; 🅿🛜) Bog-standard rooms with large bathrooms are a bit overpriced at this central option, but there's a decent restaurant (a rarity in these parts) and a competent tour company on the premises that can get you on the water at the drop of several hundred złoty.

ℹ️ Information

Tourist Office (✆89 751 4765; www.it.ketrzyn. pl; Plac Piłsudskiego 10; ⊙9am-6pm Mon-Fri, 10am-3pm Sat & Sun Jul & Aug, shorter hours rest of the year)

ℹ️ Getting There & Away

The train and bus stations are next to each other, 600m southeast of the town centre.

BUS

For the Wolf's Lair, take a service heading for Węgorzewo via Radzieje and alight at Gierłoż. At weekends it's advisable to take a taxi (30zł) from the large ul Szkolna rank in the town centre, as buses operate a why-bother-at-all kind of service. Otherwise buses run to the following towns:

Giżycko 6zł, 40 minutes, at least hourly

Olsztyn 10zł to 18zł, one to two hours, many

Święta Lipka 4zł, 20 minutes, half-hourly

Węgorzewo 12zł, 45 minutes, hourly

TRAIN

Kętrzyn has the following train services:

Gdańsk 50zł, four hours, two daily

Giżycko 8.20zł, 30 minutes, seven daily

Olsztyn 18.60zł, 1½ hours, six daily

Węgorzewo

POP 11,600

The small but busy town of Węgorzewo (ven-go-*zheh*-vo) on **Lake Mamry** is the northernmost lakeside centre for both excursion boats and independent sailors. The main town itself isn't quite on the lake shore but is linked to it by a 2km river canal.

It's less overrun by tourists than its southern cousins, except on the first weekend of August, when the town hosts a large craft fair, attracting plenty of artisans from around the region and beyond.

🍴 Sleeping & Eating

As the focus of activity is on the lake area, you won't find too many places to stay around the centre. There are dozens of pensions and larger leisure facilities spread out in the surrounding area, particularly in the lakeside suburb of Kal, but they can be tricky to reach and usually only open in summer.

Camping Rusałka

CAMPGROUND €

(✆87 427 2191; www.cmazur.pl; ul Leśna 2; per adult/tent 14/13zł; ⊙May-Sep) With its pleasant wooded grounds, a restaurant, and boats and kayaks for hire, Rusałka is a good, well-run base, though most cabins are pretty basic. It's on Lake Święcajty, 4km from Węgorzewo off the Giżycko road. Infrequent PKS buses go there in season; if you don't want to wait, take any Giżycko-bound bus to the Lake Święcajty turn-off, then walk the last 1km.

Pensjonat Nautic

GUESTHOUSE €€

(✆87 568 2585; www.nautic.pl; ul Słowackiego 14; s/d 100/150zł, apt 140-380zł; 🅿🛜) An excellent and versatile family guesthouse near the canal and the boat wharf. Rooms range from comfortable standard en suites with blue wood fittings to five amazing apartments with their own kitchenettes and terraces.

ℹ️ Information

Tourist Office (✆87 427 4009; www. wegorzewo.pl; Bul Loir-et-Cher 4; ⊙8am-5pm Mon-Fri Jul & Aug, to 4pm Mon, 7.30am-3.30pm Tue-Fri Sep-Jun)

❶ Getting There & Away

BOAT

From July to August, a single **Żegluga Mazurska** (www.zeglugamazurska.pl) boat sails from the wharf at Lake Mamry for Giżycko at 3pm.

BUS

There are no trains, so head for the bus terminal 1km northwest of the centre, from where there are services to the following towns:

Giżycko 7zł, 40 minutes, many daily

Kętrzyn 12.50zł, one hour, half-hourly

Warsaw 50zł, 5½ hours, four daily

Giżycko

POP 29,700

Positioned on the northern shore of **Lake Niegocin**, Giżycko (ghee-*zhits*-ko) is the largest sailing centre in the lakes, and the focal point of the seasonal tourist trade. It's not an aesthetically pleasing town, with a lake frontage more tacky than tasteful, but it's one of the few Masurian towns with a buzz and its huge fortress is worth at least an hour of your time.

The town started life under the Teutonic Knights but was destroyed on numerous occasions by Lithuanians, Poles, Swedes, Tatars, Russians and Germans in turn. Today it's essentially a transport hub and provisions base for the holiday homes and water-sports centres that have grown up outside the town, and for the hordes of lake-bound holidaymakers who arrive en masse in the short summer season.

◉ Sights

Boyen Fortress FORTRESS

(Twierdza Boyen; www.boyen.gizycko.pl; ul Turystyczna 1; adult/concession fortress & museum 10/5zł; ⊙9am-7pm Jul & Aug, slightly shorter hours Apr-Jun & Sep-Oct) The Boyen Fortress was built between 1844 and 1856 to protect the kingdom's border with Russia, and was named after the then Prussian minister of war, General Hermann von Boyen. Since the frontier ran north–south along the 90km string of lakes, the stronghold was strategically placed in the middle, on the isthmus near Giżycko, situated by the lake to the west of the town centre.

The fortress, which consists of several bastions and defensive towers surrounded by a moat, was continually modified and strengthened, and successfully withstood Russian attacks during WWI. In WWII it

was a defensive outpost of the Wolf's Lair, given up to the Red Army without a fight during the 1945 offensive. The fortifications have survived in surprisingly good shape, and some of the walls, bastions and barracks can safely be explored. Inside the museum you'll find a scale model of the fortress and a few odd items, such as a section of wall with a Russian soldier painted on it, used as target practice by the Prussians.

Water Tower HISTORIC BUILDING

(Wieża Ćiśień; www.wieza-gizycko.pl; cnr ul Warszawska & Wodociągowa; adult/concession 10/5zł; ⊙10am-10pm Jul & Aug, shorter hours May, Jun & Sep) Built in 1900 in neo-Gothic style, Giżycko's seven-storey Water Tower supplied the city with running water until 1997. Today the tall red-brick structure houses a cafe and memorabilia exhibition, but the main attraction is of course the views from the top, accessed by lift. The tower is located a short walk along ul Warszawska from the main Plac Grunwaldzki.

Rotary Bridge BRIDGE

(Most obrotowy; ul Moniuszki) Giżycko's working rotary bridge was built in 1889 and is the only one of its kind in the country. Despite weighing more than 100 tonnes, it can be turned by one person, and is opened six times daily to allow boats through, closing to traffic for between 20 minutes and 1½ hours each time. If you're travelling by car, circumvent the wait and take the long way round via ul Obwodowa. Pedestrians can take the footbridge a little further up the canal.

🏃 Activities

Yacht Charters

Giżycko has the largest number of yacht-charter agencies in the area, and accordingly offers the widest choice of boats. The town is also a recognised centre for disabled sailors, with regular national regattas, and many companies provide specialist equipment, advice and training.

With yachting such a huge business here, the boat-charter market is highly volatile and operators often change. The tourist office (p384) is likely to have a current list of agents (sometimes up to 40) and can provide advice.

Finding anything in July and August without advance booking can be difficult. Securing a boat in early June or late September is much easier, but shop around, as prices and conditions vary substantially and bargaining may be possible with some agents.

In July and August, expect to pay somewhere between 200zł and 500zł per day for a sailing boat large enough to sleep around four to five people. Prices depend on the size of cabins, toilet and kitchen facilities and so on, and are significantly lower in June and September – often half the high-season prices. You pay for your own petrol. A boat with skipper included costs on average 300zł per day.

Check the state of the boat and its equipment carefully, and report every deficiency and bit of damage in advance to avoid hassles on return. Come prepared with your own equipment, such as a sleeping bag, sturdy rain gear and torch.

Bełbot   BOATING
(☎87 428 0385; www.marina.com.pl) Yacht hire company with five vessels available.

Grzymała   BOATING
(☎87 428 6276; http://czarter.mazury.info.pl) Family company with seven yachts for hire.

Interjacht   BOATING
(☎660 222 880; www.interjacht.pl) Large company with many yachts and low prices.

Osmolik Romuald   BOATING
(☎602 702 524; www.osmolik.trinet.pl) Small operation with prices around 300zł per day per yacht.

Ice Sailing

The Masurian Lake district is one of Poland's coldest regions in winter; lake surfaces often freeze over from December to April. During this time the lakes support ice sailing and ice windsurfing, mostly on crisp, clear days. The tourist office (p384) has a list of operators renting boats and giving lessons.

Diving

CK Diver   DIVING
(☎602 718 580; www.ckdiver.suw.pl; ul Mickiewicza 9) Offers scuba-diving courses for all levels throughout the year, in groups or on an individual basis. Prices start at 100zł for a taster session, going up to 1600zł for advanced tuition. To find the office, walk north from Plac Grunwaldzki along al 1 Maja for around 150m, then take a left into ul Mickiewicza.

Cross-Country Skiing

Skiing on and around the frozen lake is a popular cold-weather activity. Ask the tourist office (p384) about where to hire the necessary gear.

🛏 Sleeping

The tourist office has a long list of accommodation options available in town, most of which consists of holiday cottages, pensions and private rooms. The majority only open in July and August – outside these months few places are open. Much of Giżycko's accommodation displays the pressures of mass occupation.

Hotel Cesarski   HOTEL €€
(☎87 732 7670; www.cesarski.eu; Plac Grunwaldzki 8; s/d 105/170zł; P🐾) This very comfy hotel couldn't be more central, located as it is on the main town square near the tourist office. Rooms are all creamy and cosy, but best of all is the large roof terrace where breakfast can be taken.

Gościniec Jantar   GUESTHOUSE €€
(☎734 440 291; www.jantar-gizicko.eu; ul Warszawska 10; s/d 140/190zł; P🐾) Stacked above its own traditional restaurant in the centre of town, this is a decent little guesthouse with 12 pine-filled rooms, thick rugs and personable staff. It's let down slightly by a faint tobacco odour in some of the rooms.

Hotel Wodnik   HOTEL €€
(☎87 428 3871; www.cmazur.pl; ul 3 Maja 2; s/d 175/285zł; P🐾) From the outside this looks like the worst kind of Socialist-era slab but the renovated rooms inside have only occasional reminders of Poland's yesteryear hospitality industry. Chunky radios and an overdose of woodchip wallpaper aside, the small rooms are well maintained. Book ahead as this place fills up even in midwinter. It's located just off the main Plac Grunwaldzki.

🍴 Eating

In the high season you only have to wander down to the waterfront to find dozens of temporary cafes, kiosks and snack bars catering for the holiday crowds. Outside these times you'll have to choose from the hotel restaurants and a handful of other eateries in the centre.

Kuchnia Świata   INTERNATIONAL €€
(☎87 429 2255; www.kuchnieswiata.pl; Plac Grunwaldzki 1; mains 22-48zł; ⊙10am-10pm) The best year-round place to eat in town, the 'Cuisines of the World' certainly lives up to its name, with countless reminders of

the culinary world you've left behind, such as king prawns, Greek salads and Chinese dim sum, populating the huge menu.

Bar Hornet
POLISH €€

(www.barhornet.pl; ul Unii Europejskiej 3; mains 11-35zł; ☺10am-10pm Sun-Fri, to 11pm Sat) The suitably yellow Hornet splits itself into two sections: a self-service cafeteria and a smarter sit-down restaurant. The only difference between them is the waiters, but it's nice to have a choice! The food's decent value, with a fine selection of quick eats and a salad bar, and the wooden deck is good for warm evenings.

Grota
INTERNATIONAL €€

(ul Nadbrzeżna 3a; mains 15-30zł; ☺11am-midnight summer only) Restaurants on the marina may draw crowds with their lakefront views, but Grota gets the locals' vote for its food. Wood-oven-baked pizzas and a mix of Polish and German cuisine fill the menu, and there's canalside seating in summer. To find Grota, head to the Rotary Bridge from Plac Grunwaldzki, but turn left before crossing the river; it's on the left-hand side about 150m along.

❶ Information

Main Post Office (ul Pocztowa 2; ☺8am-7pm Mon-Fri, to 2pm Sat) Three hundred metres north of Plac Grunwaldzki.

Tourist Office (☎87 428 5265; www.gizycko. turystyka.pl; ul Wyzwolenia 2; ☺8am-5pm Mon-Fri, 10am-2pm Sat & Sun Mar-May & Sep-Oct, 9am-6pm Mon-Fri, 10am-4pm Sat & Sun Jun-Aug, shorter hours Nov-Feb) Friendly, award-winning office with loads of info on the region and free internet access. Enter from Plac Grunwaldzki.

❶ Getting There & Away

BOAT

Żegluga Mazurska (www.zeglugamazurska. com) boats operate from May to September, with extra services in July and August. Services run to Mikołajki and Węgorzewo, among other destinations; check the website or the timetable at the wharf (near the train station) for sailing times and prices.

BUS

On the southern outskirts of town next to the train station, the bus terminal handles services to the following towns:

Kętrzyn 6zł, 40 minutes, at least hourly
Mikołajki 14zł to 17zł, 30 minutes to one hour, hourly

Olsztyn 12zł, two hours, many
Suwałki 20zł to 23.50zł, two to three hours, six daily
Warsaw 36zł to 53zł, 3¾ hours to 5½ hours, hourly (most services summer only)
Węgorzewo 7zł, 40 minutes, many daily

TRAIN

The train station is on the southern edge of town near the lake. Trains run to the following towns:
Białystok 38zł, 2½ hours, two daily
Ełk 13.50zł, 45 minutes, eight daily
Gdańsk 54zł, 4½ hours, two daily
Kętrzyn 8.20zł, 30 minutes, seven daily
Olsztyn 22zł, two hours, six daily
Warsaw 60zł, 5¾ hours, daily

Mikołajki
POP 3800

More intimate and scenically pleasing than Giżycko, lively lakeside Mikołajki (mee-ko-*wahy*-kee) perches on picturesque narrows crossed by three bridges. Tourism has all but taken over here, and its spruced up waterfront is filled to overflowing with promenading families and pleasure boats in summer. Like most of its neighbours, Mikołajki is a big hit with German tourists, especially those from the former GDR.

🏃 Activities

As in Giżycko, yacht hire is big business here in summer, and at least ten companies vie for the seasonal trade.

Wioska Żeglarska
BOATING

(☎87 421 6040; www.wioskazeglarskamikolajki. pl) The Wioska Żeglarska, on the waterfront, has sailing boats for hire, or staff may be able to advise you on other companies if it's booked out.

Port Rybitwa
BOATING

(☎87 421 6163; www.portrybitwa.pl) For short-term excursions, Port Rybitwa hires out low-powered motorboats from near the town's swimming beach. The owner can suggest plenty of DIY excursions on the connecting lakes.

🛏 Sleeping & Eating

Surprisingly there aren't too many hotels in Mikołajki, but the tourist office (p385) can supply a bewilderingly long list of rooms for rent (40zł to 60zł per person). However, few owners will consider single-night stays, especially during July and August; in fact most will expect you to linger at least five nights in the high season. If you're here just for a night or two, try to book ahead.

Camping Wagabunda CAMPGROUND €
(☑503 300 141; www.wagabunda-mikolajki.pl; ul Leśna 2; camp sites per person/tent 16/15zł; ☺May-Sep) The Wagabunda is the town's main camping ground. It's across the bridge from the centre and a 600m walk southwest. In addition to the camping area, it has plenty of small cabins that vary in standard and price, and bicycles, boats and canoes are available for hire.

★**Pensjonat Mikołajki** GUESTHOUSE €€
(☑87 421 6437; www.pensjonatmikolajki.pl; ul Kajki 18; s/d from 140/180zł; P🕏) In this part of Poland, accommodation is all about lake views, and if you book early here that's exactly what you'll get. But the other surprisingly contemporary rooms aren't bad either – all are fragrant with pine and boast well-maintained fittings and lemon-fresh bathrooms.

Hotel Mazur HOTEL €€
(☑87 428 2899; www.hotelmazur.pl; Plac Wolności 6; s/d 260/390zł; P🕏) Occupying Mikołajki's grandest edifice, the former town hall on the main square, the Mazur is the town's finest digs, with liberally sized and pristine bathrooms, though for these prices the pine furniture feels cheap. The wood-panelled salon and brick cellar restaurant are Mikołajki's swankiest dining nooks.

Król Sielaw GUESTHOUSE €€
(☑87 421 6323; www.krolsielaw.mazury.info; ul Kajki 5; s/d 110/165zł; 🕏) Rustic beams and twee crafts provide the usual touch of colour in these very inexpensive rooms. The country theme continues in the unpretentious fish restaurant downstairs. The lake is only a block away and there are discounts for staying more than three nights.

Restauracja Prohibicja POLISH €€
(www.prohibicjamikolajki.pl; Plac Handlowy 13; mains 14-38zł; ☺11am-11pm; 🕏) Possibly Mikołajki's best eating option has a stylishly done gangster-jazz theme. The walls are covered in pictures of famous silver-screen mobsters and celebrated

jazz musicians doing their thing, as well as photos of Polish celebs who have dined here. There's a vine-shaded terrace outside and cheap rooms upstairs.

❶ Information

Tourist Office (☑87 421 6850; www.mikolajki. pl; Plac Wolności 7; ☺10am-6pm Jun-Aug, to 6pm Mon-Sat May & Sep)

❶ Getting There & Away

BOAT

From May to September, **Żegluga Mazurska** (www.zeglugamazurska.com) boats connect Mikołajki with Giżycko – check the website for exact sailing times.

BUS

There are no trains serving Mikołajki, so that just leaves the tiny bus station on small plac Kościelny near the church at the top of the main street (ul 3 Maja), which handles services to the following towns:

Giżycko 14zł to 17zł, 30 minutes to one hour, hourly

Olsztyn 19zł, 2¼ hours, four daily (or change in Mrągowo)

Warsaw 45zł, 4½ to 5½ hours, eight daily (most summer only)

Łuknajno Reserve

The shallow 700-hectare **Lake Łuknajno**, 4km east of Mikołajki, shelters Europe's largest surviving community of wild swans (*Cygnus olor*) and is home to many other birds – 128 species have been recorded here. The 1200- to 2000-strong swan population nests in April and May but stays at the lake all summer. A few observation towers beside the lake make swan viewing possible.

A rough road from Mikołajki goes to the lake, but there's no public transport. Walk 3.5km until you get to a sign that reads '*do wieży widokowej*' (to the viewing tower), then continue for 10 minutes along the path to the lake shore. The track can be muddy in spring and after rain, so choose your shoes wisely. Depending on the wind, the swans may be close to the tower or far away on the opposite side of the lake.

Understand
Poland

Poland Today

Poland is feeling pretty good about itself these days. It was the only European country to emerge from the Great Recession of the past decade without experiencing a downturn, and a quarter century after the fall of communism, it's the acknowledged winner in the transition to democracy. That said, Poland faces new challenges, including coping with emerging regional disparities in income and opportunity.

Best on Film

Katyń (Andrzej Wajda; 2007) Moving depiction of a WWII massacre in the Katyń Forest.

Ida (Paweł Pawlikowski; 2013) A young nun-in-waiting discovers her family's hidden history; 2015 Oscar winner.

The Pianist (Roman Polański; 2002) Highly acclaimed film about life in Warsaw's WWII Jewish ghetto.

Best in Print

The Polish Officer (Alan Furst) Gripping spy novel set in Poland on the eve of WWII.

God's Playground: A History of Poland (Norman Davies) Highly readable two-volume set that covers 1000 years of Polish history.

The Painted Bird (Jerzy Kosiński) Page-turner on the travails of an orphan boy on the run during WWII.

Survival in Auschwitz (Primo Levi) Classic of Holocaust literature that hasn't lost a drop of impact.

Will Poland Ever Adopt the Euro?

When Poland joined the EU in 2004, it was taken for granted that the złoty would soon be a thing of the past. Indeed, it wasn't long ago that relatively early euro-adopters in central and eastern Europe – such as Slovenia and Slovakia – were praised for being ahead of regional-currency laggards including the Czech Republic, Hungary and Poland.

Enthusiasm for the euro began to fade during Europe's 'Great Recession' from 2008–11, when countries with their own currencies, such as Poland, appeared to fare better than countries using the euro. These countries could manipulate their interest rates and currencies to blunt the effects of falling output and demand. Greece's well-documented perils with the euro in 2015 tarnished any lustre left on those shiny euro coins.

Don't expect a euro in Poland any time soon – that's the conventional wisdom in Warsaw. President Andrzej Duda, who took office in 2015 for a five-year term, is a staunch conservative. Duda's foreign affairs adviser has said there will be no euro without a national referendum. Given the currency's poor reputation, such a vote would be unlikely to pass.

Transition Accomplished

Ever since the fall of communism in 1989, there's been a friendly rivalry between former ex-communist countries (including Poland, the Czech Republic and Hungary) to see which could complete the transition to democracy and a market-based economy most successfully. The Czech Republic had a head start: it was the Eastern bloc's leading economy during the Cold War.

The consensus among many, including the European Commission, is that Poland has emerged as the winner. Writing in 2015, a quarter century after the fall of communism, the commission said Polish living standards had more than doubled in the past 20 years – a process, it said, that accelerated when Poland joined the EU in 2004. In a graph of per capita income, the commission showed Poland had outpaced not just countries of the former Eastern bloc, but long-time EU members such as Germany and Italy.

This may come as a surprise to anyone who remembers the Cold War, when Poland was beset by chronic unrest and deep levels of public debt. Poland now finds itself confronting new problems, such as growing income inequality, but the good news is the country has overcome hurdles once viewed as insurmountable.

As part of that success, Poland is now the 10th most-visited country in Europe, with around 16 million international arrivals each year, according to the UN's World Tourism Organisation. It's well behind leader France (84 million visitors), but is the highest-placing country of the formerly communist states of central Europe.

'Poland A' vs 'Poland B'

While you're travelling around Poland, you may hear references to 'Poland A' and 'Poland B' – representing the growing divide between the country's most prosperous regions and areas that are not doing as well. The terms offer insight into how Poles see their own country and attest to ways that far-off historical events resonate in the country to this day.

While there's no universal definition, Poland A generally refers to regions of the country west of the Vistula, including cities such as Warsaw and Krakow, with relatively higher education levels, built-up economic infrastructure, and generally forward-thinking, pro-Western attitudes. Poland B refers to towns and villages to the east and south, where time appears to have stood still. Opinion polls bear out popular attitudes – citizens in Poland B tend to be more pessimistic about the future, and skew more nationalistic and conservative.

Certainly, there are geographic reasons for the differences. Areas bordering poorer states such as Belarus and Ukraine could be expected to be less dynamic than regions nearer to Germany. But there may be some history involved as well. Poland A overlaps strongly with areas that were gobbled up by Prussia (Germany) and Austria in the 19th century, when Poland was partitioned between the great powers. The area of today's Poland B was occupied largely by tsarist Russia. It seems incredible, but possible, that attitudes inculcated during that century-long occupation may have survived into modern times.

GDP (PER HEAD): **US$23,650**

INFLATION: **0.05%**

UNEMPLOYMENT: **10.3%**

LAKES: **9000**

WILD BISON: **1400**

WWII DEATHS AS % OF POPULATION: **20%**
(UK 0.9%; USA 0.2%)

if Poland were 100 people

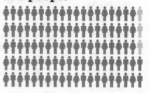

97 would be Polish
3 would be other ethnic backgrounds

belief systems
(% of population)

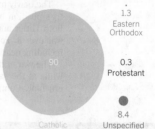

90 Catholic

1.3 Eastern Orthodox

0.3 Protestant

8.4 Unspecified

population per sq km

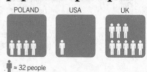

POLAND　USA　UK

= 32 people

History

It would be no overstatement to say Polish history has been characterised by a series of epic climbs, cataclysmic falls and back-from-the-brink recoveries.

The Poland that we would recognise today got its start around the first millennium, with the conversion to Christianity of Duke Mieszko I in 966. The early years, like surrounding kingdoms at that time, were filled with wars, conquests and Mongol invasions, but the kingdom thrived. The rule of Kazimierz III Wielki (Casimir III the Great, 1333–70) in the 14th century was particularly benign and brought the royal capital, Kraków, one of Central Europe's first centres of higher learning (today's Jagiellonian University) in 1364.

A major triumph came in 1410 with the defeat of the Teutonic Knights by a combined force of Poles and Lithuanians. A little over a century later, in 1569, the Poles and Lithuanians formalised their union, creating for a time Europe's largest country.

The people of Warsaw had special reason to celebrate the union, as it meant shifting the capital there from Kraków around 1600. The rest of the 17th century, though, can be written off as a wash. Poland got sucked into a series of tragic wars, including a melee with Sweden that cost the country a quarter of its territory and a third of its people.

A vastly weakened Poland in the 18th century proved too tempting for neighbours Prussia, Russia and Austria, who agreed to carve up the country among themselves, leaving Poland off world atlases until the end of WWI.

The newly independent Poland got off to a decent start, but the country's position between Germany and the Soviet Union was precarious. Both Hitler and Stalin coveted Polish territory and eventually went to war over it. Poland lost around a fifth of its population during WWII, including nearly all of the country's three million Jews.

The war ended up shifting Poland's border around 200km westward, while at the same time putting it firmly in the Soviet-controlled Eastern bloc. Communism was a period of hardship and stagnation that

National Heroes

Marshal Józef Piłsudski

Tadeusz Kościuszko

Nicolaus Copernicus

Frédéric Chopin

Marie Curie

Karol Wojtyła

Lech Wałęsa

TIMELINE	700 BC	Before AD 500	Before AD 500
	During the Iron Age, the Lusatian tribe, present on the territory of modern-day Poland, builds a remarkable fortified settlement in the town of Biskupin.	Slavs begin settling the area of present-day Poland, though the exact date of arrival of the first Slavic tribes is unknown.	Establishment of the first Polish town, Gniezno, by Lech, one of three mythical brothers who in legend founded the three Slavic nations (Poland, Ruthenia and Bohemia).

was eventually overcome as Soviet-backed regimes collapsed in Eastern Europe in 1989.

Poland has generally prospered since the fall of communism as a member of the European Union, though growth has been uneven, with big cities and the western regions of the country doing better than parts of the south and east.

Before the Poles

The lands of modern-day Poland have been inhabited since the Stone Age, with numerous tribes from the east and west calling its fertile plains home. Archaeological finds from both the Stone and Bronze Ages can be seen in many Polish museums, but the greatest example of pre-Slavic peoples resides in Biskupin: its fortified town from the Iron Age was built by the Lusatian tribe around 2700 years ago. The Celts, followed by the Germanic tribes and then the Baltic folk, all established themselves on Polish soil, but it wasn't until the coming of the Slavs that Poland began to shape itself into a nation.

Slavic Origins & the Piast Dynasty

Although the exact date of the arrival of the first Slavic tribes is unknown, historians agree Slavs began settling the area between the 5th and 8th centuries. From the 8th century onwards, smaller tribes banded together to form greater conglomerations, thus establishing themselves more fully on the lands of the future Polish state.

The country's name derives from one of these tribes, the Polanie (literally, 'the people of the fields'), who settled on the banks of the Warta River near present-day Poznań. Their tribal chief, the legendary Piast, managed to unite the scattered groups of the surrounding areas into a single political unit in the 10th century, and gave it the name Polska (later Wielkopolska, meaning Great Poland). It wasn't until the coming of Piast's great-great grandson, Duke Mieszko I, that much of Poland was united under one dynasty, the Piast.

Christianity & Conquering

After Duke Mieszko I converted to Christianity, he did what most early Christian rulers did and began conquering the neighbours. Soon the entire coastal region of Pomerania (Pomorze) fell under his sovereignty, along with Śląsk (Silesia) to the south and Małopolska (Little Poland) to the southeast. By the time of his death in AD 992, the Polish state was established within boundaries similar to those of Poland today, and the first capital and archbishopric were established in Gniezno.

By that time, towns such as Gdańsk, Szczecin, Poznań, Wrocław and Kraków already existed. Mieszko's son, Bolesław the Brave, continued

Notable Polish Kings

Kazimierz III Wielki (1333–70)

Władysław II Jagiełło (1386–1434)

Stefan Batory (1576–86)

Zygmunt III Waza (1587–1632)

Jan III Sobieski (1674–96)

HISTORY BEFORE THE POLES

966	970s	1038	1226
Poland's first recorded ruler, Duke Mieszko I, converts to Christianity, possibly as a political move against Otto the Great. It marks the formal birth of the Polish state.	Duke Mieszko I builds Poland's first cathedral at Gniezno, and a second at Poznań. The Catholic religion begins its long hold on the Polish people.	Under the rule of Piast Kazimierz I, the Polish capital is moved from Gniezno to Kraków. The city would remain the seat of royal Poland for the next 550 years.	Duke Konrad of Mazovia calls in the Teutonic Knights to help him subdue a band of pagan Prussians, allowing the Knights to gain a firm foothold on Polish soil.

Former Capitals of Poland

Gniezno

Poznań

Kraków

Płock

Lublin

Łódź

his father's work, even pushing the Polish border as far east as Kyiv. The administrative centre of the country was moved from Wielkopolska to the less vulnerable Małopolska, and by the middle of the 11th century Kraków was established as the royal seat.

When pagan Prussians, from the region that is now the northeastern tip of Poland, attacked the central province of Mazovia in 1226, Duke Konrad of Mazovia called for help from the Teutonic Knights, a Germanic military and religious order that had made its historic mark during the Crusades. The knights soon subjugated the pagan tribes but then bit the hand that fed them, building massive castles in Polish territory, conquering the port city of Gdańsk (and renaming it Danzig), and effectively claiming all of northern Poland as their own.

They ruled from their greatest castle of all, at Malbork, and within a matter of decades became a major European military power.

The Reign of Casimir III the Great

Under the rule of Kazimierz III Wielki (Casimir III the Great; 1333–70), Poland gradually became a prosperous and powerful state. Kazimierz Wielki regained suzerainty over Mazovia, then captured vast areas of Ruthenia (today's Ukraine) and Podolia, thus greatly expanding his monarchy in the southeast.

Kazimierz Wielki was also an enlightened and energetic ruler on the domestic front. Promoting and instituting reforms, he laid down solid legal, economic, commercial and educational foundations. He also passed a law providing privileges for Jews, thus establishing Poland as a safe house for the Jewish community for centuries to come. Over 70 new towns were founded, and the royal capital of Kraków flourished.

In 1364 one of Europe's first universities was established at Kraków, and an extensive network of castles and fortifications was constructed to improve the nation's defences. There is a saying that Kazimierz Wielki 'found Poland built of wood and left it built of stone'.

The Defeat of the Knights

The close of the 14th century saw Poland forge a dynastic alliance with Lithuania, a political marriage that increased Poland's territory five-fold overnight and that would last for the next four centuries. The union benefited both parties – Poland gained a partner in skirmishes against the Tatars and Mongols, and Lithuania received help in the fight against the Teutonic Knights.

Under Władysław II Jagiełło (1386–1434), the alliance finally defeated the Knights in 1410 at the epic battle of Grunwald and recovered eastern Pomerania, part of Prussia and the port of Gdańsk.

1241–42	1333	1493	Early 16th century
Mongol invasions leave Poland and much of Europe in ruin. This allows room for German settlers to move east into Poland, but also Poland to expand eastwards into Ukraine.	Kazimierz III Wielki (Casimir III the Great) assumes the throne and under his near-40-year rule, Poland gradually becomes a prosperous and powerful state, extending into areas of today's Ukraine.	Poland's lower house of parliament, or Sejm, is established. The first Sejm consists of bishops and noblemen, and is largely present to keep an eye on the monarchy.	Arts and sciences flourish under the reigns of Zygmunt I Stary and his son Zygmunt II August. This is often viewed as the kingdom's 'golden age'.

For 30 years the Polish empire was Europe's largest state, extending from the Baltic to the Black Sea.

But it was not to last. Threat of invasion became apparent towards the end of the 15th century – this time the main instigators were the Ottomans from the south, the Tatars of Crimea from the east, and the tsars of Moscow from the north and east. Independently or together, they repeatedly invaded and raided the eastern and southern Polish territories, and on one occasion managed to penetrate as far as Kraków.

Poland's Golden Age

The early 16th century brought the Renaissance to Poland and during the reigns of Zygmunt I Stary (Sigismund I the Old; 1506–48) and his son Zygmunt II August (Sigismund II Augustus; 1548–72), the arts and sciences flourished. This is traditionally viewed as the kingdom's 'golden age'.

The bulk of Poland's population at this time was made up of Poles and Lithuanians but included significant minorities from neighbouring countries. Jews constituted an important and steadily growing part of the community.

On the political front, Poland evolved during the 16th century into a parliamentary monarchy, with most of the privileges going to the *szlachta* (the feudal nobility), who comprised roughly 10% of the population. In contrast, the status of the peasants declined, and they gradually found themselves falling into a state of virtual slavery.

Hoping to strengthen the monarchy, the Sejm (an early form of parliament reserved for the nobility) convened in Lublin in 1569, unified Poland and Lithuania into a single state, and made Warsaw the seat of future debates. Since there was no heir apparent to the throne, it also established a system of royal succession based on direct voting in popular elections by the nobility, who would all come to Warsaw to vote.

Royal Republic

The 'Royal Republic' refers to the practice of 'electing' the kings by the nobility, a dubious idea that got its start when Zygmunt II August died without an heir. The decision to consider foreign candidates almost led to the unravelling of the 'republic'. For each royal election, foreign powers promoted their candidates by bargaining and bribing voters. During this period, no fewer than 11 kings ruled Poland; only four were native Poles.

The first elected king, Henri de Valois, retreated to his homeland to take up the French crown after only a year on the Polish throne. His successor, Stefan Batory (Stephen Bathory; 1576–86), prince of Transylvania, was a much wiser choice. Batory, together with his gifted commander and chancellor Jan Zamoyski, conducted a series of successful

PARTITION

The Ottoman Empire, though an ancient enemy of the Poles, was the only European power that never recognised the Partition of Poland.

battles against Tsar Ivan the Terrible and came close to forming an alliance with Russia against the Ottoman threat.

After Batory's premature death, the crown was offered to the Swede Zygmunt III Waza (Sigismund III Vasa; 1587–1632), and during his reign Poland achieved its greatest extent ever, more than three times the size of present-day Poland. Despite this, Zygmunt is best remembered for moving the Polish capital from Kraków to Warsaw between 1596 and 1609.

Eastern Interlopers & the 'Deluge'

The beginning of the 17th century marked a turning point in Poland's fortunes. The increasing political power of the Polish nobility undermined the authority of the Sejm; the country was split up into several huge private estates, and nobles, frustrated by ineffective government, resorted to armed rebellion.

Meanwhile, foreign invaders were systematically carving up the land. Jan II Kazimierz Waza (John II Casimir Vasa; 1648–68), the last of the Vasa dynasty on the Polish throne, was unable to resist the aggressors – Russians, Tatars, Ukrainians, Cossacks, Ottomans and Swedes – who were moving in on all fronts. The Swedish invasion of 1655–60, known as the Deluge, was particularly disastrous.

The last bright moment in the long decline of the Royal Republic was the reign of Jan III Sobieski (John III Sobieski; 1674–96), a brilliant commander who led several victorious battles against the Ottomans. The most famous of these was the Battle of Vienna in 1683, in which he defeated the Turks and checked their advancement into Western Europe.

The Rise of Russia

By the start of the 18th century, Poland was in decline and Russia had evolved into a mighty expansive empire. The tsars systematically strengthened their grip over the flailing country, and Poland's rulers effectively became puppets of the Russian regime. This became crystal clear during the reign of Stanisław August Poniatowski (1764–95), when Catherine the Great, empress of Russia, exercised direct intervention in Poland's affairs. The collapse of the Polish empire was just around the corner.

Poland Under Partition

During your travels in Poland, you're likely to hear reference to the 'partition', the period at the end of the 18th century when Poland was carved up between its more-powerful neighbours, Prussia, Russia and Austria. The partition period lasted all the way to the end of WWI. For 123 years Poland disappeared from world maps.

The French general Napoleon Bonaparte spent a great deal of time in Poland, and was revered by the Poles as a potential national saviour. Speaking in Italy in 1797, he personally vowed to reverse the Polish partition that had been imposed on the country by Russia.

Early 17th century	1655–60	1683	1764
Under King Zygmunt III Waza (Sigismund III Vasa), Poland achieves its greatest territorial extent ever, more than three times the size of present-day Poland.	During the 'Deluge', Poland loses a quarter of its territory, cities are plundered and the economy is destroyed. From a population of 10 million, four million succumb to war, famine and plague.	Jan III Sobieski leads a Polish force in a battle against the Ottoman Turks at the gates of Vienna. His victory saves the city, but weakens Poland's own military defences.	King Stanisław August Poniatowski assumes the throne. He is a popular but weak ruler who allows Russia's Catherine the Great to exercise direct intervention in Poland's affairs.

The partition initially led to immediate reforms and a new, liberal constitution, and Poland remained relatively stable. Catherine the Great could tolerate no more of this dangerous democracy, though, and sent Russian troops into Poland. Despite fierce resistance, the reforms were abolished by force.

Enter Tadeusz Kościuszko, a hero of the American War of Independence. With the help of patriotic forces, he launched an armed rebellion in 1794. The campaign soon gained popular support and the rebels won some early victories, but Russian troops, stronger and better armed, defeated the Polish forces within a year.

Despite the partition, Poland continued to exist as a spiritual and cultural community, and a number of secret nationalist societies were created. Since revolutionary France was seen as their major ally in the struggle, some leaders fled to Paris and established their headquarters there.

WWI & the 'Second Republic'

Though most of the fighting in WWI, at least on the eastern front, was staged on Polish land and caused staggering loss of life and livelihood, paradoxically, the war led to the country's independence.

On the one side were the Central Powers, Austria-Hungary and Germany (including Prussia); on the other, Russia and its Western allies. Since no formal Polish state existed, there was no Polish army to fight for the national cause. Even worse, some two million Poles were conscripted into the Russian, German or Austrian armies, and were obliged to fight one another.

After the October Revolution in 1917, Russia plunged into civil war and no longer had the power to oversee Polish affairs. The final collapse of the Austrian empire in October 1918 and the withdrawal of the German army from Warsaw in November brought the opportune moment. Marshal Józef Piłsudski took command of Warsaw on 11 November 1918, declared Polish sovereignty, and usurped power as the head of state.

Rise & Fall of the Second Republic

The Treaty of Versailles in 1919 that formally ended WWI called directly for the creation of a newly independent Poland, and thus the 'Second Republic' was born.

The treaty awarded Poland the western part of Prussia, providing access to the Baltic Sea. The city of Gdańsk, however, was omitted and became the Free City of Danzig. The rest of Poland's western border was drawn up in a series of plebiscites, which resulted in Poland acquiring some significant industrial regions of Upper Silesia. The eastern boundaries were established when Polish forces defeated the Red Army during the Polish–Soviet war of 1919–20.

PIŁSUDSKI

Marshal Józef Piłsudski's most famous quotation was: 'To be defeated and not to submit, that is victory; to be victorious and rest on one's laurels, that is defeat.'

1772	3 May 1791	1793	1795
First Partition of Poland at the instigation of Catherine the Great. Russia, Prussia and Austria annex substantial chunks of the country, amounting to roughly 30% of Polish territory.	The world's second written constitution (the first was in the USA) is signed in Warsaw. It places peasants under direct protection of the government, and attempts to wipe out serfdom.	Second Partition of Poland, with Russia and Prussia grabbing over half the remaining Polish territory. Poland shrinks to around 200,000 sq km and a population of four million.	The Third Partition of Poland. The country ceases to exist completely, and will only again become a republic after the end of WWI in 1918.

When God Looked the Other Way, by Wesley Adamczyk, is a gripping and terrible tale of a Polish family deported to southern Siberia in WWII.

When Poland's territorial struggle ended, the Second Republic covered nearly 400,000 sq km and had a population of 26 million. One-third was of non-Polish ethnic background, mainly Jews, Ukrainians, Belarusians and Germans.

After Piłsudski retired from political life in 1922, the country experienced four years of unstable governments until the great military commander seized power once again in a military coup in May 1926. Parliament was gradually phased out but, despite the dictatorial regime, political repression had little effect on ordinary people. The economic situation was relatively stable, and cultural and intellectual life prospered.

On 23 August 1939 a pact of nonaggression between Germany and the Soviet Union was signed in Moscow by their respective foreign ministers, Ribbentrop and Molotov. This pact contained a secret protocol in which Stalin and Hitler planned to carve up the Polish state.

PIŁSUDSKI: PATRIOT, SOLDIER, STATESMAN

All around Poland, you'll see statues bearing the stern, moustached visage of Marshal Józef Piłsudski, a controversial political figure in the 1920s and '30s who is nevertheless revered as a Polish patriot and superb military commander.

Piłsudski was born in 1867 in the Russian-occupied Vilnius region and joined the anti-tsarist movement while a teenager. He spent many of his early years in prison: five years in Siberia, a brief stint in Warsaw's Citadel, and more jail time in St Petersburg, before returning to Poland to lead the Polish Legions in WWI.

At the end of the war, Piłsudski returned to Warsaw to declare the birth of a new Polish state on 11 November 1918. Arguably, though, his greatest moment came immediately after the war when he launched a massive offensive to the east, capturing vast territories that had been Polish before the 18th-century partitions. A Soviet counteroffensive reached as far as Warsaw, but in the Battle of Warsaw in August 1920, the Polish army, under Piłsudski's command, outmanoeuvred and defeated the Red Army.

Once independent Poland was safely back on the map and a modern democratic constitution had been adopted in 1921, Piłsudski stepped down in 1922.

He reappeared on the scene four years later, however, to declare an effective coup d'état in order to rescue the country from what he saw as a political stalemate and economic stagnation. Piłsudski's sudden return spurred three days of street fighting that left 400 dead and over 1000 wounded.

After the government resigned, the National Assembly elected Piłsudski as president. He refused to take that post and opted instead for the office of defence minister, which he maintained until his death. There are few doubts, though, that it was Piłsudski who ran the country behind the scenes until he died in 1935.

Despite his dictatorial style, he was buried with ceremony among Polish kings in the crypt of Kraków's Wawel Cathedral.

1807	1810	1815	1830
Napoleon Bonaparte establishes the Duchy of Warsaw after crushing the Prussians on Polish soil. After Napoleon's defeat at the hands of the Russians, the duchy returns to Russia and Prussia.	The birth year of Frédéric Chopin, Poland's most beloved musician and a perennial favourite around the world. He's honoured by Poles but spent much of his life in France.	Congress Kingdom of Poland is established at the Congress of Vienna. The Duchy of Warsaw is swept away and Poland once again falls under the control of the Russian tsar.	First of a number of insurrections against the ruling Russians, known as the November Insurrection. Within a year the rebellion is defeated, and deportations of Poles to Siberia begin.

WWII

If Poles had been asked in the 1930s to sketch out a nightmare scenario, many would likely have said 'Germany fighting the Soviet Union over Poland', and that's more or less what happened.

The war that would vastly reshape the country started at dawn on 1 September 1939 with a massive German invasion. Fighting began in Gdańsk (at that time the Free City of Danzig) when German forces encountered a stubborn handful of Polish resisters at Westerplatte. The battle lasted a week.

Simultaneously, another German line stormed Warsaw, which finally surrendered on 28 September. Despite valiant resistance, there was simply no hope of withstanding the numerically overwhelming and well-armed German forces; the last resistance groups were quelled by early October.

Hitler's policy was to eradicate the Polish nation and Germanise the territory. Hundreds of thousands of Poles were deported en masse to forced-labour camps in Germany, while others, primarily the intelligentsia, were executed in an attempt to exterminate the spiritual and intellectual leadership.

The Jews were to be eliminated completely. At first they were segregated and confined in ghettos, then shipped off to extermination camps scattered around the country. Almost the whole of Poland's Jewish population (three million) and roughly one million other Poles died in the camps. Resistance erupted in numerous ghettos and camps, most famously in Warsaw.

WARSAW GHETTO

A Surplus of Memory: Chronicle of the Warsaw Ghetto Uprising, by Yitzhak Zuckerman, is a detailed narrative of this heroic act of Jewish resistance.

Soviet Invasion

Within a matter of weeks of the German invasion, the Soviet Union moved into Poland and claimed the country's eastern half. Thus, Poland was yet again partitioned. Mass arrests, exile and executions followed, and it's estimated that between one and two million Poles were sent to Siberia, the Soviet Arctic and Kazakhstan in 1939–40. Like the Germans, the Soviets set in motion a process of intellectual genocide.

Government-in-Exile & Homegrown Resistance

Soon after the outbreak of war, a Polish government-in-exile was formed in France under General Władysław Sikorski, followed by Stanisław Mikołajczyk. It was shifted to London in June 1940 as the front line moved west.

The course of the war changed dramatically when Hitler unexpectedly attacked the Soviet Union on 22 June 1941. The Soviets were pushed out of eastern Poland by the onslaught and all of Poland lay

You can find a library of wartime photographs chronicling the horror and destruction of the Warsaw Rising at www.warsawuprising.com.

THE WARSAW RISING

In early 1944, with German forces retreating across Poland, the Polish resistance (Armia Krajowa; AK) in Warsaw was preparing for the liberation of its city. On 1 August 1944, orders were given for a general anti-German uprising, with the intention of establishing a Polish command in the city before the Red Army swept through.

The initial 'rising' was remarkably successful and the AK, creating barricades from ripped-up paving slabs and using the Warsaw sewers as underground communication lines, took over large parts of the city. It hoped to control the city until support came from both the Allies and the Soviets. But none arrived. The Allies were preoccupied with breaking out of their beachhead in Normandy after the D-Day landings, and the Red Army, which was camped just outside the capital, didn't lift a finger. On learning of the rising, Stalin halted the offensive and ordered his generals not to intervene or provide any assistance in the fighting.

The Warsaw Rising raged for 63 days before the insurgents were forced to surrender; around 200,000 Poles were killed. The German revenge was brutal – Warsaw was literally razed to the ground, and, on Hitler's orders, every inhabitant was to be killed. It wasn't until 17 January 1945 that the Soviet army finally marched in to 'liberate' Warsaw, which by that time was little more than a heap of empty ruins.

For the Poles, the Warsaw Rising was one of the most heroic – and most tragic – engagements of the war. The events of the rising are commemorated in the Warsaw Rising Museum and the Monument to the Warsaw Rising.

under Nazi German control. The Führer set up camp deep in Polish territory, and remained there for over three years.

A nationwide resistance movement, concentrated in the cities, had been put in place soon after war broke out to operate the Polish educational, judicial and communications systems. Armed squads were set up by the government-in-exile in 1940, and these evolved into the Armia Krajowa (AK; Home Army), which figured prominently in the Warsaw Rising.

The Tide Turns

Hitler's defeat at Stalingrad in 1943 marked the turning point of the war on the eastern front, and from then on the Red Army successfully pushed westwards. After the Soviets liberated the Polish city of Lublin, the pro-communist Polish Committee of National Liberation (PKWN) was installed on 22 July 1944 and assumed the functions of a provisional government. A week later the Red Army reached the outskirts of Warsaw.

Warsaw at that time remained under Nazi German occupation. In a last-ditch attempt to establish an independent Polish administration, the AK attempted to gain control of the city before the arrival

Winston Churchill observed that 'Poland was the only country which never collaborated with the Nazis in any form and no Polish units fought alongside the German army'.

11 November 1918	28 June 1919	August 1920	12–14 May 1926
The date of the founding of the Second Republic, so named to create a symbolic bridge between itself and the Royal Republic that existed before the partitions.	The Treaty of Versailles that formally ends WWI awards Poland the western part of Prussia and access to the Baltic Sea, but leaves Gdańsk a 'free city'.	Poland defeats the Soviet Red Army in the Battle of Warsaw. The battle helps to secure large portions of land in what is now Belarus and Ukraine.	Poland's postwar experiment with democracy ends when Marshal Józef Piłsudski seizes power in a military coup, phases out parliament and imposes an authoritarian regime.

of the Soviet troops, with disastrous results. The Red Army continued its westward advance across Poland, and after a few months reached Berlin. The Nazi Reich capitulated on 8 May 1945.

At the end of WWII, Poland lay in ruins. Over six million people, about 20% of the prewar population, lost their lives, and out of three million Polish Jews in 1939, only 80,000 to 90,000 survived the war. Its cities were no more than rubble; only 15% of Warsaw's buildings survived. Many Poles who had seen out the war in foreign countries opted not to return to the new political order.

Communist Poland

Though Poland emerged from WWII among the victorious powers, it had the misfortune of falling within the Soviet-dominated Eastern bloc.

The problems started at the Yalta Conference in February 1945, when the three Allied leaders, Roosevelt, Churchill and Stalin, agreed to leave Poland under Soviet control. They agreed that Poland's eastern frontier would roughly follow the Nazi Germany–Soviet demarcation line of 1939. Six months later Allied leaders set Poland's western boundary along the

In 1944 Stalin was quoted as saying 'fitting communism onto Poland was like putting a saddle on a cow'.

MASSACRE AT KATYŃ

In April 1943, German troops fighting Soviet forces on the eastern front came across extensive mass graves in the forest of Katyń, near Smolensk, in present-day Russia. Exploratory excavations revealed the remains of several thousand Polish soldiers and civilians who had been executed. The Soviet government denied all responsibility and accused the Germans of the crime. After the communists took power in Poland the subject remained taboo, even though Katyń was known to most Poles.

It wasn't until 1990 that the Soviets admitted their 'mistake', and two years later finally made public secret documents showing that Stalin's Politburo was responsible for the massacre.

The full horror of Katyń was finally revealed during exhumations of the mass graves by Polish archaeologists in 1995–96. Here's what happened: soon after their invasion of Poland in September 1939, the Soviets took an estimated 180,000 prisoners, comprising Polish soldiers, police officers, judges, politicians, intellectuals, scientists, teachers, professors, writers and priests, and crammed them into various camps throughout the Soviet Union and the invaded territories.

On Stalin's order, signed in March 1940, about 21,800 of these prisoners, including many high-ranking officers, judges, teachers, physicians and lawyers, were transported from the camps to the forests of Katyń and other areas, shot dead and buried in mass graves. The Soviet intention was to exterminate the intellectual elite of Polish society.

No one has been brought to trial for the atrocity, as Russia states that Katyń was a military crime rather than a genocide, war crime, or crime against humanity.

1 September 1939	17 September 1939	22 June 1941	1942
The Nazis use a staged attack on a German radio station by Germans dressed as Poles as a pretext to invade Poland. WWII starts.	The Soviet Union fulfils its side of the Molotov-Ribbentrop Pact, a blueprint for the division of Eastern Europe between it and Nazi Germany, and invades eastern Poland.	Nazi Germany abrogates the Molotov-Ribbentrop Pact and declares war on the Soviet Union. This creates an uneasy alliance between Poland and the Soviet Union against their common foe.	Nazi Germany establishes 'Operation Reinhard', the name given to its plan to murder the Jews in occupied Poland, and builds secret extermination camps in Poland's far eastern regions.

Odra (Oder) and the Nysa (Neisse) Rivers; in effect, the country returned to its medieval borders.

The radical boundary changes were followed by population transfers of some 10 million people: Poles were moved into the newly defined Poland, while Germans, Ukrainians and Belarusians were resettled outside its boundaries. In the end, 98% of Poland's population was ethnically Polish.

As soon as Poland formally fell under Soviet control, Stalin launched an intensive Sovietisation campaign. Wartime resistance leaders were charged with Nazi collaboration, tried in Moscow and summarily shot or sentenced to arbitrary prison terms. A provisional Polish government was set up in Moscow in June 1945 and then transferred to Warsaw. After rigged elections in 1947, the new Sejm elected Bolesław Bierut president.

In 1948 the Polish United Workers' Party (PZPR), the country's communist party, was formed to monopolise power, and in 1952 a Soviet-style constitution was adopted. The office of president was abolished and effective power passed to the first secretary of the Party Central Committee. Poland became an affiliate of the Warsaw Pact.

Bread & Freedom

Stalinist fanaticism never gained as much influence in Poland as in neighbouring countries, and soon after Stalin's death in 1953 it all but disappeared. The powers of the secret police declined and some concessions were made to popular demands. The press was liberalised and Polish cultural values were resuscitated.

In June 1956 a massive industrial strike demanding 'bread and freedom' broke out in Poznań. The action was put down by force and soon afterwards Władysław Gomułka, a former political prisoner of the Stalin era, was appointed first secretary of the Party. At first he commanded popular support, but later in his term he displayed an increasingly rigid and authoritarian attitude, putting pressure on the Church and intensifying persecution of the intelligentsia.

It was ultimately an economic crisis, however, that brought about Gomułka's downfall; when he announced official price increases in 1970, a wave of mass strikes erupted in Gdańsk, Gdynia and Szczecin. Again, the protests were crushed by force, resulting in 44 deaths. The Party, to save face, ejected Gomułka from office and replaced him with Edward Gierek.

Another attempt to raise prices in 1976 incited labour protests, and again workers walked off the job, this time in Radom and Warsaw. Caught in a downward spiral, Gierek took out more foreign loans, but, to earn hard currency with which to pay the interest, he was forced to divert consumer goods away from the domestic market and sell them abroad.

Acclaimed Polish director Andrzej Wajda's 2007 film *Katyń* is a powerful and moving piece of work about the massacre of Polish officers in the Soviet Union on Stalin's orders during WWII. It's given added emotional impact by the fact that Wajda's own father was one of those officers.

19 April 1943	1 August 1944	27 January 1945	February– August 1945
The date of the start of the Ghetto Uprising in Warsaw. The Jewish resistance fighters hold out against overwhelming German forces for almost a month.	Start of the Warsaw Rising. The entire city becomes a battleground, and after the uprising is quelled, the Germans decide to raze Warsaw to the ground.	The Soviet Red Army liberates Germany's Auschwitz-Birkenau extermination camp. Some of the first photos and film footage of the Holocaust are seen around the world.	Poland's borders are redrawn. The Soviet Union annexes 180,000 sq km to the east, while the Allies return 100,000 sq km of Poland's western provinces after centuries of German rule.

By 1980 the external debt stood at US$21 billion and the economy had slumped disastrously.

By then, the opposition had grown into a significant force, backed by numerous advisers from the intellectual circles. When, in July 1980, the government again announced food-price increases, the outcome was predictable: fervent and well-organised strikes and riots spread like wildfire throughout the country. In August, they paralysed major ports, the Silesian coal mines and the Lenin Shipyard in Gdańsk.

Unlike most previous popular protests, the 1980 strikes were nonviolent; the strikers did not take to the streets, but stayed in their factories.

Solidarity & the Collapse of Communism

The end of communism in Poland was a long and drawn-out affair that can be traced back to 1980 and the birth of the Solidarity trade union.

On 31 August of that year, after protracted and rancorous negotiations in the Lenin Shipyard, the government signed the Gdańsk Agreement. It forced the ruling party to accept most of the strikers' demands, including the workers' right to organise independent trade unions, and to strike. In return, workers agreed to adhere to the constitution and to accept the Party's power as supreme.

Workers' delegations from around the country convened and founded Solidarity (Solidarność), a nationwide independent and self-governing trade union. Lech Wałęsa, who led the Gdańsk strike, was elected chair.

It wasn't long before Solidarity's rippling effect caused waves within the government. Gierek was replaced by Stanisław Kania, who in turn lost out to General Wojciech Jaruzelski in October 1981.

The trade union's greatest influence was on Polish society. After 35 years of restraint, the Poles launched themselves into a spontaneous and chaotic sort of democracy. Wide-ranging debates over the process of reform were led by Solidarity, and the independent press flourished. Such taboo historical subjects as the Stalin–Hitler pact and the Katyń massacre could, for the first time, be openly discussed.

Not surprisingly, the 10 million Solidarity members represented a wide range of attitudes, from confrontational to conciliatory. By and large, it was Wałęsa's charismatic authority that kept the union on a moderate and balanced course.

Learn more about the communist years at www.ipn.gov.pl, the website of the Institute of National Remembrance.

Martial Law & Its Aftermath

In spite of its agreement to recognise the Solidarity trade union, the Polish government remained under pressure from both the Soviets and local hardliners not to introduce any significant reforms.

This only led to further discontent and, in the absence of other legal options, more strikes. Amid fruitless wrangling, the economic

8 May 1945	1947	June 1956	1970
WWII officially ends with the surrender of Nazi Germany. There's great joy throughout Poland, but also apprehension as the war's end finds the country occupied by the Soviet Red Army.	Despite Stanisław Mikołajczyk – the government-in-exile's only representative to return to Poland – receiving over 80% of the vote in elections, 'officials' hand power to the communists.	Poland's first industrial strike, in Poznań. Around 100,000 people take to the streets; the Soviet Union crushes the revolt with tanks, leaving 76 dead and over 900 wounded.	West German chancellor Willy Brandt signs the Warsaw Treaty that formally recognises the country's borders. Brandt famously kneels at a monument to the victims of the Warsaw Ghetto Uprising.

crisis grew more severe. After the unsuccessful talks of November 1981 between the government, Solidarity and the Church, social tensions increased and led to a political stalemate.

When General Jaruzelski unexpectedly appeared on TV in the early hours of the morning of 13 December 1981 to declare martial law, tanks were already on the streets, army checkpoints had been set up on every corner, and paramilitary squads had been posted to possible trouble spots. Power was placed in the hands of the Military Council of National Salvation (WRON), a group of military officers under the command of Jaruzelski himself.

Solidarity was suspended and all public gatherings, demonstrations and strikes were banned. Several thousand people, including most Solidarity leaders and Wałęsa himself, were interned. The spontaneous demonstrations and strikes that followed were crushed, military rule was effectively imposed all over Poland within two weeks of its declaration, and life returned to the pre-Solidarity norm.

In October 1982 the government formally dissolved Solidarity and released Wałęsa from detention, but the trade union continued underground on a much smaller scale, enjoying widespread sympathy and support. In July 1984 a limited amnesty was announced and some members of the political opposition were released from prison. But further arrests continued, following every public protest, and it was not until 1986 that all political prisoners were freed.

The Gorbachev Impact

The election of Mikhail Gorbachev as leader in the Soviet Union in 1985, and his *glasnost* and *perestroika* programs, gave an important stimulus to democratic reforms throughout Central and Eastern Europe.

By early 1989, Jaruzelski had softened his position and allowed the opposition to challenge for parliamentary seats.

These 'semi-free' elections – semi-free in the sense that regardless of the outcome, the communists were guaranteed a number of seats – were held in June 1989, and Solidarity succeeded in getting an overwhelming majority of its candidates elected to the Senate, the upper house of parliament. The communists, however, reserved for themselves 65% of seats in the Sejm.

Jaruzelski was placed in the presidency as a stabilising guarantor of political changes for both Moscow and the local communists, but a non-communist prime minister, Tadeusz Mazowiecki, was installed as a result of personal pressure from Wałęsa.

This power-sharing deal, with the first non-communist prime minister in Eastern Europe since WWII, paved the way for the domino-like

More Reading on Poland in WWII

No Simple Victory: World War II in Europe, by Norman Davies

Rising '44: The Battle for Warsaw, by Norman Davies

Bloodlands: Europe between Hitler and Stalin, by Timothy Snyder

Between Two Evils, by Lucyna B Radlo

1978	November 1980	13 December 1981	April 1989
Karol Wojtyła, archbishop of Kraków, becomes Pope John Paul II. His election and triumphal visit to his homeland a year later dramatically increase political ferment.	Solidarity, the first non-communist trade union in a communist country, is formally recognised by the government. A million of the 10 million members come from Communist Party ranks.	Martial law is declared in Poland. It is debatable whether the move is Soviet driven or an attempt by the Polish communists to prevent Soviet military intervention. It lasts until 1983.	Poland becomes the first Eastern European state to break from communism. In round-table negotiations, Poland's opposition is allowed to stand for parliament and Solidarity is re-established.

collapse of communism throughout the Soviet bloc. The Communist Party, losing members and confidence, historically dissolved itself in 1990.

The Rise & Fall of Lech Wałęsa

In November 1990, Solidarity leader Lech Wałęsa won the first fully free presidential elections and the Third Republic of Poland was born. For Wałęsa it marked the high point of his career and for Poland the start of a very rocky rebirth.

In the first few months of the new republic, the government's finance minister, Leszek Balcerowicz, introduced a package of reforms that would change the centrally planned communist system into a free-market economy almost overnight. His economic plan, dubbed 'shock therapy' for the rapid way that it would be implemented, allowed prices to move freely, abolished subsidies, tightened the money supply, and sharply devalued the currency, making it fully convertible with Western currencies.

The effect was almost instant. Within a few months the economy appeared to have stabilised, food shortages became glaringly absent and shops filled up with goods. On the downside, prices skyrocketed and unemployment exploded. The initial wave of optimism and forbearance turned into uncertainty and discontent, and the tough austerity measures caused the popularity of the government to decline.

As for Wałęsa, while he was a highly capable union leader and charismatic man, as president he proved markedly less successful. During his statutory five-year term in office, Poland witnessed no fewer than five governments and five prime ministers, each struggling to put the newborn democracy back on track. His presidential style and accomplishments were repeatedly questioned by practically all of the political parties and the majority of the electorate.

The Country Turns to the Left

Wałęsa was defeated in the 1995 presidential election by Aleksander Kwaśniewski – a former communist. Though the election was close, it marked quite a comedown for Solidarity and for Wałęsa, its anti-communist folk hero.

With the post of prime minister in the hands of another former communist, Włodzimierz Cimoszewicz, and parliament moving to the left as well, the country that had spearheaded the anti-communist movement in Central and Eastern Europe oddly found itself with a firmly left-wing government – a 'red triangle' as Wałęsa himself had warned.

The Catholic Church, much favoured by Wałęsa during his term in the saddle, also lost out and didn't fail to caution the faithful against the danger of 'neopaganism' under the new regime.

Good Reads on the '89 Revolution

The Magic Lantern: The Revolution of '89, by Timothy Garton Ash

1989: The Struggle to Create Post–Cold War Europe, by Mary Elise Sarotte

The Year that Changed the World, by Michael Meyer

HISTORY THE RISE & FALL OF LECH WAŁĘSA

1990	1995	1999	1 May 2004
Not a great year for Polish communists. The Party dissolves, the first democratic presidential election takes place and the country becomes a free-market economy.	Former communist Aleksander Kwaśniewski defeats Lech Wałęsa for the presidency in what ends up being a humiliating climb-down for the former leader of the Solidarity trade union.	Poland becomes a member of NATO. The country has come full circle, moving from the Warsaw Pact with the former Soviet Union to an alliance with the West.	Poland joins the EU. Despite massive support, there is fear that the country is swapping one foreign governing power for another, and EU membership will spark a wave of emigration.

President Kwaśniewski's political style proved to be much more successful than Wałęsa's. He brought much-needed political calm to his term in office, and was able to cooperate successfully with both the left and right wings of the political establishment. This gained him a degree of popular support, and paved the way for another five-year term in office in the presidential election in October 2000. Wałęsa, trying his luck for yet another time, suffered a disastrous defeat, collecting just 1% of the vote this time around.

On 1 May 2004, under Kwaśniewski's presidency, Poland fulfilled its biggest post-communist foreign-policy objective, joining the European Union along with seven other countries from Central and Eastern Europe.

The Disaster at Smolensk

Outside of the traditional ups and downs of Poland's electoral politics, the year 2010 brought epic tragedy to the leadership that affected both the right and left of the political establishment and threw the entire country into prolonged sorrow.

On 10 April that year a Polish air-force jet carrying 96 people, including president Lech Kaczyński, his wife and a high-level Polish delegation of 15 members of parliament, crashed near the Russian city of Smolensk. There were no survivors. The plane had been flying in from Warsaw for a memorial service to mark the 70th anniversary of the WWII-era massacre of Polish officers at Katyń Forest.

The pilot attempted to land the plane in heavy fog at a military airport, struck a tree on the descent and missed the runway. An initial high-level Russian commission placed the blame on pilot error, though an official Polish government report, released in 2011, assigned blame to both the Polish side and to air-traffic controllers on the Russian side.

The crash brought overwhelming grief to the country and a procession of high-level funerals. However, it also served to unite the country's fractured politics – albeit briefly – and ultimately proved the strength of the country's democracy. While many leading officials were killed, there was no ensuing succession crisis.

Following the disaster, the presidency fell to parliamentary speaker Bronisław Komorowski, who promptly called for early elections. Komorowski, of the right-leaning Civic Platform party, won in a run-off against the late president's twin brother, Jarosław Kaczyński. Komorowski served as president until the elections of 2015, when he was defeated at the ballot box by the right-of-centre Andrzej Duda.

July 2006	April 2010	9 October 2011	24 May 2015
Twin brothers Lech and Jarosław Kaczyński occupy the presidential and prime minister seats respectively. Their nationalistic and conservative policies alienate many people.	President Lech Kaczyński, his wife and more than 90 others die in a tragic plane crash near the Russian city of Smolensk. The country unites in grief.	Parliamentary elections confirm the leadership of the right-leaning Civic Platform party, but the socially liberal Palikot Movement polls a historic 10% of the vote.	In the closest presidential race in Polish history, right-of-centre Law and Justice (PiS) candidate Andrzej Duda defeats incumbent Bronisław Komorowski.

Jewish Heritage

For centuries up until WWII, Poland was home to Europe's biggest population of Jews. Warsaw was the second-largest Jewish city in the world, after New York. It goes without saying that in many, many ways the saddest result of WWII was the near total destruction of this community and culture at the hands of Nazi Germany. Poland, and the world, is all the poorer for it.

Early Days

Jews began arriving in what is now Poland around the turn of the first millennium, just as the Polish kingdom was being formed. Many of these early arrivals were traders, coming from the south and east along established trading routes.

From the period of the early Crusades (around 1100), Poland began to develop a name for itself as a haven for Jews, a reputation it would maintain for centuries. At least some of the early Jewish inhabitants were coinmakers, as many Polish coins from the period bear Hebrew inscriptions.

The Enlightened Kazimierz

The Polish ruler most often associated with the growth of Poland's Jewish population is Kazimierz III Wielki (Casimir III the Great; 1333–70), an enlightened monarch who passed a series of groundbreaking statutes that expanded privileges for Jews. It's no coincidence that the Kazimierz district near Kraków and Kazimierz Dolny, both important Jewish centres, bear his name.

All was not a bed of roses and the good times were punctuated by occasional deadly pogroms, often as not whipped up by the clergy. At the time, the Catholic Church was not as fond of Jews as were the king and nobility, who relied on Jewish traders as middlemen.

The 16th century is considered the golden age of Poland's Jews; the century saw a dramatic leap in the kingdom's Jewish population, driven in part by immigration. It was during this century that the Jewish population of the Kraków district of Kazimierz began to grow. It was an independent town at the time, with a significant Catholic population. Over the centuries, it would evolve into one of Poland's most important concentrations of Jewish culture and scholarship.

Much of Europe was then an intolerant place, and Jews were being forced out of neighbouring countries. Many new arrivals were Sephardim, descendants of Spanish Jews who'd been tossed out of Spain by King Ferdinand and Queen Isabella in 1492. By the end of the 16th century, Poland had a larger Jewish population than the rest of Europe combined.

Pogroms & Partition

If the 16th century was good, the 17th century was an unprecedented disaster, both for the country and its Jewish population.

Cities with Important Jewish Heritage

Warsaw: The former Jewish ghetto

Kraków: Kazimierz and Podgórze

Lublin: The Jewish heritage trail

Łódź: The Litzmannstadt ghetto

Kazimierz Dolny: The Jewish cemetery

'If a Christian desecrates or defiles a Jewish cemetery in any way, he should be punished severely as demanded by law.' – Bolesław the Pious, inviting Jewish settlement in 1264.

The Cossack insurrection of the 1650s in neighbouring Ukraine, led by Bohdan Chmielnicki, resulted in massive pogroms and the slaughter of tens of thousands of Jews in the southeastern parts of the Polish kingdom.

The war with Sweden, the 'Deluge', laid waste to much of the kingdom. Jews found themselves caught in the middle, ruthlessly hunted by Swedes on one side and Poles on the other.

After the partitions of the 18th and early 19th centuries, conditions for Jews differed greatly depending on what area they found themselves in. In the southern and eastern parts of the country that went to Austria, Jews enjoyed a gradual move towards religious tolerance – a trend that began in 1782 under Austrian Emperor Joseph II with his 'Edict of Tolerance'. The edict formally allowed Jewish children to attend schools and universities and permitted adults to participate in various jobs outside of traditional trades, as well as to own and operate factories. These freedoms were expanded slowly, in fits and starts, to other areas of the former Polish kingdom over the 19th century.

Industrialisation in the 19th century led to higher living standards for Jews and non-Jews alike. Many Jews chose to leave the *shtetl* (small Jewish villages in the countryside) for greater opportunities in rapidly growing cities like Łódź. Urbanisation accelerated the process of assimilation, and by the 20th century, urban-dwelling Jews and Poles had much more in common than they had apart.

Any existing legal distinctions between Jews and Poles vanished after WWI with the establishment of an independent Poland, which declared everyone equal under the law regardless of religion or nationality.

A 1931 census showed Poland's Jews numbered just under three million people, or around 10% of the population.

The book *Jews in Poland: A Documentary History,* by Iwo Cyprian Pogonowski, provides a comprehensive record of half a millennium of Polish-Jewish relations.

WWII & The Holocaust

It goes beyond the scope of this section to describe in any detail the near-total slaughter of Poland's Jewish population by Nazi Germany starting in 1939. The numbers speak for themselves: of around three million Jews living in Poland in 1939, fewer than 100,000 survived the war. Whole communities, large and small, were wiped out.

In the early stages of the war, in 1940 and '41, the German occupiers forced Jews to live in restricted ghettos, such as in Warsaw, Łódź, Kraków's Podgórze neighbourhood, and scores of smaller cities around the country. In some cases, these were de facto internment camps; in others, like at Łódź, they were labour camps, harnessed directly to Germany's war effort.

Living conditions were appalling and thousands died of disease, exhaustion and malnutrition. To this day, Polish cities like Lublin, Częstochowa and Radom still bear the scars of their former ghettos; the parts of these cities where the wartime ghettos were built often remain bleak and depressed.

After Germany declared war on the Soviet Union in the summer of 1941, Nazi policy towards the Jews shifted from one of internment to that of full-scale extermination. For many, death would come quickly. By the end of 1942 and early 1943, the majority of Poland's Jewry was gone. Most of the victims were shot in the fields and forests around their villages, or deported to hastily erected extermination camps at Auschwitz-Birkenau, Treblinka, Sobibór and Bełżec.

The extermination camps at Auschwitz-Birkenau and some other places would continue on through 1944, but by then most of the victims were European Jews from outside Poland.

Most Important Holocaust Memorial Sites & Camps

Auschwitz-Birkenau

Majdanek

Bełżec

Treblinka

Sobibór

Disillusionment & Emigration

In the aftermath of WWII, many surviving Jews opted to emigrate to Israel or the USA. A small percentage decided to try to rebuild their lives in Poland, with decidedly mixed results.

It seems hard to believe now, but in the months and years after the war, there was not much sympathy in Poland for Holocaust survivors. Poland was a ravaged country, and every person to some extent had been made a victim by the war. Adding to this vitriolic atmosphere, after the war many impoverished Poles had simply asserted ownership of the homes and apartments of Jews who had been forcibly evacuated by the Nazis. In many cases, they were not prepared to give the properties back (even in the rare instances when the original owners actually survived the Holocaust).

While it must be stated that most Poles acted honourably during the war – and many gave shelter to their Jewish neighbours – this ugly strain of Polish anti-Semitism has attracted its own share of scholars and books. Among the best-known of these is Jan T. Gross' *Fear: Anti-Semitism in Poland After Auschwitz*. The low point came in Kielce in July 1946, when around 40 Jews were attacked and killed by an angry mob of Poles. The origins of the pogrom are unclear – some believe the attack was instigated by communist authorities – but for many Jews it marked a watershed in Polish attitudes. Emigration rates rose and few Jews chose to stay.

Additionally, Poland's position within the Soviet-controlled Eastern bloc greatly complicated the way the Holocaust was taught and commemorated. The Soviet Union had waged a mighty struggle to

> **Best Jewish Festivals**
> ....
> Jewish Culture Festival, Kraków
> ....
> Jewish Cultural Festival, Białystok
> ....
> Four Cultures, Łódź

READING UP ON THE HOLOCAUST

The genre of Holocaust-period literature is immense and it's not possible to mention all of the excellent titles, many written by Holocaust survivors and rich with detail. The most popular works include Thomas Keneally's *Schindler's Ark* (later retitled as *Schindler's List* and adapted as a film by Steven Spielberg), John Boyne's fictional *The Boy in the Striped Pajamas* and, of course, Anne Frank's *The Diary of a Young Girl*.

As far as historic works go, we like Laurence Rees' *Auschwitz: A New History*, which combines excellent scholarship with personal anecdote to explain how the changes in official Nazi policy during the war were felt at camps like Auschwitz-Birkenau. It sounds dry; however, it's anything but.

An occasionally overlooked masterpiece is *Fatelessness*, by Hungarian Nobel laureate Imre Kertész. The novel tells the Auschwitz story through the eyes of a 15-year-old boy separated from his family in Budapest.

In many ways, the gold standard of Holocaust survival literature remains Primo Levi's *Survival in Auschwitz* (published in some countries under the name *If This is a Man*). Levi, an Italian Jew, survived the war as a prisoner in the Monowitz camp at Auschwitz-Birkenau. It's a brilliant read, filled with honest sentiment of a young man simply trying to comprehend the insanity around him and stay alive. Levi continued writing for several decades before his death in 1987 of an apparent suicide. He returned to the theme of the Holocaust again and again in books like *The Reawakening*, *If Not Now, When?* and *The Drowned and the Saved*.

To see the camps from a Polish author's perspective, pick up a copy of Tadeusz Borowski's *This Way for the Gas, Ladies and Gentlemen*, in English translation. Borowski was not a Jew, but a political prisoner. His Auschwitz-Birkenau is a madhouse of boxing matches and brothels and filled with unlucky souls willing to risk everything simply for the chance to steal a potato.

JEWISH TOURS

Several tour companies and organisations offer guided tours to Poland's most significant Jewish heritage sights, as well as to important Holocaust destinations. Outside of the companies listed here, local tourist offices can provide information on a particular area's Jewish sights and history.

Our Roots (p434) This Warsaw-based tour group specialises in tours of Jewish sites around the city and region. It offers a standard five-hour 'Jewish Warsaw' tour for around 500zł. Other tours, including to Auschwitz-Birkenau and Treblinka, can be organised on request.

Jarden Tourist Agency (p434) Based in Kraków, this tour operator specialises in Jewish heritage tours around town. The most popular one, 'Retracing Schindler's List' (two hours by car), costs around 70zł per person for groups of four or more.

Momentum Tours & Travel (☑in the USA 305 466 0652; www.momentumtours.com; ⏰10am-4pm Mon-Fri) One of the best of many international tourist agencies that offer specialised tours of Jewish heritage sites in Poland. The company's nine-day Poland tour includes off-the-beaten-track destinations like Lublin, Kazimierz Dolny and Tarnów, among others.

defeat Nazi Germany and the official line was to milk that effort for all it was worth. To that end, the suffering of the Jews was politicised, viewed as part of a greater struggle of the working class over fascism. Even today, many Holocaust memorial sites – such as Majdanek near Lublin – remain marred by wildly overblown communist-era statuary that appear to cast the Holocaust as part of an epic battle, instead of more appropriately being memorials to honour the lives lost.

Auschwitz: The Nazis and the Final Solution is a BBC documentary that attempts to deal with the horrific events at Auschwitz-Birkenau.

Jewish Revival

The years since the collapse of the communist regime have seen a marked improvement in local attitudes towards Jewish culture and history, and what might even be termed a modest Jewish revival.

Kraków, especially the former Jewish quarter of Kazimierz, has led the way. The city's annual Jewish Culture Festival is filled with theatre, film and, most of all, boisterous klezmer music. The festival has emerged as one of the city's – and the country's – cultural highlights. In 2010, Kraków opened the doors to an impressive museum covering the Nazi-German occupation of the city during WWII, housed in the former enamel factory of Oskar Schindler, of *Schindler's List* fame.

Kazimierz itself is a mixed bag of serious Jewish remnants and cheesy-but-fun Jewish restaurants, where the *Fiddler on the Roof* theme is laid on so thick that even Zero Mostel would probably blush. Still, the energy is infectious and has exerted a positive influence on other cities, including Warsaw, Lublin and Łódź, to embrace their own Jewish heritage.

Cities with Beautiful Synagogues

Kraków (Kazimierz district)

Zamość

Oświęcim

Nowy Sącz

In the past few years, the tourist office in Łódź has marked out an important Jewish landmarks trail that you can follow through that city's former Jewish area and learn the tragic but fascinating story of what was the country's longest-surviving ghetto during the war. Lublin, too, now has a self-guided tour that highlights that city's rich Jewish heritage.

Warsaw, which was home to the biggest Jewish population and wartime ghetto, had long been a laggard in the effort to embrace the country's Jewish past, but that changed in 2014 with the opening of the impressive, interactive Museum of the History of Polish Jews.

The Arts

Poles punch above their weight when it comes to the arts. Literature and cinema are where the country excels. Poland has produced no fewer than four Nobel Prize winners in literature and several household names when it comes to film, including Andrzej Wajda, Roman Polański and Krzysztof Kieślowski.

Judging from the number of concerts and festivals around the country, the performing arts, including classical music, theatre and dance, are alive and kicking.

Literature

In Poland, as in many Central European countries, literature holds a special place in the hearts of citizens. It has served as the only outlet for resentment against foreign rule during occupation, and has often captured the spirit of a struggling country.

Novelists

The Nobel Prize for literature was first awarded in 1901, and it was only four years later that Henryk Sienkiewicz (1846–1916) became the first of four Polish writers to be so honoured. Sienkiewicz took the prize for *Quo Vadis?*, an epic novel chronicling the love affair between a pagan Roman and a young Christian girl in ancient Rome.

Novelist and short-story writer Władysław Reymont (1867–1925) won the Nobel in 1924 for *The Peasants* (Chłopi), a four-volume epic about Polish village life.

Between the wars, several brilliant avant-garde writers emerged who were only fully appreciated after WWII. They included Bruno Schulz (1892–1942), Witold Gombrowicz (1904–69) and Stanisław Ignacy Witkiewicz (also known as Witkacy; 1885–1939).

Despite penning only a handful of books, Schulz is regarded as one of Poland's leading literary lights; his *The Street of Crocodiles* is a good introduction to his ingenious, imaginative prose. As a Jew caught in the maelstrom of WWII, he stood little chance of surviving the German occupation.

The Post-WWII Generation

The postwar period presented Polish writers with a conundrum: adopt communism and effectively sell out, or take a more independent path and risk persecution.

Czesław Miłosz (1911–2004), who broke with the communist regime, offered an analysis of this problem in *The Captive Mind* (Zniewolony Umysł). Miłosz, a long-time émigré, spent the last 40 years of his life in the USA. He won the Nobel Prize in 1980 in recognition of his achievements.

Novelist, screenwriter and film director Tadeusz Konwicki (1926–2015) is another remarkable figure of the postwar literary scene. Konwicki was a teenage resistance fighter during WWII, and his pre-1989 works had communist censors tearing their hair out. He wrote more than 20 novels;

Must-
Reads by
Polish
Writers

The Painted Bird,
Jerzy Kosiński

*The Street of
Crocodiles,*
Bruno Schulz

*The Polish
Complex,*
Tadeusz Konwicki

The Captive Mind,
Czesław Miłosz

Solaris,
Stanisław Lem

---

*The Polish Way:
A Thousand-Year
History of the
Poles and their
Culture* (1988) by
Adam Zamoyski
is one of the
best accounts
of Polish culture
from its birth to
the recent past. It
is fully illustrated
and exquisitely
written.

POLISH PROSE IN EXILE

A number of Polish émigrés have made a name for themselves outside the country. Józef Teodor Konrad Nałęcz Korzeniowski (1857–1924) was born into a family of impoverished but patriotic gentry in Berdichev, now in western Ukraine. He left the country in 1874 and, after 20 years travelling the world as a sailor, settled in England. Though fluent in Polish, he dedicated himself to writing in English. He is known throughout the world by his adopted name of Joseph Conrad, and his novels (*Heart of Darkness* and *Lord Jim,* to name but two) are considered classics of English literature.

American Nobel Prize–winner Isaac Bashevis Singer (1902–91) spent his formative years in Poland before moving to the USA in 1935 in the face of rising fascism. Singer originally wrote in his native tongue of Yiddish, before translating his work into English for an American audience. Two of his most memorable stories are *Enemies, a Love Story* and *Yentl;* the latter was made into a film starring Barbara Streisand.

Despite controversy surrounding the authenticity of some of Jerzy Kosiński's works, the author (1933–91) is known for two highly regarded novels, *The Painted Bird* and *Being There*. Kosiński was born Josek Lewinkopf in Łódź and emigrated to the USA in 1957.

among novels; among the best known are the brilliant *A Minor Apocalypse* (Mała Apokalipsa) and *The Polish Complex* (Kompleks Polski).

Stanisław Lem (1921–2006) is Poland's premier writer of science fiction. Around 27 million copies of his books, translated into 41 languages, have been sold around the world. The most famous is *Solaris*.

Poetry

The 19th century produced three exceptional Polish poets: Adam Mickiewicz (1798–1855), Juliusz Słowacki (1809–49) and Zygmunt Krasiński (1812–59). Known as the Three Bards, they captured a nation deprived of its independence in their romantic work.

The greatest of the three, Mickiewicz, is to the Poles what Shakespeare is to the British, and is as much a cultural icon as a historical and creative figure. Born in Navahrudak, in what is now Belarus, he was a political activist in his youth and was deported to central Russia for five years. He left Poland in the 1830s, never to return, and served as a professor of literature in Lausanne and Paris.

Mickiewicz' most famous poem, known to all Polish schoolchildren, is the epic, book-length *Pan Tadeusz* (1834). It is a romantic evocation of a lost world of 18th-century Polish-Lithuanian gentry, torn apart by the Partition of 1795.

Interestingly, Poland's fourth and most recent Nobel Prize (in 1996) went to a poet, Wisława Szymborska (b 1923). The Swedish academy described her as 'the Mozart of poetry' with 'something of the fury of Beethoven'. For those wanting to sample her work in English, a good introduction is the volume entitled *View with a Grain of Sand,* published in 1995.

WRITERS

The website www.
polishwriting.
net is a guide
to around 20
contemporary
Polish novelists
whose works
are available
in English, and
includes short
biographies, in-
terviews, articles
and extracts from
their works.

Cinema

Though the invention of the cinema is attributed to the Lumière brothers, some sources claim that a Pole, Piotr Lebiedziński, should take some of the credit; he built a film camera in 1893, two years before the movie craze took off.

The first Polish film was shot in 1908, but large-scale film production only took off after WWI. Little work produced between the wars reached international audiences; the country's greatest contribution to world cinema at the time was actress Pola Negri (1897–1987), a star of Hollywood's silent flicks of the 1920s.

The Polish School

Polish cinema came to the fore from 1955 to 1963, the period known as the Polish School. The school drew heavily on literature and dealt with moral evaluations of the war – its three greatest prodigies, Andrzej Wajda (b 1926), Roman Polański (b 1933) and Jerzy Skolimowski (b 1938), all attended the Łódź Film School and went on to international acclaim.

Wajda produced arguably his best work during this time, the famous trilogy *A Generation* (Pokolenie), *Canal* (Kanał) and *Ashes and Diamonds* (Popiół i Diament). Since then, the tireless Wajda has produced a film every few years or so, the best of which include *Man of Marble* (Człowiek z Marmuru), its sequel *Man of Iron* (Człowiek z Żelaza), and *The Promised Land* (Ziemia Obiecana), which was nominated for an Oscar. In 2007 Wajda shot to the top of Polish cinema once again with his controversial and deeply moving film, *Katyń,* about the massacre of Polish officers by the Soviet Union in the Katyń Forest during WWII.

Polański and Skolimowski began their careers in the early '60s; the former made only one feature film in Poland, *Knife in the Water* (Nóż w Wodzie), before continuing his career in the West. The latter shot four films, of which the last, *Hands Up* (Ręce do Góry), made in 1967, was kept from the public until 1985. Skolimowski also left Poland for more receptive pastures, and while he gained an international following, it was nothing compared to the recognition Polański received. Polański's body of work includes such remarkable films as *Cul-de-Sac, Revulsion, Rosemary's Baby, Chinatown, Bitter Moon* and *The Pianist.*

After the Polish School

Poland's film-makers never again reached the heights of the Polish School after 1963, yet they continued to make exemplary works. The communist era produced a string of important directors, including Krzysztof Zanussi, Andrzej Żuławski and Agnieszka Holland, and in 1970 Marek Piwowski shot *The Cruise* (Rejs), Poland's first cult film.

One name that regularly tops the list of art-house favourites is Krzysztof Kieślowski (1941–96), the director of the extraordinary trilogy *Three Colours: Blue/White/Red*. He started in 1977 with *Scar* (Blizna), but his first widely acclaimed feature was *Amateur* (Amator). After several mature films, he undertook the challenge of making *Decalogue* (Dekalog), a 10-part TV series that was broadcast all over the world.

In 2015 the film *Ida,* by director Paweł Pawlikowski, became the first Polish feature to win the Oscar for Best Foreign Film. It's a moving story – filmed in black and white – of a young girl in training to become a nun in 1960s as she discovers her Jewish roots and the wartime fate of her family.

Music

Classical Music

The foremost figure in the history of Polish music is Frédéric Chopin (1810–49), who crystallised the national style in classical music, taking inspiration from folk or court dances and tunes such as *polonez* (polonaise), *mazurek* (mazurka), *oberek* and *kujawiak*. No one else in the history of Polish music has so creatively used folk rhythms for concert pieces, nor achieved such international recognition.

Chopin was not the only composer inspired by folk dances at the time. Stanisław Moniuszko (1819–72) used his inspiration to create Polish national opera; two of his best-known pieces, *Halka* and *Straszny Dwór,* are staples of the national opera-house repertoire. Henryk Wieniawski (1835–80), another remarkable 19th-century composer, also achieved great heights in the world of Polish music.

By the start of the 20th century, Polish artists were beginning to grace the world stage. The first to do so were the piano virtuosos Ignacy Paderewski

Don't-Miss Films by Polish Directors

The Pianist, Roman Polański

The Three Colours Trilogy, Krzysztof Kieślowski

Ashes and Diamonds, Andrzej Wajda

Katyń, Andrzej Wajda

The Double Life of Veronique, Krzysztof Kieślowski

Check out the Polish Film Institute's website at www.pisf.pl for up-to-date information on the Polish film industry.

THE ARTS MUSIC

ALL THAT JAZZ

Jazz clubs come and go, but jazz as a music form retains a passionate following in Poland. This possibly owes something to the fact that jazz was officially frowned upon by the former communist government for nearly 40 years.

Krzysztof Komeda (1931–69), a legendary pianist, became Poland's first jazz star in the postwar decades and an inspiration to many who followed, including Michał Urbaniak (violin, saxophone), Zbigniew Namysłowski (saxophone) and Tomasz Stańko (trumpet), all of whom became pillars of the scene in the 1960s. Urbaniak opted to pursue his career in the USA, and is perhaps the best-known Polish jazz musician on the international scene.

Of the younger generation, Leszek Możdżer (piano) is possibly the biggest revelation thus far, followed by several other exceptionally skilled pianists such as Andrzej Jagodziński and Włodzimierz Pawlik. Other jazz talents to watch out for include Piotr Wojtasik (trumpet), Maciej Sikała (saxophone), Adam Pierończyk (saxophone), Piotr Baron (saxophone) and Cezary Konrad (drums).

Several Polish cities hold annual jazz festivals. One of the best is Kraków's Summer Jazz Festival, held throughout July and August.

Where to Find Frédéric Chopin

Chopin Museum, Warsaw

Church of the Holy Cross, Warsaw; Chopin's heart is buried here

Warsaw University; Chopin studied here

Żelazowa Wola, Warsaw; Chopin's birthplace

(1860–1941) and Artur Rubinstein (1886–1982); the latter performed right up until his death. Karol Szymanowski (1882–1937) was another musical personality of the first half of the 20th century; his best-known composition, the ballet *Harnasie,* was influenced by folk music from the Tatra Mountains, which he transformed into the contemporary musical idiom.

Rock & Pop

Rock has a long and storied tradition in Poland, going back well before the downfall of communism in 1989. The country's first rock pioneer was Tadeusz Nalepa (1943–2007), who began his career in the late 1960s and went on to nationwide success. Other veterans of the rock-pop scene include Lady Pank, Republika, Budka Suflera, Maanam, Bajm, T. Love and Hey. Recent years have seen a rash of productions covering just about every musical genre and style from salsa to rap. Brathanki and Golec uOrkiestra are both popular groups that creatively mix folk and pop rhythms, and the likes of Wilki, Dżem and Myslovitz are keeping the country's rock traditions alive. In recent years Disco Polo – a disco-based dance music pioneered in the 1990s and unique to Poland – has made a comeback, and clubs such as Kraków's Hush Live have dedicated themselves to the style.

Painting

The country's first major painter was no Pole at all. Bernardo Bellotto (c 1721–80) was born in Venice, the nephew (and pupil) of that quintessential Venetian artist, Canaletto. He specialised in *vedute* (town views) and explored Europe thoroughly, landing the job of court painter in Warsaw during the reign of King Stanisław August Poniatowski (1764–95). An entire room in Warsaw's Royal Castle is devoted to his detailed views of the city, which proved invaluable as references during the reconstruction of the Old Town after WWII. Bellotto often signed his canvases 'de Canaletto', and as a result is commonly known in Poland simply as Canaletto.

Development of Polish Artists

Poles who became household names include Antoni Patek (cofounder of watchmakers Patek Philippe & Co), Max Factor (the father of modern cosmetics) and the four Warner brothers (founders of Warner Bros).

By the middle of the 19th century, Poland was ready for its own painters. Born in Kraków, Jan Matejko (1838–93) created stirring canvases that glorified Poland's past achievements. He aimed to keep alive in the minds of his viewers the notion of a proud and independent Polish nation, at a time when Poland had ceased to exist as a political entity. His best-known work is *The Battle of Grunwald* (1878), an enormous painting that took three years to complete. It depicts the famous victory of the united Polish, Lithuanian and Ruthenian forces over the Teutonic Knights in 1410 and is displayed in Warsaw's National Museum.

The likes of Józef Brandt (1841–1915) and Wojciech Kossak (1857–1942) also contributed to the documentation of Polish history at this time; Kossak is best remembered as co-creator of the colossal *Panorama of Racławice*, which is on display in Wrocław.

Theatre

Although theatrical traditions in Poland date back to the Middle Ages, theatre in the proper sense of the word didn't develop until the Renaissance period and initially followed the styles of major centres in France and Italy. By the 17th century the first original Polish plays were being performed on stage. In 1765 the first permanent theatre company was founded in Warsaw, and its later director, Wojciech Bogusławski, came to be known as the father of the national theatre.

In the decades after WWII Polish theatre acquired an international reputation. Some of the highest international recognition was gained by the Teatr Laboratorium (Laboratory Theatre), which was created in 1965 and led by Jerzy Grotowski in Wrocław. This unique experimental theatre, remembered particularly for *Apocalypsis cum Figuris,* was dissolved in 1984, and Grotowski concentrated on conducting theatrical classes abroad until his death in 1999.

Another remarkable international success was Tadeusz Kantor's Cricot 2 Theatre of Kraków, formed in 1956. Unfortunately, his best creations, *The Dead Class* (Umarła Klasa) and *Wielopole, Wielopole,* may never be seen again; Kantor died in 1990 and the theatre was dissolved a few years later. A new museum, Cricoteka, has opened in Kraków to celebrate his life and work.

Folk Arts

Poland has long and rich traditions in folk arts and crafts, but there are significant regional distinctions. Folk culture is strongest in the mountains, especially in the Podhale at the foot of the Tatras, but other relatively small enclaves, such as Kurpie and Łowicz (both in Mazovia), help to keep traditions alive.

Industrialisation and urbanisation have increasingly encroached on traditional customs. People no longer wear folk dress except for on special occasions, and the artefacts they make are mostly for sale as either tourist souvenirs or museum pieces. The country's many open-air folk museums, called skansens, are the best places to see what is left.

SKANSEN

THE ARTS THEATRE

A Scandinavian word referring to an open-air ethnographic museum, skansen aim to preserve traditional folk culture and architectur, in typical, mostly wooden, rural buildings (dwellings, barns, churches, mills) collected from the region. There are 35 in the country.

POST-WWII PAINTING

From the end of WWII until 1955 the visual arts were dominated by socialist realism – canvases of tractors, landscapes, peasants and factories that became, officially at least, all the rage in those days.

On a more positive note, at least from an artistic standpoint, this was also a time when poster art came to the fore, building on a tradition dating back to the turn of the century. One of the most influential artists was Tadeusz Trepkowski (1914–54), who produced his best posters after WWII. His works, and those by other poster artists, can be seen at Warsaw's Poster Museum.

From 1955 onwards, Poland's painters began to experiment with a variety of forms, trends and techniques. Zdzisław Beksiński (1929–2005) is considered one of the country's best contemporary painters; he created a mysterious and striking world of dreams in his art.

Landscape & Wildlife

With primeval forest, wind-raked sand dunes, coastal lakes, beaches, reedy islands, caves, craters, a desert, a long chain of mountains and even a peninsula called Hel, it's fair to say that Poland has one of Europe's most diverse collections of ecosystems.

Vital Stats

Area:
312,685 sq km

Countries
bordered:
seven

Total length of
border: 3582km

Number of lakes:
9300

Highest mountain:
Mt Rysy (2499m)

Longest river:
Vistula (1090km)

A Varied Landscape

Poland's bumps and flat bits were largely forged during the last ice age, when the Scandinavian ice sheet crept south across the plains and receded some 10,000 years later. This left five identifiable landscape zones: the Sudetes and Carpathian Mountains in the south, the vast central lowlands, the lake belt, the Baltic Sea in the north and the north-flowing rivers.

Southern Mountains

The southern mountains stretch from the Sudetes range in the southwest to the Tatras in the south and the Beskids in the southeast. The Sudetes are geologically ancient hills, their rounded peaks reaching their highest point at the summit of Śnieżka (1602m) in the Karkonosze range. Poland's highest point is Mt Rysy (2499m) in the Tatras, a jagged, alpine range shared with Slovakia. Indeed, the hiking trails in Tatras are integrated with those on the other side of the ridge in Slovakia, meaning you can hike across the border and pick up the same trails on the other side. To the north of the Tatra lies the lower (but much larger) densely forested range of the Beskids, with its highest peak at Babia Góra (1725m). The southeastern extremity of Poland is occupied by the Bieszczady, part of the Carpathian arc and arguably the most picturesque and lonely procession of peaks in the country.

Central Lowlands

The central lowlands stretch from the far northeast all the way south to around 200km shy of the southern border. The undulating landscape of this, the largest of Poland's regions, comprises the historic areas of Lower Silesia, Wielkopolska, Mazovia and Podlasie. Once upon a time, streams flowing south from melting glaciers deposited layers of sand and mud that helped produce some of the country's most fertile soils. As a result, the central lowlands are largely farmland and Poland's main grain-producing region. In some places, notably in Kampinos National Park to the west of Warsaw, fluvioglacial sand deposits have been blown by wind into sand dunes up to 30m high, creating some of the largest inland natural sand structures in Europe.

Fuel for the 19th-century industrial revolution was extracted from the vast coal deposits of Upper Silesia in the western part of the lowlands. The close proximity of this relatively cheap fuel encouraged the eventual growth of giant steel mills in industrial plants in this part of the country, leaving a legacy of air and water pollution (p415) that the country is still coping with – though it is making big strides.

Despite its abundance of lakes, Poland has lingering water problems, including pollution and lack of sewage treatment, though a recent European environmental study (conducted by the European Environmental Agency) said it had noticed improvements in recent years.

Water, Water, Everywhere

Not only does Poland enjoy a long stretch of the Baltic coast, it also has countless lakes and rivers, popular with yachtsmen, anglers, swimmers and divers, as well as thousands of species of flora and fauna.

POLISH ENVIRONMENTAL ISSUES

Poland has made important strides in environmental protection in recent years but continues to cope with legacy issues, including the massive deforestation that occurred during World War II and the rapid build-up of industrial output – particularly in Upper Silesia – during the communist period. This improvement can be seen particularly with respect to air pollution. A 2014 study by the European Environmental Agency (EEA) concluded that while the Polish economy had grown every year for the past two decades, this had not led to any measurable increase in emissions. In some cases (with sulphur dioxide, for example), the report said a reduction was observed.

This was seen as good news. As recently as 1992, Poland was the world's 12th-highest per capita polluter, with soot and airborne pollutants in the Katowice region alone well above acceptable health norms. Part of the answer has been de-industrialisation. The old, massive steel works at Nowa Huta, near Kraków, for example, now operate at a fraction of what they did in the 1960s and '70s. Part of the solution, as well, has been to adopt modern scrubbing technology.

The EEA report also said Poland had made noticeable progress in protecting surface and groundwater as well. Municipal waste discharge fell by 12% since 2000, while the percentage of the general population with access to water-treatment facilities grew to 70 percent. In managing agriculture runoff, the report said chemicals like nitrogen and phosphorus that flow into rivers and eventually into the Baltic Sea had decreased. Nevertheless, it said surface water quality was still lacking in some areas.

The biggest challenges, according to the EEA, remain more efficient use of material and energy resources in order to achieve economic sustainability.

Poland's Lakes

The lake zone includes the regions of Pomerania, Warmia and Masuria. The latter contains most of Poland's 9300 lakes – more than any other European country except Finland. The gently undulating plains and strings of post-glacial lakes were formed by sticky clay deposited by the retreating ice sheet. The lake region boasts the only remaining *puszcza* (primeval forest) in Europe, making Białowieża National Park and the wildlife inhabiting it one of the highlights of a visit to the country.

Some 52% of Polish territory is agricultural; almost 30% is forested.

Baltic Coast

The sand-fringed Baltic coast stretches across northern Poland from Germany to Russia's Kaliningrad enclave. The coastal plain that fringes the Baltic Sea was shaped by the rising water levels after the retreat of the Scandinavian ice sheet and is now characterised by swamps and sand dunes. These sand and gravel deposits form not only the beaches of Poland's seaside resorts but also the shifting dunes of Słowiński National Park, the sand bars and gravel spits of Hel, and the Vistula Lagoon.

Poland's Rivers

Polish rivers drain northwards into the Baltic Sea. The largest is the mighty 1090km-long Vistula (Wisła), originating in the Tatra mountains. Along with its right-bank tributaries – the Bug and the Narew – the Vistula is responsible for draining almost half of the country and is known as the 'mother river' of Poland, given its passage through both Kraków and Warsaw. The second-largest river, the Odra, and its major tributary, the Warta, drains the western third of Poland and forms part of the country's western border. Rivers are highest when the snow and ice dams melt in spring and are prone to flooding during the heavy rains of July.

Josepha Contoski's prize-winning children's book *Bocheck in Poland* is a beautifully rendered story of the relationship between white storks and Polish people.

Wildlife

Wildlife-spotters certainly have a lot to look forward to in Poland. Grazing bison in Białowieża National Park and storks nesting atop telegraph poles are easy to find; brown bears and lynx may be harder to track down. Poland's varied landscapes also provide habitats for a vast array of plants.

Animals

There is a rich bounty of zoological and ornithological treasure in Poland. Its diverse landscapes provide habitats for mammal species such as wild boar, red deer, elk and lynx in the far northeast, and brown bears and wild-cats in the mountain forests of the south. Rare bird species found in Poland include thrush nightingales, golden eagles, white-backed and three-toed woodpeckers, and hazel grouses, among 200 other species of nesting birds.

Wolves

Grey wolves are the largest members of the canine family and were once a common feature of the Polish landscape. In the days of old, wolf hunting was a favourite pastime of Russian tsars. This, and di-minishing habitats, drove their numbers down until wolves had all but disappeared in the 1990s. After specialised legislation to protect them was passed in 1998, recent wolf counts have revealed that the numbers have once again begun to climb.

Horses

Poles and horses go way back. Poland has a long tradition of breeding Arabian horses and the Polish plains were once home to wild horses. Several species of wild horse have been preserved in zoos, including the tarpan, which is extinct out of captivity. Luckily, Polish farmers used to crossbreed tarpans with their domestic horses and the small Polish kon-ik horse is the result of this mix, keeping the tarpan genes alive. Konik horses are now being used to breed the tarpan back. The hucul pony is a direct descendant of the tarpan living in the Carpathians.

Bird Life

The diverse topography of Poland is is home to diverse range of bird species. The vast areas of lake, marsh and reed beds along the Baltic coast, as well as the swampy basins of the Narew and Biebrza Rivers, support many species of waterfowl and are also visited by huge flocks of migrating geese, ducks and waders in spring and autumn. A small community of cormorants lives in the Masurian lakes.

Storks, which arrive from Africa in spring to build their nests on the roofs and chimneys of houses in the countryside, are a much-loved part of the rural scene. The expression 'every fourth stork is Polish' is based on the fact that Poland welcomes around one-quarter of Europe's 325,000 white storks each year, most of which make their summer homes in Masuria and Podlasie in the northeast.

The *orzeł* (eagle) is the national symbol of Poland and was adopted as a royal emblem in the 12th century. Several species can be seen, mostly in the southern mountains, including the golden eagle and short-toed eagle, as well as the rare booted eagle, greater spotted eagle and lesser spotted eagle. The white-tailed eagle, supposedly the inspiration for the national emblem, lives in national parks along the Baltic coast.

Plant Life

Many visitors will probably be surprised to hear that Poland contains the only surviving fragment of original forest that once covered much of prehistoric Europe. This old-growth forest of Białowieża National Park is still home to majestic five-centuries-old oak trees and a range of flora that is, quite literally, ancient.

The most common plant species in Poland is the pine, which covers 70% of the total forested area, but the biological diversity and ecological

Mt Rysy is reputed to have been climbed by Nobel laureate Marie Curie and Russian revo-lutionary Lenin (on separate occasions). A red hammer and sickle symbol is painted on a rock where the latter is believed to have rested.

STORKS

In addition to their baby-delivery service, *bociany* (storks) are also known in Poland to bring good luck. Poles will often place wagon wheels and other potential nesting foundations on their roofs to attract the white stork. Telecom-munications companies even go to lengths to ensure that their structures are stork-friendly.

BISON: BACK FROM THE BRINK

The European bison (*Bison bonasus*, *żubr* in Polish) is the largest European mammal, its weight occasionally exceeding 1000kg. These large cattle, which can live for as long as 25 years, look pretty clumsy but can move at 50km/h when they need to.

Bison were once found all over the continent, but the increasing exploitation of forests in Western Europe pushed them eastwards. In the 19th century, the last few hundred bison lived in freedom in the Białowieża Forest. In 1916 there were still 150 animals but three years later they were gone, hunted to extinction. At that time only about 50 bison survived in zoos across the world.

It was in Białowieża that an attempt to prevent the extinction of the bison began in 1929, by bringing several animals from zoos and breeding them in their natural habitat. The result is that today there a few hundred bison living in freedom in the Białowieża Forest alone and several hundred more have been sent to a dozen other places in Poland. Many bison from Białowieża have been distributed among European zoos and forests, and their total current population is estimated at about 2500.

resilience of forests are increasing thanks to the proliferation of deciduous species such as oak, beech, birch, rowan and linden. The forest undergrowth hosts countless moss and fungus species, many of the latter suitable for rich sauces or to be fried in breadcrumbs. In the highest mountain regions, coniferous forests of dwarf mountain pines are capable of resisting harsher climates, while the lowlands and highlands are hospitable for dry-ground forests and marsh forests. Distinctly Polish plants include the Polish larch *(Larix polonica)* and the birch *(Betula oycoviensis)* in the Ojców region.

Check out the English-language website www. wildpoland.com for heaps of information on wildlife spotting in Poland's national parks.

Conservation Areas in Poland

Currently 30% of Poland's land is forest, the majority of which is administered by the state. Around 23% of the country is under some sort of protection as a national park, landscape park or other type of conservation area. Entry into national parks, as well as some regional and landscape parks, normally requires an admission fee, payable at kiosks located near trailheads. Fees vary by park but typically range from 5zł to 10zł per day.

National Parks

There are 23 *parki narodowe* (national parks) in Poland, covering about 3200 sq km – about 1% of the country's surface area. Outside of a group of six in the Carpathian Mountains, they are distributed fairly evenly and therefore exhibit the full range of landscapes, flora and fauna the country possesses. Poland's oldest national park, Białowieża, was established in 1932.

Landscape Parks

In addition to Poland's national parks, the smaller and more numerous *parki krajobrazowe* (landscape parks) also play a key role in conservation efforts. As well as their aesthetic contribution, landscape parks are often of key historic and cultural value.

Of the 110 species of mammal and 424 species of bird known to inhabit Poland, 12 of each are considered threatened.

Reserves

Poland has a number of *rezerwaty* (protected reserves), usually small areas containing a particular natural feature such as a cluster of old trees, a lake with valuable flora or an interesting rock formation. Nine biosphere reserves have been recognised by Unesco for their innovative approach to sustaining various ecological elements.

Survival Guide

Directory A–Z

Accommodation

Poland has a wide choice of accommodation options to suit most budgets, including hotels, pensions and guesthouses, hostels, apartment rentals and camping grounds. Prices across all of these categories have increased in recent years, but are still generally lower than comparable facilities in Western Europe.

➡ Warsaw is the most expensive place to stay, followed by Kraków, Gdańsk and Wrocław. The further away from the big cities you go, the cheaper accommodation gets.

➡ Watch for seasonal fluctuations on rates. Summer resorts, particularly on the Baltic coast or in the mountains, have higher prices in July and August. Ski centres increase prices in winter, particularly over the Christmas and New Year holidays.

➡ Hotels in large cities often offer discounts on the weekend. Similarly, resort properties may offer lower room rates during the week.

➡ Prices normally include breakfast but not parking, which can range from 10zł a night in smaller properties to 100zł a night for garaged parking in Warsaw and Kraków.

➡ Room rates include VAT and should be the final price you pay. A small number of municipalities levy a 'tourist tax' on lodging, but this seldom amounts to more than 1zł or 2zł a night per room.

➡ Prices are quoted in *złoty*, though some larger hotels geared to foreign clients may also quote rates in euros for guests' convenience. All hotels accept *złoty* as payment.

➡ The most popular lodging website for Polish hotels is www.booking.com. Nearly all of the more popular hotels, as well as pensions and even hostels, will have a listing on the site.

Types of Rooms

Polish hotels offer a standard mix of rooms, including singles, doubles, and apartments or suites. Often hotels will also have rooms for three or four people. Hotels normally display a sign at the reception desk, listing the types of rooms and prices. Look for the following:

single room	*pokój 1-osobowy*
double room	*pokój 2-osobowy*
with bathroom	*z łazienką*
without bathroom	*bez łazienki*
basin in room only	*z umywalką*

➡ Prices for double rooms may vary depending on whether the room offers twin beds or one full-sized bed, with the latter generally more expensive.

➡ Some properties do not have dedicated single rooms, but may offer a double at a reduced rate. It never hurts to ask.

Hotels

Hotels account for the majority of accommodation

SLEEPING PRICE RANGES

Accommodation listings are grouped by price then ordered by preference. Prices listed are for an average double room in high season, with private bathroom and including breakfast.

€	less than 150zł
€€	150–400zł
€€€	more than 400zł

options in Poland, encompassing a variety of old and new places, ranging from basic to ultra-plush.

At the top end are various international and Polish hotel chains that offer high-standard accommodation to a mostly business-oriented clientele, usually at prices aimed at corporate expense accounts.

Going down the chain, there are plenty of smaller, privately owned hotels that cater to the midrange market. Many are very nice and represent excellent value, but it always pays to check the room before accepting an offer. Rates vary, but expect to pay around 160zł for a single and from 190zł for a double room.

Pensions

Pensjonaty (pensions) are small, privately run guesthouses that provide breakfast and occasionally half or full board. By and large, these are clean, comfortable and good value.

While prices vary depending on the location and comfort, they are usually cheaper than comparable hotels. Singles/doubles typically run around 130/170zł. We're big fans of Polish pensions. Our only gripe is that breakfast buffets can sometimes lack imagination (mostly simple ham and cheese plates) and they often have only instant coffee.

Hostels

Polish hostels include both the newer breed of privately owned hostels and the older, publicly run or municipal hostels. There are big differences. There are also simple, rustic mountain lodges operated by PTTK (Polish Tourist & Sightseeing Association).

PRIVATE HOSTELS

You will usually only find these in cities like Kraków, Warsaw, Zakopane, Wrocław, Poznań and Łódź. Standards are often higher than in basic youth hostels and prices are roughly the same. They typically offer shared dorm-room accommodation, with higher prices charged for rooms with fewer bunks.

→ Private hostels usually provide group kitchens, laundry facilities and sometimes a lounge and bar.

→ Beds normally come with sheets included, and rooms should have lockers to guard your things when you're not around.

→ Free wi-fi and computers are often available to surf the net, and friendly multilingual staff can help answer questions.

→ Although marketed toward backpackers, there are no age restrictions or curfews.

PUBLIC HOSTELS

Poland has around 600 *schroniska młodzieżowe* (youth hostels), which are operated by the **Polskie Towarzystwo Schronisk Młodzieżowych** (PTSM; Polish Youth Hostel Association; www. ptsm.org.pl), a member of Hostelling International (HI).

Of these, around 20% are open year-round; the rest are open in July and August only.

→ Hostels are normally marked with a sign featuring a green triangle with the PTSM logo inside, placed over the entrance.

→ Curfew is normally 10pm, and almost all hostels are closed between 10am and 5pm.

→ Facilities and conditions of public hostels differ markedly. Some hostels are in poor shape, while others are pleasant and modern.

→ Seasonal hostels are normally located in schools while pupils are on holidays, and conditions are much more basic, with some lacking showers, kitchens and hot water. Bed sheets may not be available, so bring your own.

→ Youth hostels are open to all, members and non-members alike, and there is no age limit.

PTTK & MOUNTAIN HOSTELS

The **Polskie Towarzystwo Turystyczno-Krajoznawcze** (PTTK; Polish Tourist & Sightseeing Association; www.pttk. pl) has built up a network of its own hostels, called *dom turysty* or *dom wycieczkowy*.

They are aimed at budget travellers, providing basic accommodation for hikers and backpackers. Single rooms are a rarity, but you'll always have a choice of three- and four-bed rooms, usually with shared facilities, where you can often rent just one bed (not the whole room) for around 35zł to 45zł.

PTTK also runs a network of *schroniska górskie* (mountain hostels). Conditions are simple, but prices are low and hot meals are usually available. The more isolated mountain hostels will usually try to take in all-comers, regardless of how crowded they get, which means that in high summer beds can be scarce. Many hostels are open all year, though it's best to check at the nearest regional PTTK office before setting off.

BOOK YOUR STAY ONLINE

For more accommodation reviews by Lonely Planet authors, check out http://lonelyplanet.com/hotels/. You'll find independent reviews, as well as recommendations on the best places to stay. Best of all, you can book online.

Private Rooms

Many private homes offer rooms to let for the night. These are particularly prevalent in mountain areas or places that draw large amounts of visitors. Look for signs reading 'pokoje', 'noclegi' or 'zimmer frei' in the window.

Private rooms are often a lottery: you don't know what sort of room you'll get or who your hosts will be. It's therefore a good idea to take the room for a night or two and then extend if you decide to stay longer.

➡ Private rooms may or may not offer their own bathrooms.

➡ Breakfast and other meals may be available but not included in the basic room rate. It's best to sort this out at the beginning before taking the room.

➡ Hosts are unlikely to speak English well, but will be used to accommodating guests, so communication is usually not a problem.

➡ Expect to pay 40zł for singles and from 70zł to 100zł for doubles, depending on the standard.

Short-Term Apartment Rental

A short-term apartment rental can make sense for longer stays (three days or more) in big cities such as Warsaw and Kraków. They range from simple studios to two-bedroom luxury establishments, and are often centrally located.

➡ Expect apartments to be fully equipped with towels and bed sheets. Better places may have a washing machine as well as kitchen appliances.

➡ Note payment is usually made in cash upfront or by credit card transfer over the internet. It's always a good idea to look at the property first before surrendering any money.

➡ Peer-to-peer rental sites have become popular in recent years, and large cities, including Warsaw and Kraków, now have dozens of private apartments listed on these sites.

Camping

Poland has more than 500 camping and bivouac sites registered at the **Polish Federation of Camping**

& Caravanning (☎22 810 6050; www.pfcc.eu). The sites are distributed throughout the country and can be found in all the major cities (usually on the outskirts), in many towns and in the countryside.

About 40% of registered sites are camping grounds with full facilities, including lighting, electricity, running water, showers, kitchen and caravan pitches. The remaining 60% are bivouac sites, the equivalent of very basic camp sites, usually equipped with toilets and not much else.

➡ Many places also have wooden cabins for rent, which are similar to very basic hotel rooms.

➡ Most camping grounds are open from May to September, but some run only from June to August.

➡ Fees are usually charged per tent site, plus an extra fee per person and per car. Some camping grounds levy an additional fee for electricity use.

Business Hours

Most places adhere to the following hours. Shopping centres generally have longer hours and are open from 9am to 8pm on Saturday and Sunday. Museums are usually closed on Mondays, and have shorter hours outside of the high season.

Banks 9am-4pm Mon-Fri, 9am-1pm Sat (varies)

Offices 9am-5pm Mon-Fri, 9am-1pm Sat (varies)

Post Offices 8am-7pm Mon-Fri, 8am-1pm Sat (cities)

Restaurants 11am-10pm daily

Shops 8am-6pm Mon-Fri, 10am-2pm Sat

Children

Travelling with children in Poland doesn't create any specific problems. Children

---

PRACTICALITIES

➡ **Newspapers & Magazines** Catch up on Polish current affairs at the Warsaw Voice website (www.warsawvoice. pl). Foreign newspapers can be found at Empik stores, bookshops and newsstands in the lobbies of upmarket hotels.

➡ **Radio** The state-run Polskie Radio is the main radio broadcaster, operating on AM and FM in every corner of the country; all programs are in Polish.

➡ **Television** Poland has two state-owned, countrywide TV channels: TVP1 and TVP2, the latter of which is more educational and culture focused. There are also several private channels, including the countrywide PolSat.

➡ **Smoking** Banned in all public indoor spaces, including bars and restaurants. While a few establishments defy the ban, the vast majority have complied. Most hotels are also entirely smoke-free.

➡ **Weights & Measures** Poland uses the metric system.

enjoy privileges on local transport, with accommodation and with entertainment; age limits for particular freebies or discounts vary from place to place, but are not often rigidly enforced. Basic supplies for younger children are readily available in cities. For general suggestions on how to make a family trip easier, pick up a copy of Lonely Planet's *Travel with Children*.

Customs Regulations

➤ Travellers arriving from non-EU countries can bring in up to 200 cigarettes, 50 cigars or 250g of pipe tobacco, up to 2L of non-sparkling wine, and up to 1L of spirits.

➤ Travellers arriving from an EU member state can import up to 800 cigarettes, 200 cigars or 1kg of pipe tobacco, and up to 110L of beer, 90L of wine and 10L of spirits. This is seldom checked.

➤ The export of items manufactured before 9 May 1945 is prohibited without an export permit (*pozwolenie eksportowe*). Official antique dealers may offer to help you out with the paperwork, but the procedure is bureaucratic and time-consuming.

Discount Cards

Several cities and regions offer short-term 'tourist' cards. These usually provide discounted or free admission to museums, galleries and cultural institutions. Some also provide free public transport. Cards are normally available at tourist information offices and other sales points. Check online for details.

Popular discount cards include the **Warsaw Pass** (www.warsawpass.com), **Kraków Card** (www.krakow card.com) and **Tri-City**

Tourist Card (www.gdansk4u. pl) for use in Gdańsk and Sopot.

Hostel Cards
A HI membership card can get you a 10% to 25% discount on youth-hostel prices, though some hostels don't give discounts to foreigners. Bring the card with you, or get one issued in Poland at the provincial branch offices of the PTSM in the main cities. Go to www.ptsm.org.pl to find an office.

Student Cards
Students receive great discounts in Poland, including price reductions on museum entries, as well as on some public transport. To qualify you need to be under the age of 26 and have a valid International Student Identity Card (ISIC). The website www.isic.pl has a list of hostels and establishments that honour the ISIC card. Purchase cards online or at **Almatur** (www.almatur.com. pl), which has offices in major cities.

Electricity

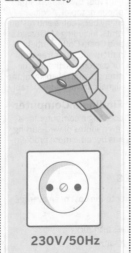

230V/50Hz

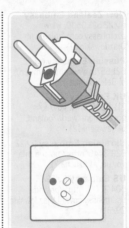

230V/50Hz

Embassies & Consulates

The website http://embassy-finder.com maintains an up-to-date list of consulates and embassies around the world. Embassies are located in Warsaw, while several countries maintain consulates in other cities in Poland.

Australian Embassy (☎22 521 3444; www.poland. embassy.gov.au; ul Nowogrodzka 11)

Belarusian Embassy (☎22 742 0990; www.poland. mfa.gov.by; ul Wiertnicza 58)

Canadian Embassy (☎22 584 3100; http://poland. gc.ca; ul Matejki 1/5)

French Embassy (☎22 529 3000; www.ambafrance-pl. org; ul Piękna 1)

German Embassy (☎22 584 1700; www.warschau. diplo.de; ul Jazdów 12)

Irish Embassy (☎22 564 2200; www.dfa.ie/irish-embassy/poland; ul Mysia 5)

Japanese Embassy (☎22 696 5000; www.pl.emb-japan. go.jp; ul Szwoleżerów 8)

New Zealand Embassy
(✆22 521 0500; www.
nzembassy.com/poland; al
Ujazdowskie 51)

Russian Embassy (✆22
621 5575; www.poland.mid.ru;
ul Belwederska 49)

UK Embassy (✆22
311 0000; www.gov.uk/
government/world/poland;
ul Kawalerii 12)

Ukrainian Embassy (✆22
629-3446; http://poland.mfa.
gov.ua; Al Szucha 7)

US Embassy (✆22
504 2000; http://poland.
usembassy.gov; Al Ujazdowskie
29/31)

Food

For an in-depth discussion
of Polish cuisine, see Eat &
Drink Like a Local (p37).

Gay & Lesbian Travellers

Homosexuality is legal in
Poland but not openly toler-
ated. Polish society is conservative and for the most
part remains hostile towards
the LGBTQ community.

The Polish gay and lesbian
scene is fairly discreet; Warsaw and Kraków are the best
places to find bars, clubs
and gay-friendly accommo-
dation, and Sopot is noted
as gay-friendly compared to
the rest of Poland. The best
sources of information for
Poland's scene are the somewhat dated http://warsaw.
gayguide.net and www.queer.
pl (in Polish).

Insurance

Insurance can cover you for
medical expenses, theft or
loss, and also for cancellation
of, or delays in, any of your
travel arrangements. There
are a variety of policies and
your travel agent can provide
recommendations.

Worldwide travel insur-
ance is available at www.
lonelyplanet.com/bookings.
You can buy, extend and
claim online anytime – even
if you're already on the road.

Always read the small
print of a policy carefully
and make sure the policy
includes health care and
medication in Poland. Some
policies specifically exclude
'dangerous activities' such as
scuba diving, motorcycling,
skiing, mountaineering and
even trekking.

Internet Access
Wi-Fi

Poland is well wired, and the
majority of hotels, above a
basic pension, offer some
form of internet access (normally wi-fi) for you to log on
with your own laptop, smartphone or tablet. Additionally,
many bars, cafes and restaurants, including McDonald's
and Costa Coffee outlets
nationwide, offer free wi-fi
for customers, though the
strength and reliability of the
signal can vary considerably.

Finding a Computer

Locating a computer for a
few minutes of web-surfing
has become more problem-
atic. Many hotels seem to
be dropping the practice of
making a computer terminal
available for guests, although
some still do, including many
private hostels. Larger hotels
will sometimes have a business centre for guests to use.

The situation with internet
cafes is much the same. As
more and more Poles pur-
chase their own computers,
the number of internet cafes
has dropped. Still, there are
some around (and we've
done our best to find them).
Other alternatives for finding
a computer include tourist
information offices, which
usually have a terminal on
hand for a few minutes of
gratis surfing, and local
libraries.

Legal Matters

Foreigners in Poland, as
elsewhere, are subject to
the laws of the host country.
While your embassy or consulate is the best stop in any
emergency, bear in mind that
there are some things it can't
do for you, like getting local
laws or regulations waived
because you're a foreigner,
investigating a crime, providing legal advice or rep-
resentation in civil or criminal
cases, getting you out of jail
and lending you money.

A consul can, however,
issue emergency passports,
contact relatives and friends,
advise on how to transfer
funds, provide lists of reliable
local doctors, lawyers and
interpreters, and visit you
if you've been arrested or
jailed.

Maps

Poland produces good quality, inexpensive maps that
can be purchased at tourist
information offices, bookstores and many large petrol
stations.

Local mapmakers **Demart**
and **Compass** both produce

EATING PRICE RANGES

The following price ranges refer to the cost of an average
main-course item.

€	less than 20zł
€€	20-40zł
€€€	more than 40zł

reliable city and hiking maps. Prices range from 14zł to 20zł per map.

You probably won't need to buy special maps for cities and tourist hot spots, but they will come in handy for smaller cities and especially on hiking and biking trips. Stock up on maps in big cities as you go along, since they may not be available locally.

Don't forget to bring along your satellite navigation system if you are driving or plan on renting a car. Polish navigation maps are usually included in most companies' European maps packages.

Money

The Polish currency is the *złoty*, abbreviated to zł and pronounced *zwo*-ti. It is divided into 100 *groszy*, which are abbreviated to gr. Banknotes come in denominations of 10zł, 20zł, 50zł, 100zł and 200zł, and coins in 1gr, 2gr, 5gr, 10gr, 20gr and 50gr, and 1zł, 2zł and 5zł. It's a stable currency that has held its own with respect to the euro and US dollar in recent years.

Keep some small-denomination notes and coins for shops, cafes and restaurants – getting change for the 100zł notes that ATMs often spit out can be a problem.

ATMs

ATMs are ubiquitous in cities and towns, and even the smallest hamlet is likely to have at least one. The majority accept Visa and MasterCard.

➡ Polish ATMs require a four-digit PIN code.

➡ Inform your bank before travelling abroad to avoid having your card blocked by bank security when overseas transactions start appearing on your account.

➡ You'll often be given the choice to convert your ATM transaction to your home currency on the spot, but you'll get a better rate if you decline the option and choose 'Polish złoty'.

Cash

Change money at banks or *kantors* (private currency-exchange offices). Find these in town centres as well as travel agencies, train stations, post offices and department stores. Rates vary, so it's best to shop around.

➡ *Kantors* are usually open between 9am and 6pm on weekdays and to 2pm on Saturday, but some open longer and a few stay open 24 hours.

➡ *Kantors* usually exchange cash only against major world currencies and neighbouring countries' currencies. The most common and easily changed are US dollars, euros and UK pounds.

➡ There's usually no commission on transactions: the rate you get is what is written on the board (every *kantor* has a board displaying its exchange rates).

Credit Cards

Visa and MasterCard are widely accepted for goods and services. The only time you may experience a problem is at small establishments or for a very small transaction. American Express cards are typically accepted at larger hotels and restaurants, though they are not as widely recognised as other cards.

Credit cards can also be used to get cash advances.

International Transfers

Have money sent to you through the **Western Union** (www.westernunion.com) money-transfer service, which is generally quick and reliable, though fees can add

up. Western Union outlets can be found in all Polish cities and most large towns.

Taxes

Poland's VAT is calculated at various rates depending on the product. The top rate is 23%. The tax is normally included in the prices of goods and services as marked.

Tipping

➡ In restaurants, tip 10% of the bill to reward good service. Leave the tip in the pouch the bill is delivered in or hand the money directly to the server.

➡ Tip hairdressers and other personal services 10% of the total.

➡ Taxis drivers won't expect a tip, but it's fine to round the fare up to the nearest 5zł or 10zł increment for good service.

➡ Tipping in hotels is essentially restricted to the top-end establishments, which usually have decent room service staff and porters, who all expect to be tipped.

Postal Services

Postal services are provided by **Poczta Polska** (www.poczta-polska.pl). In large cities there will be a dozen or more post offices, of which the *poczta główna* (main post office) will have the widest range of facilities, including (sometimes) poste restante, fax and currency exchange.

➡ Postal service is reliable. Letters and postcards sent by air take less than a week to reach a European destination and two weeks if sent anywhere else.

➡ A standard letter, including a postcard, up to 50g costs 5.20zł to mail within Europe and 5.20zł to the rest of the world. Have letters and packages weighed at the post office to ensure proper postage.

Public Holidays

New Year's Day 1 January

Epiphany 6 January

Easter Sunday March or April

Easter Monday March or April

State Holiday 1 May

Constitution Day 3 May

Pentecost Sunday Seventh Sunday after Easter

Corpus Christi Ninth Thursday after Easter

Assumption Day 15 August

All Saints' Day 1 November

Independence Day 11 November

Christmas 25 and 26 December

Telephone Services

Domestic & International Calls

Poland has dropped its former system of using city or area codes, and all telephone numbers, landline and mobile, have nine digits. Landlines are written ☑12 345 6789, with the first two numbers corresponding to the former city code. Mobile phone numbers are written ☑123 456 789.

To call abroad from Poland, dial the international access code (☑00), then the country code, then the area code (minus any initial zero) and the number. To dial Poland from abroad, dial your country's international access code, then ☑48 (Poland's country code) and then the unique nine-digit local number.

Mobile/Cell Phones

Poland uses the GSM 900/1800 network, which is compatible with the rest of Europe and Australia but not always with the North American GSM or CDMA systems; check with your service provider.

Most smartphones are multiband, meaning that they are compatible with a variety of international networks. Before bringing your own phone to Poland, check with your service provider to make sure it is compatible, and beware of calls being routed internationally (very expensive for a 'local' call).

If you have a GSM multiband phone that you can unlock (check with your service provider), it is generally cheapest and easiest to buy a Polish prepaid SIM card. They sell for as little as 10zł and can be obtained relatively quickly and painlessly at any provider shop (GSM, Orange etc). No ID is required, and top-ups can be bought at phone shops, newspaper kiosks and even some ATMs.

Even if your smartphone is not compatible or unlocked, it can still be used as a wi-fi device. To avoid any unwanted charges, simply switch your phone to 'airplane' mode on arrival, which blocks out calls and text messages, and then enable wi-fi. Also turn off your phone's 'data roaming' setting to avoid unwanted roaming fees.

Phonecards

Public phones usually require a phonecard, which you can buy from post offices and newspaper kiosks. Orange/TP cards cost 9/15/24zł for a 15-/30-/60-*impuls* (unit) card. A 60-*impuls* card is enough for a 10-minute call to the UK, or an eight-minute call to the USA.

Alternatively, buy a calling card from a private telephone service provider, such as **Telegrosik** (www.telegrosik.pl), whose international rates are even cheaper.

Time

All of Poland lies within the same time zone, GMT/UTC+1, which is the same as most of continental Europe. Polish local time is one hour

---

SHIFTING BORDERS

Poland is a member of the EU's common border area, the Schengen zone, and frontier crossings to neighbouring EU countries, including Germany, the Czech Republic, Slovakia and Lithuania, no longer involve passports or visas.

This situation does not apply for visiting Belarus, Ukraine or Russia's Kaliningrad enclave. For Belarus, most travellers will need to secure a visa in advance from a Belarusian consulate. You'll need a valid passport, photo and application. See the Belarusian foreign ministry website for details: www.mfa.gov.by.

The situation for Ukraine and Kaliningrad is mixed. For Ukraine, citizens of the EU, USA and Canada do not need a visa for stays up to 90 days, but citizens of Australia and New Zealand (at the time of writing) need to get a visa in advance. Check the Ukrainian foreign ministry website (www.mfa.gov.ua) for details.

Everyone needs a Russian visa to enter Kaliningrad, though citizens from the EU and a handful of other countries, such as Switzerland and Japan, can obtain short-term tourist visas at the border. These need to be arranged via local agencies. Travellers from other countries are best advised to check with the Russian embassy in their home capital.

ahead of London and six hours ahead of New York.

Poland observes Daylight Saving Time (DST), and moves the clock forward one hour at 2am on the last Sunday in March, and back again at 3am on the last Sunday in October.

Toilets

➡ Toilets are labelled 'toaleta' or 'WC'.

➡ Men should look for 'dla panów' or 'męski', or a door marked by an upside-down triangle.

➡ Women should head for 'dla pań' or 'damski', or a door marked with a circle.

➡ Public toilets in Poland are few and far between and often not very clean.

➡ The fee for a public toilet is usually 1zł or 2zł, collected by a toilet attendant sitting at the door. Have small change ready.

Tourist Information

Poland's official tourist information portal is www.poland. travel. It's a trove of useful information, with a large English-language section on festivals and events, accommodation, and tips on what to see and do.

On the ground, many towns have set up local tourist information offices that vary greatly in terms of usefullness and language ability, though at the very least they should be able to provide a free walking map of the city and practical advice on places to stay and eat.

Travellers with Disabilities

Poland is not well equipped for people with disabilities, even though there have been significant improvements in recent years. Wheelchair ramps are available at some upmarket hotels and restaurants, though public transport will be a challenge for anyone with mobility problems. Few offices, museums or banks provide special facilities for travellers with disabilities.

There are several useful websites for travellers with disabilities. If your Polish is up to snuff, try www.niepelno sprawni.pl for up-to-date information on the current situation for people with disabilities in Poland. In the USA, travellers with disabilities can contact the **Society for Accessible Travel & Hospitality** (www.sath.org). In the UK, a useful contact is **Disability Rights UK** (www. disabilityrightsuk.org).

Visas

EU citizens do not need visas and can stay indefinitely. Citizens of the USA, Canada, Australia, New Zealand, Israel, Japan and many other countries can stay in Poland for up to 90 days without a visa.

Other nationalities should check with their local Polish embassy or at the Polish Ministry of Foreign Affairs website (www.msz.gov.pl).

Work

Without a high standard of Polish, most people will need to arrange a job in Poland through an international company or be prepared to teach English. Teaching standards are high, however, and you'll probably need a TEFL (Teaching English as a Foreign Language) certificate to secure a job. The website **International TEFL Academy** (www. internationalteflacademy.com) offers handy tips for getting started.

Transport

GETTING THERE & AWAY

Entering the Country

Passport

EU citizens need only a valid ID to travel in Poland. For everyone else, a passport is required. Note some airlines may deny travel to passengers whose passports are within six months of expiration from date of departure.

Air

Airports & Airlines

Most international flights to Poland arrive at **Warsaw Frédéric Chopin Airport** (Lotnisko Chopina Warszawa; ☎22 650 4220; www.lotnisko-chopina.pl; ul Żwirki i Wigury 1). Warsaw has a second, smaller airport, **Warsaw Modlin Airport** (☎801 80 1880; www.modlinairport.pl; ul Generała Wiktora Thommée 1a), 35km north of the city, which handles budget flights.

Other international air gateways:

Gdańsk Lech Wałęsa Airport (☎801 066 808, 52 567 3531; www.airport.gdansk.pl; ul Słowackiego 210)

Katowice Airport (Port Lotniczy Katowice; ☎32 392 7000; www.katowice-airport.com; ul Wolności 90, Pyrzowice; ☎)

Kraków-John Paul II International Airport (KRK; ☎information 12 295 5800; www.krakowairport.pl; Kapitana Mieczysława Medweckiego 1, Balice; ☎)

Łódź Airport (www.airport.lodz.pl)

Lublin Airport (www.airport.lublin.pl)

Rzeszów Airport (www.rzeszowairport.pl)

Wrocław Airport (☎71 358 1381; www.airport.wroclaw.pl; ul Graniczna 190)

Poland's national carrier is **LOT** (☎801 703 703; www.lot.com). LOT offers regular service to Poland from throughout Europe, including from many capital cities. Outside Europe it has direct flights to/from New York, Chicago, Toronto, Tel Aviv and Beijing, among others.

Many national and major world carriers operate regular flights to Poland, normally between their national capital and/or large cities and Warsaw.

Additionally, several budget carriers service the Polish market. These usually service smaller airports such as Warsaw Modlin, Łódź, Katowice and Rzeszów, though some fly to Kraków as well.

EasyJet (www.easyjet.com)

GermanWings/Eurowings (www.germanwings.com)

Jet2 (www.jet2.com)

Norwegian (www.norwegian.com)

Ryanair (www.ryanair.com)

Wizz Air (www.wizzair.com)

Land

Border Crossings

As a member of the EU, Poland has open borders (and plenty of rail and road crossings) on its western and southern frontiers with Germany, the Czech Republic and Slovakia. Crossings with EU member Lithuania, on the northeastern end of the country, are also open.

It's a different story moving east and north into Ukraine, Belarus and Russia's Kaliningrad enclave, which form part of the EU's external border and may require **visas and advance planning** (p426).

The following is a list of 24-hour border crossings for travelling to Poland's non-EU neighbours:

Belarusian border (south to north): Terespol, Kuźnica

Russian (Kaliningrad) border (east to west): Bezledy-Bagrationowsk, Gronowo

Ukrainian border (south to north): Medyka, Hrebenne-Rawa Ruska, Dorohusk

Belarus, Lithuania, Russia & Ukraine

BUS

➡ Several coach operators link Warsaw with cities to the north and east of Poland. These include **Eurolines** (www.eurolines.pl), **Ecolines** (www.ecolines.net) and **Polski Bus** (www.polskibus.com).

➡ The best advice is to consult the online timetables for current routes and prices. Sample fares and travel times from Warsaw:

Minsk From €30, 12 hours

Vilnius From €10, eight hours

Kyiv From €40, 14 hours

➡ Ecolines runs daily to Rīga, Latvia, from where it's possible to transfer to coaches bound for St Petersburg (from €72, 24 hours).

➡ It's also possible to cross the border into Belarus by bus from the eastern city of Białystok, though service tends to be erratic. As we were researching, five buses a day ran to Hrodno (€10, two hours) in Belarus.

TRAIN

Ukraine There are overnight trains each day, from Warsaw to Kyiv (from €90, 18 hours) and from Kraków to Lviv (from €50, 11 hours). Both trains have sleeping cars. Watch timetables carefully to make sure the train bypasses Belarus and does not require a Belarusian transit visa.

Belarus & Russia There is also regular train service from Warsaw to Minsk (from €80, 10 hours). These trains are often sleeper-only, in which case a sleeping berth will be automatically included in your ticket price. The daily *Polonez* train passes through Brest and Minsk on its way to Moscow (from €130, 19 hours).

Lithuania Rail connections to Lithuania have been hampered in recent years by construction work; at the time of writing, bus travel was the best way of reach-

ing the country. In theory, there should be at least one daily train from Warsaw to Vilnius (from €25, nine hours) that runs via Suwałki (and bypasses Belarus).

Czech Republic & Slovakia

BUS

➡ Several bus companies link major Polish cities to Prague and other points in the Czech Republic.

➡ **Polski Bus** (www.polskibus.com) offers daily bus service between Warsaw (€25, 10 hours) and Prague via Wrocław (€20, five hours). The company also runs a daily service from Warsaw to Bratislava (€30, 10 hours).

➡ From Kraków, **Tiger Express** (www.tigerexpress.eu) minibus service runs to Prague (€25, six hours), as

---

FROM WESTERN EUROPE TO POLAND BY LAND

Bus

Eurolines (www.eurolines.pl) operates an extensive network of bus routes all over Western Europe. Standards, reliability and comfort vary from bus to bus but on the whole are not bad. Most buses are from the modern generation, and come equipped with air-conditioning, toilet facilities and a DVD player.

As a rough guide only, average one-way fares and journey times between some Western European cities and Warsaw are as follows:

TO	FARE (€)	TIME (HR)
Amsterdam	70	21
Brussels	70	21
Cologne	60	20
Frankfurt	70	19
Hamburg	45	17
Munich	70	20
Paris	75	27
Rome	100	27

Train

A number of German cities are linked by train (direct or indirect) with major Polish cities. Direct connections with Warsaw include Berlin, Cologne, Dresden and Leipzig. There are also direct trains between Berlin and Kraków (from €60, eight to 10 hours).

The Warsaw–Berlin route (via Frankfurt/Oder and Poznań; from €60, six hours) is serviced by several trains a day.

There are no direct trains from Brussels (Bruxelles-Nord) to Warsaw (from €100, 13½ hours); if making this trip the quickest route is via Cologne. From Paris to Warsaw (€100, 17 hours), a change is often required in Cologne.

well as to Slovak cities such as Košice (€30, six hours).

➡ From Zakopane, regional bus company Strama (www.strama.eu) runs regular coach transport to Poprad, Slovakia (€5, two hours).

TRAIN

➡ There are daily express trains from Warsaw to Prague (€50, eight hours) and Bratislava (€90, eight hours).

➡ Service between Prague and Kraków (€40, eight hours) normally requires a change in Katowice.

UK
BUS

Eurolines (www.eurolines.pl) operates between London and major Polish cities, including Warsaw (one way about €90, 26½ hours). The frequency of the service varies depending on the season. Obtain information and buy tickets from the website or any local travel agency.

TRAIN

You can travel from London to Warsaw via Brussels (20 hours). The normal 2nd-class, one-way fare is |around €150.

Sea

Ferry services connect Poland's Baltic-coast ports of Gdańsk, Gdynia and Świnoujście to destinations in Scandinavia.

Polferries (☑801 003 171; www.polferries.pl) Operates car ferries from Gdańsk Nowy Port to Nynäshamn in Sweden (adult/concession Skr680/580, 19 hours, up to four times weekly). Information, bookings and tickets can be obtained online or from travel agents.

Stena Line (☑58 660 9200; www.stenaline.pl) Operates ferries to/from Karlskrona, Sweden (adult 165zł to 195zł, concession 140zł to 165zł, 10½ to 12 hours, two or three daily). Services depart from a ferry terminal 5km

northwest of central Gdynia. Obtain information and buy tickets online.

Unity Line (☑913 595 600; www.unityline.pl) Runs daily ferries from the northwestern port of Świnoujście to Ystad, Sweden (adult 195/345zł one way/return, concession 150/276zł one way/return, seven hours). Information and tickets are available online.

GETTING AROUND

Air

LOT (☑801 703 703; www.lot.com) operates a comprehensive network of domestic routes. There are regular flights between Warsaw and Gdańsk, Katowice, Kraków, Poznań, Rzeszów, Szczecin and Wrocław. Many flights between regional cities travel via Warsaw and connections aren't always convenient.

The regular one-way fare on any of the direct flights to/from Warsaw starts at around 150zł and can reach up to 400zł and higher. Tickets can be booked and bought at any LOT office, online through the LOT website, or from travel agencies.

There's no departure tax on domestic flights.

Bicycle

Poland has great potential as a place to tour by bicycle – most of the country is flat and you can throw your bike on a train to cover long distances quickly. Camping equipment isn't essential, as hotels and hostels are usually no more than a day's ride apart, although carrying your own camping gear will give you more flexibility.

Cycling shops and repair centres are popping up in large cities, and in some of the major tourist resorts.

Likewise, the number of shops offering bike rentals is on the increase; you'll be able to hire a bike in most major

cities. The going rate for rentals is about 8/30zł per hour/day.

Road Conditions

➡ Major roads carry heavy traffic and are best avoided. Instead, plan your route along minor roads, which are usually much less crowded and in reasonable shape.

➡ Stock up on detailed hiking maps, which normally show bike trails as well as walking trails.

➡ Some drivers hug the side of the road to give cars and trucks more room to overtake, passing perilously close to cyclists. Note that in Poland cyclists are not allowed to ride two abreast.

➡ Cities are often not the most pleasant places to cycle, though many cities now have dedicated cycle paths and more are planned for the future. The main problem is drivers who often don't have much regard for two-wheeled travellers.

Taking Your Bike on the Train

Many – but not all – trains allow you to transport bikes.

➡ When buying your ticket at the station, inform the ticket seller you have a bike and they will let you know whether it's allowed on board. Online timetables usually note whether bikes are permitted.

➡ Bikes require a separate ticket, ranging in price from 7zł to 10zł, depending on the type of train.

➡ Many trains have special carriages equipped to carry bicycles and these will be marked. Other times you'll have to stow the bike in a baggage car. If the train has no baggage car, bikes are only permitted in the first and last carriages of the train. If you have to stow your bike there, try to sit near it and keep it out of the way of other passengers.

➡ Bikes cannot be taken on sleeping cars.

Security

➡ Poland is famous for bike theft. Always firmly lock your bike to a stationary object and try not to leave the bike unattended for too long.

➡ Many hotels have secure luggage rooms, which are normally fine for overnight storage; if in doubt, take your bike with you into your room.

➡ Trains pose particular risk of theft. If you have to leave your bike in a baggage car, try to sit near the car and check on your bike periodically. Lock your bike to a fixed part of the rail car if possible.

Boat

Poland has a long coastline and lots of rivers and canals, but passenger-boat services are limited and operate only in summer. There are no regular boats running along the main rivers or along the coast.

➡ Several cities, including Szczecin, Gdańsk, Toruń, Poznań, Wrocław and Kraków, have local river cruises during the summer, and a few coastal ports (Kołobrzeg and Gdańsk) offer sea excursions. There are also trips out of Elbląg to Frombork and Krynica Morska.

➡ Tourist boats are available in the Augustów area, where they ply part of the Augustów Canal.

Bus

Poland has a comprehensive bus network (far greater than the rail network) covering nearly every town and village accessible by road. Buses are often more convenient than trains over short distances, and occasionally over longer ones, when, for instance, the train route involves a long detour.

The frequency of service varies greatly: on the main routes there may be a bus leaving every quarter of an hour or so, whereas some small remote villages may get only one bus a day. Ticket prices also vary due to fierce competition between bus companies, so shop around.

Costs

Approximate fares for intercity bus journeys are as follows:

DISTANCE (KM)	FARE (ZŁ)
20	6-8
40	10-14
60	14-16
80	16-18
100	20-25
150	25-30
200	30-35
250	40-45
300	45-50

Note: while prices listed were accurate at the time of research, don't be surprised to

POLISH BUS COMPANIES

Most of Poland's bus transport is operated by the former state bus company, Państwowa Komunikacja Samochodowa (PKS), although deregulation of the bus system has made room for dozens of private operators. What this means for travellers is a broader range of options and frequent promotions.

'PKS' can be a good code word when seeking directions to bus stations – it's now a term for buses in general.

You can find details of PKS services online at its various websites, which mostly take the form of www.pks.warszawa.pl, www.pks.krakow.pl etc. Just insert the city or town you will depart from before '.pl' in the web address. If the site doesn't exist, chances are the link will redirect to a local bus company.

Most cities have a main bus station (*dworzec autobusowy PKS*) that's often located conveniently close to the train station to allow for easy transfers. Bus stations usually have only basic facilities (no left-luggage service or even a place for coffee), but most do have some sort of information counter or at least a posted timetable.

PKS has many private competitors, both locally and on the national scene. The main nationwide competitor is Polski Bus (www.polskibus.com), which runs handy long-haul services between major cities using coaches that are modern and comfortable. It has an easy-to-use English-language timetable. Another reliable competitor – also with a good online timetable and nationwide network – is Warsaw-based PKS Polonus (www. pkspolonus.pl).

Minibuses are generally more frequent and faster than their big brothers PKS and Polski Bus, and they service more routes. There is rarely any sort of information counter, but destinations are displayed on the vehicles. Minibus stations are usually in the vicinity of the main bus station. Buy tickets from the driver.

find them a few złoty different when you hit the road.

Station Timetables

➡ Timetables are posted on boards either inside or outside PKS bus terminals. The timetable of *odjazdy* (departures) lists *kierunek* (destinations), *przez* (the places passed en route) and departure times.

➡ Check any symbols that accompany the departure time. These symbols can mean that the bus runs only on certain days or in certain seasons. They're explained in the key at the end of the timetable but can be difficult to decipher.

Tickets

➡ The only place to buy PKS tickets is at the bus station itself, either from the information/ticket counter or the bus driver. If you get on the bus somewhere along the route, you buy the ticket directly from the driver.

➡ Tickets for Polski Bus and other private national bus companies can be bought online. In this case, simply print out the ticket, or save the online ticket to your smartphone or tablet and show the driver when you board the bus.

Car & Motorcycle

Automobile Associations

The **Polski Związek Motorowy** (PZM, Polish Automobile & Motorcycle Federation; ☑emergency 19 637; www.pzm.pl) is Poland's national motoring organisation. It provides a 24-hour national roadside-assistance service. If you are a member of an affiliated automobile association, it will help you on roughly the same terms as your own organisation would. If not, you must pay for all services.

Bringing Your Own Car

Many tourists bring their own vehicles into Poland. There are no special formalities: all you need is your passport (with a valid visa if necessary), driving licence, vehicle registration document and proof of third-party insurance (called a Green Card). Fines are severe if you're caught without insurance. A nationality plate or sticker must be displayed on the back of the car.

Driving Licences

Foreign driving licences are valid in Poland for up to 90 days.

Fuel

Benzyna (petrol) is readily available at petrol stations throughout the country. There are several different kinds and grades available, including 95- and 98-octane unleaded and diesel. The price of fuel can differ from petrol station to petrol station, with the highest prices typically found on major highways. Nearly all petrol stations are self-serve and accept credit cards.

Car Hire

Car-hire agencies require a passport, valid driving licence and credit card. You need to be at least 21 or 23 years of age (depending on the company).

One-way hire within Poland is possible with most companies (usually for a fee), but most will insist on keeping the car within Poland. No company is likely to allow you to take its car beyond the eastern border.

High insurance premiums mean that car hire in Poland is not cheap, and there are seldom any promotional discounts. As a rough guide only, economy models offered by reputable local companies cost about 170/900zł per day/week (including insurance and unlimited mileage). Rates at the big international agencies start at around 230/1100zł per day/ week. It's usually cheaper to book your car from abroad or over the internet.

Avis (☑22 572 6565; www.avis.pl)

Europcar (☑22 255 5600; www.europcar.com.pl)

Hertz (☑22 500 1620; www.hertz.pl)

Local Rent-a-Car (☑22 826 7100; www.lrc.com.pl; ul Marszałkowska 140) Car-hire agency offering a midsized Opel Corsa in the summer months for €43 a day, or €273 a week, including tax, collision damage waiver (CDW), theft protection and unlimited mileage.

Road Conditions

➡ Driving for long distances in Poland is no fun. Roads are crowded, and a massive effort in road building and repair in recent years has led to many detours and delays.

➡ Poland has only a few limited-access four-lane motorways, but an abundance of two- (and some four-) lane national highways. These vary greatly as to condition and speed. Often highways pass directly through the centres of towns and villages.

Road Hazards

Drive carefully on country roads, particularly at night; there are still horse-drawn carts on Polish roads. The further off the main routes you wander, the more elderly cyclists and carts, tractors and other agricultural machinery you'll encounter.

Road Rules

Road rules are similar to much of the rest of Europe. A vehicle must be equipped with a first-aid kit, a red-and-white warning triangle and a nationality sticker on the rear; the use of seat belts is compulsory. Drinking and driving is strictly forbidden – the legal blood-alcohol level

ROAD DISTANCES (KM)

	Białystok	Bydgoszcz	Częstochowa	Gdańsk	Katowice	Kielce	Kraków	Łódź	Lublin	Olsztyn	Opole	Poznań	Rzeszów	Szczecin	Toruń	Warsaw	Wrocław
Bydgoszcz	389																
Częstochowa	410	316															
Gdańsk	379	167	470														
Katowice	485	391	75	545													
Kielce	363	348	124	483	156												
Kraków	477	430	114	565	75	114											
Łódź	322	205	121	340	196	143	220										
Lublin	260	421	288	500	323	167	269	242									
Olsztyn	223	217	404	156	479	394	500	281	370								
Opole	507	318	98	485	113	220	182	244	382	452							
Poznań	491	129	289	296	335	354	403	212	465	323	261						
Rzeszów	430	516	272	642	244	163	165	306	170	516	347	517					
Szczecin	656	267	520	348	561	585	634	446	683	484	459	234	751				
Toruń	347	46	289	181	364	307	384	159	375	172	312	151	470	313			
Warsaw	188	255	222	339	297	181	295	134	161	213	319	310	303	524	209		
Wrocław	532	265	176	432	199	221	268	204	428	442	86	178	433	371	279	344	
Zielona Góra	601	259	328	411	356	422	427	303	542	453	245	130	585	214	281	413	157

is 0.02%. Police can hit you with on-the-spot fines for speeding and other traffic offences (be sure to insist on a receipt).

➡ Speed limits are 30km/h to 50km/h in built-up areas, 90km/h on open roads, 110km/h on dual carriageways and 130km/h on motorways.

➡ Headlights must be on at all times, even during a sunny day.

➡ Motorcyclists should remember that both rider and passenger must wear helmets.

Hitching

➡ *Autostop* (hitching) is never entirely safe anywhere in the world. Travellers who decide to hitch should understand that they are taking a small but potentially serious risk. Those who choose to hitch will be safer travelling in pairs, and letting someone know where they are planning to go.

➡ That said, hitching does take place in Poland; locals can often be seen thumbing a ride from one small village to the next. Car drivers rarely stop, though, and large commercial vehicles (which are easier to wave down) expect to be paid the equivalent of a bus fare.

Local Transport

Polish cities offer excellent public transport. Every large and medium-sized city will have a comprehensive *autobus* (bus) network, while some cities will also have *tramwaj* (tram) and *trolejbus* (trolleybus) systems. Warsaw is the only city with a metro.

➡ Public transport normally operates daily from around 5am to 11pm. Service is less frequent on weekends.

➡ Trams and buses are likely to be crowded during rush hour (7am to 9am and 4.30pm to 6.30pm Monday to Friday).

➡ Timetables are usually posted at stops, but don't rely too much on their accuracy.

Tickets & Fares

Each city has a slightly different system of ticketing and fares, so be prepared to watch what the locals do and do likewise.

Most cities have a fare system based on the duration of the ride, with a standard 60-minute ticket costing around 3zł. There may be slightly cheaper tickets available for shorter rides (20 or 30 minutes) and more expensive tickets for longer ones (90 minutes).

There are many common features across Polish buses and trams:

➡ There are no conductors on board buses and trams. Buy tickets beforehand and punch or stamp them in one of the little machines installed near the doors once you enter the bus or tram.

➡ Buy tickets from newspaper kiosks like Ruch or Relay or from street stalls around the central stops.

➡ Buy several tickets at once since you may find yourself at a far-flung stop with no chance to buy tickets locally.

➡ Plain-clothes ticket inspectors are always on the prowl and foreigners are not exempt.

Taxi

Taxis are easily available and not too expensive. As a rough guide, a 5km taxi trip will cost around 20zł, and a 10km ride shouldn't cost more than 35zł. Taxi fares are higher at night (10pm to 6am), on Sunday and outside the city limits. The number of passengers (usually up to four) and the amount of luggage doesn't affect the fare.

➡ Avoid unmarked pirate taxis (called 'mafia' taxis by Poles), which usually have just a small 'taxi' sign on the roof with no name or phone number.

➡ You can flag down cabs on the street or order them by phone. We recommend ordering by phone if possible, as it cuts down the chance you'll get a rogue driver.

➡ Remember to carry small bills, so you'll be able to pay the exact fare. If you don't, it's hard to get change from a driver who's intent on charging you more.

Tours

Jarden Tourist Agency (Map p132; ☑12 421 7166; www.jarden.pl; ul Szeroka

2; ⊞3, 9, 19, 24, 50) Mainly Jewish-themed tours, including two- and three-hour walking tours of Kraków's Kazimierz and Podgórze, as well as a popular two-hour driving tour of places made famous by the film *Schindler's List*. Tours are priced per person, ranging from 40zł to 90zł, depending on the number participating.

Mazurkas Travel (☑22 536 4600; www.mazurkas.com. pl; al Wojska Polskiego 27; ⊗8.30am-4.30pm Mon-Fri) Warsaw's major tour operator offers three-hour bus tours (around 140zł per person) of the major sights, plus longer trips to Kraków and themed excursions around Poland, with the added benefit of pick-up and drop-off at your hotel.

Our Roots (Map p54; ☑22 620 0556; www.our-roots. jewish.org.pl; ul Twarda 6) Specialises in tours of Jewish sites; the Jewish Warsaw tour lasts five hours and costs around 500zł. Other tours, including to Auschwitz-Birkenau and Treblinka, can be organised on request.

PTTK Mazury (Map p372; ☑89 527 5156; www.mazury pttk.pl; ul Staromiejska 1; 10-day kayaking tour per person 1190zł; ⊗9am-6pm Mon-Fri) This travel agency runs kayak tours along the country's best rivers in and around the Great Masurian Lakes, including the 10-day Krutynia River route (known as Szlak Kajakowy Krutyni), regarded as Poland's top kayaking trip. Few come away disappointed. Tours depart daily from May to October. Prices include a kayak, food, insurance, lodging in cabins and a Polish-, English- or German-speaking guide.

The 103km trip begins at Stanica Wodna PTTK in Sorkwity, 50km east of Olsztyn, and goes down the Krutynia River and Lake Bełdany to Ruciane-Nida.

Train

Poland's train network is extensive, easy to use and reasonably priced. It's likely

to be your main means of transport for covering long distances.

That said, service to many smaller cities has been cut back in recent years, which means you may find yourself relying more on buses or a combination of bus and train.

Train Companies

For years, Polish trains were administered by the state monopoly **Polskie Koleje Państwowe (PKP)**. In the past decade, the network has been broken up into different operators that manage different routes and trains. **PKP InterCity** (IC; ☑information 19 757; www.intercity.pl) runs all of Poland's express trains, including ExpressInterCity Premium (EIP), ExpressInter-City (EIC) and TLK trains. A second main operator, **Przewozy Regionalne** (PR; ☑703 202 020; www.przewozy regionalne.pl), takes care of most other trains, including relatively fast InterRegio trains and slower Regio trains.

Both networks cover the country and work in conjunction with each other. In many cases, you'll buy tickets for both at the same station ticket windows. However, they do not honour each other's tickets – buyer beware.

Timetables & Information

Rozkład jazdy (train timetables) are posted on the walls of most stations, with *odjazdy* (departures) written on yellow boards and *przyjazdy* (arrivals) on white.

➡ In addition to departure and arrival times, timetables also include initials beside the destinations to let you know what type of train is running: EIP, EIC, TLK, IR or Regio. Faster trains are marked in red and slower trains in black.

➡ The letter 'R' in a square indicates a train with compulsory seat reservations. There may also be some small letters and/ or numbers following the

Polish Railways

departure time that show whether a train runs on holidays or weekends (there should be a key at the bottom of the timetable to help you figure it out).

ONLINE TIMETABLES

There are several useful online timetables that show schedules between routes, and which usually display prices and allow you to purchase tickets online.

www.rozklad-pkp.pl Shows information for all Polish trains.

www.rozklad.sitkol.pl Another general timetable with easy-to-use instructions in English.

www.intercity.pl Displays information for high-speed express and TLK trains.

Timetables normally require Polish spellings for cities (diacritical marks are not necessary).

Tickets

There are several options for buying tickets. Most of the time you'll purchase them at train-station ticket windows. Plan to be at the station at least half an hour before the departure time of your train.

➡ Most ticket windows, but not all, accept payment with a credit card.

➡ Don't expect ticket sellers to speak English. Write down the relevant details on a piece of paper.

➡ If a seat reservation is compulsory, you'll automatically be sold a *miejscówka* (reserved-seat ticket).

➡ You can board a train without a ticket if the ticket line's not moving and the departure is imminent. Approach the conductor to pay a small supplement from 5zł to 10zł, depending on the train.

➡ Private travel companies can help organise travel times and book tickets online. One of the best of these is **Polrail Service** (☏52 332 5781; www.polrail. com).

Costs

➡ Costs for Polish trains vary greatly depending on the type of train and the distance travelled. It pays to shop around online before buying. Generally, 1st class is around

50% more expensive than 2nd class.

➜ The most expensive trains are Intercity EIP/EIC trains. Prices for these include the basic ticket price, as well as a mandatory seat reservation.

➜ As a guideline, the approximate 2nd-class fare (including compulsory seat reservation) on an EIP train from Warsaw to Kraków is 135zł for the three-hour journey. The trip from Warsaw to Gdańsk also costs 135zł for around three hours. Going down the chain of train classifications, TLK trains offer similar speeds but usually cost much less. The journey from Warsaw to Kraków on a TLK train costs 54zł and takes three hours. The journey from Warsaw to Gdańsk costs 60zł and takes five hours.

➜ The following table shows a rough approximation of fares by distance for TLK trains.

DISTANCE (KM)	FARE (ZŁ)
50	18
100	28
150	38
200	40
250	45
300	50
350	52
400	55
450	58
500	65

Discounts

➜ Children under four travel for free. Older children and students up to age 26 are usually entitled to some form of discount, but the system is complicated and seems to change year by year. Your best bet is to ask whether you qualify for a cheaper fare when you buy your ticket.

➜ If you're over 60 and planning to do a lot of

TYPES OF TRAINS

Poland's rail network has several different types of train that differ primarily by speed, cost and level of comfort. Identify the train type by the initials on station and online timetables.

ExpressInterCity Premium (EIP) This is a relatively new class of high-speed 'Pendolino' train that transits between major cities, such Warsaw, Kraków, Katowice, Wrocław and Gdańsk. Both 1st- and 2nd-class seats are available, and reservations are mandatory for both.

ExpressInterCity (EIC) One step down from EIP trains, the modern, comfortable EIC trains also run between major cities, like Warsaw–Kraków and Warsaw–Gdańsk, but are slightly less expensive. There's seating in both 1st and 2nd class, and reservations are complusory in both.

TLK (*Pociąg Twoje Linie Kolejowe;* TLK) Low-cost express trains that run between major cities at speeds approaching EIP trains, but at fares that are around 40% cheaper. TLK trains are a step down in comfort, and can be crowded. There's seating in both 1st and 2nd class; both classes require reservations. Bicycle access on TLK trains may be limited.

InterRegio (*Pociąg InterRegio;* IR) These are the standard Polish 'fast' trains running between regions, with stops at most medium-sized cities along the route. IR trains normally don't offer 1st-class seating, and no seat reservations are required.

Regio (*Pociąg Regio;* Regio/Osob) These trains are much slower as they stop at all stations along the way. These may be 2nd-class only and reservations are not required.

travelling, ask about the *karta seniora* (senior concession) card that provides a 30% discount on 1st- and 2nd-class seats. Both major Polish operators, PKP InterCity and Przewozy Regionalne, offer similar senior cards, but the two are not interchangeable.

Train Passes

If you're planning on travelling a lot, consider buying an InterRail pass. Passes are only available to those resident in Europe for at least six months and are priced in three bands: youth (under 26), adult 2nd class, and

adult 1st class. Tickets cover five/eight/10/12 days' travel within a month and range from €70 to €190. See www.interrail.net for more information.

Train Stations

Many Polish train stations are cleaning up their act these days, and stations in Kraków, Poznań and Warsaw are now attached to gleaming shopping malls. Others, such as those in Wrocław or Tarnów, are historic buildings in their own right. Most larger stations have waiting rooms, snack bars, newsagents, left luggage and toilets.

Language

Poland is linguistically one of the most homogeneous countries in Europe – more than 95% of the population has Polish as their first language. Polish belongs to the Slavic language family, with Czech and Slovak as close relatives. It has about 45 million speakers.

Polish pronunciation is pretty straightforward, as each Polish letter is generally pronounced the same way wherever it occurs.

Vowels are generally prounounced short, giving them a 'clipped' quality. Note that a is pronounced as the 'u' in 'cut', ai as in 'aisle' and ow as in 'cow'. Polish also has nasal vowels (pronounced as though you're trying to force the air through your nose), which are indicated in writing by the letters ą and ę. Depending on the letters following these vowels, they're pronounced either as an m or an n sound following the vowel, ie ą as om or on and ę as em or en.

Most Polish consonant sounds are also found in English. Note that kh is pronounced as in the Scottish loch, r is rolled and zh is pronounced as the 's' in 'leisure'. Consonants are sometimes grouped together without vowels between them, eg in pszczoła psh-cho-wa – with a bit of practice they will roll off your tongue with ease. In our pronunciation guides the apostrophe (eg in kwiecień kfye-chen') indicates that the preceding consonant is pronounced with a soft y sound.

If you read the coloured pronunciation guides in this chapter as if they were English – and not worry too much about the intricacies of Polish pronunciation – you'll be understood just fine. Note that stressed syllables are indicated with italics.

In the following phrases the masculine/ feminine, polite and informal options are included where necessary and indicated with 'm/f', 'pol' and 'inf' respectively.

WANT MORE?

For in-depth language information and handy phrases, check out Lonely Planet's *Polish Phrasebook*. You'll find it at **shop.lonelyplanet.com**.

BASICS

Hello.	Cześć.	cheshch
Goodbye.	Do widzenia.	do vee-dze-nya
Yes./No.	Tak./Nie.	tak/nye
Please.	Proszę.	pro-she
Thank you.	Dziękuję.	jyen-koo-ye
You're welcome.	Proszę.	pro-she
Excuse me./ Sorry.	Przepraszam.	pshe-pra-sham

How are you?
Jak pan/pani		yak pan/pa-nee
się miewa? (m/f pol)		shye mye-va
Jak się masz? (inf)		yak shye mash

Fine. And you?
Dobrze.		dob-zhe
A pan/pani? (m/f pol)		a pan/pa-nee
Dobrze. A ty? (inf)		dob-zhe a ti

What's your name?
Jak się pan/pani		yak shye pa-na/pa-nee
nazywa? (m/f pol)		na-zi-va
Jakie się nazywasz? (inf)		yak shye na-zi-vash

My name is ...
Nazywam się ...		na-zi-vam shye ...

Do you speak English?
Czy pan/pani mówi		chi pan/pa-nee moo-vee
po angielsku? (m/f pol)		po an-gyel-skoo
Czy mówisz		chi moo-veesh
po angielsku? (inf)		po an-gyel-skoo

I don't understand.
Nie rozumiem.		nye ro-zoo-myem

ACCOMMODATION

Where's a ...?	Gdzie jest ...?	gjye yest ...
campsite	kamping	kam-peeng
guesthouse	pokoje gościnne	po-ko-ye gosh-chee-ne
hotel	hotel	ho-tel
youth hostel	schronisko młodzieżowe	skhro-nees-ko mwo-jye-zho-ve

KEY PATTERNS

To get by in Polish, mix and match these simple patterns with words of your choice:

When's (the next bus)?
Kiedy jest (następny autobus)? — kye·di yest (nas·temp·ni ow·to·boos)

Where's (the market)?
Gdzie jest (targ)? — gjye yest (tark)

Do you have (something cheaper)?
Czy jest (coś tańszego)? — chi yest (tsosh tan'·she·go)

I have (a reservation).
Mam (rezerwację). — mam (re·zer·va·tsye)

I'd like (the menu), please.
Proszę (o jadłospis). — pro·she (o ya·dwo·spees)

I'd like to (hire a car).
Chcę (wypożyczyć samochód). — khtse (vi·po·zhi·chich sa·mo·khoot)

Can I (take a photo)?
Czy mogę (zrobić zdjęcie)? — chi mo·ge (zro·beech zdyen·chye)

Could you please (write it down)?
Proszę (to napisać). — pro·she (to na·pee·sach)

Do I need (a guide)?
Czy potrzebuję (przewodnika)? — chi po·tshe·boo·ye (pshe·vod·nee·ka)

I need (assistance).
Potrzebuję (pomoc). — po·tshe·boo·ye (po·mots)

Do you have a ... room?	*Czy jest pokój ...?*	chi yest po·kooy ...
single	*jedno-osobowy*	yed·no-o·so·bo·vi
double	*z podwójnym łóżkiem*	z pod·vooy·nim woozh·kyem

How much is it per ...?	*Ile kosztuje za ...?*	ee·le kosh·too·ye za ...
night	*noc*	nots
person	*osobę*	o·so·be
air-con	*klimatyzator*	klee·ma·ti·za·tor
bathroom	*łazienka*	wa·zhyen·ka
window	*okno*	ok·no

DIRECTIONS

Where's a/the ...?
Gdzie jest ...? — gjye yest ...

What's the address?
Jaki jest adres? — ya·kee yest ad·res

Could you please write it down?
Proszę to napisać. — pro·she to na·pee·sach

Can you show me (on the map)?
Czy może pan/pani mi pokazać (na mapie)? (m/f) — chi mo·zhe pan/pa·nee mee po·ka·zach (na ma·pye)

at the corner/ traffic lights	*na rogu/ światłach*	na ro·goo/ shfyat·wakh
behind ...	*za ...*	za ...
in front of ...	*przed ...*	pshet ...
left	*lewo*	le·vo
near ...	*koło ...*	ko·wo ...
next to ...	*obok ...*	o·bok ...
opposite ...	*naprze-ciwko ...*	nap·she-cheef·ko ...
straight ahead	*na wprost*	na fprost
right	*prawo*	pra·vo

EATING & DRINKING

I'd like to reserve a table for ...	*Chciałem/am zarezerwować stolik ...* (m/f)	khchow·em/am za·re·zer·vo·vach sto·leek ...
(two) people	*dla (dwóch) osób*	dla (dvookh) o·soob
(eight) o'clock	*na (ósmą)*	na (oos·mom)

I don't eat ...	*Nie jadam ...*	nye ya·dam ...
eggs	*jajek*	yai·ek
fish	*ryb*	rib
(red) meat	*(czerwonego) mięsa*	(cher·vo·ne·go) myen·sa
poultry	*drobiu*	dro·byoo

What would you recommend?
Co by pan/pani polecił/poleciła? (m/f) — tso bi pan/pa·nee po·le·cheew/po·le·chee·wa

What's in that dish?
Co jest w tym daniu? — tso yest v tim da·nyoo

I'd like the menu, please.
Proszę o jadłospis. — pro·she o ya·dwo·spees

That was delicious!
To było pyszne. — to bi·wo pish·ne

Cheers!
Na zdrowie! — na zdro·vye

Please bring the bill.
Proszę o rachunek. — pro·she o ra·khoo·nek

Key Words

bottle	*butelka*	boo·tel·ka

bowl	*miska*	*mee·ska*
breakfast	*śniadanie*	shnya·da·nye
cold	*zimny*	*zheem·ni*
cup	*filiżanka*	fee·lee·zhan·ka
dinner	*kolacja*	ko·la·tsya
fork	*widelec*	vee·de·lets
glass	*szklanka*	shklan·ka
grocery	*sklep spożywczy*	sklep spo·zhiv·chi
hot	*gorący*	go·ron·tsi
knife	*nóż*	noosh
lunch	*obiad*	o·byad
market	*rynek*	ri·nek
menu	*jadłospis*	ya·dwo·spees
plate	*talerz*	ta·lesh
restaurant	*restauracja*	res·tow·rats·ya
spoon	*łyżka*	wish·ka
vegetarian	*wegetariański*	ve·ge·ta·ryan'·skee
with ...	*z ...*	z ...
without ...	*bez ...*	bes ...

Meat & Fish

beef	*wołowina*	vo·wo·vee·na
chicken	*kurczak*	*koor·*chak
cod	*dorsz*	dorsh
duck	*kaczka*	*kach·*ka
fish	*ryba*	ri·ba
herring	*śledź*	shlej
lamb	*jagnięcina*	yag·nyen·*chee·*na
lobster	*homar*	ho·mar
mackerel	*makrela*	ma·*kre·*la
meat	*mięso*	myen·so
mussels	*małże*	mow·zhe
oysters	*ostrygi*	os·*tri·*gee
prawns	*krewetki*	kre·*vet·*kee
pork	*wieprzowina*	vyep·sho·*vee·*na
salmon	*łosoś*	wo·sosh
seafood	*owoce morza*	o·*vo·*tse mo·zha
trout	*pstrąg*	pstrong
tuna	*tuńczyk*	*toon'·*chik
turkey	*indyk*	een·dik
veal	*cielęcina*	chye·len·*chee·*na

Fruit & Vegetables

apple	*jabłko*	*yabw·*ko
apricot	*morela*	mo·*re·*la
bean	*fasola*	fa·*so·*la
cabbage	*kapusta*	ka·*poos·*ta
carrot	*marchewka*	mar·*khef·*ka
cauliflower	*kalafior*	ka·*la·*fyor
cherry	*czereśnia*	che·*resh·*nya
cucumber	*ogórek*	o·*goo·*rek
fruit	*owoc*	o·vots
grapes	*winogrona*	vee·no·*gro·*na
lemon	*cytryna*	tsi·*tri·*na
lentil	*soczewica*	so·che·*vee·*tsa
mushroom	*grzyb*	gzhib
nut	*orzech*	o·zhekh
onion	*cebula*	tse·*boo·*la
orange	*pomarańcza*	po·ma·*ran'·*cha
peach	*brzoskwinia*	bzhosk·*fee·*nya
pear	*gruszka*	*groosh·*ka
pepper (bell)	*papryka*	pa·*pri·*ka
plum	*śliwka*	*shleef·*ka
potato	*ziemniak*	zhyem·nyak
strawberry	*truskawka*	troos·*kaf·*ka
tomato	*pomidor*	po·*mee·*dor
vegetable	*warzywo*	va·*zhi·*vo
watermelon	*arbuz*	ar·boos

Other

bread	*chleb*	khlep
cheese	*ser*	ser
egg	*jajko*	*yai·*ko
honey	*miód*	myood
noodles	*makaron*	ma·*ka·*ron
oil	*olej*	o·ley
pasta	*makaron*	ma·*ka·*ron
pepper	*pieprz*	pyepsh
rice	*ryż*	rizh
salt	*sól*	sool
sugar	*cukier*	*tsoo·*kyer
vinegar	*ocet*	o·tset

SIGNS

Wejście	Entrance
Wyjście	Exit
Otwarte	Open
Zamknięte	Closed
Informacja	Information
Wzbroniony	Prohibited
Toalety	Toilets
Panowie	Men
Panie	Women

Drinks

beer	piwo	pee·vo
coffee	kawa	ka·va
(orange) juice	sok (pomarańczowy)	sok (po·ma·ran'·cho·vi)
milk	mleko	mle·ko
red wine	wino czerwone	vee·no cher·vo·ne
soft drink	napój	na·pooy
tea	herbata	her·ba·ta
(mineral) water	woda (mineralna)	vo·da (mee·ne·ral·na)
white wine	wino białe	vee·no bya·we

EMERGENCIES

Help!	Na pomoc!	na po·mots
Go away!	Odejdź!	o·deyj

Call the police!
Zadzwoń po policję! zad·zvon' po po·lee·tsye

Call a doctor!
Zadzwoń po lekarza! zad·zvon' po le·ka·zha

There's been an accident.
Tam był wypadek. tam biw vi·pa·dek

I'm lost.
Zgubiłem/am się. (m/f) zgoo·bee·wem/wam shye

Where are the toilets?
Gdzie są toalety? gjye som to·a·le·ti

I'm ill.
Jestem chory/a. (m/f) yes·tem kho·ri/ra

It hurts here.
Tutaj boli. too·tai bo·lee

I'm allergic to (antibiotics).
Mam alergię na (antybiotyki). mam a·ler·gye na (an·ti·byo·ti·kee)

SHOPPING & SERVICES

I'd like to buy ...
Chcę kupić ... khtse koo·peech ...

I'm just looking.
Tylko oglądam. til·ko o·glon·dam

Can I look at it?
Czy mogę to zobaczyć? chi mo·ge to zo·ba·chich

How much is it?
Ile to kosztuje? ee·le to kosh·too·ye

That's too expensive.
To jest za drogie. to yest za dro·gye

Can you lower the price?
Czy może pan/pani obniżyć cenę? (m/f) chi mo·zhe pan/pa·nee ob·nee·zhich tse·ne

There's a mistake in the bill.
Na czeku jest pomyłka. na che·koo yest po·miw·ka

ATM	bankomat	ban·ko·mat
credit card	karta kredytowa	kar·ta kre·di·to·va
internet cafe	kawiarnia internetowa	ka·vyar·nya een·ter·ne·to·va
mobile/cell phone	telefon komórkowy	te·le·fon ko·moor·ko·vi
post office	urząd pocztowy	oo·zhond poch·to·vi
tourist office	biuro turystyczne	byoo·ro too·ris·tich·ne

TIME & DATES

What time is it?
Która jest godzina? ktoo·ra yest go·jee·na

It's one o'clock.
Pierwsza. pyerf·sha

Half past (10).
Wpół do (jedenastej). fpoow do (ye·de·nas·tey)
(lit: half to 11)

morning	rano	ra·no
afternoon	popołudnie	po·po·wood·nye
evening	wieczór	vye·choor
yesterday	wczoraj	fcho·rai
today	dziś/dzisiaj	jeesh/jee·shai
tomorrow	jutro	yoo·tro
Monday	poniedziałek	po·nye·jya·wek
Tuesday	wtorek	fto·rek
Wednesday	środa	shro·da
Thursday	czwartek	chfar·tek
Friday	piątek	pyon·tek
Saturday	sobota	so·bo·ta
Sunday	niedziela	nye·jye·la
January	styczeń	sti·chen'
February	luty	loo·ti
March	marzec	ma·zhets
April	kwiecień	kfye·chyen'
May	maj	mai
June	czerwiec	cher·vyets
July	lipiec	lee·pyets
August	sierpień	shyer·pyen'
September	wrzesień	vzhe·shyen'
October	październik	pazh·jyer·neek
November	listopad	lees·to·pat
December	grudzień	groo·jyen'

NUMBERS

1	jeden	ye·den
2	dwa	dva
3	trzy	tshi
4	cztery	chte·ri
5	pięć	pyench
6	sześć	sheshch
7	siedem	shye·dem
8	osiem	o·shyem
9	dziewięć	jye·vyench
10	dziesięć	jye·shench
20	dwadzieścia	dva·jyesh·chya
30	trzydzieści	tshi·jyesh·chee
40	czterdzieści	chter·jyesh·chee
50	pięćdziesiąt	pyen·jye·shont
60	sześćdziesiąt	shesh·jye·shont
70	siedemdziesiąt	shye·dem·jye·shont
80	osiemdziesiąt	o·shem·jye·shont
90	dziewięćdziesiąt	jye·vyen·jye·shont
100	sto	sto
1000	tysiąc	ti·shonts

TRANSPORT

Public Transport

When's the ... (bus)?	Kiedy jest ... (autobus)?	kye·di yest ... (ow·to·boos)
first	pierwszy	pyerf·shi
last	ostatni	os·tat·nee
next	następny	nas·temp·ni

boat	statek	sta·tek
bus	autobus	ow·to·boos
plane	samolot	sa·mo·lot
taxi	taksówka	tak·soof·ka
ticket office	kasa biletowa	ka·sa bee·le·to·va
timetable	rozkład jazdy	ros·kwad yaz·di
train	pociąg	po·chonk

A ... ticket (to Katowice).	Proszę bilet ... (do Katowic).	pro·she bee·let ... (do ka·to·veets)
one-way	w jedną stronę	v yed·nom stro·ne
return	powrotny	po·vro·tni

What time does it get to ...?

O której godzinie przyjeżdża do ...? o ktoo·rey go·jee·nye pshi·yezh·ja do ...

Does it stop at ...?
Czy się zatrzymuje w...? chi shye za·tshi·moo·ye v ...

Please tell me when we get to ...
Proszę mi powiedzieć gdy dojedziemy do ... pro·she mee po·vye·jyech gdi do·ye·jye·mi do ...

Please take me to (this address).
Proszę mnie zawieźć pod (ten adres). pro·she mnye za·vyeshch pod (ten ad·res)

Please stop here.
Proszę się tu zatrzymać. pro·she shye too za·tshi·mach

Driving & Cycling

I'd like to hire a ...	Chcę wypożyczyć ...	khtse vi·po·zhi·chich ...
4WD	samochód terenowy	sa·mo·khoot te·re·no·vi
bicycle	rower	ro·ver
car	samochód	sa·mo·khoot
motorbike	motocykl	mo·to·tsikl

Is this the road to ...?
Czy to jest droga do ...? chi to yest dro·ga do ...

Where's a service station?
Gdzie jest stacja benzynowa? gjye yest sta·tsya ben·zi·no·va

How long can I park here?
Jak długo można tu parkować? yak dwoo·go mozh·na too par·ko·vach

I need a mechanic.
Potrzebuję mechanika. po·tshe·boo·ye me·kha·nee·ka

I've had an accident.
Miałem/am wypadek. (m/f) myow·em/am vi·pa·dek

diesel	diesel	dee·zel
leaded	ołowiowa	o·wo·vyo·va
petrol/gas	benzyna	ben·zi·na
unleaded	bezołowiowa	bes·o·wo·vyo·va

QUESTION WORDS

What?	Co?	tso
When?	Kiedy?	kye·di
Where?	Gdzie?	gjye
Which?	Który/a/e? (m/f/n)	ktoo·ri/ra/re
Who?	Kto?	kto
Why?	Dlaczego?	dla·che·go

LANGUAGE TRANSPORT

GLOSSARY

The following is a list of terms and abbreviations you're likely to come across in your travels through Poland. For other food and drink terms, see page 438.

aleja or Aleje – avenue, main city street; abbreviated to al in addresses and on maps
apteka – pharmacy

bankomat – ATM
bar mleczny – milk bar; a sort of basic self-service soup kitchen that serves very cheap, mostly vegetarian dishes
bazylika – basilica
bez łazienki – room without bathroom
biblioteka – library
bilet – ticket
biuro turystyki – travel agency
biuro zakwaterowania – office that arranges private accommodation
brama – gate
britzka – horse-drawn cart

Cepelia – a shop network selling artefacts made by local artisans
cerkiew (cerkwie) – Orthodox or Uniat church(es)
cukiernia – cake shop

Desa – chain of old art and antique sellers
dom kultury – cultural centre
dom wycieczkowy – term applied to PTTK-run hostels; also called *dom turysty*
domy wczasowe – workers' holiday homes
dwór – mansion

góra – mountain
gospoda – inn, tavern, restaurant
grosz – unit of Polish currency, abbreviated to gr; plural groszy; see also *złoty*

jaskinia – cave

kancelaria kościelna – church office
kantor(s) – private currency-exchange office(s)
kawiarnia – cafe
kemping – camping
kino – cinema
kolegiata – collegiate church
komórka – literally, 'cell'; commonly used for cellular (mobile) phone
kościół – church
księgarnia – bookshop
kwatery agro-turystyczne – agrotourist accommodation
kwatery prywatne – rooms for rent in private houses

miejscówka – reserved-seat ticket
muzeum – museum

na zdrowie! – cheers!; literally, 'to the health'
noclegi – accommodation

odjazdy – departures (on transport timetables)
ostrów – island
otwarte – open

park narodowy – national park
parking strzeżony – guarded car park
pchać – pull (on door)
pensjonat(y) – pension or private guesthouse(s)
peron – railway platform
piekarnia – bakery
PKS – Państwowa Komunikacja Samochodowa; former state-run company that runs most of Poland's bus transport
Plac – Sq
poczta – post office
poczta główna – main post office
pokój 1-osobowy – single room
pokój 2-osobowy – double room
przechowalnia bagażu – left-luggage room

przez – via, en route (on transport timetables)
przyjazdy – arrivals (on transport timetables)
PTSM – Polskie Towarzystwo Schronisk Młodzieżowych; Polish Youth Hostel Association
PTTK – Polskie Towarzystwo Turystyczno-Krajoznawcze; Polish Tourist & Countryside Association

rachunek – bill or check
riksza – bicycle rickshaws
rozkład jazdy – transport timetable
Rynek – Town/Market Sq

sanktuarium – church (usually pilgrimage site)
schronisko górskie – mountain hostel, providing basic accommodation and meals, usually run by the PTTK
schronisko młodzieżowe – youth hostel
Sejm – the lower house of parliament
skansen – open-air ethnographic museum
sklep – shop
stanica wodna – waterside hostel, usually with boats, kayaks and other water-related facilities
stare miasto – old town/city
Stary Rynek – Old Town/Market Sq
stołówka – canteen; restaurant or cafeteria of a holiday home, workplace, hostel etc
święty/a (m/f) – saint; abbreviated to Św
szopka – Nativity scene

teatr – theatre
toalety – toilets

ulica – street; abbreviated to ul in addresses (and placed before the street name); usually omitted on maps
Uniat – Eastern-rite Catholics

wódka – vodka; the number one Polish spirit

z łazienką – room with bathroom

zajazd – inn (sometimes restaurant)

zamek – castle

zdrój – spa

złoty – unit of Polish currency; abbreviated to zł; divided into 100 units called grosz

Food Glossary

bażant – pheasant

befsztyk – beef steak

befsztyk tatarski – raw minced beef accompanied by chopped onion, raw egg yolk and often chopped dill, cucumber and anchovies

botwinka – soup made from the stems and leaves of baby beetroots; often includes a hard-boiled egg

bryzol – grilled beef (loin) steak

budyń – milk pudding

chłodnik – chilled beetroot soup with sour cream and fresh vegetables; served in summer only

ciastko – pastry, cake

ćwikła z chrzanem – boiled and grated beetroot with horseradish

dorsz – cod

dzik – wild boar

gęś – goose

gołąbki – cabbage leaves stuffed with minced beef and rice, sometimes also with mushrooms

grochówka – pea soup, sometimes served z grzankami (with croutons)

indyk – turkey

kaczka – duck

kapuśniak – sauerkraut and cabbage soup with potatoes

karp – carp

knedle ze śliwkami – dumplings stuffed with plums

kopytka – Polish 'gnocchi'; noodles made from flour and boiled potatoes

kotlet schabowy – a fried pork cutlet coated in breadcrumbs, flour and egg, found on nearly every Polish menu

krupnik – thick barley soup containing a variety of vegetables and small chunks of meat

kurczak – chicken

leniwe pierogi – boiled noodles served with cottage cheese

łosoś wędzony – smoked salmon

melba – ice cream with fruit and whipped cream

mizeria ze śmietaną – sliced fresh cucumber in sour cream

naleśniki – crepes; fried pancakes, most commonly z serem (with cottage cheese), z owocami (with fruit) or z dżemem (with jam), and served with sour cream and sugar

pieczeń cielęca – roast veal

pieczeń wieprzowa – roast pork

pieczeń wołowa – roast beef

pieczeń z dzika – roast wild boar

placki ziemniaczane – fried pancakes made from grated raw potato, egg and flour; served ze śmietaną (with sour cream) or z cukrem (with sugar)

polędwica po angielsku – English-style beef; roast fillet of beef

pstrąg – trout

pyzy – ball-shaped steamed dumplings made of potato flour

rosół – beef or chicken (z wołowiny/z kury) bouillon, usually served z makaronem (with noodles)

rumsztyk – rump steak

ryż z jabłkami – rice with apples

sałatka jarzynowa – 'vegetable salad'; cooked vegetables in mayonnaise, commonly known as Russian salad

sałatka z pomidorów – tomato salad, often served with onion

sarna – deer, venison

schab pieczony – roast loin of pork seasoned with prunes and herbs

serem i z makiem – dumplings with cottage cheese/poppy seeds

śledź w oleju – herring in oil with chopped onion

śledź w śmietanie – herring in sour cream

stek – steak

surówka z kapusty kiszonej – sauerkraut, sometimes served with apple and onion

sztuka mięsa – boiled beef with horseradish

zając – hare

zrazy zawijane – stewed beef rolls stuffed with mushrooms and/or bacon and served in a sour-cream sauce

zupa grzybowa – mushroom soup

zupa jarzynowa – vegetable soup

zupa ogórkowa – cucumber soup, usually with potatoes and other vegetables

zupa pomidorowa – tomato soup, usually served either z makaronem (with noodles) or z ryżem (with rice)

zupa szczawiowa – sorrel soup, usually served with hard-boiled egg

Behind the Scenes

SEND US YOUR FEEDBACK

We love to hear from travellers – your comments keep us on our toes and help make our books better. Our well-travelled team reads every word on what you loved or loathed about this book. Although we cannot reply individually to your submissions, we always guarantee that your feedback goes straight to the appropriate authors, in time for the next edition. Each person who sends us information is thanked in the next edition – the most useful submissions are rewarded with a selection of digital PDF chapters.

Visit **lonelyplanet.com/contact** to submit your updates and suggestions or to ask for help. Our award-winning website also features inspirational travel stories, news and discussions.

Note: We may edit, reproduce and incorporate your comments in Lonely Planet products such as guidebooks, websites and digital products, so let us know if you don't want your comments reproduced or your name acknowledged. For a copy of our privacy policy visit lonelyplanet.com/privacy.

OUR READERS

Many thanks to the travellers who used the last edition and wrote to us with helpful hints, useful advice and interesting anecdotes:

A Alyssa Donald, Aneta McNally, Arie van Oosterwijk, Assen Totin **B** Brian Mooney **D** Daniëlle Wolbers, David Bourchier, Debbie Greenlee **E** Elaine Silver, Emlyn Williams **G** Gillian Gardiner **J** Jalle Daels **K** Kingsley Jones **L** Lars Walter, Lucas Szymansk, Łukasz Patejuk **M** Marcia Anton, Marcus Hinske, Marie Neumann, Mark Wenig, Mathieu Gendaj, Mikolaj Stasiewicz **N** Nicolas Combremont **P** Peter Divine **R** Reinhart Eisenberg **S** Stefan Görke

AUTHORS' THANKS

Mark Baker

I would like to thank the many people who took me under their wing along the way, with a special mention for Olga Brzezińska, Magdalena Krakowska and Anna Czerwinska.

Marc Di Duca

Huge thanks go to parents-in-law Mykola and Vira for looking after the boys while I was away, and to my wife Tanya for holding the fort. Also much gratitude goes to the staff at tourist offices across the region but in particular those in Gdańsk, Świnoujście, Sopot, Olsztyn and Grudziądz.

Tim Richards

My intricate journey through forests and cities was eased by the good nature of the Polish people, who cheerfully answered questions and endured my imperfect command of their language. Thanks in particular to the staff of local tourist offices, who were always helpful. Gratitude also to Poland's rail companies, whose trains took me all over the place (and were quite punctual). Thanks too to those restaurants who were happy to tinker with Polish classics to meet my new-found vegetarianism. *Dziękuję!*

ACKNOWLEDGMENTS

Climate maps data adapted from Peel MC, Finlayson BL & McMahon TA (2007) 'Updated World Map of the Koppen-Geiger Climate Classification', *Hydrology and Earth System Sciences*, 11, 1633-44.

Cover photograph: St Mary's Basilica, Kraków, in winter, Witold Skrypczak / Getty Images ©

THIS BOOK

This is the 8th edition of Lonely Planet's *Poland* guidebook and was researched and written by Mark Baker, Marc Di Duca and Tim Richards. The previous edition of the guide was also written by the same writers, while the 6th edition was written by Tim Richards, Neal Bedford, Steve Fallon and Marika McAdam.

This guidebook was produced by the following:

Destination Editor Gemma Graham

Product Editors Elizabeth Jones, Amanda Williamson

Cartographer Valentina Kremenchutskaya

Book Designer Wendy Wright

Assisting Editors Sarah Bailey, Imogen Bannister, Victoria Harrison, Rosie Nicholson, Christopher Pitts, Jeanette Wall

Cover Researcher Naomi Parker

Language Content Branislava Vladisavljevich

Thanks to Jane Grisman, James Hardy, Andi Jones, Catherine Naghton, Karyn Noble, Lauren Wellicome, Tracy Whitmey

Index

Map Legend

Sights

- Beach
- Bird Sanctuary
- Buddhist
- Castle/Palace
- Christian
- Confucian
- Hindu
- Islamic
- Jain
- Jewish
- Monument
- Museum/Gallery/Historic Building
- Ruin
- Shinto
- Sikh
- Taoist
- Winery/Vineyard
- Zoo/Wildlife Sanctuary
- Other Sight

Activities, Courses & Tours

- Bodysurfing
- Diving
- Canoeing/Kayaking
- Course/Tour
- Sento Hot Baths/Onsen
- Skiing
- Snorkelling
- Surfing
- Swimming/Pool
- Walking
- Windsurfing
- Other Activity

Sleeping

- Sleeping
- Camping

Eating

- Eating

Drinking & Nightlife

- Drinking & Nightlife
- Cafe

Entertainment

- Entertainment

Shopping

- Shopping

Information

- Bank
- Embassy/Consulate
- Hospital/Medical
- Internet
- Police
- Post Office
- Telephone
- Toilet
- Tourist Information
- Other Information

Geographic

- Beach
- Gate
- Hut/Shelter
- Lighthouse
- Lookout
- Mountain/Volcano
- Oasis
- Park
- Pass
- Picnic Area
- Waterfall

Population

- Capital (National)
- Capital (State/Province)
- City/Large Town
- Town/Village

Transport

- Airport
- Border crossing
- Bus
- Cable car/Funicular
- Cycling
- Ferry
- Metro station
- Monorail
- Parking
- Petrol station
- S-Bahn/S-train/Subway station
- Taxi
- T-bane/Tunnelbana station
- Train station/Railway
- Tram
- Tube station
- U-Bahn/Underground station
- Other Transport

Note: Not all symbols displayed above appear on the maps in this book

Routes

- Tollway
- Freeway
- Primary
- Secondary
- Tertiary
- Lane
- Unsealed road
- Road under construction
- Plaza/Mall
- Steps
- Tunnel
- Pedestrian overpass
- Walking Tour
- Walking Tour detour
- Path/Walking Trail

Boundaries

- International
- State/Province
- Disputed
- Regional/Suburb
- Marine Park
- Cliff
- Wall

Hydrography

- River, Creek
- Intermittent River
- Canal
- Water
- Dry/Salt/Intermittent Lake
- Reef

Areas

- Airport/Runway
- Beach/Desert
- Cemetery (Christian)
- Cemetery (Other)
- Glacier
- Mudflat
- Park/Forest
- Sight (Building)
- Sportsground
- Swamp/Mangrove

OUR STORY

A beat-up old car, a few dollars in the pocket and a sense of adventure. In 1972 that's all Tony and Maureen Wheeler needed for the trip of a lifetime – across Europe and Asia overland to Australia. It took several months, and at the end – broke but inspired – they sat at their kitchen table writing and stapling together their first travel guide, *Across Asia on the Cheap*. Within a week they'd sold 1500 copies. Lonely Planet was born.

Today, Lonely Planet has offices in Franklin, London, Melbourne, Oakland, Beijing and Delhi, with more than 600 staff and writers. We share Tony's belief that 'a great guidebook should do three things: inform, educate and amuse'.

OUR WRITERS

Mark Baker

Kraków, Małopolska, Carpathian Mountains Prague-based journalist and free-lance writer Mark Baker first visited Poland as a student in the mid-1980s while the country was still part of the Eastern bloc and has returned many times over the years. He has worked as a writer and editor for the Economist Group, Bloomberg News and Radio Free Europe/Radio Liberty. In addition to contributing to the Lonely Planet guide to *Poland* and writing Lonely Planet's pocket guide to *Kraków*, he's the author of Lonely Planet guides to *Prague & the Czech Republic*, *Romania & Bulgaria*, *Slovenia* and the Baltic countries. Mark also wrote the Planning and Survival sections of this book.

Marc Di Duca

Gdańsk & Pomerania, Warmia & Masuria Marc has been criss-crossing the post-Communist world for the past quarter of a century, the last decade as a full-time travel writer. The author of several guides to Poland, the country's north is one of his favourite corners of Eastern Europe. When not stalking Copernicus across the white sand of the Baltic, packing on pounds with cheesecake and Polish pizza and attempting to ask for railway tickets to Szczecin, Marc lives between Kent and West Bohemia with his wife, Tanya, and two sons.

Read more about Marc at:
http://auth.lonelyplanet.com/profiles/madidu

Tim Richards

Warsaw, Mazovia & Podlasie, Silesia, Wielkopolska Tim taught English in Kraków in the 1990s, and was fascinated by Poland's post-communist transition. He's returned repeatedly for Lonely Planet, deepening his relationship with this beautiful, complex country. In 2011 Tim released a Kindle ebook collecting his media articles about Poland, *We Have Here the Homicide*. When not on the road for Lonely Planet, Tim is a freelance journalist in Melbourne, Australia, writing about travel and the arts. You can find his blog and social media contacts at www.iwriter.com.au.

Read more about Tim at:
http://auth.lonelyplanet.com/profiles/timrichards

Published by Lonely Planet Publications Pty Ltd
ABN 36 005 607 983
8th edition – March 2016
ISBN 978 1 74220 754 4
© Lonely Planet 2016   Photographs © as indicated 2016
10 9 8 7 6 5 4 3 2 1
Printed in China